HISTORICAL DICTIONARIES OF AFRICA
Edited by Jon Woronoff

1. *Cameroon,* by Victor T. Le Vine and Roger P. Nye. 1974. *Out of print. See No. 48.*
2. *The Congo,* 2nd ed., by Virginia Thompson and Richard Adloff. 1984. *Out of print. See No. 69.*
3. *Swaziland,* by John J. Grotpeter. 1975.
4. *The Gambia,* 2nd ed., by Harry A. Gailey. 1987. *Out of print. See No. 79.*
5. *Botswana,* by Richard P. Stevens. 1975. *Out of print. See No. 70.*
6. *Somalia,* by Margaret F. Castagno. 1975. *Out of print. See No. 87.*
7. *Benin (Dahomey),* 2nd ed., by Samuel Decalo. 1987. *Out of print. See No. 61.*
8. *Burundi,* by Warren Weinstein. 1976. *Out of print. See No. 73.*
9. *Togo,* 3rd ed., by Samuel Decalo. 1996.
10. *Lesotho,* by Gordon Haliburton. 1977. *Out of print. See No. 90.*
11. *Mali,* 3rd ed., by Pascal James Imperato. 1996.
12. *Sierra Leone,* by Cyril Patrick Foray. 1977.
13. *Chad,* 3rd ed., by Samuel Decalo. 1997.
14. *Upper Volta,* by Daniel Miles McFarland. 1978.
15. *Tanzania,* by Laura S. Kurtz. 1978.
16. *Guinea,* 3rd ed., by Thomas O'Toole with Ibrahima Bah-Lalya. 1995.
17. *Sudan,* by John Voll. 1978. *Out of print. See No. 53.*
18. *Rhodesia/Zimbabwe,* by R. Kent Rasmussen. 1979. *Out of print. See No. 46.*
19. *Zambia,* 2nd ed., by John J. Grotpeter, Brian V. Siegel, and James R. Pletcher. 1998.
20. *Niger,* 3rd ed., by Samuel Decalo. 1997.
21. *Equatorial Guinea,* 3rd ed., by Max Liniger-Goumaz. 2000.
22. *Guinea-Bissau,* 3rd ed., by Richard Lobban and Peter Mendy. 1997.
23. *Senegal,* by Lucie G. Colvin. 1981. *Out of print. See No. 65.*
24. *Morocco,* by William Spencer. 1980. *Out of print. See No. 71.*
25. *Malawi,* by Cynthia A. Crosby. 1980. *Out of print. See No. 84.*
26. *Angola,* by Phyllis Martin. 1980. *Out of print. See No. 52.*
27. *The Central African Republic,* by Pierre Kalck. 1980. *Out of print. See No. 51.*

28. *Algeria,* by Alf Andrew Heggoy. 1981. *Out of print. See No. 66.*
29. *Kenya,* by Bethwell A. Ogot. 1981. *Out of print. See No. 77.*
30. *Gabon,* by David E. Gardinier. 1981. *Out of print. See No. 58.*
31. *Mauritania,* by Alfred G. Gerteiny. 1981. *Out of print. See No. 68.*
32. *Ethiopia,* by Chris Prouty and Eugene Rosenfeld. 1981. *Out of print. See No. 56.*
33. *Libya,* 3rd ed., by Ronald Bruce St John. 1998.
34. *Mauritius,* by Lindsay Riviere. 1982. *Out of print. See No. 49.*
35. *Western Sahara,* by Tony Hodges. 1982. *Out of print. See No. 55.*
36. *Egypt,* by Joan Wucher King. 1984. *Out of print. See No. 67.*
37. *South Africa,* by Christopher Saunders. 1983. *Out of print. See No. 78.*
38. *Liberia,* by D. Elwood Dunn and Svend E. Holsoe. 1985. *Out of print. See No. 83.*
39. *Ghana,* by Daniel Miles McFarland. 1985. *Out of print. See No. 78.*
40. *Nigeria,* 2nd ed., by Anthony Oyewole and John Lucas. 2000.
41. *Côte d'Ivoire (The Ivory Coast),* 2nd ed., by Robert J. Mundt. 1995.
42. *Cape Verde,* 2nd ed., by Richard Lobban and Marilyn Halter. 1988. *Out of print. See No. 62.*
43. *Zaire,* by F. Scott Bobb. 1988. *Out of print. See No. 76.*
44. *Botswana,* 2nd ed., by Fred Morton, Andrew Murray, and Jeff Ramsay. 1989. *Out of print. See No. 70.*
45. *Tunisia,* 2nd ed., by Kenneth J. Perkins. 1997.
46. *Zimbabwe,* 2nd ed., by Steven C. Rubert and R. Kent Rasmussen. 1990. *Out of print. See No. 86.*
47. *Mozambique,* by Mario Azevedo. 1991. *Out of print. See No. 88.*
48. *Cameroon,* 2nd ed., by Mark W. DeLancey and H. Mbella Mokeba. 1990.
49. *Mauritius,* 2nd ed., by Sydney Selvon. 1991.
50. *Madagascar,* by Maureen Covell. 1995.
51. *The Central African Republic,* 2nd ed., by Pierre Kalck; translated by Thomas O'Toole. 1992.
52. *Angola,* 2nd ed., by Susan H. Broadhead. 1992.
53. *Sudan,* 2nd ed., by Carolyn Fluehr-Lobban, Richard A. Lobban Jr., and John Obert Voll. 1992. *Out of print. See No. 85.*
54. *Malawi,* 2nd ed., by Cynthia A. Crosby. 1993. *Out of print. See No. 84.*
55. *Western Sahara,* 2nd ed., by Anthony Pazzanita and Tony Hodges. 1994.

56. *Ethiopia and Eritrea,* 2nd ed., by Chris Prouty and Eugene Rosenfeld. 1994. *Out of Print. See No. 91.*
57. *Namibia,* by John J. Grotpeter. 1994.
58. *Gabon,* 2nd ed., by David E. Gardinier. 1994.
59. *Comoro Islands,* by Martin Ottenheimer and Harriet Ottenheimer. 1994.
60. *Rwanda,* by Learthen Dorsey. 1994.
61. *Benin,* 3rd ed., by Samuel Decalo. 1995.
62. *Republic of Cape Verde,* 3rd ed., by Richard Lobban and Marlene Lopes. 1995.
63. *Ghana,* 2nd ed., by David Owusu-Ansah and Daniel Miles McFarland. 1995.
64. *Uganda,* by M. Louise Pirouet. 1995.
65. *Senegal,* 2nd ed., by Andrew F. Clark and Lucie Colvin Phillips. 1994.
66. *Algeria,* 2nd ed., by Phillip Chiviges Naylor and Alf Andrew Heggoy. 1994.
67. *Egypt,* 2nd ed., by Arthur Goldschmidt Jr. 1994. *Out of print. See No. 90.*
68. *Mauritania,* 2nd ed., by Anthony G. Pazzanita. 1996.
69. *Congo,* 3rd ed., by Samuel Decalo, Virginia Thompson, and Richard Adloff. 1996.
70. *Botswana,* 3rd ed., by Jeff Ramsay, Barry Morton, and Fred Morton. 1996.
71. *Morocco,* 2nd ed., by Thomas K. Park. 1996.
72. *Tanzania,* 2nd ed., by Thomas P. Ofcansky and Rodger Yeager. 1997.
73. *Burundi,* 2nd ed., by Ellen K. Eggers. 1997.
74. *Burkina Faso,* 2nd ed., by Daniel Miles McFarland and Lawrence Rupley. 1998.
75. *Eritrea,* by Tom Killion. 1998.
76. *Democratic Republic of the Congo (Zaire),* by F. Scott Bobb. 1999. (Revised edition of *Historical Dictionary of Zaire,* No. 43)
77. *Kenya,* 2nd ed., by Robert M. Maxon and Thomas P. Ofcansky. 2000.
78. *South Africa,* 2nd ed., by Christopher Saunders and Nicholas Southey. 2000.
79. *The Gambia,* 3rd ed., by Arnold Hughes and Harry A. Gailey. 2000.
80. *Swaziland,* 2nd ed., by Alan R. Booth. 2000.

81. *Republic of Cameroon,* 3rd ed., by Mark W. DeLancey and Mark Dike DeLancey. 2000.
82. *Djibouti,* by Daoud A. Alwan and Yohanis Mibrathu. 2000.
83. *Liberia,* 2nd ed., by D. Elwood Dunn, Amos J. Beyan, and Carl Patrick Burrowes. 2001.
84. *Malawi,* 3rd ed., by Owen J. Kalinga and Cynthia A. Crosby. 2001.
85. *Sudan,* 3rd ed., by Richard A. Lobban Jr., Robert S. Kramer, and Carolyn Fluehr-Lobban. 2002.
86. *Zimbabwe,* 3rd ed., by Steven C. Rubert and R. Kent Rasmussen. 2001.
87. *Somalia,* 2nd ed., by Mohamed Haji Mukhtar. 2002.
88. *Mozambique,* 2nd ed., by Mario Azevedo, Emmanuel Nnadozie, and Tomé Mbuia João. 2003.
89. *Egypt,* 3rd ed., by Arthur Goldschmidt Jr. and Robert Johnston. 2003.
90. *Lesotho,* by Scott Rosenberg, Richard Weisfelder, and Michelle Frisbie-Fulton. 2004.
91. *Ethiopia, New Edition,* by David H. Shinn and Thomas P. Ofcansky. 2004.

Historical Dictionary of Ethiopia
New Edition

David H. Shinn
Thomas P. Ofcansky

Historical Dictionaries of Africa, No. 91

The Scarecrow Press, Inc.
Lanham, Maryland • Toronto • Oxford
2004

SCARECROW PRESS, INC.

Published in the United States of America
by Scarecrow Press, Inc.
A wholly owned subsidiary of The Rowman & Littlefield Publishing Group, Inc.
4501 Forbes Boulevard, Suite 200, Lanham, Maryland 20706
www.scarecrowpress.com

PO Box 317
Oxford
OX2 9RU, UK

British Library Cataloguing in Publication Information Available

Library of Congress Cataloging-in-Publication Data

Shinn, David Hamilton.
  Historical dictionary of Ethiopia / David H. Shinn, Thomas P.
Ofcansky.— New ed.
    p. cm. — (historical dictionaries of Africa ; no. 91)
  Rev. ed. of: Historical dictionary of Ethiopia and Eritrea / by
Chris Prouty and Eugene Rosenfeld. 2nd ed. c1994.
  Includes bibliographical references.
  ISBN 0-8108-4910-0 (alk. paper)
  1. Ethiopia—History—Dictionaries. I. Ofcansky, Thomas P., 1947– II. Prouty,
Chris. Historical dictionary of Ethiopia and Eritrea. III.
Title. IV. Series.
  DT381 .S55 2004
  963'.003—dc22

                                                          2003020859

Contents

Editor's Foreword *Jon Woronoff*   ix

List of Acronyms and Abbreviations   xi

Maps   xiv

Chronology   xix

Introduction   xlvii

THE DICTIONARY   1

Appendix   417

Bibliography   423

About the Authors   633

Editor's Foreword

Looking back over Ethiopia's recent past, there seems to have been little more than a ceaseless and incomprehensible series of calamities. An apparently solid empire was truncated by civil war, then ravaged by smaller insurrections throughout its territory, with the conservative (more accurately, reactionary) imperial regime replaced by the revolutionary (and rather anarchic) left-wing Derg, only to shift gradually to a somewhat more centrist government but ruling over a highly fragmented society. Yet, even then, the military engaged in a pretty useless—if ultimately victorious—interstate war with Eritrea. The economy, once fairly promising, collapsed after collectivization, decentralization, resettlement, and the gratuitous destruction of warfare, with the people periodically afflicted by famine and dirt poor in the best of times. Yet, Ethiopia finally seems to be making steadier progress than before, and its inhabitants and outside observers can only hope this continues.

Will it? Nobody knows what lies ahead. So let us try a simpler question. Why did it all happen? Actually, it was much less senseless than appears when one looks back far enough, to the time when Ethiopian kingdoms emerged, fought against one another and were pitted against external foes (Muslim raiders and the Italians), and coalesced in an empire and sovereign state. Much of what happened recently was history in reverse, Ethiopia breaking apart along fault lines that always existed and could not withstand too much pressure. This is why this *Historical Dictionary of Ethiopia* stands out among all those in the African series. It not only tells us about the current situation, which cannot be understood without numerous references to the last few decades, which in turn cannot be properly grasped unless seen in the context of earlier centuries, even millennia. Thus, a particularly large dictionary section, but none too large for what it has to do, a helpful introduction, necessary to put things in place, a very long list of acronyms for obvious reasons, and a fairly comprehensive bibliography.

Despite so many negative aspects, there is no question that Ethiopia remains one of the most interesting, even intriguing countries in Africa. It is not only rich in history, it is rich in culture, and it is rich in ethnic diversity. This brings out the best in passive observers who spent several years compiling an amazingly enlightened book. David H. Shinn took a keen interest in exploring many aspects, writing them up individually, and putting the pieces together. This is not the first time for Thomas Ofcansky, who conducts research with the U.S. Department of State and has already coauthored the *Historical Dictionary of Tanzania* and the *Historical Dictionary of Kenya*. David Shinn's background is more pragmatic; he held a string of diplomatic postings from the 1960s on and eventually served as U.S. ambassador to Ethiopia from 1996 to 1999. Both authors have also written and lectured academically, but what makes them different and this volume special is the wealth of hands-on experience.

Jon Woronoff
Series Editor

Acronyms and Abbreviations

AAPO	All Amhara People's Organization
AAU	Addis Ababa University
AESM	All-Ethiopian Socialist Movement
AETU	All Ethiopia Trade Union
AEUP	All Ethiopian Unity Party
AFCC	Armed Forces Coordination Committee
AFROMET	Association for the Return of the Maqdala Ethiopia Treasures
AIDS	Acquired immune deficiency syndrome
ALF	Afar Liberation Front
ANDM	Amhara National Democratic Movement
AOI	Africa Orientale Italiana
CA	Constituent Assembly
CC	Constitutional Commission
CELU	Confederation of Ethiopian Labor Unions
CETU	Confederation of Ethiopia Trade Unions
CMS	Church Missionary Society
CO	Colonial Office
COPWE	Commission for Organizing the Party of the Working People of Ethiopia
DPPC	Disaster Preparedness and Prevention Commission
EAF	Ethiopian Air Force
EAL	Ethiopian Air Lines
ECA	Economic Commission for Africa
EDORM	Ethiopian Democratic Officers' Revolutionary Movement
EDU	Ethiopian Democratic Union
EECMY	Ethiopian Evangelical Church Mekane Yesus
EFFORT	Endowment Fund for the Rehabilitation of Tigray

EFPJA	Ethiopian Free Press Journalists' Association
ELF	Eritrean Liberation Front
ELM	Eritrean Liberation Movement
EOPRS	Ethiopian Oppressed People's Revolutionary Struggle
ENDF	Ethiopian National Defense Forces
ENLF	Ethiopian National Liberation Force
EOC	Ethiopian Orthodox Church
EPDM	Ethiopian People's Democratic Movement
EPLF	Eritrean People's Liberation Front
EPRDF	Ethiopian People's Revolutionary Democratic Front
EPRP	Ethiopian People's Revolutionary Party
ERCS	Ethiopian Red Cross Society
ESAF	Enhanced Structural Adjustment Facility
ESM	Ethiopian Student Movement
ETA	Ethiopian Teachers' Association
ETC	Ethiopian Telecommunications Corporation
ETU	Ethiopia Trade Union
EU	European Union
EWNHS	Ethiopian Wildlife and Natural History Society
FGM	Female genital mutilation
FO	Foreign Office
GDP	Gross domestic product
GNP	Gross national product
HIV	Human immunodeficiency virus
HPR	House of Peoples' Representatives
IBT	Imperial Board of Telecommunications
ICRC	International Committee of the Red Cross
IDA	International Development Association
IEP	Imperial Ethiopian Police
IES	Institute of Ethiopian Studies
IMF	International Monetary Fund
LRB	Labor Relations Board
MIDROC	Mohamed International Development Research and Organization Companies
MLLT	Marxist-Leninist League of Tigray
NCHP	National Committee on Harmful Practices
NCTPE	National Committee on Traditional Practices of Ethiopia

NGO	Nongovernmental organization
NLC	National Literacy Campaign
NLCCC	National Literacy Campaign Coordinating Committee
NPV	Net present value
OAU	Organization of African Unity
OETA	Occupied Enemy Territory Administration
OLF	Oromo Liberation Front
ONLF	Ogaden National Liberation Front
OPDO	Oromo People's Democratic Organization
PMAC	Provisional Military Administrative Council
POMOA	Provisional Office for Mass Organizational Affairs
PRGF	Poverty Reduction and Growth Facility
REST	Relief Society of Tigray
RRC	Relief and Rehabilitation Commission
SAF	Structural Adjustment Facility
SEM	Swedish Evangelical Mission
SIM	Sudan Interior Mission
SLF	Sidamo Liberation Front
SNA	Somali National Army
SNNPR	Southern Nations, Nationalities, and People's Region
TF	Trust Fund
TGE	Transitional Government of Ethiopia
TPLF	Tigray People's Liberation Front
TWA	Transcontinental and Western Airlines
UN	United Nations
UNDP	United Nations Development Program
UNESCO	United Nations Educational, Scientific, and Cultural Organization
UNHCR	United Nations High Commissioner for Refugees
UNMEE	United Nations Mission to Ethiopia and Eritrea
UNSC	United Nations Security Council
U.S.	United States
VAT	Value-added tax
WPE	Workers' Party of Ethiopia
WSLF	Western Somalia Liberation Front

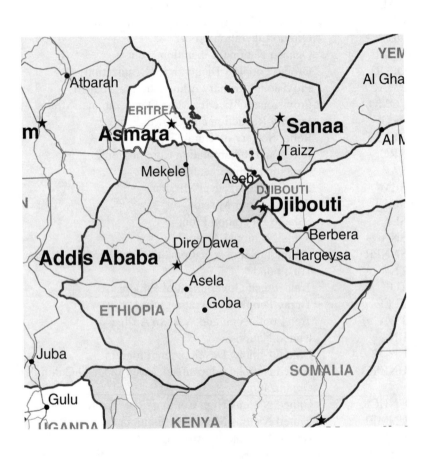

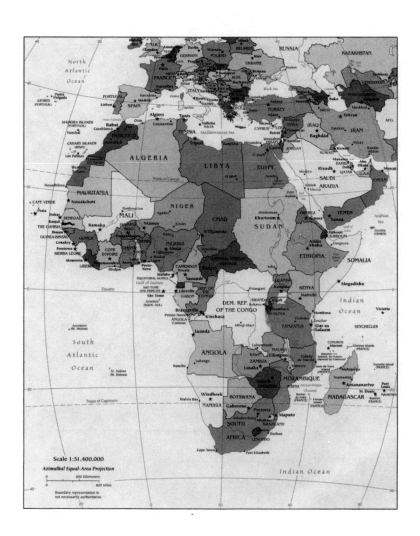

Disputed territory

100 Kilometers
50
0

100 Miles
50
0

Eritrean-Ethiopian boundary is not
authoritative. Locations of Badme
and Zela Ambesa relative to the
boundary are not known.

Sudan

Red

Sea

Eritrea

Sawa

Massawa

Asmara

Yemen

Teseney

Barentu

Hadish Adi

Yirga

Tsorona

Zela Ambesa

Badme

Sheraro

Himora

Inda Silase

Aksum

Adigrat

Mek'ele

Ethiopia

Assab

Bure

Tanu
Hayk

Djibouti

300 Kilometers
300 Miles

Saudi Arabia

Asmara

Eritrea

Yemen

Sudan

Area of
main map

Djibouti

Gulf of
Aden

Addis
Ababa

Ethiopia

Somalia

Uganda

Kenya

Indian
Ocean

(R02705)

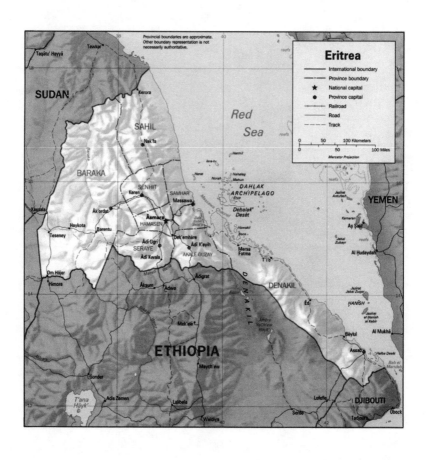

Provincial boundaries are approximate.
Other boundary representation is not
necessarily authoritative.

Eritrea

— International boundary
---- Province boundary
★ National capital
● Province capital
+ Railroad
— Road
---- Track

0   50   100 Kilometers
0   50   100 Miles
Mercator Projection

Taqatu' Hayya   Tawkar

SUDAN

Kerora

SAHIL

Red
Sea

reefs

BARAKA

Nak'fa

Isra-tu

Harat   Norah   Mahun

Nahaleg

Hermil

DAHLAK
ARCHIPELAGO

SENHIT
Keren

Kassala

Ak'ordat   SAMHAR
Massawa

Dehalak
Desêt

Baca

YEMEN

Kamaran

Aş Salif

Haykota   Barentu

Asmara
HAMASEN

Howakil

Jebel
Zukayr

Teseney

Adi Ugri

Dek'emhare

Adi K'eyih   Mersa
Fatma

reefs

Al Hudaydah

SERAYE

Adi Kwala   AKALE GUZAY   Ti'o

Om Hajer

Himora

Adigrat

Aksum   Adwa

D E N A K I L

DENAKIL

Jazira
Jabal Zuqar

Al Hudaydah

Ed

HANISH

Jazira
Jabal
al Hanish
al Kabir

Mek'ele

Adinu
Techicw
Hayk'

Baylul   Al Mukhā

Assab   Hatta Dese

ETHIOPIA

Maych'ew

Gonder

T'ana
Hāyk'

Adis Zemen

Lalibela

Weldiya

Serdo   Lofefle

Tadjoura

Bab el
Mandeb

DJIBOUTI

Obock

Chronology

3000 B.C.	The word *Ethiopia*, which means "land of the burnt faces," is known widely, but the country itself remains a mystery.
1000 B.C.	Immigrants from the Arabian Peninsula begin settling on the Red Sea's African coast and the Ethiopian plateau.
975 B.C.	Menelik I, son of Solomon and the Queen of Sheba and Ethiopia's first emperor, is born.
A.D. 100–300	Kingdom of Axum emerges.
c.340	Ezana, king of Axum, embraces Christianity.
524	Emperor Kaleb crosses the Red Sea and conquers Yemen, destroys the Jewish kingdom of Humyar, and liberates the local Christians.
590	Persian army expels the Axumites from Yemen.
615	Prophet Mohammed urges his followers to immigrate to Axum. The following year, a group of at least 132 Muslims arrives in the kingdom.
702	Ethiopia attempts to invade the Hijaz by occupying the port of Jidda.
1516–1846	Ottoman Turks conquer and rule over the coastal and some lowland areas.

1530–1532	Muslim leader Ahmad ibn Ibrahim al Ghazi conquers much of Ethiopia and establishes Islam as one of the country's major religions.
16 November 1841	Britain concludes a treaty of friendship and commerce with Sahle Selassie, negus of Shoa, Ifat, and the Galla.
1846–1875	Egypt gains control of previously administered Turkish areas and expands the territory under its control.
2 November 1849	Britain and Ethiopia conclude a treaty of friendship and commerce. Outbreak of the Anglo-Ethiopia war (1868) results in the treaty's termination.
21 August 1867	Queen Victoria announces that Britain will send a military expedition to Ethiopia.
20 May 1868	Sultan of the Ottoman Empire transfers Massawa to Egypt.
18 September 1875	Egyptian army, under the command of Rauf Pasha, occupies Harar.
15 March 1883	Italy concludes a treaty of peace and friendship with Mohamed Hanfari, the sultan of Asab and chief of the Danakils. Among other things, the treaty provides for the free transport of Italian goods from Asab and Aussa and the Red Sea coast.
21 May 1883	Italy and Shoa conclude a treaty of peace and friendship that provides for the appointment of diplomatic and consular officers.
3 June 1884	Ethiopia, Britain, and Egypt sign the Hewett Treaty, which seeks to normalize relations between the three countries.
5 February 1885	Italian rear admiral Paolo Caimi announces that Italy has taken possession of Massawa.

1 May 1887 Italy imposes an arms blockade on Ethiopia.

7 July 1887 Italy concludes a convention with Mohamed Hanfari, the sultan of Asab and chief of the Danakils, that abolishes the slave trade.

20 October 1887 Italy and Ethiopia conclude a treaty of friendship that pledges the former to refrain from annexing any Ethiopian territory.

2 May 1889 Italy and Ethiopia conclude a treaty of friendship and commerce. The treaty fixes the boundary between Italian and Ethiopian territory and allows for the free transport of arms and ammunition through the port of Massawa en route to Menelik II's forces.

1 January 1890 Italy proclaims Eritrea a colony.

19 July 1895 Germany issues a decree forbidding the export of arms and ammunition from its East African possessions to Somalia and Ethiopia.

26 October 1896 Italo-Ethiopian treaty defines the frontier between Ethiopia and Italian Eritrea.

20 March 1897 Franco-Ethiopian treaty defines the boundary between French Somaliland (now Djibouti) and Ethiopia.

14 May 1897 Anglo-Ethiopian treaty defines the boundary between Ethiopia and British Somaliland (now Somaliland).

10 July 1900 Italy and Ethiopia conclude a treaty that delimits the frontier between Eritrea and Ethiopia.

15 May 1902 Menelik II concludes a treaty with Britain, according to which Ethiopia promises not to undertake any work across the Blue Nile, Lake Tana, and the Sobat River that would interfere with the flow of waters into the Nile River.

27 June 1903	Anglo-Ethiopian treaty defines the boundary between Sudan and Ethiopia.
27 December 1903	Treaty to Regulate Commercial Relations between the U.S. and the king of Ethiopia concluded in Addis Ababa. Its term is 10 years.
7 March 1905	Ethiopia and Germany conclude a treaty of friendship and commerce.
13 December 1906	Britain, France, and Italy conclude the Tripartite Treaty, which divides Ethiopia into spheres of influence.
6 December 1907	Britain and Ethiopia conclude a treaty that defines the borders between British East Africa (now Kenya), Uganda, and Ethiopia.
19 December 1907	First resident U.S. consul general established in Addis Ababa.
6 December 1907	Anglo-Ethiopian treaty defines the border between Ethiopia and British East Africa (now Kenya).
16 May 1908	Italo-Ethiopian treaty defines the borders between Ethiopia and Italian Eritrea and between Ethiopia and Italian Somaliland.
3 October 1935	Italy invades Ethiopia without a declaration of war.
5 October 1935	American president Franklin Delano Roosevelt enacts an arms embargo on Ethiopia and Italy. On 29 June 1936, he terminates the arms embargo.
9 May 1936	Italy announces the annexation of Ethiopia and declares the king of Italy as its emperor.
17 March 1937	League of Nations fails to act on Haile Selassie's request to appoint an inquiry commission to investigate Italian war crimes in Ethiopia.

8 April 1941 Eritrea placed under British Military Administration pending an international decision about the territory's fate.

15 September 1941 Britain establishes an East Africa Command that comprises Ethiopia, Eritrea, former Italian-ruled Somalia (now Somalia), British Somaliland (now Somalia), Kenya, Zanzibar (now part of Tanzania), Tanganyika (now Tanzania), Uganda, Nyasaland (now Malawi), and Northern Rhodesia (now Zambia).

28 November 1941 British War Office announces the end of the East African campaign.

1 December 1942 Ethiopia declares war on Germany, Italy, and Japan.

1 July 1943 Ethiopia and the Soviet Union agree to establish diplomatic relations.

9 August 1943 Ethiopia and the U.S. sign a lend-lease treaty.

30 November 1943 Italy's government of Premier Pietro Badoglio nullifies King Victor Emmanuel's title as emperor of Ethiopia.

13 February 1944 Haile Selassie meets U.S. president Roosevelt aboard the USS *Quincy* on Bitter Lake, Egypt. The two leaders discuss Ethiopia's role in drafting the UN charter and in the peace conference with the Axis powers; Ethiopia's need for access to the sea and greater control over the Addis Ababa–Djibouti Railway; economic aid to purchase military, transportation, and communications equipment; and support for the return of the Ogaden and the annexation of Eritrea.

27 August 1944 Haile Selassie issues a decree that prohibits foreign church missions from operating or seeking converts in areas predominantly populated by members of the Ethiopian Orthodox Church.

17 May 1945	Ethiopia and the U.S. open the first radio-telegraph circuit between the two countries.
6 September 1945	Sinclair Oil Corporation announces that it has received an exclusive 50-year exploration concession from Haile Selassie.
27 December 1945	Ethiopia signs the Bretton Woods Agreement authorizing the creation of the International Monetary Fund and the World Bank for Reconstruction and Development.
25 March 1946	Kenneth Royall, undersecretary of war, announces that the U.S. has given Ethiopia a $1 million credit to purchase surplus American military supplies in the Middle East.
25 May 1949	Ethiopia and the U.S. sign an agreement for the final settlement of Addis Ababa's lend-lease account. Under its terms, Ethiopia agrees to pay $200,000 for lend-lease goods of civilian value.
1 June 1949	Ethiopia is the first country to ratify the UN Convention against Genocide.
29 January 1950	Ethiopia refuses to recognize a UN Trusteeship Council decision (27 January 1950) to allow Italy to administer Somalia as a trust territory for 10 years. Ethiopia objects to the appointment of Guglielmo Nas as Somalia's governor because he had participated in the Italian-Ethiopian War and had been considered a war criminal by the Allies.
2 December 1950	UN General Assembly passes Resolution 390 to federate Eritrea with Ethiopia as an autonomous territory under the sovereignty of the Ethiopian crown.

6 December 1950   Ethiopia and Italy announce that they have agreed to "forget the past" and resume diplomatic and economic relations.

14 June 1951   U.S. and Ethiopia sign an agreement to initiate a Point Four Program, a Harry Truman administration project to increase American aid to the Third World.

21 July 1951   Ethiopian special tribunal in Addis Ababa sentences eight men, including former president of parliament Bitwoded Negash, for plotting to assassinate Haile Selassie and planning to create an Ethiopian republic.

15 May 1952   Ethiopia and the U.S. sign a Point Four technical aid agreement.

15 September 1952   British administration ends in Eritrea and sovereignty is transferred to the Ethiopian imperial government.

22 May 1953   U.S. and Ethiopia conclude a military assistance agreement. Under its terms Washington provides a Military Assistance Advisory Group and supplies to the Ethiopian armed forces in exchange for basing rights.

6 August 1953   Ethiopia and the U.S. sign a friendship and economic assistance treaty.

14 May 1954   Haile Selassie grants the U.S. 99-year military base rights in Ethiopia.

15 February 1957   Haile Selassie accuses Egypt of trying to subvert Ethiopian Muslims against the Coptic Christian majority. He appeals for greater U.S. military aid to thwart Cairo's plans to create an Egypt-dominated Greater Somalia.

11 March 1957   U.S. vice president Richard Nixon arrives in Addis Ababa and asks Haile Selassie for permission to build a U.S. military communications center outside Asmara and port facilities at Massawa.

17 February 1959 Ethiopia declares that it does not oppose the UN's plan to unite British and Italian Somalia.

1 September 1961 *Shifta* chieftain Hamid Idris Awate fires the first shot of the Eritrean liberation struggle against Ethiopia.

14 November 1962 Haile Selassie abrogates the federation with Eritrea, dissolves the Eritrean National Assembly, and makes Eritrea the 14th province of Ethiopia.

22 November 1963 Ethiopia and Kenya sign a mutual defense pact under which they would come to one another's assistance if attacked by a third party (i.e., Somalia). The pact came into existence upon Kenya's independence (12 December 1963). On 27 December 1963, both countries ratified the pact.

16 September 1966 Haile Selassie declares that Djibouti is an "integral part" of Ethiopia.

11 March 1969 Bomb explodes on an EAL Boeing 707 at Frankfurt, causing more than £2 million in damage and injuring several German cleaning women. On 15 March 1969, ELF claims credit for the attack.

9 September 1969 ELF abducts the U.S. consul general in Asmara and lectures him about its goals before setting him free.

9 June 1970 Ethiopia and Kenya sign a treaty delimiting their border.

18 October 1970 Testimony made public by the Department of State and the Department of Defense discloses that the U.S. had entered into an "unpublished agreement" with Ethiopia to equip and train the 40,000-man Ethiopian army and to oppose any threats to Ethiopia's territory. In exchange, the U.S. received permission to expand Kagnew Station.

23 October 1973   Ethiopia severs diplomatic relations with Israel.

27 June 1974   Derg established.

12 September 1974   Derg deposes Emperor Haile Selassie and seizes power.

30 November 1974   Derg announces that Haile Selassie had signed a letter authorizing the transfer of his personal and family fortune, estimated at $1.5 billion, to the government to aid drought and famine victims.

1 January 1975   Derg nationalizes banks, insurance companies, and other financial institutions.

3 February 1975   Derg nationalizes 72 enterprises and orders state participation in 29 others.

7 February 1975   Derg issues a Declaration on the Economic Policy of Socialist Ethiopia, which identifies areas of the economy reserved for the government, for joint ventures between the government and private capital, and for private enterprise.

4 March 1975   Derg issues Proclamation No. 31, which nationalizes all rural land, establishes a Peasant Association as a new government organ and mass organization, and allows farming households usufruct over as many as 10 hectares.

22 March 1975   Derg formally abolishes the monarchy.

20–21 April 1975   Derg arrests some 20 officers and civilians for plotting to free deposed Emperor Haile Selassie and overthrow the military government.

26 July 1975	Derg issues Proclamation No. 27, which nationalizes all urban land but allows individuals to own one house and up to 500 square meters for residential purposes.
31 July 1975	Ethiopia renounces any territorial ambitions over Djibouti at OAU.
12 September 1975	ELF attacks U.S. communications facility at Kagnew. Rebels kill nine people and wound 23 others. ELF takes eight men hostage, including two Americans.
30 September 1975	Derg declares a state of emergency.
19 January 1976	U.S. agrees to help modernize the Ethiopian army by supplying new tanks, patrol craft, and advanced infantry weapons.
5 July 1976	Government amends the penal code by introducing penalties of death for anyone who established a relationship with antirevolutionary organizations in or out of Ethiopia.
30 January 1977	Sudan announces that it will support the Eritrean rebels against Ethiopia.
25 February 1977	U.S. announces that it will reduce military aid to Ethiopia because of escalating human rights violations.
23 April 1977	Ethiopia terminates its military relationship with the U.S. by closing Kagnew Station, the American consulate in Asmara, U.S. Information Service offices throughout Ethiopia, the U.S. Military Assistance Advisory Group office, and a U.S. Navy medical research center. On 27 April 1977, the U.S. responds by terminating arms shipments to Ethiopia.
6 May 1977	Ethiopia and the former Soviet Union sign several economic and technical protocols.

29 May 1977	Ethiopia expels the American and British defense attachés.
9 March 1978	Somali president Siad Barre announces the unilateral withdrawal of Somali National Army units from the Ogaden.
20 November 1978	Ethiopia and the Soviet Union sign a 20-year treaty of friendship and cooperation.
21 January 1979	ELF and the EPLF conclude a unity agreement.
25 June 1979	Ethiopia issues a directive ordering collectivized farming.
15 November 1979	Ethiopia and East Germany conclude a treaty of friendship and cooperation. On 14 August 1980, the two countries ratify the treaty.
23 August 1981	At a meeting in Aden, the presidents of Ethiopia, Libya, and South Yemen sign a treaty of friendship and cooperation covering economic, political, and military issues.
12 September 1985	Ethiopia celebrates the 10th anniversary of the overthrow of Haile Selassie. The festivities cost $100–200 million.
19 December 1985	Ethiopia and the U.S. sign an agreement whereby the former agrees to compensate American companies for property nationalized after the 1974 revolution.
18 September 1987	Ethiopia's 14 provinces are redivided into 25 administrative regions and five autonomous regions.
6 April 1988	Mengistu Haile Mariam orders all foreign relief organizations, with the exception of UNICEF, to cease operations in Tigray and Eritrea.

15 May 1988	Mengistu Haile Mariam declares a state of emergency in Tigray and Eritrea.
1 March 1989	TPLF announces that Tigray has been liberated.
7–19 September 1989	Ethiopia and EPLF hold peace talks in Atlanta, Georgia, under the auspices of the International Negotiating Network chaired by former U.S. president Jimmy Carter. The two sides agree to continue negotiations and to adopt a 13-point procedural agenda.
17 September 1989	Last Cuban troops arrive in Havana after evacuating Ethiopia.
3 November 1989	Ethiopia and Israel resume diplomatic relations after a 16-year break.
20–29 November 1989	Ethiopia and EPLF open a second round of peace talks in Nairobi. The two sides agree on a series of procedural issues that clear the way for substantive negotiations to begin in early 1990.
11 December 1989	East Germany announces that it has stopped all arms deliveries to Ethiopia.
8 February 1990	After a truce of nearly nine months, fighting resumes in Eritrea along a 124-mile (200-kilometer) front from Asmara to Keren.
28 February 1990	U.S. acknowledges that the 1952 Ethiopian-Eritrean federation was not in accordance with the wishes of the Eritrean people.
5 March 1990	Mengistu abandons Marxism and announces sweeping political, economic, and social reforms to unite the country.
20–29 March 1990	Third round of peace talks between Ethiopia and EPLF in Rome break down over the latter's insistence that "substantive talks" involve EPDM.

| 21 March 1990 | Soviet ambassador to Sudan, Valery Sukhin, announces that, as of early February 1990, all Soviet military advisers had been withdrawn from combat areas in Ethiopia. |

21 March 1990 Soviet ambassador to Sudan, Valery Sukhin, announces that, as of early February 1990, all Soviet military advisers had been withdrawn from combat areas in Ethiopia.

1–21 April 1990 Ethiopia and ELF hold peace talks in North Yemen (now Yemen). Both parties agree on procedural matters, opening the way for substantive talks.

1 May 1990 In his traditional May Day speech, Mengistu announces that he has survived nine attempts on his life.

19 May 1990 Ethiopian Supreme Court sentences 12 generals to death for complicity in the 16 May 1989 coup attempt against Mengistu. Two other generals are given long prison terms. On 21 May 1990, the executions are carried out.

23 June 1990 Mengistu admits his government is "on the verge of collapse."

13 July 1990 *New York Times* reports that Ethiopia has suspended emigration of Falashas to Israel to force Tel Aviv to supply Addis Ababa with more military aid.

17 January 1991 EPRDF convenes its first congress.

15–17 April 1991 Coalition of Ethiopian Democratic Forces is founded in the U.S.

26 April 1991 Mengistu reconstitutes his government by replacing hard-liners with more liberal officials and agreeing to discuss the possibility of a cease-fire with the country's rebel groups. The rebels refuse the offer.

27 April 1991 State Council establishes a national campaign supreme command to mobilize civilians to fight alongside the army and militia.

11 May 1991	*Izvestiya* announces the closure of the Soviet Navy's base in the Dahlak archipelago.
24 May 1991	EPLF occupies Asmara.
27 May 1991	EPRDF captures Addis Ababa and establishes an interim government. London peace talks open between Ethiopian government and TPLF, EPLF, and OLF under the chairmanship of Herman Cohen, U.S. assistant secretary of state for African affairs.
6 June 1991	Acting head of state Meles Zenawi announces the formation of a provisional government with Tamrat Layne, head of the EPDM, as prime minister.
7 June 1991	New Ethiopian government announces the closure of all security services associated with the Mengistu regime.
15 June 1991	Ethiopia's interim government announces the creation of a rehabilitation commission attached to the Ministry of Defense to help disbanded troops to resume a peaceful life.
19 June 1991	Ethiopia's interim government announces that it will disband the Ethiopian army and seek to prosecute some former soldiers and officials for war crimes and human rights violations.
1–5 July 1991	Conference on Peace and Democracy held in Addis Ababa. Hundreds of delegates from about 25 groups attend the meeting. They establish the Transitional Government of Ethiopia, elect an 87-member Council of Representatives, and recognize Eritrea's right to determine its political future by an internationally supervised referendum.
3 July 1991	Ethiopia announces that it will allow Eritrea to vote on independence within two years.

8 August 1991 Djibouti returns 22 military aircraft whose pilots had fled Ethiopia after the collapse of the Mengistu regime.

27 August 1991 OLF and the EPRDF conclude a peace agreement.

24 September 1991 World Bank announces that it intends to normalize relations with Ethiopia.

10 October 1991 Ethiopian Human Rights Council established.

24 October 1991 Ethiopia and Sudan sign treaty of friendship and cooperation.

2 November 1991 Canada announces that it will provide $3.1 million to Ethiopia to rehabilitate former soldiers and refugees.

19 November 1991 Ethiopia and Kenya sign a treaty of friendship and cooperation.

17 December 1991 Ethiopia appeals for 1.28 million tons of emergency food relief for 1992 for some 7.4 million famine victims.

4 January 1992 Ethiopia and Eritrea sign an agreement whereby the former is allowed to the Asab as a "free port."

16 January 1992 Council of Representatives approves draft decree on the formation of the special attorney general's office that has the authority to prosecute war criminals who had served in the Mengistu regime. Government issues proclamation (no. 8/92) formalizing the formation of a new army and police force.

10 February 1992 U.S. removes Ethiopia from the "Marxist-Leninist List." Ethiopia is eligible to use Export-Import Bank services.

5 June 1992 U.S. grants Ethiopia $95.2 million to help rebuild the country's shattered economy.

23 June 1992 OLF withdraws from the transitional government. The following day, OLF initiates military operations against the transitional government.

18 September 1992 Ethiopian National Assembly endorses appointment of special prosecutors to bring to trial hundreds of former government officials who were jailed after the overthrow of the Mengistu regime.

11 January 1993 U.S. provides $5 million for the rehabilitation of former Ethiopian soldiers.

23–25 April 1993 Eritrea holds a referendum on the question of independence. Some 99.8 percent of those who participate vote for independence.

29 April 1993 Ethiopia recognizes Eritrea's referendum.

24 May 1993 Eritrea proclaims its independence.

12 July 1993 Ethiopia adopts a population policy that seeks to harmonize the population growth rate with the country's capacity for development and to implement a nationwide family planning program.

20 July 1993 Ethiopia and Eritrea conclude a friendship and cooperation agreement that establishes a Joint Ministerial Commission and pledges both countries to cooperate in the cultural, foreign affairs, defense, economic, scientific, social, technical, and transportation sectors.

22 September 1993 Ethiopian-Eritrean Joint Ministerial Commission opens in Asmara. By the time the meeting ends on 27 September, the two countries conclude 25 agreements in the political, economic, and social sectors.

27 September 1993   Ethiopia and Eritrea conclude Transit and Port Service Agreement whereby the two countries agree that the Eritrean ports of Asab and Massawa will serve as transit points for goods originating from and destined to Ethiopia.

23 October 1993   Germany cancels Ethiopia's $126 million arms debt to the former East Germany.

15 November 1993   Ethiopia and the U.S. sign an economic and technical cooperation agreement.

18 December 1993   Ethiopian government refuses to participate in a "peace and reconciliation" conference organized by opposition groups in Addis Ababa.

7 February 1994   Former U.S. president Carter mediates talks between the Ethiopian government and various opposition groups at the Carter Center. They fail to produce any agreements.

23 February 1994   Ethiopia unsuccessfully appeals to Zimbabwe to extradite Mengistu so he can be tried for crimes.

22 March 1994   Ethiopia accuses Libya, Syria, and Iraq of providing support to the secessionist ONLF.

20 April 1994   Ethiopia and Eritrea sign a security and military affairs agreement.

13 May 1994   Ethiopian-Eritrean Joint Ministerial Commission ends in Addis Ababa. The two countries sign a communiqué that promises to improve economic cooperation.

20 June 1994   Britain agrees to provide $3.79 million to help train Ethiopian policemen.

27 October 1994   Ethiopian government formally charges Mengistu and 72 other former officials with genocide and human rights violations.

13 December 1994   Special Prosecutor's Office begins trial of 73 former Derg officials, only 47 of whom appear in court. In four days of hearings, the court arraigns them on 211 counts of mass murder, torture, and forced disappearance.

26 June 1995   Egyptian president Hosni Mubarak survives an assassination attempt in Addis Ababa.

20 November 1996   After running out of fuel, an EAL Boeing 767 (flight 961) crashes near the Comoros islands. Three individuals had attempted to hijack the plane.

17 January 1997   Merid Azmatch Asfa Wossen, Ethiopia's one-time crown prince who crowned himself the country's 226th emperor in 1988, dies in exile in the U.S. On 2 February 1997, he is buried in Addis Ababa's Trinity Cathedral.

22 January 1997   Sileshi Semaw discovers stone tools along the Ethiopia-Kenya border dating back 2.5 million years. The find pushes back the frontier of the first-known use of tools by prehumans by 200,000 years.

24–25 November 1997   Italian president Oscar Luigi Scalfaro meets with Prime Minister Meles. He apologizes for the Italian invasion and occupation of Ethiopia (1935–1941) and promises to return the Axum obelisk. Scalfaro is the first Italian head of state to visit Ethiopia since before World War II.

13 March 1998   Ethiopia and Italy conclude a defense cooperation agreement whereby the latter will provide training and supplies for the Ethiopian army and air force.

25 March 1998   Ethiopia announces that the first provincial trials of suspects accused of taking part in the Red Terror open in Harar.

28 March 1998 Russian government delegation visits Ethiopia for the first time since the downfall of the Mengistu regime. Issues discussed by the two countries include the debt built up during the Mengistu years (1974–1991), business and investment opportunities, and prospects for political cooperation.

16 April 1998 Ethiopia unveils plans to open new universities in Amhara, Oromia, South Ethiopia, and Tigray.

12 May 1998 Ethiopian-Eritrean War begins as Eritrean troops occupy Badme town and several other locations along its border with Ethiopia. Bilateral and multilateral donors react by suspending more than $1 billion in aid to Ethiopia.

13 May 1998 Ethiopia stops using the Eritrean ports of Asab and Massawa and terminates all EAL flights to Asmara.

3 June 1998 U.S.-Rwanda-brokered peace plan fails to end the Eritrean-Ethiopian border dispute.

12 June 1998 Ethiopia announces that it intends to deport those Eritreans who are considered a threat to national security.

17 June 1998 Five Ethiopian opposition movements in exile (Afar Revolutionary Democratic Unity Front, Coalition of Ethiopian Democratic Forces, Gambella National Democratic Alliance, Southern Ethiopian People's Democratic Coalition, and Tigray Alliance for National Democracy) issue a statement that urges all Ethiopians to support the war against Eritrea.

12 September 1998 Government releases 31 generals and other senior military and Worker's Party of

Ethiopia officials who had been among the 2,000 arrested in 1991 and charged with genocide.

22 November 1998   *Ethiopian Herald* reports that the government has formulated a $710 million five-year plan to increase national health coverage.

16 April 1999   Eritrea deports 40,943 Ethiopians.

6 May 1999   Prime Minister Meles denounces the "blackmail" of the World Bank and IMF in his opening address to the Economic Commission for Africa conference in Addis Ababa.

7 May 1999   Ethiopian minister of finance Sufian Ahmed admits that the war with Eritrea is jeopardizing donor funding.

27 May 1999   Ethiopia's DPPC announces that because of an ongoing famine in several areas, the country requires 360,000 tons of food aid for 4.6 million people.

22 September 1999   U.S. announces that more than five million Ethiopians are affected by food shortages due to drought and the ongoing border conflict with Eritrea.

10 November 1999   Ethiopian court finds former Derg officials Getachew Terbaa and Kebede Kebret guilty of torture and murder. The two, who probably are living overseas, are sentenced to death in absentia. About half of the 5,200 former Derg administrators and military officers accused of similar crimes remain in custody.

24 November 1999   Ethiopia and the American firm Sicor conclude an agreement for a $1.4 billion venture to develop natural gas fields in the Ogaden near the Somali border.

22 December 1999   Ethiopian deputy prime minister and minister of defense Tefera Walwa travels to Moscow to discuss Ethiopia's debt for military supplies acquired during the Mengistu regime. The two nations fail to settle this issue.

3–5 March 2000   Ethiopian-Sudanese joint ministerial commission, meeting in Khartoum, agrees to build a railway between Port Sudan and Moyale. There are two options.

16 March 2000   Federal Supreme Court sentences former deputy prime minister and defense minister Tamrat Layne to 18 years, imprisonment on charges of corruption and misuse of power.

31 March 2000   UN appeals for $200 million worth of food aid for an estimated 12 million people facing imminent starvation in the Horn of Africa, some 8 million of whom are in Ethiopia.

1 April 2000   Addis Ababa rejects an offer by Asmara to use the port of Asab to deliver food aid to Ethiopian famine victims as a "public relations gimmick."

21 April 2000   London-based International Institute for Strategic Studies estimates that Ethiopia's 1999 defense budget totaled $467 million, up from about $140 million prior to the start of the war with Eritrea.

17 May 2000   UN Security Council adopts Resolution 1298, which imposes a one-year arms embargo on Ethiopia and Eritrea.

18 June 2000	Ethiopia and Eritrea sign a cessation of hostilities agreement in Algiers.
7 July 2000	Ethiopia's DPPC announces that the number of people affected by the current drought and humanitarian crisis has reached 10.5 million.
29 August 2000	Russian president Vladimir Putin signs a decree barring Russian arms sales to Ethiopia and Eritrea. Nevertheless, Russia continues to sell arms to both countries.
24 October 2000	World Bank announces that Ethiopia's total foreign debt is $5.5 billion.
24 October 2000	Ethiopian United Patriotic Front, Ethiopian United Democratic Patriotic Movement, Ethiopian United Democratic Forces Front, and Benishangul People's Liberation Movement agree to unite under the name Ethiopian People's Patriotic Front and to fight to overthrow the Meles regime.
30 October 2000	UN Secretary General Kofi Annan appoints Major General Patrick Cammaert (Dutch) as UN Mission to Ethiopia and Eritrea commander. He commences his duties on 1 November 2000.
8 December 2000	House of People's Representatives approves the proposed peace treaty with Eritrea.
12 December 2000	Ethiopian prime minister Meles Zenawi and Eritrean president Isaias Afeworki sign peace agreement in Algiers ending 30 months of war.
10 January 2001	U.S. fails to persuade the UN Security Council to lift arms embargo against Ethiopia and Eritrea.
10 February 2001	Ethiopia and Djibouti agree to a new tariff structure at the Port Autonome International de Djibouti.

15–18 March 2001 TPLF Central Committee convenes a meeting in Mekele, where a group of hard-liners, led by Minister of Defense Seye Abraha, attacks Prime Minister Meles for abandoning TPLF principles. However, the Central Committee voted 17–12 in Meles' favor after the hard-liners walk out of the meeting.

24 March 2001 Prime Minister Meles denounces a plot by a TPLF "dissenting group" that criticized him for being too liberal toward Eritrea and following Western formulas for improving the economy.

4 April 2001 Ethiopia begins notifying the families of soldiers who were killed in the war with Eritrea.

5 April 2001 Ethiopia and the Paris Club sign a debt-relief agreement canceling and rescheduling 67 percent of the $430 million debt Ethiopia was due to pay creditors until 31 March 2004.

17–18 April 2001 University students and jobless youths riot in Addis Ababa. Police kill at least 41 people (the government maintains only 31 are killed) and injure some 250 others.

23 April 2001 Independent Ethiopian newspapers claim police have jailed about 2,300 people in the wake of the riots in Addis Ababa. The government maintains that this number is grossly inflated.

11 May 2001 Office of the Special Public Prosecutor announces that the trials of defendants indicted on charges of genocide and crimes against humanity will be concluded over the next three years.

29 May 2001 Russia cancels $4.8 billion of debt run up by the Mengistu regime. This sum constitutes 80 percent of Ethiopia's total debt to Russia.

22 June 2001	President Negaso Gidada resigns from the EPRDF after clashing with Prime Minister Meles during an acrimonious debate within the EPRDF's Central Committee.
11 August 2001	Almaz Meko, speaker of Ethiopia's upper house of parliament, arrives in the U.S. and seeks political asylum because she fears government retribution for her outspoken support of the Oromo people.
8 October 2001	Both houses of parliament unanimously elect 77-year-old Girma Wolde-Giorgis as president. Two days later, he goes to Saudi Arabia for medical attention.
15 October 2001	Council of People's Representatives passes legislation that establishes a National Security Council.
30 October 2001	Germany forgives more than half of Ethiopia's $24 million debt.
2 November 2001	Ninth Bench of the Federal First Instance Court nullifies a charge filed by 10 TPLF members who had been expelled from the party during a power struggle with Prime Minister Meles.
12 November 2001	IMF announces that Ethiopia has become eligible for debt relief under the World Bank–IMF Heavily Indebted Poor Countries Initiative.
23 November 2001	Ethiopian News Agency announces that Ethiopia's foreign debt has declined to $5.2 billion. In 1999, Ethiopia's foreign debt was $10.2 billion.
3 December 2001	Ethiopia and Russia sign a friendship and cooperation agreement.

7 December 2001	House of People's Representatives passes legislation that will enable Ethiopia to export apparel and other products to the U.S. under the Africa Growth and Opportunity Act.
10 December 2001	Border Commission begins hearing the cases of Ethiopia and Eritrea in The Hague.
11 December 2001	Ethiopian Ministry of Health announces that there are about one million AIDS orphans in Ethiopia.
17 December 2001	Ethiopia and the U.S. sign a debt reduction and rescheduling agreement that amounts to a savings of some $100 million annually over the next 20 years.
12 April 2002	Ethiopia and Djibouti conclude an agreement on the utilization of Djibouti port.
8 July 2002	Ethiopia (Lieutenant General Samora Yonus) and Russia (General Anatoly Kvashnin) sign a military cooperation agreement.
26 July 2002	UNDP announces that Ethiopians are as poor now as they were 20 years ago and per capita income is the same as it was in the early 1980s. According to the UN's Human Development Index, Ethiopia is the world's sixth poorest country.
10–19 October 2002	Ethiopia sponsors a meeting of 25 delegates from 15 Eritrean opposition groups to create an alternative government in anticipation of the downfall of President Isaias.
15 October 2002	Ethiopian, Sudanese, and Yemeni officials meet in Sanaa to discuss "regional security issues." Eritrea denounces the three countries as an "Axis of Belligerence."

6 November 2002   Prime Minister Meles dissolves Addis Ababa's city council for incompetence. A new transitional authority will govern the capital until a new city council is elected in 2005.

12 November 2002   WFP warns that 10 million to 14 million Ethiopians will require food aid in 2003.

26 November 2002   Ethiopia announces that all 1,568 Eritrean prisoners of war have been freed.

2 December 2002   EAL suspends flights to Israel after one of its planes is forced to land at a military installation because of questions over security at Bole International Airport.

5 December 2002   Prime Minister Meles meets President George W. Bush and several other senior American government officials to discuss issues including the global war on terrorism.

29 January 2003   U.S. cancels nearly $29.2 million in debt. Ethiopia agrees to use the money saved from this debt write-off to support the country's Poverty Reduction Strategy.

18 March 2003   U.S. announces that Ethiopia and 29 other nations have joined the "coalition of the willing" that supports Washington's policy toward Iraq.

20 March 2003   Ethiopia grants the U.S. military flyover rights and access to its military bases to support the global war on terrorism.

1 April 2003   Ethiopia announces that it will deploy 950–1,000 troops to Burundi as part of the African Union's African Mission in Burundi.

15 April 2003   Ethiopia announces that it will become one of the first African countries to manufacture antiretroviral drugs to treat HIV/AIDS patients.

12 May 2003   Eritrea announces that any further dialogue about the Eritrea-Ethiopia Boundary Commission's border decision is "unthinkable."

27 May 2003   Prime Minister Meles brands the Eritrea-Ethiopia Boundary Commission's border decision as "wrong and unjust."

2 June 2003   WFP announces that it is facing a $90 million shortfall for its emergency operations to feed some 12.5 million Ethiopians who are in danger of starvation.

12 June 2003   *Nature* magazine reports that the three 160,000-year-old skulls that had been found in 1997 in a valley bordering the Awash River are probably "immediate ancestors of anatomically modern humans."

23 June 2003   U.S. announces that it will provide $100 million to Ethiopia, Kenya, Tanzania, Uganda, and Djibouti to improve their counterterrorism capabilities.

10 July 2003   U.S. announces that it will conduct a three-month antiterrorism course for Ethiopian troops at Hurso Military Training Camp, northwest of Dire Dawa.

20 August 2003   Ethiopia announces that it will deploy peacekeeping troops to Liberia.

15 September 2003   United Ethiopian Democratic Forces, a coalition of 15 opposition groups that had been established in the U.S., begins operations in Ethiopia.

8 October 2003   UN Population Fund reports that Ethiopia's population has reached 70.7 million, the third largest number in Africa after Nigeria and Egypt.

9 October 2003   Eritrea rules out further negotiations with Ethiopia over the border demarcation process because of an impasse over the status of Badme and Irob.

9 October 2003   Berlin-based Transparency International ranks Ethiopia 92 out of 133 countries in its annual corruption report.

24 October 2003   UN announces that the demarcation of the Ethiopia-Eritrea border has been postponed as a result of Addis Ababa's rejection of some parts of the Eritrea-Ethiopia Boundary Commission's ruling.

4 November 2003   The defense trial of Mengistu Haile Mariam, who is facing genocide charges, begins in Addis Ababa, and 37 senior Derg officials appear in court to answer charges about their involvement in the Red Terror campaign.

Introduction

Ethiopia is a country rich in history, varied in topography, ethnicity, and climate, and blessed with physical beauty. Although briefly occupied militarily by Italy, Ethiopia never experienced colonial rule. Its proud national character and relatively undeveloped infrastructure reflect the absence of a colonial past. Ethiopia is the third most populous country on the African continent. Due in part to its large and fast-growing population, Ethiopia on a per capita basis is one of the poorest countries in the world. It lacks major mineral or oil wealth. With the important exception of coffee, most of its agricultural output goes to feed its people. In recent decades, Ethiopia has been a food-deficient country and has experienced periodic famines.

Ethiopian history is well documented and often linked to the Ethiopian Orthodox Church (EOC) and occasional competition with Islam. Today, both religions and a smaller group of Protestants affect the lives of all but a small minority of Ethiopians. The borders of Ethiopia have waxed and waned over the centuries, reaching their current limits minus Eritrea only about 100 years ago. The core of Ethiopia, or Abyssinia as it was often called, has been the highlands in the central and northern part of the country. Ethiopia has two principal cultural groups: those people who live in the highlands and are primarily settled agriculturists and those who live in the lowlands, many of whom are pastoralists.

LAND AND PEOPLE

Ethiopia is the center of the Horn of Africa and shares a boundary with Djibouti, Eritrea, Kenya, Somalia, and Sudan. The borders with Somalia and Sudan are about 1,000 miles (1,609 kilometers) long while those with the other three countries are considerably shorter. At 435,000 square miles (1,126,645 square kilometers), Ethiopia is larger than California and Texas combined. In 1993, Ethiopia lost its Red Sea coastline when Eritrea became independent; it is now a landlocked country.

Ethiopia's bedrock constitutes part of the earth's first continent of Gondwanaland, of which Africa is the largest intact remnant. The Great Rift Valley running from the southwest border to Djibouti dissects the country. A massive highland plateau covers most of Ethiopia to the north and west of the Rift. A smaller highland plateau extends into a significant part of Ethiopia south and east of the Rift. Lakes punctuate the Rift Valley floor in the south and center while the Awash River and Danakil Depression are the main features in the north central area.

Ethiopia has more than 20 mountains in excess of 13,000 feet; Mount Dashen in the Simien Mountains is the fourth highest in Africa. At the other extreme is the Danakil Depression, one of the hottest places on Earth at 410 feet (125 meters) below sea level. Ethiopia boasts one of the world's larger lakes, Lake Tana, and a small part of another, Turkana, known as Lake Rudolph until 1975, most of which is in neighboring Kenya. Ethiopia is blessed with rivers, the most important being the Blue Nile, which flows for 850 miles (1,370 kilometers) through Ethiopia and Sudan before joining the White Nile at Khartoum, the capital of Sudan. The Blue Nile and several other Ethiopian tributaries contribute 86 percent of the water that ultimately reaches the Aswan Dam in Egypt. Ethiopia's other major rivers are the Awash, Omo, and Wabe Shebelle. Ethiopia has significant hydropower potential.

Generally poor in natural resources, Ethiopia does produce modest quantities of gold and has small reserves of platinum, copper, and potash. There are large reserves of unexploited natural gas located in the politically unstable and isolated Ogaden Region inhabited by Somalis. Some of the rich oil fields now being exploited in neighboring Sudan may extend across the border into Ethiopia. Much of Ethiopia's soil is seriously degraded. Only an estimated 12 percent of the land is arable, about 40 percent is permanent pasturage, and 25 percent consists of generally sparse forests and woodlands. The remainder has minimal productive value.

Located north of the equator, Ethiopia has many different climates that are determined largely by varying altitude. The capital, Addis Ababa, which is about 8,000 feet (2,438 meters) above sea level, has a temperate climate throughout the year. There is usually very little rain in the capital from October through May. Rain is often heavy and occasionally continuous for several days at a time from June through September. Temperatures can be icy cold in the high Simien and Bale mountain ranges. Much of the highlands experiences a temperate climate like that found in Addis Ababa while some of the lowlands have torrid temperatures. As one climbs from the lowlands to the highlands, the temperature and rainfall change accordingly. The timing and quantity of the rain are the keys to Ethiopia's grain production.

In 2003, Ethiopia's population was about 70 million people, making it the third most populous country on the continent after Nigeria and Egypt. Due in part to the imprecise impact of human immunodeficiency virus/acquired immune deficiency syndrome (HIV/AIDS), estimates of the population growth rate range between 2.4 and 2.8 percent. Life expectancy at birth is dropping. The estimates vary between 42 and 45 years. About 17 percent of Ethiopia's population now lives in an urban setting, a relatively low figure even for a developing country.

Ethiopians speak more than 70 languages as mother tongues; a few are spoken by many millions and some by only a few thousand persons. Most of the languages fall within three families—Semitic, Cushitic, and Omotic—of the Afro-Asiatic super language family. The other languages are in the Nilo-Saharan super language family.

Amharic is the most important of the Ethio-Semitic languages. The official language, it is used widely in government and business and serves as the lingua franca for most of the country. There are parts of Ethiopia where the indigenous people speak little if any Amharic, especially in Somali and Afar regions and other peripheral areas. Tigrinya, spoken by the Tigray people, is the second most widespread Ethio-Semitic language. The Gurage speak seven different Ethio-Semitic languages. Small numbers of Ethiopians speak Tigre, which is related to Tigrinya. Two other groups that speak Ethio-Semitic languages are the Harari and the Argobba.

Oromiffa is the most important Cushitic language in Ethiopia. The Oromo live in both the highland and lowland parts of Ethiopia. Several Cushitic-speaking groups live in the far south, the most numerous being the Konso. The Somali, Afar, and Saho, all Cushitic-speaking peoples, share a pastoral tradition. Sidamo is often used to describe a group of languages, the most important being Sidamo and Hadya-Libido.

There are six groups of Agew Cushitic speakers in the central highlands.

Many small groups that speak languages of the Omotic family live between the lakes of southern Ethiopia's Rift Valley and the Omo River. There are as many as 80 different groups, although some of them speak dialects of the same language. The Wolaytta-speakers are the most numerous followed by those who speak Gemu-Gofa. Of the four language groups represented in Ethiopia, the smallest number of people speak a Nilo-Saharan language. The most important of these are Nuer and Anuak, spoken by persons who live along the border with Sudan in the southwest. The Kunema and Nara speakers are located in western Tigray. The Berta and the Gumuz live along the central part of the border with Sudan.

Ethiopia's ethnic groups correspond roughly to these language groups. The most numerous are the Oromo at about 40 percent of the population. Amhara account for perhaps 25 percent, Tigrayans about 7 percent, Somali 6 percent, and Afar 4 percent. The various Sidamo peoples probably constitute about 9 percent and the Gurage about 2 percent. Many small groups make up the remainder. Historically, the Amhara have held a disproportionate amount of political power while the Oromo have been underrepresented. Tigrayans are now in a particularly strong position in the central government.

The EOC was usually a central part of the power structure during periods of Amhara and Tigrayan rule. Relations between Christians and Muslims have historically been both cordial and hostile. Islamic leaders have not forgotten that Ethiopia gave refuge to members of the Prophet's family in the seventh century. At the same time, there is the legacy of the Islamic invasion of Ethiopia in the 16th and 19th centuries. There was a close EOC-state link until the overthrow of the imperial government (1974), when left-wing revolutionaries disestablished the EOC and declared all religions equal. The current government repaired relations with the EOC and has tried hard to develop harmonious relations with both Muslims and Protestants.

The Amhara and Tigrayans are almost entirely Ethiopian Orthodox. The Oromo are mainly Muslim, but have significant numbers of Orthodox and Protestants. The Somali and Afar and smaller related groups are almost entirely Muslim. Many of the Omotic-speaking peoples in the south are followers of indigenous practices, but Protestant missionaries have made some inroads. The small ethnic groups along the Sudan border tend to be Muslim. There are also a few pockets of Roman Catholics scattered about Ethiopia. Ethiopian Orthodox and Muslims probably account for about 45 percent each of the population. Protestantism may have reached almost 5 percent of the population while animists account for the remainder.

HISTORY

Recent discoveries in the Rift Valley of hominid (i.e., erect-walking human ancestors) teeth and bone fragments date back about 4.5 million years. Ethiopia may be the origin of humankind, although more recent findings in Chad put this in doubt. These discoveries are known as *Australopithecus ramidus*. The partial skeleton of the more famous Lucy, also found in Ethiopia's Rift Valley, is known scientifically as *Australopithecus afarensis* and dates back 2.9 to 3.4 million years.

Linguistic evidence suggests that both Cushitic and Omotic speakers were living in Ethiopia by about 7000 B.C. Northern Ethiopia probably established contact with southwestern Arabia across the Red Sea by 2000 B.C. Persons from Arabia began to arrive in Ethiopia by the first millennium B.C., bringing with them Semitic speech, writing, and a stone building tradition. From these contacts the Ge'ez language, a forerunner of Amharic, developed. The newcomers joined with indigenous inhabitants, producing a pre-Axumite culture.

A unique African civilization emerged at the beginning of the first millennium A.D. in the northern highlands of Ethiopia and Eritrea. Axum, located in present-day Tigray Region, flourished for almost seven centuries and became one of the most powerful kingdoms of the ancient world. Thriving on trade, the Axumite state was strongest between the third and sixth centuries. The kingdom extended across the Red Sea into southern Arabia and west into Sudan's Nile Valley. Axum was rich, well organized, and technically and artistically advanced. It produced coinage in bronze, silver, and gold and erected extraordinary monuments. Christianity came to Ethiopia during this period.

Islam from the Arabian Peninsula had a significant impact on Axum during the seventh and eighth centuries. Islam's expansion in Egypt and the Levant reduced Axum's influence and hastened the church's isolation.

Trade and the economy declined and hard times set in. Power in Ethiopia shifted southwards. Military colonies drawing on Axumite culture, the Semitic language and Christianity began to develop around the Agaw population. By the 10th century, a post-Axumite Christian kingdom emerged in the central northern highlands and extended to the Red Sea. During the 11th and 12th centuries, this culture expanded throughout that part of Ethiopia inhabited by the Amhara people.

In about 1137, the Zagwe dynasty, based in the Agaw district of Lasta, came to power. Strong Christians, the Zagwe built the rock-hewn churches of Lalibela. But unhappiness with rule from Lasta developed in Eritrea and Tigray and among the Amhara. About 1270, an Amhara noble, Yekuno Amlak, overthrew the last Zagwe leader and proclaimed himself as king. He restored the Solomonic dynasty, which claimed descent from Axum and King Solomon in ancient Israel. According to Ethiopian tradition, the lineage of Axumite kings originated with the offspring of an alleged union between Solomon and the Queen of Sheba. Shoa Province became the geographical and political center of the Christian kingdom under Yekuno Amlak. A succession of Amhara leaders expanded the territory under their control. Zara Yakob, who reigned from 1434 to 1468, was one of the most important kings to further this expansion.

Islamic raids from the Somali port of Zeila plagued Christian Ethiopia during the 1490s. Although the Ethiopians put the raids down, Ahmad ibn Ibrahim al Ghazi, known as "Gran the Left-Handed," led a jihad against Ethiopia early in the 16th century designed to end Christian power. By 1532, he had overrun most of eastern and southern Ethiopia. The Ethiopians, aided by a Portuguese force, defeated the Muslim army and killed Gran in 1543. Weakened by the Muslim attacks, the Ethiopian highlands became pressured to the south and southeast by migrations of the pastoral Oromo, who also had penetrated into the highlands.

Emperor Fasilidas, who reigned from 1632 to 1667, reasserted central authority and reinvigorated the Solomonic monarchy. Ruling from Gondar, Ethiopia experienced a flowering of architecture and art. Successive Gondar kings relied upon Oromo military units to counter challenges to their rule. Gondar became consumed with court intrigue and faced a serious challenge from Tigray. The central government self-destructed and emperors became little more than puppets in the hands of rival feudal lords and their armies. From 1769 until 1855, the central kingdom ceased to exist as a coherent entity.

Crowned emperor in 1855, Tewodros II was the first leader of what is generally known as modern Ethiopia. Ruling from the natural fortress of Maqdala, Tewodros II established a national army and worked to reform the land system, abolish slavery, and promote Amharic as the national language in place of Ge'ez. Tewodros II imprisoned several British functionaries in his court at Maqdala. A large British force defeated Tewodros II, who committed suicide (1868) and left a disorganized kingdom. His demise weakened Ethiopia and encouraged the European powers to consider colonizing Ethiopia.

Following Tewodros II's suicide, Yohannes IV, a Tigrayan, became emperor (1872). Yohannes IV defeated Egyptian forces that advanced on Ethiopia from Eritrea. In 1888, a large Islamic army of Mahdists attacked Ethiopia from Sudan, sacking Gondar and burning many of its churches. The following year, Yohannes defeated the Mahdist forces at Metemma on the Sudanese border but died in the battle.

In 1889, Menelik II claimed the throne and within 10 years established control over much of present-day Ethiopia. He located the capital at Addis Ababa and embarked on military conquests to the south that more than doubled the size of the empire. European powers, especially Italy, began to cast a covetous eye on Ethiopia. In 1885, Italian forces invaded Tigray from Eritrea. During a pitched battle the following year near the Tigrayan capital of Adwa, Menelik humiliated the Italian forces, inflicting the first defeat on a European power by an African army.

Following Menelik's death in 1913, his grandson briefly held power, to be replaced soon after by Menelik's daughter. Ras Tafari Makonnen, later to become emperor, served as the prince regent. In 1926, he took control of the government and signed a 20-year friendship agreement with Italy. Crowned emperor in 1930, Ras Tafari Makonnen took the name Haile Selassie. He introduced the first written constitution and encouraged reforms and modernization of the country.

Although Italy reaffirmed its friendship treaty with Ethiopia in 1934, it provoked an incident the same year at Wal Wal in Ethiopia's Somali-inhabited Ogaden region bordering Italian Somalia. Benito Mussolini concluded this was enough of an excuse to attack Ethiopia without a declaration of war. The Fascists invaded Ethiopia from their bases in Eritrea and Italian Somalia. The League of Nations declared Italy an aggressor but took no effective action. Superior Italian armaments and the use of chemical weapons overwhelmed the Ethiopians, who had difficulty obtaining adequate weapons. Ethiopian forces fought on for seven months. On 2 May 1936, Haile Selassie went into exile in Britain and Italian forces entered Addis Ababa.

Italy merged Ethiopia with Eritrea and Somalia to create the new colonial territory of Africa Orientale Italiana (Italian East Africa). Ethiopians resisted Italian rule; Mussolini's response was brutal. The outbreak of World War II changed the course of events in Ethiopia. Italy's declaration of war against Britain led the latter to provide assistance to Ethiopian patriots operating along the Sudan-Ethiopia border. Britain launched attacks against the Italians, one of which was led by Haile Selassie. On 5 May 1941, the emperor and his forces entered Addis Ababa. Until March 1951, the British Military Administration remained in Ethiopia but the emperor was responsible for internal affairs.

During the postwar period, Haile Selassie focused on reconstruction and reform. His government established a national bank, airline, currency, and university. He was less successful at land reform and most land remained in the possession of the nobility and the church. The government was autocratic with real power in the emperor's hands. Some Ethiopians considered the pace of modernization too slow and nearly overthrew the emperor while he was visiting Brazil in 1960. Although the coup ultimately failed, it put into question the ability of the imperial system to withstand the political changes sweeping through Africa.

The two regions posing the greatest challenge to the empire were Eritrea and the Somali-inhabited Ogaden. In 1952, the United Nations installed an autonomous Eritrean government linked to Ethiopia through a loose federal structure under the emperor's sovereignty. In 1962, the Eritrean Assembly, many of whose members had been accused of taking bribes, voted unanimously to change Eritrea's status to a province of Ethiopia. This decision energized Eritrean groups that already opposed incorporation into Ethiopia. An armed conflict between these groups and Ethiopian forces plagued Haile Selassie and his successor until the Eritreans achieved military victory almost 30 years later. The new independent government in Somalia also challenged Ethiopian control over the Ogaden.

Near the end of his rule, Haile Selassie faced increasing pressure from students and other groups for faster reform. Inflation and corruption persisted at a time when Haile Selassie was growing old and being isolated by his advisers. The final straw was a famine in 1972–1974,

INTRODUCTION • lv

causing the death of as many as 200,000 peasants. The government mishandled the famine and tried to hide it from the outside world. On 12 September 1974, a group of left-wing military officers known as the Derg took advantage of the situation by deposing the emperor and seizing power. Major Mengistu Haile Mariam emerged as the leader of the Derg. He embarked on a socialist path and made preparations to launch a new offensive against the growing threat of Eritrean secession.

The Derg nationalized all land, abolished tenancy, and put peasants in charge of enforcement. Internal political groups began to challenge Mengistu for control of the revolution. He dealt severely with this opposition. The most famous campaign, known as the Red Terror, occurred in 1977–1978 and resulted in the death of up to 100,000 political opponents. This coincided with a growing threat in the Ogaden from an indigenous Somali liberation group supported by neighboring Somalia. Mengistu obtained military support from the Soviet Union and Cuba to end the Ogaden War. In the meantime, a new challenge developed in Tigray—the Tigray People's Liberation Front (TPLF).

As Ethiopia became more closely allied to the Soviet Union, it announced that its single political party was a genuine communist party and the government took on the trappings of a Marxist-Leninist state. A horrific famine followed the drought of 1984–1985 in which hundreds of thousands of Ethiopians died. War with the Eritreans and the TPLF aggravated the disaster. Food production continued to decline. The economy was in free fall by the late 1980s as the Eritreans and TPLF continued their military victories. In 1989, the numerous Ethiopian opposition groups united to form the Ethiopian People's Revolutionary Democratic Front (EPRDF). In 1991, pressure from the EPRDF and the Eritreans caused the Mengistu government to fall. Ethiopian-Eritrean relations remained cordial until 1998, when a conflict broke out along their border. Following a huge military buildup in both countries and tens of thousands of casualties, Ethiopia won a decisive military victory in 2000. A United Nations force is monitoring the border area.

GOVERNMENT AND POLITICS

In 1991, Meles Zenawi emerged as the leader of a transitional government in Ethiopia. Isaias Afwerki assumed control of Eritrea and established a provisional government that remained in effect until 1993, when the Eritreans voted for independence. Ethiopia accepted the new Eritrean government, causing Ethiopia to become a landlocked country with the loss of the Eritrean coastline. In 1994, Ethiopians elected a Constituent Assembly and adopted a constitution for the Federal Democratic Republic of Ethiopia. In 1995, elections for the national parliament and regional legislatures took place. Most opposition parties boycotted them, ensuring a landslide victory for the EPRDF.

National legislative elections take place every five years; they were last held in 2000 and are not scheduled again until 2005. The people directly elect the 548 members of the House of People's Representatives (lower house). State assemblies choose the 117-member House of Federation (upper house). In 2000, candidates representing the ruling EPRDF won 483 of the 548 lower-chamber seats. Regional parties won 46 seats and independents 8 seats with the remainder not specified. The House of People's Representatives nominates the president, who is then elected by a two-thirds vote during a joint session with the House of Federation. The president holds office for six years. Although the president serves as chief of state, his role is largely ceremonial.

The prime minister is the head of government and, together with the Council of Ministers, holds the highest executive powers. The prime minister is a member of, and is elected by, the House of People's Representatives for a five-year term. Meles Zenawi has held this position since 1995. The prime minister is the chief executive, chairman of the Council of Ministers, and commander in chief of the armed forces. The prime minister appoints most senior officials to the federal government and is in charge of the country's foreign policy.

Real executive power on key policy issues lies with the EPRDF, an umbrella organization for a number of essentially ethnic-based political parties. The major parties that comprise the EPRDF are the Tigray People's Liberation Front (TPLF), the Amhara National Democratic Movement (ANDM), and the Oromo People's Democratic Organization (OPDO). The TPLF, which played the primary role in overthrowing the Mengistu regime, holds a disproportionate amount of power. There is usually considerable discussion within the EPRDF, however, before it makes key decisions.

Opposition political parties have existed since the fall of the Derg in 1991. The leadership of one important organization, the Oromo Liberation Front (OLF), is now in exile and dedicated to the overthrow of the

EPRDF government. Other parties continue to operate within Ethiopia. They include the All Amhara People's Organization (AAPO), now the All Ethiopia Unity Party (AEUP), Coalition of Alternative Forces for Peace and Democracy, Ethiopian Democratic Union (EDU), and Ethiopian National Democratic Party. The EPRDF controls radio and television and much of the written media. There are, however, opposition newspapers, some of which are outspoken in criticism of the government.

Ethiopia's federal system of government has two sets of courts and jurisdictions. There is a three-tiered federal system. At the bottom are the Federal High and Federal First Instance Courts, which are established as necessary by the House of Peoples' Representatives. At the top of the structure is the Federal Supreme Court, which is established automatically by the constitution. Each region or state also has a three-tiered system of State Supreme, High, and First Instance courts.

Ethnic federalism is the most radical and controversial EPRDF policy. Each region or state has its own executive branch headed by a president and supported by functional department heads. Ethiopia has nine ethnically based regions or states and two chartered cities. The regions are Afar; Amhara; Benishangul/Gumuz; Gambela; Harar; Oromia; Somali; Southern Nations, Nationalities and People's Region (SNNPR); and Tigray. The two chartered cities are Addis Ababa and Dire Dawa. The regions and chartered cities are divided into 68 zones; each zone has its own administrative structure that reports to the regional government. The zones are subdivided into 526 districts, known locally as *woredas*, which also have administrative responsibilities. The districts are further subdivided into thousands of *kebeles* or neighborhood/rural organizations. Regional governments can raise their own revenue; the kebeles have the authority to create local militias.

ECONOMY

The EPRDF believes that the agricultural sector should be the driving force for the rest of the economy. It has emphasized new technology, use of fertilizer, improved seed, and extension services. Other EPRDF policies include improved taxation administration, the establishment of a competitive financial system, increased private investment, and poverty reduction. Structural reforms include modernizing monetary management, improving inter-bank operations, strengthening the soundness of smaller banks, and upgrading management of the state-owned Commercial Bank of Ethiopia.

The structure of Ethiopia's economy has changed little in recent years. Agriculture continues to contribute more than 50 percent of gross domestic product (GDP). Industry's contribution to GDP has remained static at about 10 percent. The service sector has increased to about 25 percent of GDP from 20 percent during the Derg. The distributive sector remains at about 10 percent. Ethiopia's real GDP under the EPRDF has grown on average at a rate of about 6 percent annually. The per capita GDP growth rate has averaged about 2.6 percent in recent years. The Ethiopian economy has performed modestly under the EPRDF. Perhaps the biggest surprise is the fact that the economy has done as well as it has in spite of a $3 billion expenditure on a war with Eritrea.

Ethiopia is divided into two major agricultural zones, the highlands and the lowlands. The highlands constitute about 40 percent of the land area and the lowlands 60 percent. About 25 percent of the land area is intensively or moderately cultivated. Animals graze on most of the remainder, although some areas are so steep, eroded, and/or lacking in water that they serve virtually no agricultural purpose. Farming techniques are generally backward but becoming more progressive. In the final analysis, the rains or lack thereof determine the size and quality of the food crop. The major cereal crops are teff (used in making *injera*), wheat, barley, corn, millet, and sorghum. Pulses are the second most important element in the national diet.

The most important cash crop is coffee. As many as 15 million Ethiopians depend on the production, processing, trade, and transport of coffee for their livelihood. Other cash crops include cotton, sugar, tea, tobacco, and khat, a mild stimulant that is illegal in the United States. Livestock contribute an estimated 30–35 percent of agricultural GDP and about 15 percent of overall GDP. Cattle account for 70 percent of this value, sheep and goats 14 percent, and poultry 13 percent. Ethiopia may have as many as 80 million head of livestock and 60 million fowl.

Ethiopian exports total almost a $1 billion. Five products—coffee, hides and skins, oil seeds, pulses, and vegetables—account for about 80 percent of total export earnings. Coffee alone traditionally provides about two-thirds of the merchandise export earnings, although a 60 percent drop in coffee prices from 1997 to 2001 has decreased its importance. Most Ethiopian exports go to Germany, Japan, Djibouti, Saudi Arabia, France, Britain, and Italy. Capital and consumer goods account for two-thirds of imports and semi-finished products for most of the rest. The dollar cost of imports is about $1.25 billion and includes fuel, fertilizer, vehicles, machinery, electrical products, metal, metal products, and cereal. The principal sources of supply are Saudi Arabia, Italy, the United States, and Japan.

Ethiopia has a relatively underdeveloped road system although there have been significant improvements in recent years. Ethiopia has about 18,000 miles (28,968 kilometers) of road. Since the closure of the Ethiopia-Eritrea border in 1998 and the loss of the port of Asab, the most important route for commerce is the one between Addis Ababa and the Gulf of Aden port of Djibouti. The only railroad in Ethiopia connects Addis Ababa and Djibouti. As a landlocked country, Ethiopia has no port but still retains a merchant marine of 12 ships. Ethiopian Airlines is one of the largest and most efficient in Africa with service throughout Africa and flights to Asia, Europe, and the United States. The telecommunications system is rudimentary and remains under government control. There are about 400,000 telephones in the country and several thousand Internet subscribers.

FUTURE PROSPECTS

Ethiopia has experienced almost constant conflict since the early 1960s except for the 1991–1998 period and since 2000. This conflict has detracted from the ability of successive governments to concentrate on economic development and poverty reduction. It has also contributed to Ethiopia's inability to produce enough food to feed its people. Until Ethiopia completes a sustained period with no significant conflict, it will not be able to improve the situation for the average Ethiopian. New problems include the negative financial implications of the expensive war with Eritrea, the urgency to demobilize many tens of thousands of soldiers and reintegrate them into society, and a schism within the EPRDF over past and future policies. Added to these problems are the continuing failures of Ethiopia to grow enough food, low coffee prices that adversely impact foreign exchange earnings, and a high population growth rate even as the HIV/AIDS epidemic ravages the country.

The challenges facing Ethiopia are huge. But they are not insurmountable. Except for some relatively minor security concerns along the border with Somalia and occasional threats from the Oromo Liberation Front, Ethiopia is now conflict free and has an opportunity to focus on economic development. Internal EPRDF political differences seem to be nearing resolution. The Ethiopian people are hardworking and the leadership is capable and generally progressive. There have been major improvements since 1991 in Ethiopia's infrastructure; most projects even continued without interruption during the 1998–2000 war with Eritrea. Ethiopia's partners in development have returned in force following peace with Eritrea. Relations with neighboring countries, except for Eritrea, are generally good. Ethiopia has proven that it has one of the strongest military organizations on the continent. It is, albeit belatedly, taking seriously the threat posed by HIV/AIDS. If Ethiopia can avoid new internal and external conflicts, it can make real progress in the coming years.

The Dictionary

– A –

ABAY. *See* BLUE NILE.

ABBADIE, ANTOINE D' (1810–1897). French-Irish astronomer, explorer, geodetist, geographer, physician, numismatist, philologist, and scientist. Born in Dublin on 3 January 1810. Abbadie received his early education from a governess. After passing his baccalaureate exams (1827), he enrolled in the University of Toulouse. In 1828, Abbadie's family moved to Paris, where he pursued legal and scientific studies.

In 1836, the French Academy of Sciences commissioned Abbadie to go to Brazil, where he conducted geodesic and magnetic surveys. In 1838, he traveled to **Massawa** via Cairo and the **Red Sea** with his younger brother Arnaud-Michel d'Abbadie (1815–1893). On 28 May 1838, the two arrived in **Gondar**, where they met with Liq Atsqu, an Ethiopian judge and legal scholar.

Antoine and Arnaud then parted company. The latter went to the region south of the **Blue Nile** and, during one of his expeditions, visited the river's source. Meanwhile, Antoine returned to Europe on a diplomatic mission to Britain and France on behalf of Sahle Dingel, **Ras Alula Qubi**, and other concerned officials who feared Egyptian encroachment in western Ethiopia.

The brothers reunited at Massawa to plan another journey to Gondar. However, a shooting accident required Antoine to get medical treatment in Aden and Cairo. Arnaud returned to the Blue Nile to conduct further explorations. In June 1842, Antoine finally arrived in Gondar and subsequently visited the Kingdom of **Enarya**, south of the Blue Nile. The local king, Abba Bagibo, arranged for Antoine to journey to **Kafa** kingdom. After returning to Gondar, Antoine learned

Amharic and studied and copied many religious manuscripts. In 1848, the brothers left Ethiopia for good.

Antoine spent the rest of his life carrying on research about his Ethiopian travels. His exploits earned widespread public recognition. In 1850, Antoine was made a Knight of the Legion of Honour. He also was elected a member of the Academy of Sciences (1867) and of the Bureau des Longitudes (1978). He died on 19 March 1897 and left his estate to the Academy of Sciences of Paris.

ABBA SALAMA, ABUNA (c. 1818–1867). Abuna of the **Ethiopian Orthodox Church** (EOC). Born in Egypt as Indriyas and educated in the Coptic Church and the Protestant mission in Cairo. In the early 1820s, he was elected and consecrated bishop of Ethiopia with the name Salama.

In 1841, he arrived in Ethiopia and quickly immersed himself in the political and ecclesiastical intrigues during the closing years of the **Zamana Masafent**. Salama supported **Dajazmach Webe Hayla Maryam,** who ruled the **Tigray region** and Semen (1831–1855), against **Ras Alula Qubi,** who controlled much of central and northern Ethiopia. In the religious arena, he supported the Qibat doctrine of the Ewostatian monks who believed Christ's nature was human and divine. The EOC regarded Qibat as heresy. As a result of this dispute, Salama spent most of his first 12 years in Ethiopia in exile in Tigray, where parts of the local population accepted the Qibat.

In 1854, Kassa Haylu arranged a reconciliation between Salama and the EOC. On 11 February 1855, Salama crowned Kassa Emperor **Tewodros II**. In return, Tewodros II expelled the Roman Catholic **missionaries** and allowed him to have a greater say over internal ecclesiastical affairs. Cooperation between the two ended in 1856, when the emperor's men arrested Salama, who subsequently threatened to excommunicate Tewodros II's supporters. The Egyptian patriarch of Alexandria, Qerlos, secured a temporary truce between Salama and Tewodros II. However, relations between the two soon deteriorated over the question of the EOC's landholdings. In 1864, Tewodros imprisoned Salama at Magdala, where he died on 25 October 1867. *See also* BASILIOS, ABUNA; EWOSTATEWOS; MATEWOS, ABUNA; PAULOS GEBRE-YOHANNES, ABUNA; TEWOFLOS (THEOPHILOS), ABUNA.

ABEBE AREGAI, RAS (1903–1960). Police officer, **patriot** commander, and government administrator. Born on 18 August 1903 in **Axum**. Abebe received a church education and private tutoring in **Amharic** and Ethiopian law and administration. He also attended Tafari Makonnen School in **Addis Ababa** before becoming a member of the staff of Tafari Makonnen's (later **Haile Selassie**). In 1930, Abebe joined the police. By the outbreak of the **Italian-Ethiopian War**, he was police chief of Addis Ababa with civil authority over the city. Unable to preserve law and order after Haile Selassie fled the capital on 2 May 1936, Abebe departed for **Shoa,** where he became an important symbol of Ethiopia's resistance to Italy. Abebe organized patriot fighters in **Ankober**, Gindeberet, Marabatie, and Menz, an area that went from the **Blue Nile** to the Kassam River. Italian attempts to defeat or co-opt him failed.

After liberation, he returned to Addis Ababa, where Haile Selassie confirmed the rank of **ras** that his followers had earlier conferred upon him. The emperor also named him governor of Addis Ababa (1941). Subsequent government appointments included the governorships of Sidamo (1941–1942) and **Tigray** (1943–1947). Abebe then served as minister of war (1947–1949), minister of interior (1949–1955), minister of defense (1955–1960), and chairman of the **Council of Ministers** (1957–1960). On 16 December 1960, Mengistu Newaye, commander of the **Imperial Body Guard** and one of the chief plotters during the **coup attempt (1960)**, shot and killed Abebe who had remained loyal to the emperor.

ABEBE BIKILA. *See* MARATHON AND DISTANCE RUNNERS.

ABETO. *See* IMPERIAL TITLES.

ABUNA (ABUNE). An Arabic word for "Our Father" that refers to the head of the **Ethiopian Orthodox Church**.

ABYE ABABA (1918–1974). Born of a **Shoan** family in **Addis Ababa** and educated at the Holeta (Genet) Military Academy. Abye fought with the **patriots** alongside British forces (1941). In 1942, he married **Haile Selassie**'s second daughter, Princess Tsehai, who died in childbirth the same year. His close relationship to the emperor ensured that he had a good career. Abye's posts included governor of **Wollega**

Province (1942–1943), acting minister of war (1943–1947), minister of war (1949–1955), ambassador to Paris (1955–1958), minister of justice (1958–1961), emperor's representative to Eritrea (1959–1964), and minister of interior (1961–1964). Between 28 February and 22 July 1974, he served as minister of defense and chief of staff. The **Derg** subsequently jailed and then executed him on 23 November 1974. *See also* BLOODY SATURDAY.

ABYSSINIA. In common usage, particularly by foreigners, until the end of **World War II**, Abyssinia was interchangeable with Ethiopia. Abyssinia comes from a corruption of the Arabic word *habesh,* which means "mixed breed." The Habeshat people from the southwest coast of Arabia and Yemen colonized the west coast of the **Red Sea**, now Eritrea and northern Ethiopia. Abyssinia makes its first appearance in a European book written in 1211 by the English writer Gervase of Tilbury. Strictly speaking, Abyssinians are only those people who live roughly in the area coincident with the former Axumite State, which controlled the northern **highlands** for the first seven centuries A.D.

References to Abyssinia experienced a renaissance during the **Italian-Ethiopian War** and Italian military occupation (1936–1941). Many foreign accounts of these events called the country Abyssinia despite the fact that the Abyssinian **population** inhabited a minority of the territory. Most Ethiopian authors and intellectuals preferred Ethiopia as the country designation. The government was known as the Imperial Ethiopian Government. All official postage stamps printed by the Ethiopian government beginning in 1894 and until the present time show Ethiopia as the name of the country. Ethiopia is a more suitable term to describe all the ethnic and **language** groups living within the country's present borders. Abyssinia is now rarely used.

ACQUIRED IMMUNE DEFICIENCY SYNDROME. *See* HUMAN IMMUNODEFICIENCY VIRUS/ACQUIRED IMMUNE DEFICIENCY SYNDROME (HIV/AIDS).

ADAL SULTANATE. The Adal sultanate (also called an emirate or state) was located in the southeastern part of the **Horn of Africa** east of the **Ifat sultanate**. In 1298, Marco Polo made one of the earliest western references to *Adal* in his *Travels. Adal* is a term that was sometimes vaguely used to refer to the Muslim **population** in the **lowlands** east of the highland Christian empire. Adal included much of the **Awash River** basin north to Lake Abbe on the current Ethiopian-Djiboutian border and the lowlands between **Shoa** Province and the port of Zeila in present-day Somaliland near the border with Djibouti. Zeila, which was inhabited by Arabs, **Somalis**, and **Afars**, was originally the center of Adal power. Shoa Province was dependent on Ifat and Adal, which contained the trade routes to ports on the Gulf of Aden. In 1415, the Christian **highlanders** defeated the sultan of Ifat; Adal then became the most important Muslim power east of the Christian empire.

In 1445, the Sultan of Adal challenged Emperor **Zara Yakob**'s rule over the sultanate. Zara Yakob won a major battle against the sultan and reintegrated Adal into the empire. Adal was virtually independent during the reign of **Baeda Mariam** (1468–1478). Baeda Mariam's son marched into Adal about 1478 and sacked the capital of Dakar but was soon set upon by a much larger Adal army and was lucky to escape with his life. There followed a period of mutual military incursions by Muslim and Christian forces. In 1517, **Lebna Dengel** won a major military victory over the sultan of Adal. This event coincided with the Portuguese destruction of Zeila in the same year. In 1520, the Muslims sought to regroup by moving their capital from Dakar to **Harar**. Adal and Zeila clawed their way back to importance.

The most important figure in Adal's history was **Ahmad ibn Ibrahim al Ghazi**. He lived initially in Harar but moved with some followers to Hubat outside Harar. Ahmad defeated the sultan in battle, returned to Harar, and appointed himself ruler. His followers gave him the title of imam. Ahmad had considerable popular support, easy access to firearms, religious fanaticism, and enormous leadership skills. His well-armed troops overran **Dawaro**, Bali, **Hadeya**, Ganz, Waj, Fatagar, and Ifat. His victories only came to an end when 400 Portuguese soldiers came to the aid of Emperor **Galawedos** and killed Ahmad on 21 February 1543. Adal rule quickly collapsed and Galawedos reestablished Christian rule in much of the area that had been captured by Ahmad. There was, however, more conflict between Adal and the Christian empire that continued through the reign of Sarsa Dengel (1564–1597).

By this time, the great **Oromo** migration was having a major impact on Adal. The Oromo reached the old capital of Dakar and almost to Harar, which survived as an independent state. In 1577, Adal moved its capital northeast to Awssa to escape the Oromo. Already exhausted by conflict with the Ethiopian highlands, Adal was in no condition to keep out the Oromo, who occupied much of Adal by the early 17th century. The Oromo were pressuring Awassa by mid-century. Adal effectively ceased to exist. *See also* AFAR REGION; HADEYA KINGDOM; OGADEN; SOMALI REGION.

ADAL TESSEMMA, RAS. *See* TAKLA HAYMANOT.

ADDIS ABABA. (2,638,500; estimated 2002 **population**.) Ethiopia's capital and the country's largest city. As a result of the severe **famine** and **food** shortages in rural areas in 2002–2003, there has been a major movement of people to the capital. Consequently, its population may have temporarily reached more than four million by early 2003.

The date of the city's establishment remains a matter of dispute. Some authorities maintain that Addis Ababa was created in 1886. According to another account, **Menelik II**, who was living at his capital in **Entoto**, a hill above present-day Addis Ababa, decided in 1887 to relocate to a slightly warmer, less windy and lower elevation. Addis Ababa's hot springs also were an attraction. Menelik II reportedly moved to Addis Ababa, which means "new flower," at the beginning of 1889. He was, however, crowned emperor near the end of 1889 at Entoto. Menelik II's personal physician indicated that the real beginning of Addis Ababa occurred in 1891 when the first stone house was built and the emperor distributed land to individuals to develop the new town. Visiting Addis Ababa in 1896, Augustus Wylde described it as a "conglomeration of hamlets." Writing a year later, Count Gleichen said the capital gave the appearance of a "gigantic camp." For a study of this period of the city's history, see Peter P. Garretson's *History of Addis Ababa from Its Foundation in 1886 to 1910*.

Addis Ababa grew rapidly in subsequent years. By 1910, the population had reached an estimated 60,000 to 70,000. Most estimates prior to the **Italian-Ethiopian War** indicated the population was about 100,000. There were a surprising number of foreigners included in these figures. More than a thousand foreigners lived there in 1910.

That figure grew to an estimated 2,000 to 2,500 just before the Italian invasion. By 1935, Addis Ababa had experienced major changes. A visiting foreign correspondent, Patrick Balfour, said it looked like a town from the American Midwest built on hills. Also, the numerous eucalyptus trees planted at the turn of the century were dense throughout the city. During the Italian occupation (1936–1941), the **Africa Orientale Italiana** administration undertook a massive modernization program. Some of the more notable accomplishments included the construction of a network of paved roads, a clean water supply, and a hydroelectric plant. There also was a renovation program for the central district, known as Arada to the Ethiopians and the Piazza to the Italians. During the **Derg** period (1974–1991), officials erected numerous Soviet-style monuments to the people.

Today, Addis Ababa is noisy, sprawling and vibrant. It has a moderate climate although there are frequent and sometimes heavy rains from June through August. Despite its large size and heavy vehicular traffic, it still has the flavor of a smaller town with goats, donkeys, and humanity competing with vehicles for space. Addis Ababa became the headquarters for the United Nations **Economic Commission for Africa** (1958) and the Organization of African Unity (now the **African Union**) (1963). The city hosts a number of museums, the most important being the National Museum and the Ethnological Museum. The Sheraton Hotel is one of Africa's most magnificent hotel and restaurant complexes.

ADDIS ABABA ACCORD (1972). Landmark treaty, brokered by **Haile Selassie** and the World Council of Churches, that marked a high point in Ethiopia's regional influence. On 27 February 1972, Ezboni Mondiri Gwonza, who represented the Southern Sudan Liberation Movement, and Mansour Khalid, Sudan's minister of foreign affairs, signed the accord in **Addis Ababa**. The agreement established autonomy and religious rights for the Southern Sudanese within a unified Sudan. It also created federalism by forming the Southern Sudan Provisional Government, Nile Provisional Government, Anyidi Revolutionary Government, the Sue River Revolutionary Government, and Sudan-Azania Government, all of which incorporated specific ethnic groups. However, the southern Sudanese **diaspora** undermined the accord by accusing those southerners who remained in the south and formed political parties of collaborating with Khartoum. In 1983, growing Islamic radicalism and a deteriorating **economy** caused Sudanese president Jaafar Nimieri to abrogate the accord. This action led to the creation of the Sudanese People's Liberation Movement/Army and other rebel groups who claimed to be fighting for self-determination, democracy, and religious rights. *See also* FOREIGN POLICY; KOKA DAM DECLARATION.

ADDIS ABABA–DJIBOUTI RAILWAY. The railway is 480 miles (781 kilometers) long. The majority of the track (412.5 miles; 660 kilometers) is in Ethiopia. On 9 March 1894, **Alfred Ilg** received a concession from **Menelik II** to establish the Paris-based Compagnie Impériale des Chemins de Fers Ethiopiens and to build a railway from Djibouti to the White Nile via **Harar** and **Entoto**. On 27 April 1896, France authorized the railway's construction in Djibouti. On 22 July 1901, the first train service operated between Djibouti and Douanle and, on 24 December 1901, the first train arrived in **Dire Dawa**. On 7 June 1917, the single-track railway reached **Addis Ababa**, after stopping at 38 stations.

The **Italian-Ethiopian War** and subsequent Italian occupation of Ethiopia (1936–1941) caused serious damage to the railway. During 1946–1947, Ethiopia, with French aid, re-equipped and modernized the railway and rebuilt bridges that Italian troops had destroyed. On 4 May 1946, Ethiopian and French Railway Company officials signed an agreement whereby the latter assumed control of the Ethiopian section of the railway while Addis Ababa became responsible for the administration of Dire Dawa, the Railway Reserve, and the region northwest of the railway. On 12 November 1959, France and Ethiopia concluded an agreement that moved the Compagnie Imperiale des Chemins de Fers Ethiopiens from Paris to Addis Ababa.

In recent years, the railway has suffered from neglect and occasional attacks by brigands or rebel groups like the **Oromo Liberation Front**. On 12 November 1993, France announced that it had concluded a $13,765,000 agreement with Ethiopia for the railway's rehabilitation. On 1 December 1994, the French Development Agency approved an aid package for track repair and technical assistance. There also were subsequent pledges from the European Union and the **World Bank**.

However, such activities failed to resolve all the railway's problems. Nevertheless, it played a vital role during the **Ethiopian-Eritrean War**, especially after Eritrea had barred Addis Ababa from using its ports. During the first half of 1999, for example, the railway registered a 43 percent increase in freight shipments. By the turn of the century, maintenance and management problems continued to plague the railway. *See also* ECONOMY; TRANSPORTATION.

ADDIS ABABA UNIVERSITY. *See* EDUCATION, UNIVERSITY.

ADULIS. *The Periplus of the Erythraen Sea*, written by a Greek sailor sometime in the first century A.D., was the first historical document that mentioned the ancient Axumite port of Adulis. Adulis, which was located some 31 miles (49 kilometers) south of **Massawa** in present day Eritrea, was first settled in the sixth century B.C. The port's trade links extended to the Mediterranean, Middle East, and Indian subcontinent. Its main exports included slaves, ivory, tortoise shell, rhinoceros horn, apes, hippopotamus hides, and obsidian. Imported goods included cloth, glassware, tools, gold and silver jewelry, copper, iron, and steel.

The eighth-century growth of **Islamic** power gradually diminished trade in the **Red Sea**. As a result, Adulis and other coastal ports lost their economic influence. This in turn reduced revenues to the Axumite state, which could no longer maintain its control over trade routes. Diminished revenues reduced the capabilities of its **armed forces** and weakened its control over lucrative trade routes. **Axum** therefore sought new markets in the rich, grain-growing areas of **Agaw** country. By the ninth century, the kingdom had established itself as far south as the Beshlo River. Meanwhile, Adulis had been sacked and the port had lost its former glory forever.

ADWA (ADOWA, ADUA). Long the capital of eastern **Tigray**, Adwa was an important commercial center linking the Ethiopian **highlands** to the **Red Sea**. Its importance in the 16th century caused the Portuguese Jesuits to establish their headquarters at Fremona. Nineteenth-century European travelers regularly passed through Adwa. Britain, British-occupied Egypt, and Ethiopia signed a tripartite treaty, known as the **Hewett Treaty**, at Adwa on 3 June 1884. Italian encroachment from Eritrea resulted in the seizure of Adwa in 1890. This penetration culminated in the **Battle of Adwa**.

Today, Adwa is a quiet commercial and **education** center situated in the midst of beautiful mountains. It resumed a strategic importance following the 1998 outbreak of the **Ethiopian-Eritrean War**. Adwa is the location of the two important churches of Enda Selassie built by Emperor **Yohannes IV** and Enda Medhane Alem with its famous wall paintings dating from the first decade of the 19th century. Having a strong local culture that valued education made the people in and around Adwa strong proponents of Tigrayan nationalism. Prime Minister **Meles Zenawi** and numerous other **Tigray People's Liberation Front** leaders were born in Adwa or its environs. *See also* BARATIERI, ORESTE; TIGRAY PEOPLE AND LANGUAGE.

AFAR LIBERATION FRONT (ALF). On 3 June 1975, the ALF, led by Sultan Ali Mirah, declared an armed struggle against the **Derg** to defend the **Afars** and their land. During its early years, the ALF received support from the **Eritrean Liberation Front** but opposed the **Tigray People's Liberation Front** (TPLF) because of its conviction that Afar land in **Tigray** was an integral part of **Afar Region.**

After 1977, the ALF ceased to be an active military force as a result of an Ethiopian offensive in the **Danakil Depression**. However, in 1985, Habib Ali Mirah, son of the Sultan who then was living in Saudi Arabia, resumed the ALF's political and military activities with Saudi support. The rebels focused their attention on Abno in the Lake Abbe region along the Djibouti border. In 1989, the TPLF abandoned its claims to Afar land in Tigray. This decision facilitated cooperation with the ALF.

After the Derg's downfall (1991), the ALF supported the **Ethiopian People's Revolutionary Democratic Front** (EPRDF) and attended the 1991 London Conference to help ensure the establishment of a democratic government. On 25–28 November 1991, some 3,000 ALF delegates attended a national conference, where Sultan Ali Mirah indicated that the Afar nation would seek separation from Ethiopia. Relations soon deteriorated as the ALF maintained that the EPRDF was waging an undeclared war against the Afar. On 16 December 1995, the EPRDF sought to marginalize the ALF by ordering military units to besiege the home of Sultan Ali Mirah.

Nevertheless, the ALF participated in the 1995 elections for Afar Region's council but, because of internal squabbling, won only 12 of 48 seats. The ALF also suffered from an internal dispute between Habib Ali Mirah, who was hostile toward **Meles Zenawi**'s government, and his pro-EPRDF brother Hanfareh Ali Mirah, who was president of Afar Region. By the turn of the century, the ALF continued to call upon the international community to pressure the EPRDF not to lead Ethiopia to internal war.

AFAR PEOPLE AND LANGUAGE. There are approximately two million Afars who live in a triangle-shaped region between Djibouti, Eritrea, and Ethiopia. More than one million Afars live in Ethiopia. These nomadic peoples are organized into the four Sultanates of Tadjourah (Djibouti), Rahaital (Eritrea and Djibouti), Baylul (Eritrea), and Aussa (Ethiopia). There are more than a hundred clan families among the Ethiopian Afars. Apart from the sultanate divisions, the Afars also are characterized by a distinction between noble (Asaimara or Red) and commoner (Adoimara or White) groups. Both classes comprise several tribal confederacies and tribes that are not always territorially distinct. The nobles are said to descend from peoples in the Ethiopian **highlands** who imposed themselves on the Afars as the Abyssinians expanded their territory in the 16th century. Following subsequent intermarriage, it is often difficult to distinguish between nobles and commoners. Tribes in both classes claim descent from Arabia.

The Afars are a Cushitic-speaking people who call their **language** Cafar-af. It is classified along with **Somali** and Afar Oromo with the lowland east Cushitic language family. Afar and Saho constitute the northernmost east Cushitic languages

The northern Afar tribes were under **Tigray**'s rulers in earlier years while those in the center and south, with whom the Shoan kings had to remain on good terms to ensure the safety of their caravans to the coast, were generally independent. The most important Afar sultanate, which emerged in the 16th century, was that of Aussa on the **Awash River**. It eventually extended its influence over all of southern Afar territory. In the belief that the sultan of Aussa had become an ally of the Italians, **Menelik II** sent an army against him in 1895 and forced the sultan to pay tribute. Highland Ethiopian forces did not penetrate Aussa, however, until 1944, when they captured the sultan and brought him to **Addis Ababa,** where he died. The office then went to an Afar kinsman who maintained a semi-independent sultanate tributary to the government in Addis Ababa. Even this degree of autonomy disappeared after the 1974 revolution.

Islam as practiced by the Afar takes the form of Sufism. Although the Afar may be unorthodox, they hold Islam in high regard. Orthodox observance among the nomads is still marked by the persistence of pre-Islamic Cushitic religious practices. Orthodoxy is stronger in the sultanate of Aussa. Cushitic figures are transfigured into Islamic saints and some Cushitic customs persist such as the use of sorcery to cure the sick and widespread use of amulets.

Most Afars are seminomadic pastoralists whose existence is dependent on livestock. During years of normal rain, Afar move their herds from a home base within a radius of 32 miles (20 kilometers) and seldom more than 80 miles (50 kilometers). During times of severe climate stress, they are forced to move their herds up to 240 miles (150 kilometers) to find sufficient water and pasturage. Afar markets are well known for their livestock. The production of salt also remains an important part of the **economy** for some Afar. The introduction of irrigated **agriculture** since the 1960s along the Awash River has resulted in a group of settled agriculturists. Cohabitation between pastoralists and farmers presents some challenges. Many Afars believe that the introduction of irrigation and the resultant formation of small towns with a large number of highland migrant workers have undermined their culture.

The Afars have generally cordial relations with the **Tigrayans** and **Amhara people** who live on their western border. Their interaction with **Oromo** to the south is usually friendly although occasional altercations occur over grazing rights. There is a serious problem, however, between the Afars and the Somali Issas who border them on the east. The Issas are well armed and challenge the Afars for rangeland and even access to the Awash River and other tributary rivers. Conflict among the Afar clans is not especially serious, but regularly occurs. Kassa Negussie Getachew describes the Afar in *Among the Pastoral Afar in Ethiopia. See also* AFAR LIBERATION FRONT; AFAR REGION; OGADEN; SAHO PEOPLE AND LANGUAGE; SOMALI REGION.

AFAR REGION. According to the 1994 **census**, there were 1.1 million people in Afar Region, which is one of the poorest and least developed of Ethiopia's nine regions. Only 5 percent of the **population** has access to adequate **health** care. Afar borders Eritrea and Djibouti at its northern extremity and includes territory along both sides of the **Awash River** to the town of Awash at its southern end. Assaita, the capital, is a small, dusty town isolated in the center of the region. Divided into five zones and 29 *weredas* or districts, Afar Region borders **Tigray** and **Amhara Regions** in the west, **Oromia Region** in the south and **Somali Region** in the east. The northern part of Afar includes the **Danakil Depression**, Ethiopia's lowest and hottest point. It is a desertlike area with thorn bushes and occasional acacias. The Awash Valley in the southern part of the region contains vegetation more typical of the steppe. Several million years ago, the region was lush, tropical, and, according to recent **paleoanthropological** evidence, possibly the location of the first hominids.

In 1996, the government began to build a new capital at Samara along the main highway that is formed after the roads from the ports of Djibouti and **Asab** meet in northern Afar. This project is moving slowly, probably set back by the closure of the border with Eritrea following the outbreak of the conflict between the two countries in 1998. The road remained critical to Ethiopia, however, as most of its imports and exports passed through Djibouti following the loss of access to Asab in Eritrea. Trucking along the road has a major impact on the Afar region's **economy**. The other components of the economy are livestock, salt production and irrigated agricultural projects along the Awash River. *See also* AFAR LIBERATION FRONT; AFAR PEOPLE AND LANGUAGE; OGADEN.

AFEWERK TEKLE (1932–). The most famous of Ethiopia's current artists. Born in October 1932 in **Ankober**. In 1947, Afewerk went to Britain to study mining engineering, but soon realized his talent lay in art and attended the Central School of Arts and Crafts in London and then the University of London. In 1954, he returned to **Addis Ababa** and arranged a one-man show that was the first significant art exhibition in post–World War II Ethiopia. His first major commission was the decoration of Saint George's Cathedral, where he worked on murals and mosaics for more than three years. Afewerk subsequently did the stained glass windows for the **Harar** Military Academy and several sculptures. His work adorns postage stamps, playing cards, ceremonial dress, posters, murals, mosaics, and paintings. One of Afewerk's best known works is the set of stained glass windows in the entrance of Africa Hall, the Addis Ababa headquarters of the United Nations **Economic Commission for Africa (ECA)**. His most famous painting is *The Meskel Flower*, a painting of a young Ethiopian **woman** in formal dress. Afewerk Tekle has received numerous international awards and exhibited his art throughout Ethiopia and in numerous foreign countries. *See also* ZERIHUN YETMGETA.

AFRICA HALL. *See* ECONOMIC COMMISSION FOR AFRICA.

AFRICA ORIENTALE ITALIANA (AOI). On 1 June 1936, Rome issued a decree that organized its East African territorial holdings into the AOI, which was divided into five provinces (Eritrea, **Amhara**, **Harar**, Oromo-Sidama, and Somalia). Each province had a military Governor who reported to the Viceroy in **Addis Ababa**, the seat of the AOI, which was about 666,000 square miles (1,726,657 square kilometers) with an estimated **population** on 1 May 1939 of 12.1 million people. During its brief existence, the AOI had five viceroys, including Marshal **Pietro Badoglio** (9 May 1936–22 May 1936), **Rodolfo Graziani** (22 May 1936–21 December 1937), **Amedeo di Savoia, Duke of Aosta** (21 December 1937–19 May 1941), Pietro Gazerra (23 May 1941–6 July 1941), and Guglielmo Nasi (6 July 1941–27 November 1941).

The AOI's administrative system included Italian residents and vice-residents at the district level. Italians courts operated the **judiciary** that based its decisions on Italian law. However, although there was a provision to use Ethiopian laws to settle disputes among Ethiopians, Italian courts dealt with all criminal cases while military courts assumed responsibility for all political and military offenses. There was no common taxation system in the AOI. In Eritrea and Somalia, the native population paid some taxes while in Ethiopia some of the Italian residents in richer regions imposed contributions in kind.

The AOI was short-lived. By 1941, Ethiopia, with help from Britain and South Africa, had defeated Italy and had been reconstituted as an independent state. All other parts of the AOI were under the **British Military Administration**. *See also* ASKARI; BLACK LIONS; GIDEON FORCE; IMRU HAILE SELASSIE; MISSION 101; PATRIOTS; WORLD WAR II.

AFRICAN UNION. In November 1961, Ethiopia first suggested creating an organization of African states at the 16th session of the United Nations General Assembly. In January 1962, **Addis Ababa** again raised the issue at the Lagos Conference of African Heads of State and prepared a draft of the Organization of African Unity (OAU) charter. In May 1963, **Haile Selassie** then convened the Pan African Conference of Heads of State in Addis Ababa. On 25 May 1963, 30 nations signed the Charter of African Unity.

This document enjoined member states to promote "unity and solidarity" among African states, cooperation to improve the lives of all Africans, sovereignty and independence, the eradication of colonialism, international cooperation, respect for one another's sovereign equality, noninterference in the internal affairs of states, peaceful settlement of disputes, nonaligned foreign policies, and opposition to assassination and subversion.

The OAU's organizational structure included the Assembly of Heads of State and Government, Council of Ministers, General Secretariat (based in Addis Ababa), specialized commissions (e.g., Defense Commission; Mediation, Conciliation, and Arbitration Commission; Commission of Fifteen on **Refugees**; Economic and Social Commission; and Educational, Scientific, Cultural, and Health Commission), and autonomous specialized agencies (e.g., Pan-African **Telecommunications** Union, Pan-African Postal Union, Pan-African News Agency, Union of African National Television and Radio Organizations, Union of African Railways, Organization of African Trade Union Unity, and Supreme Council for Sports in Africa). The OAU has had seven secretaries-general.

Throughout its existence, the OAU suffered from inadequate resources. Nevertheless, it made some notable contributions. Its Coordinating Committee for the Liberation of Africa organized international support and channeled financial and military aid to various African liberation movements and anti-apartheid groups. The OAU also supported various peacekeeping missions and efforts to resolve

African conflicts and border disagreements, including those between Somalia and Ethiopia and Kenya and the **Ethiopian-Eritrean War**. Additional activities included promotion of African culture, support for African refugees, endorsement of economic and social development, and efforts to harmonize Africa's transport and communications sectors.

On 2–3 March 2001, the OAU summit in Sirte, Libya agreed to establish the African Union. According to the Constitutive Act of the African Union, the organization also will be headquartered in **Addis Ababa**. Eventually, there will be a pan-African parliament. *See also* FOREIGN POLICY; KETEMA YIFRU.

AGAW PEOPLE AND LANGUAGE. The Agaw, who may number a half million, are known by several names, including Agau, Agew, Agow, and Awi. Unassimilated communities are concentrated in Semien, **Wag**, and Lasta north of **Lake Tana**. A large isolated Agaw community also remains unassimilated in an area called Agaw Meder south of Lake Tana. Although their **agricultural** practices are similar to those of the **Amhara people**, the Agaw tend to be poorer. Those who live in the **Tekeze River** valley have no history of local craftsmen and rely on neighboring areas for their markets. Their Cushitic **language** is called Awingi, which is one of three Agaw dialects together with **Kemant** and **Kumfel**. Nearly all Agaw speak **Amharic** as a second language.

Along with the Kemant and Kumfel, the Agaw probably are the unassimilated remnants of the Agaw farmers who occupied the northwest **highlands** before the Semitic-speaking peoples dominated them during the last millennium B.C. They were pushed from the highlands to the hot Tekeze River valley and its tributaries north of Lake Tana. They probably survived as a separate group in this area because the Amhara, who prefer the plateaus, were not interested in living in the inhospitable lowlands. In the fifth and sixth centuries, they were subject to Christian **missionary** activity and eventually became strong Christians. During the ninth and 10th centuries, the Agaw were constantly at war with the Abyssinian kings. In the early 12th century, an Agaw chief called Marara or Mara founded the **Zagwe Dynasty** with a capital at Adafa not far from **Lalibela** in the Lasta Mountains. During the 17th and 18th centuries, most Agaw living south and east of Lake Tana were absorbed into Amhara society through a combination of military and missionary effort. *See also* SUSNEYOS.

AGRICULTURE. Agriculture is the backbone of Ethiopia's **economy**. It contributes about 45 percent to the gross national product, employs more than 85 percent of the work-force, and accounts for about 90 percent of the value of exports. The country is divided into two major agricultural zones—the **highlands** and the **lowlands**. The highlands constitute about 40 percent of the land area and the lowlands 60 percent. About 25 percent of the land is cultivated intensively or moderately. Animals graze on most of the remainder, although some areas are so steep, eroded and/or lacking in water that they serve virtually no agricultural purpose.

Farming practices vary according to vegetation zones and the tradition of different ethnic groups. The most common way of tilling the field is by oxen or cattle that pull a crude wooden plow fitted with iron tips. Mechanized plowing is rare. It is not uncommon to see farmers working small plots using hoes or even sharpened sticks to break up the soil. The farmers then spread seeds and plow them under. There is growing use of fertilizer. The rains or lack thereof ultimately determine the crop's size and quality. There is very little irrigated agriculture. When the crops fail, farmers kill off livestock to survive. When the livestock are gone, they are dependent on foreign assistance and wild plants and roots.

In the 1960s, commercial farming began. Following a brief period of modest growth, the **Derg** nationalized the commercial operations and converted them to state farms. Most of these operations performed poorly and the **Ethiopian People's Revolutionary Democratic Front** (EPRDF) gave some of them to local farmers and privatized others. Of the original 26 state farms, there are now only about a dozen remaining. The EPRDF is encouraging large-scale commercial farming, but results have been modest. Access to good land is the main obstacle. Investors must identify land that is not already being used by others. This forces them to the low, hot, disease-ridden parts of Ethiopia where there is still unoccupied land.

Ethiopia grows 146 crops for **food**. The major cereal crops are teff (used in making *injera*), wheat, barley, corn, millet, and sorghum.

Pulses are the second most important element in the national diet and a principal source of protein. Niger seed, flaxseed, and sesame are widely cultivated. Castor beans, rapeseed, peanuts, safflower, and sunflower seeds are a less significant part of the diet. *Ensete*, also known as the false banana, is an important food source in the southern and southwestern highlands. Fruits and vegetables grow well in parts of Ethiopia but consumption tends to be low because of their high cost. Common vegetables include onions, green beans, peppers, squash, and cabbage. Ethiopia produces a variety of citrus, bananas, mangoes, and papaya.

The most important export and cash crop is **coffee**, which provided about two-thirds of the merchandise export earnings until the recent drop in coffee prices. Other cash crops include **cotton**, sugar, tea, and tobacco, most of which are consumed domestically. Five agricultural products—coffee, hides and skins, oil seeds, pulses, and fruits and vegetables—account for about 80 percent of Ethiopia's export earnings. **Khat** production is also becoming increasingly important. Livestock contribute an estimated 30–35 percent of agricultural gross domestic product (GDP) and about 15 percent of overall GDP. Cattle account for 70 percent of this value, sheep and goats 14 percent, and poultry 13 percent. Camels, mules, and horses make up the balance. Ethiopia may have as many as 80 million head of livestock and 60 million of poultry. *See also* LAND TENURE; PEASANT ASSOCIATIONS.

AHMAD IBN IBRAHIM AL GHAZI (1506–1543). Also known as "Gran the Left-Handed." Imam and rebel leader who facilitated the 16th-century Muslim conquest of Ethiopia. Born in the **Adal sultanate**, an emirate in the **lowlands** east of **Shoa** Province. Gran subsequently killed Adal's sultan, Abu Bakr, but allowed the royal line to continue. He refused to accept the title of sultan but instead adopted the Islamic title of imam. His refusal to acknowledge the supremacy of **Lebna Dengel** caused a war that led to the Muslim conquest of much of Ethiopia. During the 1526–1540 period, he enjoyed his greatest military successes. On 10 February 1541, 400 Portuguese soldiers, under the command of Christovãro da Gama (son of Vasco), arrived in **Massawa** to help the emperor repulse the Muslim invaders. On 21 February 1543, **Galawedos** ordered his 9,000-man Ethiopian-

Portuguese army to attack Gran's 15,000-man army near **Lake Tana**. Within days, Galawedos had scored a decisive victory. On 25 February 1543, Gran sustained a mortal wound during the Battle of Wayna Daga, in western **Bagemder**. The Ethiopians severed his head and displayed it throughout the surrounding countryside. *See also* ISLAM.

AIR FORCE. Ethiopian military **aviation** dates from 1929, when **Ras Tafari Makonnen**, later **Haile Selassie**, purchased four French biplanes and hired two French pilots. By the outbreak of the **Italian-Ethiopian War**, the Ethiopian Air Force (EAF) consisted of 13 aircraft and four pilots. After **World War II**, Haile Selassie sought to expand and professionalize the EAF by using Swedish instructors and establishing a flying school. In 1947, the emperor contracted a Swedish training team, equipped with 18 Saab trainers and two Saab-17 light bomber squadrons, to develop the EAF. He also named a Swedish general to command the EAF, an arrangement that continued until 1962, when Brigadier General Asefa Ayene assumed command. In 1960, the United States delivered a squadron of F-86F Thunderjets. Between 1966 and the early 1970s, the United States provided the EAF with Northrop F-5A/B/E fighters. By 1970, Ethiopia had one of the most proficient air forces in Africa. In 1977, the Soviet Union started providing aircraft and instructors to the EAF. During the second **Ogaden War (1977–1978)**, the EAF quickly destroyed its Somali counterpart. By the late 1980s, the EAF had become vital to the **Derg**'s war against the **Tigray People's Liberation Front** and the **Eritrean People's Liberation Front**. By early 1991, the EAF included 4,500 officers and airmen and some 150 combat aircraft but it suffered from low morale and internal divisions.

After it seized power (1991), the **Ethiopian People's Revolutionary Democratic Front** (EPRDF) abolished the air force and imprisoned all officers and pilots down to the rank of major (Eritrea did the same). In 1995, the EPRDF sought to rebuild the EAF with Israeli assistance and recruited former TPLF fighters for pilot training. However, the amount of resources devoted to this project was comparatively small, especially when compared to the monies allocated to the Ethiopian National Defense Force.

The outbreak of the **Ethiopian-Eritrean War** led to a significant escalation of the government's interest in the EAF's rebirth. The EAF quickly established a 10–1 advantage in aircraft over the Eritrean Air Force. The Ministry of Defense also contracted about 300 Russian officers and instructors to improve the EAF's capabilities. Major General Kasienko Anatoly Vasilievich, former chief of military operations in the Ural Region, went to Ethiopia as senior military adviser to the general Staff. By the end of the war, the EAF had become one of the strongest air forces in sub-Saharan Africa. *See also* ARMED FORCES.

AKLILU HABTE-WALD (1908–1974). Politician, prime minister, and adviser to **Haile Selassie**. Born on 12 March 1912 in **Addis Ababa**. He was educated at the Ecole Impériale **Menelik II**, the French Lyceé in Alexandria, and the Sorbonne, Paris (1930–1936). During the **Italian-Ethiopian War**, Aklilu remained in Europe and worked as secretary and chargé d'affaires at the Ethiopian legation in Paris (1936–1940). After returning to Ethiopia (1941), he joined the Foreign Office and served in several senior-level diplomatic positions, including vice-minister of the pen (1942–1943), vice-minister and then acting minister of foreign affairs (1943–1949), and minister of foreign affairs (1949–1958 and 1960–1961). Some of Aklilu's more notable **foreign policy** achievements included negotiating the **Anglo-Ethiopian Agreement (1944)**, signing the United Nations Charter on Ethiopia's behalf (1949), and helping to persuade the UN General Assembly to vote in favor of the **Ethiopian-Eritrean Federation Act** (1952).

In November 1957, Aklilu's political career began when he became deputy prime minister and remained minister of foreign affairs. In 1958, he asked to be relieved of the latter portfolio and was put in charge of the Royal Secretariat. However, the following year, he returned to the Ministry of Foreign Affairs and continued as deputy prime minister.

After the **coup attempt (1960)**, Aklilu became prime minister (1961–1974). During this period, he gradually gained control over the day-to-day administration of the government with the emperor's acquiescence. Apart from appointing ministers, Aklilu formulated economic planning policies and new legislation. His close identification with the emperor proved to be his undoing. In February 1974, he resigned as prime minister, thus paving the way for the military's accession. On 24 November 1974, the **Derg** executed Aklilu without trial along with 51 other leading political and military figures. *See also* BLOODY SATURDAY.

AKOBO RIVER. *See* SOBAT RIVER.

ALABA PEOPLE AND LANGUAGE. Nearly 100,000 Alaba people live in the **Rift Valley** southwest of Lake Shala. The Bilate River separates them from the **Kambata** to the west. The **Hadiyya** reside to the north and south. Kulito is their major market town. A map contained in M. Legrand's *Voyage Historique d'Abissinie*, which was published in 1628, shows a kingdom of Alaba. About 1830, Sheikh Kana, a descendant of the famous Nur Husain, introduced the Shafi'i school of **Islam** to the Alaba. Today there are also Christian Alaba. The Alaba speak an east Cushitic **language**. It has 81 percent lexical similarity with Kambata, 64 percent with **Sidama**, 56 percent with **Libido,** and 54 percent with Hadiyya.

ALAMAYU (ALEMAYEHU, ALEMAYYEHU) (1861–1879). Son of **Tewodros II**. Before committing suicide as a result of his defeat in the **Anglo-Ethiopian War**, Tewodros II asked his wife to ensure that Alamayu received an education in Britain. **Robert Napier** and Alamayu returned to London together. Captain Charles S. T. Speedy, who had served as an **Amharic** interpreter on Napier's headquarters staff, then assumed responsibility for Alamayu's welfare. After living with Speedy on the Isle of Wight and in India, Alamayu attended Cheltenham College and Rugby. In 1879, he entered the Royal Military College at Sandhurst but performed poorly. His supporters, who included Queen Victoria, hoped that he would receive a commission in an Indian regiment. Unfortunately, he developed pleurisy and died on 14 November 1879. Queen Victoria ordered that Alamayu be buried at Saint George's Chapel at Windsor.

AL-AMOUDI, MOHAMED HUSSEIN ALI (1941–). Chairman of the Mohamed International Development Research and Organizations Companies (MIDROC) holding company. Born in Weldiya, a town in **Wollo Province,** and educated in **Dese**. In 1965, al-Amoudi emigrated to Saudi Arabia. In 1984, he returned to Ethiopia and worked in the import-export business with the support of senior **Derg** officials like Prime Minister Fikre Selassie Wogderes (1987–1989) and **Tesfaye Gebre Kidan**, the second most powerful man in the government. Al-Amoudi also formed the al-Tad company, which specialized in car rentals, construction work, and travel agencies.

After the **Ethiopian People's Revolutionary Democratic Front** (EPRDF) seized power (1991), he ousted his partner, Tadele Yidnekatchew, and integrated the al-Tad company into the newly formed MIDROC, which opened businesses in the **agricultural**, **banking**, car sales, construction, industrial, insurance, and mining sectors. By the late 1990s, al-Amoudi, as MIDROC chairman, had become Ethiopia's largest foreign investor with more than $500 million invested in virtually all sectors of the **economy**. In late 2002, he and his two brothers created Trust Protection and Personnel Services, a security company that offers industrial and personal security and fire protection.

Apart from his numerous charitable activities, al-Amoudi has shown his generosity by providing aid to the state, especially during the **Ethiopian-Eritrean War**. He also helps development activities in **Tigray Region**, the home of **Meles Zenawi** and numerous other influential senior government officials. Such largess has enabled al-Amoudi to deflect criticism from his adversaries. *See also* ENDOWMENT FUND FOR THE REHABILITATION OF TIGRAY.

ALEQA. Chief of priests; lay administrator. *See also* GEBRE-HANNA GEBRE-MARIYAM, ALEQA.

ALGIERS AGREEMENT (2000). On 18 June 2000, Ethiopia and Eritrea signed a Cessation of Hostilities Agreement in Algiers as a first step to reaching a comprehensive peace agreement. On 28 July 2000, the first group of United Nations peacekeeping military liaison officers arrived in **Addis Ababa** and Asmara to prepare the way for the deployment of the **United Nations Mission to Ethiopia and Eritrea** (UNMEE). On 4 November 2000, Major General Patrick Cammaert (Netherlands) arrived in Asmara to assume command of UNMEE.

On 12 December 2000, Ethiopia and Eritrea signed the Algiers Agreement, thereby ending the **Ethiopian-Eritrean War**. The Algiers Agreement sought to prevent a renewal of hostilities by implementing a three-phase strategy. First, it asked the **Organization of African Unity** (OAU) to investigate and then publish a report about the events that led to the conflict. In particular, the Algiers Agreement directed the OAU to focus on Ethiopia's claim that Eritrea had invaded its territory on 6 May 1998 and Eritrea's accusation that Ethiopian cross-border raids in July and August 1997 put the two countries on the road to war. Second, the Algiers Agreement established a mechanism to demarcate the disputed border after a UN peacekeeping force had deployed to the border to monitor the ceasefire. A five-man boundary commission, sitting in The Hague, was responsible for the final adjudication of the border. Third, the Algiers Agreement called for the creation of a neutral claims commission, also headquartered in The Hague, to adjudicate the cases of Eritreans expelled from Ethiopia and Ethiopians expelled from Eritrea.

On 20 December 2001, five opposition parties (**All Amhara People's Organization**, Council of Alternative Forces for Peace and Democracy in Ethiopia, Ethiopian Democratic Union Party, Ethiopians' Democratic Party, and Oromo National Congress) sent a letter to United Nations Secretary General Kofi Annan that rejected the Algiers Agreement. These parties maintained that a nationwide referendum would have to approve any territorial adjustments. The ruling **Ethiopian People's Revolutionary Democratic Front** ignored the petition.

ALL AMHARA PEOPLE'S ORGANIZATION (AAPO). *See* ALL ETHIOPIA UNITY PARTY.

ALL-ETHIOPIAN SOCIALIST MOVEMENT (AESM). Also, known in **Amharic** as MEISON. In August 1974, Ethiopian students abroad established the Voice of the Masses group and a weekly newspaper entitled *Voice of the Masses*. In early 1975, the leadership returned to Ethiopia and, in April 1976, changed its name to AESM. Along with the **Ethiopian People's Revolutionary Party** (EPRP), the AESM mounted an anti-**Derg** campaign. Ironically, the *Voice of the Masses* supported Derg policies such as imprisoning the aristocracy, nationalizing their assets, suspending the **constitution**, and deposing **Haile Selassie**. AESM and the EPRP goals included the reinstatement of democratic rights to the "broad masses" and the handing over of power by the Derg to a provisional people's government. On 28 July 1977, the AESM ordered some of its members to withdraw from official forums such as the Joint Front of the Ethiopian Marxist–Leninist Organizations and to go underground. **Mengistu Haile Mariam** responded to the challenge by unleashing the **Red Terror**. Within months, the Derg had executed hundreds of its leaders and had jailed AESM leader Haile Fida and several of his associates, all of whom were subsequently executed.

ALL ETHIOPIA TRADE UNION. *See* LABOR UNIONS.

ALL ETHIOPIA UNITY PARTY (AEUP). In November 1991, **Asrat Woldeyes** (chairman), Hailu Shawel, and Nekea Tibeb formed the All Amhara People's Organization (AAPO) to facilitate the creation of a unitary state as opposed to the ethnic federalist system that had been created by the **Ethiopian People's Revolutionary Democratic Front** (EPRDF) after its May 1991 takeover. The AAPO opposed Eritrean secession and unsuccessfully tried to derail that country's independence referendum. Although dominated by the **Amhara people**, the AAPO claims it is a national party because it includes some other nationalities and has the support of the **Ethiopian Orthodox Church** and the **Ethiopian Teachers' Association**. Until its dissolution on 6 December 1975, the **Confederation of Ethiopian Labor Unions** also supported the AAPO.

During the first months of its existence, the AAPO established a network of offices throughout parts of Ethiopia, including **Gojam**, **Gondar**, northern and southern **Shoa** Province, and South **Wollo**. The party also had offices in **Dire Dawa**, **Harar**, and other Ethiopian towns and eventually in Europe and North America. After Asrat's death in 1999, Nekea Tibeb became AAPO chairman but he alienated many members in Europe and North America. On 12 November 2000, the AAPO nominated and subsequently elected Hailu Shawel, who had been minister of state farms in **Mengistu Haile Mariam**'s government, as its new chairman. Hailu Shawel healed the rift within the AAPO and, in early December 2000, announced that the party would "reluctantly" participate in the upcoming national elections. By 2001, the AAPO had joined an anti-EPLF coalition that included the **Oromo Liberation Front** and the Ethiopian Medhin Democratic Party.

On 14 August 2002, a group of AAPO officers announced that it had changed the party's name to the AEUP. According to the party's executives, the name change had arisen from the need to create a strong, multi-ethnic national party. The AEUP also blamed the **Ethiopian People's Revolutionary Democratic Front** for the secession of Eritrea from Ethiopia and for the loss of **Asab** port. Some AAPO leaders refused to go along with the new party. As of late 2002, this faction remained weak and ineffectual as the AEUP controlled the party's offices and bank account and had secured recognition from the national election board. The AEUP leadership dismissed from the party the pro-AAPO All Amhara People's Relief and Development Association based in Washington, D.C. *See also* HUMAN RIGHTS; TAYE WOLDE SEMAYAT.

ALULA QUBI, RAS (1827–1897). Trusted general of **Yohannes IV**, governor of Mareb Mellash, and chief architect of military resistance to Egyptian and Italian encroachment in Ethiopia. Born in Marerraivé, a small village about 15 miles (24 kilometers) south of Abbi-Addi, the capital of **Tigray's** Tamben District. He was educated by Mamher Walda-Giyorgis in the church at Mannawê.

Ras Alula began his career as a *nagadras*, or chief customs officer. He became a confidant of Yohannes IV, who, after seizing power in 1871, made him a major in his army. Ras Alula played a key role in thwarting Egypt's attempts to conquer northern Ethiopia. On 23 September 1885, he defeated Mahdist forces at Uthman Digna. On 26 January 1887, he defeated an Italian force at the **Battle of Dogali**. On 15 February 1897, he died from wounds sustained in a battle with his rival Ras Hagos.

ALVARES, FRANCISCO (14??–1542). Portuguese priest, **missionary**, and traveler. In 1515, Alvares accompanied Duarte Galvão, Portugal's ambassador designate, to Ethiopia. In 1517, Galvão died on Kameran Island off the Yemeni coast. Alvares then agreed to serve as chaplain of the first Portuguese diplomatic mission to Ethiopia (1520–1527). On 9 April 1520, the mission, which was under the command of Rodrigo de Lima, arrived in **Massawa**. In 1533, Alvares presented Pope Clement VII (1478–1534) with several letters from **Lebna Dengel**. He remained in Rome until his death.

AMAN MIKAEL ANDOM (1924–1974). Soldier, politician, and chairman of the **Provisional Military Administration Council** (PMAC) (12 September 1974–17 November 1974). Eritrean by birth and educated at an American school in Khartoum. Aman gained his initial military experience as a **patriot** during the Italian occupation of Ethiopia (1936–1941). After liberation, he became a regular soldier and attended courses at Cadet College (Khartoum), and Camberley and the Royal Military College, Sandhurst. Aman quickly established a reputation for being a good commander and an advocate for the common soldier. During the **Ogaden War (1964)**, he commanded the Third Division and earned the sobriquet "Lion of the Ogaden." However, **Haile Selassie** sacked Aman for contravening an order to refrain from initiating military action on Somali territory. From May 1964 to July 1965, he served as Ethiopian military attaché in Washington, D.C. After returning to Ethiopia in 1965, the emperor appointed him to the Senate, where he became a critic of government policies. In July 1974, Haile Selassie, realizing that his liberal credentials might help to offset growing military unrest, appointed Aman chief of staff of the **armed forces** and subsequently minister of defense. However, this tactic failed to prevent the monarchy's demise.

On 12 September 1974, Aman became the PMAC's chairman. He also received a promotion to lieutenant general and became chairman of the **Council of Ministers**. Aman continued to hold the chief of staff and minister of defense portfolios. The **Derg** had hoped he would be a puppet leader but Aman proved to be a strong, charismatic, and contentious official. Such attributes put him on a collusion course with the Derg's leadership. After only three and a half months in power, the Derg sacked Aman for being a radical and "dictatorial" leader. On 23 November 1974, he died in a shoot-out with the Derg's security guards. Other accounts maintain that he had committed suicide. *See also* BLOODY SATURDAY; ITALIAN-ETHIOPIAN WAR.

AMBA. An *amba* is a flat-topped mountain or plateau that is sometimes virtually inaccessible because of steep sides in all directions. It is a typical geological formation in the Ethiopian **highlands**. Peasant farmers often situate their fields and associated villages on an *amba* to enhance protection from potential invaders. The **Debre Damo** monastery is located on a typical amba. It is about 0.6 (1 kilometer) in diameter and equipped with wells, cisterns, and fields on top. It can only be reached by climbing a rope up the face of a rock cliff. Ambas also have been important in Ethiopian military history as soldiers often used them as a natural fortification.

AMDA TSEYON (12??–1344). Emperor (1314–1344). Son of Wedem Arad (reigned 1299–1314). Amda Tseyon took the throne as Gabra Masqal (Slave of the Cross). Ironically, his relations with the **Ethiopian Orthodox Church** were stormy. During the early years of Amda Tseyon's reign, some monks accused him of fornicating with his father's concubine and two of his sisters and subsequently criticized him for marrying three wives. The emperor excommunicated his critics and his military exploits soon overshadowed his objectionable personal behavior.

His initial campaigns were against **Tigray** and rebellious tribes in **Damot, Gojam**, and **Hadiyya**. After conquering these regions, Amda Tseyon organized the fractious provinces into more easily governed smaller jurisdictions. The emperor's victories enabled him to control lucrative trade routes from Sudan to **Massawa**, from the Central Provinces through southern Shoa to Zeila, and from the southern provinces through **Shoa** to Zeila. Amda Tseyon's most notable military exploits were against the Muslim monarchs of Yefat, **Adal**, and Somalia. *See also* AHMAD IBN IBRAHIM AL GHAZI; DAMOT.

AMEDEO DI SAVOIA, DUKE OF AOSTA (1898–1942). Viceroy of **Africa Orientale Italiana** (AOI) (21 December 1937–19 May 1941). Born on 21 October 1898 in Turin and educated at Britain's prestigious Eton school. Aosta, who was the cousin of the king of Italy, Emmanuel (1869–1947), spent his early career in the Italian army and air force.

As viceroy, Aosta inherited a difficult situation in Ethiopia because of the harsh policies of his predecessor, **Rodolfo Graziani**. Upon assuming office, he introduced a policy of greater cooperation with the Ethiopians. Among other things, Aosta closed the hated military tribunals, abolished serfdom, authorized the appointment of Ethiopians to minor administrative posts, and released 1,000 detainees at

Danane. These conciliatory gestures reduced but failed to eliminate Ethiopian opposition to the Italian occupation. Aosta initially pursued a vigorous military policy. On 4 August 1940, for example, Italian forces invaded and subsequently occupied British Somaliland (now Somaliland). However, chronic materiel shortages, growing opposition by the **patriots**, and a looming allied offensive convinced Aosta to adopt a limited strategy of defending selected redoubts. After the allied invasion of AOI in January 1941, an Italian counteroffensive failed to materialize. On 19 April 1941, Aosta surrendered at **Amba Alagi**. On 3 March 1942, he died of tuberculosis in a prisoner-of-war camp in Kenya.

AMHARA PEOPLE. Although not the most numerous people in Ethiopia—the **Oromo** have that distinction—when reference is made to Ethiopia most outsiders think of the Amhara. In the past, when foreigners referred to **Abyssinians** they usually meant the Amhara. In fact, however, Abyssinian was a reference to both the Amhara and the **Tigrayan** people in the central and northern **highlands**. For most of Ethiopia's history, the Amhara ruled the country. Ethiopia significantly expanded its borders under the leadership of an Amhara, Emperor **Menelik II**, from 1889 to 1913. Throughout the imperial regime, which ended with the overthrow of Emperor **Haile Selassie** in 1974, the Amhara dominated the government and the country's culture. The Amhara, not a European colonial power, created the modern Ethiopian state. The Amhara constitute about 25 percent of Ethiopia's **population** of 67 million and their language, **Amharic** or Amharigna, is the lingua franca of virtually all educated Ethiopians and even many non-Amhara with little or no formal education. As a result of commerce and service in local government administration over the years, Amhara are found in virtually every sizable town in Ethiopia. They are concentrated, however, in the central highlands surrounding **Lake Tana** and extending south and east to **Shoa**, Wollo, and **Addis Ababa**.

The best analysis of the Amhara is Donald N. Levine's *Wax and Gold*. He describes them as practical peasants, austere religionists, and spirited warriors. Levine suggests their highest achievements are military success, governmental organization, and the development of unique aspects of their **language** and **poetry**. The ambiguity contained in the language affects the fabric of Amhara life. Most Amhara are agriculturists who live in a rural setting. Their life revolves around a small homestead consisting of from one to a half dozen small round structures built of wattle and capped with conical thatched roofs. The peasant usually works the land in the vicinity of the homestead. There may be a cluster of households that include married brothers or other relatives. Every household also will depend on a market within a one-day walk for regular supplies of **food** and household items. Major market days usually occur once a week. The market links the peasant to a wider group.

Traditionally, the district headman was the primary link with governmental administration. The **Derg** regime largely supplanted the district headman with the establishment of the *kebele* that is linked to the political party. The **Ethiopian People's Revolutionary Democratic Front** continued this mechanism for political control. The **Ethiopian Orthodox Church** is the final major link between the Amhara peasant and broader society. The peasant follows the ritual requirements of the church and contributes a small quantity of grain to it annually. Like most peasant societies, the Amhara tend to be conservative. *See also* AMHARA REGION.

AMHARA REGION. Covering an area of 65,927 square miles (170,752 square kilometers) in northwestern Ethiopia, Amhara Region is a high plateau punctuated by even higher mountains. On its western edge, the topography tapers off as it approaches the border with Sudan. Amhara Region has a **population** of more than 13.8 million, according to the 1994 **census**. Its ethnic composition is about 92 percent Amhara, 3 percent **Oromo**, 3 percent Agaw, and includes small numbers of Kemant and other peoples. About 81 percent belong to the **Ethiopian Orthodox Church** and 18 percent are Muslim. There is a small number of Protestants. The regional capital, **Bahir Dar**, is located at the south end of **Lake Tana**. Other major towns in the region are **Gondar**, **Dese**, Debre Birhan, Debre Markos, Kombolcha, and Weldiya. It is divided administratively into 10 zones. Approximately 90 percent of the population lives in a rural **environment**. Together with **Tigray Region**, Amhara forms the core of ancient **Abyssinia**.

Many of Ethiopia's major **tourist** attractions are found in Amhara Region. The source of the **Blue Nile** is to the southeast of Lake Tana and the Blue Nile Falls are located outside Bahir Dar and just south of the lake. Most of the length of the Blue Nile is located in Amhara Region. Structures from the 17th century are frequently visited at the former capital of **Gondar**, to the north of Lake Tana. The carved rock churches of **Lalibela** well to the east of Lake Tana are a must visit. The Simien Mountains to the north of Gondar include Ethiopia's highest peak, Mount Ras Dashen. These mountains also provide a home for the rare gelada baboon, Walia ibex, and Simien fox.

AMHARIC. Descended from the old South Arabic, Amharic or Amharigna belongs to the Afro-Asiatic **language** family and the Semitic subgroup that includes Arabic, Hebrew, and Assyrian. It is the mother tongue of the **Amhara people**, Ethiopia's official language, and the lingua franca for educated Ethiopians and those involved in commerce. Under the current federal system of government, regional officials can determine the language used in the lower levels of the **educational** system. In addition to **Amhara Region**, the residents of **Southern Nations, Nationalities and People's Region**, **Gambela Region**, and **Benishangul/Gumuz Region** selected Amharic. Amharic and English are taught as second and third languages at later stages in the school systems of the other regions. Despite its widespread use, there are areas of Ethiopia, particularly in rural settings, where it is not used. This is especially true in much of **Somali** and **Afar Regions**.

Amharic developed as the vernacular language in the Amhara **highlands** while **Ge'ez** served until recently as highland Ethiopia's literary language. Even today, Ge'ez is used to some extent in the **Ethiopian Orthodox Church**. Job Ludolf, a German scholar, published the first Amharic grammar more than 300 years ago. In the 16th and 17th centuries, written Amharic received a temporary boost when Jesuit **missionaries** used it in their unsuccessful propaganda to convert the Ethiopian Orthodox to **Catholicism**. Following the expulsion of the Jesuits, Ge'ez regained its literary supremacy until the middle of the 19th century when Amharic publications began to appear. For centuries, Amharic also was the language used by the imperial government. At the end of the 19th century, the stationing of

Amharic-speaking administrators throughout the empire expanded the language's use. Today, it serves as the literary language as well as the vernacular.

There are relatively few and insignificant dialectal variants of Amharic. There are some distinctions between the Amharic spoken in **Gojam** and that used in **Shoa** Province. Amharic syntax is involved and devoid of all Semitic conceptions. The verb is found at the end of the sentence and subordinate clauses precede the main clause. The vocabulary retains many words of Semitic origin but also has added numerous words of Cushitic stock. Enormously expressive and subject to minute nuance, Amharic embodies the concept of "wax and gold" or two semantic layers. The apparent meaning of the words is called "wax" while the subtle or hidden significance of the words is known as "gold." Many insist that it is impossible to speak the language properly until you master the ambiguities of "wax and gold." *See also* AMHARA PEOPLE.

AMHA SELASSIE I. *See* ASFA WOSSEN MERIDAZMATCH.

ANFILLO PEOPLE AND LANGUAGE. The Anfillo, also known as the southern Mao, number only about 1,000 and live in the Anfillo forest west of Dembi Dolo not far from the Sudanese border. Scholars believe that the term Anfillo derives from the name of a late-17th-century village of the same name. The ruling class has **Sidama** physical characteristics and may have come from **Kafa**. They are divided into exogamous clans and have a hereditary King or chief who has supreme authority over the people. Social and political organization is modeled after the Sidama. Their supreme being is Yere or Yeretsi. The Anfillo speak a north Omotic **language** that has 53 percent lexical similarity with **Shakacho**. The older members still speak Anfillo while the younger ones generally speak Afan Oromo. *See also* KAFICHO PEOPLE AND LANGUAGE.

ANGLO-ETHIOPIAN AGREEMENT (1944). On 19 December 1944, Britain and Ethiopia concluded this treaty, which was valid for two years, after which termination was possible upon three months' notice. It was a revised version of the **Anglo-Ethiopian Agreement and Military Convention (1942)**. Under its terms,

Ethiopia agreed that the **Ogaden** and the **Reserved Areas** should remain under the **British Military Administration**. In exchange, the British waived their right to diplomatic precedence, abandoned their military privileges, and relinquished control of the **Addis Ababa–Djibouti Railway**. The treaty also placed the head of the British military mission under the Ethiopian minister of war's control.

ANGLO-ETHIOPIAN AGREEMENT AND MILITARY CONVENTION (1942). On 31 January 1942, Britain and Ethiopia concluded this treaty that was valid for two years after which termination was possible upon three months' notice. According to its terms, Britain recognized Ethiopia as a "free and independent state" and promised "to help" **Haile Selassie** organize a government. To finance government operations, Britain promised to provide £1.5 million for the first year and £1 million for the second year. If both countries agreed to extend the treaty Britain would pay £0.5 million for the third year and £0.4 million for the fourth year.

The Anglo-Ethiopian Agreement and Military Convention also imposed some restrictions on Ethiopian sovereignty. **Addis Ababa** acknowledged that the British representative was the doyen of the diplomatic corps. Haile Selassie permitted a British military mission to train the Ethiopian **armed forces** and agreed to appoint British advisors, a British commissioner of **police**, judges, magistrates, police officers, and inspectors. Moreover, the emperor agreed to allow the British to police Addis Ababa and to station their military forces anywhere in Ethiopia, consult with them before appointing any other foreign advisors, and exempt British citizens from the jurisdiction of Ethiopian courts. The British retained control of the **Addis Ababa-Djibouti Railway** and the territory it occupied, the radio station, and the telephone system. The treaty's most important clause left the British in control of the **Ogaden** and the **Reserved Areas**, a strip of land adjacent to British Somaliland (now Somaliland). On 25 May 1944, Haile Selassie gave the required three months' notice to terminate the agreement, which was replaced by the **Anglo-Ethiopian Agreement (1944)**.

ANGLO-ETHIOPIAN TREATY (1897). *See* RODD MISSION.

ANGLO-ETHIOPIAN WAR (1867–1868). On 26 July 1867, the British government decided to send a military expedition to Ethiopia. On 21 October 1867, 291 vessels landed **Robert Napier**'s force in Ethiopia. The expedition included about 13,000 troops (4,000 Europeans and 9,000 Indians) organized into four British and 10 Indian infantry battalions, a British cavalry squadron, four Indian horse regiments, five artillery batteries, a rocket brigade, and eight companies of sappers and miners (one British and 7 Indian). **Tewodros II**'s force numbered some 10,000 soldiers.

On 10 April 1868, British and Ethiopian forces clashed at Aroge and, on 13 April 1868, the British stormed Magdala. During the nine-month campaign, the British suffered 35 killed in action and 333 wounded while some 700–800 Ethiopians lost their lives and approximately 1,500 sustained wounds. The expeditionary force also freed two diplomats and 58 other European hostages and 215 Ethiopians, 36 of whom were princes or senior chiefs. Some had been incarcerated for as long as 30 years. On 18 June 1868, the last British expedition troops departed Ethiopia. The cost of the operation totaled £8.6 million.

One of the campaign's most controversial aspects concerned Napier's decision to ship Ethiopian cultural treasures back to Britain. Included in the booty were more than 1,000 **Ge'ez** and **Amharic** manuscripts, 350 of which ended up in the British Museum. Individual officers and soldiers also took manuscripts and other valuable artifacts back to Britain. Ethiopia continues to seek the return of all these items. *See also* ASSOCIATION FOR THE RETURN OF THE MAQDALA ETHIOPIAN TREASURES.

ANKOBER. A natural fortress located on the edge of the **Rift Valley** about 108 miles (175 kilometers) northeast of **Addis Ababa**, Ankober flourished during the **Era of the Princes** as the capital for five kings of **Shoa** Province. Amha Yesus conquered the Ankober region and ruled there for 30 years. His son, **Asfa Wossen**, succeeded him and ruled from 1775–1808. Another notable king at Ankober was **Sahle Selassie**, who ruled from 1813–1847 and was the grandfather of **Menelik II**. At its peak, Ankober may have had a **population** of 25,000. In the early 13th century, Ankober became important as a strategic location in the struggle between rulers of the **highlands** and **lowlands**. It was economically significant because it controlled the trade from the lowlands and the **Red Sea** port of Zeila. In 1886, Menelik II moved his capital to **Entoto** and then Addis Ababa. As a result, Ankober's importance declined although it continued to be used as an arms and treasure store and a place of political detention. Changes in trade and trade routes contributed to the fall of Ankober. In 1892, artisans restored the churches. Today, there are a few scattered farms on Ankober's original site. The only historical remains are the churches of Maryam, constructed by Asfa Wossen, and Mikael, built by Sahle Selassie. All that is left of Sahle Selassie's palace is a circular stone wall.

ANTONELLI, PIETRO (1853–1901). Italian explorer, diplomat, and politician. Born on 29 April 1853 in Rome. Antonelli was one of the most influential Europeans in Ethiopia, primarily because of the series of agreements and treaties he signed with **Menelik II**. He began his Ethiopian career in 1879–1881, when he visited **Shoa** Province, **Gojam**, and **Wollega Province**. On 27 March 1881, he signed a contract with Menelik II whereby the latter would receive 2,000 Remington rifles in exchange for his promise to open trade relations with Italy via the port of **Asab**. In November 1881, Antonelli returned to Italy. Within a few months, he had persuaded Rome to honor the contract and had convinced influential Italian businessmen and industrialists that Ethiopia was a lucrative market.

In June 1882, Antonelli departed Italy with instructions to solidify relations with Menelik II. During a stopover at Asab, he concluded a treaty with Mohammed Hanfari, the sultan of Aussa, to open a trade route from Asab, through the sultan's territory, to Shoa. On 21 May 1882, Antonelli and Menelik II signed a 10-year treaty of friendship and commerce. Among other things, the treaty provided for the establishment of diplomatic relations, freedom of movement of goods and men from one country to the other, and reciprocal most-favored-nation treatment. On 21 May 1885, Antonelli persuaded Menelik II to sign another treaty at **Ankober** that led to the establishment of diplomatic relations between Italy and Shoa. In recognition of his accomplishments, Antonelli became resident diplomatic agent at Menelik II's court (1885–1889).

After the Italian occupation of **Massawa** on 3 February 1885, Menelik II became suspicious of Rome's intentions toward

Ethiopia. However, Antonelli's presence helped to prevent a rupture in Italian-Shoan relations. On 20 October 1887, he and Menelik II signed an agreement whereby Italy promised to supply 5,000 Remington rifles within six months and to refrain from annexing any Ethiopian territory. In return, Menelik II pledged not to use the arms against Italian interests. However, Antonelli failed to convince Menelik II to oppose **Yohannes IV** who had been resisting Italian territorial encroachments in northern Ethiopia. On 2 May 1889, he and Menelik II signed the **Treaty of Wichale**, whereby Italy recognized him as emperor of Ethiopia in exchange for approval of its occupation of Adi Johannes, Adi Nefas, Asmara, Halai, and Soganeiti.

On 24 November 1894, he received an appointment as minister to Buenos Aires; on 21 November 1897, he was transferred to Rio de Janeiro. Antonelli died on 11 January 1901.

ANUAK PEOPLE AND LANGUAGE. Found in Ethiopia's **Gambela Region** and across the border in Sudan. In 1991, **missionaries** estimated that there were some 26,000 Anuak in Ethiopia and about 52,000 in Sudan. Part of the East Sudanic **language** family, Anuak is close to Acholi and Luo in Uganda. The Nilotic Anuak, who call themselves *Anyuaa*, live along the Baro, Alworo, and Gilo Rivers and on the right bank of the **Akobo River**. Their main concentration is in Gambela town. According to Anuak tradition, they have a common origin with the Shilluk and their ancestors came from the southwest. Most Anuak are agriculturists who raise corn and sorghum. Others engage in fishing, animal husbandry, and hunting. The Anuak speak a Nilotic language known as Anyua. Many are evangelical Christians who resist recruitment into the **armed forces** as they do not believe in fighting people they do not know. They have a long history of conflict with the **Nuer**. Ethiopians from the **highlands** captured many Anuak as **slaves** until the government abolished the practice. The most thorough account of the Anuak is E. E. Evans-Pritchard's *Political System of the Anuak of the Anglo-Egyptian Sudan*.

ARAYA SELLASIE YOHANNES (1870–1888). Son and heir to **Yohannes IV**. He was educated privately. In September 1883,

Yohannes IV arranged the marriage of Araya to Menelik's (later **Menelik II**) daughter, **Zawditu** in an effort to preserve peace and reinforce national unity. As part of the dowry, Menelik ceded northern Wollo to Araya who then became governor of **Wollo** (1883–1886) and subsequently governor of **Bagemder** and Dembea (1886–1888). Yohannes IV's strategy of uniting the houses of Tigray and **Shoa** failed as his son died from smallpox in Makele, while he was returning from the Battle of Saati.

ARBORE PEOPLE AND LANGUAGE. Several thousand Arbore people live north and east of Lake **Chew Bahir** and west of the Weyito River in South Omo zone. The Arbore believe that Arbore is the name of the first ancestor of the people and that they always have lived in this territory. On the other hand, they may have migrated from territory now inhabited by the **Konso**. They are traders and travel great distances. They once had a monopoly on the Ethiopian ivory trade.

Traditionally, they had hereditary chiefs assisted by elders. Their huts are slightly oval in shape and the framing is done with carefully arranged grass-lined poles. Arbore men wear an amulet belt and virgins wear heavy iron bracelets around their ankles. They resemble the **Boran** with their aluminum jewelry. Arbore town is located where several ethnic boundaries converge. They regularly marry with other peoples. The Arbore speak an east Cushitic **language**, but Konso is the lingua franca.

ARENDRUP, SØREN ADOLPH (1834–1875). Danish soldier and mercenary. Born in Frederikshaven, Denmark. In 1859, he received a commission in the Danish army and eventually was promoted to first lieutenant in the artillery (1863). In 1874, Arendrup, suffering from consumption, went to Egypt, entered the Egyptian army as a lieutenant colonel, and served under General (Fariq) Charles Pomeroy Stone (1824–1887), an American soldier who was chief of the Egyptian general staff. On 10 September 1875, he departed Cairo with three infantry battalions, three mountain artillery battalions, and a cavalry troop. On 17–18 September 1875, Khedive Ismail Pasha (1830–1895) issued a series of orders to gain control over all territory between the **Nile River** and the Indian Ocean. One of these directives instructed Arendrup to proceed to **Massawa**, assume command of a 2,500-man Egyptian army, and extend the khedive's influence into the Ethiopian **highlands**. On 16 November 1875, Arendrup died leading his troops during the **Battle of Gundet**.

ARGOBBA PEOPLE AND LANGUAGE. The Argobba are divided into northern and southern groups. They inhabit a long chain of settlements, some connected to one another and others scattered among Christian **Amhara people** or Muslim **Oromo**. Argobba villages are situated on hilltops, which explains why they are interspersed with Amhara and Oromo. The northern Argobba number about 25,000 and live near **Ankober**. Their villages include Aliyu Amba and Ch'ano. This area has been the crossroads for important trade routes that brought the Argobba into contact with the Amhara, Oromo, and **Afar**. There are some 15,000 southern Argobba who live 31 miles (50 kilometers) south of **Harar** between the Besidimo and Gobelli valleys that cut across the eastern slopes of Mount Hakim. In 1108, the northern Argobba converted to **Islam** and probably were an extension of the **Ifat sultanate**. By the 16th century, most southern Argobba, who also are Muslims, settled at their present location, apparently just ahead of the Oromo migration.

The southern Argobba and Oromo were once enemies. They traditionally traded with the **Somalis** and **slavery** flourished among them. Both Argobba groups engage in **agriculture** and raise livestock. The southern Argobba grow sorghum, corn, **coffee**, and **khat**. The staple crop of the northern Argobba is teff. Argobba is a Semitic language in the south **Ethiopic** family. It has high lexical similarity with **Amharic**. Southern Argobba is disappearing in favor of Afan Oromo, while Amharic is replacing northern Argobba. Nevertheless, the Argobba are trying to encourage recognition of their separate identity.

ARIMONDI, GIUSEPPE EDOARDO (1846–1896). Italian military officer. Born on 26 April 1846 in Savigliano (Cuneo), Italy. He served as commander of the Erythrean troops and commandant of Tigre. Arimondi played a significant role in three major Italian military campaigns during the last years of the 19th century. On 21 December 1893, he commanded a 2,402-man force that defeated an invading 10,000-man Dervish army at Agordat. Italian losses totaled only 232 troops while the Dervishes lost some 2,000 men. On 7 December 1895, Arimondi participated in the **Battle of Amba Alage**, during which a victorious 30,000-man Ethiopian army killed or wounded more than 2,000 Italian soldiers. During the 1 March 1896 **Battle at Adwa**, Arimondi commanded the Central Column, which included the first Infantry Brigade, first Company of the fifth Native Battalion, and the eighth and 11th Batteries. He died leading his troops against the Ethiopians.

ARI PEOPLE AND LANGUAGE. At least 110,000 Ari reside in the south Omo area of southwestern Ethiopia. The Kara and **Banna** people live to the south and the **Mursi**, **Dime**, and **Basketo** to the west. The **Gofa** are to the north and the **Male** to the east. The principal towns of Ari territory are Jinka, Gazer, and Metser. There are various legends concerning their origins that seem to differ according to their clan. They were only conquered and considered part of Ethiopia beginning with the rule of **Menelik II**. The Ari are primarily **agriculturists** living in permanent villages. They grow a variety of subsistence crops and two major cash crops—**coffee** and cardamom. They also raise livestock and engage in handicrafts and beekeeping. There is significant trade with neighboring ethnic groups. Ari territory is divided into nine independent territorial subdivisions each with its own hereditary leader called *babi*. Before Ari land fell under Ethiopian control, the babi was the supreme authority who performed judicial, military, administrative, economic, and ritual functions. The Ari are patrilineal.

Most Ari follow traditional beliefs although a significant minority belongs to the **Ethiopian Orthodox Church** or **Protestant** churches. Traditional beliefs include worship of ancestors and male and female deities. The Ari speak Araf, a member of the Omotic **language** family. There has been considerable confusion in placing Araf because it resembles Cushitic and Nilotic languages as well as Omotic ones. There are five dialects in Araf. The language elaborately describes the people's activities and experiences. The Ari have a rich heritage of songs, stories, proverbs, and riddles. The vast majority of the Ari speak Araf in the home and the market. An estimated 15 percent are literate. Gebre Yintiso published a useful study entitled *The Ari of Southwestern Ethiopia*.

ARK OF THE COVENANT. According to the Old Testament, the children of Israel built the Ark of the Covenant to hold the Tablets of Law God gave to Moses on Mount Sinai. Following the settlement of the Jews in **Jerusalem**, Solomon built a temple to house the ark. This treasured artifact of the Jewish faith disappeared after the Babylonians destroyed Solomon's temple in 587 B.C.

Followers of the **Ethiopian Orthodox Church** believe the Ark of the Covenant is locked in a building on the compound of the Saint Mary of Zion Church in **Axum**. In 1665, **Fasilidas** built the existing church that replaced a much older one destroyed by **Ahmad ibn Ibrahim al Ghazi** in 1535. Only the official guardian is permitted to enter the building and no one is allowed to see the ark. Several persons have constructed plausible theories to support the belief that the ark resides in Saint Mary of Zion. The best known account is Graham Hancock's *The Sign and the Seal*, which posits that angry priests removed the ark from Jerusalem before the Babylonians destroyed Solomon's temple. He dates the ark's arrival in Axum several centuries after Solomon during the reign of **Ezana** in the fourth century A.D. He notes that priests in the monastery of Tana Kiros on a **Lake Tana** island claim to have records stating that the ark was kept there for 800 years before it went to Axum. However, one of the leading Axum scholars, Stuart Munro-Hay, is skeptical that the Ark of the Covenant resides there.

ARMAH. Ruler of Axumite kingdom (c. seventh century A.D.). Armah was one of the most important personalities in Ethiopia's early history. In 615, 11 men and four **women** who were followers of the Prophet Mohammed fled from Arabia and sought refuge in **Axum**. Armah welcomed the **refugees** and placed them under his protection. This act of kindness ensured that Axum maintained good relations with the expanding Islamic world. He also had harmonious ties with South Arabia, despite the fact that Axum no longer occupied that region. This enabled him to control commercial traffic in the **Red Sea**. *See also* ISLAM.

ARMED FORCES. The armed forces have played a significant role in Ethiopia for some 2,000 years. One of the most important aspects of the country's military history concerned the duality of centrally controlled units attached to the imperial government and regional armies that were loyal to provincial lords.

At the beginning of Ethiopia's modern era in the mid–19th century, the country's rulers sought to modernize and to professionalize the armed forces. **Tewodros II**, for example, adopted a hierarchical chain of command and **military titles** equivalent to western ranks. He also paid soldiers a salary and manufactured weapons. **Yohannes IV** established a reputation as a fearsome military leader by defeating the Egyptians at the **Battle of Gundet** and the **Battle of Gura**. In 1896, **Menelik II** scored a decisive military victory over the Italians at the **Battle of Adwa**, an event that remains a hallmark in the history of the armed forces. In 1897, he turned the **Fitawrari** into the minister of war. **Haile Selassie** accelerated the development of the armed forces. On 30 January 1935, the Imperial government opened the **Haile Selassie I** Military School at Genet. A Swedish military mission operated the facility. The outbreak of the **Italian-Ethiopian War** resulted in the near destruction of the armed forces but an irregular force of **patriots** continued to fight for Ethiopia's liberation.

During the post-war period, the Emperor reestablished the armed forces with the help of the **British Military Administration** and sought aid from numerous western countries, the most significant of which was the United States. On 25 September 1953, Haile Selassie created the Imperial Ministry of National Defense that unified the Imperial Ethiopian Army, the **Air Force**, and the **Navy**. In May 1959, the emperor established the Imperial Territorial Army as an auxiliary force that also provided military training to civil servants. He also created an air force, navy, numerous Western-operated military training schools, and a close military relationship with the United States.

During the **Derg** period (1974–1991), the armed forces, which had been an adjunct of state power, became more closely identified with the increasing militarized government. The Soviet Union (now Russia) supplied the armed forces with modern weaponry, training, and advisors. This relationship, along with a significant intervention by Cuban combat troops, enabled the Derg to score a decisive military victory during the **Ogaden War (1977–1978)**. However, growing opposition by the **Tigray People's Liberation Front** (TPLF) and the **Eritrean People's Liberation Front** (EPLF) eventually doomed Ethiopia's increasingly brutal and isolated regime.

According to the **Ethiopian People's Revolutionary Democratic Front** (EPRDF), the Derg had recruited some 1,112,000 soldiers during its time in power. However, only 530,000 survived, the rest being killed, wounded, or reported missing. According to Derg figures, there were only 300,000 killed or wounded. The EPRDF also reported that the Derg had purchased 227 fighter aircraft, 1,700 tanks, 1,600 armored vehicles, and 4,000 artillery pieces. The cost of this equipment was approximately $8.5 billion.

During its first years in power, the EPRDF sought to transform its guerrilla force into a conventional army and to implement a **demobilization campaign** for the TPLF, the defeated Derg army, and the **Oromo Liberation Front**. After the outbreak of the **Ethiopian-Eritrean War**, the government embarked on a massive buildup for the Ethiopian National Defense Forces (ENDF). By the end of the war, the ENDF personnel strength was an estimated 350,000 organized into three military regions each with a corps headquarters (each corps had two divisions and one reinforced mechanized brigade). There also was a strategic reserve division of six brigades in Addis Ababa. The ENDF inventory included more than 300 T-54/-55, T-62 tanks, an estimated 200 reconnaissance and armored personnel vehicles, 300 artillery pieces, 50 multiple rocket launchers, and 370 surface-to-air missiles. The ENDF also had an unknown number of mortars, air defense guns, antitank weapons, and rocket launchers. *See also* ANGLO-ETHIOPIAN WAR; ASKARI; BATTLE OF AMBA ALAGE; BATTLE OF AMBA ARADAM; BATTLE OF AYSHAL; BATTLE OF COATIT; BATTLE OF DOGALI; BATTLE OF EMBABO; BATTLE OF KUFIT; BATTLE OF METEMMA; BLACK LIONS; COUP (1977); COUP ATTEMPT (1960); COUP ATTEMPT (1976); COUP ATTEMPT (1989); IMPERIAL BODY GUARD; ITALIAN-ETHIOPIAN WAR; MENGISTU HAILE MARIAM; OGADEN WAR (1964); PEOPLE'S MILITIA; PEOPLE'S PROTECTION BRIGADES; RED STAR CAMPAIGN; WORLD WAR I; WORLD WAR II.

ARMED FORCES COORDINATION COMMITTEE. *See* DERG.

ARNOUX, PIERRE (1822–1882). French trader and gunrunner. Born on 3 March 1822 in Nice. In September 1874, Arnoux arrived in

Shoa Province with a complex scheme to enhance Franco-Shoan relations by opening a route to Central Africa via Obock and Shoa, introducing western medicine, training Shoans in modern agricultural and industrial techniques, and improving the capabilities of the Shoan government and military. Although Arnoux failed to achieve all these goals, he gained the confidence of **Menelik II** by supplying arms to his forces. The emperor sent him to Europe to establish relations with Britain, Egypt, France, and the papacy. On 23 June 1881, Arnoux became the African director of the Franco-Ethiopian Company. In October 1881, he established a colony with 20 local workers and 25 Europeans, 18 of whom were Frenchmen. However, relations with the indigenous population were unstable. Fighting eventually broke out and, on 3 March 1882, Danakil tribesmen stabbed Arnoux to death.

ARSI PEOPLE AND LANGUAGE. *See* OROMO PEOPLE AND LANGUAGE.

ART. Ethiopia has a rich artistic tradition, virtually all of it until recently linked to Christianity. The earliest existing examples are decorative art in churches constructed in the eighth or ninth century of the post-Axumite period. The **Zagwe dynasty** of the 12th and 13th centuries witnessed the construction of the **rock-hewn churches** at **Lalibela**, all of which contained works of art. The 14th and 15th centuries are known for illustrated religious manuscripts, additional rock churches, and a style of art characterized by geometrical design, enlarged hands and eyes, and an absence of scenery. **Dawit I** commissioned an illustrated version of the *Miracles of Mary* and is associated with one of the period's most beautiful illustrated books, the *Gospel of the Monastery of Saint Gabriel*. Dawit I also brought artists from Venice to Ethiopia. In the 15th century, an artist monk from Venice named Nicolo Brancaleon adapted the international Gothic style to icon paintings, book illustrations, and church decorations.

The 16th-century arrival of the Jesuits had less influence on painting than it did on architecture. In the 17th century, **Fasilidas** commissioned numerous illustrated books dominated by yellows and reds. The Gondarine style spread throughout the **highlands**. The 18th-century painters abandoned geometric patterns and contrasting colors and emphasized painting with gradations of tone and color. In the 18th and 19th centuries, Ethiopian art lost much of its spiritual content. Artists adopted new western models whereby science replaced tradition. This Second Gondarine period tried to blend two incompatible elements, the perfect illusion of life and the old techniques and tradition of Ethiopian artists. Ethiopian painters continued, however, to serve the **Ethiopian Orthodox Church** into the 20th century.

Secular painting was rare until scenes of royal hunting, state processions, and funerals started appearing in the 18th century. Even these paintings formally belonged to the church. In the first half of the 18th century, the **negus** of **Shoa** commissioned paintings of military expeditions to adorn his prayer books. In the early 20th century, war scenes remained popular artistic subjects. In the mid–20th century, popular art further developed with a focus on religious and historical themes. The story of the **Queen of Sheba** and her meeting with King Solomon, Saint George slaying the dragon, and the **Battle of Adwa** became the most popular. Perhaps as a result of this rich artistic tradition there are many fine Ethiopian secular artists today. The best known is **Afewerk Tekle**; copies of his work can be seen throughout Ethiopia. Tibebe Terfa is another well-known contemporary abstract artist. Two of the best references are *Ethiopian Art* by the Walters Art Museum and *Ethiopian Icons* by Stanislaw Chojnacki.

ASAB (ASEB, ASSAB). Next to **Massawa**, Asab was Ethiopia's most important **Red Sea** port. On 2 December 1961, **Haile Selassie** inaugurated a newly completed port of Asab, which had an annual capacity of 800,000 tons, docks for four ships of up to 15,000 tons each or seven smaller vessels of up to 10,000 ships. After the **Eritrean People's Liberation Front** defeated the **Derg** (1991), Asab became part of Eritrea. However, Ethiopia enjoyed free access to the port. At the outbreak of the **Ethiopian-Eritrean War**, Asmara terminated this arrangement and Ethiopia has not used the port as of 2003.

ASFA WOSSEN, MERIDAZMATCH (1916–1997). Eldest son of **Haile Selassie** and Itegue Menen. Born on 27 July 1916 in **Harar**. Educated at Entoto Technical and Vocational School and at the palace with an expatriate tutor. He also pursued spiritual lessons at Saint Mark's Church. Appointed crown prince in 1930, he took the added title of governor general of **Wollo Province** and the traditional title of **Shoan** princes, "Merid Azmatch." Asfa Wossen accompanied the emperor to Britain following the Italian occupation of Ethiopia (1936–1941). For the next five years, he pursued tutorials in political science and public administration in Liverpool University. In 1940, Asfa Wossen enrolled at the Saint George Military Academy near Khartoum and earned the rank of lieutenant. Following Italy's defeat in Ethiopia (1941), Asfa Wossen returned to Ethiopia, with the rank of lieutenant general and joined **Fitawrari** Birru Wolde Gabriel in **Gondar** as supreme commander of the Ethiopian Army. Together with the British, they defeated the remnants of the Italian army in Ethiopia. Until 1945, Asfa Wossen administered Wollo and **Bagemder Provinces**. In 1948–1973, Asfa Wossen headed the **Ethiopian Red Cross Society,** a position that enabled him to travel extensively within Ethiopia and overseas.

While Haile Selassie was visiting Brazil, a group of disaffected Ethiopian soldiers who had previously organized a clandestine Council of the Revolution launched an unsuccessful **coup attempt (1960)**. They took the crown prince into custody and announced a new government with him as constitutional monarch. Asfa Wossen announced that he supported the coup, but later maintained that the coup instigators had forced him to make the statement. The failed coup cast a shadow over Asfa Wossen who never subsequently held a significant government position. However, according to the **constitution**, he remained in line to succeed **Haile Selassie** as emperor. After suffering a stroke in 1972, he went to Switzerland for medical care and subsequently moved to London.

When the **Derg** overthrew Haile Selassie in 1974, it proclaimed the recuperating Asfa Wossen as emperor of Ethiopia. The crown prince denounced the Derg's 23 November 1974 **Bloody Saturday** massacre of 60 senior imperial government officials. The Derg, in turn, revoked its proclamation of Asfa Wossen as emperor, adding that the Solomonic dynasty had come to an end. Asfa Wossen then returned to London and formed a government in exile. On 6 April 1988, this government and the Crown Council proclaimed him Emperor Amha Selassie I. On 23 October 1989, he moved to the United States to further coordinate efforts to restore a constitutional monarchy. In 1992, Amha Selassie I announced that he planned to return to Ethiopia to discuss his status with the **Ethiopian People's Revolutionary Democratic Front.** However, ill health doomed this effort. On 17 January 1997, he died in Virginia. On 2 February 1997 Amha Selassie I was buried next to his two brothers at the Holy Trinity Cathedral in **Addis Ababa.**

Asfa Wossen married his first wife, Princess Wolete Israel Seyoum, in 1932. The eldest daughter from this marriage, Princess Ejigayehu, died in a Derg prison in 1977. In 1945, the crown prince married Princess Medferiash Worq Abebe. The couple had four children: Princess Mariam Senna, Princess Sihin, Prince Zara Yakob, and Princess Sifrash Bizu. Asfa Wossen also left 11 grandchildren and two great-grandchildren.

ASHENAFI KEBEDE (1938–1998). One of Ethiopia's leading ethnomusicologists. Born in **Addis Ababa** in 1938. Ashenafi developed an interest in music while a student at Haile Selassie I elementary school and the **Harar** Teacher Training School. He taught music at **Haile Selassie I University** and the Addis Ababa YMCA. He received a B. A. in music (1962) from the University of Rochester's Eastman School of Music and returned to Addis Ababa to serve as director of the Yared School of Music (1963–1968). He then received an M.A. (1969) and Ph.D. (1971) in ethnomusicology from Wesleyan University. Ashenafi was assistant director and director of the ethnomusicology program at Queens College, City University of New York, and then professor of music, director of the Center for African American Culture at Florida State University, and executive officer of Ethius, Inc., an international organization promoting the arts.

Ashenafi published a novel entitled *Confession* in 1964. His publications in music include *The Grammars of Music* in **Amharic** (1966), a recording called *The Music of Ethiopia: Azmari Music of the Amharas* (1969), *African Music in the Western Hemisphere* (1972), and *The Bowl-Lyre of Northeast Africa. Krar: The Devil's Instrument* (1977). He also produced *The Sacred Chant of Ethiopian Monotheistic Churches: Music in Black Jewish and Christian Communities* (1980), *Modern Trends in Traditional Secular Music of Ethiopia* (1976), and *Roots of Black Music: The Vocal Instrumental* *and Dance Heritage of Africa and Black America* (1982 and 1995). His final work in progress was *Secular Verse and Poetry in Ethiopian Music*. He was best known as a scholar and teacher but also composed numerous compositions. He frequently used ambiguity and the oblique in his compositions, song texts, and **poetry**. On 8 May 1998, he died in Tallahassee, Florida.

ASKARI (ASCARI). Eritreans who served in the Italian colonial infantry. During 1890–1941, more than 130,000 Eritreans served as askaris. Italian officers believed that askaris were excellent but expendable soldiers. As a result, the askaris usually saw more action and suffered greater casualties than their Italian counterparts. Until 1935, the voluntary military service attracted recruits because of the pay, educational opportunities, the prospect of foreign service, and postretirement employment in the colonial administration. However, regulations barred Eritreans from rising above the rank of sergeant.

Askaris participated in several important Italian military campaigns. In the **Battle of Adwa**, 7,104 askaris participated in the fighting while another 1,600 remained in a rear camp. During the campaign, 2,261 askaris were killed and 958 wounded. About 1,000 askaris became prisoners of war. The Ethiopians behaved abominably to prisoners and wounded askaris. **Menelik II** ordered many prisoners to be emasculated and freed 406 askaris only after their right hand and left foot had been amputated. During 1907–1910, two askari battalions of 600 men each served in Somalia. Between 1911 and 1932, some 60,000 askaris served in Libya. In early 1934, Italy started assembling an army to invade Ethiopia. To support this effort, the colonial administration introduced conscription. By the beginning of the **Italian-Ethiopian War**, there were 60,200 askaris in the Italian colonial army. Most askaris served in the first, second, or third colonial divisions but some belonged to other units and the irregular militias called bandas. The number of askari casualties during the Italo-Ethiopian War remains a matter of controversy but tens of thousands certainly had been killed, wounded, or taken prisoner. *See also* BATTLE OF AMBA ARADAM; WORLD WAR II.

ASRAT. In 1893, **Menelik II** instituted this land **taxation** for farmers who wanted to pay the government one-tenth of their crops instead of quartering soldiers. Local elders or officials determined the amount of tax each farmer had to pay. *Asrat*, which went by different names in different parts of Ethiopia, remained in force until the dissolution of **Africa Orientale Italiana**. **Haile Selassie** eventually imposed more specific tax levies.

ASRAT WOLDEYES (1928–1999). Physician and chairman of the **All Amhara People's Organization** (AAPO). Born on 28 June 1928 in **Addis Ababa**. In 1931, Asrat's family moved to **Dire Dawa**. After an unsuccessful assassination attempt against Rodolfo Graziani on 19 February 1937, Italian soldiers killed his father, Woldeyes Altaye, and many other Ethiopians. After liberation (1941), Asrat graduated from Addis Ababa's Tafari Makonnen School as its best student. He continued his education at Victoria College (Egypt), and then studied medicine at Edinburgh University.

In 1956, Asrat returned to Ethiopia and served as a general practitioner in the former Prince Tsehai Hospital, where he later became hospital director. In 1961, he returned to Edinburgh, where he specialized in surgery. In 1965, Asrat helped establish a medical faculty as part of the **Haile Selassie I University** where he later served as dean and professor of surgery. He also was **Haile Selassie**'s personal physician and treated **Mengistu Haile Mariam**'s family. Asrat was a founding member of the Ethiopian Medical Association, a Fellow of the Royal College of Surgeons of Scotland and of England, and a member of the British Medical Association, East African Surgical Association, and International College of Surgeons (U.S.).

Until 1991, Asrat taught at **Addis Ababa University** and devoted himself to creating and advancing medical institutions that served the **population**, especially the poor and disadvantaged. In November 1991, he became head of the AAPO. On 27 June 1994, Asrat received a two-year jail sentence for armed conspiracy against the government. In October 1994, he got a six-month sentence for writing a letter to a court claiming that he had failed to receive a fair trial. In December 1994, a court sentenced Asrat to a further three years in jail for inciting an armed rebellion at a rally in Debre Berhan. Sustained efforts by prominent Ethiopians and many international **human rights** organizations failed to obtain his release from prison on medical grounds. The Ethiopian authorities did not provide him with adequate health care and only as his condition worsened did they release him. On 27 December 1998, Asrat departed Ethiopia for medical treatment in Britain and then in the United States. On 14 May 1999, he died at the University of Pennsylvania Medical Center from complications associated with hypertension and diabetes mellitus, both of which had been exacerbated by the time he had served in prison.

ASSOCIATION FOR THE RETURN OF THE MAQDALA ETHIOPIAN TREASURES (AFROMET). Established on 14 April 1999. AFROMET seeks to persuade Britain to return the countless artifacts and manuscripts that British forces had taken from Magdala during the **Anglo-Ethiopian War**.

The history of these items is a complicated issue. According to the custom of the day, all nations, including Britain and Ethiopia, recognized the principle of plunder. British troops therefore felt free to loot the treasures (e.g., crosses, manuscripts, and other religious and historical objects). British military authorities then transported the treasure on 15 elephants and nearly 200 mules to the nearby Dalanta plain and, on 20–21 April 1868, held a two-day auction to raise "prize money" for the soldiers. The sale raised some £5,000.

Richard Holmes, assistant in the British Museum's Department of Manuscripts, bought 350 Ethiopian manuscripts. The Royal Library, Windsor Castle acquired six manuscripts. The Bodleian Library (Oxford), Cambridge University Library, and John Rylands Library (Manchester) purchased nearly 200 manuscripts. Other London-based institutions that received some of the loot included the South Kensington Museum (later the Victoria and Albert Museum), the Museum of Mankind, and the National Army Museum.

In 1872, 1924, and 1965, the British government returned at least four items (e.g., one of **Tewodros II**'s two crowns and his royal cap and seal as well as a copy of the *Kebra Nagast*). However, the bulk of the treasure remains in Britain, where opinion is divided about what to do with the items. Some maintain that Ethiopia lacks the conservation capabilities to care for them while others fear that corrupt Ethiopian officials would sell them. Others maintain that Britain should return the treasure to Ethiopia.

ATBARA RIVER. (500 miles; 805 kilometers long.) The Atbara River rises in the mountains west and northwest of **Lake Tana**. One of its

Ethiopian tributaries, the Angereb River, joins the Atbara in Sudan. The main branch, sometimes called the Gwany River in Ethiopia, crosses into Sudan just north of the border town of **Metemma** where it becomes known as the Atbara. The **Tekeze**/Setit River is the true upper source of the Sudan Atbara River and joins it at Tomat in Sudan. The Atbara River then enters the **Nile River** north of Khartoum, at the town of Atbara. The Tekeze/Setit and Atbara together provide 13 percent of the Nile River's water reaching Egypt. On 15 April 1891, Britain, representing the interests of Egypt and Sudan, and Italy concluded the Rome Protocol that determined the Atbara River's boundaries.

ATSE. *See* IMPERIAL TITLES.

ATSME GIYORGIS (1821–1914). Court official and historian. Born at Harramba in **Ankober** and educated at several monastic schools. Atsme learned Arabic from Muslim traders at Farré, a town in Adal **lowlands**. The European **missionaries Gugliemo Massaia** and **Justin De Jacobis** taught Atsme Latin and persuaded him to convert to Roman **Catholicism**.

Atsme began his career by carrying official correspondence between **Menelik II** and his governors. The emperor also ordered him to conduct a survey of the political-military situation in **Harar** in preparation for a military campaign against that town. Disguised as a Moslem merchant, Atsme lived in Harar for three months compiling his report for Menelik II who occupied the town in 1887.

Just before he signed the **Treaty of Wichale** on 2 May 1889, the Emperor received a warning from Atsme about the duplicitous language in Article XVII. Menelik II responded angrily to Atsme's criticism by ordering the confiscation of his house and property. When he realized that Atsme had been right, Menelik II offered him a title and a senior government position in Harar. Atsme declined the offer but remained loyal to the emperor.

Throughout his career, Atsme wrote numerous manuscripts about Ethiopia's culture, history, and people but only two of them survived. One is a history of the **Oromo** people and the other is a biography of the Virgin Mary. Apart from his academic interests, Atsme also helped foreign missionaries to expand their teaching activities and facilitated the establishment of customs houses in eastern Ethiopia.

AUSTRALOPITHECUS AFARENSIS. *See* PALEOANTHROPOL-
OGY.

AVIATION. Air transport in Ethiopia began on 18 August 1929, when
the first airplane arrived in **Addis Ababa**. Great distances, mountainous terrain, a country divided by the **Rift Valley,** and an underdeveloped road system required that Ethiopia invest heavily in an air
transport system. Ethiopia also has the distinction of being the country where one of the first if not the first airplane was built in Africa.
The plane, named by Emperor **Haile Selassie** after his daughter
Princess Tsehai, was assembled in 1935. Airplane aficionados around
the world dubbed the plane "Ethiopia I" or the "Airplane of the **Negus**." A German, Ludwig Weber of Frieburg, was the first pilot to fly
the plane. Italy took the plane during its occupation of Ethiopia; it
now resides in Italy's aviation museum. In 1946, Ethiopia launched
Ethiopian Airlines. Ethiopia is a founding member of the International Civil Aviation Organization, which helped establish a civil aviation school in Addis Ababa (1951).

   In 1957, the American Export-Import Bank extended a $24 million
line of credit for the construction, improvement, and enlargement of
Ethiopia's aviation facilities. Ethiopia, then including Eritrea, developed a network of 33 airports by 1960; 25 were in use year round. By
1991, the number of Ethiopian towns that had air service had reached
45. The **Ethiopian People's Revolutionary Democratic Front** government has emphasized the expansion and improvement of airfields
and airport facilities. In recent years, there have been major improvements or expansions at **Mekele**, **Bahir Dar**, **Gondar**, **Lalibela**,
and Addis Ababa among others. In January 2002, Addis Ababa's Bole
International Airport opened a modern, new terminal that can process
3,000 passengers an hour. Today, there are 12 airports with paved
runways. Eight have airstrips of at least 8,000 feet (2,438 meters).
There are about 75 airports with unpaved runways; 19 of the airstrips
are at least 5,000 feet (1,524 meters). *See also* TRANSPORTATION.

AWARAJA. Amharic term for an administrative unit that is comprised
of several *woredas* and is immediately below a province. Approximately equivalent to a county. The term is not in common use today.
See also KEBELE.

AWASA (AWASSA). (87,600; estimated 2002 **population.**) The capital of present-day **Southern Nations, Nationalities, and People's Region** and the capital of former Sidamo Province. Located via paved road 168 miles (275 kilometers) south of **Addis Ababa** on the edge of **Lake Awasa**, part of the city is protected by a dike. A vibrant city, it is near a major **coffee**-growing area and known for the variety of **bird life** attracted by Lake Awasa. The city has an **agricultural** college, teacher training college, and a nursing institute. The predominant people living in the area are the **Sidama**. **Protestantism** is strong in the city and surrounding area following many decades of **missionary** activity.

AWASH RIVER. (434 miles; 695 kilometers long.) The Awash River, which is one of Ethiopia's major rivers, begins about 40 miles (65 kilometers) northwest of Melka-Kunture in the Worke massif and terminates at Lake Abbe on the Ethiopian-Djiboutian border. The Akaki and Holeta Rivers feed the Awash near its source. The Awash makes a semicircular bend first southeast and then northeast. It reaches the **Danakil Depression** through a breach in the eastern escarpment of the plateau beyond which it is joined by its major tributary, the Kessem River. This part of the Awash is about 197 feet wide (60 meters) and just over 3 feet (1 meter) deep in the dry season and 49 to 59 feet (15 to 18 meters) during the rainy season when it floods the plains along both banks. Its waters, which never reach the Gulf of Tadjura, end in a chain of salt lakes in the Danakil desert.

The Awash forms the southeastern boundary of Awash National Park. The dramatic Awash Falls are located near the park. The river below the falls offers a popular one or two-day rafting trip where one can see spectacular **bird life** and vervet and colobus monkeys. The river irrigates an area of about 24,000 square miles (60,000 square kilometers), which affords the farmers the opportunity to grow **cotton**, dates, maize, and tobacco and to tend livestock. The opening of the Awash I (1960), Awash II (1966), and Awash III (1968) hydroelectric generating facilities, which have a combined capacity of 107,200 kilowatts, is an important part of Ethiopia's electricity grid. *See also* HYDROPOWER.

AWINGI PEOPLE AND LANGUAGE. The Awingi are often included among the **Agaw**. They number about 500,000 and reside south of **Lake Tana** in scattered parts of Agaw Midir and Metekel zones. They are also sometimes called **Damot** in the belief that they had migrated from the old Damot Province in southeast Ethiopia under pressure from the **Oromo**. Today, the Awingi are **agriculturists**. They speak a Cushitic **language** that is separate from Agaw and most Awingi speak **Amharic** as a second language.

AXUM (AKSUM). The *Periplus of the Erythraean Sea*, a Greek document of the late first century A.D., describes the region ruled from Axum and suggests that the city, located in present-day **Tigray Region**, was already important at that early date. The *Periplus of the Erythraean Sea* also notes that the **Red Sea** port of **Adulis**, near today's **Massawa** in Eritrea, was part of the Axumite Kingdom. Axum engaged in Red Sea commerce and trade with the Roman Empire, India, and Ceylon (now Sri Lanka). In the first several centuries A.D., Axum dominated the region and thrived on trade and **agriculture**. Stone palaces had a distinctive architectural style.

In the late third century, the prophet Mani wrote that Axum was one of the world's four great kingdoms. King **Ezana** (reigned c. 303–356), who was Axum's first Christian monarch, called himself king of Axum, Saba, Salhen, Himyar, Raydan, Habashat, Tiamo, Kasu, and the **Beja** tribes. Saba, Salhen, Himyar, and Raydan refer to two of the Yemeni kingdoms and the palaces in their respective capitals. Habashat is **Abyssinia** and Tiamo may be the old Di'amat. Kasu is Meroe in the biblical Kush in modern Sudan and the Beja tribes still live in Sudan.

In the early sixth century, King Kaleb expanded the Axumite kingdom in Yemen and parts of Arabia. A sixth-century Greek visitor to Axum wrote of a four-towered palace of the king of Ethiopia. Even today, there are impressive remains at Axum, especially the royal tombs and their markers, the stelae or obelisks. Cut from a type of granite, they may represent a kind of stairway to heaven for Axum's dead rulers. At the base there are granite plates with carved wine cups for offerings to the deceased's spirit. The Axumites produced their own coinage from about the late third century until the seventh century, when Axum's power began to wane. The coins first used Greek and later a combination of Greek and **Ge'ez.** In the late sixth century, the Persians conquered Yemen. Not long after, Axum lost control of

AYELE GEBRE (1896-

the Red Sea trade to the Roman Empire and India. With the **Islam** about 640, the Roman or Byzantine Empire no longer had access to the Red Sea and Indian Ocean and their ships ended visits to Adulis. Axum became a doomed and forgotten place. Muslim states took control of the coastal areas, blocking Ethiopia's foreign trade.

Portuguese chaplain **Francisco Alvares** provided the first extensive description of Axum, having spent eight months in the town during his 1520–1526 visit to Ethiopia. He documented some structures, especially the original Saint Mary of Zion Church that probably was destroyed by **Ahmad ibn Ibrahim al Ghazi**. Subsequent visitors to Axum wrote about a town that looked much like it does today. Among the most important ruins are King Ezana's park, King Basen's tomb, King Kaleb's palace, the Mai Shum reservoir, the Pantaleon Monastery, Mary of Zion Church, Dongar or the queen of Sheba's palace, and the stelae fields. Exciting archaeological work is continuing by the Italian Rodolfo Fattovich and the American Kathryn Bard. Stuart Munro-Hay and David Phillipson have written extensively and authoritatively about Axum. Italy has agreed to return to Ethiopia the Axum Obelisk, now in Rome, which it removed from the country in 1937.

AYELE GEBRE (1896–1960). Civil servant, diplomat, government minister, crown councilor, and senator. Born in Garamulata, Hararge and educated at the Capuchin Mission in **Harar**, where Ras Tafari Makonnen, later **Haile Selassie**, also was a student. Ayele began his career in **Dire Dawa** by working for the **Addis Ababa–Djibouti Railway**. He then served in that town's post office and later became subdirector and director of customs. In 1928, Ayele received an appointment as acting head of customs in **Addis Ababa**. The following year, he became director of the municipality of Addis Ababa. In 1932, Ayele served as head of the Special Court.

During and after the **Italian-Ethiopian War**, he collaborated with the Italians by helping to develop the local **judiciary** and by participating in the search for those responsible for the failed 19 February 1937 assassination attempt against **Rodolfo Graziani**. Despite his cooperation, he became a prisoner in Asinara, Italy. In 1939, Italy repatriated Ayele to Ethiopia. Haile Selassie, his longtime friend, overlooked his wartime relationship with the Italians and appointed him minister of justice. In 1944, he became envoy extraordinary and minister plenipotentiary and reopened the Ethiopian legation in London. During 1947–1955, Ayele served as deputy governor of Hararge. He then returned to Addis Ababa, where he again became minister of justice. Thereafter, he worked as crown councilor and senator. On 16 December 1960, security forces killed him and other hostages who were being held by the plotters of the **coup attempt (1960)**. *See also* AFRICA ORIENTALE ITALIANA.

– B –

BADOGLIO, PIETRO (1871–1956). Italian general, first viceroy of Ethiopia and **Africa Orientale Italiana** (9 May 1936–22 May 1936), Duke of **Addis Ababa**, Marquis of Sabotino, and statesman. Born in Grazzano Monferrato (now Grazzano Badoglio) on 11 September 1894. Educated at the Turin military academy. Badoglio first saw active military service during the **Battle of Adwa**. During the 1911–1912 Italo-Turkish war, he served in the Italian campaign in Tripoli. In **World War I**, Badoglio participated in the capture of Monte Sabotono, an action that established his military reputation.

After World War I, he became a senator and then went as special envoy to Romania and later the United States. During 1924–1935, Badoglio served as Ambassador to Brazil. In June 1935, he became marshal of Italy and then chief of the general staff of the army. Badoglio's next assignment was as governor of Libya (1928–1933).

On 17 November 1935, Badoglio replaced **Emilio De Bono** as commander in chief of Italian forces in East Africa. After reorganizing Italian military forces, he quickly completed the conquest of Ethiopia by employing ruthless tactics and using **chemical weapons** against the **patriots** and noncombatant civilians. Badoglio's victory at the **Battle of Amba Aradom** broke Ethiopian resistance in the strategically important northern **highlands**. Badoglio then served as viceroy of **Abyssinia** for a few weeks before returning to Italy, where he received a hero's welcome.

During **World War II**, he was chief of the general staff. However, in 1940, Badoglio resigned because of his disgust with Mussolini and the Fascists. After Mussolini resigned on 25 July 1943, Badoglio became prime minister, a post he held until 1944. On 1 November 1956, he died in Grazzano Monferrato.

BAEDA MARIAM I (c. 1446–1478). Son of **Zara Yakob** and emperor of Ethiopia (1468–1478). Little is known about Baeda's early life except that he spent much of his youth in Debre Berhan, his father's capital in northern **Shoa** Province. After becoming emperor, he banished the royal princes and imprisoned them at **Amba** Geshen in Shoa Province. Baeda also assumed command of the army and appointed new rulers to the provinces. His greatest legacy concerned the many churches he built in his kingdom.

BAGEMDER PROVINCE. Bagemder was one of the administrative divisions during the **Haile Selassie** government. The **Derg** renamed it Gondar Province. The principal towns in Bagemder were **Gondar** and **Debre Tabor**. Virtually all of **Lake Tana** was in the province. Following a reorganization of the regions by the **Ethiopian People's Revolutionary Democratic Front**, Bagemder today consists of north and south Gondar zones and some of Wag Hamra zone in **Amhara Region**. As part of the northern Amhara highlands, Bagemder played a major role throughout Ethiopian history. Gondar's establishment as a permanent capital in 1636 by Emperor **Fasilidas** began Bagemder's golden era. Gondar's importance declined following **Iyasu II**'s death (1755). During the subsequent **Era of the Princes**, the empire ceased to exist as a centrally administered polity.

BAHIR DAR (BAHAR DAR). (121,700; estimated 2002 **population**.) Ethiopia's seventh largest city and capital of **Amhara Region**. Located some 358 miles (578 kilometers) northwest of **Addis Ababa** and situated on **Lake Tana**'s southern shore. Bahir Dar is a thriving commercial center and jumping off point for **tourists** visiting the nearby Blue Nile Falls and Lake Tana's island monasteries. Although the **Blue Nile**'s true source is in the hills southwest of Bahir Dar and flows into Lake Tana, the river empties from the lake on the city's outskirts. Bahir Dar also is becoming an important **banking** and **educational** center and has one of the country's most centrally located and important airports.

Although Bahir Dar gives the impression of a fairly new city, it became important in the 16th and 17th centuries when Ethiopian leaders established temporary capitals in the vicinity of Lake Tana. During the reign of Emperor **Susneyos** (1607–1632), the Jesuits unsuccessfully tried to impose **Catholicism** in the area. One Jesuit building can still be seen in the compound of Saint George's Church.

BAISO PEOPLE AND LANGUAGE. Numbering only about 1,000, the Baiso people live on several small islands in Lake Abaya and small communities on the west side of the lake. They have avoided extinction for at least 1,000 years. They are **agriculturists**, fishermen, weavers, and hippo hunters. They speak an east Cushitic **language**, although most Baiso are bilingual in **Wolaytta**.

BAKAFA (1694–1730). Emperor of Ethiopia (1721–1730). Son of **Iyasu I**. Also known as Atsma-Giyorgis, Adbar Tsaga II, and Masih Tsaga. After his father's death (1706), Bakafa was jailed on Ama Waheni, near **Gondar**. He escaped twice and took refuge among the **Oromo**. After recapture, Bakafa remained imprisoned until Emperor Dawit III's death (1721). On 21 May 1721, he was crowned emperor at Gondar. Bakafa gradually reasserted Imperial authority, especially in **Tigray**; eroded the nobility's power, and established control over the provinces by appointing Governors loyal to him. He also suppressed rebellions by people of **Damot** in **Gojam** and those in Lasta, south of **Lalibela**. Throughout his reign, Bakafa enjoyed the support of the military and the masses but the nobility hated him. Apart from these political and military exploits, Bakafa facilitated a cultural revival, especially with regard to the arts, architecture, and **literature**. Illness forced him to live the last two years of his life in seclusion. Bakafa died on 19 September 1730.

BAKER, SAMUEL WHITE (1821–1893). Explorer, traveler, and sportsman. Born on 8 June 1821 in London. Baker was educated at a private school in Rottingdean, then attended College School, Gloucester (1833–1835) and subsequently studied under the Reverend Henry Peter Dunster, a private tutor in Tottenham (1838–1840). He finished his education in Germany. During the next 16 years, Baker lived and worked in Mauritius, Ceylon (now Sri Lanka), eastern Europe, and Asia Minor (1858–1860).

On 15 April 1861, Baker undertook a trip up the Nile River to Korosko. He and his wife, Florence, then went to Kassala near the Sudanese-Ethiopian border to explore the Nile River's eastern tributaries. Baker spent five months exploring the Setit River, a tributary of the **Atbara River**, and hunting big game largely with the Hamran Arabs. He also explored other tributaries of the Atbara, including the Bahr-er-Salam and the Angareb, and then traveled along the Rehad to its confluence with the **Blue Nile**. After completing this phase of the expedition, Baker marched to Khartoum, where he arrived on 11 June 1862.

The results of this 14-month journey, while not overly significant, were nevertheless impressive. He discovered that the Nile River's sediment was due to its Ethiopian tributaries. Additionally, Baker gained experience as an African explorer, mastered Arabic, and learned to use astronomical instruments that were vital for determining geographical locations. These skills facilitated his travels throughout East Africa (1863–1864).

On 14 October 1865, Baker arrived in Britain where he became active in local affairs and published books such as the *Exploration of the Nile Tributaries of Abyssinia, Ismailia*, and *The Nile Tributaries of Abyssinia, and the Sword Hunters of the Hamran Arabs*. On 30 December 1893, he died of a heart attack at Sandford Orleigh, near Newton Abbot.

BALCHA ABBA NEFSO (1862–1936). Military leader and provincial governor. Born in **Gurage**. He was educated by priests and received his primary education at the imperial court. As a young boy, Balcha had been wounded, captured, and castrated in one of **Menelik II**'s military campaigns. **Ras Makonnen Walda Mikael** successfully petitioned the emperor for his guardianship. After serving Ras Makonnen as an *ashker* (servant), he received a posting to Menelik II's palace and eventually became the Imperial Court's Treasurer. Balcha achieved fame and notoriety during the **Battle of Adwa**, when he replaced a dead cannoneer and used the weapon with great effectiveness against the Italians. After the war, Balcha received the title of **dajazmach**.

His administrative career began shortly thereafter when he received an appointment as governor of Sidamo Province (1898–1908).

Subsequent posts included governor of **Harar** and Sidamo Province (1910–1914 and 1917–1928). Balcha had a mixed record as governor. He paid no taxes to the central government, refused to outlaw **slavery**, and regularly exploited the peasantry. On the other hand, Balcha improved provincial administration and cooperated with Indian traders to establish relatively competent credit and marketing systems.

Balcha also was no stranger to court politics. In 1916, he participated in the downfall of **Lij Iyasu Mikael** and defeated his forces at Harar. His frequent clashes with **Ras** Tafari Makonnen, later **Haile Selassie**, eventually caused his dismissal (1928). Balcha then retired to a monastery (1928–1935). After the outbreak of the **Italian-Ethiopian War**, he rejoined the military and died fighting the Italians on 6 November 1936 (some sources maintain that he died on 5 November).

BALE MOUNTAINS. The Bale Mountains, which include the Bale Mountain **national park**, contain Africa's most extensive Afro-alpine habitat. Much of the area is a vast moorland that varies between 5,000 feet (1,500 meters) and 13,000 feet (3,960 meters) in altitude. Its mountains are the source of the **Wabe Shebelle** and the **Genale** Rivers. The Bale Mountains boast Ethiopia's second highest peak, Tullu Deemtu, at 14,360 feet (4,377 meters). Bale is home to the rare mountain nyala and Simien fox among the 60 species of mammals in the area. There also are some 260 species of **bird life** and unusual flora. The road from Goba, the principal town in the Bale Mountains, up the Sanetti plateau and down the Harenna escarpment reaches 13,200 feet (4,000 meters), making it the highest all-weather road in Africa.

BAMBASSI PEOPLE AND LANGUAGE. The Bambassi, also known as the northern Mao, number more than 5,000 and reside in the Dabus (Yabus) area of **Benishangul/Gumuz Region** near Bambesi town. The **Berta** live to the north and the **Oromo** in all other directions. They are divided into exogamous clans; each clan recognizes only the authority of the clan head. The Bambassi do not have chiefs. They live in both beehive and cylindrical huts. Their supreme being, Yere or Yeretsi, lives in a serene heaven. They speak a north Omotic **languag**e of the Mao family that has a 31 percent lexical similarity with other Omotic languages and some connection with **Hozo**. Some Bambassi speak Afan Oromo or Arabic, but virtually none speaks **Amharic**.

BANKING. Modern banking began on 10 March 1905, when **Menelik II** authorized the establishment of the Bank of **Abyssinia**, which was an affiliate of the National Bank of Egypt. The Bank of Abyssinia, which officially opened on 16 February 1906, performed poorly until the railway reached **Addis Ababa** (1917) and stimulated trade. The economic upturn allowed the bank to register profits in 1919, 1920, and from 1924 onwards. Shareholders received an average 4 percent return on their investments. The bank also opened numerous branch offices, including **Harar** (1906), **Dire Dawa** (1908), Gore (1912), and **Dese** (1920). The bank also established a transit office in Djibouti (1920). Growing criticism that the Bank of Abyssinia was inefficient, foreign controlled, and purely profit motivated eventually led to its demise (1931).

On 29 August 1931, an imperial decree established the Bank of Ethiopia, which assumed responsibility for all of the Bank of Abyssinia's branch offices. The Ethiopian government owned 60 percent of the bank's total shares and the minister of finance exercised authority over all bank transactions. The Bank of Ethiopia, which issued the **currency**, opened a branch office in **Debre Tabor** and an agency in **Gambela**.

After the outbreak of the **Italian-Ethiopian War**, the Bank of Ethiopia closed its doors. Italy opened branches of its main banks (e.g., Banco d'Italia, Banco di Roma, Banco di Napoli, and Banca Nazionale del Lavoro) in many of Ethiopia's main towns. After liberation, these banks ceased operations with the exception of Banco di Roma and Banco di Napoli, both of which maintained offices in Asmara. From 1 July 1941 to 14 February 1942, Barclays Bank offered banking services, largely for British military personnel, in Addis Ababa. On 14 February 1942, the **British Military Administration** closed all Italian banks and sent their assets to the British controller of banks in Asmara.

On 15 April 1943, the State Bank of Ethiopia commenced operations with the authority to act as Ethiopia's central bank and to issue banknotes and coins as the Ministry of Finance's agent. By the time it ceased operations in December 1963, the State Bank of Ethiopia had established 21 offices in Ethiopia, a branch office in Khartoum, and a transit office in Djibouti.

The Ethiopian Monetary and Banking Law (1963) separated the functions of central and commercial banking by creating the National Bank of Ethiopia and the Commercial Bank of Ethiopia, both of which opened their doors in January 1964. The legislation also authorized foreign banks to operate in Ethiopia providing Ethiopians owned at least 51 percent of the shares of each foreign bank. Other important financial institutions included Imperial Savings and Home Ownership Public Association, the Savings and Mortgage Corporation of Ethiopia, and Agricultural Bank. In 1951, the Investment Bank replaced the Agricultural Bank; in 1965, the Investment Bank changed its name to the Ethiopian Investment Corporation Share Company. In 1970, the government established the Agricultural and Industrial Bank, which assumed responsibility for the assets and liabilities of the Development Bank and Investment Corporation of Ethiopia.

In 1974, the **Derg** nationalized the **economy**. As part of that process, the government reduced the number of banks. In 1976, for example, three privately owned banks (Addis Ababa Bank, Banco di Roma, and Banco di Napoli) merged to form Ethiopia's second largest bank called the Addis Ababa Bank, which had 34 branch offices and 480 employees. On 2 August 1980, the government issued proclamation No. 184 that ordered the Commercial Bank of Ethiopia to take over the Addis Ababa Bank, thus forming Ethiopia's sole commercial bank with 128 branch offices and 3,633 employees. The proclamation also created the Housing and Savings Bank. Proclamation No. 158 (1979) replaced the Agricultural and Industrial Bank with the Agricultural and Industrial Development Bank. By the time of the Derg's downfall (1991), there were only three banks in Ethiopia (National Bank of Ethiopia, Commercial Bank of Ethiopia, and Agricultural and Industrial Development Bank).

The Monetary and Banking Proclamation (1994) liberalized the banking sector. Consequently, several privately owned banks started operations, including the Awash International Bank (1994), Dashen Bank (1995), Bank of Abyssinia (1996), Wegagen Bank (1997), United Bank (1998), and Nib International Bank (1999).

Despite this significant policy change, the banking sector remained plagued by problems. In January 2002, the government arrested more than 40 senior Central Bank of Ethiopia employees for **corruption**. On 3 October 2002, the **Economic Commission for Africa** criticized Addis Ababa for allowing Ethiopians to invest only within the largely government-owned banking and insurance sectors. *See also* DEBT; INTERNATIONAL MONETARY FUND; WORLD BANK.

BANNA PEOPLE AND LANGUAGE. The Banna or Bena people live east of Mago **National Park**, to the north of the **Hamer,** and to the south of the **Ari**. The area they inhabit includes a cool mountainous area around Chari mountain near Kako town and continuing to a hot savanna near Dimeka. They intermarry with the Ari and Hamer while Banna **women** marry the **Tsamai** to the east. Their basic diet consists of cereals, beans, and milk. Although a separate ethnic group, they speak virtually the same south Omotic **language** that the Hamer speak. They number about 60,000 and engage primarily in **agriculture** supplemented by pastoralism, gathering, and hunting. Several thousand are Christian, mainly members of the **Kale Hiwot Church**. The Banna have their own king.

BARATIERI, ORESTE (1841–1901). Italian general. Born on 13 November 1841 in Condino, near Venice. Baratieri served as a captain of volunteers under Giuseppe Garibaldi (1807–1882) in the Battle of Capua (1860). He then became a member of parliament. In 1872, he joined the regular army.

Baratieri's African experience included a tour in Eritrea (1887–1891) and service as commander of Italian troops in Africa (1891) and governor of Eritrea (1892–1896). On 17 July 1894, Baratieri commanded a 2,500-man mobile column, which marched 125 miles (201 kilometers) in four days and captured Kassala, Sudan, from the Mahdists. His next major campaign occurred on 28 December 1894, when he and 3,500 **askaris** occupied **Adwa** after **Ras Mangasha Yohannes** refused to surrender and fled the scene. On 13–14 January 1894, Baratieri's troops finally defeated Mangasha's forces at the **Battle of Coatit**.

His next campaign occurred in December 1894, when he relieved a besieged Italian garrison at a fort called Halai. Some of the Ethiopians fled into **Tigray**'s interior and joined Mangasha. Baratieri ordered Mangasha to give up the "rebels" and to use his remaining troops to attack the Dervishes at Gedaref. After Mangasha rebuffed the ultimatum, he and some 3,500 askaris occupied Adwa without a fight on 29 December 1894. Baratieri returned to Italy where he received a hero's welcome and promised to destroy **Menelik II**'s army.

His hopes for further glory were dashed at the **Battle of Adwa**. On 21 March 1896, the Italian authorities ordered that Baratieri be tried on criminal charges for poor planning of the Adwa campaign and for abandoning his campaign during the retreat of Italian forces from Adwa. A court subsequently acquitted him of any criminal wrongdoing but indicated that it deplored the fact that he was "so entirely unfit to cope with the exigencies of the situation." Shortly thereafter, he retired from the army. On 7 August 1901, Baratieri died in Sterzing, Tirol, Austria-Hungary.

BARO RIVER. *See* SOBAT RIVER.

BASILIOS, ABUNA (1891–1970). Patriarch of the **Ethiopian Orthodox Church** (EOC). Born Gebre Giyorgis, he became a monk of **Debre Libanos**. In 1933, Basilios went to **Jerusalem**, where he took charge of Ethiopian churches and monasteries in that city. After the outbreak of the **Italian-Ethiopian War**, he returned to Ethiopia and served as a chaplain during the Battle of Maichew. Basilios subsequently returned to Jerusalem but maintained contact with the resistance movement. In 1948, he was ordained a bishop. Two years later, Basilios became an archbishop and assumed responsibility for church administration and management of church properties. On 28 June 1959, the Egyptian Coptic patriarch Kyrillos IV appointed Basilios as EOC patriarch. In this capacity, he did little to modernize the EOC but concentrated on serving **Haile Selassie**. In October 1970, the international media announced his death. *See also* ABBA SALAMA, ABUNA; COPTIC ORTHODOX CHURCH OF ALEXANDRIA; MATEWOS, ABUNA; PAULOS GEBRE-YOHANNES, ABUNA; TEWOFLOS.

BASKETO PEOPLE AND LANGUAGE. Some 100,000 Basketo people live on the east bank of the **Omo River** in North Omo zone between the **Dime** to the south and the **Malo** to the north. In 2000, the **Southern Nations, Nationalities and People's Region** accorded the Basketo special *woreda* status. The Basketo breed cattle and were once known for hunting elephants. They speak an Omotic **language** in the Ometo family that has 61 percent lexical similarity with **Oyda**, a nearby people. Very few Basketo speak any language other than Basketo.

BASKETRY. *See* HANDICRAFTS.

BATTLE OF ADWA (1–2 MARCH 1896). Known by the Italians as the Battle of Abba Garima, from the mountain of that name. The Battle of Adwa is one of the most significant military events in Ethiopian history as it temporarily halted Italy's penetration of the country. Additionally, **Adwa** became an important chapter in European colonial history, as it was the first time an African force scored such a major victory against a European army.

The events that led to the Battle of Adwa are well documented. In 1889, Italy supported the accession of **Menelik II**. However, Ethiopian-Italian relations soured after the Emperor renounced the **Treaty of Wichale,** which had established an Italian protectorate over his kingdom. On 6–8 December 1891, Italy therefore concluded the Convention of Mareb with Menelik II's rival, **Mangasha Yohannes**, who ruled **Tigray**. Unfortunately for Rome, in June 1894, the two Ethiopian leaders concluded a secret alliance against Italy known as the Convention of **Entoto**. Six months later, Ras Mangasha launched an unsuccessful rebellion at Batha Agos against the Italians in the province of Okule-Kusai, a region that he previously had controlled. To prevent further unrest, the Italians occupied Adwa.

Menelik II, who feared an expansion of Italian colonial power, led an estimated 100,000 Ethiopian troops against an Italian force, which numbered about 17,700 (10,596 Italians and 7,104 **askaris**) troops. Early on the morning of 1 March 1896, the battle commenced. Within a few hours, the poorly coordinated Italian campaign crumbled. The Italians lost 261 officers, 2,918 noncommissioned officers and men, and 954 missing and presumed dead, for a total of 6,123 deaths. Additionally, 2,261 askaris lost their lives. The wounded included 470 Italians and 958 askaris. The Ethiopians lost between 5,000 and

6,000 men. Another 8,000 were wounded. Major Generals **Giuseppe Arimondi** and Vittorio Dabormida lost their lives while Major General Albertone was taken prisoner. The Italian government charged **Oreste Baratieri**, the overall commander, with criminal negligence. A court subsequently acquitted him but noted that he was "unfit" for command.

The battle was the greatest military disaster in European colonial history. When news of the Ethiopian victory reached Italy, there was rioting throughout the country that claimed many lives, including at least 100 in Milan. The crisis also brought down the government of Premier Francesco Crispi (1819–1901).

On 9 April 1896, Rome sued for peace and, on 26 October 1896, Italy and Ethiopia concluded a peace agreement. The Adwa victory remains a national **holiday** in Ethiopia. *See also* ARMED FORCES.

BATTLE OF AMBA ALAGE (ALAGI) (7 DECEMBER 1895). The origin of this battle lay in Italy's determination to expand its East African empire. On 9 October 1895, the Italians scored a victory over **Ras Mangasha Yohannes** at Debre Aila. Shortly thereafter, **Oreste Baratieri** annexed **Tigray**. **Menelik II**, who feared that Rome aimed to establish a protectorate over Ethiopia, sought to avoid a confrontation by reaching an understanding with the Italians. In October 1895, he dispatched **Ras Makonnen Walda Mikael** to Zeila to open peace negotiations but the Italians rejected this overture. Menelik II responded by raising a 30,000-man largely **Oromo** army and deploying it to Amba Alage in southern Tigray.

On the morning of 7 December 1895, this force clashed with an Italian column commanded by Major Pietro Toselli (1841–1896). During the six-hour battle, the Ethiopians killed more than 2,000 troops, including Toselli. Near the end of the fighting, General **Giuseppe Arimondi** arrived with reinforcements. The Ethiopians also decimated this column but Arimondi and about 400 soldiers escaped to **Mekele**, where he left the wounded with the Italian garrison. He and his troops then continued their retreat to Edaga Hamus, south of Adigrat. Ethiopia's victory at Amba Alage boosted morale, destroyed the notion of European invincibility, and helped lay the groundwork for the **Battle of Adwa**.

BATTLE OF AMBA ARADAM (10–15 FEBRUARY 1936). Key battle in Italy's campaign to conquer the northern **highlands**. By 4 February 1936, Italian air and ground forces, under the command of **Pietro Badoglio**, had used 280 cannons and 170 aircraft to bomb Ethiopian positions along a 250-mile front between **Dese** and Amba Aradam, a strategically important flat-topped mountain southeast of Mekele. The minister of war, **Ras** Mulugueta, had deployed 35,000–40,000 troops to Amba Aradam. His forces had 400 machine guns, 10 cannons, and a few antiaircraft guns. On 10 February 1936, Badoglio launched an offensive that included three divisions (Sabauda, Pusteria, and January 3rd) from I Corps and two divisions (Sila and March 23rd) from III Corps. The Assietta and Eritrean divisions remained in reserve. Using an encircling movement, the Italians quickly defeated the Ethiopians and occupied Amba Aradam on 15 February 1936. The following day, Ras Mulugueta and 50 of his men fled Amba Aradam. During 17–19 February, Badoglio's forces pursued the remnants of the Ethiopian army. During this operation, the Italian Air Force (Regia Aeronautica) flew 546 raids, dropped 396 tons of bombs, and fired 30,000 rounds of machine gun ammunition. On 27 February 1936, Raya-Galla *shiftas* killed Ras Mulugueta. Italian casualties, including dead and wounded, totaled 36 officers, 621 Italian soldiers, and 145 **askaris**. The Ethiopians lost an estimated 20,000 troops.

BATTLE OF AYSHAL (29 JUNE 1853). The origins of this conflict began in 1852, when Kassa Haylu refused an order to join **Ras** Ali II (reigned 1831–1853) of Yeju, who controlled most princes and regions of northern Ethiopia, for his perennial military expedition against **Gojam**. In retaliation, **Dajazmach** Goshu Zewde of Gojam, an ally of Ras Ali II, clashed with Kassa's army at the Battle of Gur Amba (27 November 1852). Ras Ali II. Along with his army and government, fled **Gondar** and went to **Debre Tabor**, where he called up additional troops from **Wollo**, Yeju, **Tigray**, and Gojam. He then returned to Gondar which Kassa had occupied. After a victory at the Battle of Takusa (12 April 1853), Kassa burned Debre Tabor. On 29 June 1853, Kassa's army destroyed Ras Ali II's **Oromo** cavalry in one of the costliest battles during the **Era of the Princes**. Ras Ali II retreated to Yeju, where he died in 1856.

BATTLE OF COATIT (KO'ATIT, KEWATIT) (13–14 JANUARY 1895). This battle occurred because of Italy's determination to establish a presence in Ethiopia. To achieve this goal, Italian officials had been conducting independent talks (1891–1892) with **Tigray**'s **Ras** Mengesha Seyoum (1887–1960), **Yohannes IV**'s nephew and later adopted son. In June 1894, he went to **Addis Ababa** to receive **Menelik II**'s pardon for his indiscretions.

On 15 December 1894, Bahta Hagos, the Italian-supported governor of Akkele Guzay, revolted and proclaimed the independence of his province from foreign rule. On 18 December 1894, Italian soldiers killed Bahta Hagos outside Halai. **Oreste Baratieri**, the Italian Governor of **Eritrea**, suspected that Ras Mengesha, with Menelik II's support, had engineered the revolt. He therefore marched on **Adwa** but quickly withdrew because he lacked the capabilities to confront the rebels.

Ras Mengesha pursued him back across the **Mereb River** into Eritrea, where the two sides clashed at Coatit. The Italian force included 3,883 soldiers (66 Italian officers and 105 Italians in the ranks, 3,684 **askaris**, 28 cavalrymen armed with lances, and one mountain battery with four guns). The Italians lost three officers and 92 troops while two officers and 227 troops were wounded. Ras **Mangasha Yohannes**, who commanded a force of some 10,000 soldiers, was also unprepared for the campaign. After the Italians had killed about 1,500 of his troops and wounded some 3,000 others, he withdrew to Tigray. The indecisive outcome of the battle not only ensured that tensions between Italy and Ethiopia remained high but also helped to lay the groundwork for the **Battle of Adwa**.

BATTLE OF DOGALI (26 JANUARY 1887). Known in Ethiopia as the Battle of Tedale. The events that led to the Battle of Dogali began in the mid-1880s, when Italy started consolidating its presence around **Massawa**. **Yohannes IV** relied on **Ras Alula Qubi** to stop this advance. In January 1886, Ras Alula therefore occupied the village of Wa, west of Zula. However, on 23 November 1886, General Carlo Géne overran Wa. Ras Alula responded by arresting the members of an Italian exploration party led by Count Augusto Salimbeni and offering to free them if Italian soldiers evacuated Wa. Géne refused and not only reinforced Wa but also deployed troops to Saati. On 25 January 1887, Ras Alula launched an unsuccessful campaign against Saati. Nevertheless, Géne, who feared another Ethiopian attack, abandoned Saati, Wa, and Arafali. However, on 26 January 1887, a 20,000-man Ethiopian force surprised and nearly destroyed a 524-man Italian contingent (only 80 wounded troops survived), commanded by Lieutenant Colonel De Cristoforis who had been transporting supplies to the Saati garrison, near the village of Dogali. After the battle, Ras Alula informed the Italians that peace was possible only if they remained in their own territory. Unfortunately, the Italian government dispatched more troops to East Africa.

In retrospect, the Battle of Dogali was one of the most significant events of the late 19th century because of the enmity it created between Ethiopia and Italy. The confrontation also started a series of events that eventually led to the **Battle of Adwa**.

BATTLE OF EMBABO (7 JUNE 1881). The origins of this battle lay with the competition between Menelik (later **Menelik II**) and **Adal Tessemma** to gain control of the **Oromo** territories in the Gibe River vicinity. On 20 January 1881, **Yohannes IV** sought to avoid a confrontation by crowning Adal Tessemma, afterwards known as **Takla Haymanot**, as **negus** of **Gojam** and **Kafa**. This strategy failed as Menelik sent **Ras Gobana Dachi** to collect tribute from Goma and Kafa while Takla's deputy was in the region. Their two forces briefly fought at Dilaloin Nonno. The matter then escalated to the level of Menelik and Takla.

On 7 June 1881, their armies clashed at Embabo in northwest **Wollega Province** in a fierce, daylong battle with both kings taking part in the fighting. Menelik's **Shoan** army wounded and captured Takla and decimated his army by killing more than half its troops. Menelik's losses included 913 killed and 1,648 wounded, and in the looting that followed another 50 men were killed.

The Shoan victory had long-term implications for Ethiopia. Between 1882 and 1886, Menelik secured the submission of several Oromo leaders, including Kumsa Moroda of Leqa Naqamte, Jote Tullu of Leqa Qellam, and Abba Jifar II of **Jimma**. The rulers of other Gibe River territories and of **Ilubabor** also eventually acknowledged Menelik's supremacy. The loyalty of these territories ensured that Menelik had a steady source of revenue that made him the only serious contender for Yohannes IV's throne.

BATTLE OF GUNDET (16 NOVEMBER 1875). The origins of this battle lay in the decline of Ottoman rule in Egypt and the emergence of Viceroy Mohammed Ali (c. 1769–1849) and his grandson Ismail Pasha (1830–1895), both of whom were committed to expanding Egyptian influence in the **Horn of Africa**. To achieve this goal, Ismail Pasha sought to improve his army's capabilities by enlisting the services of foreign officers, including several veterans of the American Civil War (1861–1865) and by cultivating good relations with Menelik (later **Menelik II**). On 17–18 September 1875, he issued a series of orders to gain control over all territory between the **Nile River** and the Indian Ocean. One of these orders directed the deployment of an Egyptian column, under the command of **Søren Adolph Arendrup**, to Ethiopia. **Yohannes IV** responded to these machinations on 23 October 1865 by declaring war against Egypt.

According to Colonel William McEntyre Dye, an American in the khedive's service, the Egyptian force included 2,500 troops (others maintain that there were 3,000). Yohannes IV's army nearly massacred the entire column as only a few Egyptians managed to escape. The emperor's troops also captured some 2,500 Remington rifles, 14 artillery pieces, and rocket stands, ammunition, various other supplies, and 20,000 **Maria Theresa thalers**. Ethiopian losses amounted to about 550 dead and 400 wounded.

After his victory, Yohannes IV considered the war with Egypt finished and demobilized much of his army. However, the khedive remained committed to an expansionist policy in Ethiopia. His subsequent actions led to another disaster at the **Battle of Gura**.

BATTLE OF GURA (8–9 MARCH 1876). After the disastrous defeat at the **Battle of Gundet**, Egypt deployed a much larger military force to Ethiopia. In February 1876, a 20,000-man Egyptian army crossed the Mereb River and built forts at Gura and Kayakor. **Yohannes IV** responded by issuing a call to arms to defend Christian Ethiopia against the Muslim invader. With the exception of **Shoa** Province, all of Christian Ethiopia responded. According to some sources, 200,000 Ethiopians volunteered for military service. The Battle of Gura ended Egypt's territorial ambitions in Ethiopia. *See also* LORING, WILLIAM WING.

BATTLE OF KUFIT (23 SEPTEMBER 1885). Located 40 miles (64 kilometers) from Kassala, Sudan. The origin of this battle began with the machinations of Amir Uthman abu Bakr Diqna (c. 1846–1926), a Mahdist leader who was active in eastern Sudan. **Ras Alula Qubi** correctly assumed that he posed a threat to the **Massawa**-Keren-Asmara triangle. On 21 August 1885, the Mahdists gained control of Kassala, a town that could be used as a base from which to launch an attack against Ethiopia. Ras Alula responded to this development by organizing his army. On 23 September 1885, about 10,000 Ethiopians clashed with a Mahdist force of approximately the same size. The Ethiopians killed numbered some 40 officers and 1,500 men, with 300–500 wounded. Estimates of the number of Mahdists killed vary between 3,000 and 10,000. Ras Alula's victory stabilized the Ethiopian-Sudanese border but, more importantly, safeguarded Ethiopia's independence.

BATTLE OF MAGDALA. *See* ANGLO-ETHIOPIAN WAR.

BATTLE OF METEMMA (9 MARCH 1889). The events that led to this battle began in January 1886, when Mahdist forces invaded Dembea and killed its governor, Shum Dahna Fanta. The Mahdists then marched on Chilga, burned the Mahbere Selassie monastery, and butchered all its monks. **Yohannes IV** retaliated by ordering the mobilization of some 100,000 soldiers under the command of Negus **Takla Haymanot**. The army deployed to **Metemma** and then descended on Galabat and scored a decisive victory over the Mahdist force that numbered about 16,000 troops. Despite Galabat's strategic importance, the emperor's army returned to the **highlands** because of the growing Italian threat in northern Ethiopia.

BATTLE OF SAGLE. *See* IYASU MIKAEL, LIJ.

BEGA PEOPLE AND LANGUAGE. Closely related to the **Gumuz**, the Bega are concentrated south of the **Blue Nile** along the Didessa and Dabus Rivers where they are intermingled with the far more numerous **Oromo**. They also are found across the border in Sudan and in neighboring **Gojam**. *Bega* means "people" and their Nilo-Saharan **language** is called literally Bega-ear. The Bega are organized on territorially based clan and subclan lines. In the late 1800s, they migrated from Go-jam to their present area of concentration south of the Blue Nile. Farming is the main occupation of the Bega. They believe in a mythical creator known as Rebba, who knows, hears and sees all. Patrick Wallmark has a chapter on the Bega in the *Peoples and Cultures of the Ethio-Sudan Borderlands* edited by M. Lionel Bender.

BEJA. The Beja peoples reside in Sudan but are believed to have been under the loose control of the Axumite empire, at least in its early years. King **Ezana** sent his two brothers to put down a rebellion by the Beja who had launched periodic attacks against Axumite power. In the late seventh century, a powerful Beja tribe invaded the Axumite empire from the north, laying waste to the countryside in the process. The expansion of the Beja nomads forced foreign traders to flee **Red Sea** coastal towns and thus contributed to the decline of **Axum**'s trade with the civilized world.

BENCH PEOPLE AND LANGUAGE. The Bench are also called the Gimira and the Dizu. They number more than 80,000 in the vicinity of Mizan Teferi. The **Kaficho** reside to the north, the **Sheko** to the west, and the **Me'en** to the south and east. Some have converted to Christianity, but many retain their traditional religious beliefs that includes a sky god known as C'ai. One of the Kafa kings who reigned from about 1675 to 1710 is thought to have incorporated or reincorporated the Bench into the **Kafa**. The Bench live in the forest and raise wheat, barley, corn, and sorghum. They speak a north Omotic **language** in the Gimira family that has several dialects.

BENISHANGUL/GUMUZ REGION. Benishangul/Gumuz is one of Ethiopia's most isolated and least developed regions, with an estimated **population** of only 500,000. It includes part of what was known during **Haile Selassie**'s monarchy as **Wollega Province** and borders southern Sudan's Upper Nile area. It now has three zones, 20 *woredas*, and two special woredas. The Sudan People's Liberation Army periodically uses the Benishangul/Gumuz Region as a staging ground for attacks into neighboring Sudan. A refugee camp for southern Sudanese fleeing the Sudanese civil war is located at Sherkole, about halfway between Asosa, the regional capital, and Kurmuk, on the Ethiopian-Sudanese border. Due to the absence of paved roads, Benishangul/Gumuz Region is often cut off for days at a time from the rest of Ethiopia during the rainy season. The Beles River divides the region roughly into a northern and southern section; there is no way to drive directly between the two sections even during the dry season.

Residents living along the Sudanese border speak several Nilo-Saharan **languages** including **Berta**, **Gumuz**, and **Bambassi**. **Amharic**, **Boro**, **Ganza**, and Kunfal also are spoken. The region's official **language** is Amharic, but Arabic also informally serves this purpose. The **Derg** government forcibly resettled many Ethiopians from other parts of the country in the region. Many, especially those sent from the **highlands**, died of diseases. Some remain to the present day and are successful farmers. The region grows excellent fruit, especially mango. Principal **food** crops include beans, maize, millet, Niger seed, peanuts, sesame, and sorghum.

BERHANU BAYEH (1937–). Lawyer and member of **Mengistu Haile Mariam**'s inner circle. Born in **Gojam**. In 1959, Berhanu entered **Harar** Military Academy as an officer cadet. After graduation, he received a posting to the airborne division in **Nazret** (1963). Two years later, Berhanu entered law school at **Addis Ababa University**. In 1967, he became a lecturer at Harar Military Academy. In 1974, Berhanu joined the **Armed Forces Coordination Committee** as the Harar Military Academy's representative. From 1974 until July 1976, he served as chairman of the **Derg**'s Legal Committee. Berhanu then became head of the Foreign and Political Affairs Committee but, in December 1976, returned to the chairmanship of the Legal Committee. In February 1977, he became head of the newly established Foreign Affairs Committee and then of the **Commission for Organizing the Party of the Working People of Ethiopia** Foreign Affairs Department. On 19 April 1983, Mengistu appointed him minister of labor and, on 12 September 1984, Berhanu became a politburo member of the **Workers' Party of Ethiopia**. On 26 October 1984, he became chairman of the Aid Coordination Department of the Natural Disaster Relief Committee.

Apart from his official duties, Berhanu held periodic discussions (1976–1979) with the **Eritrean Liberation Front** and the **Eritrean**

People's Liberation Front but they failed to end rebel activities. After the **Derg**'s fall (1991), Berhanu, who had become minister of foreign affairs, sought refuge in the Italian embassy in Addis Ababa.

BERTA PEOPLE AND LANGUAGE. Berta origins are unclear. They may have come from southern Sinnar in Sudan. Insecurity in the **lowlands** may have caused their migration to the Ethiopian **highlands**. Known also as Bertha, Barta, and by the Arabic designation of **Benishangul**, the Berta number more than 50,000 in Sudan and Ethiopia. The Berta live along the Ethiopia-Sudan border from **Metemma** in the north to the Dabus River in the south. The Berta are **agriculturists** and breed small black pigs. Their huts are cylindrical with a conical roof, supported by a single center pole. The inside walls are plastered with red clay. Men and **women** wear a skin or piece of leather between the legs attached to the waist by a belt. Berta women wear rings on the ankles, in the nose, ears, and hair and on their wrists and neck. The men wear boar tusks around the neck and brass or iron bracelets on the arms. The Berta paint their bodies with red ochre and have numerous scar tissues on the face, arms, trunk, and sometimes legs.

The Berta supreme being has no cult. They offer sacrifices to a malignant spirit who is thought to live in a man, especially if he is deformed. Increasingly, the Berta have become Muslim. A Nilo-Saharan **language**, Berta is an isolated dialect cluster consisting of a number of dialects spoken by the Berta, the Jebelawin, the Watawit, and others. Useful information on the Berta is found in Ernesta Cerulli's *Peoples of South-West Ethiopia and Its Borderland* and a chapter by Alessandro Triulzi in *Peoples and Cultures of the Ethio-Sudan Borderlands,* edited by M. Lionel Bender.

BETA ISRAEL. *See* FALASHAS.

BIANCHI, GUSTAVO (1845–1884). Italian explorer. In 1878, Bianchi arrived in Ethiopia as part of a mission commanded by Pellegrino Matteucci. During the course of his travels, Bianchi visited **Debre Tabor**, Dembea, and **Gondar**. After the Matteucci mission returned to Italy (1879), he remained in Ethiopia and explored **Shoa** Province, **Oromo**, and **Gojam** territories. In October–November 1883,

Bianchi, acting on behalf of the Società Italiana di Commercio con Africa, unsuccessfully sought to persuade **Yohannes IV** to sign a commercial treaty with Italy. After departing the emperor's court, Bianchi, two of his colleagues (Gherardo Monari and Cesare Diana), and 11 Ethiopians set off for the **Red Sea** coast via the **Danakil Depression**. On 7 October 1884, **Afar** warriors massacred the party at the well of Tio, near Lake Alabad.

BIRALE PEOPLE AND LANGUAGE. The Birale people now number less than 100 and are nearly extinct as a separate ethnic group. There is one remaining village in south Omo zone on the west bank of the Weito River north of Lake **Chew Bahir**. The Birale are wedged between the **Tsamai** people to the west and the **Konso** to the east. They are **agriculturists** and hunters. The older Birale speak an unclassified Afro-Asiatic **language**. The others conduct their affairs in Tsamai.

BIRD LIFE. Ethiopia's proximity to the equator and great habitat diversity gives it one of the richest avifaunas in Africa. There are about 860 species, of which 16 are found only in Ethiopia and 13 can be seen only in Ethiopia and Eritrea, and three are shared only with Somalia. Of the 860 species, almost 700 are believed to be resident while the others are migrants. Of the 10 bird families endemic to the African mainland, eight are found in Ethiopia. Although birds exist throughout the country, areas of special interest include the **Rift Valley** lakes, Awash and Bale **National Parks**, and the river valleys. Birds endemic to Ethiopia include Harwood's francolin (*Francolinus hardwoodi*), found in the valleys and gorges of the upper **Blue Nile** system; Prince Ruspoli's Turaco (*Turaco ruspolii*), found in the juniper forests of southern Ethiopia; Abyssinian longclaw (*Macronyx flavicollis*), found in the western and southern **highlands;** and Stresemann's bush crow (*Zavattariornis stresemann*), found in a small area in southern Ethiopia.

The study of ornithology in Ethiopia has a long and rich background. **James Bruce** has extensive bird notes in the appendix to the fifth volume of *Travels to Discover the Source of the Nile in Egypt, Arabia, Abyssinia and Nubia* published in 1790. **Henry Salt**'s journey to Eritrea and northern Ethiopia in 1809–1810 resulted in an ornithological appendix in *A Voyage to Abyssinia, and Travels into the*

Interior of That Country. In 1832, Edward Ruppell made the first visit to **Abyssinia** for the purpose of cataloging bird species. In 1839–1843, Théophile Lefebvre, A. Petit, and Quartin-Dillon collected many birds while P. V. Ferret and J. G. Galinier did likewise from 1840–1842. In 1842–1844, Paul Wilhelm von Wurttenberg collected birds in central and northeastern Africa. Theodor von Heuglin, perhaps the most important name in Ethiopian ornithology, spent about 12 years in the field observing, collecting, and publishing papers on his observations. His work, published in German in 1869 and 1871, became the basis for all future study. Marquis Antinori, Ragazzi, and Leopoldo Traversi (1876–1887) were the first to make extensive collections in **Shoa** Province. Muzioli's work in **Tigray** and Blundell and Lovat's journey through Somaliland and southern Oromoland added considerably to what is known about the distribution of birds. Arthur Donaldson Smith (1866–1939) contributed more ornithological information about the area between southern Somaliland, Jubaland, and **Lake Rudolf**.

In the early 1900s, the most important contributions to knowledge of Ethiopian avifauna came from the expeditions of Carlo von Erlanger, Oscar Neumann, and Graf von Zedlitz. An American expedition led by Childs Frick traveled from Djibouti to **Addis Ababa** and then through the Rift Valley continuing into Kenya in 1911–1912. Frick then presented the collection to the Smithsonian Institution and Herbert Friedmann, curator of birds, published the results in 1930 as *Birds Collected by the Childs Frick Expedition to Ethiopia and Kenya Colony*. In 1926–1927, William Hudson Osgood led the Field Museum-*Chicago Daily News* Abyssinian Expedition whose other members included Louis Agassiz Fuertes, Jack Baum, Alfred M. Baily, and C. Suydam Cutting. During his 2,000 mile (3,218 kilometers) expedition throughout southern and northern Ethiopia, Osgood collected nearly 2,000 mammal and 2,000 bird specimens. Thirty-six species are threatened and could become extinct before the end of the 21st century unless proper conservation action is taken. The main threat is **deforestation** and the destruction of grasslands and wetlands. The government has designated a network of conservation areas and the **Ethiopian Wildlife and Natural History Society** is working to preserve threatened species. *See also* TOURISM; WILDLIFE.

BIRR. *See* CURRENCY.

BITWODED. Literally beloved. Equivalent to earl in European nobility.

BLACK LIONS. Ethiopian resistance to Italian forces began almost immediately after the outbreak of the **Italian-Ethiopian War (1935–1936)**. The Black Lions dominated the early resistance movement. Its members included students from the Holeta (Genet) Military Academy and foreign-educated Ethiopians. The Black Lions were somewhat critical of Emperor **Haile Selassie** for leaving the country. The president of the Black Lion organization was Dr. Alamawarq Bayyana, a veterinary surgeon educated in Britain. There was an executive committee and a training council headed by Lieutenant Colonel Balay Hayla-Ab, an officer of Eritrean origin from the Holeta (Genet) Military Academy.

The Black Lions had a 10-point constitution. One of the points asserted the supremacy of the political over the military command. There also were injunctions against the harassment of the peasantry and abuse of prisoners of war. It urged members to accept death rather than capture and expressed ultimate loyalty to the emperor. The Black Lion organization convinced **Ras Imru Haile Selassie**, who tried to organize an Ethiopian government in western Ethiopia, to join the movement. He led a resistance force toward **Addis Ababa**. Harassed by the local **Oromo** population, the march turned into a tragedy. In late 1936, his force surrendered to the Italians at the Gojeb River in **Kafa**. The Black Lion organization then collapsed and the Italians liquidated many of its members. Nevertheless, the Black Lions and other Ethiopian **patriots** had a common goal to remove the Italians. This opposition was a major setback to Italian rule. *See also* GIDEON FORCE; MISSION 101; SANDFORD, DANIEL ARTHUR; WINGATE, ORDE.

BLOODY SATURDAY (23 NOVEMBER 1974). During its first months in power, the **Derg** was split between hard-liners, led by **Mengistu Haile Mariam**, who wanted to pursue a military victory over Eritrean separatists, and moderates, who favored a negotiated settlement of the dispute. This crisis, coupled with a wider power struggle in the Derg, led to a decision to execute the most influential moderates.

Those executed for "gross abuse of power" included **Aklilu Habte Wolde** (prime minister), Ras Asrate Kassa (crown councilor), **Lij Makonnen Endakatchew** (prime minister), Ras Mesfin Seleshi (enderassie), Lieutenant-Colonel Tamirat Yegezu (enderassie), Ato Akale Work Habte Wolde (minister), Tesfaye Gebre-Egzy (minister), Ato Mulatu Debebe (minister), Ato Abebe Retta (minister), Dajazmach Legessie Bezu (enderassie), Dajazmach Sahlu Defaye (enderassie), Dajazmach Solomon Abraha (enderassie), Dajazmach Worku Wolde Amanuel (Enderassie), Dajazmach Worku Enqu Selassie (Enderassie), Dajazmach Amero Abebe (Enderassie), and Dajazmach Kebede Ali (enderassie), and Dajazmach Kifle Ergetu **(senator).**

Those executed for "gross abuse of authority" included Colonel Solomon Kedir (chief of security), Afenigus Abeji Debalke (judge), Ato Yilma Aboye (courtier), Ato Tegegn Yetesha-Work (vice minister), Ato Solomon Gebre Mariam (vice minister), Ato Hailu Teklu, Lij Haile Desta (**Ethiopian Red Cross Society** official), Beleta Admassu Retta (courtier), **Fitawrari** Demisse Alamerew (**awaraja** governor), Fitawrari Amede Aberra (awaraja governor), Fitawrari Taddesse Enqu Selassie (awaraja governor), Lieutenant-General Abiye Abebe (minister), Lieutenant-General Keble Gebre (minister), Lieutenant-General Dressie Dubale (commander, ground forces), Lieutenant-General Abebe Gemeda (commander, **Imperial Body Guard**), Lieutenant-General Yilma Shebeshi (**police** commissioner), Lieutenant-General Haile Bykedagn (commander, ground forces), Lieutenant-General Assefa Ayene (minister), Lieutenant-General Belete Abebe, Lieutenant-General Isayas Gebre Selassie (senator), Lieutenant-General Assefa Demissie (aide-de-camp of the emperor), Lieutenant-General Debebe Haile Mariam (enderassie), Major-General Gashaw Kebede, Major-General Seyoum Gedle Giorgis, Major-General Tafesse Lemma, Major-General Mulugetta Wolde Yohannis, Brigadier-General Wondimu Abebe, Brigadier-General Girma Yohannis, Rear Admiral **Iskander Desta** (vice-commander of the **Navy**), Colonel Yalem-Zewde Tessema, Colonel Tassew Mojo, Colonel Yegezu Yimer, Major Berhanu Metcha, Captain Molla Wakene, and Ato Nebiye-Luel Kifle (security chief).

Those executed for "plotting to incite civil war" included Captain Belaye Tsegaye, Captain Demissie Sheferaw, Captain Wolde Yohannis Zergaw, Lance Corporal Tekle Haile, and Private Bekele Wolde Giorgis.

Those executed for "breach of military oath" included Lieutenant-General **Aman Mikael Andom** (chairman of the Derg and **Council of Ministers**, minister of defense, and chief of staff of the **armed forces**), Lieutenant Tesfaye Tekele (Derg member), and Junior Aircraftman Yohannes Fitiwi (Derg member).

On 24 November 1974, the Derg released an official statement entitled "A Major Political Decision" that acknowledged these executions. These executions discredited the Derg domestically and internationally and led to a deterioration in relations between **Addis Ababa** and Washington, D.C.

BLUE NILE. (850 miles long; 1,370 kilometers.) Known locally as the Abay or Abbai, the Blue Nile is one of the world's most famous and important rivers. Numerous explorers sought its source while others tried to follow it from **Lake Tana** into Sudan. In 1771, Scottish traveler **James Bruce** claimed to be the first European to discover the Blue Nile's source. His self-proclaimed discovery is, however, disputed by others. Alan Moorehead's best seller entitled *The Blue Nile* popularized the river's history.

The fact that the Blue Nile provides 59 percent of the water reaching the Aswan Dam in Egypt underscores its importance. Without the Nile, Egypt would cease to exist as we know it today. There have been periodic strains in Egyptian-Ethiopian relations over the use of water from the Blue Nile and other Ethiopian tributaries that provide a total of 86 percent of the Nile River's water. Several groups have rafted major sections of the Blue Nile. *National Geographic* sponsored the most recent expedition (1999), which Virginia Morell has recounted in *Blue Nile: Ethiopia's River of Magic and Mystery.*

Although many believe that Lake Tana is the source of the Blue Nile, it actually begins south of Lake Tana near Sekela in the **Gojam highlands**. It flows for 67 miles (112 kilometers) due north and enters the south side of Lake Tana. The Blue Nile escapes from Lake Tana through a deep crevice at the southeast corner of the lake. During flood stage, the Blue Nile's power is so strong that it virtually holds back the water reaching Khartoum from the White Nile. A brief distance from Lake Tana is one of Ethiopia's major attractions—the

Blue Nile or Tis Isat (smoke of fire) Falls. Actually a series of falls 145 feet (45 meters) high, they extend 1,300 feet (400 meters) across at the height of the rainy season.

The Blue Nile has many tributaries before it reaches the Sudan border near Bumbadi and joins the Roseires Reservoir. The Beshilo River rises near Magdala and drains southern **Wollo**. The Jema River starts near **Ankober** and drains northern and northwestern **Shoa** Province. The Muger River takes rainwater from north and northwest of **Addis Ababa**. The Didesa River, the largest of the Blue Nile tributaries, rises in the Kafa Hills. The Dabus River runs near the western edge of the plateau escarpment and parallel to the Sudan border. All these tributaries entering from the left side of the Blue Nile are perennial. The tributaries entering the right side of the Blue Nile rise mostly on the western side of the plateau have steep slopes and tend to be torrential in the rainy season. The Beles River rises southwest of Lake Tana and reaches the Blue Nile before it enters Sudan. The Dinder River begins west of Lake Tana and flows well into Sudan before joining the Blue Nile south of Wad Medani. The source of the Rahad River is also west of Lake Tana; it enters the Blue Nile just north of Wad Medani. The Dinder and Rahad are insignificant in the dry season.

BORAN PEOPLE AND LANGUAGE. The pastoral Boran, who are the southern branch of the **Oromo** people, call themselves Boorana. They once inhabited the territory from the escarpment north of Dilla in Ethiopia to the Ewaso Ngiro River near the foot of Mount Kenya. However, pressure from **Somalis** along the Genale River in the east, Arsi to the northeast, and Guji to the northwest has largely confined them to an area from Ethiopia's Dirre plateau, Liban, and Badha escarpment to the Golba plains that run from the base of the Ethiopian escarpment to Kenya's Isiolo District.

All Boran share a common identity but recognize regional identities. A Boran man without cattle cannot perform his social obligations, marry, or participate in rituals. In effect, he loses his Boran identity. Over the centuries, the Boran developed a pastoral system that successfully controlled the **population** of people and livestock that could live on the relatively arid land. However, occasional droughts have had a disastrous impact on the Boran.

Boran contact and trade with **Somalis** dates back at least to the 1500s. Competition for scarce grazing and water resources periodically has led to conflict between the two peoples. Somali Darod were particularly aggressive in attacking the Boran on their eastern borders. By 1897, **Menelik II** had conquered the Boran people, primarily to counter the threat of British forces advancing from the south. Ethiopia then established a system of indirect rule among the Boran. The Anglo-Ethiopian demarcation of the Ethiopian/Kenyan frontier divided the Boran between two countries.

Boran society is based on a rigid *gada* age-set system; each set moves through stages of life and responsibility together. The Boran speak a dialect of Afan Oromo. A Cushitic **language**, it is closer to the Afan Oromo spoken by the Arsi and Guji Oromo than it is to western or eastern Afan Oromo. *See also* OGADEN.

BORO PEOPLE AND LANGUAGE. The Boro constitute an enclave of about 7,000 related people who live among the **Amhara people** southwest of **Lake Tana** and near the source of the **Blue Nile**. The grouping includes the Boro and Gamila who speak the Amuru, Wambera, Gamila, and Guba dialects. The **language** is north Omotic and has 46 percent lexical similarity with **Shakacho**, which suggests that the people migrated from the southwest. Most Boro speak **Amharic** as a second language.

BRAIN DRAIN. Like most developing countries, Ethiopia has lost many of its skilled and professional people as a result of emigration. The impact has been particularly severe in the fields of science, engineering, and medicine. Prior to the 1974 revolution, the brain drain was not a serious issue for the country. Virtually all Ethiopians who attended university in the country remained at the completion of their work and the vast majority of those who studied abroad returned to Ethiopia. According to one study, only one Ethiopian physician was working outside the country as recently as 1972. The environment created by the **Derg** as a result of political persecution and the **Red Terror** was a major turning point. It caused a significant migration of highly skilled Ethiopians that continues to the present day, although the reasons for the exodus have changed somewhat.

There are no reliable, long-term statistics for documenting Ethiopia's brain drain. Anecdotal information since 1974 is, however, consistently depressing. During 1980–1991, some 22,700 students studied abroad and only 5,777 or about 25 percent returned to Ethiopia. The **Addis Ababa University** (AAU) academic vice president's annual report for the 1983–1984 academic year noted that more than 300 academic staff had been sponsored for study leave in previous years. Only 22 of them or seven percent returned to AAU. Twenty AAU staff from the physics faculty went abroad for study in the 1970s and 1980s. All 20 remained outside the country.

Of the Ethiopian students sent abroad for study between 1968/1969 and 1995–1996 academic years, 35 percent failed to return to Ethiopia. A study of four government organizations, including AAU, also indicated that out of every 100 professionals sent overseas for training between 1982 and 1997, 35 failed to return. A 2000 report stated that of the 600 AAU academic staff who were sent abroad during the previous 20 years for further studies, only 200 returned. Those trained in medicine were the least likely to return and the higher the level of education, the greater the probability they remained in their adopted country. The primary destinations were Australia, Europe, the Gulf States, North America, and South Africa.

Other political factors that have contributed to the post-1991 brain drain included continuing **human rights** problems and political arrests under the **Ethiopian People's Revolutionary Democratic Front**, favoritism based on ethnic affiliation, and the **Ethiopian-Eritrean War**. Economically, there are low salaries, **poverty**, a poor standard of living, and limited educational opportunities. In the professional ranks, there are few advancement opportunities, difficulty in putting advanced training to work, lack of research funds, limited Internet connectivity, low institutional morale, and poor management practices.

The West's willingness to accept Ethiopians and others from the Third World—particularly in the communications, educational, and medical fields—has exacerbated the brain drain. As yet, however, the west has failed to acknowledge the brain drain as a serious impediment to third world development. Indeed, special employment visa programs offered by countries like Britain and the United States contribute to the brain drain. *See also* EDUCATION, PRIMARY AND SECONDARY; EDUCATION, UNIVERSITY.

BRITISH MILITARY ADMINISTRATION (BMA). *See* OCCU-PIED ENEMY TERRITORY ADMINISTRATION.

BRUCE, JAMES (1730–1794). Scottish explorer. Born at Larbert in Stirlingshire on 14 December 1730. Bruce attended Harrow (1742–1746) and Edinburgh University (1747–1748). After marrying Adriana Allan, a wine merchant's daughter, he joined her father's business. In 1757, Bruce traveled to Spain, where he learned Arabic and became interested in the east. Bruce later served as consul general in Algiers (1763–1765).

In September 1769, Bruce, who was deeply interested in the origins of the Nile River, arrived in **Massawa** in preparation for a journey to Ethiopia. On 15 February 1770, he arrived in the imperial capital **Gondar**. On 4 November 1770, he reached the source of the **Blue Nile** at Geesh, which is located about 100 miles (161 kilometers) south of **Lake Tana** and 250 miles (402 kilometers) south of Gondar. In late December 1771, Bruce departed Ethiopia en route to Britain via Sudan and Egypt. En route, he stopped in France (1773), where he gave an account of his Ethiopian experiences to the French naturalist Comte de Buffon (1707–1788) and was received by the French court. In 1774, Bruce arrived in London. Initially, his reception was cordial but an increasing number of people doubted the veracity of his many tales about Ethiopia.

In 1776, an embittered Bruce returned to Scotland and, in 1780, began to write a five-volume account of his exploits entitled *Travels to Discover the Source of the Nile in Egypt, Arabia, Abyssinia, and Nubia*. The book, published in 1790, was a best seller and was translated into French and German by the end of the year. Despite this success, many readers condemned Bruce as a fraud and charlatan who had manufactured many of his accounts of life in Ethiopia. Humiliated and outraged, he retired to his Scottish estate, where he died on 27 April 1794. Fifty years later, the public acknowledged his achievements and accepted his work as accurate. Today, scholars view his *Travels* as one of the most important Western studies ever written.

BULATOVICH, ALEXANDER XAVIERYERICH (1870–1919). Russian soldier, explorer, and monk. Born on 8 October 1870 in Orel, Russia. Educated at the Alexandrovskiy Lyceum in Saint Petersburg

(1884–1891). On 28 May 1891, Bulatovich enlisted in the Second Calvary Division's Life-Guard Hussar Regiment. On 7 April 1896, he received a posting to the Russian Red Cross Mission to Ethiopia. On 24 July 1896, the 61-man mission arrived in **Addis Ababa** to provide medical care to Ethiopian soldiers who had been wounded in the **Battle of Adwa**.

During the performance of his duties, Bulatovich made a positive impression on **Menelik II,** who invited him to accompany a three-month Ethiopian military expedition to the Baro River. The mission, which departed Addis Ababa on 10 November 1896, sought to consolidate Ethiopia's western frontier. Bulatovich also made two other trips to explore the Angar River and the Didepa valley. On 8 April 1897, Menelik II welcomed his return to Addis Ababa and on 2 May 1897, Bulatovich departed Ethiopia for Russia.

On 5 October 1897, he returned to Ethiopia in advance of the arrival of a Russian diplomatic mission. Shortly thereafter, **Ras** Wolda Giyorgis, governor of **Kafa**, asked Bulatovich to accompany him on an expedition to establish Ethiopian authority at **Lake Rudolf**. On 8 January 1898, Bulatovich departed Addis Ababa for Kafa Province, where Wolda had assembled a 16,000-man army. In less than two weeks, the force had grown to 30,000 troops. After arriving at Lake Rudolf on 7 April 1898, Wolda annexed some 18,000 square miles (28,968 square kilometers). Menelik II subsequently awarded Bulatovich a gold shield for his services during the expedition. On 26 June 1898, he left Addis Ababa for Saint Petersburg. In 1911, Bulatovich, who had become a monk, made his last trip to Addis Ababa in an unsuccessful attempt to persuade Menelik II to authorize the establishment of a Russian Orthodox monastery in Ethiopia. After returning to Russia, he served with the 16th Advanced Detachment of the Red Cross during **World War I**. On the night of 5–6 December 1919, bandits murdered Bulatovich in Lutsikovka.

BURJI PEOPLE AND LANGUAGE. The Burji people, who number more than 80,000, live in a mountainous area southeast of Lake Chama. Their name comes from the town of Burji; they call themselves Bambala. The **Konso** and **Dirasha** peoples border them on the west, the **Koorete** people on the north, and the **Boran Oromo** on the south and east. The Burji are divided into several clans, the most numerous being the Rashe people. Their origin is unknown although they may be ancestors of the Boran in Liban. Burji is a special *woreda* in the **Southern Nations, Nationalities and People's Region**. The capital is Soyama. The Burji Peoples' Democratic Union won one seat to the **House of Peoples' Representatives** in the **elections (2000)**.

The land is fertile and the climate generally healthy. The Burji raise animals and engage in terraced **agriculture**. They once had an age-grade system that has largely disappeared. They live in beehive-style huts built on stonewalled terraces. Burji wear a skin cape over their shoulders. Burji or Bambala is an east Cushitic **language** that has its closest lexical similarity with **Sidamo**. A small community of Burji also lives in Kenya.

BURTON, SIR RICHARD FRANCIS (1821–1890). Anglo-Irish soldier, explorer, author, linguist, and Orientalist. Born on 19 March 1821 in Torquay and educated at Trinity College, Oxford (1840–1842). During 1842–1849, Burton served in the Indian army. In 1853, he journeyed to Mecca disguised as a Muslim. In October 1854, he and Lieutenant John Hanning Speke, Indian army, arrived in Aden in preparation for an expedition to the **Horn of Africa**. On 29 October 1854, Burton departed Aden for the two-day journey to Zeila. On 3 January 1855, he entered **Harar** town for a 10-day visit. During that time, Burton gathered an array of social, economic, political, cultural, and linguistic information, all of which appeared in his *First Footsteps in East Africa*. He went on to become one of the world's greatest explorers. Burton died on 20 October 1890 in Trieste.

BUSSA PEOPLE AND LANGUAGE. Several thousand Bussa people live west of Lake Chamo and east of the Weyito River at the south end of North Omo zone. They live on the mountain slopes of deciduous forests. They are **agriculturists** who practice terrace farming, and their social system still retains elements of the *gada* age-set system. Outsiders have given the Bussa numerous other names. They speak an east Cushitic **language** that has 78 percent lexical similarity with **Gawwada**, 61 percent with **Tsamai,** and 51 percent with **Konso**.

– C –

CALENDAR. Although most countries operate under the Gregorian calendar, Ethiopia still uses the Julian calendar, which has 13 months. For this reason, **tourist** information often describes Ethiopia as a country with 13 months of sunshine. Use of the Julian calendar puts the Ethiopian year about eight years behind the Gregorian year. The months correspond as follows:

Ethiopian Julian Months	Gregorian Calendar
Meskerem (New Year)	September 11–October 10
Tikimt	October 11–November 9
Hidar	November 10–December 9
Tahsas	December 10–January 8
Tir	January 9–February 7
Yakatit	February 8–March 9
Maggabit	March 10–April 8
Miyazya	April 9–May 8
Ginbot	May 9–June 7
Sene	June 8–July 7
Hamle	July 8–August 6
Nehasa	August 7–September 5
Pagume	September 6–10

CAMERON, CHARLES DUNCAN (c. 1826–1870). British officer and diplomat. Cameron, who served in the British army (45th Foot) (1846–1851), spent the early part of his career in South Africa performing a variety of administrative, political, and military duties. He rejoined the military during the Crimean War (1853–1856) and subsequently held two posts in Russia as vice-consul (1858–1859).

In 1860, Cameron received an appointment to Ethiopia. However, it was not until 9 January 1862 that he arrived in **Massawa** to succeed **Walter Plowden** as British consul. Shortly afterwards, Cameron accompanied the Grand Duke of Saxe-Cobourg on a trip to the interior. On 23 June 1862, he arrived in **Gondar** and subsequently delivered a royal letter and presents from Queen Victoria to **Tewodros II**. On 29 October 1862, the emperor dispatched a letter, through Cameron, to Queen Victoria in which he solicited permission to send a diplomatic mission to Britain. Tewodros II also asked for help to enable his envoys to pass through Egyptian territory, prevent Egyptian penetration of the **Red Sea**, purchase firearms, and build roads.

On 4 January 1864, the emperor imprisoned Cameron and his party as he had received no reply from Queen Victoria. Upon hearing this news, the British government quickly drafted a reply to Tewodros II's letter. In February 1866, Hormuzd Rassam, British resident at Aden, delivered the letter to the emperor, who released Cameron and his colleagues. However, he later rearrested them in hopes of convincing Britain to send foreign artisans to Ethiopia.

However, after receiving a false report that a British company had agreed to build a railway in Sudan, the emperor ordered the captives to be taken to his mountain fortress a Magdala. This action laid the groundwork for the **Anglo-Ethiopian War**. In July 1868, Cameron returned to Britain and retired on a pension. He died on 30 May 1870 in Geneva.

CATHOLICISM. In 1520, Father **Francisco Alvarez** arrived in Ethiopia with a Portuguese mission led by Dom Roderigo Da Lima. Emperor **Lebna Dengel** (reigned 1508–1540) sent two letters to the pope during this five-year visit that sought recognition for Ethiopia and emphasized that the country was waging endless wars against a neighboring Muslim state encouraged by other Muslim states. Emperor **Galawedos** wrote to the Portuguese king for Catholic priests to minister to Portuguese soldiers who had been sent to help the Christians deal with **Islamic** incursions. In Portugal, the letters were misunderstood and interpreted as a request by the emperor for priests to convert him and his subjects. The Portuguese and the pope entrusted this effort to the Society of Jesus. Although the emperor later clarified this misunderstanding, the Jesuits persisted in their desire to convert Ethiopians to Catholicism. The Jesuits first tried to convince the Ethiopians to replace the bishop appointed in Alexandria with a Roman patriarch.

In March 1603, Father Pedro Paez (1564–1622), a Spaniard by birth, arrived in Ethiopia to convert the Orthodox to Catholicism. By 1612, he had converted a number of followers who engaged in public debates about church practices with the Orthodox clergy. Emperor **Susneyos** (reigned 1607–1632) converted to Catholicism, thereby convincing Paez that Catholicism had been implanted in Ethiopia. In 1622, another Jesuit, Manoel de Almeida, arrived and wrote extensively about Ethiopia during his 11-year stay. **Jeronimo Lobo** was a Jesuit priest in Ethiopia at about the same time. In 1625, Afonsus Mendez (1579–1639) arrived in Ethiopia and received the emperor's support. The following years, Susneyos enthroned Mendez as patriarch and, by 1630, the number of Jesuit priests in Ethiopia had grown to 34. In 1632, Susneyos abdicated in favor of his son, **Fasilidas** (reigned 1632–1667), who immediately restored the **Ethiopian Orthodox Church**. Although a new proclamation allowed Catholics to practice their faith, there was a violent reaction against those Ethiopians who had converted to Catholicism.

Catholic interest in Ethiopia did not end with the abortive Susneyos experience. Emperor Yostos (reigned 1711–1716) secretly harbored three Capuchin **missionaries** for their wisdom and advice. His successor, Dawit III (reigned 1716–1721), promptly executed them. In 1752, Empress Mentewwab invited three Franciscans to Gondar but they were banished after EOC officials had discovered them. An Ethiopian convert to Catholicism, Father Tobias Gebre Egziabeher, was ordained a bishop and enjoyed the protection from 1790 to 1797 of political figures including Emperor Hezekiah (reigned 1789–1784).

In 1838, Catholic missionary efforts resumed when Lazarist Father **Giuseppe Sapeto** went to **Adwa** as chaplain for two Basque explorers. He developed good relations with the local clergy and encouraged the Lazarists to become more active. In 1839, Monsignor **Justin de Jacobis**, accompanied by Father Luigi Montuori, arrived in Adwa as the new prefect apostolic of Ethiopia. After learning the language and having some initial success, Tigray's local ruler banished de Jacobis (1848) only to readmit him two years later. The Lazarists shifted their activity from Adwa to Akala Guzay on the eastern rim of the plateau. De Jacobis planned to expand into the central provinces and visited **Gondar** in 1854. Regional politics intervened. The Catholic clergy's most distinguished indigenous member, Father Gabra Mikael, challenged the political and church leadership in the Gondar area. This led to his merciless beating and death in 1855, an event de Jacobis witnessed. The Catholics then became embroiled on the wrong side of palace politics to support French interests. Although Catholicism thrived in locations such as Bogos, it increasingly ran into conflict with Emperor **Tewodros II**. De Jacobis died in 1860. His legacy was to establish indigenous Catholicism in Ethiopia but he achieved no mass conversions. When he died, there were several thousand Catholics in eight parishes served by about 20 indigenous priests.

While the Lazarists were active in **Tigray**, the Capuchins led by Bishop **Gugliemo Massaia** established themselves among the **Oromo** of southwest Ethiopia in 1846. Unlike the Lazarists who worked with the **Ge'ez** rite, the Capuchins encouraged Latin rite and practices. In 1863, Massaia left the southwest and crossed the **Blue Nile** and was prohibited from returning to the southwest. In 1869, Menelik (later **Menelik II**), who was in conflict with Emperor **Yohannes IV** (reigned 1872–1889), granted Massaia property at Finfine near present-day **Addis Ababa**. By 1878, Massaia was virtually an éminence grise to Menelik. As a result, Yohannes IV expelled Massaia from Ethiopia (1880). The Capuchins had earlier retreated to the southeast near **Harar** where they continued their work in the late 19th century. There was virtually no Catholic missionary activity in the southwest until the arrival of the Consolata fathers in the 1920s.

Today, there are eight Catholic jurisdictions in Ethiopia—five apostolic vicariates, two dioceses, and one prefecture. One principal Catholic zone of Semitic peoples includes the Archdiocese of Addis Ababa and the Diocese of Adigrat in Tigray Region. The second comprises the **Oromo**, **Gamo-Gofa**, and other peoples of southern Ethiopia. The church is effectively divided into two parts on the basis of ethnic groups and rites. The total number of Catholics in Ethiopia today is probably well under a half million. Useful background on the Catholic Church in Ethiopia can be found in *Priests and Politicians* by Donald Crummey, *The Missionary Factor in Ethiopia* edited by Getatchew Haile, Aasulv Lande, and Samuel Rubenson, *The Ebullient Phoenix* by Kevin O'Mahoney, *Church and State in Ethiopia 1270–1527* by Taddesse Tamrat, *The Survival of Ethiopian Independence* by Sven Rubenson, and *The Romance of the Portuguese* by C. F. Rey.

CENSUS. Ethiopia has conducted a census twice in its history. The first, which began on 11 October 1984, cost about $20 million and involved

68,000 enumerators and 13,000 superiors. By the time of its demise in 1991, the government of **Mengistu Haile Mariam** had not yet published the second volume of the 1984 census results.

On 6 June 1996, Abdulahi Hassen, secretary general of the Census Committee, released preliminary census figures for **Addis Ababa** and three regional states. According to Abdulahi Hassen, the capital's **population** totaled approximately 2.3 million, which represented a 3.8 percent annual growth rate since the 1984 census.

Tigray Region had a **population** of more than 3.2 million. Most were Orthodox Christians (95.5 percent). About 4.1 percent were Muslims and 0.4 percent were **Catholics**. Tigray's ethnic composition was largely Tigrayan (94.8 percent) but there also were **Amhara** (2.6 percent), Eritrean (0.9 percent), and modest numbers of **Saho** and Agaw-Kamyr.

Amhara Region had a **population** of some 14.4 million inhabitants. Most were Orthodox Christian (81.5 percent). Approximately 18.1 percent were Muslims. Amhara's ethnic composition was largely Amhara (92.2 percent), **Oromo** (3 percent), Agew (2.7 percent), and modest numbers of Kemant and Kamyr.

Harari Regional State, which includes only **Harar** and its immediate vicinity, had only 139,000 inhabitants. More than half of these were town dwellers. Most were Muslims (60.3 percent). Some 38.2 percent were Orthodox Christian. Harari's ethnic composition was largely Oromo (52.3 percent), Amhara (32.6 percent), Harari (7.1 percent), and **Gurage** (3.2 percent).

CHAMBER OF DEPUTIES. *See* PARLIAMENT.

CHARA PEOPLE AND LANGUAGE. The Chara, also called the Ciara and Cara, number about 15,000 and reside just north of the **Omo River** on the western edge of north Omo zone. On the northeast is the ancient **Konta** Kingdom. The Chara are **agriculturists**. They practice traditional religion; their supreme being is Yero. They also worship several minor deities and breed and venerate serpents. They speak an Omotic **language** of the Ometo-Gimira family. It has 54 percent lexical similarity with **Wolaytta**. Although they use Chara in village and family life, some are bilingual in Wolaytta and others in **Kafa**.

CHEMICAL WEAPONS. Italy's use of chemical weapons during the **Italian-Ethiopian War (1935–1936)** reflected the weakness of the international community and the duplicity of some of the major powers. On 17 January 1926, the **League of Nations** Geneva Protocol, which Italy had ratified on 3 April 1928, banned the use of mustard gas (diclorodietilsulphur). However, Rome eventually ignored the protocol and, on 10 October 1935, **Rodolfo Graziani** first ordered his troops to employ chemical weapons against **Ras** Nasibu's troops at Gorrahei. During the following months, Italy frequently used chemical weapons against Ethiopia. In response to growing international criticism, Benito Mussolini initially denied Italy used chemical weapons but later justified using them as retaliation for Ethiopian atrocities against Italian soldiers.

After liberation (1941), the allied powers thwarted Ethiopia's efforts to prosecute Italian war criminals. On 29 October 1943, London created the United Nations War Crimes Commission but excluded Ethiopia for fear it would initiate proceedings against **Pietro Badoglio**, who had used chemical weapons against Ethiopian forces. However, after Mussolini's downfall, he switched loyalties and became Italy's prime minister and a valuable ally against the Axis powers.

On 20 May 1946, **Haile Selassie** issued an imperial decree that created the Ethiopian War Crimes Commission to prosecute senior Italian officials who had sanctioned the use of chemical weapons and had committed other war crimes such as torturing and executing Ethiopian prisoners and citizens during the Italian-Ethiopian War. On 22 July 1946, the Ethiopian Ministry of Foreign Affairs sent a letter to the United States, the secretary-general of the League of Nations, the International Tribunal (Berlin), and the British Legation in **Addis Ababa** that urged them to institute proceedings against Italian war criminals. All these initiatives failed, largely because Britain and the United States did not want to alienate the Italian government, which supposedly was an important ally in the West's determination to contain the Soviet Union.

Although Addis Ababa ceased its efforts to bring Italian war criminals to justice, the chemical weapons issue remained a subject of concern. During 23–26 November 1997, for example, Italian president Oscar Luigi Scalfaro made the first visit to Ethiopia by an Italian head of state since the Italian-Ethiopian War. Among other things, he acknowledged his country's "mistakes and guilt" for attacking Ethiopia. On 3 May 2001, Ethiopia accused Italy of breaking international law by refusing to disclose the location of chemical weapons depots. Addis Ababa also announced that Italy had stockpiled about 80,000 tons of chemical weapons in Ethiopia during the 1935–1936 period but admitted that it had no idea how much remained in the country. *See also* HUMAN RIGHTS.

CHEW BAHIR. This lake, which has no outlet, is located in the southernmost part of Ethiopia's **Rift Valley** and within the Chew Bahir Wildlife Reserve. It is famous for its fluctuating water level and expanse. In the 1960s, the lake contained about 1.2 miles (1.9 kilometers) of open water but for the rest of the 20th century it was a mere swamp.

Throughout much of the 19th century, the lake attracted numerous European explorers and hunters. During an 1887–1888 expedition, Hungarian sportsman Count Samuel Teleki von Szek (1845–1915) named it Lake Stephanie in honor of the wife of Austrian crown prince Rudolf. The Ethiopian government subsequently changed the name to Chew Bahir. In 1895, the American explorer Arthur Donaldson Smith (1866–1939) virtually circumnavigated the lake. By the time an Anglo-American expedition reached Lake Stephanie (1900), it had dried up and life around it had died off. Today, this seasonal lake varies between a flooded marsh during the rainy season and a dry lakebed that can be driven on during the dry season. When it has water, oryx and gazelles sometimes frequent the area.

CHURCH MISSIONARY SOCIETY (CMS). In 1830, Samuel Gobat and Christian Kugler, two German **missionaries** employed by the London-based Anglican CMS, arrived in Ethiopia. They pursued ambiguous but overly aggressive policies by seeking to control pagan tribes and members of the **Ethiopian Orthodox Church** (EOC). The missionaries also denigrated traditional customs like fasting and veneration of the Virgin Mary and the saints. Such tactics, particularly the criticism of Ethiopian devotion to the Virgin Mary, undermined the CMS mission. **Johann Krapf** unsuccessfully solicited British political or military intervention to ensure the success of its strategy. By 1843, all CMS missionaries had returned home or had been expelled from Ethiopia.

In 1855, a CMS team, led by **Johann Martin Flad** and Krapf, returned to Ethiopia. **Tewodros II** welcomed the missionaries but told the pair that he wanted them to develop Ethiopia and to refrain from all evangelical activities. The CMS mission complied and undertook road-building projects, repaired thousands of broken muskets, and forged heavy artillery. The emperor eventually allowed the missionaries to preach to the **Falashas** but insisted that converts had to be baptized into the EOC. In 1863, Tewodros II imprisoned all foreign missionaries and many Europeans. After the **Anglo-Ethiopian War**, all the captives regained their freedom. *See also* MISSIONARIES; PROTESTANTISM.

CLIMATE. Ethiopia has three climatic zones, the *Dega* (cold), *Woina Dega* (temperate), and *Quolla* (hot). The Dega zone starts at an elevation of just over 8,000 feet (2,450 meters) and has average temperatures of 50–60° Fahrenheit (10–16° Celsius). This zone is characterized by some medium-sized trees and a few high-mountain forests. The lower reaches serve as pasture and for cultivation of cereals. The Woina Dega zone includes a large part of Ethiopia's **highlands** or plateau country. The altitude varies between 5,900 and 8,000 feet (1,800 to 2,450 meters) and the temperature ranges on average from 60–68° Fahrenheit (16–20° Celsius). This is the most productive part of Ethiopia and includes most of the **coffee** crop. The Quolla zone includes altitudes of less than 5,900 feet (1,800 meters) and has temperatures in the higher locations of 68–82° Fahrenheit (20–28° Celsius). The temperatures are much hotter at the lower altitudes.

In the temperate highlands, including **Addis Ababa**, there are usually a few light scattered rains during the February–May period. The true rainy season occurs from June through September, when about 80 percent of the precipitation falls. These rains normally stop during the last 10 days of September and the dry season begins. The western and southwestern highlands receive the heaviest rain, between 60 and 70 inches (150 and 175 centimeters) annually. Addis Ababa has an annual rainfall of 50 to 60 inches (125 to 150 centimeters) while lower areas of the country receive only 10 to 20 inches (25 to 50 centimeters). The driest parts of Ethiopia may go for a year with little or no rain.

COFFEE. Believed to be the original home of arabica coffee, Ethiopia produces one of the world's best **highland** coffees. Coffee was possibly taken many years ago across the **Red Sea** to Yemen for large-scale planting; the Ottoman Turks introduced it into Europe from Arabia. This gave it the name *arabica*. More than 60 percent of Ethiopia's foreign exchange income traditionally derives from coffee exports and an estimated 15 million Ethiopians depend on their livelihood from the production, processing, trade, and transport of coffee. Peasant farmers grow and harvest an estimated 96 percent of the coffee crop, which is usually processed in peasant cooperatives. Some of the coffee actually grows wild and much of it is consumed domestically. As a result, there are no reliable estimates for coffee area, production, and yields. State farms produce no more than 4 percent. In fiscal year 2001, Ethiopia exported 110,000 tons of coffee and earned about $170 million. As a result of the sharp drop in the world price of coffee, this represented a 40 percent decrease in the total value of Ethiopian coffee exports. Ethiopia's share of the global export market for coffee is less than 3 percent. In late 1999, the International Coffee Organization approved various projects to increase coffee production and improve marketing.

The main coffee-producing regions are **Oromia** and the **Southern Nations, Nationalities, and People's Region**, although there are isolated coffee-growing areas elsewhere, such as near **Harar**. Using extension services, the government is encouraging the introduction of coffee in **Amhara**, **Benishangul/Gumuz**, **Tigray**, and **Gambela Regions**. The main threat to increased production is coffee berry disease, which results in a loss of 20 to 30 percent of total annual production. Germany is the largest importer of Ethiopian coffee. Although an increasing percentage of Ethiopian export coffee is now washed, the majority remains sun dried. This brings a lower price in a world market that has been saturated in recent years, further driving down the price Ethiopia receives. Some of Ethiopia's most prized varieties, however, are available in Western specialty coffee shops such as Starbucks. Ethiopians pride themselves on their elaborate coffee ceremony that accompanies most celebrations and meals in Ethiopian restaurants worldwide.

COMMISSION FOR ORGANIZING THE PARTY OF THE WORKING PEOPLE OF ETHIOPIA (COPWE). On 17 December 1979, the Provisional Military Administrative Council issued Proclamation 174, which established COPWE, with **Mengistu Haile**

Mariam as chairman. The party's objectives included disseminating Marxist-Leninist dogma throughout society, liquidating feudalism, imperialism, and bureaucratic capitalism, and guiding Ethiopia's people to socialism and communism.

On 16–19 June 1980, COPWE held its first congress to politicize and organize the people and to restructure and strengthen groups like the All Ethiopia Trade Union and the All Ethiopia Peasants' Association. The congress also established the Revolutionary Ethiopian Youth Association and the Revolutionary Ethiopian Women's Association. By the eve of COPWE's second congress, some 1.3 million Ethiopians had held elective posts in these organizations.

On 3–6 January 1983, some 1,600 people (seven attendees belonged to the party's Executive Council, 91 served on the Central Committee, and 26 others were Central Committee alternative members) attended COPWE's second congress. Mengistu told the delegates that although there were about 6,500 COPWE cells in Ethiopia, additional recruitment was necessary, especially among the working class. He also reviewed the country's economic problems and noted that **agricultural** production had declined from 4.7 percent in 1979–1980 to 2.4 percent in 1980–1981, to 2 percent in 1981–1982. Lastly, Mengistu expelled 34 COPWE members for activities incompatible with the organization's objectives. At the end of the congress, COPWE issued a communiqué that ordered the creation of the **Workers' Party of Ethiopia** (WPE).

On 6–11 September 1984, COPWE held its third and last congress in Addis Ababa. On 6 September 1984, the congress dissolved COPWE and, on 12 September 1984, created the WPE. *See also* DERG; LABOR UNIONS; PEASANT ASSOCIATIONS.

CONFEDERATION OF ETHIOPIAN LABOR UNIONS. *See* LABOR UNIONS.

CONFEDERATION OF ETHIOPIAN TRADE UNIONS. *See* LABOR UNIONS.

CONSTITUTION (1931, 1955, 1987, and 1994). When he ascended the throne, **Haile Selassie** sought to establish a reputation as a modern and enlightened leader. To achieve this goal, the emperor granted a constitution without any public pressure. However, Haile Selassie ensured that he would be the main beneficiary of the constitution. Minister of Finance Bäjerond Täklä-Hawariyat drafted the constitution, portions of which he borrowed from the Imperial Japanese Constitution (1889). On 16 July 1931, the emperor proclaimed Ethiopia's first constitution. The document's 55 articles assigned all government power to the emperor and established a Senate (Yaheg Mawossena Meker-beth) and a Chamber of Deputies (Yaheg Mamria Meker-beth). Haile Selassie appointed members of the Senate from among the nobility and local chiefs, who then selected members of the Chamber of Deputies.

On 4 November 1955, the emperor proclaimed Ethiopia's second constitution, which contained 131 articles and introduced several reforms. Some of the more important changes included ministerial responsibility to **Parliament**; the expansion of the Chamber of Deputies; the introduction of free, universal, and secret suffrage; the extension of the franchise to **women**; the independence of the **judiciary**; recognition of civil rights for all Ethiopians and the inclusion of a bill of rights; and the suppression of feudal practices. Haile Selassie retained the right to conduct foreign affairs, dissolve the Chamber of Deputies, appoint cabinet ministers and judges, and issue emergency decrees. Critics maintained that important parts of the constitution remained undemocratic. In particular, the Chamber of Deputies included 60 members elected on a restricted franchise and chosen largely by official nomination. Also, Haile Selassie reserved the right to nominate the 30 senators.

After its creation in 1984, the **Workers' Party of Ethiopia** (WPE) gave priority to drafting and implementing a new constitution that would inaugurate the People's Democratic Republic of Ethiopia. In March 1986, the government formed a 343-member Constitutional Commission (CC) to draft a new constitution based on the principle of scientific socialism. The 122 full and alternate members of the WPE Central Committee dominated the deliberations about the nature and scope of the proposed constitution. In June 1986, the WPE Central Committee issued a 120-article draft constitution. The government printed and distributed one million copies to **kebeles** and **peasant associations** throughout Ethiopia. Over the next two months, there were government-sponsored discussions about the draft at some 25,000 locations. Much of the talk focused on issues such as **taxation**, the role of religion, marriage, polygamy, citizenship rights, and the organization of **elections**. However, the draft failed to address the nationality problem and the right to self-determination. The government claimed that the citizenry had submitted more than 500,000 suggested revisions but the WPE Central Committee made only 95 amendments to the original draft. On 1 February 1987, the government held a constitutional referendum. About 96 percent of the 14 million eligible voters actually voted. Approximately 81 percent endorsed the constitution while some 18 percent opposed. One percent of the ballots were invalid. On 22 February 1987, the constitution took effect. The final document, which consisted of 17 chapters and 119 articles, committed the government to facilitating the country's economic development by implementing the Program for the National Democratic Revolution. Critics maintained that the constitution was little more than an abridgement of the 1977 Soviet constitution. However, there were two important differences between the two constitutions. Under the Ethiopian constitution, the Office of the President theoretically shared power, and the country was a unitary state rather than a union of republics.

On 8 December 1994, the **Ethiopian People's Revolutionary Democratic Front** adopted a new constitution. This constitution provided for a president as chief of state and a prime minister as head of government. The bicameral parliament included the 117-seat Council of the Federation, which represented the ethnic interests of the regional governments, and the 548-seat Council of People's Representatives whose members are popularly elected and who in turn elect the President. The party in power designates the Prime Minister. On 8 December 1994, the 548-member Constituent Assembly ratified the constitution that provided for the establishment of a federal government and the division of the country into **Afar Region; Amhara Region; Benishangul/Gumuz Region; Gambela Region; Harar Region; Oromia Region; Somali Region; Southern Nations, Nationalities, People's Region;** and **Tigray Region**. The two chartered cities are **Addis Ababa** and **Dire Dawa**. The constitution also contained a controversial clause that provided for regional autonomy including the rights of secession. On 22 August 1995, the Council of People's Representatives and the Federal Council adopted the new constitution, thereby creating the Federal Democratic Republic of Ethiopia. *See also* NATIONAL CHARTER.

COPTIC ORTHODOX CHURCH OF ALEXANDRIA. The Copts were the first Christian **missionaries** in Africa. Merchants from Egypt introduced Christianity to **Axum** in the fourth century and to Sudan in the sixth century. There also were Coptic missionary activities in India, Europe, and the Middle East. In the 19th century, missionaries established modern Coptic schools in Egypt. The Coptic **language** is the last stage of the ancient Egyptian language and is important for the study of biblical and pharaonic history. There are several million Copts in Egypt today and small numbers in Sudan, the Middle East, and even Europe and North America. The Coptic Orthodox Church is a member of the World Council of Churches. It maintains cordial ties with the **Ethiopian Orthodox Church** (EOC).

Egypt's Coptic Orthodox Church has had a long relationship with Ethiopia. Even today, some people inaccurately refer to followers of the EOC as Copts. In the first century, Christianity spread in Egypt despite Roman persecution. By the year 200, the Nile delta had many Christian converts. In the fourth century, Alexandria was the center of Christian theological studies.

In 325, the First Ecumenical Council of Nicaea sat and dealt with several significant theological issues. Among them was the canon that rendered the church in Ethiopia subject to the authority of the occupant of the patriarchal throne of Alexandria. Only the patriarch of Alexandria could consecrate the metropolitan of Ethiopia, who must be a Copt or Egyptian Christian. In the fourth century, Patriarch Athanasius (c. 293–373) consecrated **Frumentius** as the first bishop to the see of Axum (Ethiopia). Known as **Abuna Abba Salama** or "Father of Peace," Frumentius baptized the royal family and ordained priests. As a result of this situation, a bishop who knew neither **Ge'ez,** the liturgical language, nor **Amharic**, the popular language, governed the Ethiopian church.

The patriarch of Alexandria continued to appoint a non-Ethiopian as the bishop of the Ethiopian church until 1950, when a native Ethiopian, Abuna **Basilios**, ascended the metropolitan seat. He received authority to consecrate bishops and, in 1959, received the title of patriarch of the Ethiopian Orthodox Church. Stuart C. Munro-

Hay has produced the most thorough account of relations between Alexandria and the Ethiopian church in a book entitled *Ethiopia and Alexandria: The Metropolitan Episcopacy of Ethiopia.*

CORRUPTION. Corruption has plagued Ethiopia since time immemorial. This is not surprising in a country that pays unusually low wages and where the wage earner is expected to support a large extended family. Popular opposition to corruption was one of the reasons that contributed to the downfall of **Haile Selassie.** The **Derg** jailed or executed imperial officials and ordinary Ethiopians suspected of corruption. However, many Derg officials enriched themselves by engaging in corrupt practices.

Since coming to power (1991), the **Ethiopian People's Revolutionary Democratic Front** has sought to eliminate corruption. Several officials including a former deputy prime minister actually have been convicted. On 16 March 2000, for example, the Federal Supreme Court sentenced Deputy Prime Minister and Defense Minister Tamrit Layne to 18 years' imprisonment for corruption and misuse of power (he had been in jail since 1997). In 2001, the **police** arrested several prominent businessmen and bankers on corruption charges. By early 2003, these cases had yet to come to trial and it was unclear whether the charges will be upheld in court. The Berlin-based Transparency International, the only international nongovernmental organization devoted to combating corruption, prepares an annual corruption perception index. The rankings are based on the perception of corruption obtained in international surveys by business persons and risk analysts. In 2002, Transparency International ranked 102 countries. Ethiopia was tied with the People's Republic of China and the Dominican Republic in 59th place or just below the midway point.

COTTON. The cotton sector is the largest industrial **agricultural** and **handicraft** employer in the Ethiopian **economy**. The principal cotton producing areas are in the Middle Awash, Lower Awash, North Omo, Gambela, Humera, North Gondar, and Tendaho areas. During the **Derg** period, cotton relied heavily on state farms and was the largest contributor to gross domestic product. Since the fall of the Derg, cotton production has been slowly moving from state farms to private farms and peasant farmer production. By the 1993–1994 production year, state farms produced only 22 percent or 13,100 metric tons of cotton while the peasant sector accounted for 60 percent or 36,400 metric tons. Private farms produced 18 percent or 11,100 metric tons of Ethiopia's total production of 60,600 metric tons in 1993/94.

Cotton yields are declining for several reasons. The state farms are not efficient. Cattle and increased salinity have damaged fields. New agricultural liberalization policies have allowed farmers to use land for any crop, which has encouraged a move to more profitable ones or livestock. Imports have driven down the price of cotton, thus further discouraging local production. In addition, Ethiopia's textile **industry** is not competitive and is in need of modernization. Ethiopia does not currently grow enough cotton to meet domestic needs.

COUNCIL OF MINISTERS. Established in 1907 by **Menelik II** to assist him as poor health and a recent stroke had limited his capacity to govern his empire. He appointed important men to the Council of Ministers, initially nine and eventually 11, but they split into factions and failed to manage the monarchy's affairs effectively. Following Menelik's death in 1913, his grandson **Lij Iyasu Mikael** became regent at age 15. Factionalism continued to plague the Council of Ministers. In 1916, a group of **Shoan** nobles and high church officials deposed Lij Iyasu Mikael. Menelik II's daughter **Zawditu** became empress while **Ras** Tafari Makonnen, later to reign as **Haile Selassie**, became regent. The young Ras Tafari Makonnen ruled in concert with several elder statesmen until the death of the empress (1930). Although Haile Selassie had a Council of Ministers until the outbreak of the **Italian-Ethiopian War (1935–1936)**, its members served at his pleasure and were reluctant to act in his absence. Governance occurred in the palace and a minister's role depended on his relationship with the emperor.

After liberation (1941), Haile Selassie returned to **Addis Ababa** and quickly reestablished his authority. The Ministers Order of 1943 reestablished the Council of Ministers and created the position of prime minister. Nevertheless, the emperor's role remained supreme. In fact, the most important ministerial position was the minister of the pen, a successor of the ancient office of *Tsahafe T'ezaz*, which sent out the emperor's orders. Although the prime minister presided over the Council of Ministers, he tended to function as the chief of staff to the emperor for administrative matters. Following a 1966 reorganization, the prime minister received authority to select the other 19 ministers. However, the government continued to function largely on the basis of personal relations between the emperor and his senior officials until a group of military officers seized power in 1974.

The **Derg** increased the power of the state apparatus and ruled initially as a junta dictatorship. It retained a few ministers from the Haile Selassie government. Real power resided with the officers who seized power. Twelve Derg departments were in charge of different areas of government activities. Individual government agencies were responsible to the cabinet and the relevant Derg department. A few ministers held considerable power, such as the minister of public and national security, Tesfaye Wolde-Selassie, a close ally of **Mengistu Haile Mariam**. By the early 1980s, the Leninist principle of democratic centralism governed the relationship between the lower and upper layers of the government and mass organizations.

In 1987, the Derg introduced a new **constitution** and created the People's Democratic Republic of Ethiopia, whose Marxist-Leninist institutions took over from the military regime. The transfer of power to civilian institutions was largely cosmetic; the same people remained in power. Loyalty to the leader of the **Workers' Party of Ethiopia** (WPE) was the characteristic feature of power. As president and general secretary of the WPE, Mengistu was head of government and had leverage over the policymaking functions of the Council of Ministers. In addition, the prime minister could convene the Council of Ministers only when the president thought it was necessary for him to do so. This tended to make the prime minister an assistant to the president. The new constitution gave authority to the Council of Ministers to develop economic plans and the budget with the assistance of other organizations. They then went to the **National Shengo** for approval.

With Mengistu's overthrow in 1991, the **Ethiopian People's Revolutionary Democratic Front** established a Transition Period Charter designed to run the government for two and a half years, culminating with a constitution and national assembly. A National Conference elected **Meles Zenawi** as president of the **Transitional Government of Ethiopia** (TGE). Meles appointed his prime minister and the TGE established a 17-member multiethnic Council of

Ministers that ran individual ministries until a new government took power after adoption of a new constitution on 8 December 1994.

Under the constitution, the prime minister is the head of government and, together with the Council of Ministers, holds the highest executive powers. The prime minister is a member of, and elected from, the House of Peoples' Representatives for a five-year term. Meles Zenawi has held this position since the first national **elections (1995)**. The prime minister is the chief executive, chairman of the Council of Ministers, and commander in chief of the **armed forces**. There is a deputy prime minister who has no constitutionally specified task except to carry out responsibilities specifically entrusted to him by the prime minister.

Upon nomination by the prime minister, the House of Peoples' Representatives appoints the members of the Council of Ministers or cabinet. The Council of Ministers is responsible to the prime minister and the House of Peoples' Representatives. Each minister is in charge of a government ministry such as justice, education, or foreign affairs and is, therefore, responsible for routine government business under the purview of that ministry. The key task of the ministers is the formulation of the federal budget. The ethnic background of ministers and deputy ministers generally reflects the ethnic composition of Ethiopia. Ministers are chosen on the basis of competence and/or ethnic identification. Most tend to be technocrats. Only rarely do ministers have their own political power base. *See also* ELECTIONS (1957); ELECTIONS (1961, 1965, 1973); ELECTIONS (1987); ELECTIONS (1992); ELECTIONS (1994); ELECTIONS (2000); PARLIAMENT.

COUNCIL OF REPRESENTATIVES. *See* MELES ZENAWI; NATIONAL CHARTER; PARLIAMENT; TRANSITIONAL GOVERNMENT OF ETHIOPIA.

COUP (1977). The events that culminated in this concerned a disagreement between **Mengistu Haile Mariam** and **Derg** chairman **Teferi Bante** about the direction of the Ethiopian revolution. Mengistu wanted to eliminate troublesome groups such as the **Ethiopian People's Revolutionary Party** (EPRP), the **Ethiopian Democratic Union** (EDU), and the **Eritrean Liberation Front** (ELF). Teferi favored reconciliation and urged all groups to set aside personal and ideological differences for the good of the nation. The two also disagreed about how to deal with problems like urban terrorism, national unity, and how to form an alliance of progressive forces to thwart foreign and domestic counterrevolutionary efforts.

A crisis between the two finally erupted on 3 February 1977, when there was an hour-long shoot-out at **Menelik II**'s Grand Palace in **Addis Ababa**. Mengistu's henchmen, commanded by Lieutenant Colonel Daniel Asfaw, killed Teferi, Lieutenant Colonel Hirui Haile Selassie, Lieutenant Colonel Asrat Desta, Captain Tefera Deneke, Captain Alemayehu Haile, Captain Moges Wolde-Mihael, and Corporal Haile Belay. Other fatalities included Colonel Daniel and Senaye Likke, who had been the leader of the **Workers' League**.

On 4 February 1977, Mengistu addressed some 200,000 Ethiopians at a rally in Addis Ababa and condemned those who had been killed and the EPRP, EDU, and ELF as enemies of the revolution. On 11 February 1977, Mengistu became head of state and succeeded Teferi as Derg chairman.

COUP ATTEMPT (1951). *See* NEGASH BEZABEH.

COUP ATTEMPT (1960). On 13 December 1960, Brigadier General Mengistu Newaye (1916–1961), commander of the **Imperial Body Guard**, and his younger brother Germané Newaye (1924–1960), governor of Jijiga Province, occupied the imperial palace in **Addis Ababa**. Their supporters included Major General **Mulugeta Buli**, former Imperial Body Guard commander and personal chief of staff to the emperor; Brigadier General Tsigué Dibou, chief of **police**; Lieutenant Colonel Workineh Gebeheyu (c. 1925–1960), chief of security; and Getachew Bekelé, acting minister in the Marine Department; and parts of the Imperial Body Guard's rank and file.

On 14 December 1960, the rebels detained Crown Prince **Asfa Wossen** (1916–1997), announced the overthrow of Emperor **Haile Selassie** (1892–1974), who was in Brazil on a state visit, and appointed Crown Prince Asfa Wossen (1916–1980) as the new emperor. The rebels also appointed **Ras Imru Haile Selassie** (1892–1980), Haile Selassie's cousin, as premier for a government that advocated an 11-point socialist and nationalist program under a constitutional monarchy. Major-General Merid Mengesha (1912–1966), chief of staff of the

armed forces, and Major-General Kebede Gebré, chief of ground forces, opposed the rebels. The rebels sought to avoid a battle by opening negotiations with these two loyalist officers through the U.S. military attaché. However, Merid and Kebede used the interlude to gather reinforcements.

On 15 December 1960, Merid announced that troops had deployed throughout Addis Ababa and called on all Ethiopians to remain loyal to the emperor. The following day, he declared that the coup had failed. On 17 December 1960, countless thousands of Ethiopians lined the streets to welcome the emperor's return. However, fighting continued on the outskirts of Addis Ababa for several days. On 21 December 1960, the authorities captured Getachew while Mulugeta, Tsigué, Workineh committed suicide. On 24 December 1960, soldiers killed Germané and captured Mengistu.

On 12 January 1961, the emperor pardoned all Imperial Body Guard privates and noncommissioned officers who had participated in the coup but indicated that officers would be placed on trial. On 28 March 1961, a court ordered Brigadier General Mengistu to be hanged and sentenced Captain Kiflé Woldé Mariam and Lieutenant Degafe Tedla to 15 and 10 years' imprisonment respectively. On 30 March 1961, Mengistu was hanged in a public square in Addis Ababa. The failed coup attempt resulted in numerous casualties in the armed forces (29 killed; 43 wounded) and the Imperial Body Guard (174 killed; 800 wounded) and among the civilian population (121 killed; 442 wounded). At least seven foreigners also died in the fighting.

COUP ATTEMPT (1976). The events surrounding the coup attempt are murky. Indeed, it is unclear whether it was a genuine coup attempt or an internal purge. On 10 July 1976, news of the incident emerged to the effect that Sisay Habte and Brigadier General Getachew Nadew, commander in chief and martial-law administrator in Eritrea, had launched an unsuccessful coup. On 13 July 1976, the **Derg** announced that Getachew had been shot dead while resisting arrest and that 19 others had been executed after being condemned to death by a special military court.

COUP ATTEMPT (1989). By early 1989, the Ethiopian army had become demoralized because of a successful joint **Eritrean People's**

Liberation Front/Tigray People's Liberation Front military operation in northern Ethiopia. As a result of this successful offensive, the Ethiopian army on 27–28 February 1989 abandoned **Mekele**, the last government-controlled town in Tigray. On 16 May 1989, a group of disaffected generals responded to these developments by attempting to overthrow **Mengistu Haile Mariam** after he had departed Ethiopia on a state visit to East Germany. The major conspirators included Major General Merid Negusie (**armed forces** chief of staff), Major General Amha Desta (**Air Force** commander), and Fanta Belay (minister of industry). On 21 May 1990, Ethiopia announced that 12 senior military officers had been executed for taking part in the coup attempt.

General Kumlachew Dejene (deputy commander of the 2nd Revolutionary Army, Asmara), the only coup plotter to have escaped to the west, claimed that the Ethiopian authorities arrested, executed, or removed 680 Ethiopian military officers.

CROSSES. The cross of the Crucifixion is central to Ethiopian culture and religion, especially in the **Ethiopian Orthodox Church**. Historically, the most important processional crosses continue to play a fundamental role in liturgical processions, church services, and sacramental ceremonies. Displayed on festive occasions, they are carried like triumphal standards in religious processions. The processional cross has a hollow shaft that is mounted on a staff so that it is visible from considerable distances. They are normally cast from metal. Artisans often created the earliest processional crosses in bronze by the lost wax process. The artisan shaped the cross in wax and then covered it in clay and fired it. The wax melted during the firing process and flowed out of a hole in the clay mold. When filled with molten metal, the mold formed it in the shape of the original wax version.

Hand crosses belong to individual priests and play a fundamental role in the healing of souls. Priests extend them to be kissed by their parishioners as they administer benedictions and absolutions. The metal ones are usually made of silver, brass, or iron that has been hammered into shape. Some are carved from wood. Iron crosses are usually simple and slender while brass and silver crosses may be ornate and engraved with abstract patterns. The oldest surviving hand crosses date back to the 17th century although they were used earlier.

The most common cross is the ornamental neck variety. A cord from the neck usually suspends the cross. It demonstrates that an individual is Christian and is believed to offer protection to the wearer. In the 15th century, **Zara Yakob** decreed that all Christians should wear a neck cross and they have been in common use ever since. Many 19th-century crosses were made from the silver in **Maria Theresa thalers**. Most modern crosses have very little silver content. Crosses come in many shapes and designs, some of which are quite intricate. A few crosses incorporate an ear wax pick in the design so that they serve a double function.

CUNNINGHAM, ALAN GORDON (1887–1983). British soldier. Born on 1 May 1887 in Edinburgh and educated at Cheltenham College and the Royal Military Academy, Woolwich. In 1906, Cunningham received a commission in the Royal Artillery. After duty on the western front during World War I, he served in the Straits Settlements; attended Naval Staff School and the Imperial Defense College; and taught at the Small Arms School, Netheravon. In 1937, Cunningham became commander, Royal Artillery and, in 1937, received a promotion to major general to command the fifth Anti-Aircraft Division.

After the outbreak of **World War II**, he commanded several infantry divisions. In 1940, Cunningham became general officer commanding East Africa to help liberate Ethiopia. In January 1941, the campaign started with the forces of Major General **William Platt** advancing from Sudan and Cunningham's army, which consisted of four brigades comprised mainly of East, South, and West African troops, deploying from Kenya. On 25 February 1941, Cunningham's forces captured Mogadishu and, on 29 March 1941, entered **Harar**. On 5 April 1941, his troops liberated **Addis Ababa**. Cunningham and Platt then converged on **Amba** Alagi, where **Amedeo di Savoia,** Duke of Aosta, commander of Italian forces, surrendered on 16 May 1941. In two months, Cunningham and his troops traveled 1,700 miles (2,736 kilometers), liberated almost 400,000 square miles of territory, and took some 50,000 prisoners, while suffering only 500 casualties.

After the war, Cunningham served in Northern Ireland, Palestine, and Transjordan. After retiring, he remained active in military and academic circles. On 30 January 1983, Cunningham died in Tunbridge Wells. *See also* ITALIAN-ETHIOPIAN WAR.

CURRENCY. The first coinage in Ethiopia took place in **Axum** in the third century. Axum minted more than 500 different types of coins in gold, silver, bronze, and copper. As Axum's power declined, the minting of coins ended in about the eighth century. Barter replaced coins as the medium of exchange. Articles of clothing, **food**, agricultural implements, decorative ornaments, **cotton** cloth, small iron bars, cartridges, and bars of salt or *amole*, as it was called, replaced coins for many years.

Primitive coins minted in **Harar** were in use locally beginning in 742, interrupted by periods of nonuse. The production of Harari currency ceased with the occupation of the city by **Menelik II**. One of the last coins struck at Harar was called a Mahalek in silver and dated 1892.

The Maria Theresa dollar, known as the thaler in Austria, was first minted in Vienna in 1751 and named after Austrian Empress Maria Theresa. It was 80 percent pure silver. In the late 18th century, Arab traders probably introduced the Maria Theresa thaler to Ethiopia and, by the mid–19th century, it had become the most widely acceptable form of currency. Before 1935, the coinage of Menelik II and **Haile Selassie** failed to dislodge the thaler. During the **Italian-Ethiopian War** (1935–1936), there were some 50 million thalers in circulation. The Italians brought the master dies of the thaler to Ethiopia so that they could increase production. During their occupation of Ethiopia (1936–1941), the Italians replaced the thaler with the Italian lira. However, Ethiopians had no confidence in the lira and continued using the thaler. With the defeat of the Italians in 1941, the **British Military Administration** introduced the East African shilling. Ethiopians used it concurrently with the Maria Theresa thaler until abolished by the Currency and Legal Tender Proclamation on 23 July 1945. After **World War II** ended, the Ethiopian government collected the thalers and sent them to the United States to be melted down for use as 50-cent silver coins in Ethiopia.

An imperial proclamation of 20 May 1945, brought into effect on 23 July 1945, introduced a new currency and conferred on the Ethiopian State Bank the sole right to issue banknotes and coins. The dollar bank note was divided into 100 cents. Its value was set at 40 cents United States. Other denominations included 5, 10, 20, 50, 100, and 500 dollar banknotes. Ethiopia minted copper coins worth 1/100, 1/20, 1/10, and 1/4 of a dollar and a silver coin worth 50 cents. The Ethiopian State Bank decreed that in the future the thaler and the East African shilling would be accepted only at their silver value.

On 20 September 1976, the **Derg** regime replaced the imperial dollar with the birr. The new bank notes included denominations of 100, 50, 10, 5, and 1 birr and coins of 1, 5, 10, 25, and 50 cents. The Derg valued the birr at 2.07 to the U.S. dollar. The current government retained the birr but issued new currency on 8 November 1997 to coincide with the issuance of the nakfa in Eritrea. In 1993, the rate of the birr was five to the U.S. dollar. In 2003, the exchange rate was about 8.25 birr to the U.S. dollar.

– D –

DAJAZMACH (DEJAZMATCH). *See* MILITARY TITLES.

DAMOT. Damot was an ancient province located south of the **Blue Nile** and between it and the Gibe River. The **Sidama** or **Wolaytta** people, who lived on the empire's southwestern border probably were Damot's original inhabitants. In early medieval times, contact between Damot and the northern **highlands** developed. One of the **Zagwe dynasty**'s rulers sent an expedition from his capital at Roha to Damot. Initially a pagan land, it was apparently the location of important **Ethiopian Orthodox Church (EOC) missionary** activity. According to some accounts, a famous pagan chief known as Mota Lame or Motalami ruled Damot in the first half of the 13th century. At the urging of Saint Tekle Haymanot (c. 1215–1313), Mota Lame reportedly converted to Christianity and built churches throughout Damot. Emperor **Amda Tseyon** incorporated Damot into the empire and expanded Christian missionary activity. Damot also produced gold and engaged in **slavery**.

Emperor **Zara Yakob** put Damot under the supervision of one his daughters and later assumed personal control over the province.

When the governor of neighboring **Hadeya Kingdom** rebelled against imperial rule, Damot remained loyal. **Baeda Mariam**, successor to Zara Yakob, decentralized imperial rule and placed Damot under a local ruler. By the early 16th century, Damot was a large province and an important source of gold and slaves. The former came principally from **Enarya** and the latter from Enarya and Bizamo. Damot's importance was its strategic position along trade routes. Despite earlier Christian missionary efforts, Damot remained inhabited primarily by pagans in the early 16th century. It was also a popular location for detaining political prisoners.

At the time of the Islamic invasion led by **Ahmad ibn Ibrahim al Ghazi** in the early 16th century, Damot was part of the empire and provided soldiers for Emperor **Lebna Dengel's** (reigned 1508–1540) forces. In 1531, Ahmad defeated Lebna Dengel in Damot and appointed his own governor of the province. Damot returned to imperial rule after Ahmad's death. In 1548, Emperor **Galawedos** sent a punitive expedition to Damot and returned in 1555, when he issued his famous *Confession of Faith* that defined the EOC's main principles. Emperor Sarsa Dengel (reigned 1564–1597) maintained close links with Damot, which provided him with troops for the 1588 campaign against the Turks at **Massawa**. By the late 16th century, the **Oromos** were beginning to push into Damot and eventually conquered the province. The Oromos assimilated some of the local population while others retreated across the Blue Nile to **Gojam,** where they settled as a distinct community. Much later, **Iyasu II** (reigned 1730–1755) depended on Oromo support when a rebellion broke out in Damot soon after his coronation.

After some of Damot's inhabitants crossed the Blue Nile to escape the Oromo, the term Damot also came to be applied to the new area of settlement north of the Blue Nile near present-day Debre Markos. The migrants in the new Damot remained close to the Empire and resisted attempts by Jesuit missionaries to implant **Catholicism**. An army formed by Emperor Susneyos (reigned 1607–1632), who converted to Catholicism, eventually subdued the Damots and forced them to accept Catholicism. Soldiers from the new Damot helped **Fasilidas** (reigned 1632–1667) to defeat a rebel who had marched on **Gondar**. Subsequently, the Gondarine rulers frequently visited new Damot and the name appears regularly in the chronicles of the Gondarine period.

DANAKIL DEPRESSION. An irregular triangle-shaped basin located in the northern part of **Afar Region**, the Danakil Depression is about 400 miles (640 kilometers) long and 150 miles (240 kilometers) wide. The depression descends as much as 377 feet (115 meters) below sea level. It is one of the hottest places on Earth; temperatures soar to 140° Fahrenheit (60° Celsius). Coastal hills in neighboring **Eritrea** drain inland into saline lakes from which commercial salt is extracted. Because it has long been considered one of Africa's most inhospitable places due to the **climate**, topography, and fierceness of the **Afar** clans residing there, early explorers usually gave it a wide berth. No European member of three separate expeditions that explored the depression in the late 1800s ever returned. In 1928, British mining engineer Ludovico Mariano Nesbitt was the first European to explore the area extensively and live to write about his exploits in the *Geographical Journal* and a book entitled *Desert and Forest: The Exploration of Abyssinian Danakil.*

DANCE. Ethiopian **music** and dance are closely linked. The earliest tradition of religious dance goes back to the Old Testament. The solemn procession of the *tabot*, accompanied by singing and dancing, rattling of the *sistra,* and beating with prayer sticks typifies religious dance. Dancing in church or at religious festivals acquired an Orthodox as well as an Ethiopian character. European travelers have recorded this dance since the 14th century.

Religious dance is especially evident during major ceremonies such as Timket. The *debtaras* or church musicians face each other in two long lines. They wear a white turban and a toga with embroidered borders. In one hand they hold a staff crowned with a cross and in the other a sistrum whose jingling lends rhythm to the intoning chant. Two or three drummers are nearby. The debtaras begin softly and advance with rhythmic swaying from side to side, shifting the balance to one foot as the other lifts off the ground. The prayer sticks are moved back and forth, up and down, then raised high and swayed from one side to the other. The beating of the drums quickens, sistrums jingle louder, and the pitch rises. As the lines of the debtaras approach nearer to one another, the atmosphere becomes electric. Suddenly the sound and movement stop with the sticks, faces, and bodies of the debtaras straining toward the sky.

Folk or ethnic dances are as varied as Ethiopia's ethnic groups. Ethiopians living in the valleys and hot plains tend to have boisterous and lively dances. Persons who live in the high plateau are more restrained in their movements. Intricate footwork or body movements are not typical of Ethiopian folk dancing. A common characteristic is the vigorous jumping, thumping of the feet and swaying from side to side. Among highland **women**, movement of the body from the waist to the knees is frowned upon. Movements of the head and neck and facial expressions are the most important component of the highland dance. One of the most popular dances in the **highlands** is the *eskeesta* or shoulder dance. The shoulders move in a series of motions forwards and backwards while the head moves from one shoulder to another. The motions are accompanied by a sharp drawing of air through the teeth, making a sound resembling the word eskeesta.

The **Gurage** are well known for their harvest dance that replicates the motions used in harvesting crops. Tribes from southern Ethiopia are famous for their rhythmic and exciting dances. The men may wield spears and make fearsome facial expressions. The people around **Axum** dance a subdued style and the women show great modesty. The **Somali** of the **Ogaden** perform a vigorous and manly dance. The men wear colorful towels around their legs and a shirt of matching color. The women wear a skirt of striped cloth over which is a long tunic. They drape their heads in a white scarf.

All social occasions offer an opportunity for dancing. Both men and women perform the nuptial dance at the time of arrival of the bride at the home of the groom. Young girls in the traditional white dress perform the flower dance house to house on Ethiopian New Year. A form of dance **drama** is popular in rural **Tigray Region** where performers narrate a story through conventional gestures.

DARGE SAHLA SELASSE (c. 1830–1900). Soldier, government administrator, and adviser to **Menelik II**. In 1849, Darge helped conquer the areas around **Entoto**. He became a prisoner of war during **Tewodros II**'s campaign against **Shoa** Province (1855). British forces freed Darge during the **Anglo-Ethiopian War**. His nephew, Menelik II, then appointed him **dajazmach** and governor of Shoa's Marha Beta Province. After pacifying northwest Shoa, Darge became a **ras** and, in October 1878, governor of Salale district. In 1886, he commanded a successful military campaign in Arsi that culminated in the Battle of Azule. As governor of Arsi, Darge ensured that the region became a good source of revenue and agricultural products. He also participated in Menelik II's campaign to capture **Harar**. During his later years, Darge was one of Menelik II's most trusted counselors and a staunch opponent of **slavery**. He died on 22 March 1900.

DASANETCH PEOPLE AND LANGUAGE. The Dasanetch people live on the east and west side of the lower **Omo River** and along the west side of upper **Lake Turkana** extending into Kenya. They are known by many names including Geleb or Geluba in Ethiopia and Marille or Merile in Kenya. They number perhaps 30,000. They tend to be a pastoral people and define wealth in terms of their cattle and to some extent sheep and goats. From the late 1890s until about 1903, Ethiopian troops repeatedly invaded Dasanetch lands. Surviving Dasanetch fled to the south and along the western side of Lake Turkana. The Dasanetch eventually returned to their lands and made peace with the highland Ethiopians, who withdrew from the area and did not return until the 1920s. At about the same time, there also was a major war between the Dasanetch and the Turkana in Kenya that resulted in an expansion of Dasanetch territory. The **language** spoken by the Dasanetch is part of the east Cushitic group in the Afro-Asiatic language family. Two detailed studies of the people are Claudia J. Carr's *Pastoralism in Crisis: The Dasanetch and Their Ethiopian Lands,* and Uri Almagor's *Pastoral Partners: Affinity and Bond Partnership among the Dassanetch of South-West Ethiopia.*

DAWARO. Dawaro became part of the Christian empire in early medieval times. Although European maps from the 16th and 17th century do not always agree where Dawaro was located, they generally place it east of present-day Bale in southeast Ethiopia. **Amda Tseyon** occupied Dawaro, but the local governor, Haydara, challenged imperial rule in the late 1320s. Amda Seyon retaliated by capturing Haydara and laying waste to the state. During this period, Dawaro had an estimated 20,000-man cavalry and a 15,000-man infantry. Emperor **Zara Yakob** (reigned 1434–1468) appointed a governor of Dawaro, suggesting that it was part of the Christian empire at that time. During Zara Yakob's rule, Dawaro supported a rebellion in **Hadeya**

kingdom. After suppressing the rebellion, he stationed many troops there. Dawaro remained under Imperial rule during the reign of **Baeda Mariam**. In the late 15th century, there was considerable competition between Christian and Muslim **missionaries**. Trade routes linked Dawaro to **Shoa** Province in the north and Bale to the south or west.

Because of its relative proximity to the **Adal sultanate**, the Christian Dawaro was one of the first to experience the Islamic campaigns of **Ahmad ibn Ibrahim al Ghazi**. After an initial raid into Fatagar in 1526–1527, Ahmad made several forays into Dawaro. Initially, he encountered fierce opposition. Learning of a much larger planned invasion, Emperor **Lebna Dengel** recruited soldiers from all parts of the empire. Ahmad won an initial but costly victory in 1529 at Shembera Kore (Swamp of the Chickpeas), about 50 miles (80 kilometers) east of present-day **Addis Ababa**. After some other tentative military successes, Ahmad decided to occupy Dawaro. In 1531, he defeated Lebna Dengel's army and laid waste to much of Dawaro. Ahmad initially accepted tribute from the defeated Dawaro leaders so that he could focus on the defeat of Lebna Dengel elsewhere. Faced with continuing military threats from Ahmad's forces, the Dawaro's 50 Christian nobles converted to **Islam**. About 1540, Ahmad appointed his son, Nasradin, to take charge of Dawaro's government.

Lebna Dengel's son, **Galawedos**, resumed the fight against Ahmad in Dawaro. Both sides scored early victories. After Ahmed's death (1543), his soldiers in Dawaro made an all-out effort to defeat Galawedos but his troops crushed them. Galawedos then proceeded to Dawaro and constructed a palace at Agraro. There were, however, continuing problems between Muslims and Christians in Dawaro. In 1547 or 1548, Galawedos assigned one of his principal commanders as governor of Dawaro. By 1559, the uneasy peace in the area began to disintegrate. There also were increasing incursions by the **Oromo** who invaded much of Dawaro. In 1579, Emperor Sarsa Dengel (reigned 1563–1597) wanted to repel the Oromo but gave up the plan when his chiefs appeared uninterested. There were no subsequent efforts to contest Oromo occupation of Dawaro.

DAWIT I. Emperor of Ethiopia (1380–1412). Son of Emperor Newaya Krestos. As one of the most powerful monarchs in medieval Ethiopia,

Dawit I facilitated the growth of Christianity throughout his empire. Supposedly, he brought a remnant of the True **Cross** from **Jerusalem**. Dawit I also battled against **Islam**, particularly in the **Adal sultanate** and fought a successful campaign against the **Falashas** who had rebelled in the **Simien Mountains**. Apart from his military prowess, Dawit I was a skilled diplomat in his handling of the **Ewostateswos**. He also sent diplomatic missions to Egypt (1386) and Europe (1402). About a year before his death, Dawit I abdicated and is believed to have died in a riding accident. He is buried on Dek Island in **Lake Tana**.

DAWIT YOHANNES (1953–). Speaker of the House of Peoples' Representatives. Born in **Addis Ababa** and educated at the Ras Tafari Makonnen School and the **Haile Selassie I University** (1972–1974). While a university student, Dawit became one of the founders of the Ethiopian Communist Party. After the overthrow of **Haile Selassie**, he lived in exile in Sudan, Italy, France, and the United States (1979–1991). In 1989, Dawit attended the founding congress of the **Ethiopian People's Revolutionary Democratic Front** (EPRDF) and joined the Ethiopian People's Democratic Front (EPDM), one of the parties that belonged to the EPRDF. After the **Derg**'s collapse (1991), he moved to Ethiopia and served in the Legal Affairs Department, the transitional **parliament**, and the Election Commission. After the EPDM transformed itself into the Amhara National Democratic Movement (ANDM) in January 1994, Dawit became part of the party's leadership. In January 1995, he became a member of the ANDM politburo. In August 1995, Dawit became Speaker of the House of Peoples' Representatives; as of 2003, he still held this post. Dawit was instrumental in bringing Internet access to Ethiopia.

DAWRO PEOPLE AND LANGUAGE. *See* GAMO-GOFA-DAWRO PEOPLES AND LANGUAGES.

DAWUD IBSA AYANA (1952–). Chairman of the **Oromo Liberation Front** (OLF) (1999–). Born in Abuna village, Horro Guduru district, **Wollega**. Dawud attended primary and secondary school in Shambu. After graduation (1966), he received a scholarship to General Wingate High School and then attended **Haile Selassie I University**

(1970–1971), where he participated in the students' movement against **Haile Selassie**. Dawud became one of the first members of the Association of Oromo University Students in **Addis Ababa**. During 1974–1976, he participated in the **Zemacha** campaign. In 1977, Dawud was elected to the OLF's Central Committee. From October 1977 to December 1979, he was imprisoned by the **Derg**. He returned to Addis Ababa University during the 1979–1980 academic year. Before finishing his studies (statistics), Dawud fled to Sudan (1980) and joined OLF units operating from that country. A few months later, he received basic military training in Eritrea. In April 1981, Dawud commanded the OLF unit that started the armed struggle in Wollega Province. In December 1981, the **Derg** poisoned and then tortured him for several months. From August 1982 to December 1986, he was jailed at Kerchele prison without charge. Dawud eventually escaped and rejoined the OLF. In 1988, he was elected to the OLF's Central Committee and the Executive Committee. Until 1991, Dawud headed the OLF's Military Department. In 1998, he was reelected to the OLF's Executive Committee and, in 1999, became the OLF's chairman. *See also* OROMO PEOPLE AND LANGUAGE.

DE BONO, EMILIO (1866–1944). Born on 19 March 1866 in Cassano d'Adda, Milan. In 1878, De Bono attended the Military College of Milan and then enrolled in the Military School. In 1888, he served in Eritrea. In 1912, De Bono became chief of the general staff of the Department of Libya. He fought in **World War I** without much distinction. After the armistice, he joined the Fascists in Italy and helped to organize Benito Mussolini's march on Rome (1922). After a tour as governor of Tripolitania (1925–1928), De Bono became minister for the colonies (1929–1935).

On 10 January 1935, he became high commissioner of East Africa. On 3 October 1935, in command of a force of more than 100,000 troops, De Bono crossed the Mareb River into Ethiopia along a 40-mile front without a declaration of war. On the right, the second Army Corps, under the command of General Pietro Maravigna advanced toward **Adwa**. In the center, General Pirzio Biroli commanded the Eritrean Corps, which marched to the Enticho mountains. On the left, General Ruggero Santini's first Army Corps moved on

Adigrat. The unpreparedness of the Ethiopians enabled Italian forces to occupy several important towns, including Adigrat, Inticho, and Daro Tacle (4 October); Adwa (6 October); **Axum** (15 October); and **Mekele** (8 November). Another setback occurred on 10 October 1935, when Haile Selassie Gugsa, commander of the Makele sector, defected to the Italians.

On 11 November 1935, Mussolini ordered De Bono to advance from Mekele to **Amba** Alagi. De Bono refused and, on 17 November 1935, **Pietro Badoglio** replaced him as commander in chief of Italian forces in East Africa. On 10 January 1944, the Fascist Grand Council executed De Bono for alleged treason.

DEBRE DAMO. The Debre Damo monastery, believed to date from the sixth century, is located on a high plateau 30 miles (48 kilometers) from **Axum** on the road to Adigrat. It can only be reached by ascending a 50-foot cliff with the help of a rope lowered by monks living at the monastery. **Women** are not permitted to visit. It is thought that **Abuna** Aregawi, one of nine saints who came from Syria in the sixth century, passed through the area and concluded this was an appropriate location to live a solitary life. Legend suggests that Abuna Aregawi first reached the location when a serpent at the command of God reached down and lifted him safely to the top.

The church of Abuna Aregawi, built in the Axumite style before the ninth century, is probably Ethiopia's oldest intact church. The church's beams and ceilings are decorated with carved wooden panels depicting several animals, most of which can no longer be found in the area. The monastery also contains a collection of some of the best manuscripts presently existing in Ethiopia. The church of Abuna Aregawi has had a profound impact on the **literature** of the **Ethiopian Orthodox Church**. The site also contains a secondary church, monastic dwellings, water cisterns, and hermit caves.

In addition to its important contribution to religious history, Debre Damo, because of its inaccessibility, served as a place of detention for male members of the Axumite royal dynasty so they would be unable to conspire against the ruling monarch. Debre Damo also was a refuge for Emperor **Lebna Dengel** and Queen Seble Wengel, who fled the invading forces of **Ahmad ibn Ibrahim al Ghazi** in the 16th century. Lebna Dengel died at Debre Damo in 1540.

DEBRE LIBANOS. Located 71 miles (115 kilometers) north of **Addis Ababa**, Debre Libanos is the site of a monastery founded about 1275 by Saint Tekle Haymanot. Descended from a family of Christian immigrants, Saint Tekle Haymanot studied at **Debre Damo** monastery in **Tigray** before settling with his disciples at Debre Asbo, as the site was originally known. According to legend, Saint Tekle Haymanot moved into a cave that had previously been inhabited by a magician. He turned part of the cave into a church dedicated to Saint Mary and stood praying on one leg for seven years without interruption until the other leg withered and fell off. A bird brought him one seed once a year for sustenance. For his devotion, God gave him three sets of wings as a substitute for his lost leg. He is usually shown in pictures with one leg and wings. One of Ethiopia's most revered saints, Saint Tekle Haymanot is credited with the spread of Christianity throughout the **highlands**. There is no trace of the original monastery, a casualty of the Muslim-Christian wars. Since the time of Saint Tekle Haymanot, Debre Libanos periodically has served as **Shoa** Province's principal monastery. Today, Debre Libanos, which operates five religious schools, is one of Ethiopia's largest and most important monasteries.

Emperor Yeshaq (reigned 1412–1427) built the first large church at the site. His younger brother, Emperor **Zara Yakob** (reigned 1434–1468), used the monastery for the propagation of his radical religious policies and renamed the location Debre Libanos. The monastery was apparently rebuilt in the early 16th century; **Ahmad ibn Ibrahim al Ghazi** destroyed it in 1531, after massacring a large number of monks. The center of the kingdom soon moved to the **Lake Tana** area and eventually to **Gondar**. Many in the Debre Libanos order followed the court and the monastery became much less significant. A few of the Gondarine kings visited Debre Libanos. It became an important monastic site again by the time of King Sahle Selassie (reigned 1813–1847). Emperor **Yohannes IV** visited the monastery in 1878 and had a new church built there. Emperor **Menelik II** subsequently rebuilt it once again.

In February 1937, Debre Libanos suffered another massacre following an attempt in Addis Ababa on the life of Fascist Italian viceroy General **Rodolfo Graziani**. Debre Libanos was long suspected as a hotbed of rebel activity that gave shelter to Graziani's assailants. Consequently, between 21 and 26 May 1937, General Pietro

Maletti supervised the executions of 449 monks and laymen. The Italians exiled those who survived to Danane, Somalia. Following this action, Graziani wrote to Benito Mussolini that "the monastery is closed—definitely." Some say that the human bones exposed on a hillside above the church are those of persons massacred by Graziani's forces. Like other aspects of the history of Debre Libanos, this may be legend.

In 1963, Emperor **Haile Selassie** authorized the construction of the eighth and present church of Saint Tekle Haymanot. Visitors can enter the church and climb up to the saint's cave. Only men can enter the monastery. What is commonly known as a 17th-century "Portuguese Bridge" is located close to Debre Libanos. However, **Menelik II**'s uncle **Ras** Darge, who was governor of Salale, actually built the bridge in the 19th century. Another attraction is the small village of Fiche. Situated near the edge of a cliff, it offers a spectacular view of the Jema valley, the **Blue Nile** gorge, and the mountains of eastern and southeastern **Gojam**.

DEBRE TABOR. (28,400; estimated 2002 **population**.) Capital of **Bagemder Province**. Located about 62 miles (100 kilometers) northwest of **Bahir Dar** on the Chinese-built road to Weldiya. **Ras** Gugsa Mersa, the **Oromo** ruler of Bagemder (1803–1825) and one of Ethiopia's most powerful political figures, founded Debre Tabor and used it as his administrative center. The town remained the seat of power for three of Ras Gugsa's sons and his more famous grandson, Ras Alula Qubi, who was elected by a council of the clan in 1831 when he was 13 years old. In the early 1800s, Ras Gugsa built Tabor Eyesus Church, which is located on a hill outside of Debre Tabor. During part of the 19th century, Debre Tabor served as Ethiopia's capital. **Tewodros II** abandoned the capital at **Gondar** in favor of Debre Tabor, a strategically better location. **Yohannes IV** resided briefly at Debre Tabor before making his capital at **Mekele** in **Tigray Region**. Earlier, the important Yejju Oromo dynasty, which was originally Muslim but eventually became Christian, held power in Bagemder Province. Little remains in Debre Tabor of its prestigious past.

DEBRE ZEIT (DEBRE ZEYIT, DEBRE ZEYT). (92,900; estimated 2002 **population**.) Ethiopia's 10th largest city. Known to the local

Oromo population as Bishoftu. Near the town is the site where, in 1529, **Ahmad ibn Ibrahim al Ghazi** won a victory over **Lebna Dengal**'s troops. Since 1945, Debre Zeit, which is 30 miles (48 kilometers) from **Addis Ababa**, has been the home of the Ethiopian **Air Force**'s main base and the Air Force Training School. The Pan-African Veterinary Center and the Agricultural Research Center also are located in the town. Debre Zeit is a popular weekend resort for Addis Ababa's elite, who are drawn to the region's six crater lakes (Aranguade, Chalaklaka, Bishoftu, Bishoftu Guba, Hora Arsedi, and Kilole).

DEBT. Ethiopia, one of the world's poorest countries, has $5.6 billion of debt following a reduction of debt to Russia from $5.9 billion to $1.3 billion. As a percent of gross domestic product (GDP), Ethiopia's total debt increased from almost 40 percent in the **Derg**'s last days to a high of 91 percent in 1993–1994. By 1996–1997, total debt had dropped to 64 percent of GDP. Three factors explain the phenomenal increase over a short period of time. The 1992 devaluation of the Ethiopian birr inflated its denominated debt by the same proportion as the devaluation. The government also took on new debt. Arrears began to appear in Ethiopia's debt repayment schedule, adding to the total debt. Multilateral institutions account for about 54 percent of the long-term debt and bilateral lenders 44 percent. Commercial lenders hold only 2 percent. More than 80 percent of the debt is on concessional terms.

Historically, Ethiopia's growth rate has exceeded the cost of borrowing and debt service obligations were honored without straining the **economy** or foreign exchange reserves. Even excluding loans for military purchases, the correlation between economic growth and debt turned negative during the Derg regime. Between 1974 and 1986, external debt increased at four times the annual average rate of GDP growth and arrears began in 1989. In the **Ethiopia People's Revolutionary Democratic Front**'s (EPRDF) early years, the debt burden increased significantly but then began to decline. During the **Ethiopian-Eritrean War**, debt stock increased at an annual rate of 22.5 percent.

Ethiopia is now one of about 24 countries scheduled to benefit from the Heavily Indebted Poor Countries (HIPC) initiative, which is designed to reduce debt burden. In late 2001, the **International Monetary Fund** (IMF) and the **World Bank** decided that Ethiopia was eligible for assistance under this program. If it meets the conditions, Ethiopia will receive a debt relief of $1.3 billion in net present value (NPV) under the HIPC. In NPV terms, the World Bank's International Development Association (IDA) will provide $463 million. The IMF will provide $34 million, bilateral creditors $482 million, and commercial lenders $30 million. This represents 47 percent of Ethiopia's total debt after it has received debt relief under traditional programs. This will allow Ethiopia to save $96 million annually until 2021 in debt-service obligations. Ethiopia's total debts will be reduced to only 150 percent of its exports, down from about 350 percent prior to this relief. Debt servicing as a percentage of exports will also be cut in half from 16 percent to about 7 percent by 2003.

Ethiopia will begin to benefit from substantial relief when it has completed several reform measures within a three-year time frame, including implementation of a **Poverty** Reduction Strategy Paper, attainment of macroeconomic stability, measurable improvements in governance and public expenditure management, reform of the financial sector, and introduction of a value-added tax by January 2003. Ethiopia must also show improvement in girls' enrollment in primary school, achieve higher levels of immunization, and take measures to combat **human immunodeficiency virus/acquired immune deficiency syndrome.**

DEBTARA. *See* DANCE; ETHIOPIAN ORTHODOX CHURCH.

DEFORESTATION. Deforestation and, as a result, soil erosion are serious problems in Ethiopia. Since the 17th century, accounts by travelers to Ethiopia suggest that trees covered a significantly larger part of the country in earlier times. By the early 19th century, the main areas of settlement were denuded of trees. Disappearance of forests contributed to the decline in **wildlife**. In 1900, natural forests covered an estimated 42 million hectares of Ethiopia's total land area. In the 20th century, Ethiopia's **population** grew rapidly, causing farmers to clear more land for cultivation and families to cut more wood for fuel. Ethiopians used additional wood for building material. There was also increased population pressure in pastoral areas and more animals per acre.

A 1958 study of land under cultivation as compared with a 1976 study, suggested that the acreage had doubled in less than 20 years. According to a 2000 study by the Ethiopian Agricultural Research Organization, the country was losing up to 200,000 hectares of forest annually due to growing demand for firewood and agricultural and grazing land. On 14 September 2000, Ethiopia announced that it had developed a national forestry research strategy to revive the country's depleted forests. Despite this and other conservation efforts, the country's forests remained in critical danger.

On 7 January 2002, the United Nations Emergency Unit issued a study that concluded that less than 3 percent of Ethiopia is now covered with trees. It said much of the destruction of Ethiopia's forests had taken place in the last 40 years. The report was critical of Ethiopia's feeble efforts to protect state forests and encourage reforestation projects. The majority of remaining forests are in the southwest; the **highlands** and low-altitude pastoral areas are especially devoid of trees. The environmental trend in the hot, low-lying pastoral regions is a not-so-gradual change from bush to savanna to semiarid land. This situation contributes enormously to soil erosion and increases the prospect for drought and **famine**. *See also* ENVIRONMENT.

DE JACOBIS, JUSTIN (GIUSTINO) (1818–1860). Italian **missionary**. Born on 9 October 1800 in San Fele, Luciana. On 17 October 1818, De Jacobis entered the Congregation of the Lazarists in Naples. On 12 June 1824, he was ordained a priest in Brindisi. During the early years of his career, De Jacobis served at Oria and Monopoli. In 1839, he became superior in Lecce and then in Naples, where he worked with the sick during a cholera epidemic (1826–1837).

In 1839, De Jacobis received an appointment as prefect apostolic and missionary to **Adwa**. He established **Catholic** missions, schools for training native clergy, and a college and seminary at Guala. In 1849, De Jacobis became vicar apostolic of **Abyssinia**. His accomplishments and those of his colleagues like **Giuseppe Sapeto** and **Guglielmo Massaia** caused the **Ethiopian Orthodox Church** (EOC) to ban Catholicism and to close all Catholic facilities. Some EOC clergy called for the death of De Jacobis, who became an underground missionary. By 1853, he had consecrated 20 priests, converted some

5,000 Ethiopians, and reopened the college at Guala. **Tewodros II** imprisoned De Jacobis for several months and then exiled him to the area of Halai in what is now Eritrea. On 31 July 1860, he died of fever on the side of a road near Halai.

DEMOBILIZATION CAMPAIGN (1991–1994). On 14 June 1991, the **Transitional Government of Ethiopia** (TGE) embarked on a massive demobilization campaign for the defeated **Derg** army and the **Oromo Liberation Front** (OLF) by establishing an autonomous government office called the Commission for the Rehabilitation of Members of the Former Army and Disabled War Veterans. The commission created seven regional offices and 36 district offices to organize and coordinate demobilization and reintegration activities. An advisory council assisted the commission and acted as a liaison with government ministries.

The commission adopted a two-step strategy for the demobilization campaign. Phase I, which lasted from June to December 1991, included transport of ex-soldiers to their place of origin, emergency food rations, and a cash grant for each soldier and his dependents. The commission also held discussions with local communities about the needs of returning troops. By late January 1992, the commission had demobilized Ethiopia's entire army of nearly 500,000, despite the reluctance of some donors to support the process.

In March 1992, donors accepted Phase II of the demobilization campaign. The **World Bank**'s Emergency Relief and Recovery Program became a major conduit of funds for ex-soldiers. Some bilateral donors established their own projects in collaboration with the commission or channeled their resources through various nongovernmental organizations. Phase II focused on the needs of the ex-soldier and his family, including **education**, employment, **health**, and housing. A majority returned to rural areas to farm and received assistance in obtaining land and credit. Many received health support and vocational training. Donor aid sought to improve the **agriculture** sector by distributing seeds, fertilizers, and plastic tubing for **coffee** seedlings. During Phase II (1992–1994), the commission demobilized some 22,200 OLF fighters.

DERG. **Amharic** word for "committee" that scholars often use to identify the entire period of **Mengistu Haile Mariam**'s regime

(1974–1991). Established on 27 June 1974, the Derg began to evolve on 12 January 1974, when the Territorial Army's 4th Brigade mutinied at Negele in Sidamo Province. Over the next few weeks, discontent spread to other military units and the **armed forces** disintegrated into several competing factions, the most significant of which was the **Armed Forces Coordination Committee** (AFCC) headed by Colonel Alem Zewd. The AFCC alienated many in the military by arresting disgruntled officers and supporting government policies.

In early June 1974, a group of junior officers broke away from the AFCC and established a new organization called the Coordinating Committee of the Armed Force, **Police**, and Territorial Army. They elected then major Mengistu Haile Mariam as chairman and Major Atnafu Abate as vice-chairman of the committee, which became known as the Derg. Initially, the Derg coexisted and often competed with the government. On 8 July 1974, the Derg issued its first policy statement, known as *Itopya Tikem* (Ethiopia First). This document promised, among other things, to implement socialism and national unity but promised loyalty to the monarchy. Over the coming weeks, the Derg became increasingly confident and determined to rule Ethiopia. On 12 September 1974, the Derg abolished the monarchy. On 15 September 1975, the Derg assumed the name **Provisional Military Administrative Council** under the chairmanship of Lieutenant General **Aman Mikael Andom**. *See also* COMMISSION FOR ORGANIZING THE PARTY OF THE WORKING PEOPLE OF ETHIOPIA; FIKRE SELASSIE WOGDERES; HUMAN RIGHTS; NATIONAL DEMOCRATIC REVOLUTION; PROVISIONAL OFFICE FOR MASS ORGANIZATIONAL AFFAIRS; RED TERROR; WORKERS' PARTY OF ETHIOPIA.

DESE (DESSIE, DASE, DESSYE). (123,200; estimated 2002 **population**.) Ethiopia's fifth largest city. Located in central Ethiopia 246 miles (397 kilometers) north of **Addis Ababa** on the road to **Mekele** and situated on an escarpment above the **Rift Valley**.

In 1882, **Yohannes IV** founded Dese after sighting a comet, which prompted him to build a church on the site called Dese-Amhaigna (My Joy). In 1888, Dese became the capital of **Ras** Mikael Ali Abba Bula of Wollo, an **Oromo** chief who had converted to Christianity under **Yohannes IV** 10 years earlier. On 3 August 1917, supporters of **Lij Iyasu Mikael** attacked and briefly occupied Dese until government forces retook the town.

After **World War I**, Dese undertook several modernization projects, including the opening of a Bank of Abyssinia branch office (1920), the establishment of the Princess Sehin School (1928), and the construction of a small hospital operated by the Seventh-Day Adventists. On 28 November 1935, **Haile Selassie** left Addis Ababa for Dese, where he established his headquarters; however, advancing Italian forces eventually forced him to leave Dese for exile in Britain. On 15 April 1936, Italian forces entered Dese and occupied Ras Mikael's palace.

The mountainous topography around Dese constrained its ability to expand. As a result, most growth and new **industry** occurred in Kombolcha, a town of about 50,000, located on the plain below Dese, which is 16 miles (26 kilometers) away. Kombolcha also is astride one branch of the main truck route from the ports of **Asab** and Djibouti.

Today, Dese is an important market center that trades in beeswax, civet, **coffee**, durra (sorghum), hides, honey, and leopard skins. Local industries include silver working, tanning, and weaving. Dese also is well known for its nightclubs and Asmari bars where Asmari singers play one-stringed instruments.

DEVELOPMENT AND LITERACY THROUGH COOPERATION CAMPAIGN. *See* ZEMACHA.

DIASPORA. Chronic instability, civil war, and the repressive **Derg** regime caused significant numbers of Ethiopians to leave the country or remain abroad if they had departed before the monarchy's downfall (1974). In addition to those living in Kenya, Somalia, and Sudan, there are large communities in Canada, Italy, and the United States. Smaller numbers reside in Britain, France, Germany, Netherlands, and the Scandinavian countries. Although new arrivals in Western countries tend to work in lower-paying jobs, some professionals have been successful in the private, educational, and health care sectors. Nearly all **Falashas** have emigrated to Israel. *See also* BRAIN DRAIN.

DIME PEOPLE AND LANGUAGE. Numbering several thousand people, the Dime or Dima live on the bank of the **Omo River** in the northern part of south Omo zone, to the west of the **Ari people** and to the east of the **Me'en**. The **Basketo** live to the north and the **Suri** to the south. Five kings once ruled the Dime. They use stone but no mortar to build the cylindrical walls of their huts. Ornaments worn by men include thick bronze or wooden bracelets and feathers and strings of small shells and beads on the head. They make large perforations in the lower lobe of the ear to insert wooden pegs or spiral-shaped earrings. The Dime are well known for their ironwork. They speak a south Omotic **language** that has 47 percent lexical similarity with **Banna**. They tend not to speak the language of neighboring peoples.

DIRASHA PEOPLE AND LANGUAGE. Also known as the Gardulla and Gidole people, they number several thousand and live southwest of Lake Chamo and north of the **Konso people**. There are five subgroups among the Dirasha. They have their own special *woreda*. The Dirasha grow **cotton** and practice terrace farming. They traditionally observed a *gada* age-set system, which has weakened, and had a hereditary paramount chief before being conquered by the **highlanders**. They traditionally believed in a supreme being who was the creator and father of men. The Dirasha speak an east Cushitic **language** called Dirashigna that has 55 percent lexical similarity with Konso. It is part of a dialect chain with Konso and **Bussa**, the language of the people to the north. Many Dirasha are bilingual in Konso or Afan Oromo.

DIRE DAWA. (208,700; estimated 2002 **population**.) Ethiopia's second largest city. The population is mixed ethnically, although **Somalis** and **Oromos** predominate.

Established in 1902, when the **Addis Ababa–Djibouti Railway** workers reached that point on the line. It was an alternative to **Harar**, which is located nearby in the Chercher Mountains, where the cost of building a railway was too high. Today, Dire Dawa is Ethiopia's most economically important urban hub after **Addis Ababa**.

Historically, Dire Dawa's **economy** depended largely on smuggling but this is now declining. Growth sectors include **tourism** (based primarily on the two yearly Saint Gabriel festivals and Dire Dawa's proximity to **Harar**) and the export of **khat** (mainly to Djibouti), **coffee** from Hararge, and other **agricultural** goods. The city also grows sizable quantities of fruit and vegetables, especially beans; and operated several small **industries**. Dire Dawa retains some Italian influence in its architecture. Situated in the **lowlands**, it tends to be hot, dusty and dry.

DISASTER PREPAREDNESS AND PREVENTION COMMISSION (DPPC). Originally known as the Relief and Rehabilitation Commission, which was established in June 1974 after the outbreak of **famine** in **Wollo** and **Tigray**. Over the next two decades, the commission underwent several reorganizations. In August 1995, Proclamation No. 10/1995 established the DPPC. Its mission was to prevent humanitarian disasters by eliminating the causes of such catastrophes, build the capacity necessary to alleviate damages resulting from disasters, and ensure the timely arrival of human assistance to suffering **populations**. By 2003, the DPPC had had little impact on the recurring cycles of drought, although it has been effective in preventing serious **famine**.

DIZI PEOPLE AND LANGUAGE. About 25,000 Dizi people live in the vicinity of Maji town to the west of Omo **National Park**. In fact, the Dizi are often called Maji. To further confuse the issue, the term Maji is often used to refer to a group of distinct peoples. The **Me'en** live to the north and east of the Dizi while the **Kacipo-Balesi** reside to the southwest and the **Suri** to the south. The Me'en have assimilated substantial numbers of Dizi over the years. The Dizi traditionally have had a hierarchical chiefdom structure. The Dizi cultivate terraced slopes intensively with millet, teff, and corn. They also raise cattle, sheep, and fowl. Some Dizi have converted to Christianity, but many follow traditional religious beliefs that include a sky god and local spirits. Although they do not worship the sky god, they make periodic animal sacrifices to appease his anger when someone dies. Dizi is a north Omotic **language** that is related to **Sheko** and **Nayi**, languages spoken by peoples who live well to the north of the Dizi.

DORZE PEOPLE AND LANGUAGE. Although the Dorze number only several thousand and occupy a small area in north Omo zone, they are well known for their weaving skills and unique huts. The Dorze reside in the Guge hills west of Lake Abaya at an altitude of about 9,500 feet (2,900 meters). They are clustered around the town of Chencha, which is often cold and misty and reached by a spectacular switchback road from the valley floor. Chencha was once the capital of Gamo-Gofa before the capital moved to Arba Minch. The Dorze have a reputation as being among the best **cotton** weavers in Ethiopia. The *shamma* cloth, white *gabbi* robes, and brightly colored *netalas* produced by the Dorze are highly prized. The **women** normally spin the cotton and the men weave the cloth. The Dorze are skilled subsistence farmers and experienced in the use of terracing. They also grow *ensete*, vegetables, and tobacco near their huts. The Dorze live in beehive-style huts that are nearly two stories high. The spacious interior includes a large fireplace for cooking and heating. Although supported largely by hardwood poles and woven bamboo, the huts are sufficiently sturdy that they usually last a lifetime. It is believed the Dorze have lived in the area for at least 500 years. They speak an Omotic **language** in the Ometo family. It has a high lexical similarity with **Gamo**, **Gofa**, and **Wolaytta**.

DRAMA. Ethiopians use gestures, facial expressions, and dramatic dialogue in normal conversation. Humorous skits are common in most villages. But drama in the modern sense is a fairly recent development. The **Ethiopian Orthodox Church** has long enacted plays associated with the life of Christ. The first Western-style drama occurred after the turn of the 20th century, when Tekle Hawariat produced and directed an **Amharic**-language comedy based on Aesop's fables. Emperor **Menelik II** reportedly watched the play. Other pioneers in the field of drama were Melaku Begosew, Fitwarari Cherinet, and Yeftahae Negussie.

In the post–World War II era, Tekle Hawariat wrote a historical play called *Theodore* while Kebede Mikael wrote *Hannibal* and translated classics such as *Romeo and Juliet*. Balambaras Asheber Gabre-Hiwot produced *The Queen of Sheba* and *Love Never Dies*. In the early 1960s, Tsegaye Gabre Medhin adapted to Amharic such classics as Molier's *Tartuffe* and Shakespeare's *Othello*. **Mengistu Lemma**, Tesfaye Gassesse, and Taezazu Hayle came of age at the same period. Following the 1974 **Derg** revolution, drama tended to focus on political themes and was subject to censorship. In 1978, **Addis Ababa University** established a Department of Theatrical Arts. It has not recovered even after the Derg's downfall (1991). Despite its large population, **Addis Ababa** only has six professional theaters. Leelai Demoz, born in Britain to Ethiopian parents, has produced several world-class works, performed on Broadway, and acted at London's National Theater and Washington's Kennedy Center. Drama and the theater are still not particularly important elements of Ethiopian social life. *See also* LITERATURE; POETRY.

– E –

ECONOMIC COMMISSION FOR AFRICA (ECA). Established in 1958 by the United Nations and headquartered in **Addis Ababa.** The ECA is one of five regional commissions that reports to the UN Economic and Social Council (ECOSOC) through the Conference of African Ministers Responsible for Economic and Social Development and Planning. The ECA has a mandate to support the economic and social development of its 53 African member states, foster regional integration, and promote international cooperation for Africa's development. The ECA, which has a staff of about 850, helped to establish the African Development Bank (ADB). It facilitated the establishment of a number of sub-regional organizations, including the Economic Community of West African States (ECOWAS) and the Preferential Trade Area for Eastern and Southern Africa, now known as the Community of Eastern and Southern Africa. The ECA built about 30 technical institutions to buttress Africa's socioeconomic development. The ECA also played an important role in the development of economic strategies such as the Lagos Plan of Action and the Cairo Agenda for Re-launching Africa's Development. A Ghanaian, K. Y. Amoako, has been the ECA's executive secretary since 1995.

Emperor **Haile Selassie** worked hard to bring the ECA to Addis Ababa. He agreed to build the headquarters, known as Africa Hall, in downtown Addis Ababa near Meskel Square. Completed in 1961, it is still used and noted for the huge stained glass window by Ethiopian artist **Afewerk Tekle** and entitled "Africa: Past, Present, and Future."

It is one of the world's largest stained glass windows, covering more than 1600 square feet (150 square meters). The stained glass represents the struggle and aspirations of the African people. The ECA outgrew Africa Hall, and, in 1984, the African states began to lobby the United Nations to build a huge conference facility in Addis Ababa. Located behind Africa Hall, this state-of-the-art center is now one of the most sophisticated and spacious in Africa.

ECONOMY. The structure of Ethiopia's economy has changed little since the **Ethiopian People's Revolutionary Democratic Front** (EPRDF) came to power (1991). **Agriculture** continues to contribute more than 50 percent of gross domestic product (GDP). The average share for agriculture over the last 20 years has been about 55 percent. **Industry**'s contribution to GDP has remained relatively static at about 10 percent. The service sector, on the other hand, has increased to about 25 percent of GDP from 20 percent during the **Derg**. The contribution of the distributive sector has remained static at just over 10 percent.

Ethiopia's real GDP under the EPRDF has grown on the average at a rate of about 6 percent annually. The per capita GDP growth rate has been about 2.6 percent, which compares favorably with a 1.9 percent rate during the last 10 years of the Derg. Ethiopia's economic situation deteriorated sharply in 1999–2000 as a result of a severe drought, the 1998–2000 **Ethiopian-Eritrean War**, a major worsening of its terms of trade associated with lower **coffee** export prices, and the steep rise in petroleum import prices. In spite of this situation, the **International Monetary Fund** (IMF) reported that real GDP growth reached 7.5 percent in 2000–2001 while inflation turned negative, reflecting a bumper cereal crop and large inflows of **food** aid. This strong showing occurred in spite of an expenditure of $3 billion by Ethiopia to finance the conflict with Eritrea.

The Ethiopian Economic Policy Research Institute offered a more dismal picture of the economy, citing a sharp drop in foreign investment, a reduction in **tourism**, the high cost of the war, costs associated with rerouting imports and exports, and higher **debt**. Ethiopian reserves dropped from about $500 million in 1997 to less than $400 million in 2000. The Institute concluded, however, that Ethiopia continues to have a reasonable GDP growth rate. The IMF suggested the debt-service ratio would fall from 19 percent in 1999–2000 to 15 percent in 2002/2003 and 9 percent by 2009–2010. It further expected the ratio to drop to an average of 7.5 percent beyond that.

Gross domestic savings averaged 7.2 percent during the Derg and 6.9 percent during the EPRDF. There is a steady trend, however, suggesting that some of the measures taken by the EPRDF to encourage savings are beginning to work. While gross fixed capital formation as a percent of GDP declined sharply during the last 11 years of the Derg, it has made a healthy recovery under the EPRDF, averaging over 15 percent and doing best in recent years. Because the low savings ratio could not finance this increase in investment, the resource gap widened from an average of 7.1 percent of GDP during the Derg to about 8.7 percent under the EPRDF. This resulted in an increase of the debt burden during EPRDF stewardship.

The value of Ethiopian exports totals almost $1 billion, a figure that rose steadily in the 1990s. The increased value of exports has been greater in services than in merchandise, although the latter still constitutes more than half the total. Coffee alone provided about two-thirds of the merchandise export earnings. The export of manufactured goods accounts for only about 4 percent of the total by value and has been declining. Ethiopia has one of the lowest export per capita rates in the world. Most Ethiopian exports go to Germany, Japan, Djibouti, Saudi Arabia, France, Britain, and Italy.

As a percentage of GDP, imports are running at over 20 percent and the trend was upward during the 1990s. Ethiopia has experienced a large balance of payments deficit in eight of the last 10 years. Capital and consumer goods account for two-thirds of the total and semi-finished products for most of the rest. Imports are about $1.25 billion if the extraordinary military purchases during the recent war are excluded. Major imports include fuel, fertilizer, vehicles, machinery and electrical products, metal and metal products, and cereal. The principal sources of supply are Saudi Arabia, Italy, the United States, and Japan. China, North Korea, Russia, and many of the former Soviet republics were important sources of military equipment during the conflict with Eritrea.

Unemployment is more than 30 percent in urban areas. Underemployment may reach as high as 70 percent when agricultural work declines on a seasonal basis. The high unemployment rate, especially among young high school graduates, contributes significantly to the crime rate in urban areas.

The Ethiopian economy has performed modestly under the EPRDF. Its successes stem from the positive effect of dismantling the most suffocating anti-private-sector policies of the Derg regime and generous support from the donor community. High growth rates in industry and services are largely due to the recovery made from the unusually low level during the last years of the Derg. The agricultural sector did not perform as well as expected. This is not surprising in view of several bad harvests due to drought and, in some high-altitude locations, an excess of rain. Perhaps the biggest surprise, however, is the fact that the economy has done as well as it has in spite of the $3 billion expenditure on the war with Eritrea. Military expenditures are declining and Ethiopia is moving rapidly to demobilize large numbers of soldiers. The best compilations of economic data for Ethiopia are the *Annual Report on the Ethiopian Economy* prepared by the Ethiopian Economic Association and *Ethiopia: The Dynamics of Economic Reform* by Kinfe Abraham. *See also* BANKING; BRAIN DRAIN; CURRENCY; ENDOWMENT FUND FOR THE REHABILITATION OF TIGRAY; HYDROCARBONS; HYDROPOWER; LABOR UNIONS; POVERTY; TAXATION; ZEMACHA.

EDEN, SIR ANTHONY (1897–1977). British politician. Born on 12 June 1897 in County Durham and attended Sandroyd School, Eton, and Christchurch, Oxford. In 1923, Eden was elected to Parliament, and in June 1935 he became minister without portfolio for **League of Nations** affairs. After the outbreak of the **Italian-Ethiopian War (1935–1936)**, Eden maintained that the League of Nations should apply sanctions against Rome. During the war, he repeatedly said that he would welcome the reappearance of an independent Ethiopia and would recognize **Haile Selassie**'s claim to the throne. However, on 4 February 1941, Eden, who had become foreign secretary, told Haile Selassie that Ethiopia's independence would be restored but that Britain would offer a "temporary measure of guidance and control." Thus, on 6 April 1941, London approved the establishment of the **British Military Administration** in Ethiopia. On 31 January 1942, Britain and Ethiopia concluded the **Anglo-Ethiopian Agreement and Military Convention** that recognized the latter's independence but placed many restrictions on its sovereignty. After an illustrious government career, Eden died on 14 January 1977 at his home in Wiltshire.

EDUCATION, PRIMARY AND SECONDARY. Religious instruction organized by the **Ethiopian Orthodox Church** was the only formal education in Ethiopia until the early 1900s. The first public school opened in **Addis Ababa** in 1907; by the mid-1930s, there were only about 8,000 students in 20 public schools. By 1952, the number had grown to 60,000 students in 400 primary schools, supplemented in the 1960s by 310 mission and privately owned schools with an enrollment of 52,000. The **Derg** significantly expanded primary school enrollment, which grew to 2.5 million in the mid-1980s. It crept up to 2.7 million by the mid-1990s, about 28 percent of Ethiopia's total potential primary school population and about 21 percent of its total female population. Ethiopia's primary school enrollment now stands at about 30 percent. Junior secondary schools increased from 1,000 in the mid-1980s to over 1,200 in the mid-1990s while senior secondary schools grew from 260 to 330 in the same period. Enrollment remained, however, static.

The quality of primary and secondary school education continues to be a problem. Schools are generally understaffed and poorly equipped. Laboratories are virtually nonexistent in some secondary schools. The physical infrastructure of many schools, especially in rural areas, is well below standard. The **Ethiopian People's Revolutionary Democratic Front**'s ethnic federalism policy permits the regions to determine the principal **language** of instruction in primary school. **Afar, Oromia, Somali,** and **Tigray Regions** have selected the predominant indigenous language. Other regions continue to use **Amharic**. All schools teach English at a certain point, but the quality of instruction has declined due to the significant increase in the number of students in school and the decrease in native English-speakers from organizations like the Peace Corps.

The educational system has long been a manufacturer of an unemployable cadre of students rather than provider of skilled manpower. It tends to be theory focused and is not designed to link theoretical knowledge to practical issues. Civic education traditionally has not been an important part of the curriculum. Nor is the system designed to develop openness, assertiveness, and creativeness among students.

The number of vocational and technical schools remains low but is beginning to show signs of growth. The government also is devoting a greater share of its budget to education. It increased from about 10 percent in the mid-1980s to 15 percent in the mid-1990s. *See also* EDUCATION, UNIVERSITY.

EDUCATION, UNIVERSITY. On 20 March 1950, **Haile Selassie** established the University College of Addis Ababa with fewer than a hundred students and nine Canadian Jesuit faculty members who had been primary and secondary school teachers in Ethiopia. On 27 February 1951, the emperor formally opened the college, which accommodated 150 students. The college had a 7,000-volume library and a faculty of arts and a faculty of science. In 1952, the university administration added an engineering faculty and an **agriculture** college at Alemaya, near **Harar**. In 1954, a college started operations in **Addis Ababa** and a public **health** college opened in **Gondar**. On 18 December 1961, the authorities established Haile Selassie I University, which incorporated the University College of Addis Ababa and several other institutions. The university had more than 1,000 students. After the monarchy's abolition on 22 March 1975, officials changed the name to Addis Ababa University (AAU).

Over the next several decades, AAU steadily expanded. By 2001, there were 19,149 students, including 7,702 in continuing education, and 871 faculty members. Apart from a college of social sciences, AAU included faculties of business and economics, education, law, medicine, science, technology, and veterinary medicine. There also was an institute of language studies and schools of graduate studies, information studies, and pharmacy. Other institutions included the **Awasa** College of Agriculture, Bahir Dar Teacher's College, and Gondar College of Medical Science.

In 1958, the Piae Matres Nigritiaell (Comboni Sisters) opened the Holy Family University Institute in Asmara, with Italian as the medium of instruction. The Eritrean government (1959), Superior Council of the Institute of Italian Universities (1960), and Imperial government (1964) recognized the university. In 1964, Addis Ababa changed the name from the Holy Family University Institute to the University of Asmara and adopted English as a medium of instruction alongside Italian. Other significant milestones included becoming a chartered university

(1968), adopting English as the sole medium of instruction (1975), and coming under the Ethiopian Commission for Higher Education. In 1990, Addis Ababa, fearing the emergence of a radical student movement, disbanded the University of Asmara and moved the staff and movable property to Ethiopia. After the downfall of **Mengistu Haile Mariam** (1991), the Provisional Government of Eritrea reestablished the university and adopted an ambitious rehabilitation program.

By 2002, other higher-earning institutions included the Alemaya University of Agriculture (founded 1952; achieved university status 1985) which had 182 faculty members and 1,730 day and 1,008 evening students. The Jimma College of Agriculture (founded 1952) had 65 faculty members and 500 students, and the Polytechnic Institute (founded 1963) had 57 faculty members and 350 students. The Yared National School of **Music** (founded 1967) had 120 students. There also was the Gondar College of Medical Sciences, which had been established in 1954 as the Public Health College. Beginning in the late 1990s, several small private colleges opened their doors. *See also* BRAIN DRAIN; EDUCATION, PRIMARY AND SECONDARY; TAYE WOLDE SEMAYAT.

ELECTIONS (1957). Ethiopia's first general elections (12 September–10 October 1957) that elected a 210-member Chamber of Deputies. In accordance with the **constitution**, the elections were held by universal, direct, and secret ballot. All Ethiopians over the age of 21 were eligible to vote except for individuals who had been deprived of civil rights or imprisoned on criminal charges. Candidates, who had to have the support of at least 50 registered voters, had to be at least 25 years old and Ethiopian nationals by birth. They also had to own unmovable property worth at least 1,000 Ethiopian dollars or movable property worth 2,000 Ethiopian dollars.

For electoral purposes, the government divided the country into 95 districts each containing about 200,000 inhabitants. Two deputies represented each district. Cities with a **population** of more than 30,000 were entitled to one deputy, plus an additional deputy for each 50,000 inhabitants in excess of 30,000. Candidates campaigned on their personal records, as there were no political parties. A total of 491 candidates stood for the 210 seats. The total number of votes cast was 3,015,260 out of an electorate of about 6 million.

On 1 November 1957, the Chamber of Deputies met for the first time (officials had confirmed the election of 190 members while 20 electoral results were still outstanding). On the same day, **Haile Selassie** appointed 35 members to the Senate. Most were government officials. The prime minister, **Makonnen Endakatchew**, served as president of the Senate (1957–1961). *See also* PARLIAMENT.

ELECTIONS (1961, 1965, 1969, 1973). After the **elections (1957)**, the monarchy conducted four parliamentary elections. On 17 June–12 July 1961, some 2,850,200 (13.5 percent) out of a **population** of approximately 21,160,000 voted. The figures for the 23 June–12 July 1965 elections included 3,203,100 (14.1 percent) voters out of a population of about 22,700,000. In the 1969 elections, some 3,674,000 (14.8 percent) out of a population of approximately 27,770,000 Ethiopians voted. During the 23 June–7 July 1973 elections, 4,234,000 (16.2 percent) out of a population of 26,190,000 voted. More than 1,500 candidates contested seats in the 250-member **Chamber of Deputies.** Property requirements for candidates debarred much of Ethiopia's population from standing for **parliament**.

ELECTIONS (1987). On 14 June 1987, Ethiopia conducted an election for the members of the new 835-seat **National Shengo**. Although the candidates did not have to be members of the **Workers' Party of Ethiopia** (WPE), they had to be nominated by the party, the **armed forces**, or some mass organizations like **labor unions**. Some 2,250 candidates had been nominated, with 81 percent of the 835 seats being contested by three candidates. One or two candidates contested the other 19 percent of the seats. Military activity by the **Tigray People's Liberation Front** and the **Eritrean People's Liberation Front** disrupted voting in **Tigray** and Eritrea. Nevertheless, out of 17,768,000 registered voters, 16,085,900 actually voted at one of more than 22,000 polling stations. The WPE and its allied parties won 795 seats while independent parties secured 35 seats. On 9 September 1987, the National Shengo was inaugurated. The following day, **Mengistu Haile Mariam** was elected president of the **Provisional Military Administrative Council**.

ELECTIONS (1992). On 8 June 1992, the **Oromo Liberation Front** (OLF) and 17 other political organizations unsuccessfully petitioned the electoral commission to postpone the elections until discriminatory and irregular activities had been resolved and the **armed forces** had redeployed to their bases as agreed. After the **Ethiopian People's Revolutionary Democratic Front** (EPRDF) refused to accommodate these demands, many groups boycotted the elections, including the OLF, **All Amhara People's Organization**, National Democratic Union, Islamic Front for the Liberation of Oromia, Gideo People's Democratic Organization, and Ethiopian Democratic Action Group.

On 21 June 1992, Ethiopia conducted elections for the new regional councils that also were known as national local administrations. Some 33 million people were eligible to vote, and 62 "nations, nationalities and political organizations" had registered candidates. Voting occurred in 11 of Ethiopia's 14 regions as instability had prevented voting in **Afar Region**, **Somali Region**, and **Harar** town. The EPRDF won 1,108 of 1,147 regional assembly seats. The **Transitional Government of Ethiopia** (TGE) claimed the elections represented a "significant step" toward establishing a democratic political order. Opposition groups, however, denounced the elections and accused the EPRDF of undemocratic behavior.

There were 250 foreign election monitors from Africa, Asia, Europe, the Middle East, North America, and international agencies such as the United Nations Development Program, the **Organization of African Unity**, and the European Community. The monitors concluded that some of the claims of electoral malpractice were, at least in part, justified. The EPRDF and its allies won 90 percent of the votes cast. On 10 July 1992, political groups that had been signatories to the 22 July 1991 **National Charter** demanded that the regional election results be annulled. In the same month, the TGE established a board to investigate the alleged electoral errors, but the election results never were altered.

ELECTIONS (1994). On 5 June 1994, Ethiopia conducted its first national election to select a 544-seat Constituent Assembly (CA). This body aimed to approve a constitutional framework for a decentralized political system based on a voluntary union between the country's different ethnic regions. According to the National Election Board, 14,698,103 (64.5 percent) of 16,797,143 registered voters actually voted at one of Ethiopia's 26,659 polling stations. The **Ethiopian**

People's Revolutionary Democratic Front and its allied parties won 463 CA seats; other organizations secured 81 CA seats. There were 148 foreign election monitors from Asia, Europe, the United States, and international agencies such as the United Nations Development Program. There also were 448 elected Ethiopian monitors. *See also* CONSTITUTION.

ELECTIONS (1995). On 7 May 1995, Ethiopia conducted an election for a 548-seat **parliament**. Of 21,337,379 registered voters, 19,986,179 actually voted. The **Ethiopian People's Revolutionary Democratic Front** and its allied parties won 483 seats while opposition groups secured 54 seats. There were 11 unconfirmed seats. On 22 August 1995, the parliament was sworn in, thereby replacing the **Transitional Government of Ethiopia**, which had ruled the country since 1991.

ELECTIONS (2000). On 30 March 2000, the National Election Board announced that some 26,000 polling stations had registered 20,250,000 voters. On 14 May 2000, the elections were held and, on 17 June 2000, the National Election Board announced that the **Ethiopian People's Revolutionary Democratic Front (EPRDF)** had achieved a "landslide victory" by winning 467 of the 548 seats in the lower house of **parliament** (House of People's Representatives). The EPRDF also was assured of a majority in the 100-seat upper house (House of Federation). On 31 August 2000, the elections in the **Somali Region** finally were held for the House of Federation, the House of People's Representatives, and the regional council. The elections had been postponed because of drought.

ENARYA. Long famous for gold production, this ancient territory was located north of the Gojeb River and west of the **Omo River** and **Janjero Kingdom**. Also known as Inar'it, Enarya came under northern Ethiopian influence in the late **Axumite** or early medieval period. In the first half of the ninth century, an Axumite ruler reportedly traveled to the province. By the early 13th century, Enyara was part of **Damot**. Following the restoration of the **Solomonic Dynasty** in 1270, Enyara became part of the dominion of the King of **Abyssinia** under a viceroy. By the early 15th century, it paid tribute in gold to the Abyssinian king.

When war with the Muslims broke out during the reign of Emperor **Lebna Dengel** (reigned 1508–1540), Enyara was largely animist but much affected by the imam's war with the emperor. Early in the conflict, many fighters from Enarya joined Lebna Dengel's army. At this time, the viceroy was a **slave** from Damot who had submitted to the Muslims. The territory accepted Islamic suzerainty and avoided occupation. Soon after the Imam's death in 1543, Emperor **Galawedos** dispatched an army to Enarya, where it encountered strong opposition and apparently failed. Enarya then fell prey to the **Oromo**, who conquered it between 1550 and 1570. Part of it was settled by the Limmu Oromo and became known as Limmu-Enarya to distinguish it from the rest, which remained for a time under Islamic rule. Emperor Sarsa Dengel (reigned 1563–1597) reestablished loose Abyssinian rule and Christianity in Enarya. Emperor **Susneyos** deployed a large army to Enarya to subdue a local prince. Isolated from Abyssinian rule and surrounded by the Oromo, Enarya continued to pay occasional tribute to Susneyos until his abdication in 1632. Enarya's special relationship with the Christian kingdom ended and there was increasing internal dissent. Christianity and **Islam** faded and the Oromo took control of the entire territory. Emperor **Iyasu I** marched to Enarya and recognized the status of two rival chiefs. This provided an element of independence for Enarya for a brief time. In the early 19th century, Islam returned and Enarya increasingly came under Oromo rule.

ENDAKATCHEW MAKONNEN (1926–1974). Son of **Makonnen Endakatchew**, politician, and diplomat. Born in September 1926 in **Addis Ababa** and educated at Haile Selassie Secondary School, University of Exeter, and Oriel College, Oxford University. After returning to Ethiopia, Endakatchew joined the Ministry of Foreign Affairs and, in 1953, became chief of protocol. In 1955, he was Ethiopia's representative at the Bandung Conference. In 1958, Endakatchew left the Ministry of Foreign Affairs to become vice-minister of education (1958–1959). He then served as ambassador in London (1959–1961), minister of commerce (1961–1966), Ethiopia's permanent representative to the United Nations (1966–1969), and minister of communications, telegraphs, **telecommunications** and post (1969–1974). On 28 February 1974, **Haile Selassie** appointed Endakatchew prime minister. In April 1974, he announced sweeping reforms that included a provision that government would assume control of uncultivated land, pay compensation to the owner, and give it to others for farming. On 22 July 1974, the **Derg** sacked Endakatchew. On 13 November 1974, the Commission of Inquiry into **Corruption** and Maladministration by Government Officials found him guilty of gross abuse of authority. On 23 November 1974, the Derg executed him and 28 others.

ENDOWMENT FUND FOR THE REHABILITATION OF TIGRAY (EFFORT). Established in August 1995. EFFORT, which operates as a public endowment, is an umbrella organization for companies operated by the **Tigray People's Liberation Front** (TPLF). The multimillion-dollar organization operates businesses in the fields of **agriculture**, services, and **industry**. Examples of EFFORT companies include Addis Pharmaceuticals, Guna Trading Company, Hiwot Agricultural Mechanization, Mega Advertising Enterprise, Radio Fana, and Trans-Ethiopia Company. The private sector complains that EFFORT companies receive unfair advantages and force private companies out of business. In late 2002, EFFORT announced plans to create Ethiopia's first private television station. The current EFFORT Board of Directors chairman is Minister of Foreign Affairs **Seyoum Mesfin**. The EFFORT general manager is TPLF insider Sebhat Nega. *See also* ECONOMY; TIGRAY REGION.

ENHANCED STRUCTURAL ADJUSTMENT FACILITY (ESAF). *See* INTERNATIONAL MONETARY FUND.

ENSETE. Better known as the false banana, *ensete* is a staple **food** for the **Gurage** and **Sidama** peoples living south of **Addis Ababa**. Persons unfamiliar with ensete often mistake it for the banana plant. It has no edible fruit; the stem and root are used to make flour. That part of the plant transformed into flour is chopped and beaten into a white pulp and then buried in an underground pit where it ferments for at least one month. The result is a sticky, rather tasteless, unleavened bread with modest nutritional value. It also makes a chewy porridge. On the other hand, ensete has some important advantages. The flour stores well and the plant is resistant to drought. Those parts of Ethiopia that rely heavily on ensete for food have often been able to avoid the worst impact of periodic **famines**. The Gurage and Sidama use the fibers of the ensete for rope and the leaves for thatching roofs. It is a versatile plant and significant food source. *See also* AGRICULTURE.

ENTOTO. Site on the north edge of **Addis Ababa** at one of the highest points in the city. **Menelik II** established his fourth capital at Entoto. He named it after an early capital that had existed in the area before the **Islamic** invasions led by **Ahmad ibn Ibrahim al Ghazi** in the 16th century. Emperor **Lebna Dengel**, a powerful ruler in the 16th century, reputedly had a residence at the site. Menelik II's decision to settle at Entoto symbolized his determination to make Ethiopia as great as it was in Lebna Dengel's days. He also believed that he was fulfilling an old prophecy that a great-grandson of Lebna Dengel would rebuild the site. Menelik II first built a palace. After his marriage to **Taytu Betul** (1883), she supervised construction of Entoto Maryam Church. In 1885, Menelik II dedicated a second church to the archangel Raguel.

Menelik II built Entoto as a fortress that was not especially suitable as a peacetime capital. Due to its high altitude, Entoto was cold and windy much of the year, difficult to reach, and lacked an adequate supply of drinking water. Eventually, firewood ran out in the vicinity of Entoto and Menelik II moved the capital down the hill and near the hot springs of Finfine, near the center of present-day Addis Ababa. In 1889, he returned to Entoto Maryam Church to be crowned emperor. After Menelik II's death (1913), Taytu moved to a house next to the church and remained there until her death (1918). Today, the Entoto Maryam Church and a small museum inside the church compound are open to visitors. Saint Raguel's church is located less than a mile away.

ENVIRONMENT. In addition to **deforestation**, Ethiopia faces a host of other environmental problems. Soil erosion, caused by a combination of deforestation, **population** growth, clearing of land for **agriculture,** and overgrazing, results in the annual loss of between one and two billion tons of soil. Salinization and chemical degradation of soil, caused primarily by the use of fertilizer, are additional problems. Some research indicates that 4 percent of the country's land area has lost its ability to produce **food** and more than 70 percent has been seriously eroded. The major form of soil erosion is rill erosion caused by running water after heavy rain. Crop cultivation contributes to the problem. Environmental degradation of land was especially acute during the **Derg** regime, when the government cut more trees and cleared more land for agricultural production.

Industrial pollution has been less serious because of the low level of industrialization. Except for **Addis Ababa**, air pollution is not yet a major problem and industrial waste in water is only beginning to receive attention. The main sources of industrial waste are the food, beverage, tobacco, textile, leather-tanning, paper, and chemical and sugar industries. In 1997, the Chemical Society of Ethiopia and Ethiopian Private Industries Association initiated a program to deal with this issue, particularly the discharge of effluents into the Akaki River near Addis Ababa.

Environmental awareness has increased significantly in the past 25 years. In 1988, the government agreed upon a national conservation strategy. The **constitution (1994)** deals with environmental concerns. In 1997, the government adopted the Federal Environmental Policy of Ethiopia. Ethiopia's current environmental policy recognizes that the country must adopt a holistic and integrated approach that relies on a bottom-up participatory process. Ethiopia has a National Environmental Protection Authority and a host of other government and nongovernmental organizations devoted to environmental issues. The Environmental Protection Council advises the government on policy matters. A shortage of financial resources to solve these problems has resulted in minimal progress beyond the planning and policy stage.

ERA OF THE PRINCES. Also, known as the Era of the Judges or Zamana Masafent. These terms define the 1769–1850 period when the central government had collapsed and political power had devolved to the provinces of **Amhara**, **Shoa**, and **Tigray**. However, internal instability restricted Amhara's ability to defend Ethiopia against external enemies such as Egypt and Italy. Shoa refrained from engaging in internal political struggles with Amhara and Tigray but expanded its power southwards and established trade that produced an abundance of **coffee** and **slaves**. Tigray played a decisive role in reestablishing an Imperial government and defeating the Italians at the **Battle of Adwa**.

During the Era of the Princes, foreign influence also grew in Ethiopia as Turks supplied weapons to Tigrayan rulers who used them to seize power. An influx of European **missionaries** unsuccessfully sought to convert Ethiopians but succeeded in increasing their awareness about the potential of modernization and technological advancements.

ERITREAN-ETHIOPIAN FEDERATION ACT (11 September 1952). During the immediate post–**World War II** era, Ethiopian **foreign policy** focused on the disposition of Italian colonies. Eritrea was of particular interest as much of it had belonged to Ethiopia prior to the late 19th century. Eritrea also offered land-locked Ethiopia access to the sea.

During February–April 1950, the United Nations (UN) Commission for Eritrea undertook a fact-finding mission to Asmara, **Addis Ababa**, Cairo, and Rome. On 29 June 1950, the commission, which had failed to reach a unanimous agreement about Eritrea's future status, presented three separate reports to the UN General Assembly. The first, supported by the commission's Burmese and South African delegates, recommended a three-year transition period after which Eritrea would become a self-governing unit in a federation with Ethiopia. The second, advocated by the commission's Norwegian delegate, proposed an Eritrea-Ethiopia union with western Eritrea remaining under British administration until its inhabitants decided whether they wanted to join Ethiopia or Sudan. The last, devised by the commission's Pakistani and Guatemalan delegates, suggested that Eritrea become independent after a 10-year period under UN trusteeship.

On 2 December 1950, the UN General Assembly adopted Resolution 390 (V), which provided for Eritrea's federation with Ethiopia as an autonomous, self-governing entity. The resolution also brought into force the Eritrean constitution that had been ratified by the Eritrean Representative Assembly (10 July 1952) and approved by the UN commissioner (9 August 1952) and ratified by **Haile Selassie** (11

August 1952). Under the resolution's terms, Ethiopia would be responsible for Eritrea's defense, foreign policy, and finances. On 11 September 1952, Haile Selassie ratified the Act of Federation, and, on 15 September 1952, the British authorities relinquished control of Eritrea.

The Act of Federation was short-lived, primarily because the imperial government failed to abide by its provisions. The Eritrean constitution established ethnic and religious equilibrium by choosing Tigrinya and Arabic as official **languages**, allowing parents to choose the language of education for their children, and ensuring Christian-Muslim parity in the civil service.

Addis Ababa eventually eliminated Arabic from state education and reduced the number of Muslims in public sector jobs. Moreover, Ethiopia harassed leaders of the Eritrean independence movement, banned political parties (1955) and **labor unions** (1958), changed the name Eritrean Government to Eritrean Administration (1959), and imposed Ethiopian law. On 14 November 1962, the Ethiopian **parliament** and the pro-monarchy Eritrean Assembly made Eritrea a province of Ethiopia by unanimously voting its federal status. Shortly thereafter, Addis Ababa banned the use of Tigrinya in education in favor of **Amharic**, Ethiopia's official language.

ERITREAN LIBERATION FRONT (ELF). Formed in Cairo on 10 July 1960 by Idris Mohamed Adem, Idris Osman Galadewos, and several other former Islamic political leaders who had gone into exile after the **Ethiopian-Eritrean Federation**. The founders supported an armed struggle for liberation in Eritrea. In late 1961, the ELF launched its first attack. By 1965, the ELF had become the principal opposition to Ethiopian rule in Eritrea. An escalation of ELF military activities resulted in the imposition of martial law (1971).

However, tension between Muslim and Christian ELF members split the ELF and resulted in the creation of the Christian-dominated **Eritrean People's Liberation Front** (EPLF). Ideological, political, and personal differences also caused the ELF to split. In 1969, the ELF fractured into three splinter groups called the People's Liberation Front, ELF–People's Liberation Front, and ELF-Ubel. All these organizations received funds from Arab countries.

In the early 1970s, ELF-EPLF clashes further weakened the former, and, by 1975, the latter had become the predominant group opposing Ethiopian rule in Eritrea. By 1977, the ELF had an estimated 23,000 members. However, in 1977–1978 and again in 1985, reformist elements broke away from the ELF and established splinter groups such as the ELF–People's Liberation Front–Revolutionary Council, ELF–Unified Organization, and ELF–Revolutionary Council. These desertions destroyed the ELF, although some factions like the ELF–Revolutionary Council remained modestly active. *See* also ERITREAN LIBERATION MOVEMENT.

ERITREAN LIBERATION MOVEMENT (ELM). In November 1958, five Muslim Eritreans in Port Sudan established the ELM. Their aim was to build an organization that would free Eritrea of Ethiopian rule. Early recruitment efforts were confined to Muslim communities. However, the ELM quickly discovered widespread discontent among Eritrea's Christian community. The ELM therefore started recruiting Eritreans under the policy that "Muslims and Christians are brothers." Apart from Eritrea, the ELM also organized cells in Ethiopia, Sudan, and Saudi Arabia.

In 1960, the ELM held its first and last congress in Asmara. About 40 delegates elected a 13-man general command (11 Muslims and two Christians). The organization decided to focus on organizing and politicizing the Eritrean population and on infiltrating the **police** and government in preparation for a coup. To achieve these goals, the ELM solicited aid from neighboring countries.

The **Eritrean Liberation Front** rejected an ELM request to form a united front and, in May 1965, disarmed a small ELM unit in Ela Tada, killing six of its members in the process. The ELM never recovered from this incident and soon disappeared from the scene.

ERITREAN PEOPLE'S LIBERATION FRONT (EPLF). The EPLF grew out of strategic and tactical disagreements within the largely Muslim **Eritrean Liberation Front** (ELF). In 1972, a rebel faction called the Eritrean Liberation Forces–Ubel, commanded by Isaias Afeworki, joined in a coalition with the Eritrean Liberation Forces–People's Liberation Forces. In 1972, the two groups united under the name People's Liberation Forces. In March 1976, the field commanders of the People's Liberation Forces started calling themselves the Eritrean People's Liberation Forces. On 23–31 January 1977, this organization held its first congress and changed its name to the EPLF. Its ideology fused Eritrean nationalism with populist Marxism.

The EPLF's organizational structure and policies reflected a strong Marxist influence but stopped short of calling for creation of a Marxist–Leninist state. It demanded redress of Ethiopian **human rights** violations against Eritreans. The EPLF also formed an alliance with ELF factions and conducted a campaign that almost resulted in a military victory against the Ethiopian **armed forces**. In 1977, Ethiopia counterattacked and forced the EPLF from **Massawa**, after the Soviet Union had come to the rescue of the **Derg** regime. The EPLF regrouped in the north, where it remained for a decade. Its victory over government forces during the disastrous **Red Star Campaign** (1981–1982), which was the largest military operation carried out by the Derg, marked a turning point in the conflict that eventually led to **Mengistu Haile Mariam**'s downfall.

At the EPLF's second congress (1987), Isaias Afeworki replaced Ramadan Nur as General Secretary and revised most oi its Marxist-Leninist positions. The EPLF began to emphasize the need for a unified Eritrean nation and Ethiopia's illegal occupation of Eritrea. By 1988, the EPLF had a conventional army with tanks and other weaponry captured from Ethiopian garrisons. In 1988, it began a steady push south and, in 1990, captured Massawa. In May 1991, the EPLF occupied the capital of Asmara and the port of **Asab**. The EPLF announced a two-year waiting period, which was followed by a referendum in which the Eritrean people voted for independence. At its third congress (1994), the EPLF changed its name to the People's Front for Democracy and Justice in hopes of embracing all Eritreans. A growing number of Eritreans and some international observers believe this effort failed largely because the Eritrean government had refused to share power. *See also* ETHIOPIAN-ERITREAN WAR.

ETHIOPIAN AIRLINES (EAL). In late 1945, the Ethiopian government and Transcontinental and Western Airlines (TWA) began negotiations to establish a commercial **aviation** company in Ethiopia. On

8 September 1945, TWA representatives signed an agreement in **Addis Ababa** with Ethiopia's foreign affairs adviser, American John Spencer. The original contract provided for TWA management and operating responsibility with financing from the Ethiopian government. Ethiopia initially appointed half of the airline's board of directors and TWA the other half. On 1 February 1946, EAL's first five planes, U.S. government surplus Douglas C-47 Skytrain transports, flew into Addis Ababa. On 8 April 1946, EAL began international service from Addis Ababa to Cairo via Asmara. Demand for additional aircraft grew quickly when EAL extended its network in the late 1940s to Nairobi, Port Sudan, and Bombay. In 1950, EAL purchased two Convair 240 aircraft for international flights.

In 1957, EAL appointed Captain Alemayehu as the first Ethiopian aircraft commander. To support a growing route structure, EAL added three Douglas DC-6B Cloudmasters in 1958. In 1962, EAL entered the jet age by purchasing two Boeing 729Bs and by opening Bole International Airport in Addis Ababa. In 1965, EAL changed its legal structure from a corporation to a share company. The TWA-EAL contractual relationship reflected the reality of Ethiopianization by 1966, when the fourth renewal of the original 1945 agreement called for an Ethiopian deputy general manager. The 1970 renewal resulted in the appointment of an Ethiopian general manager and changed the role of TWA from EAL manager to adviser. In 1975, TWA terminated its 30-year association with EAL. In 1982, EAL began purchasing Boeing 727s and added de Havilland Canada DHC-5 Buffaloes for use in its domestic service. On 1 June 1984, EAL's first Boeing 767 arrived at Bole International Airport. EAL also added de Havilland Canada DHC-6 Twin Otters and ATR-42s to its domestic routes.

On 26 July 2002, Ethiopian Airlines announced that it had decided to buy 12 Boeing airplanes (six B737-700s and six B767-300ERs) to replace its older B737-200s and B767-200s over the next four years. The deal also included purchase rights for an additional five B737s and three B777s. By late 2002, EAL's fleet consisted of five Fokker 50s, two ATR-42s, three De Havilland Canada DHG-6 Twin Otters, three Boeing 737s, four Boeing 757s, five Boeing 767s, and three aircraft for cargo and nonscheduled service. About the same time, the airline officials finalized plans to build a new air cargo terminal and maintenance hangar. Bole International Airport also opened a new passenger terminal.

By its 57th anniversary in 2003, EAL serviced numerous African (e.g., Abidjan, Accra, Bamako, Brazzaville, Bujumbura, Cairo, Dar-es-Salaam, Djibouti, Entebbe, Harare, Hargeisa, Johannesburg, Khartoum, Kigali, Kilimanjaro, Kinshasa, Lagos, Lilongwe, Lomé, Luanda, Nairobi, N'djamena, and Zanzibar), Asian (e.g., Bangkok, Beijing, Bombay, Hong Kong, Karachi, Mumbai, and New Delhi), European (e.g., Amsterdam, Copenhagen, Frankfurt, London, and Rome), Middle Eastern (e.g., Dubai, Jeddah, Riyadh, and Tel Aviv), and North American (e.g., Newark, N.J., and Washington, D.C.) destinations. EAL also has an extensive domestic route network. Despite its reputation for profitability and reliability, EAL has not existed without problems. Due to regional political differences, it has had its share of actual or attempted airplane hijackings. One hijacking resulted in the disastrous 20 November 1996 crash of a Boeing 767 off the Comoro Islands in the Indian Ocean.

ETHIOPIAN DEMOCRATIC UNION (EDU). Originally known as the Ethiopian National Democratic People's Union. In March 1975, Lieutenant General Iyasu Mengesha, an Eritrean who had been former chief of staff of Ethiopia's **Kagnew Battalion** that deployed to the Congo on a United Nations peacekeeping mission and former Ethiopian ambassador to Britain, established the EDU in London. Other important EDU leaders included **Ras** Mengesha Seyoum, grandson-in-law of **Haile Selassie** and great-grandson of **Yohannes IV**, and Brigadier General Nega Tegegn, grandson-in-law of Haile Selassie. Originally, EDU members belonged to the landed **Amhara** aristocracy and elements loyal to Haile Selassie, and advocated the creation of a constitutional monarchy.

The party created a 17-member supreme council at its London headquarters. After realizing that the emperor would not be restored, the EDU abandoned its royalist agenda. In December 1975, the party started its newspaper, *EDU Advocate*. In mid-1976, it published *Aims and Objectives of EDU*, which included removing the **Derg**, uniting all resistance movements, finding a "sincere and credible" solution to the war in **Eritrea,** and establishing an "enlightened, progressive, and democratic regime" for Ethiopia.

In mid-May 1976, the EDU, which was divided into area political bureaus, announced that it had started military operations in northern Ethiopia to sever the Ethiopian **armed forces'** lines of communication with Eritrea. By 1977, the EDU had about 10,000 members. On 13 January 1977, the EDU, with support from Sudan and the **Eritrean Liberation Front**, took **Metemma**, near the Sudanese border, and Humera. However, subsequent attempts to overrun **Gondar** town failed. The EDU also clashed with the **Tigray People's Liberation Front** but, by 1979, had been defeated.

After the Derg's fall (1991), relations between the EDU and the **Ethiopian People's Revolutionary Democratic Front** (EPRDF) were frosty as the former failed to receive an invitation to the 1–5 July 1991 Peace and Democracy Conference in **Addis Ababa**. Also, on 31 January 1992, some 25,000 **Mekele** residents demonstrated against the government's trial of Mengesha Seyoum for committing "injustices" against the Tigrayan people.

Eventually, however, part of the EDU joined the EPRDF coalition while another wing joined the Washington, D.C.–based, anti-EPRDF Coalition of Ethiopian Democratic Forces. In 1993, the latter complained to the United Nations about the "sham referendum" that led to Eritrea's independence and, in 2002, registered its displeasure about the Ethiopia-Eritrea border demarcation for disowning Ethiopian people from their sovereign territories. During the 1990s, the EDU's small military wing periodically conducted operations against the EPRDF in Gondar region in northern Ethiopia.

ETHIOPIAN EMPLOYERS' ASSOCIATION. *See* LABOR UNIONS.

ETHIOPIAN-ERITREAN WAR (1998–2000). This conflict rivaled the **Ogaden War (1977–1978)** as one of the bloodiest in the **Horn of Africa**. The war's origins lay in the troubled relationship between the **Tigray People's Liberation Front** (TPLF) and the **Eritrean People's Liberation Front** (EPLF). Ideological differences centered on the EPLF's Third World Marxist orientation and its support of the former Soviet bloc as strategic allies, while the TPLF embraced Maoism and Albanian-style Marxism and harbored suspicions about Moscow's goals in the Horn of Africa. By May 1985, disagreements about military and political tactics resulted in a termination of mutual cooperation. However, in March 1989, the TPLF and EPLF resumed military cooperation as the **Derg**'s growing weakness convinced them that victory was at hand. In May 1991, the regime collapsed and **Mengistu Haile Mariam** fled to Zimbabwe.

Shortly after this victory, tensions resurfaced between the two groups. During 1991–1992, Eritrea expelled some 120,000 Ethiopians, the majority of whom had belonged to the **armed forces** while a sizable number were civilians who had lived in Eritrea all their lives. The immediate events that led to the outbreak of this conflict began in August 1997, when Eritrea announced that it had decided to introduce its own **currency**, the nakfa, in lieu of the Ethiopian birr that it had used since it gained independence (1993). Asmara then suggested that the nakfa be on parity with the birr and that it be circulated freely on both sides of the border. In October 1997, Ethiopia rejected this proposal and maintained that all trade between the two countries would be conducted in hard currency. By the time the nakfa had become legal tender in December 1997, Ethiopia had issued new birr notes to prevent Eritrea from redeeming the old currency. The two nations subsequently severed all trade and communications links while, in December 1997, Asmara imposed a partial trade ban on Ethiopia.

The other factor that divided Ethiopia and Eritrea concerned territorial disagreements along their common border. In August 1997, there was a brief skirmish in the Bada region of the southern Eritrean–northern **Danakil Depression**. On 13 November 1997, the two countries sought to restore stability to this area by holding their first Joint Border Commission meeting in Asmara. Despite this encouraging sign, potential territorial disputes existed in numerous other places, including Alitena, Badme, Bure, Humera, Tsorona, and Zala Ambessa. After an armed clash in the Badme region on 6 May 1998, Ethiopia and Eritrea convened another Joint Border Commission meeting two days later in **Addis Ababa**. The two nations concluded an agreement to defuse the tense situation.

However, on 12 May 1998, the war began when about 9,000 Eritrean troops organized into three brigades invaded Badme and parts of Sheraro. According to Ethiopia, the 6 and 12 May 1998 operations displaced more than 24,000 people and destroyed 12 schools, a veterinary clinic, and fertilizer and grain stores. Addis Ababa responded by deploying some 200,000 troops along its northern border.

On 22 May–11 June 1998, the first round of heavy ground fighting occurred around Badme, Sheraro, and Zala Ambessa, and in the south for control of the road to **Asab** port. This campaign also included modest air operations. On 5–6 June 1998, four Ethiopian **Air Force** MiG-23s bombed Asmara International Airport in two separate sorties. The Eritrean Air Force attacked **Mekele**, killing 51 and wounding another 132 civilians.

Over the coming months, both nations replenished their arsenals by buying considerable amounts of weapons from China, North Korea, Russia and many of the former Soviet republics, and various other nations. There also were some significant Ethiopian military operations. On 23–26 February 1999, for example, Addis Ababa launched "Operation Sunset," which resulted in the capture of Badme. Diplomatic efforts by the **Organization of African Unity**, the Union of African Parliaments, Algeria, the United States, and the United Nations to end the conflict proved unsuccessful.

On 12 May 2000, the Ethiopian armed forces launched an offensive that involved some 200,000 troops and large numbers of artillery, helicopter gunships, and jet fighter bombers. The three-pronged attack resulted in the occupation of Barentu (18 May), Zala Ambessa (25 May), and Senafe (26 May). This offensive broke the back of the Eritrean armed forces. On 18 June 2000, Ethiopia and Eritrea concluded a **Cessation of Hostilities Agreement** in Algiers.

On 17 July 2001, Abebe Teferi, economic consultant at the Office of the Prime Minister, announced that Ethiopia had spent $3 billion in the war with Eritrea. He also indicated that the conflict had unleashed massive devastation with staggering human costs, demolished the country's social and physical infrastructure, and diverted a great portion of the economically active **population**. On 6 December 2000, the World Bank announced that it had approved two loans worth $400.6 million to help Ethiopia rebuild after its war with Eritrea. On 12 December 2000, the two countries finally ended their war by signing the **Algiers Agreement**.

There is no precise accounting of the war fatalities. On 22 June 2001, Eritrean president Isaias Afeworki announced that the war had claimed 19,000 Eritrean troops. Other sources suggest that the number of fatalities was much higher. According to **Tsadkan Gebre Tensae**, for example, Eritrea lost 67,000 soldiers. On 8 April 2002, the Voice of the Democratic Path of Ethiopian Unity, an opposition radio station, announced that 123,000 Ethiopian soldiers had died during the conflict and that each family that lost a relative would receive a $350 indemnity. Eritrea estimated that Ethiopia lost 100,000 troops. During a 2001 visit to London, Major General Samora Yenus (1955–) told a meeting of Tigrayans of 60,000 deaths. However, Tsadkan maintains that only 34,000 troops were killed in the war.

ETHIOPIAN EVANGELICAL CHURCH MEKANE YESUS (EECMY). The EECMY had a difficult beginning as it tried to establish itself in a country where the predominant **Ethiopian Orthodox Church** (EOC) had close ties to the government. The Lutheran evangelical movement that began in the western part of Ethiopia finally became a national church in 1959. However, it was not until 1969 that the EECMY became legally registered. The registration occurred in the face of continuing opposition from the EOC patriarch, who argued that the EECMY was not "Ethiopian" and could not be registered as a church. As a compromise, it initially became the Evangelical Church Mekane Yesus in Ethiopia. The EECMY consists of congregations organized into synods and is today one of the country's largest **Protestant** movements. Its followers are concentrated in southwest Ethiopia, especially among the **Oromo**, **Sidama**, and **Kambata**. Lutheran **missionary** activity in Ethiopia dates back to the early 20th century. German, Danish, Swedish, Finnish, and Norwegian organizations have been especially prominent and continue to work closely with the EECMY.

In addition to its evangelical work, the EECMY supports development efforts and **famine**-relief activities. In cooperation with the Lutheran World Federation, the EECMY began joint relief operations in 1985 in response to widespread famine. In 1988, it became the first religious organization in Ethiopia to implement a **human immunodeficiency virus/acquired immune deficiency syndrome** prevention and control programs. It also has developed small-scale irrigation projects and reforestation programs. Emmanuel Abraham's *Reminiscences of My Life* documents the history of the EECMY. Oyvind M. Eide's *Revolution and Religion in Ethiopia: 1974–85* discusses the persecution of the EECMY during the **Derg** regime.

ETHIOPIAN MEDHIN DEMOCRATIC PARTY. *See* GOSHU WOLDE.

ETHIOPIAN NATIONAL DEFENSE FORCE. *See* ARMED FORCES.

ETHIOPIAN NATIONAL LIBERATION FRONT (ENLF). On 27 June 1971, the ENLF held its founding congress and, in August 1971, announced its intention to overthrow **Haile Selassie**'s "feudal regime" and to create a "progressive republic" based on a decentralized union comprised of autonomous regions. The ENLF also supported agrarian reform, land distribution to peasants, freedom of the press, release of political prisoners, and the right to organize political parties and professional groups. The ENLF promised a **foreign policy** guided by nonalignment and support for African unity.

The ENLF, headed by Chairman Hassen Sorra, maintained an office in Aden, South Yemen (now Yemen). Its presence in Ethiopia was minimal and ineffective. In 1976, the South Yemeni government, which had established good relations with **Mengistu Haile Mariam**'s government, closed the ENLF office in Aden, thereby ending the ENLF's brief history.

ETHIOPIAN OPPRESSED PEOPLE'S REVOLUTIONARY STRUGGLE (EOPRS). Founded by Baro Tomsa, who had been one of the organizers of the University Students Union of **Addis Ababa**. On 19 December 1975, the EOPRS, which initially was known as the Ethiopian Oppressed Peoples Party, announced its program to destroy feudalism and establish a People's Democratic Republic. The party's supporters included **Oromo** and other oppressed nationalities. The EOPRS also pledged to create a free-market **economy**, eliminate ethnic hatred, implement a land reform program, and establish a People's Assembly.

Several factors contributed to the EOPRS's undoing. Ideologically, it was closely aligned to the **All-Ethiopian Socialist Movement** (AESM), which opposed the **Derg**. The EOPRS opposed a second round of the **Red Terror**. In June 1978, the Joint Front of Marxist-Leninist Organizations suspended the EOPRS because of its critical attitude. The **Revolutionary Flame** approved this action, claiming that the EOPRS had failed to support the AESM, promoted narrow nationalism, supported Somalia's invasion of Ethiopia, and maintained contacts with the **Ethiopian People's Revolutionary Party** and the **Oromo Liberation Front** (OLF). The Derg subsequently arrested many EOPRS officials, while those who managed to escape fled to rural areas, where some may have joined the OLF. Baro Tomsa was found dead in the countryside; many believe he had been executed by the Derg. *See also* OGADEN WAR (1977–1978); PROVISIONAL OFFICE FOR MASS ORGANIZATIONAL AFFAIRS; WORKERS' LEAGUE.

ETHIOPIAN ORTHODOX CHURCH (EOC). Founded in the fifth century, the EOC belongs to the group of Oriental Orthodox churches that includes the Egyptian Coptic Church, Syrian Jacobite Church, Mar Thoma Church of India, and Armenian Orthodox Church. These churches are similar in many respects to the Greek or other Orthodox churches. However, the Oriental group does not accept the dogmas of the Fourth Ecumenical Council held in Chalcedon (451). The Oriental churches maintain the Orthodox doctrine of the Trinity as articulated in the First Ecumenical Council at Nicaea (325) and confirmed by the Second Council in Constantinople (387).

The Chalcedonian creed affirms the doctrine of the two natures, according to which Jesus Christ possessed a human nature and a divine nature. The followers of Chalcedon asserted the Jesus of history and the Christ of faith. The bishop of Rome and the patriarch of Constantinople accepted this formula. The patriarch of Alexandria and his followers, including the Ethiopians, rejected the formula. Those who accepted the position at Chalcedon are known as diophysites or two natures. Those opposed to the Chalcedonian formula are called monophysites or one nature (i.e., Jesus Christ had only a combined divine-human nature).

In the fourth century, Christianity came to Ethiopia through Alexandria. The patriarch of Alexandria appointed **Frumentius** as the first bishop in Ethiopia. Non-Ethiopians continued to be appointed by the patriarch of Alexandria until 1959, when the first native Ethiopian, **Abuna Basilios**, ascended to the metropolitan seat. On 28 June 1959, the Egyptian patriarch Kyrillos IV declared the EOC autocephalous, thus allowing the EOC to become independent of the Egyptian church for the first time since the fourth century. In 1970, **Abuna Tewoflos** succeeded Basilios as patriarch.

Although many EOC practices are similar to those of the Greek Orthodox Church, there are differences. There are Judaic features in the EOC, which retains the distinction between clean and unclean meats, priestly dances with drums, and reverence for Saturday, the Sabbath, as well as for Sunday. Each EOC possesses a so-called **Ark of the Covenant**. This is similar to the ark of a Jewish synagogue where the Torah is kept. The EOC practices circumcision eight days after birth as a local custom rather than a religious rite.

The EOC's religious **calendar** consists of 12 months of 30 days each. Five or six days are added to a 13th month to adjust it to the solar year. According to this calendar, 7 January is the date of Christ's birth and Easter usually comes two weeks later than the Gregorian Easter. The Ethiopian liturgy is derived from that of the Coptic saint Cyril and its recitation requires at least two priests and three deacons. Most Ethiopian churches are round and contain three concentric parts: the outer ambulatory where the hymns are sung, the nave where Communion is administered, and the inner circle where the Tabot or Ark of the Covenant rests. Some larger churches are built on the basilica pattern. **Women** enter the right side only, separated from the men.

The Ethiopian **cross** is most frequently on the pattern of a Greek cross but with frequent decorative designs and is widely used in services and processions. The umbrella is also a religious object carried in processions. It is not for rain or shade but is a mark of distinction. An orange umbrella is used at funerals and a red one at weddings. EOC monks belong to the order of Saint Anthony the Hermit. The New Testament contains 35 books, the 27 familiar to other Christian churches and an additional collection of eight called the Sinodos.

For the average Ethiopian, the priest is the most important member of the clergy. Most priests come from the peasantry. They usually have limited education, most of it acquired during training. Priests are ranked according to their learning and some acquire far more religious knowledge than others. The priest's primary duty is to celebrate the Eucharist. Young boys become deacons by joining a church school and living with their teachers. After about four years of study, the diocesan bishop ordains them deacons. Monks are laymen, usually widowers, who have devoted themselves to a pious life. Other monks lead a celibate life while young and commit themselves to advanced religious education. Nuns, who are relatively rare, usually are older women who perform largely domestic tasks in the churches. *Debtaras* are priests who have lost their ordination because they are no longer ritually pure or individuals who have chosen not to enter the priesthood. They often have a wider range of learning and skill than what is required for a priest. Debtaras act as choristers, poets, herbalists, astrologers, fortunetellers, and scribes.

Almost half of Ethiopia's 70 million people belong to the EOC. Relations with Ethiopia's large **Islamic** community are generally cordial. The EOC experiences competition and even occasional conflict with the much smaller but fast-growing **Protestant** movement, especially the evangelicals. The EOC believes that the evangelicals are trying to convert their followers. This has led to several incidents in recent years. There are 32 EOC dioceses in Ethiopia and others elsewhere in Africa, **Jerusalem**, the Caribbean, Latin America, North America, Europe, and Australia. The current patriarch is **Abuna Paulos Gebre-Yohannes**, who studied at Yale and Princeton Universities. *See also* ABBA SALAMA; COPTIC ORTHODOX CHURCH OF ALEXANDRIA; DAWIT I; MATEWOS; MUSIC AND INSTRUMENTS.

ETHIOPIAN PEOPLE'S REVOLUTIONARY DEMOCRATIC FRONT (EPRDF). In May 1988, the **Tigray People's Liberation Front** (TPLF) and the Ethiopian People's Democratic Movement, which in January 1994 was renamed the Amhara National Democratic Movement, formed the EPRDF. In January 1989, the EPRDF adopted its constitution and a joint leadership and opened its membership to all democratic organizations.

On 10 March 1989, the TPLF convened its third congress. Apart from passing several anti-**Derg** resolutions, the delegates pledged their loyalty to the EPRDF. The organization's charter sought to create a democratic government, eliminate imperialism and feudalism, establish a people's government based on people's councils, and guarantee **human rights** and self-determination for all Ethiopians. In May 1990, the Oromo People's Democratic Organization (OPDO) and the Ethiopian Democratic Officers' Revolutionary Movement (EDORM) joined the EPRDF but the latter was eventually disbanded.

On 17–23 January 1991, the EPRDF held its first congress. A total of 624 delegates—representing the TPLF, OPDO, EPDM, and the

Ethiopian Democratic Officers' Revolutionary Movement—attended the meeting. They discussed numerous issues, including peace, democracy, nationalities, and social and economic development. The delegates also adopted a new constitution and established a 53-member council.

On 20–25 December 1994, the second EPRDF congress convened in Awasa. Apart from reexamining the EPRDF's political, economic, social, and foreign policy programs, the attendees devised a five-year Plan for Peace, Democracy, and Development, prepared for the election of a democratic government, and approved the membership of the Southern Ethiopian People's Democratic Front. Several smaller ethnic-based political parties subsequently affiliated with the EPRDF.

The third EPRDF congress, which opened in December 1997 in **Jimma**, evaluated the progress of the Plan for Peace, Democracy, and Development and approved a policy that allowed national and private sector investment in the electric, **telecommunications**, and defense sectors.

The fourth EPRDF congress, which ended on 16 September 2001 in **Jijiga**, reelected **Meles Zenawi** as its chairman and elected Adisu Legese as vice-chairman. The delegates also appointed a 140-member council, a 36-member executive committee, and an eight-member control commission.

By 2003, critics had become increasingly skeptical about the EPRDF's performance. The lack of progress on issues like the **economy**, human rights, **corruption**, power sharing, democratization, and land reform has alienated a growing number of Ethiopians. Initially, Prime Minister Meles remained convinced that his strategy for resolving these problems eventually would succeed. However, on 4 June 2003, the EPRDF announced plans to transform itself into a unitary party. Under this scheme, the EPRDF's principal parties (TPLF, Amhara National Democratic Movement, OPDO, and Southern Ethiopian People's Democratic Front) would be dissolved, thus ending the ethnic federalism experiment within the party.

ETHIOPIAN PEOPLE'S REVOLUTIONARY PARTY (EPRP). On 2–9 April 1972, the EPRP held its founding congress in exile. Its program supported the overthrow of **Haile Selassie**, an end to the feudal system, and the creation of a popular democratic republic. In July 1974, the EPRP leadership returned to Ethiopia and launched a weekly newspaper called *Democracia* that outlined its strategy for ending military rule and creating a people's government.

In 1973–1974, the **Eritrean People's Liberation Front** provided military training to some of its members. Disagreement between the EPRP and **Mengistu Haile Mariam**'s supporters about how to implement the **National Democratic Revolution** caused the two groups to clash. On 11 September 1976, the **Provisional Military Administrative Council** (PMAC) denounced the EPRP as a "subversive and anti-revolutionary" organization that had committed economic and industrial sabotage and had allied itself with imperialists and Eritrean secessionists. In October 1976, the EPRP announced that the PMAC's **Red Terror** campaign had resulted in the deaths of at least 1,225 of its members and had tortured hundreds of others. In retaliation, the EPRP launched an armed struggle called the White Terror against the government in **Addis Ababa** and other cities. Those who survived joined the organization's rural wing, which maintained a base in Assimba, **Tigray**, near Adigrat. By 1977, the EPRP had some 47,000 members. Nevertheless, in March 1978, the **Tigray People's Liberation Front** (TPLF) scored a decisive military victory over the EPRP. Surviving EPRP personnel fled to Sudan, thus ending the organization's influence in Ethiopia.

In 1984, the EPRP held its second congress in the liberated area of Quara and adopted a new program that called for the creation of a federal, multiparty, and pluralistic system; democratic **elections**; and a mixed **economy**. The EPRP sought to unite with all anti-Derg forces and formed an alliance with the **Ethiopian Democratic Union** and joined the Washington, D.C.–based Coalition of Ethiopian Democratic Forces. However, the TPLF opposed cooperation with the EPRP.

After the Derg's downfall (1991), the **Ethiopian People's Revolutionary Democratic Front** sought to eliminate EPRP influence by mounting military operations against its members in **Gondar** and **Gojam** and by outlawing the party. In 1993, the EPRP attended an opposition Peace and Reconciliation Conference in Paris. A few months later, the EPRP attended the Ghion Peace and Reconciliation Conference in Addis Ababa but the **police** arrested all the delegates.

On 21–26 August 2001, the party held its third congress, which paid homage to its leaders and members who have disappeared at the hands of the TPLF and urged its followers to champion democracy, **human rights**, and an end to ethnic politics and discrimination. Kiflu Tadesse documented the EPRP's history in a two-volume study entitled *The Generation*. *See also* ALL ETHIOPIAN SOCIALIST MOVEMENT; DERG; ETHIOPIAN OPPRESSED PEOPLE'S REVOLUTIONARY STRUGGLE; PROVISIONAL OFFICE FOR MASS ORGANIZATIONAL AFFAIRS; REVOLUTIONARY FLAME; WORKERS' LEAGUE.

ETHIOPIAN RED CROSS SOCIETY (ERCS). On 8 July 1935, **Haile Selassie** issued an imperial proclamation that established the ERCS under the government's control. Ethiopia's minister of foreign affairs, **Heruy Walda Selasse**, agreed to become ERCS president. Shortly afterwards, Ethiopia signed the Geneva Red Cross Convention, thus becoming the 48th member state of the International Red Cross.

The outbreak of the **Italian-Ethiopian War (1935–1936)** put the ERCS in the line of fire as it repeatedly came under attack from Fascist forces. The ERCS ceased operations during the Italian occupation but returned in 1948 when the crown prince of Ethiopia became the president of the society. The ECRS initially focused on providing information about missing Italians and then founded a training school for nurses that was attached to the Haile Selassie I Hospital. The ERCS provided free medical treatment for needy individuals and established a blood bank.

In recent years, the ERCS has created a new structure that emphasizes development issues and a reduction in dependency on foreign aid. The ERCS also cooperated with the International Committee of the Red Cross (ICRC) on the repatriation of Ethiopians from Eritrea following the outbreak of the **Ethiopian-Eritrean War** (1998). The ERCS has worked with the ICRC and the Red Crescent Societies to provide assistance to drought-affected Ethiopians. In 2001, the ERCS assisted in countering an outbreak of meningitis. In 2002, Shimelis Adugna, president of the ERCS, announced that the organization would do everything possible to deal with the **human immunodeficiency virus/acquired immune deficiency syndrome** in Ethiopia.

ETHIOPIAN STUDENT MOVEMENT (ESM). Some Ethiopian students expressed their support for the **coup attempt (1960)**. Several Ethiopian student organizations such as the University Students' Union of **Addis Ababa**, Ethiopian Student Union of North America, and World-Wide Federation of Ethiopian Students constituted the ESM. By the late 1960s and early 1970s, the ESM had emerged as a coordinated Marxist opposition organization to the imperial government. In 1969, university students chose Tilahun Gizaw as president. He advocated violent revolution to establish a people's government. A student paper, *Struggle*, advocated the removal of the imperial regime. In 1974, the ESM played a role in the overthrow of the **Haile Selassie** government. The student movement gave rise to two radical political organizations, which acted independently of the ESM: the **Ethiopian People's Revolutionary Party** (EPRP) and the **All Ethiopian Socialist Movement** (Meison). By the late 1970s, the revolution had consumed the student movement and it disappeared. Following the **Derg**'s collapse (1991), student activism returned to **Addis Ababa University**, where there have been sporadic protests and closures of the campus. Fentahun Tiruneh documented the ESM in *The Ethiopian Students: Their Struggle to Articulate the Ethiopian Revolution*.

ETHIOPIAN STUDIES. There is an active international group of scholars devoted to the study of Ethiopia's long and unique history. The First International Conference of Ethiopian Studies took place in Rome (1959). Manchester, England, hosted the second conference (1963), while the third occurred in **Addis Ababa** (1966). The goal is to have every third conference in Ethiopia. The 14th International Conference was held in Addis Ababa (2000). It coincided with the 50th anniversary of the founding of **Addis Ababa University**. Topics covered included archaeology, history, anthropology, sociology, linguistics, **literature**, sociology, law, philosophy, religion, politics, fine **arts**, economics, and environmental studies. More than 200 specialists from around the world attended. Conference proceedings normally are available a year or two after the conclusion of the conference. The institute published the three volume proceedings in 2002. The 15th International Conference of Ethiopian Studies took place in Hamburg, Germany (2003).

ETHIOPIAN TEACHERS' ASSOCIATION (ETA). There are two ETAs. The first was founded in 1948 and the second was created in 1993. The current government recognizes the new ETA as the official **labor union** representing teachers in Ethiopia. On 8 May 1997, **police** shot and killed ETA vice president Assefa Maru, supposedly while he was trying to escape arrest. The police had suspected him of supporting the Ethiopian National Patriotic Movement. Others maintained that the government had trumped up charges to remove him from the national scene. On 10 June 1999, a court sentenced **Taye Wolde Semayat**, ETA chairman, to 15 years' imprisonment. He regained his freedom in 2002 and vowed to continue his union work.

ETHIOPIAN WILDLIFE AND NATURAL HISTORY SOCIETY (EWNHS). In September 1966, conservationists established the EWNHS in **Addis Ababa**. The non-profit-making EWNHS seeks to increase the public's awareness of the need to preserve Ethiopia's natural resources, promote the interests of the country's fauna, flora, and natural **environment**, and support legislation to protect these resources. Some recent EWNHS initiatives include the Important Bird Area Project, Plant Locally and Nurture Trees, School's Environmental Education Project, and Environmental Education Support Publications. The EWNHS also publishes a scientific journal called *Walia* and an educational magazine, *Agazen*, in English and **Amharic**. *See also* BIRD LIFE; NATIONAL PARKS; WILDLIFE.

ETHIOPIC. Ethiopic is a syllabic writing system whose origins most experts believe are South Arabian or Sabaean. Inscriptions on monuments from northern Ethiopia indicate that the system is at least 3,000 years old. The system flourished primarily in the Ethiopian **highlands** and has at least five functions: philosophy, astronomy, numerology, grammar, and aesthetics. Ethiopic **literature** has a logical and intricate grammar. The writing system is used for Ethiopian and Eritrean **languages** such as Ge'ez, Tigre, Tigrinya, and Amarinya. Ayele Bekerie's *Ethiopic: An African Writing System* provides a detailed account of the subject.

EWOSTATEWOS (EUSTATHIUS) (1273–1352). Tigrayan monastic evangelist who advocated spiritual independence and isolation from corrupting state influences. To advance his religious beliefs, Ewostatewos established a community at Seraye (Serae) and expected his followers to grow their own **food**, a significant departure from the traditional practice whereby clerics received sustenance from the peasantry. He also accused the secular clergy of loose morality, condemned Christians who engaged in **slavery,** and abolished animistic and pagan religious practices and ceremonies. Followers of Ewostatewos celebrated the Sabbath on Saturday and Sunday, a custom that brought them into conflict with the traditional Ethiopian clerics and the Alexandrian patriarch. His opponents, relying on the Alexandrian church's 13th-century anathematization of Old Testament customs, subsequently declared him a deviant. In about 1337, Ewostatewos fled to Cyprus, **Jerusalem**, and Egypt, and finally settled in Armenia, where he died.

His followers remained in Ethiopia and moved to remote border regions to avoid persecution by church officials. Their monasteries and communities flourished and built Debre Bizen in Hamasien and Gunda Gunde in northwest **Tigray. Dawit I** sought to suppress the Ewostatewans by jailing some of their leaders. The emperor's strategy failed as the Ewostatewans formed a mass movement against the established order. In 1403, Dawit I freed those who had been incarcerated and decreed that the Ewostatewans were free to celebrate their Sabbath if they abandoned their confrontational tactics. Dawit I's successor, **Zara Yakob**, continued a policy of cooperation. In 1450, he supervised the Council of Debre Mitmak (Metmaq) in **Shoa** Province, which resolved the conflict with the Ewostatewans by authorizing them to observe the Sabbath on Saturday and Sunday. In turn, the Ewostatewans accepted the Holy Orders and episcopal discipline. *See also* ABBA SALAMA; ETHIOPIAN ORTHODOX CHURCH.

EZANA (date of birth and death unknown). Negus of **Axum**. Received a Christian and Greek education and ascended the throne sometime between A.D. 320 and 325. Ezana's armies conquered Kush (subsequently known as Meroe) and extended his kingdom to include much of what is now Ethiopia and parts of Somalia and Sudan. His two brothers, Adephas and Sayzana, played a significant role in the campaigns against various ethnic groups in what is now northern and northwestern Ethiopia. Ezana also facilitated considerable economic growth throughout his kingdom, in part by opening a trade route to Egypt. As a result, many Greek traders moved to Ethiopia and traded in gold, hides, ivory, spices, and tortoiseshell. These Greek merchants paved the way for the introduction of Christianity. Ezana supported their efforts by sending his tutor, **Frumentius**, to Alexandria to inform Patriarch Athanasius (c. 293–373) that Ethiopia was ready for Christianity. Supposedly, Ezana died fighting during a military campaign in western Ethiopia. He and Sayzana are saints in the **Ethiopian Orthodox Church** and their lives are celebrated every 14 October.

– F –

FALASHAS. The Falashas or Ethiopian Jews referred to themselves, while they were living in Ethiopia, as Beta Israel (House of Israel). Most lived in the **Gondar** vicinity and to the west and north toward the Sudan border. Their religion was a primitive form of Judaism based on the Old Testament and the Book of Jubilees. Falashas did not speak Hebrew; they spoke **Amharic** or Tigrinya, depending on the location of their villages. They did not have knowledge of the basic rabbinical writings such as the Talmud and the Mishnah. Major villages had a synagogue and at least one priest. They used a complex ceremonial calendar based on the solar and lunar years. They observed major Jewish holidays and fasts. They kept the Sabbath in an orthodox manner according to the Old Testament. Falasha **literature** and the Torah were written in **Ge'ez**, an early south Semitic **language**.

The origin of the Falashas is obscure. They claim they are Jews who came to Ethiopia with Menelik I, the alleged son of King Solomon and the Queen of Sheba. Others believe they migrated to Ethiopia when the Hebrews left Egypt during the Exodus or are descended from Jews who came after the destruction of the First or the Second Temple. Still others argue they are indigenous Agau people who converted to Judaism. Their name probably comes from the **Ethiopic** *fallasa*, which means "to emigrate." There are secondhand references to the Falashas by travelers to Ethiopia dating back to the ninth century. The explorer **James Bruce** aroused the Western world's curiosity about the Falashas when he mentioned them in his 18th-century travel account about the region. By the early 20th century, pro-Falasha groups had sprung up in various countries. Although more than 50 years old, one of the most authoritative accounts of this subject is Wolf Leslau's *Falasha Anthology*.

In 1975, Israel recognized the Falashas as Jews. This soon led to an organized effort by groups in Israel, the United States, and elsewhere to bring the Falashas to Israel. Due to a combination of civil war and **famine** in Ethiopia, significant numbers of Falashas took refuge in neighboring Sudan in the mid-1980s. Their plight became difficult. Between 21 November 1984 and 5 January 1985, a U.S.-Israeli program known as "Operation Moses" transported about 10,000 Falashas via commercial flights from Khartoum to Israel. As the physical condition of the remaining Falashas in Ethiopia worsened, the United States secretly arranged on 28 March 1985 for a fleet of nine C-130s to pick up the remaining Falashas in eastern Sudan. Known as "Operation Sheba," this one-day effort transported almost 1,000 Falashas to Israel. Following negotiations with **Mengistu Haile Mariam**'s regime, Israel, on 25 May 1991, launched "Operation Solomon," an airlift under the command of Major-General Amnon Shahak. The operation involved the Israeli Air Force (18 C-130s and six Boeing 707s) and El Al Airlines (eight Boeings). Within 33 hours the airlift mounted 41 sorties that transported 14,324 Falashas to Israel.

By 2003, virtually all the Falashas, about 80,000, had immigrated to Israel. They have not adapted easily to their new home. According to some reports, 77 percent of the Falashas in Israel are unemployed. However, several thousand Feles Mora Ethiopians who claim they are descended from Jews who were forcibly converted to Christianity more than 100 years ago continue to seek entry to Israel. In early 2003, the Israeli cabinet reversed an earlier policy by agreeing to admit some 17,000 Feles Mora. *See also* DIASPORA.

FAMINE. Ethiopia has been subject to famine going back many centuries. The earliest evidence of famine comes from an account about Abba Joseph, the 52nd patriarch of Alexandria (831–849). During his reign, the Abune of the **Ethiopian Orthodox Church** appointed by him, Abba Yohannes, was expelled from the country. This expulsion reportedly resulted in a famine. The Ethiopian emperor at the time appealed to the patriarch for the return of Abba Yohannes. Upon his return, rains miraculously occurred. The second recorded famine occurred in the 12th century. There are numerous written references to subsequent famines in Ethiopia. Accounts from the 13th and 14th centuries suggested that most Ethiopians regarded famines as punishment from God. Six famines ravaged the country in the 16th century and the first decade or so of the 17th century. Lack of rain caused some of them while invasions of locusts accounted for others.

Several major famines occurred after the founding of **Gondar** in 1636. There were serious famines in 1668 and 1706. Two successive plagues of locusts said to cover "the land like a fog" ate all of the grain in 1747 and 1748. Others occurred in 1752, 1772–1773, and 1788–1789. A famine devastated people and livestock in **Shoa** Province (1828–1829). Epidemics of disease such as influenza, typhus, dysentery, smallpox, and cholera frequently accompanied famines.

The great Ethiopian famine of 1888–1892 is perhaps the best documented until the 20th century. The beginning of the famine coincided with **Yohannes IV**'s death (1889). Many Ethiopians, especially those in his home province of **Tigray**, considered it an act of God. The causes of the famine predated, however, his death and can be attributed to an outbreak of rinderpest, a harvest failure, and plagues of locusts and caterpillars. It began in the north and advanced southwards. As many as 90 percent of the cattle died. A harvest failure followed, resulting in a steep rise in the price of **food**. By 1892, famine had spread throughout central and western Ethiopia. Several epidemics accompanied the famine. Although there are no reliable statistics on the number of human deaths, some observers believe that one-third of the **population** died. There was evidence of depopulation throughout both rural and pastoral areas. The famine had important political implications in that it permitted **Menelik II**'s forces to move southward with greater ease and seize new territory. It also emboldened the Italians to expand their control from the **Red Sea** coast into Tigray. Richard Pankhurst documented this subject in *The History of Famine and Epidemics in Ethiopia Prior to the Twentieth Century.*

With the passage of time, famines have occurred in Ethiopia at shorter intervals. Population growth has certainly contributed to this situation. From 1270 until 1855, famines occurred approximately every 22 years. Since 1855, they have affected the country about every eight years. Since the 1980s, there has been a famine somewhere in Ethiopia every four or five years.

Peasant farmers producing at the subsistence level historically have constituted about four-fifths of the population. It does not require a very negative event to push large numbers of them into a severe food-deficit situation. Ethiopia experienced terrible famines in 1972–1973 and 1983–1985. Mishandling of the 1972–1973 famine contributed to **Haile Selassie**'s downfall (1974). Major resettlement efforts by the **Derg** contributed to the harshness of the 1983–1985 famine. The number of drought-affected people between 1981 and 1995 ranged from a minimum of 2.53 million in 1987 to a high of 7.85 million in 1992. Famine returned to parts of Ethiopia in 1999–2000 and again in 2002–2003.

In recent years, foreign food aid has covered a significant percentage of total food needs. The government sought to contend with recurring drought and famines by creating an Early Warning System (1976), Emergency Food Security Reserve (1982), National Disaster Prevention and Management Policy (1993), **Disaster Preparedness and Prevention Commission (DPPC)** (August 1995), and National Disaster Prevention and Preparedness Fund (4 July 2000).

The DPPC, which plays the lead role in combating famines, has sought to increase crop production and long-term development and to improve disaster preparedness capabilities by strengthening the Food Security Reserve Administration. The DPPC also seeks to increase the food reserve to a level required to supply food to an average of 4.5 million people at any one time. Getachew Diriba presented a detailed analysis of the famine issue in *Economy at the Crossroads: Famine and Food Security in Rural Ethiopia.*

FASILIDAS (?–1667). Emperor (1632–1667). Son of **Susneyos**. The greatest challenge that faced Fasilidas was the religious turmoil caused by the growing influence of Catholic **missionaries** in Ethiopia. In 1622, Susneyos proclaimed **Catholicism** the state religion. However, Fasilidas rejected this decision and worked to eliminate the Catholic presence. Seela Krestos, Susneyos's brother, opposed his views and activities. This controversy eventually erupted into warfare. On 2 June 1632,

Susneyos scored a victory over anti-Catholic Ethiopians at the battle of Wayna-Dega, which resulted in at least 8,000 deaths. Susneyos, over-wrought by the devastation, restored the **Ethiopian Orthodox Church** and abdicated (1632) in favor of Fasilidas.

After becoming Emperor, he expelled the Jesuits from his court and then imprisoned and subsequently executed Seela Krestos. Fasilidas also sought to prevent other European missionaries from entering Ethiopia by concluding agreements with the Muslim pashas of Suakin and **Massawa** and Yemen's imams whereby they promised to execute European missionaries who entered their territories. Such tactics helped to retard the growth of European missionary influence in Ethiopia.

Fasilidas's other major accomplishment was his decision to move the Imperial capital from **Shoa** Province to **Gondar**, where he built an impressive palace. On 18 October 1637, Fasilidas died in Azazo and was succeeded by his son Yohannes I.

FELES MORA. *See* FALASHAS.

FEMALE CIRCUMCISION. The National Committee on Traditional Practices of Ethiopia (NCTPE) conducted a 1998 survey that indicated almost 73 percent of the female population had undergone female genital mutilation (FGM). This was down from an estimated 90 percent of the female population in 1990. The practice is most prevalent among Muslims and **Ethiopian Orthodox Church** members. Clitoridectomies typically occur seven days after birth and consist of excision of the labia. Infibulation, the most extreme and dangerous but less frequent form of FGM, is performed sometime between the age of eight and the onset of puberty. Ethiopian law does not specifically prohibit FGM, but the **Ethiopian People's Revolutionary Democratic Front** discourages the practice and supports the NCTPE. The government also has a public information campaign in public schools and health clinics to discourage FGM. At a 1998 conference on traditional practices, Ethiopian Christian and Muslim authorities agreed that FGM has no foundation in the Bible or the Koran. Although the practice remains widespread in Ethiopia, the country has made considerable progress in reining in FGM. The Ethiopian Women Lawyers' Association has called for legislation against FGM and led protests against the practice, including a 2001 rally by nine **women**'s rights groups in **Addis Ababa**. *See also* HEALTH.

FIKRE SELASSIE WOGDERES (c. 1940–). Secretary general of the **Derg** and prime minister. After attending elementary (1952–1959) and secondary (1960–1963) school, Fikre became an **air force** cadet (1964). In June 1974, he joined the Derg as an air force representative and, the following month, became a member of the Derg's Social Affairs Committee. In April 1976, he joined the **Workers' League** and, later in the year, the **Revolutionary Flame**.

In February 1977, Fikre became a member of the Derg's Standing Committee and secretary general of the **Provisional Military Administrative Council**. In December 1979, he joined the Central Committee of the **Commission for Organizing the Party of the Working People of Ethiopia** and became head of the Ideological Department and a member of the Defense and Security Committee. In April 1983, Fikre was named deputy chairman of the **Council of Ministers**. In 1984, he joined the politburo and the Central Committee of the **Workers' Party of Ethiopia**. Between 10 September and 7 November 1989, Fikre served as prime minister.

Throughout his career, he managed to maintain a degree of independence vis-à-vis other Derg members. However, despite the fact that he was the Derg's second most senior person, he had limited power, as he never cultivated a group of party supporters. After it seized power (1991), the **Ethiopian People's Revolutionary Democratic Party** jailed him on charges of crimes against humanity.

FILM. Ethiopia does not have a well-developed cinema industry. During the **Derg** era, there was a government film institute but the **Ethiopian People's Revolutionary Democratic Front** disbanded the effort, arguing that filmmaking should be privately funded. Haile Girima, a professor at Howard University in Washington, D.C., is perhaps Ethiopia's best-known director. He produced *Harvest 3000 Years* (1976), *Adwa: An African Victory* (1999), *Sankofa* (1993), and *Imperfect Journey* (1994). Another filmmaker, Solomon Bekele, made an award-winning film about love crossing the barriers of class and wealth called *Aster*. Yemane Demissie added a full-length film in **Amharic** called *Tumult*, a thriller about an aristocrat turned revolutionary who masterminds a coup d'état against the Ethiopian monarchy. Ermias Woldeamlack (1964–) directed one of the most recent Ethiopian films called *The Father*, a 28-minute production that portrays the horrors of the **Red Terror** during the Derg regime. In November 2000, Ermias first screened the film at South Africa's Sithengi film and television market. In August 2001, *The Father* won the best debut movie at the Ghanaian Aniwa film festival and the Silver Award at the Zanzibar film festival. In 2003, Mekdela Film Works produced a film called *Mezez* written and directed by Million Ayele. It is a romantic suspense story.

FISSEHA DESTA (c. 1942–). Vice president of Ethiopia (1987–1991). A Tigrayan born in **Addis Ababa**. Attended elementary school and Haile Selassie I High School in Addis Ababa. Fisseha then entered **Harar** Military Academy (1962). After graduation, he received a posting to the first Division, **Imperial Body Guard**. In 1971, Fisseha entered **Addis Ababa University**. After joining the **Derg**, he served as a member of the Administration Subcommittee (1974–1977) and as joint head of the Administration and Legal Affairs Subcommittee (1977–1978). In 1976, Fisseha was a founding member of the **Revolutionary Flame**. In 1978, he became the Derg's deputy secretary general. In December 1979, Fisseha became a member of the **Commission for Organizing the Party of the Working People of Ethiopia** (COPWE) and head of the Administration and Justice Department. In 1980–1983, he served as deputy senior minister without portfolio and deputy chairman of the **Council of Ministers**. In 1984, Fisseha became a politburo member in the **Workers' Party of Ethiopia** and chairman of the Administration, Justice, and Defense Committee. On 10 September 1987, **Mengistu Haile Mariam** appointed him vice president. After the Derg's fall (1991), Fisseha made no attempt to flee Ethiopia. The **Ethiopian People's Revolutionary Democratic Front** detained him on charges of committing atrocities. *See also* ARMED FORCES; HUMAN RIGHTS; JUDICIARY.

FITAWRARI. *See* MILITARY TITLES.

FLAD, JOHANN MARTIN (1831–1915). German **missionary**. Born on 17 January 1831 in Udingen, Württemberg, Germany. Educated as a missionary at Saint Chrischona Missionary Institute in Basel, Switzerland. Flad began his career with the Basel Mission. In 1854, he went to **Jerusalem** to continue his studies under the Anglican bishop **Samuel Gobat**, who wanted to reintroduce missionaries to Ethiopia to resume the work he had started in 1826 but which had been stopped with the expulsion of missionaries. On 20 January 1855, Flad, accompanied by **Johann Ludwig Krapf**, departed for Ethiopia, thus beginning a career that lasted six decades.

During 1861–1915, he served with the London Society for the Promotion of Christianity Amongst the Jews. Apart from working among the **Falasha**, Flad helped to establish a school at Avora, near **Gondar** (1856), and a missionary station at Kobula, north of **Lake Tana**. He also translated the Old Testament and numerous other religious and educational works into **Amharic**. In the **Anglo-Ethiopian War**, Flad acted as a diplomatic intermediary between **Robert Napier** and **Tewodros II**. Flad died on 1 April 1915 in Korntal bei Stuttgart. *See also* PROTESTANTISM.

FLAG. The concept of a national flag is an imported idea. In about 1897, the Ethiopians sewed together three pennons of red, green, and yellow that had been in use for some years. This eventually gave rise to the first national flag. The three colors appeared in various positions for the next 25 years until a flag of three horizontal stripes (green on top, yellow in the middle, and red on the bottom) of equal size became the agreed-upon version. The green stands for fertility, prosperity, and hope. The yellow indicates gold and faith and is sometimes interpreted as religious freedom. The red refers to blood and suggests that Ethiopia's children will shed their blood for their country. The center of the flag contained the Imperial insignia of the lion until the **Derg** deposed **Haile Selassie** (1974).

After the 1974 revolution, the Derg replaced the imperial insignia with a crest depicting a lion at the bottom, then a temple of **Axum** under a five-pointed red star and the wording "People's Democratic Republic of Ethiopia." With the downfall of the Derg (1991), the **Ethiopian People's Revolutionary Democratic Front** returned to a plain flag with green, yellow, and red horizontal stripes. It subsequently added to the center of the flag a blue circle containing a symbol representing the sun—a yellow pentagram from which emanate four yellow rays.

FOOD. Ethiopian food is almost as varied as the country's different ethnic groups. Traditional **highland** food consists of a huge, spongy, and slightly fermented pancake-like bread called *injera* and many vegetable- and meat-based *wat* dishes. Typically, one serves the injera, which is made from a local grain known as teff, on a mesob or basketlike table. Ethiopians do not use utensils but break off pieces of injera and then pick up some of the wat with the injera.

The wat resembles spiced stew; some versions are exceedingly hot. Lamb, beef, and chicken are the most commonly used meats in wat. Vegetable wat is especially popular during Lent. Other specialties are *kitfo* or minced raw meat, usually beef or lamb, that is warmed in a pan with a little butter and hot pepper; and *tere sega* or pieces of raw, blood-red meat. Although Western-style soft drinks and beer are popular, many Ethiopians drink *tej* or locally made honey wine. There also is a local and foul-tasting beer called *tella* made from millet or maize. The Ethiopian hostess usually caps a formal meal with an elaborate **coffee** ceremony by roasting the beans in a pan, grinding them with a mortar and pestle, brewing the mix with hot water, and serving the strong coffee in small cups. Ethiopian restaurants are now found around the world; they serve the traditional highlands food described above.

FOREIGN POLICY. During the pre-Axumite period, Ethiopia had contact, mainly trade, with Egypt, South Arabia, and India dating back several millennia B.C. In the fourth century A.D., the link with Egypt became important when the patriarch of the **Coptic Orthodox Church of Alexandria** consecrated an Egyptian Christian as the first bishop of the see of **Axum**, a practice that continued until the mid–20th century.

In the late 14th century, relations with Europe began with a visit by a Florentine trader, Antonio Bartoli. In the early 15th century, a Sicilian, Pietro Rambulo, followed and returned many years later to Sicily with an Ethiopian priest on a diplomatic mission from **Zara Yakob**. In the meantime, Ethiopia had sent Rambulo on a diplomatic mission to India and China. France dispatched the first European embassy to Ethiopia. In the 15th century, many European adventurers, mainly Italians and Portuguese, arrived in Ethiopia to seek political influence and economic opportunity.

Apprehension about expansion of the Ottoman Turks in the **Red Sea** caused the Ethiopians to focus on the importance of firearms and to open relations with the Portuguese, who were rivals to the Turks. By the time a Portuguese mission arrived in Ethiopia in 1520, the concern had abated and the Ethiopian emperor detained the delegation for six years. This ill-timed Ethiopian decision was followed in 1526 by an Islamic invasion led by **Ahmad ibn Ibrahim al Ghazi**. **Lebna Dengel** appealed for Portuguese military help. Although the 400 Portuguese soldiers did not arrive in **Massawa** until 10 February 1541, they helped Lebna Dengel's successor to defeat the invaders. Soliciting support from, and making alliances with, outside powers to protect the Ethiopian **highlands** became a hallmark of Ethiopian foreign policy and has continued to the present day. Portuguese Jesuit **missionaries** continued their involvement in Ethiopia until well into the 17th century. Their efforts to convert members of the **Ethiopian Orthodox Church** to **Catholicism** resulted in their expulsion. Relations with Europe remained strained until the 19th century. On the other hand, unofficial contact between Ethiopia and Europe continued in the 17th and 18th centuries with the Dutch, French (French physician **Charles-Jacques Poncet**), and British (Scottish explorer **James Bruce**).

In the 18th century, Ethiopia improved relations with Europe by exchanging letters with the British and the French. **Tewodros II**, fearing Egyptian encroachment and a continuing threat from the Ottomans, sought British help. When this failed, he imprisoned two British envoys. The British responded by sending a military expedition that overran much of the Ethiopian highlands and captured the Emperor's citadel, causing him to commit suicide. **Yohannes IV** established good relations with Britain and other European nations. Faced with an invasion by the Egyptians in the 1870s, he unsuccessfully appealed for help from several European countries. Yohannes IV defeated the Egyptian forces at the **Battle of Gundet** (1875) and the **Battle of Gura** (1876) on his own and then signed the **Hewett Treaty** in 1884 with Britain and Egypt to stabilize Ethiopia's western border.

In 1889, **Menelik II** signed the **Treaty of Wichale** with Italy, according to which Rome recognized Menelik II's claim to the Ethiopian throne while Menelik II acknowledged Italian sovereignty over Eritrea. Italy subsequently claimed that the Treaty of Wichale also accorded it protectorate status over Ethiopia, an assertion denied by the emperor. Most European powers accepted Italy's interpretation. Italy attempted to assert its control over the country in 1896 by sending an army that was soundly defeated in the **Battle of Adwa**. Italy then recognized the annulment of the Treaty of Wichale and Menelik II again accepted Italian sovereignty over Eritrea.

By the early 20th century, a small diplomatic corps had arisen in **Addis Ababa** that included legations from Austro-Hungary, Belgium, Britain, France, Germany, Italy, Russia, and Turkey. This was also a period of Ethiopian territorial expansion to the east and south. In 1903, the United States sent a mission to Ethiopia. Menelik II sought to modernize and develop Ethiopia by bringing in advisers from many countries. On 13 December 1906, Britain, France, and Italy concluded the **Tripartite Treaty**, which partitioned Ethiopia into three spheres of economic influence (i.e., a British sphere in the **Blue Nile** and **Lake Tana** areas, a French sphere in the hinterland of the Somali coast, and an Italian sphere in the vast stretch from Eritrea in the north to Italian Somalia in the south). Concerned about the intentions of these three countries, Ethiopia briefly showed sympathy for Germany and Turkey during **World War I**. In 1923, Ethiopia joined the **League of Nations**, but Britain and Italy persuaded the League to ban the export of firearms by member states to much of Africa, including Ethiopia. In 1926, Britain and Italy pressured Ethiopia to grant them economic concessions. In 1928, **Ras** Tafari Makonnen, later **Haile Selassie**, negotiated a 20-year treaty of peace and friendship with Italy, and Ethiopia began establishing a number of legations in foreign countries.

However, Italy remained determined to invade Ethiopia and avenge its defeat at the Battle of Adwa. Haile Selassie's protestations before the League of Nations were to no avail as the **Italian-Ethiopian War (1935–1936)** resulted in the rapid conquest of Ethiopia. The only countries that did not recognize the Italian occupation were the Soviet Union, the United States, Mexico, and New Zealand. In 1941, Ethiopian **patriots** with the help of British and Allied forces defeated Italy. Haile Selassie returned, supported by the **British Military Administration** until after the end of **World War II**. The postwar era began with a close relationship between Ethiopia and the United States.

The latter initiated major military and economic assistance programs in return for a major communications base outside Asmara. At the request of the United States, Ethiopia sent troops in support of the United Nations **police** action in Korea, and Haile Selassie could generally be relied upon to support U.S. and Western positions during the Cold War.

At the same time, Ethiopia was active in the nonaligned movement and a strong supporter of Pan-Africanism. With the creation of the **Organization of African Unity** (1963), it was only natural to locate its headquarters in Addis Ababa. Since 1945, the Middle East also had been an important part of Ethiopia's foreign policy. Haile Selassie tried to maintain a delicate balance between good relations with the Arabs and support for the new Israeli state. He managed cordial relations with neighboring Sudan and Kenya but found himself in regular conflict with Somalia, which claimed all of southeastern Ethiopia. Foreign policy under Haile Selassie was predicated on a belief in collective security and support for international organizations and a combination of peaceful coexistence and strong defense.

Ethiopia's foreign policy changed dramatically with the overthrow in 1974 of Haile Selassie and the arrival of a left-wing military junta. Relations worsened with Sudan and Somalia. The **Eritrean People's Liberation Front** (EPLF) stepped up its war of independence against Ethiopia. Relations with the West and particularly the United States began to deteriorate. In 1977, the **Derg** asked the United States to leave the communications base outside Asmara. The **Ogaden War (1977–1978)** resulted in the temporary loss of most of the **Ogaden**. Ethiopia's eventual victory over Somalia resulted from an influx of Soviet arms and advisers and some 15,000 Cuban troops. By this time an anti-American group, disappointed by the end of American military assistance, had risen to power in the Derg. Ethiopia effectively switched the previous alliance with the United States for one with the Soviet Union and the Eastern Bloc while Washington supported Somalia, an erstwhile Soviet ally. China also tightened its relationship with the Derg government. Ethiopia's new policy became known as "proletarian internationalism" and was little more than an appendage of Soviet policy. When the Soviet Union began to unravel in the late 1980s, Ethiopia made some halfhearted and ineffectual efforts to improve relations with the West. However, these overtures were too late. In 1991, the **Ethiopian People's Revolutionary Democratic Front** (EPRDF), led by the **Tigray People's Liberation Front** (TPLF) and the EPLF, overturned **Mengistu Haile Mariam**'s regime.

The TPLF, the core of the EPRDF, began as a Marxist-Leninist organization. But it had some pragmatic leaders who, watching the Soviet Union's collapse, realized it needed good ties with the West to gain economic assistance and **debt** relief. From the beginning, the EPRDF emphasized its good relationship with the United States and the European Union (EU) member countries. It also has maintained close links with China and has been careful not to ignore key countries like Russia, Canada, and a few others in Europe that are not EU members. Ethiopia values its association with the **International Monetary Fund** and the **World Bank**. As with previous Ethiopian governments, it relies on a strong defense to deal with potential problems from neighbors. It attaches considerable importance to maintaining security along all of its borders, including, if necessary, cross-border military action.

Ethiopia also showed, as it has done on several occasions in past centuries, that it would spare no expense or loss of life in defending its territory. The **Ethiopian-Eritrean War** (1998–2002) is a case in point. In 1996, the EPRDF issued a major statement that set forth its foreign policy strategy. According to the document, the EPRDF would seek to promote policies that protected national interests and sovereignty; promoted noninterference in the internal affairs of other states; facilitated economic union with neighbors and other African countries; and supported the peaceful solution of international disputes. Kinfe's Abraham's *Ethiopia from Empire to Federation* contains a useful analysis of Ethiopian foreign policy.

FORESTRY. *See* DEFORESTATION.

FRUMENTIUS (c. 300–c. 360). First bishop of Ethiopia. Born in Tyre. Credited with bringing Christianity to Ethiopia. At an early age, Frumentius and his brother, Aedesius, traveled to India under the care of Meropius, a merchant of Tyre. On the return journey, the ship landed at a **Red Sea** port, which probably was **Adulis**. Local warriors killed Meropius and the ship's crew but spared the two brothers and took them to **Axum**'s ruler, who made Aedesius his cupbearer and Frumentius his steward. When the ruler died, his queen made the brothers coregents. Frumentius used his position to build churches for local Roman merchants.

After reaching their majority, the brothers received permission to leave Ethiopia. Aedesius returned to Tyre, where he was ordained presbyter, but Frumentius went to Alexandria and convinced the patriarch, Athanasius (c. 293–373), to help spread Christianity in Ethiopia. Athanasius also consecrated Frumentius as bishop.

After Frumentius returned to Ethiopia in 333 (other sources maintain that he returned in 327 or 330) as bishop of Axum, he became known as Abba Salama (father of peace). Emperor **Ezana** supported his efforts and established Christianity as the state religion of Ethiopia. After the Arian schism (356) had split Christendom, the pro-Arian Emperor Constantius II (317–361), ruler of the Roman Empire (356–361), asked the Ethiopian emperors to send Frumentius to Egypt to test his loyalty. There is no evidence that they responded to this request. Nothing is known of Frumentius's later activities. In the 16th century, Portuguese Jesuits in Ethiopia honored Frumentius by establishing their headquarters at a place they called Fremonia, near **Adwa**.

– G –

GADA. *Gada* is a way of life for the **Oromos**. It consists of two underlying concepts: gada-sets or age-sets and gada-grades. The gada-sets are the first 40 years of life through which all males pass in five eight-year initiation periods. The grades are the stages through which all males enter the gada system 40 years after their fathers. The gada age classification system is similar to age-sets practiced by the Masai, Kikuyu, and **Nuer**. Its use of generations as an organizing principle makes it different from other age-sets. Members of gada age-sets share the same status and perform their rites of passage together. The grades are the stages of development through which the groups pass. Government based on gada contains principles of checks and balances to avoid subordination and exploitation, periodic succession, balanced opposition, and power-sharing between higher and lower political structures. Gada is at the center of Oromo culture and civilization.

While gada is a strong symbol of Oromo ethnic identity, it may be developing multiple meanings. An Oromo nationalist tends to see gada as something around which all Oromo should identify because it is at the core of Oromo culture and a symbol of pan-Oromo national political identity. This is part of a concerted effort in recent years to shift the role of gada as a symbol of Oromo identity to gada as a political practice. There is a growing tendency for Oromo nationalists to call for gada democracy as a replacement for **Tigrayan** or **Amhara** "imperialism." There are numerous analyses of the meaning and importance of gada by experts such as Asmaron Legesse, Lemmu Baissa, P. T. W. Baxter, and Marco Bassi.

GALAWEDOS (?–1559). Emperor (1540–1559). Son of **Lebna Dengel**. He acceded to the throne when the kingdom was under attack by the **Islamic** leader **Ahmad ibn Ibrahim al Ghazi** and his followers. Galawedos therefore spent much of his time fighting Muslim armies from the **Adal sultanate**. On 10 February 1541, 400 Portuguese soldiers, under the command of Christovãro da Gama (son of Vasco), arrived in **Massawa** to help the emperor repulse the Muslim invaders. However, Gran's army killed or captured at least 280 Portuguese soldiers. Nevertheless, on 21 February 1543, Galawedos defeated the Muslims and killed Gran. In 1545, the emperor expelled all Muslims from Bale.

Despite these setbacks, Gran's nephew, Nur ibn Mujahid, pledged to prolong the war against Galawedos. In 1550, the emperor's army sacked the Muslim stronghold of **Harar,** but Nur continued to launch attacks against Ethiopia. To make matters worse for Galawedos, Ottoman Turks seized Massawa and Arkiro and made periodic military forays into northern Ethiopia, oftentimes with the support of the emperor's rivals. In 1559, Nur invaded Fatajar. Galawedos ignored his advisers who urged him to avoid a precipitous battle and lure the Muslim leader deeper into Ethiopia before launching an attack. Instead, he ordered an immediate assault on Nur's army. On 24 March 1559, Muslim forces killed Galawedos, who was succeeded by his younger brother Minas (reigned 1559–1563).

GALLA. Galla is the term applied by outsiders to the **Oromo** people until it was dropped from scholarly discourse about 1970. The Oromo never called themselves Galla. The Ethiopian ecclesiastic Abba Bahrey wrote in 1593 a *History of the Galla.* This account and subsequent European writings that consistently referred to the Galla kept the term alive. Galla has the connotation of being a stranger, outsider, or subject, although the word's etymology remains a mystery. According to one account, Galla refers to the Oromo word *galaa,* a term that the **Amhara** misunderstood. Others suggest that the word has only a geographic meaning, citing the Gala River in **Gurageland**. Some have argued the word comes from the Phoenician *galah*, meaning "to wander." In some Indo-European **languages** Galla means "blackness." Whatever the origin, the Oromo consider it derogatory.

GAMBELA (GAMBELLA) REGION. Ethiopia's smallest region with a **population** of only about 200,000. The **Ethiopian People's Revolutionary Democratic Front** carved Gambela out of what was previously known as **Ilubabor Province**. In 1936, the Italians captured and occupied Gambela. In 1941, British and Ethiopian forces retook Gambela, which then became part of Sudan (1951), but returned to Ethiopia five years later. Southern Sudan surrounds about half of Gambela. In 1902, Ethiopia and the Anglo-Egyptian Sudan (now Sudan) determined the international boundaries. The capital, also known as Gambela, is located on the Baro River, which joins the **Sobat River** at the Sudan border and continues to the White Nile at Malakal. In an earlier era, there was extensive barge and river traffic during the rainy season between Gambela and Khartoum. The long-running civil war in Sudan and silting of the Baro and Sobat Rivers ended this trade.

Gambela Region is one of Ethiopia's most backward, although Gambela town has an excellent all-weather airstrip. The civil war in southern Sudan has affected Gambela Region more than the rest of Ethiopia. That part of the region that juts into Sudan has been crossed periodically by troops from the Sudan People's Liberation Army and South Sudan Independence Movement as they maneuvered for position. Gambela Region hosts three southern Sudanese **refugee** camps at Bonga in the eastern part of the region, at Fugnido to the south of Gambela town, and at Dimma. The United Nations High Commissioner for Refugees has long maintained a branch office in Gambela town. Most refugees are Sudanese (e.g., **Anuak**, **Nuer**, Dinka, Shilluk, and Uduk).

Gambela Region's westernmost part can be reached only by air because of insecurity due to Sudan's civil war and the presence of a
large swampy area that lacks an all-weather road. Government control over the zonal capitals of Jikao and Akobo, both on the Sudan
border, is sometimes problematic. The two principal ethnic groups in
the region are the Anuak and the Nuer, who occasionally fight one
another. The region's population is 40 percent Nuer, 27 percent Anuak, 24 percent **highlanders**, and the remainder small ethnic groups.
The Anuak depend on **agriculture** and the Nuer on livestock. Some
Nuer in Gambela Region also have been linked to the South Sudan
Independence Movement, which is primarily a Nuer movement.

Most Ethiopian maps and tour guides suggest that Gambela **National Park** continues to function. However, Sudanese rebels and local
hunters have killed most of the **wildlife**. Moreover, the park is located
in an unsafe part of the region and lacks a **tourist** infrastructure.

GAMO-GOFA-DAWRO PEOPLES AND LANGUAGES. The Gamo,
Gofa, and Dawro are three closely related peoples who live to the northwest of Lake Abaya and Lake Chamo. The **Wolaytta** and **Dorze** live to
the east; the **Kaficho**, **Nayi**, **Chara**, and **Malo** to the west; the **Oromo**
to the north; and the **Ari**, **Oyda**, **Maale**, **Bussa**, and **Zayse-Zergulla** to
the south. The Gamo number about 500,000, the Dawro about 275,000,
and the Gofa well over 150,000. The principal town in their area is Arba
Minch. The Gofa and Dawro had their own kings. In the early 1890s,
Menelik II conquered the last Gofa king, Kamma or Qanna, and his
wife and son converted to Christianity. The Gamo had a system of
chiefs. In the 16th century, the Oromo occupied Gamo and neighboring
kingdoms ruled over them in the centuries leading up to the time Menelik II seized control. The Dawro, who are also known by the derogatory
term Kullo, are 16th-century refugees from the Muslim **Dawaro** to the
east. At one time, the kingdom paid tribute to the king of **Kafa**. Their
last king, Kanta, was in power as late as 1887.

Gamo territory is densely populated, well supplied with water, and
intensively cultivated. All these groups rely on the cultivation of *ensete*. They grow oats, barley, millet, teff, potatoes, **cotton**, **coffee**, and
lentils. They breed cattle and engage in beekeeping. They live in beehive-shaped huts that have a characteristic noselike projection. Most
Gamo nominally belong to the **Ethiopian Orthodox Church** (EOC)

but **Protestant** churches recently have made inroads among them. For those who still practice traditional beliefs, the supreme being is called Waga. The supreme being of the Gofa is Tsuossa. The most important Gofa deity is Tala, a spirit of the **Omo River**. The Gofa also venerate a particular tree that they plant inside the enclosure of new families. The Dawro grow coffee and cotton and raise cattle. Most Dawro today are EOC members or Protestants. The supreme being of those who follow traditional beliefs is Tosa. There are reports of old, ruined Christian churches where the Dawro live.

Gamo, Gofa, and Dawro are separate Omotic dialects in the Ometo family. Gamo has more than 80 percent lexical similarity with Gofa, Wolaytta, and Dorze; more than 70 percent with Dawro; and more than 40 percent lexical similarity with Koorete and Maale. Dawro has more than 70 percent lexical similarity with Gofa, Dorze, and Gamo; 80 percent with **Wolaytta**; and more than 40 percent with **Koorete** and Maale. The government is developing joint educational materials for all three groups.

GANZA PEOPLE AND LANGUAGE. The Ganza, sometimes mistakenly called the Koma or **Komo**, constitute a small number of people who live in an enclave near Mount Manga and the Dota River south of the Dabus (Yabus) River. The **Berta** live to the west, **Boro** to the north, **Gumuz** to the east, and **Oromo** to the south. The Ganza speak a north Omotic **language** of the Mao family that is related to but separate from **Hozo** and distinct from Gumuz. The nearly extinct Ganza language has a 14 percent lexical similarity with Omotic languages and 6 percent with Mao.

GAWWADA PEOPLE AND LANGUAGE. Gawwada refers to several small, related ethnic groups that live southwest of Lake Chamo. They number about 75,000 and include the Dihini, Gergere, Gollango, Gorose, and Harso. They are **agriculturists** who live on mountain slopes and practice terraced cultivation. They retain an age-set social system and are probably related to the **Konso**. They speak an east Cushitic **language**. Gawwada has 78 percent lexical similarity with **Bussa**, 73 percent with **Tsamai**, and 41 percent with Konso. The Gawwada dialects are closely related. Educated Gawwada and their leaders use **Amharic**, Afan Oromo, and Konso as a second language.

GEBRE-HANNA GEBRE-MARIYAM, ALEQA (c. 1804–1902). Born about 1804 near **Debre Tabor** in **Bagemder Province**. As the son of a clergyman, he learned to read psalms, sing church chants, and recite *qene* **poetry**. As a result of this proficiency, Empress Menen requested his services to teach her to recite prayers in Ge'ez. She also arranged additional church education for Gebre-Hanna in **Gondar** and then gave him the title of **aleqa**, head of a large church or monastery. Gebre-Hanna administered the churches around Gondar and became an expert in the interpretation of the *Fitha Nagast* or Law of Kings, which was Ethiopia's primary code of law until recently. Gebre-Hanna was close to **Tewodros II**, and served as an administrator of justice under **Yohannes IV**.

The apex of Gebre-Hanna's career came when he served in **Menelik II**'s court. Apart from enhancing his reputation as a master of qene poetry, he helped the **Ethiopian Orthodox Church** to interpret the Old and New Testaments. Gebre-Hanna also invented a new style of church **dance** called *Tekle,* which he named after his only son. It became popular and spread from Debre Tabor to **Shoa** Province and **Tigray**. He became known for speaking double entendre, referred to as "wax and gold," and using puns and expressions that had a deeper meaning than first appeared to be the case.

GEDEO PEOPLE AND LANGUAGE. The Gedeo people, also known as the Darasa, number more than a half million and live to the east of Lake Abaya. The **Sidama** reside to the north and the **Oromo** live on their other borders. They are divided into seven clans. The principal town is Dilla. They cultivate **coffee**, *ensete*, corn, and tobacco. Before coming under control of **highland** Ethiopians, the Gedeo had a hereditary oligarchy. Following Ethiopian occupation, a chief ruled a particular zone supported by minor chiefs. The Gedeo live in round huts with conical roofs that are divided into rooms. They believe that snakes are immortal and that the devil is diffused throughout nature. Old phallic steles made of basalt have become cult objects. Some have the sun and the Southern Cross carved on the western side. Today, the Gedeo are a mixture of Christian, Muslim, and followers of their traditional beliefs. The Gedeo speak an eastern Cushitic **language**. It has 60 percent lexical similarity with Sidamo, 57 percent with **Alaba**, 54 percent with **Kambata**, and 51 percent with **Hadiyya**. It serves as their literary language.

GE'EZ (GI'IZ, GHEEZ). The Semitic **language** of the **Axumite** empire. In the first century A.D., immigrants from South Arabia settled along the Ethiopian coastline and in the **highlands**, bringing with them the Sabaean language and script. This language eventually evolved into Ge'ez. The process by which Ge'ez became a different language no longer intelligible to traders from the **Red Sea**'s east coast was gradual. Several important phonetic and morphological changes took place in the language during this transformation. The Ge'ez dictionary resembles that of South Arabian but many words received new and special meaning. Ge'ez is written from left to right. In the eighth century, the decline of the Axumite empire began and was followed a century or two later by the eclipse of Ge'ez as a spoken language. Ge'ez continued to thrive, however, as Ethiopia's literary and ecclesiastical language. In fact, the classical period of Ge'ez **literature** was between the 13th and 17th centuries, hundreds of years after Ge'ez had ceased being the common spoken language of highland Ethiopians.

From the end of the first millennium until recently, Ge'ez functioned in Ethiopia in a manner similar to that of Latin during the Middle Ages. It was considered the only worthy language for literary work. The use of Ge'ez in churches and monasteries led to a fairly high rate of literacy in Ethiopia. Under **Zara Yakob**, for example, there was a flowering of Ge'ez literature. The language also is important to scholars because the Axumites used Ge'ez to keep the royal chronicles and other official and religious records. Indeed, the large number of Ge'ez manuscripts forms the basis of the world's understanding of Ethiopia's early history. Today, the use of Ge'ez is confined to the **Ethiopian Orthodox Church**.

GELASSA DILBO. General secretary of the **Oromo Liberation Front** (OLF) (1992–1999) and secretary general of United Liberation Forces of Oromia (1999–). Born in Horo Gudru, **Wollega Region**. His real name is Yohannis Benti. After the **Derg** seized power (1974), Gelassa dropped out of **Addis Ababa University** and enrolled in the Yekatit 66 Political School. He subsequently left this school and went to eastern **Harar**. On his return to **Addis Ababa**, Gelassa became associated with Negede Gobezie, leader of the pro-Derg **Meison** party. During 1975–1977, he belonged to the **Ethiopian Oppressed People's Revolutionary Party**, which was part of the **Provisional Office**

for Mass Organizational Affairs. After **Mengistu Haile Mariam** severed the Derg's relationship with Meison, Gelassa resigned, went to Sudan, and joined the OLF. After the **Ethiopian People's Revolutionary Democratic Front** (EPRDF) came to power (1991), he joined the OLF delegation that participated in the 1–5 July 1991 Peace and Democracy Conference in Addis Ababa.

The OLF then joined the **Transitional Government of Ethiopia** and held four ministerial portfolios (**Agriculture**, **Education**, Information, and Trade) and 21 seats in the **Council of Ministers**. However, on 17 June 1992, the OLF withdrew from the EPRDF-led government and the **Elections (1992)**, claiming that Prime Minister **Meles Zenawi** had failed to live up to his agreement to allow the OLF to operate freely and to ensure a free and fair election. During 1992–1998, Gelassa served as the OLF's general secretary, operating out of Germany. In November 1999, he resigned, ostensibly because of poor health; however, many OLF members maintained that he had lost his position because of poor leadership skills. Thereupon Gelassa became secretary general of the United Liberation Forces of Oromia.

GENALE RIVER. (375 miles; 600 kilometers long.) The Genale River rises to the west of the **Bale Mountains** and flows southeast until it reaches Dolo Odo near the Ethiopia-Kenya-Somalia tripoint. The Genale continues into Somalia, where it is known as the Juba, and disappears in the sands near the Indian Ocean coast. During the rainy season, the Genale's upper tributaries are mountain torrents and have spectacular waterfalls. Its main tributaries are the Welmel, Mena, and Weyb Rivers, all of which are fed by the Bale Mountains and are unimpressive in the dry season. The Dawa River, which rises west of Lake Abaya and flows roughly parallel to the Genale, joins it where it enters Somalia and becomes the Juba. In the upper reaches dense jungle-like growth lines the Genale, behind which are hills covered in thornbush. In the lower reaches, the Genale flows through a low, grass-covered plain.

GERAZMACH. *See* MILITARY TITLES.

GERMANE NEWAY (1904–1960). Civil servant and coup plotter. Born in **Addis Ababa** and educated at the Tafari Makonnen School, Haile

Selassie I Secondary School, University of Wisconsin, and Columbia University. While in the United States, Germane served as president of the Ethiopian Students' Association. In 1954, he returned to Ethiopia and received an appointment as governor of Walamo district in **Sidamo** Province. During his tenure, Germane earned a reputation as a reformer by establishing schools and increasing social services. These activities put him on a collision course with the aristocracy that financed Germane's reforms. A coalition of rich landowners arranged his transfer to Addis Ababa as titular governor of **Jijiga**.

His light duties enabled Germane to attend extension courses at the **University College of Addis Ababa** and, more importantly, to meet other students, some of whom were military officers who had become disenchanted with the monarchy. According to the government, Germane hatched a coup plot that included land nationalization, the disestablishment of the **Ethiopian Orthodox Church**, and the assassination of senior government officials.

After launching the **coup attempt (1960)**, Germane created a revolutionary Council to implement his program. Before the suppression of the coup, he killed 14 captives. On 24 December 1960, Germane committed suicide while resisting loyalist forces. The following day, his body was hanged outside Addis Ababa's Saint George's Cathedral.

GIDEON FORCE. On 6 November 1940, Major **Orde Wingate**, Royal Engineers, arrived in Khartoum and started to organize an army that he called Gideon Force. The unit eventually comprised 50 British officers, 20 British noncommissioned officers, the second Ethiopian battalion (800 troops), and a Sudan Defense Force Frontier battalion (800 troops).

On 20 January 1941, Gideon Force crossed into Ethiopia at Um Idla, where **Haile Selassie** joined Gideon Force. Less than four months later, on 5 May 1941, Wingate accompanied the emperor on his triumphant return to **Addis Ababa**. On 1 June 1941, General **Alan Gordon Cunningham**, fearing that Wingate would get involved in Ethiopian politics, informed him that Gideon Force no longer officially existed.

GILO RIVER. *See* SOBAT RIVER.

GIMIRA-SPEAKING PEOPLES. Originally Gimira was the name given by the **Oromo** and **highland** Ethiopians to several ethnic groups in southwest Ethiopia who speak one of the Gimira dialects. The Europeans adopted Gimira as a linguistic term and it also came into use incorrectly as the name of a single ethnic group. The Gimira-speaking peoples include the **Sheko**, **Dizi**, **Nayi**, and **Bench** ethnic groups. Over the years, these and related peoples have been known by a wide variety of names, adding confusion to the use of the term Gimira. Today, some scholars separate the Gimira-Bench speakers from the Gimira-Maji speakers—the Sheko, Dizi, and Nayi.

GIRMACCHEW TEKLE-HAWARIYAT (1915–1987). The son of **Tekle-Hawariyat Tekle-Mariyam**. Born on his father's farm at Hirna in Hararge Province on 21 November 1915. Educated in **Dire Dawa**, **Addis Ababa**, and Paris. In 1935, Girmacchew returned to Ethiopia and fought in the **Italian-Ethiopian War (1935–1936)**. However, the Italians captured him and sent him to Italy, where he spent seven years in prison. In about 1942, Girmacchew returned to Ethiopia and served as director general of the Office for Newspapers. Girmacchew then began a diplomatic career, holding posts as director general for Europe in the Ministry of Foreign Affairs, chargé d'affaires (Sweden and Brazil), and ambassador (Italy and the former West Germany). In 1961, he returned to Ethiopia and served in several senior positions, including minister of information, governor of **Ilubabor Province**, minister of **agriculture**, minister of **health**, and crown councilor. During this period, Girmacchew also wrote a play called *Tewodros* and the novel *Araya*. Imprisoned during the **Derg** period, he was eventually released for medical reasons and died on 5 November 1987.

GOBANA DACHI (DACI, DATCHE), RAS (1821–1889). Aristocratic **Oromo** general who helped **Menelik II** expand his empire. Born in 1821 in Aman, Wegda, **Shoa** Province. Little is known about Gobana's early career. In 1865, he opposed a pretender to the throne. Gobana then joined Menelik's (later Menelik II) service after the latter had escaped from prison in Magdala and had become **negus** of Shoa. Menelik rewarded him by giving him the office of Agafari, an influential position that enabled him to receive and introduce visitors to Menelik II.

By 1876, Gobana had assembled a formidable army, thanks in part to the acquisition of some 1,000 Remington rifles from **Yohannes IV**'s troops who had passed through his territory (1876). During the next two years, he reconquered regions around what is now **Addis Ababa**. Menelik acknowledged Gobana's triumphs by conferring the title of **ras** upon him (1878). Gobana subsequently subjugated **Gurage** and much of southwestern and western Ethiopia. In 1881, he defeated **Takla Haymanot** at the **Battle of Embabo**. His many military successes and growing popularity among the **Oromos** concerned Menelik II, who restricted him to the governorship of **Wollega**. Despite this setback, Gobana remained loyal to Menelik II and, in 1885, scored a decisive victory over Sudanese dervishes on his western boundary. On 3 July 1889, Gobana died after three days' illness in **Entoto**.

GOBAT, SAMUEL (1799–1879). Swiss Lutheran and then Anglican **missionary**. Born on 26 January 1799 in Crémines, Bern, Switzerland. Educated at the Basle Missionary Institution, the Missionary Institute of Paris, and the **Church Missionary Society** (CMS) in London. During his studies, Gobat acquired a knowledge of Arabic, **Amharic**, and **Ge'ez**.

On 28 December 1829, he arrived at **Massawa** with a CMS party that included fellow missionary Christian Kigler and a German carpenter named Christian Aichinger. Gobat remained in Ethiopia until 6 February 1833, when he went to Europe for a prolonged visit. In 1834, he returned to Ethiopia accompanied by fellow missionary Carl Wilhelm Isenberg. During his years in Ethiopia, Gobat, unlike many of his missionary colleagues, sought to accept indigenous customs. His attempts to establish a stable and productive relationship with the **Ethiopian Orthodox Church** (EOC) was less than successful largely because of the suspicion and hostility of the EOC clergy. In 1836, illness forced Gobat to return to Europe. He documented his time in Ethiopia in a *Journal of Three Years' Residence in Abyssinia*.

He subsequently served in Malta (1839–1845), where he supervised an Arabic translation of the Bible. In July 1846, Gobat was ordained an Anglican priest. A few days later, on 5 July 1846, he was consecrated bishop of **Jerusalem**. Until his death on 11 May 1879 in

Jerusalem, Gobat worked tirelessly to spread Christianity and to improve the lives of his followers by building schools, hospitals, and orphanages in places such as Bethlehem, Jerusalem, Nablus, and Nazareth.

GOBATO PEOPLE AND LANGUAGE. The Gobato occupy a tiny enclave of perhaps 1,000 persons in the Didessa River valley north of Gimbi. The **Gumuz** reside to the north and the **Oromo** to the east, south, and west. They speak a Nilo-Saharan **language** in the **Berta** family. Many are bilingual in Afan Oromo.

GOFA PEOPLE AND LANGUAGE. *See* GAMO-GOFA-DAWRO PEOPLES AND LANGUAGES.

GOJAM (GOJJAM). Gojam was one of the administrative divisions during the **Haile Selassie** government and the **Derg** period. The **Ethiopian People's Revolutionary Democratic Party** substantially redrew the regional boundaries. What was previously known as Gojam is today three zones in **Amhara Region** (i.e., East Gojam, West Gojam, Agaw) and Metekel in **Benishangul Region**. Most of Gojam's border was the **Blue Nile** as it swung southwest and then west from **Lake Tana** to the Sudan border. Gojam's two major towns are **Bahir Dar** and Debre Markos. Gojam has been an important part of Ethiopia's **highlands** history and the expansion of Christianity. In 1316–1317, Emperor **Amda Seyon** established control over Gojam. The people of Gojam have a reputation for independence and not taking kindly to authority.

GONDAR (GONDER). (142,100, estimated 2002 **population**.) Ethiopia's fourth largest city and the country's capital for almost 200 years during the 17th and 18th centuries. Gondar, which today is one of Ethiopia's premier **tourist** attractions, is situated on a basaltic ridge some 7,500 feet (2,286 meters) above the sea, about 21 miles (34 kilometers) northeast of **Lake Tana**. The Angerab and Qaha Rivers flow from the ridge to below the town and onwards to the lake.

In the early 16th century, Gondar was a small village. In 1636, Emperor **Fasilidas** established his capital in Gondar, which was near three commercially and strategically important crossroads. One ran across the **Blue Nile** into the southwest, which contained civets, gold, ivory, and **slaves**. The second went northeast to **Massawa**, and the third ran west to Sudan and Egypt. All served as transit routes for imports such as textiles, manufactured goods, and firearms. Muslim traders monopolized much of this commerce while Gondar's Christian rulers controlled political power. By the time of the emperor's death (1667), the town's population had reached some 25,000.

By the end of **Iyasu II**'s (1730–1755) reign, Gondar's glory days were over. Thereafter, the town suffered greatly from the civil wars. In 1868, **Tewodros II** burned 41 of Gondar's churches. In 1888, the Mahdists from Sudan sacked and burned the city. After the British pacification of Sudan (1886–1889), there was a revival of trade between Gondar and the Blue Nile regions. The inhabitants included Muslims and **Falashas**. The **economy** flourished as local **industry** produced **cotton**, cloth, gold and silver ornaments, copper wares, fancy articles in bone and ivory, excellent saddles, and shoes.

The cultural and economic renaissance that took place during the Gondarine era continued beyond the city's decline as a political capital. The 200-year Gondarine period is one of the most fascinating in Ethiopia's history and left a rich legacy of unique architecture. Unlike Ethiopia's other buildings, Gondar's castles and palaces resembled, with some modifications, medieval European fortresses, the style of architecture being the result of the Portuguese presence in the country. Portuguese craftsmen remaining after the expulsion of the Jesuits (1633) probably contributed to the construction of Fasiladas Palace, a two-story castle constructed of brown basalt stone.

In 1941, the British bombed the Italian military headquarters in the castle area. However, the original structures are surprisingly well preserved despite these attacks. Following **Bahir Dar**'s designation as the regional capital, Gondar became a zonal capital. In October 1954, the imperial government established the Public Health College in Gondar.

The town's **economy** has not prospered in recent years. Periodic water shortages also are a chronic problem. On the positive side, it is the location of a major branch of the **Addis Ababa University** system, has a modern new airport, and is the major city in **Amhara Region** linked to western **Tigray Region** and the Sudan border. Following the normalization of relations with Sudan in the late 1990s and growing interest in the use of Port Sudan, Gondar is Ethiopia's first large city on the road from Port Sudan and may experience an economic revival.

GORGORA. Located on **Lake Tana**'s northern shore. During the reign of **Susneyos**, old Gorgora served as Ethiopia's temporary capital. The remnants of his palace, built in 1614, are still visible. Located on a peninsula, old Gorgora is usually visited by boat. Gorgora has strong historical ties to **Gondar**. In 1626, new Gorgora was founded. Small and dominated by the Marine Authority compound, it has a weekly ferry connection with **Bahir Dar** at the south end of Lake Tana. **Mengistu Haile Mariam** maintained a guesthouse in Gorgora. The 17th-century Church of Debre Sina is located nearby.

GOSHU WOLDE (1942–). Soldier and cabinet minister. Born in Gore, **Ilubabor Province**. After elementary school in Gore, Goshu went to **Addis Ababa** and enrolled in the Haile Selassie I Secondary School. In 1960–1963, he attended the **Harar** Military Academy, where he graduated at the top of his class in academic and military subjects and received a special sword of honor from the emperor. Goshu continued his military studies at the Royal Marine School, Devon (1966), Officer Training School, Salisbury (1967), and Frunze Academy, Moscow (1977). In 1969–1972, he studied law at **Haile Selassie I University** and then attended Yale University Law School on a fellowship.

Goshu's military career included assignments as instructor at Harar Military Academy (1963–1978), a member of the Ethiopian Commission for Defense Studies, and a member of the United Nations Operation in the Congo. In 1968, he established and commanded the Ethiopian Marine Corps.

After the **Derg** seized power (1974), Goshu entered the government and served as minister of education and chairman of the **National Literacy Campaign** (1978–1983) and foreign minister (1983–1986). In October 1986, he resigned from the government to protest the Derg's harsh policies. Goshu then went to the United States, where he became a Peace Fellow at the U.S. Institute for Peace, Washington, D.C. (1988–1990). On 21–22 March 1992, he helped to found the

Ethiopian Medhin Democratic Party in Alexandria, Virginia, to advance the cause of political pluralism and democracy in Ethiopia. Goshu's association with the **Mengistu Haile Mariam** regime undermined potential support for Medhin. As a result, his efforts to build a common front against what he termed the **Tigray People's Liberation Front/Eritrean People's Liberation Front** dictatorship failed. In August 1996, Goshu resigned from Medhin for personal reasons, but critics maintained that he was sacked for embezzling funds.

On 22 February 2003, the Paris-based *Indian Ocean Newsletter* reported that Goshu had joined Cheru Terefeis, an Atlanta, Georgia, businessman. The two proposed to abandon the armed struggle against **Addis Ababa** and to adopt a new political platform through a possible alliance with the Ethiopian Democratic Party. This split Medhin, as a faction led by Seyoum Gelaye, the party's president, pledged to continue fighting for a change of government in Ethiopia. On 26 April 2003, the *Indian Ocean Newsletter* declared that Goshu had created a new party called Medhin Congress, with the goal of returning to Ethiopia to lead a "pacifist and legal" battle against the **Ethiopian People's Revolutionary Democratic Front**.

GRAZIANI, RODOLFO (1882–1955). Soldier, colonial governor, and viceroy of **Africa Orientale Italiana** (AOI) (22 May 1936–21 December 1937). Born on 11 August 1882 in Follettino, Frosinone, a town in central Italy near Rome. Educated in Rome. In 1903, Graziani joined the Italian army and served with the First Pomegranates of Sardinia. He subsequently received postings to Eritrea (1908–1913) and Libya (1914, 1930–1934). Graziani then served as governor of Italian Somalia (1935–1936), from where he launched an offensive into Ethiopia. On 8 May 1936, his troops occupied **Harar**. Two weeks later, Graziani replaced **Pietro Badoglio** as the AOI's viceroy.

During June–July 1936, Italian dictator Benito Mussolini ordered Graziani to execute all captured Ethiopian guerrillas, use poison gas to end the Ethiopian rebellion, and implement a policy of "terror and extermination" against the Ethiopian rebels and their supporters. Graziani complied and quickly became known as the "hyena" and "butcher of **Addis Ababa**." By February 1937, he had eliminated the remnants of Ethiopia's **armed forces**. However, the **patriots** continued to oppose the Italian presence in Ethiopia.

On 19 February 1937, two Eritreans (Abraha Deboueh and Moges Asgedom) hurled grenades at Graziani, who had been at a palace reception. He sustained minor injuries. On 19–21 February 1937, the Italians retaliated by massacring thousands of Ethiopians. On 1 March 1937, Graziani, who recently had been released from the hospital, ordered additional executions in Harar and elsewhere. On 26 December 1937, Mussolini, who realized that such tactics had failed to improve the security situation, recalled Graziani and named **Amedeo di Savoia,** Duke of Aosta, as the new viceroy.

On 31 October 1939, Graziani returned to office as army chief of staff. On 28 June 1940, Mussolini transferred him to Libya to command the invasion of Egypt, but Graziani retired after the British victory in Cyrenaica at Beda Fomm. In 1943, he joined the Nazi-led occupation government of Italy. He remained active in supporting neo-Fascists in Italy until his death in Rome on 11 January 1955. *See also* CHEMICAL WEAPONS.

GREATER SOMALIA. Greater Somalia is a term associated with Mogadishu's attempts to incorporate the **Somali**-inhabited regions of neighboring Djibouti, Ethiopia, and Kenya into a Greater Somalia governed by Mogadishu. Somali dictator Siad Barre (1969–1991) underscored this goal by providing support to rebel groups like the **Western Somalia Liberation Front** and the **Ogaden National Liberation Front** and subsequently by deploying the Somali National Army into the **Ogaden**. Such adventurism led to the **Ogaden War (1964)** and the **Ogaden War (1977–1978).** Despite Barre's downfall and the collapse of the Somali nation-state, Ethiopia remains concerned that a reunified Somalia would advocate a Greater Somalia policy. Additionally, Ethiopia fears that Somali-based Islamic extremist groups like al-Ittihad al-Islami (Unity of Islam) will stir up trouble in the Ogaden. As a result, **Addis Ababa** seeks to keep its neighbor weak and divided by occasionally deploying units from its **armed forces** into Somalia to support its clients and by providing financial and military aid to Somali warlords, who are continually battling one another for economic and political gain. *See also* SOMALI PEOPLE AND LANGUAGE; AFAR REGION; HAUD; ISLAM; SOMALI REGION.

GULT. A **land tenure** system among the **Amhara**, **Tigrayans**, and, with modifications, other groups. The emperor or his representative granted *gult* rights to people as a reward for service to the kingdom or to the **Ethiopian Orthodox Church** or monasteries as endowments. A holder of gult rights usually collected tribute, a portion of which went to the emperor, and demanded labor from those on the land over which he held rights. In 1975, the **Derg** abolished the gult system.

GUMUZ PEOPLE AND LANGUAGE. The Gumuz live on both sides of the Ethiopia-Sudan border. They extend south from the border town of **Metemma** into **Gojam** and east toward **Gondar** town. They number perhaps 100,000, the majority living inside Ethiopia and others in Sudan. Over the years, expansion by neighboring ethnic groups reduced the area traditionally inhabited by the Gumuz. Crops grown by the Gumuz include cereals, vegetables, sesame, and tobacco. **Women** work in the fields and have a right to half the crops. The Gumuz also raise cattle, sheep, goats, and fowl. They hunt with a bow and arrow and women do the fishing. The Gumuz are polygynous. They paint their bodies with red ochre, perforate the nose, and make two or three horizontal cuts on the cheeks. The Gumuz are almost blue black in appearance. They believe in spirits and the power of the souls of evil men. They venerate trees and bury their dead immediately after death. Gumuz is a Nilo-Saharan **language** that belongs to the isolated Koma language group, which tends to reflect few Nilotic affinities. It has numerous dialects.

GURAGE PEOPLE AND LANGUAGE. Constituting about 2 percent of Ethiopia's population, the Gurage are essentially of **Sidama** stock, and Sidama tribes once inhabited the area where they now live. In the seventh century, the Sidama were decimated or absorbed by groups from the northern **highlands** and later by **Oromo** moving west and north. Additional 14th-century invasions by Semitic Ethiopians from the northern highlands led to the ancestors of present-day Gurage. Over centuries, the Sidama and Semitic invaders intermarried to produce the Gurage; their physical characteristics tend to resemble those of the Sidama. The Gurage speak Guragina, a Semitic **language** influenced by Sidama, a Cushitic substratum language of South Ethiopic. There are numerous dialects that correspond roughly to the political and geographical divisions of Gurage tribes.

Today, the Gurage are concentrated in a relatively small area to the west of Lakes Zwai, Langano, and Shala. Most are herders or farmers. Their **food** and culture are linked closely to the *ensete* or false banana plant. Gurage huts are especially distinctive and sometimes have attractively decorated doors. The Gurage have developed a reputation as particularly clever businesspeople and are skilled in crafts. They are also generally hardworking and many are seasonal laborers in the highlands. Most remain, however, stuck in **poverty**. They are Christian, Muslim, or animist, depending on the area where they live. Two of the most authoritative studies on the Gurage are William A. Shack's *The Gurage: A People of the Ensete Culture* and Gabreyesus Hailemariam's *The Guragüe and Their Culture.*

– H –

HADDIS ALEMAYEHU (c. 1910–2003). Born in the Debre Marcos district of **Gojam** Province on 15 October 1910, Haddis grew up with his mother, as his father worked away from home as a priest and took another wife. He received a *qene* education in traditional **poetry**. Haddis then attended several schools in **Addis Ababa**, including the Swedish Mission school (1925–1927), Tafari Makonnen School, and Ecole Impériale Menelik II. He wrote his first play during this period. In the early 1930s, Haddis returned to Gojam, where he worked as a customs clerk and school headmaster before moving to a teaching position at Debre Marcos. Haddis fought during the **Italian-Ethiopian War (1935–1936)** until he was captured and sent to the island of Ponzo in the western Mediterranean and then to the island of Lipari, near Sardinia. Freed by Allied forces, Haddis returned to Ethiopia (1943).

After brief stints in the Department of Press and Propaganda and Ministry of Foreign Affairs, he became the Ethiopian consul in **Jerusalem** (1945–1946). Haddis then served as a delegate to the International Telecommunications Conference in Atlantic City, New Jersey (1946). Afterwards, he received a posting to the Ethiopian mission in Washington, D.C., and at the United Nations (1946–1950). His next assignment was at the Ethiopian Ministry of Foreign Affairs (1950–1956), first as director general and then as vice minister. During 1956–1960, Haddis served as Ethiopia's representative to the UN.

Upon his return to Ethiopia, Haddis briefly worked as minister of education (1960) followed by appointment as ambassador to Britain and the Netherlands (1960–1965). After his recall to Ethiopia, Haddis, who was not in good health, preferred not to reenter government service. Reluctantly, he agreed to become minister of planning and development (1965–1966) and also served in the Ethiopian Senate (1968–1974). During the first two years of the **Derg** regime, Haddis served as a member of the "advisory body" that had been created to replace the dissolved **parliament**. However, he declined the Derg's offer to become prime minister, thus removing himself from any meaningful role in government.

In the meantime, he had revived his literary career. In 1965, he published *Fikir Eske Mekabir*, his most famous novel, about love in feudal Ethiopia. He subsequently published several other novels in **Amharic**. In 1999, **Addis Ababa University** awarded Haddis an honorary doctorate for his literary accomplishments. H died on 6 December 2003.

HADEYA KINGDOM. The Hadeya or Hadya kingdom was located in southwestern Ethiopia and inhabited by people known today as the **Hadiyya**. The *Kebra Nagast*, which contains the history of the Solomonic line of Ethiopian kings and has been in existence for a thousand years, claims that Menelik I made war on the Hadeya. Although this is not necessarily a true reflection of history, it suggests that northern Ethiopians were aware of the Hadeya at an early date. In the 14th century, Hadeya probably became part of the Ethiopian empire during the reign of Emperor **Amda Seyon**. Hadeya, which was capable of raising a 40,000-man cavalry and at least twice as many foot soldiers, soon rebelled against the emperor, who deployed soldiers to restore peace and capture its king. Many men from Hadeya then joined Amda Seyon's troops. Hadeya was geographically small and its economy depended on **agriculture** and **slavery**. Its inhabitants used iron as a primitive form of **currency**.

During the reign of Emperor **Zara Yacob**, there were new political problems in Hadeya. The governor and local chiefs refused to pay taxes to the emperor, who designated new officials and sent them to Hadeya with a large army. The new governor brought the severed head of the recalcitrant former governor to Zara Yacob, who eventually established his authority over Hadeya. His successor, **Baeda Mariam I**, strengthened his ties with the kingdom by marrying Eleni, the daughter of the governor of Hadeya. This marriage linked the nominally Muslim kingdom of Hadeya with the Christian Ethiopian empire. Eleni subsequently played a major role in Ethiopian statecraft and helped bring together the Hadeya and Ethiopian dynasties. In the 1520s, Emperor **Lebna Dengel** led an expedition to Hadeya and ordered the construction of many churches and monasteries. With the help of the **Ethiopian Orthodox Church**, he reestablished Hadeya as a tributary state.

By 1531, the Muslim forces of **Ahmad ibn Ibrahim al Ghazi** reached Hadeya and gained the loyalty of the local Muslim ruler, who provided Ahmad and his senior commander with a daughter and sister respectively to cement the link. Following Ahmed's defeat and death (1543), Emperor **Galawedos**, with Portuguese support, once again brought Hadeya under Imperial control. The Hadeya ruler, a chief called Aze, joined with other nobles in a conspiracy against Emperor Sarsa Dengel (reigned 1564–1597). In 1568–1569, the emperor led an army to Hadeya and slaughtered many of Aze's soldiers. Aze eventually surrendered and received a pardon but continued to engage in treachery and was killed. In the early 17th century, a Muslim chief called Sidi ruled Hadeya. By this time, **Oromo** migrations were having a major impact on the kingdom, although it maintained its distinct identity. By the late 17th century, the king of Hadeya had submitted to the rule of **Abyssinia** and many people embraced Christianity.

HADIYYA PEOPLE AND LANGUAGE. Known by a variety of other names including Hadya and the derogatory Gudella, the Hadiyya number about one million and live in a mountainous area between the Bilate and **Omo** Rivers. The **Gurage** and **Libido** reside to the north, the **Yem** to the west, and the **Kambata** and **Alaba** to the south and east. The Hadiyya have one of Ethiopia's highest **population** densities. Until the late 17th century, they lived in an independent **Hadeya kingdom**. The inhabitants were either assimilated by the **Oromo** or moved to their present homeland. Until the late 19th century, the backbone of their **economy** was cattle and barley. Following extensive military campaigns against the Hadiyya between the 1870s and the 1890s, **Menelik II** incorporated them into the Ethiopian empire. A key element of Hadiyya culture was *Fandano*, a socioreligious system that determined their way of life until the mid–20th century.

Today, the Hadiyya cultivate barley, sorghum, *ensete*, corn, and vegetables. Ensete is now a staple part of the diet and provides the flour to make bread. Although the early ruling class was nominally Muslim, it has been only since the mid–20th century that most Hadiyya converted to **Islam** or Christianity. Fandano has largely disappeared, although some Hadiyya have retained their traditional religious beliefs, which include the cult of the ancient pagan sky god known as Wa'a. They sacrifice animals to Wa'a, worship the spirits of trees, and attach great importance to rainmakers. According to tradition, any Hadiyya who kills an enemy or large animal has the right to smear his head with butter. The Hadiyya National Democratic Organization elected one person to the **House of Peoples' Representatives** in 2000. Hadiyya is an east Cushitic **language** that has 82 percent lexical similarity with Libido, 56 percent with Kambata, 54 percent with Alaba, and 53 percent with Sidamo.

HAILE GEBRESELASSIE. *See* MARATHON AND DISTANCE RUNNERS.

HAILE SELASSIE (1892–1975). Heir apparent and regent plenipotentiary (27 September 1916–2 November 1930), **negus** (7 October 1928–2 November 1930), and last emperor (3 April 1930–12 September 1974) of the 3,000-year-old Ethiopian monarchy. Born **Lij** Tafari Makonnen on 23 July 1892, at Ejersa Goro, near **Harar**. After learning **Ge'ez** and the psalms of David, he studied under a French-speaking tutor named Abba Samuel, who belonged to the French Capuchin mission in Harar.

Tafari began his public career on 1 November 1905, when his father, **Ras Makonnen Walda Mikael**, conferred the title of **dajazmach** on him and appointed him governor of Gara-Muletta in Harar Province. In 1906, Tafari returned to **Addis Ababa** and enrolled in the Ecole Impériale Menelik II. On 9 May 1906, he became titular governor of Selale, which enabled him to continue his studies. Subsequent appointments as governor included Darrassa, **Sidamo** Province (April 1908), Harar (3 March 1910), and Kefe (13 August 1916). On 27 September 1916, Empress **Zawditu Menelik** proclaimed Tafari heir apparent and regent plenipotentiary and promoted him to **ras**.

During his regency, Tafari assumed responsibility for the country's **foreign policy**. On 23 August 1928, he succeeded in securing Ethiopia's admission to the **League of Nations**. On 16 April 1924, Tafari departed Addis Ababa on a tour that included stops in Egypt, Palestine, France, Belgium, Luxembourg, Holland, Germany, Sweden, Italy, Britain, and Greece. After returning to Addis Ababa on 4 September 1924, he continued to work toward enhancing Ethiopia's standing in the world. On 2 August 1928, Tafari concluded a 20-year treaty of friendship with Italy.

Domestically, he took an important step to stabilize Ethiopia on 22 October 1916, when, along with **Fitawrari** Habte Giyorgis (1851–1926), **Kassa Halyu**, Tafari led an army that defeated a force commanded by **Mikael Ali Abba Bula**, who was seeking to restore his son, **Iyasu Mikael**, to the throne. He also took steps to end **slavery** as a precondition for membership in the League of Nations. Tafari supported numerous modernization projects, including an initiative to open schools in Addis Ababa and other towns and cities.

On 7 October 1928, Empress Zawditu crowned him negus. At the same time, conservative elements in the palace lost their influence and ability to protect the monarch. As a result, Empress Zawditu lost control of the government. Thus, Tafari consolidated his power in Addis Ababa. However, he found it difficult to pacify the provinces. Ras Gugsa Wale (1877–1930), governor of **Bagemder Province** and a particularly troublesome adversary, neglected to undertake a military campaign against **Lij** Iyasu Mikael. As a result, Tafari defeated and killed Ras Gugsa at the Battle of Wadia on 31 March 1930. Two days later, Empress Zawditu died, thereby paving the way for Tafari's accession to the throne. On 2 November 1930, he was coronated under the name Haile Selassie I.

Between his coronation and the outbreak of the **Italian-Ethiopian War (1935–1936)**, the emperor continued efforts to modernize Ethiopia. Among other things, he approved the **constitution (1931)** that created a bicameral **Parliament**, with a Senate appointed by the monarch from among the nobility and a Chamber of Deputies nominated by the Senate. However, the Parliament, which had little real power, served only as a consultative council. By the time of the Italian invasion, it largely had ceased to exist. Another major undertaking focused on the establishment and training of modern **armed**

forces. To achieve this goal, Haile Selassie recruited Belgian instructors for the **Imperial Body Guard** and Swiss officers to train the army. There also was one threat to the emperor. In 1932, Lij Iyasu escaped from detention at Fitche and endeavored to reach Debre Marcos, where he planned to issue a proclamation reclaiming the throne. However, elements loyal to Haile Selassie quickly captured the pretender and sent him back to jail.

After a period of exile in Britain after the Italian invasion of Ethiopia, the emperor returned to East Africa and helped to organize the resistance. In 1941, he reclaimed the throne and, for the next several decades, continued to pursue his modernization strategy. On 19 August 1950, Haile Selassie told the *Christian Science Monitor* that his main priorities included expanding **education**, **telecommunications**, and employment. He reorganized the local administration, ostensibly to improve efficiency but also to increase his power at the expense of the local nobility.

Politically, the **Ethiopian-Eritrean Federation** expanded the Ethiopian empire but led to a 30-year insurgency that eventually claimed some 65,000 lives. The United States became a major source of military and economic aid and, in return, received Kagnew Station in Asmara, an installation that served as a listening post for Africa and the Middle East.

The **coup attempt (1960)** shook the monarchy to its foundation. His declining popularity fueled speculation that the emperor's days were numbered. In 1973, his position worsened after he dismissed the existence of a large-scale **famine**. The armed forces and workers also became more restive as evidenced by a series of military mutinies and labor strikes. On 12 September 1974, the **Derg** deposed Haile Selassie.

On 27 August 1975, government officials announced that he had died in captivity of "circulatory failure" after prostate surgery. Actually, the Derg had executed him for failing to disclose information about his foreign bank accounts. After seizing power in 1991, the **Ethiopian People's Revolutionary Democratic Front** revealed the truth about Haile Selassie's death. On 5 November 2000, the emperor's remains were interred in a crypt inside Trinity Cathedral, Addis Ababa, as several thousand Ethiopians witnessed the ceremony. The current government stayed away, reminding Ethiopians of the emperor's "oppression and brutality." To this day, scholars continue to debate whether Haile Selassie was a medieval autocrat or a modern reformer or a combination of the two.

HAILE SELASSIE I UNIVERSITY. *See* EDUCATION, UNIVERSITY.

HAMER PEOPLE AND LANGUAGE. The Hamer people are one of Ethiopia's smaller but more distinctive ethnic groups. Numbering perhaps 35,000, the Hamer occupy a large area in South Omo that stretches north of **Lake Turkana** from the **Omo River** to Lake **Chew Bahir**. Dimeka and Turmi are typical Hamer towns. Traditionally, the Hamer were pastoralists and still take pride in their cattle, although **agriculture** now plays a greater role in their subsistence. They speak an Omotic **language**. Hamer **women** are noted for their elaborate body decoration. They adorn themselves with thick plaits of ochre-colored hair hanging in a heavy fringe, leather skirts decorated with cowries, beaded bands hanging from their waists, and copper bracelets fastened around their arms. They also make thick welts on their body by cutting themselves and treating the wound with ash and charcoal. Men undergo body scarring and paint themselves with white chalk paste before a **dance** or ceremony. Clay hair buns on the head of some men suggest they killed a person or dangerous animal within the past year. One of the most important events in Hamer culture is the bull-jumping ceremony in which the initiate has to jump from the back of one bull to that of 30 others lined up in a row and then repeat the feat several times.

HANDICRAFTS. Ethiopia's handicrafts are as rich and varied as the numerous ethnic and cultural groups that produce them. Ethiopians use wood for practical implements such as tools, utensils, and furniture. The simple wooden plow is ubiquitous in the central and northern **highlands** while the digging stick is more common in the southern areas. A round, bored stone fits over the haft of the digging stick to give it weight and durability. Ethiopians fashion wood into many hand tools, drinking vessels, butter jars, spoons, combs, meat boards, foot washers, chairs, beds, stools, drink stands, chests, etc. The **Oromo** who live around **Jimma** and **Wollega** are famous for their distinctive stools and chairs and elaborate carved beds. They carve each stool and chair from a single piece of wood. Carved wooden neck rests are popular in various parts of the country, especially the south and lowland areas. They permit their owners to rest or sleep on the ground without disturbing their hair. Folding wooden bookstands are popular among both Christian and Muslim Ethiopians. Richly decorated, they are used for study and carrying holy books. Carved wooden statuary is not as highly developed in Ethiopia as it is in many other parts of Africa. The **Konso** tribe is well known, however, for its woodcarvings that symbolize the achievements of an individual after death.

Ethiopian potters are mostly **women** and receive little respect for their handiwork. The quality of the pottery is often very low. This was not always the case. Ethiopians produced exquisite pottery in ancient **Axum** and apparently used a proper kiln. Pottery styles are similar throughout the central and northern highlands. There is greater variation in the south and southwest. In parts of **Gambela** and Wollega, the potters make an attractive range of globular pots, often intricately decorated. Although virtually all of the **Falasha** Jews have left for Israel, their tradition of primitive ceramic statuary continues near **Gondar**. Modeled in black terra cotta, the small statuettes depict the life of people and animals.

Leather is widely used in handicrafts. The nomads of the eastern and northern deserts and inhabitants of the Omo valley wear leather skirts. They also rely on leather water bags and buckets. Leather is used for the baskets slung on the side of donkeys and camels for carrying water and dry goods. Ethiopians make shoes and baby carriers from leather. Leather thongs are in common use for binding, and leather often covers basketry, pottery, or wooden containers to give them more strength. Cowhides even serve as bedding and roofing material in some areas.

Weaving in **cotton** and wool takes place throughout highland Ethiopia. Wool from highland sheep becomes blankets, hats, bags, and mats. Ethiopians spin cotton into thick and lumpy togas worn by both men and women in the cold highlands. It also becomes fine cloth for producing the beautiful national dress of highland women. The dress designs and colorful borders vary from one location to another but they all reflect superior craftsmanship. The **Dorze** people in particular are associated with expert weaving. They live in a small area of the Gemu-Gofa highlands and speak their own dialect of **Sidamo**. Dorze has become synonymous with weaver as a result of their expertise. Working in a cottage **industry**, housewives spin the cotton and then pass it on to a weaver for making clothes.

Basketry takes many forms in Ethiopia. Ethiopians make numerous items from woven reeds, grass, and even string. Highland shepherds avoid the driving rain by taking cover under woven-straw hooded coats that can be worn like a coat or used as a shelter. Farmers use woven-reed or -straw winnowing and drying trays, some patterned with colored grasses. Woven baskets are common throughout the highlands. Ethiopians near **Kafa** make baskets from bamboo, palm, and *ensete* leaves and fibers. In parts of Kafa, the coil building technique is augmented by flat strand weaving to produce raffia mats, bags, and screens. Near Jimma round lunch boxes and large clothesbaskets are a specialty. The **Gurage people** produce a wide range of wickerwork, including furniture, fences, granaries, mats, bags, and baskets.

The most famous baskets in Ethiopia, however, come from **Harar**. Made mostly of grass and straw, they are characterized by several ingenious geometric patterns woven into the coils and accentuated by bright, contrasting colors. Harar basketry is always made by continuous coils of grass bound with transverse fibers of various colors and designs. The resulting designs are normally geometric, but floral patterns also occur. Harar baskets come in many shapes and sizes. Harari also make dishes, plates, and decorative wall covers. The most famous of the Harar basket forms is the table or *mesob*, which is designed to serve *injera*. The table is made of a wide, shallow, colorful basket with a low conical lid mounted on a hollow, tapering pedestal. Diners sit around the mesob and eat off the top of the "table."

Metalworking takes place throughout most of Ethiopia. Plowshares, hoe tips, knives, swords, spearheads, and daggers are common products. The shape of spearheads varies greatly from place to place. Ethiopians produce a wide range of spears designed for use on horseback. Since the 19th century, the local metalworking industry has produced swords for use by horse cavalry. Ethiopians usually use a low dome furnace with a double bellows of goatskin or camel bladder for smelting. Raymond A. Silverman's *Ethiopia: Traditions of Creativity* is a good illustrated account of handicrafts.

HARAR (HARER). (96,700, estimated 2002 **population**). Located about 327 miles (523 kilometers) east of **Addis Ababa** and situated on a granite hill (5,500 feet; 1,680 meters) in the **Rift Valley**'s eastern escarpment. Harar, the old part of which is surrounded by a high stonewall and flanked by 24 towers, dominates the desert plain from the **Danakil Depression** in the north to Somalia in the south. Harar is **Islam**'s fourth holiest town after Mecca, Medina, and **Jerusalem** and, during the 17th and 18th centuries, was an important center of Islamic scholarship and at one point had 99 mosques.

Some sources suggest that Arab immigrants from Yemen established Harar in the seventh century. In 1521, the Sultan of Adal, probably fearing possible attacks by the Turkish or Portuguese navy, moved his government from the Gulf of Aden port of Zeila to Harar. Soon thereafter, **Ahmed ibn Ibrahim al Ghazi** killed Abu Bakr Mohammed and seized the city. Decades of war followed, with Ethiopian Christians suffering many depredations.

Sir **Richard Burton**'s 1885 visit to Harar disguised as a Muslim nearly cost him his life as it was more difficult to evade detection as a non-Muslim in Harar than was the case during his journey to Mecca. During 1875–1885, Egypt occupied Harar. At its height, the Egyptian garrison and civil population numbered some 6,500 persons. On 25 April 1885, the last Egyptian departed Harar. However, the town did not return to government control until 13 January 1887, when **Menelik II**'s forces occupied the city. The French poet and adventurer **Arthur Rimbaud** late in the 19th century spent the final decade of his life in Harar.

For much of its early history, Harar was an important commercial crossroads. Ethiopian, Armenian, and Greek traders controlled the shipment of merchandise, especially **cotton** goods, into southern Ethiopia and the export of camels, cattle, **coffee**, ghee, guns, ivory, **khat**, mules, and skins and hides. In recent years, however, **Dire Dawa**'s **economy** has surpassed that of Harar.

After Tafari Makonnen, later **Haile Selassie**, became governor of Harar (1905), his father, **Ras Makonnen Walda Mikael**, built a palace for him outside Harar's walls. Since then, the "new town," has grown considerably and has overwhelmed the "old town," which has suffered from deterioration over the centuries. Currently, there is little architecture left that is more than 125 years old. Nevertheless,

Harar remains a major **tourist** destination because of its medieval walls and pleasant climate. In addition to the walls, points of interest include Arthur Rimbaud's house and the home where Haile Selassie lived as a child.

During the Haile Selassie and **Derg** periods, Harar was the capital of Hararge Province. Under the 1995 **constitution**, Harar and the surrounding area received the status of one of Ethiopia's regions. Although Hararis are a minority of the population in Harar, they have their own ethnic identity, **language**, and culture. *See also* ADAL SULTANATE.

HARRIS, WILLIAM CORNWALLIS (1807–1848). Soldier, diplomat, engineer, and explorer. Baptized on 2 April 1807 in Wittersham, Kent, and educated at a military school. In 1823, Harris became an engineer in Bombay. Over the next seven years, he served in similar posts in Candeish and Deesa. In 1836–1838, Harris explored parts of Southern Africa. In January 1838, he returned to India and resumed his career as an engineer.

In 1841–1843, Harris commanded an expedition to Ethiopia that sought to establish relations with the kingdom of **Shoa**. His superiors also directed him to gather commercial and scientific information and to investigate **slavery**. On 16 November 1841, he concluded a treaty of friendship and cooperation with **Sahle Selassie**, **negus** of Shoa, **Ifat**, and the **Galla**. Harris accompanied Sahle Selassie on various military campaigns to the **highlands** and **lowlands** and spent more than a year exploring **Ankober** and Angolala. One of his lasting impressions was that the **Ethiopian Orthodox Church** opposed the country's social and economic development. Harris relates his experiences and observations in his three-volume *Highlands of Ethiopia*, an essential study for understanding the early British penetration of Ethiopia.

In 1846, Harris returned to India where he eventually became superintending engineer for the northern provinces (1848). On 9 October 1848, he died of "lingering fever" in Surwur, near Poona.

HAUD. (25,000 square miles; 65,000 square kilometers in area.) The Haud is a strip of prime grazing land along the Ethiopia-Somaliland border. Traditionally, about half of Somaliland's population crossed annually into the Haud for seasonal grazing. Inhabited by Somalis, the Haud together with Ethiopia's **Ogaden** region has been central to Somalia's post-independence irredentist claims against Ethiopia.

Among other things, the **Anglo-Ethiopian Treaty (1897)** delimited the frontier between British Somaliland (now Somaliland) and Ethiopia. Neither country consulted **Somali** elders or solicited their views about the border adjustment. The Haud was the most important area, from the Somali perspective, to come under Ethiopian administration as a result of the treaty. It placed part of the Haud in Somaliland and part in Ethiopia. The grazing grounds to the northwest of the Haud and adjacent to the boundary of British Somaliland and French Somaliland (now Djibouti) became known as the **Reserved Areas**. By 1935, an Anglo-Ethiopian Boundary Commission had demarcated the boundary.

On 1 June 1936, after the fall of **Addis Ababa**, Rome established **Africa Orientale Italiana**, which created a single administration in most of the Somali-inhabited area in the Ogaden and Italian Somalia (now Somalia). After Italy's defeat (1941), London set up a **British Military Administration** (BMA) in most of the **Horn of Africa**'s Somali-inhabited areas. In 1945, **Haile Selassie**, fearing the possibility that London would support the creation of a separate Somali state that would include the Ogaden, claimed Italian Somalia as a "lost province." In Italian Somalia, the nationalist Somali Youth League rejected this claim and demanded unification of all Somali-inhabited areas, including those in Ethiopia.

On 24 July 1948, Britain and Ethiopia concluded a protocol whereby the former agreed to evacuate the greater part of the Ogaden that was restored to Ethiopian jurisdiction but preserved the BMA in the Haud and Reserved Areas. The 29 November 1954 Anglo-Ethiopian Agreement reaffirmed the 1897 treaty and set a withdrawal date (28 February 1955) of BMA liaison officers from the Haud and Reserved Areas. Another provision guaranteed the right of tribes in Ethiopia and British Somaliland to cross the frontier to graze their animals. Continued disagreement between Addis Ababa and Mogadishu over the Ogaden's status accounted for the **Ogaden War (1964)**, **Ogaden War (1977–1978)**, and numerous border clashes. *See also* see GREATER SOMALIA, ITALIAN-ETHIOPIA WAR, OCCUPIED ENEMY TERRITORY ADMINISTRATION, RODD MISSION, OGADEN, and SOMALI REGION.

HAYLU TAKLA HAYMANOT, RAS (1868–1951). Governor of **Gojam** and businessman. In 1896, Haylu began his career as governor of Mecha, a district south of **Lake Tana**. After the death of his father (1901), **Negus Takla Haymanot**, Haylu became governor of Gojam while other chiefs received the rest of his father's territories. He sought to recover these lands by accusing the chiefs of conspiring against **Menelik II**. After learning that Haylu had lied, the emperor sentenced him to death but later commuted the sentence to a five-year prison term.

In 1910, he regained his freedom, married into the royal family, and received an appointment as **ras** and resumed his duties as governor of Gojam. During his tenure, Haylu introduced monetary **taxation**, sold offices, levied his own customs fees, and required corvée on his farms that grew cash crops. He used this revenue to modernize his capital, Debre Markos, and to invest in his taxicab fleet and rental properties in **Addis Ababa**. A tribunal eventually found him guilty of mendacity, **corruption**, tax evasion, and treason. Many believed his real crime concerned his opposition to **Haile Selassie**'s efforts to centralize the government and to ensure that traditional rulers were subordinate to the monarchy. The emperor freed him just before the outbreak of the **Italian-Ethiopian War (1935–1936)**. After liberation (1941), Haylu remained in Addis Ababa. He received a comfortable pension and resumed his business career. After a long illness, he died on 2 May 1951 and was buried in Debre Markos.

HEALTH. The first recorded foreign medical practitioner to arrive in Ethiopia was João Bermudes, a barber-surgeon from Portugal, who accompanied the Portuguese embassy of 1520–1526. Numerous other medical experts of different nationalities followed. In the early 19th century, Western medicine expanded significantly. By the late 19th century, **Menelik II** underscored the importance of Western medicine by having a pharmacy and clinic at his palace. Several Italian doctors visited the country and, in 1896, the Russian Red Cross sent a medical mission to Ethiopia. The following year, the Russians established Ethiopia's first hospital. In the late 19th century, missionary doctors, nurses, and midwives also brought modern medicine to Ethiopia. **Warqnah Ishete**, a small child who was orphaned during the **Anglo-Ethiopian War**, went to India and attended the Lahore

Medical College and eventually went to Edinburgh University for further studies. Warqnah joined the British Medical Service in India (1887). At Menelik II's urging, he returned to Ethiopia in 1899. Richard Pankhurst documented Ethiopia's early medical history in *An Introduction to the Medical History of Ethiopia.*

Haile Selassie, both during his period as regent and later as emperor, consolidated the medical advances begun by Menelik II. The old Menelik II hospital, which had been staffed only by nurses, added professional administrators and trained doctors. **Missionaries**, especially those with the United Presbyterian Church of North America, stepped up their efforts in the field of health and medicine. A few hospitals and clinics appeared in the regions before the outbreak of the **Italian-Ethiopian War (1935–1936)**. Italy took over the medical system during the occupation and tended to favor care for Europeans. In 1948, Ethiopia created the Ministry of Public Health to begin the process of confronting the country's many health problems. In 1954, the government established the **Gondar** Public Health College, which is now one of three major medical universities. During the imperial period, the number of hospitals and clinics increased from 48 in 1930 to 240 in 1955. By the end of the monarchy (1974), Ethiopia had 650 health stations, 93 health centers, and 84 hospitals with 8,624 beds.

Expansion of the health sector was a **Derg** priority. Shortly after seizing power, **Mengistu Haile Mariam** announced that smallpox had been eradicated. By 1988, the Ministry of Health reported that there were 1,916 health stations, 140 health centers, and 86 hospitals with 11,000 beds. The annual output of health professionals had increased from 766 during the last years of Haile Selassie's regime to 1,627. A 10-year health plan (1985–1994) sought to strengthen all health services by increasing the number of hospital beds, health stations (3,600), and health centers (360). Such improvements were never fully realized as the government spent an increasing amount of money to ensure domestic security and to sustain the **armed forces.**

The **Ethiopian People's Revolutionary Democratic Front** (EPRDF) continued the struggle to end Ethiopia's long history of endemic disease, epidemics, and **famine** that have debilitated large segments of the **population**. Sadly, the majority of Ethiopians remain in a poor state of health. Several factors account for this. Rivers and lakes are the source of water for most Ethiopians. This water is often unsafe; it is estimated that only 25 percent of the rural population and 75 percent of the urban population have access to clean water. Malnutrition is widespread in much of Ethiopia even during a good crop year. Recurrent bouts of drought and famine magnify the problem. Health services are concentrated in the urban areas. Only about 60 percent of the population has access to any kind of health service and it is often of low quality. There is one doctor for every 40,000 Ethiopians and 87 hospitals with only 12,000 beds for 70 million people. The health care infrastructure has been crippled by more than three decades of conflict, underfunding, and neglect. Efforts to improve the situation are under way, but it will take decades to meet the challenge. Government expenditures on health care as a percentage of total expenditure, for example, increased from 3.5 percent in 1986–1987 to 4.9 percent in 1995–1996.

The primary killing diseases in Ethiopia are perinatal-maternal conditions, acute respiratory infection, malaria, nutritional deficiency for children, diarrhea, tuberculosis, and **human immuno-deficiency virus/acquired immune deficiency syndrome** (HIV/AIDS). There is wide regional variation in the pattern of diseases. Malaria, for example, is endemic in at least 70 percent of Ethiopia but does not generally occur in the higher altitudes. Although HIV/AIDS is the major killer in Ethiopia today, malaria remains the highest killer of children. Schistosomiasis and yellow fever also tend to be concentrated at lower altitudes. Venereal disease is more common in urban areas, where prostitution contributes to the problem. HIV/AIDS is increasing at a rapid rate, and, as of 2003, as many as four million people may be infected. Because of its large population, Ethiopia now has the world's third highest number of HIV-positive persons. Ethiopia is making progress on some diseases. Only about three million children have not yet been vaccinated against polio, and there have been no reported cases of polio in the past three years. The basic problem remains that Ethiopia is a poor country with a large population and relatively few medical and health personnel. *See also* ASRAT WOLDEYES; BRAIN DRAIN; BULATOVICH, ALEXANDER XAVIERY-ERICH; ZERVOS, JACOVOS G.; LAMBIE THOMAS A.; MELAKU BEYAN; WOMEN; FEMALE CIRCUMCISION.

HERUY WALDA SELASSE (1878–1938). Author, historian, civil servant, and adviser to **Haile Selassie**. Born on 7 or 8 May 1878 in Gabra Giyorgisi, Marahabete, **Shoa** Province, and educated in church music and **poetry** and European **languages**. Heruy began public life as a secretary in **Menelik II**'s palace. In 1911, Heruy traveled to Britain as a member of the Ethiopian delegation that attended King George V's coronation. In 1916, he served as director general in the **Addis Ababa** municipality, a position that enabled him to become close to the crown prince and the empress.

After **World War I**, Heruy accompanied an Ethiopian delegation to Britain and the United States "to congratulate the victors." In 1921, he became Chief Judge of the special court concerning disputes between Ethiopians and foreigners. In 1923, Heruy accompanied a delegation that went to Geneva on the occasion of Ethiopia's admission to the **League of Nations**. The following year, he went with **Ras** Tafari Makonnen, later Haile Selassie, on the latter's tour of foreign capitals.

After returning to Ethiopia, Heruy was a special adviser to Ras Tafari and then director general of the Ministry of Foreign Affairs. On 20 April 1931, he became minister of foreign affairs. On 1 October 1931, Heruy undertook a diplomatic mission to Japan, where he visited numerous towns, universities, and churches. Two years later, he became ambassador to Japan. Despite his busy schedule, Heruy agreed to become the first president of the **Ethiopian Red Cross Society** after its formation on 8 July 1935.

After the outbreak of the **Italian-Ethiopian War**, he went into exile with Haile Selassie. Apart from his government work, Heruy authored some 28 books, edited the civil and ecclesiastical code, and translated the New Testament into **Amharic**. He died on 29 September 1938 at the emperor's residence in Bath, England. There were unsubstantiated rumors that Heruy had committed suicide after the emperor had discovered that he had carried on a secret correspondence with the Italians.

HEWETT, WILLIAM NATHAN WRIGHTE (1834–1888). British naval officer. Born on 12 May 1834 in Brighton. In 1847, Hewett entered the Royal Navy and served in the Burmese War (1851). Over the next several decades, his postings included Crimea, West Africa,

North America, West Indies, China, and the East Indies. During the 1882 Egyptian War, Hewett commanded British naval operations in the **Red Sea**. On 6 February 1884, he landed at Suakin, where he became the khedive's governor.

Shortly thereafter, Hewett went to Ethiopia to arrange the evacuation of Egyptian troops from Sudan. On 7 April 1884, he departed **Massawa** for **Adwa**. His party included Mason Bey, an American-born adventurer who became the khedive's governor of Massawa; Captain Charles S. T. Speedy, who had served as an **Amharic** interpreter during the **Anglo-Ethiopian War**; and some 150 officers and escorts. On 26 May 1884, **Yohannes IV** arrived in Adwa and immediately received Hewett. On 3 June 1884, the emperor, Hewett, and Mason signed an agreement known as the **Hewett Treaty**, which ended the long-standing enmity between Egypt and Ethiopia and sought to improve relations with Britain and Egypt. After leaving Ethiopia, Hewett served as commander of the Channel fleet (1886–1888). He died on 13 May 1888.

HEWETT TREATY. The only treaty **Yohannes IV** ever signed with a foreign power. Concluded between Britain, Egypt, and Ethiopia on 3 June 1884; also known as the Tripartite Treaty (not to be confused with the 1906 **Tripartite Treaty** between Britain, France, and Italy). The Hewett Treaty was one of the most important documents Ethiopia ever signed with a foreign power insofar as it ended the enmity between Egypt and Ethiopia that had resulted in at least 16 battles during the 1832–1876 period. The treaty also sought to normalize relations with Britain and Egypt.

The treaty provided for the free transit of goods through **Massawa** to and from Ethiopia (Article I), the restoration of the Egyptian-occupied Bogos region to Ethiopia (Article II), the withdrawal of Egyptian troops from Amedib, Kassala, and Sanhit (now Keren) (Article III), Egypt's promise to facilitate the future appointments of **Abunas** for Ethiopia (Article IV), and the mutual extradition of criminals between Egypt and Ethiopia (Article V).

The Hewett Treaty had a short life as Ethiopia's interests clashed with those of Britain and Egypt. Yohannes IV believed that the treaty entitled Ethiopia to occupy Massawa once Egyptian forces had evacuated the port. However, Britain did not trust the emperor and feared that, once in Massawa, Ethiopia would seek to gain control of the strategically important **Red Sea** coastline. To thwart possible Ethiopian expansionism, Britain informed Italy that it would have no objection to its occupation of Massawa, which occurred on 5 February 1885.

HIGHLANDS. There often are references to "highland" Ethiopia or "highlanders." This term has geographical, historical, and political meaning despite the fact that it is not precisely defined. For example, **Tigrayans** and **Amhara** are generally considered to be highlanders. Historically, the highlands refers to the northern highland provinces of **Tigray**, **Gondar**, **Gojam**, **Wag**, Lasta, northern **Shoa** Province, and much of highland Eritrea, which tended to share a common political and social structure, **land tenure** system, culture, and **religion**. One of the cultural characteristics of highlanders is a desire for secrecy and in earlier times an element of xenophobia. There is also a history of trying to exercise strong political control from the center. One of the major factors in the long independence of the highlands is the fact that outsiders found the highland topography so difficult to conquer.

Geographically and culturally, the lower-lying western fringes of Tigray, Gondar, and Gojam do not qualify as highlands. At the same time, southern Shoa and significant parts of **Ilubabor**, **Kafa**, Bale, Arsi, and the mountain range from **Harar** to Asela do qualify as highlands. Although there are important distinctions among highland peoples and one should not put too much emphasis on the differences between people who live in the highlands and those who live in lower elevations, it still remains a useful way to differentiate certain characteristics. The highlands normally begin above 5,000 feet (1,525 meters) altitude. *See also* LOWLANDS.

HOARE-LAVAL PLAN. On 7–8 December 1935, British foreign secretary Sir Samuel Hoare (later Lord Templewood) and French foreign minister Pierre Laval met secretly in Paris. The two diplomats concocted a scheme to end the **Italian-Ethiopian War**, avoid allied conflict with Italy in East Africa, and defuse a possible confrontation at the **League of Nations** with Italy. Their plan involved Ethiopia ceding part of the **Ogaden** to Italy. It also acknowledged a virtual Italian protectorate in southern Ethiopia with the exception of **Ilubabor Province** and the Baro salient. In return, Ethiopia would receive an outlet to the sea at **Asab** and a land corridor through the **Danakil Depression** to the port.

The plan aroused considerable protest in the British House of Commons and the press. On 18 December 1935, Hoare resigned and **Anthony Eden** subsequently became foreign secretary. On 22 January 1936, Laval also resigned. These dramatic events caused an uproar among states whose security depended on the League of Nations because Britain and France had violated their covenant by discussing Ethiopia's dismemberment after Italy had committed an act of war. For this reason, many scholars maintain that the Hoare-Laval Plan was the League of Nations' death warrant.

HOLIDAYS, RELIGIOUS. Ethiopia celebrates numerous Ethiopian Orthodox and Muslim holidays, some of which are treated as festivals. The dates follow the standard Gregorian **calendar** rather than the Julian calendar used in Ethiopia. *Leddet* or Christmas occurs on 7 January and involves attendance at an all-night church service beginning the previous evening. On Christmas Day it is common to play traditional games and observe horse racing. *Timkat* takes place on 19 January and is the most colorful festival of the year. Also known as Epiphany, it celebrates the baptism of Christ. The celebration begins on the eve of Timkat with colorful processions. In the three-day event, the priests remove the *tabots* (symbolizing the **Ark of the Covenant** containing the Ten Commandments) from each church and bless the water of the pool or river where the celebration of Christ's baptism occurs the next day. The third day is devoted to the Feast of Saint Michael the Archangel, one of Ethiopia's most popular saints. Ethiopians wear their finest clothes, consume traditional **food** and drink, and give gifts to children.

Ethiopian Orthodox faithful fast from the Thursday evening before Good Friday until the Easter service on Sunday. Orthodox Easter or *Fasika* ends a 55-day vegetarian fast. Good Friday and Easter can fall in March or April. Ethiopian New Year, also known as *Enkutatash* or "gift of jewels," is on 11 September. According to legend, when the Queen of Sheba returned from **Jerusalem**, her chiefs welcomed her back by replenishing her treasury with jewels. The holiday includes the Feast of Saint John the Baptist. After dark on New Year's Eve, Ethiopians light fires outside their houses.

Meskel or "Finding of the True Cross" is second in importance to Timkat. The feast commemorates the discovery by Empress Helena, the mother of Constantine the Great (c. 274–337), of the cross used to crucify Jesus. The event first took place in the year 326 during March but is now celebrated on 27 September. Many rites observed during the festival are connected to the legend of Empress Helena. Yellow daisies or Meskel flowers, which are prolific in the **highlands** at this time of year, are prominent in the ceremonies. The festival begins by planting a tree on Meskel eve in the town square or village marketplace. Bonfires also are a hallmark of the celebration.

Although it is not an official holiday, many Ethiopian Orthodox celebrate the Feast of Saint Gabriel or Kullubi. The 19th day of each Ethiopian month is devoted to Saint Gabriel, the archangel who protects homes and churches, but the most colorful celebrations occur on 28 July and 28 December. The December festivities culminate in a pilgrimage to Saint Gabriel's Church at Kullubi. **Ras Makonnen Walda Mikael** founded a small church at Kullubi to thank Archangel Gabriel for Ethiopia's victory at the **Battle of Adwa**. In 1962, **Haile Selassie** built the cathedral, which continues to attract worshipers and **tourists**. The festival of the church of Maryam Zion is unique to **Axum** and occurs in late November. The church tabot, said by many to be the original Ark of the Covenant, is brought out, accompanied by singing and dancing.

The dates for **Islamic** holidays change each year as they are determined by the lunar calendar. Those officially recognized as holidays in Ethiopia are Eid al-Fitr (end of Ramadan), Eid al-Adha, and the birthday of the Prophet Mohammed. Ramadan is one of the 12 months of the lunar calendar. It is the month in which the first Koranic verses were revealed to Mohammed and in which Mohammed's small band of followers achieved the first important military success at the battle of Badr (624). Muslims are required to refrain from eating, smoking, drinking, and pleasures of the flesh from first to last light during Ramadan. Each day of Ramadan ends with *fitr* or the breaking of the fast. The Eid al-Fitr feast marks Ramadan's final day, after which life for Muslims returns to normal. Eid al-Adha or festival of the sacrifice commemorates Abraham's willingness to sacrifice his son. Ethiopia also celebrates the Prophet Mohammed's birthday.

HOLIDAYS, SECULAR. Ethiopia celebrates four secular holidays. The first is Victory of Adwa Day and takes place on 2 March. It commemorates **Menelik II**'s victory over the Italians at the **Battle of Adwa** (1896). Ethiopian **Patriots** Victory Day, also known as Liberation Day, celebrates the Allied occupation of **Addis Ababa** on 6 April 1941. Like most nations, Ethiopia observes International Labor Day on 1 May. The final secular holiday occurs on 28 May and marks the fall of the **Derg** (1991).

HORN OF AFRICA. A geopolitical term that includes at a minimum Ethiopia, Sudan, Eritrea, Djibouti, and Somalia. The Horn of Africa takes its name from the point of Somalia that juts into the Gulf of Aden and the Indian Ocean. These five countries are about the size of Europe. Although Kenya and Uganda are usually considered part of East Africa, they also have important commercial and political links to the countries of the Horn of Africa and are sometimes included for discussion purposes. All seven countries are members of the regional development and political organization known as the Intergovernmental Authority on Development (previously known as the Intergovernmental Authority on Drought and Development). In 1994, the Bill Clinton administration sought to deal with the unrelenting conflicts and **food** shortages in a 10-country region by creating the Greater Horn of Africa Initiative, which added Tanzania, Rwanda, and Burundi to the mix. Although the initiative fell short of expectations, the term "Greater Horn" has become part of the lexicon.

Separated by the **Red Sea** from the Arabian Peninsula, the Horn links Africa to the Middle East through a combination of its Judeo-Christian and Islamic legacies. The Horn is dominated numerically by Cushitic-speaking peoples who live in the **lowlands** and foothills while Semitic-speaking peoples of the Ethiopian and Eritrean **highlands** have traditionally held political power in those two countries. Although the discovery of oil in Sudan may change the equation, all the countries are poor, subject to periodic and sometimes devastating **famine**, and are not well endowed with natural resources.

During the past 50 years, the Horn has been one of the world's most troubled regions. Except for a 10-year hiatus, civil war has raged in Sudan since 1955. Although Eritrea finally concluded successfully a long-standing war of independence from Ethiopia in

1991, the **Ethiopian-Eritrean War (1998–2000)** plunged them back into conflict. It took Ethiopian liberation groups 17 years to overthrow the **Derg**, which, in turn, had deposed **Haile Selassie** in a bloody coup in 1974. Ethiopia also fought the **Ogaden War (1964)** and **Ogaden War (1977–1978)** with Somalia. Several less significant security issues continue to confront Ethiopia. Until recently, Djibouti was plagued by a civil war by three militant **Afar** groups that had organized themselves under the banner of the Front pour la Restauration de l'Unité et de la Démocratie. After a horrible civil war, the Siad Barre government collapsed in 1991, and Somalia has been a failed state ever since. Various countries in the Horn periodically join together to put pressure on a third country, only to change the alignment after several years. The Horn desperately needs an extended period of peace so that economic development can proceed unimpeded.

HOUSE OF FEDERATION. *See* PARLIAMENT.

HOUSE OF PEOPLES' REPRESENTATIVES. *See* PARLIAMENT.

HOUSING. *See* SHELTER.

HOZO PEOPLE AND LANGUAGE. The Hozo live in a small enclave near the village of Begi (Beigi) near the Sudan border between the Dabus (Yabus) and Daka Rivers. The **Seze** live to the north, the **Kwegu** to the west, and the **Oromo** to the south and east. Some 3,000 Hozo live in about 50 villages. They speak an Omotic **language** that is related to but separate from **Bambassi**. Afan Oromo is the lingua franca, although Hozo have some negative attitudes toward the language. Very few Hozo speak **Amharic** or Arabic.

HUMAN IMMUNODEFICIENCY VIRUS/ACQUIRED IMMUNE DEFICIENCY SYNDROME (HIV/AIDS). In 1985, Dr. Seyoum Ayehunie, who was associated with African AIDS Initiative, diagnosed Ethiopia's first HIV/AIDS case. However, the Ethiopian Ministry of Health has claimed that it had recorded the first HIV/AIDS case the previous year. Since the mid-1980s, the disease has spread rapidly among Ethiopia's 70 million **population**. By late 1993, Ethiopia's National AIDS Prevention and Control Office estimated that 43,000 people had AIDS, although hospitals had reported only 8,735 cases, and up to 500,000 people had the HIV virus, which causes the disease. By late 2001, there were an estimated 2.7 million Ethiopians infected with HIV/AIDS. This places Ethiopia behind South Africa and India worldwide. More than 7 percent of the sexually active population is HIV positive. The death toll since the outbreak of HIV/AIDS has been more than two million. An estimated one million children have lost one or both parents to the disease. Average life expectancy in Ethiopia could fall to 39 years as a result of HIV/AIDS.

As it became increasingly obvious that HIV/AIDS was taking a serious toll on Ethiopians, domestic and international nongovernmental organizations formulated several **health** and prevention programs. Ethiopian medical authorities, in conjunction with officials from various donor nations, devised a strategy to help control the spread of this disease by improving Ethiopia's ability to diagnose and treat sexually transmitted diseases. Medical authorities also created AIDS education units, promoted the use of condoms, encouraged behavioral research to understand how awareness causes behavioral change, and monitored the spread of AIDS and the transmission of the HIV virus. Despite such laudable activities, the country's lack of commitment and resources hampered efforts to combat the disease.

By 1999, President **Negaso Gidada** had become an active government spokesman for HIV/AIDS. The patriarch of the **Ethiopian Orthodox Church**, **Abuna Paulos Gebre-Yohannes**, launched a major prevention campaign using the church's vast resources. Donor countries like the United States also participated in the anti-HIV/AIDS campaign. The Packard Foundation adapted some of its population program to the HIV/AIDS pandemic. In April 2000, **Addis Ababa** created a National HIV/AIDS Council and obtained a $60 million low-interest loan from the **World Bank**.

There are many challenges facing the control of HIV/AIDS in Ethiopia. The country's **transportation** and **telecommunications** infrastructure is limited and/or backward. The health care system is fragile and poorly equipped. The human capacity problem in the health sector is even more serious. There is one doctor for every 40,000 Ethiopians and those doctors tend to be concentrated in **Addis Ababa** and other major towns. The biggest obstacle to establishing an effective anti-HIV/AIDS strategy is the stigma attached to the disease. Although there is a willingness to discuss HIV/AIDS openly as a national health problem, there is an enormous reluctance to acknowledge it at the personal level. Persons found through blood donations to be HIV positive, for example, are normally not told of their condition.

Ethiopia's efforts to combat HIV/AIDS focuses primarily on prevention and communication. Anti-HIV/AIDS clubs are common in the high schools, and the media are encouraged to talk about the issue. There has been little attention, however, to HIV/AIDS counseling, and treatment with antiretroviral drugs was not even legal until 2001. The Ethiopian **armed forces** and **Ethiopian Airlines** have devised programs to help come to terms with this problem. The HIV-positive incidence in the armed forces is less than in the general population. The fact remains, however, that Ethiopia has been late in tackling the problem, and this will have a negative impact on social and economic development before the rate of increase starts to decline. *See also* HEALTH.

HUMAN RIGHTS. When viewed from the perspective of the United Nations Declaration of Human Rights, Ethiopia's human rights record traditionally has been poor. Beginning with the imperial government, all Ethiopian governing systems have had a strong authoritarian streak and have shown little concern for human rights as they are understood in Western liberal democracies. The worst abuses in the past century occurred during the Italian occupation (1936–1941) and the **Derg** regime (1974–1991). Both periods witnessed mass arrests, torture, summary executions, random shootings, and massacres to ensure political control. The Italians also used **chemical weapons** on noncombatants.

Although the situation has improved somewhat since the **Ethiopian People's Revolutionary Democratic Front** (EPRDF) came to power in 1991, the country's human rights record remains poor. However, on 10 October 1991, the EPRDF permitted the establishment of the Ethiopian Human Rights Council. This organization has been critical of the EPRDF's human rights practices. Other groups like Amnesty International and Human Rights Watch also have criticized Ethiopia's human rights record. The EPRDF, which prefers to focus on the progress made since the Derg's fall, is highly defensive about public criticism.

In the **elections (2000)**, most opposition political parties competed, but due to lack of funds, unequal access to government-controlled **media**, and weak political organization, they contested only 20 percent of the seats to the federal **parliament**. The EPRDF and affiliated parties won 518 of the 547 seats. According to international and local observers, the elections were generally free and fair in most areas although there were serious irregularities in the **Southern Nations, Nationalities, and People's Region**. The chairman of the Southern Ethiopian People's Democratic Coalition claimed that government forces had killed at least 11 supporters in the period leading up to the elections.

Ethiopia's **judiciary** is weak, understaffed, and overburdened but continues to show signs of independence. It has also made progress in reducing a huge backlog of cases. On 12 July 1999, for example, the High Court in **Addis Ababa** handed down its first verdict in the mass trial of more than 5,000 members of the former Marxist regime, all of whom had been charged with crimes against humanity. The court sentenced former minister of agriculture Geremew Deble to eight years in prison.

According to the 2001 human rights report on Ethiopia issued by the U.S. Department of State, security forces committed a number of extrajudicial killings and occasionally beat and mistreated detainees. Arbitrary arrest and detention and prolonged pretrial detention remained problems. The government continued to detain persons suspected of sympathizing with or being members of the **Oromo Liberation Front**. Thousands of suspects remained in detention without charge. The Special Prosecutor's Office has charged more than 5,000 persons with crimes during the Derg regime. Some of the accused persons have been indicted and arraigned, and testimony of victims is being heard in open court. Most detainees have been held in custody for seven or eight years awaiting trial and judgment. There has been no improvement in longstanding poor conditions in prisons.

Police often ignore the law regarding search warrants. The government has restricted freedom of the press and continued to detain or imprison journalists. On 9 April 2002, the Paris-based Reporters sans Frontières announced that the Ethiopian authorities had jailed three journalists just weeks after Ethiopian prisons had been declared free of journalists. Journalists continue to practice self-censorship although there is a surprising amount of reporting highly critical of government policies. There also have been some improvements in the registration process for nongovernmental organizations and the atmosphere in which they work. The government has yet to establish the new Human Rights Commission and the Office of the Ombudsman. The government generally respects freedom of **religion**. Those incidents that occur tend to reflect problems at the local level.

Discrimination and violence against **women** and abuse of children are long-standing societal problems that the government tries to discourage. It also supported efforts to eliminate the widespread practice of female genital mutilation and other harmful traditional practices. The exploitation of children for economic and sexual purposes together with child labor remains a problem. There are occasional reports of forced labor, including forced child labor, **slavery**, and trafficking in persons. *See also* FEMALE CIRCUMCISION.

HYDROCARBONS. Ethiopia currently does not produce any hydrocarbons and imports two million metric tons annually at a cost of about $221 million. Most imports come from Saudi Arabia and the Gulf states. In 2003, Sudan began supplying some of Ethiopia's import requirement. There is an estimated 68 million cubic meters of natural gas in the politically troubled **Ogaden** of **Somali Region**. Deposits at the Calub field are thought to be especially rich. So far, no company has been willing to develop these reserves due to security concerns. Between 1930 and 1974, the U.S. Sinclair Oil Company prospected for oil in the Ogaden. In 1991 and 1994, the International Petroleum Corporation conducted explorations in **Gambela Region**. The Afar Company of Oklahoma received a concession to explore in the upper **Rift Valley**. In 2002, Ethiopia signed an agreement with a Canadian company, Pinewood, to prospect for oil in **Gambela Region**, which borders oil-rich Sudan. Ethiopia has coal deposits of almost 300 million tons. *See also* ECONOMY; HYDROPOWER.

HYDROPOWER. Ethiopia has an enormous hydropower potential (650 billion kilowatt hours [KWH] per year), but the lack of resources retards development of this valuable asset. It currently generates only about 1.2

billion KWH of electricity annually. As a result, Ethiopia has one of the lowest levels of per capita electrical consumption in the world. More than 90 percent of the energy consumed in Ethiopia comes from biomass fuels used primarily for cooking. Almost half of Ethiopia's hydropower potential is on the **Blue Nile**. Other significant contributing rivers are the **Omo**/Gibe, Baro, Akobo, **Tekeze**, **Genale,** and **Wabe Shebelle**.

In 1932, **Haile Selassie** authorized Ethiopia's first hydropower project south of **Addis Ababa** on the **Akaki River**. With a 6-megawatt capacity, this project created Lake Aba Samuel. However, the lake above the dam became choked with water hyacinth and it has not produced any power since 1970. In 1953, the government completed a project at Tis Abay on the Blue Nile near **Lake Tana** that had an 11.5-megawatt capacity.

Koka Dam, built with funds from the Italian Reparation Fund to Ethiopia for damages incurred during the **Italian-Ethiopia War**, began operation on 3 May 1960 on the **Awash River**. The facility quickly became the major electricity supplier for Addis Ababa and surrounding area. Koka Dam, which was Ethiopia's first major dam, has a 43.2-megawatt capacity. In 1962, the government created the Awash Valley Authority to act as an umbrella organization for numerous **agricultural**, agroindustrial, and hydroelectric enterprises. Projects in 1966 and 1971, known as Awash II and Awash III, each added 32 megawatts to Koka Dam's capacity. In 1973, the government commissioned a 100-megawatt plant on the Fincha River east of Addis Ababa. This project created Lake Chomen.

During the **Derg** regime, progress continued toward developing Ethiopia's hydropower capabilities. In 1989, the government commissioned hydropower projects at Melka Wakena (1989) with a 153-megawatt capacity and at Sor (1990) with a 5-megawatt capacity. With a hydropower potential of 15,000 to 30,000 megawatts, it had exploited only 360 megawatts or less than 2 percent of its potential as of 1997. Today, Fincha produces 39.5 percent of Ethiopia's hydropower; Tis Abay 28.3 percent; Melka Wakena 18.4 percent; Awash I, II, and III 13 percent; and small plants the remainder.

Development of hydropower is a priority for the current government. To achieve its goals, Ethiopia, along with the Nile basin's other riparian states, agreed to form the Technical Cooperation Committee for the Development and Environmental Protection of the Nile Basin (1992). In 1999, all these nations joined the Nile Basin Initiative, which also sought to harness the Nile River's hydropower potential.

By the early 21st century, the Ethiopian Electric Power Corporation had four major hydroelectric projects under way. On 31 May 2002, the China National Water Resources and Hydropower Engineering Corporation won the bidding to undertake a five-year, $224 million Gilgel Gibe project on the Tekeze River with a 180-megawatt capacity. There also were plans, under the aegis of the Eastern Nile Subsidiary Action Program, for two hydropower projects at Kara Dobi (Blue Nile) and Baro/Akobo/Bir Rivers that will generate about 300 megawatts. These were the first of 46 projects that Ethiopia has proposed under the Eastern Nile Subsidiary Action Program. There would be new facilities at Tis Abay II (75-megawatts), near the Blue Nile Falls, and Gojeb (153-megawatts), a major tributary of the Omo River. The fourth project aimed to rehabilitate the 100-megawatt generator at Fincha, which drains into the Blue Nile, and add a 15-megawatt unit. On 15 August 2001, Ethiopia also announced that it intended to launch a $400 million plan to build 13 power generating dams and an irrigation development project. Despite such efforts, experts maintained that Ethiopia had to increase its power generation capabilities by 25 times to meet the projected needs in 2040. *See also* ECONOMY; ENVIRONMENT; HYDROCARBONS.

– I –

IFAT SULTANATE. Ifat was located to the northwest of **Shoa** Province and became part of the Ethiopian empire in early medieval times. This Muslim territory was important because of its strategic position on the trade routes between the central **highlands** and the sea, especially the port of Zeila in present-day Somaliland. Many pastoralists who lived in the **lowlands** also passed through Ifat to graze their animals in the highlands. There were constant conflicts involving the Ethiopian highlands and Muslim Ifat. Ifat's first known ruler was Sultan Umar ibn Dunya-huz, who probably was appointed by Emperor Yekuno Amlak (reigned 1270–1285). There were periodic challenges to Ethiopian rule. About 1320, there was a disagreement between Emperor **Amda**

Seyon and the sultan that resulted in an invasion of many Muslim areas by the emperor's forces. In 1332, there was a more serious challenge that some described as a jihad. The rulers of neighboring **Dawaro** and **Hadeya kingdom** joined the **Islamic** uprising. After several battles, Amda Seyon's troops persevered, thus maintaining Imperial rule over the territories. Ifat was the richest of Ethiopia's Muslim provinces. One of the reasons for this wealth was the production of **khat**, which already was being exported to Yemen. Ifat had an infantry of about 20,000 and cavalry of some 15,000.

Amda Seyon's son, Newaya Krestos (reigned 1344–1372), followed his father's rule but became embroiled in internal Ifat politics. The situation failed to improve during the reign of his successor, Newaya Maryam (reigned 1372–1382). By the 1370s, Ifat engaged in constant warfare against the emperor's forces. For a while the sultan of Ifat had a number of military successes. Emperor **Dawit I** (reigned 1380–1412) sent a large army to Ifat and defeated the Sultan's forces. In 1415, the emperor's forces killed Sultan Sad ad-Din.

This was a turning point in Ifat's history. The empire restored control over the sultanate and its army harassed the Muslim forces for the next 20 years, causing their power to wane. The independent Ifat Sultanate soon came to an end and was largely assimilated into the Shoa-based Christian empire. Emperor Zara Yakob (1434–1468) placed Ifat under a governor and stationed imperial troops there. His successor, **Baeda Mariam**, allowed Ifat to have more autonomy but continued imperial control. By the early 16th century, Ifat had been reintegrated into the empire and many residents embraced Christianity, although those living in the lowlands near the **Awash River** remained predominantly Muslim.

Ifat reemerged as a problem during the time of **Ahmad ibn Ibrahim al Ghazi** in the neighboring **Adal sultanate**. In 1531, Ahmad's Muslim forces defeated the emperor's forces in Ifat. Ahmad entrusted Ifat's government to Awra'i Abun, who feared that he could not hold the territory against a concerted imperial counterattack. Awra'i won an initial battle against the imperial forces but had not secured all of Ifat. The Muslim rulers could not depend on Ifat's residents, many of whom had become Christians. Following Ahmad's death (1543), there was a rebellion against Ifat and the territory returned to imperial control. Under Emperor **Susneyos**, Ifat remained an appendage of Shoa but had been largely occupied by **Oromos** during the great migration.

ILG, ALFRED (1854–1916). Swiss engineer and counselor to **Menelik II**. Born on 30 March 1854 in Frauenfeld, Switzerland, and educated at Zurich Polytechnic. In April 1879, Ilg went to Ethiopia to work as a craftsman and to train Ethiopian workers. He became one of Ethiopia's first photographers. Some of his early accomplishments included building a modern bridge over the **Awash River**, constructing Menelik II's palaces in **Addis Ababa** and **Entoto**, and installing the first piped water system in Ethiopia. On 9 March 1894, Menelik II gave Ilg a concession to build and operate the **Addis Ababa–Djibouti Railway**.

In 1894, Ilg warned Menelik II of Italian plans to invade Ethiopia. After the **Battle of Adwa**, the European powers became more interested in Ethiopia, prompting Menelik II to appoint Ilg chancellor of state on 27 March 1897. His duties included receiving foreign representatives and writing diplomatic correspondence. Ilg played a significant role in the post-Adwa negotiations that led to a peace agreement with Italy. He also concluded treaties with Britain, France, and several other countries. Ilg received the title **Bitwoded**, the highest rank ever given to a foreigner. In 1906, Ilg retired from the emperor's service. On 7 January 1916, he died of a heart ailment in Switzerland.

ILUBABOR PROVINCE. Ilubabor was one of the administrative divisions during the **Haile Selassie** government and the **Derg** period. It bordered Sudan and the principal towns were **Gambela**, Gore, and Metu. After the **Ethiopian People's Revolutionary Democratic Front** reorganized the regions, what was previously Ilubabor is today most of **Gambela Region** and part of Ilubabor zone in **Oromia Region**. Ilubabor did not loom large in Ethiopian history because **Menelik II** did not incorporate it into the empire until the mid-1880s. Ilubabor remained an isolated part of Ethiopia that received minimal central government assistance.

IMPERIAL BODY GUARD. Also referred to as the Imperial Guard prior to 1929. In 1917, **Ras** Tafari Makonnen, later **Haile Selassie**, formed the Imperial Guard, which was formally under army command but reported directly to the emperor. In 1929, he engaged

Belgian military advisers to train the renamed Imperial Body Guard. Some cadets received training at France's Saint Cyr Academy. By February 1933, the Imperial Body Guard consisted of 2,100 infantry troops and 150 horsemen. By 1960, the Imperial Body Guard numbered about 6,000 personnel who were organized into nine infantry battalions equipped with light armored vehicles. The Imperial Body Guard Cadet Training Center trained officers.

Imperial Body Guard members participated in the **Italian-Ethiopian War** while its **Kagnew Battalion** served under the United Nations Command in Korea and its Tekele Brigade served in the Republic of Congo. The Imperial Body Guard also engineered the **coup attempt (1960)**. Haile Selassie ordered the execution of **Mengistu Neway**, the Imperial Body Guard commander, and reorganized the force to prevent further unrest. During **Bloody Saturday**, the **Derg** executed several Imperial Body Guard officers.

IMPERIAL TITLES. Prior to the monarchy's abolition, the primary imperial titles, with their Western equivalents, included negus nagast (king of kings) and atse (emperor). The emperor bore the title Conquering Lion of Judah and Elect of God. Nigiste nagast (queen of kings) referred to a reigning empress, who bore all the titles of a reigning emperor except atse. An empress consort (wife of a reigning emperor) bore the title of itege. Princes who were the emperor's sons or grandsons in the male line bore the title leul. Princesses who were the emperor's daughters or granddaughters in the male line or spouses of princes bore the title lielt. Grandsons in the female line generally bore the title lij, as did much of the senior aristocracy. Granddaughters in the female line bore the title emebet but generally received the title lielt upon marriage. All the emperor's sons and grandsons bore the additional title of abeto. The heads of the Houses of **Tigray** and **Gojam** and certain members of the House of **Shoa** Province also were princes with the title of leul, often in combination with the title of ras (equivalent to duke). The rulers of **Bagemder Province**, Gojam, **Shoa**, and **Wollo Province** frequently held the title of negus (king). **Yohannes IV** was the last emperor to use the title king of Zion. Most titles were not hereditary and were bestowed at the emperor's discretion. *See also* MILITARY TITLES.

IMRU HAILE SELASSIE, RAS (1892–1980). Prince, soldier, diplomat, and cousin of **Haile Selassie.** Born in November 1892 in **Shoa** Province. Educated in the household of **Ras Makonnen Walda Mikael**, the father of Ras Tafari Makonnen, later **Haile Selassie**, and at a church in Jarso outside **Harar** followed by instruction from **Catholic** teachers. He continued his education in **Menelik II**'s palace and the Ecole Impériale Menelik II in **Addis Ababa**. In 1909, Imru became the head of a small subdistrict in **Sidamo** Province and then continued to Jarso where he became governor. In 1913, he married Princess Rosemary Tsige-Mariyam; they had seven daughters and one son. During the **coup attempt (1916)** against **Lij Iyasu**, Imru supported Ras Tafari Makonnen.

Empress **Zawditu Menelik** and Regent Ras Tafari rewarded Imru by installing him as governor of Harar Province (1918–1929). During his tenure, Imru earned a reputation as a reformer by restructuring **taxation** laws, counteracting the influence of the local nobility, and supporting Tafari's progressive policies. Imru subsequently served as governor of **Wollo Province** (1929–1932), where he dealt with the aftermath of a **famine** and restored law and order. He also served as governor of **Gojam** Province (1932–1935), where he instituted reforms and received the title of ras for his performance. On 1 May 1936, Haile Selassie appointed him regent and commander in chief of the Ethiopian army. Imru also led the **patriots'** resistance movement during the **Italian-Ethiopian War**. Imru carried on the fight against the Italians after Haile Selassie had appointed him regent and had fled the country. In early March 1936, the Italians defeated Imru's army. In late 1936, Imru surrendered and the Italians interned him at Ponzo Island, where he wrote the first of his three novels.

In 1943, Allied troops freed him and he returned to Ethiopia. He served briefly as governor of **Bagemder**, where he clashed with the emperor and conservative landowners over the land reform question. Haile Selassie responded to this crisis by sending Imru to the United States as ambassador (1946–1954). Still seen by many Ethiopians as too progressive, he then served as ambassador to India (1954–1960) and the Soviet Union (now Russia) (1961).

Although he was not associated with the failed **coup attempt (1960)** against Haile Selassie, his progressive ideas did not serve him well in the subsequent political environment. Nevertheless, Imru continued to engage in political debates, especially on land reform, until the end of Haile Selassie's reign.

The **Derg** not only held Imru in high esteem for his liberal views but also decided not to detain him. As the only aristocrat never jailed, he continued to enjoy the respect of the **armed forces** until his death from natural causes in Addis Ababa on 17 August 1980. The Derg gave him a state funeral.

INDUSTRY. Prior to the 1974 revolution, foreigners established and/or owned most of Ethiopia's 273 manufacturing enterprises. The **Derg** nationalized virtually all of these companies. The **Ethiopian People's Revolutionary Democratic Front** is slowly returning them to private hands. Ethiopia's manufacturing sector contributes only about 3 percent of gross domestic product (GDP) and accounts for only about 4 percent of total exports by value. These rates are among the lowest in the world. The contribution of all industry to GDP slipped from 12 percent in 1980 to 10 percent in 1995. Although the number of manufacturing establishments in the mid-1990s was well over a million, only 642 firms employed 10 or more persons and used power machines. The remainder included cottage, informal, small-scale, and **handicraft** industries.

About 40 percent of all the small-scale, cottage, and handicraft enterprises are engaged in the **food** and beverage sector. One-third of the cottage and handicraft industries involve textiles while about one-third of the small-scale activities are in metalworking and weaving. Enterprises that employ 10 or more persons focus primarily on food and beverages, furniture and fixtures, nonmetallic mineral products and leather goods. All of the small-scale, cottage, handicraft, and informal industries are privately owned. About one-third of the large-scale industries are government owned. Approximately 45 percent of all the value added originates from manufacturing in **Addis Ababa**. **Oromia Region** accounts for another 37 percent. *See also* ECONOMY.

INSTITUTE OF ETHIOPIAN STUDIES (IES). Founded in 1963, the IES conducts, promotes, and coordinates research and publications about Ethiopia. It gives special attention to the humanities and to preserving Ethiopia's cultural heritage. The IES also organizes conferences on Ethiopian studies, manages a museum, and oversees a library with some 94,000 books, 17,000 manuscripts, 38,000 photographs, and innumerable religious icons and other artifacts. The IES also has documents written in Adare, a **language** spoken only within the walls of **Harar**. The 14th International Conference of Ethiopian Studies convened in **Addis Ababa** in 2000.

The IES's principal publication is the *Journal of Ethiopian Studies*, which has been published continuously since 1963, usually twice per year. The journal's editorial board is composed of prominent scholars and an international advisory board. The IES also publishes a quarterly bulletin that updates members on its activities. The Society of Friends of the IES supports the organization.

Dr. Richard Pankhurst served as the IES's first director (1963–1975) and remains active in the organization. Professor Stanislaw Chojnacki initiated a collection of Ethiopian books and artifacts and was the first librarian and curator of the IES's museum (1963–1975). The IES experienced a difficult time during the **Derg** regime (1974–1991) and published the *Journal of Ethiopian Studies* only once per year during most of that era. On 24 September 2001, the IES announced the beginning of a fundraising campaign to build a new $5 million library. The Society of Friends of the Institute of Ethiopian Studies, established in 1968, has played a major role in this endeavor. The old library, once **Haile Selassie**'s palace, would remain a museum. As of 2003, Professor Baye Yimam was the Institute's director.

INTERNATIONAL MONETARY FUND (IMF). The IMF, which Ethiopia joined on 27 December 1945, makes loans to member nations when they experience balance-of-payments difficulties. These loans often have conditions that require substantial internal economic adjustments by the recipient. These programs are called Structural Adjustment Facility (SAF), Trust Fund (TF), Enhanced Structural Adjustment Facility (ESAF), and **Poverty** Reduction and Growth Facility (PRGF). Ethiopia has benefited from all of these programs.

However, relations between the IMF and Ethiopia have not always been cordial. There were strained relations between Ethiopia and the IMF/**World Bank** during the **Derg**'s early years. In 1998, the

IMF/World Bank suspended aid to Ethiopia following the outbreak of the **Ethiopian-Eritrean War.** In 2000, Prime Minister **Meles Zenawi** visited IMF headquarters and convinced the organization to resume development assistance to Ethiopia.

The IMF operates on the basis of special drawing rights (SDR). The IMF determines the SDR's **currency** value daily by summing the values in U.S. dollars, based on market exchange rates, of a basket of four major currencies. From 1992 until early 2002, the IMF disbursed about 138 million SDRs to Ethiopia under PRGF, SAF, ESAF, and TF arrangements. During the same period, Ethiopia made repayments of about 34 million SDRs. The latest IMF financial agreements with Ethiopia include a SAF in 1992 for 49 million SDRs that expired in 1995. It was fully drawn down. In 1996, the ESAF approved 88 million SDRs that expired in 1999; Ethiopia drew 29 million SDRs from this account.

In 2001, the IMF and Ethiopia signed a PRGF for 100 million SDRs. It expires in 2004, and as of early 2002, Ethiopia had drawn 59 million SDRs from the account. A 2002 IMF assessment of the PRGF noted that Ethiopia, following the end of the conflict with Eritrea, had resumed its economic reform efforts and had reconfirmed its commitment to poverty reduction within a framework of macroeconomic stability. It described Ethiopia's economic performance as satisfactory, adding that most quantitative criteria and benchmarks had been met. To mitigate the impact of continued deterioration in the trade terms for Ethiopia and the 11 September 2001 terrorist attack on New York and Washington, D.C., the IMF agreed to augment Ethiopia's access under the PRGF arrangement by 10 percent of quota. *See also* ECONOMY.

ISKANDER DESTA (1934–1974). Member of the royal family and naval officer. Born on 6 August 1934 in **Addis Ababa** and educated primarily in Britain. In 1955, Iskander, a grandson of the emperor, became deputy commander of the newly formed Ethiopian Imperial **Navy** under **Haile Selassie**, who was commander in chief of all **armed forces**. Despite his affiliation with the royal family and his reputation of being a "vigorous and progressive" commander, Iskander was a minor figure in the imperial government. Some sources suggest that Iskander was a possible successor to Haile Selassie, but others maintain that the emperor distrusted him and therefore never gave him significant government responsibilities. As a result, Iskander frequently performed minor representational duties such as serving on the International Christian Fellowship's executive committee and attending the Prince Henry the Navigator celebrations in Lisbon and a royal wedding in Brussels (1960). During a minor armed forces revolt on 25–26 February 1974, he temporarily fled the main naval base at **Massawa** and sought refuge in Djibouti, where he remained for a few weeks. On 8 March 1974, he resumed his duties in Addis Ababa. On 23 November 1974, the **Derg** executed Iskander and 59 others in what is now known as the **Bloody Saturday** massacre.

ISLAM. Ethiopia has a long exposure to Islam and has lengthy borders with Sudan and Somalia, two predominantly Islamic countries. In the early seventh century, a group of Arab followers of Islam in danger of persecution by local authorities in Arabia took refuge in the **Axumite** kingdom of the Ethiopian **highlands**. As a result of this generosity, the Prophet Mohammed concluded that Ethiopia should not be targeted for jihad.

Subsequent Ethiopian contact with Islam was less cordial. In the late 15th century, Islamic raids from the Somali port of Zeila plagued the highlands. In the first half of the 16th century, the Islamic threat became more serious when **Ahmad ibn Ibrahim al Ghazi** rallied a diverse group of Muslims in a jihad to end Christian power in the highlands. After early Muslim successes, the Ethiopians finally defeated them (1543). In 1875, the khedive of Egypt tried unsuccessfully to overrun Ethiopia. The last major, organized threat from Islam occurred in 1888, when the forces of the Mahdi in the Sudan sacked the former capital of **Gondar** and burned many of its churches.

Islam expanded gradually in Ethiopia, especially in the country's lower-lying parts. Most Ethiopian Muslims are not of Arab descent but belong to indigenous ethnic groups such as the **Oromo**. The authorities always treated Islam as a secondary religion and discriminated against Muslims. There were, however, only brief periods when Christian rulers tried to suppress Islam. There were other occasions, especially the period of rule from Gondar in the 17th century, when Muslim communities enjoyed considerable autonomy. Ethiopian Muslims generally are not receptive to Islamic fundamentalism. They tend to identify first with their ethnic kin and constitute a benign religious group. They are geographically intermixed throughout the country except for overwhelming concentrations in **Somali**- and **Afar**-inhabited regions.

The 1994 **census** indicated there were 14.3 million Muslims in Ethiopia or about 29 percent of the total **population**. In a recent survey of Islamic populations around the world, the International Population Center at San Diego State University estimated Ethiopia's Muslim population at 29 million. The same survey noted that Ethiopia, along with Morocco, had the world's 11th largest Muslim population. If the survey's figures are accurate, it means "Christian" Ethiopia has more Muslims than Saudi Arabia, Sudan, or Iraq. Ethiopia's current population is probably more than 45 percent Muslim. Useful books on this topic include Ulrich Braükamper's *Islamic History and Culture in Southern Ethiopia* and J. S. Trimingham's *Islam in Ethiopia*. *See also* AFAR PEOPLE AND LANGUAGE; AFAR REGION; OGADEN; SOMALI REGION.

ITALIAN EAST AFRICA. *See* AFRICA ORIENTALE ITALIANA.

ITALIAN-ETHIOPIAN WAR (1935–1936). The major factors that led to Italy's invasion of Ethiopia included a desire to avenge the humiliating defeat at the **Battle of Adwa** and a desire to enhance its international reputation by acquiring a colonial empire. In late 1935, Italian dictator Benito Mussolini deployed 207,000 Italian troops equipped with 150 aircraft, 700 field pieces, and 150 tanks.

On 3 October 1935, General **Emilio De Bono** attacked Ethiopia from Eritrea and General **Rodolfo Graziani** invaded from Italian Somalia. The Ethiopian **armed forces** were no match for the highly mechanized Italian army. During the campaign's first days, Italian forces occupied Adigrat, **Adwa**, Dolo, Enticcio, Gerlogubi (7 October), and **Axum** (15 October). Within six months, the Italians, who employed vicious tactics such as the use of **chemical weapons**, had defeated the Ethiopians, despite the fact that on 7 April 1936, **Haile Selassie** issued an imperial proclamation that called to arms every Ethiopian male capable of military service. Eventually, Ethiopia had some 350,000 soldiers under arms, but they lacked the capabilities to mount a credible defense as only about of quarter of them had received military training and weapons were in short supply. On 5 May 1936, Marshal **Pietro Badoglio** and his troops occupied **Addis Ababa**.

According to Italian government statistics, between 1 January 1935 and 31 May 1936, its army sustained 1,148 killed (regular troops and Blackshirts), 125 deaths as a result of wounds, 31 missing in action, and 1,593 **askaris** killed in action. Other fatalities included 453 workmen. According to the Ethiopian government, at least 275,000 of its soldiers died during the war. *See also* BLACK LIONS.

ITEGE. *See* IMPERIAL TITLES.

IYASU I (1658–1706). Emperor (1682–1705) and son of **Yohannes I**. Also known as Adyam-Saggad I. After the death of his eldest brother Yostos (1676), Iyasu inherited his house, wealth, and position as governor of Semen. He also became governor of **Gojam**. Shortly afterwards, Iyasu argued with his father about religious matters. In 1680, he left **Gondar** and sought refuge with the **Oromo**. **Abuna** Sinoda eventually reconciled the two and Iyasu returned to Gondar. However, he lost his Gojam governorship but retained the Semen governorship.

After Yohannes I died on 19 July 1682, Iyasu became emperor and fought numerous military campaigns against the Oromos (e.g., 1684, 1685, 1686, 1688, 1690–1691, 1696, 1699, 1700, and 1705). He also undertook expeditions to the north and northwest of his empire. He died on 13 October 1706 on the island of Tchekla Mamzo. After his death, the monarchy became increasingly unstable.

IYASU II (1723–1755). Emperor (1730–1755). Also known as Adeyam Saggad or as Berhan Saggad. Son of Emperor **Bakafa**. As Iyasu II succeeded his father while still a young boy, the queen regent, Mentewab, dominated the country during most of his reign. Chronic political instability, caused largely by the growing power of the feudal lords, characterized Iyasu II's reign. He launched an unsuccessful military campaign against the Funj kingdom in what became Sudan's **Blue Nile** Province. Iyasu II is best remembered for the churches he built at Qusqwam and Azazo, both of which were close to **Gondar**. He also built a palace in Gondar. Iyasu II's second wife was an **Oromo** chief's daughter named Webi. The couple had a son named

Iyoas, who eventually succeeded his father, thus beginning nearly a century of Oromo domination. Iyasu II died on 26 June 1755 in Gondar.

IYASU MIKAEL, LIJ (1896–1935). Emperor (12 December 1913–27 September 1916). Son of **Menelik II**'s daughter, Shewa Regga, and **Ras** Mikael of **Wollo Province**. Born on 3 February 1896 and educated by private French and German tutors. He also attended the Ecole Impériale Menelik II in **Addis Ababa**.

In April 1916, Lij Iyasu announced his conversion to **Islam**. The conversion unleashed a storm of opposition in Ethiopia. On 27 September 1916, a group of **Shoan** aristocrats issued a proclamation that deposed the emperor because, in their view, he had committed apostasy and treason. **Abuna Matewos** also excommunicated him from the **Ethiopian Orthodox Church**. Lij Iyasu responded by organizing an army in **Harar** and then marching toward Addis Ababa. At Mieso, a place midway between Harar and Addis Ababa, a government force drove the emperor's troops back to Harar. On 9 October 1916, **Dajazmach Balcha Abba Nefso** and his soldiers entered Harar, looted the city, and killed several hundred Muslims. Lij Iyasu retreated toward **Jijiga** and then into the **Danakil Depression**.

Negus Mikael, the emperor's father, sought to restore his son to the throne by deploying an 80,000-man army against the Shoan force. At Tora Mesk, northeast of Addis Ababa, Mikael scored a victory over the Shoans who were defending **Ankober**. On 27 October 1916, the Shoans clashed with Mikael's army at Sagle, north of Addis Ababa. After several hours of fighting that caused some 10,000 casualties, the Shoans succeeded in capturing Mikael and his camp.

Meanwhile, Iyasu left Ankober and, on 8 November 1916, arrived in **Dese**. After the Shoans occupied Dese on 10 December 1916, the deposed emperor fled to Magdala. In August 1917, government forces again defeated Iyasu in Dese and Magdala. He then fled to the eastern **lowlands** where he remained at large for nearly four years. Finally, on 28 January 1921, loyalist forces captured Iyasu and, on 21 May 1921, delivered him to Ras Tafari Makonnen, later **Haile Selassie**, in Dese. On 7 November 1935, Lij Iyasu died in captivity at Garamulata near Harar.

– J –

JANJERO KINGDOM. Janjero's first kings belonged to a dynasty called Halman Gama and claimed to be of **Abyssinian** origin. The first written mention of the kingdom appeared in a victory song of Emperor Isaac (1414–1429) where it is called Zenjaro. In 1613, one of the Janjero kings received Jesuit Father Antonio Fernandez, who wrote a fanciful account of his visit. In the 19th century, only a few European explorers visited Janjero. The kingdom remained isolated until Ethiopian highlanders conquered it in 1894. The last king, Abba Bagibo, initially fled to **Gurage** country but eventually submitted to Emperor **Menelik II** in **Addis Ababa**. The king's son, Abba Cabsa, became a Christian and eventually Ethiopia's minister in Rome.

The Janjero kingdom was located between the Gibe River on the west and the **Omo River** on the east. It included a narrow mountain chain rising to more than 10,000 feet (3,084 meters) altitude. Mount Bor Ama is the chain's highest mountain. Although the capital's original name is uncertain, by the mid-1950s, the present-day town of Fofa was the center of government. The **Yem** or Yemma people controlled Janjero. The nearby **Oromo** called them *zenjaro*, which means "baboon" in the Oromo language. Before the Ethiopian government conquered the Yem, they were exclusively pagans and engaged in human sacrifice. They worshiped two pillars of bronze, allegedly the remains of an ancient temple, which were washed with human blood every year. They also worshiped the Gibe River's crocodiles and sacrificed human beings to the crocodiles if the king fell ill. **Slavery** existed from an early period. The king could take persons of either sex from their homes and sell them into slavery or force them to work for him. The king or *tato* belonged to the royal Mwa clan of the Yem. The principal court official was the commander of the royal enclosure, who was in charge of the king's guard. G. W. B. Huntingford offers a good summary of the kingdom in *The Galla of Ethiopia, The Kingdoms of Kafa and Janjero.*

JERUSALEM. According to Ethiopian legend, Menelik I, the son of King Solomon and the **Queen of Sheba**, took the **Ark of the Covenant** from **Jerusalem** to **Axum**. In the late Axumite period, Ethiopian pilgrims began to visit Jerusalem and eventually established a permanent colony in that city.

Almost immediately, Jerusalem became an important part of the **Ethiopian Orthodox Church**'s (EOC) doctrine. In 1189, the Egyptian ruler Salah ad-Din (known in the West as Saladin), captured Jerusalem. Although a Muslim, Saladin was favorably disposed toward Ethiopia's Christians. He granted them Jerusalem's Chapel of the Invention of the Cross in the Church of the Holy Sepulchre and a station in Bethlehem's Grotto of the Nativity. As a result, Ethiopian pilgrimages to Jerusalem became frequent. **Amda Seyon** is the first among Ethiopia's Emperors whose names are recorded as benefactors of the Ethiopian community's library collection in Jerusalem. In 1442, Emperor **Zara Yakob** also sent a book to the Ethiopian community in Jerusalem.

In 1924, Regent **Ras** Tafari Makonnen, later **Haile Selassie**, made a trip to Europe, which he began by spending Easter in Jerusalem. Apart from visiting the holy places, he reached an agreement with the Greek Patriarch for improving access to the Ethiopian chapel in the Church of the Holy Sepulchre. Following the outbreak of the **Italian-Ethiopian War**, he returned to Jerusalem as Emperor Haile Selassie and continued to Britain, where he went into exile.

Jerusalem remains important to the EOC, which owns monasteries and chapels in the city and which has an archbishop for the Ethiopian religious community. There is even an Ethiopia Street in Jerusalem.

JIJIGA. (38,100, estimated 2002 **population**.) The capital of **Somali Region**. A small seasonal river known as Jerer passes through Jijiga, which is located on a vast plain. Its name is taken from an **Oromo** word *jig-jiga* or "friable," meaning that the soil makes well construction difficult. In the early 1890s, Jijiga began as a fort for the **Abyssinian** chief Bangussie, who used it as part of his system for collecting customs duties on goods coming from Somaliland. In 1900, the Abyssinians won a major military victory at Jijiga when they defeated an attack by Mohamed ibn Abdulle Hassen, also known as the "Mad Mullah." In the early 20th century, Jijiga developed as an administrative center. **Amhara**, **Somali**, and Indian merchants then populated the town. Today, Jijiga is primarily a Somali town with a large market that is full of contraband from Somaliland. There continue to be occasional security incidents, perpetrated largely by groups such as the **Ogaden National Liberation Front,** in and around Jijiga, which still has the reputation of a wild frontier town. Nega Mezlekia's *Notes from the Hyena's Belly* offers a descriptive account of Jijiga.

JIMMA ABBA JIFAR, KINGDOM OF. The kingdom of Jimma Abba Jifar was an internally autonomous state from 1830 to 1932 and covered, at its height, an area of 8,000 square miles (13,000 square kilometers). Abba Jifar I ruled from 1830 to 1855. The palace of its last important king, Abba Jifar II, who ruled from 1878 to 1932, is located at Jiren outside of **Jimma Town**. Situated on a hill, the palace at Jiren was ideal for detecting the movement of opponents. While it was an independent kingdom, Jimma reportedly had relations with India, Egypt, Saudi Arabia, and other African and Middle Eastern countries. It exported gold, **coffee**, honey, civet, ivory, and articles of wood and animal skin while it imported weapons, ornaments, jewelry, and industrial goods.

In 1884, Abba Jifar II agreed to pay tribute to **Menelik II**. At that point, the kingdom of Jimma Abba Jifar lost its independence and its administration shifted to Jimma Town. By taking this step, however, Abba Jifar II avoided the harsh reprisals experienced by his neighbors who refused to pay tribute, and he gained a reputation for wealth and greatness. **Agriculture** and coffee production flourished. **Haile Selassie** assumed control of Jimma upon Abba Jifar II's death (1932). Herbert S. Lewis wrote a thorough history of the kingdom entitled *A Galla Monarchy*.

JIMMA (JIMA) TOWN. (112,500, estimated 2002 **population**.) Ethiopia's eighth largest city and the largest in western Ethiopia. Located some 210 miles (335 kilometers) west of **Addis Ababa**. Originally, Jimma was the capital of the former **Kafa** Province and an important market known as Hermata during the **kingdom of Jimma**. During the Italian occupation of Ethiopia (1936–1941), Jimma served as a regional center. Fascist buildings from that period continue to attract some architectural historians. Today, Jimma serves only as a zonal capital in **Oromia Region**. Although located in an important **coffee**-growing area, Jimma has not prospered in recent years as it attracts few **tourists** and little investment. Jimma remains famous for production of the three-legged Jimma stool.

JUDICIARY. The *Fetha Nagast*, a legal text written in **Ge'ez** in the 13th century, formed the basis of traditional Ethiopian jurisprudence. In 1942, **Haile Selassie** established Ethiopia's law courts under the Administration of Justice Proclamation. The judiciary included a Supreme Imperial Court, a High Court of 12 divisions, provincial courts, regional courts, communal courts, and subcommunal courts (*atbia dagna*). There also were special Muslim, military, and ecclesiastical courts.

The **Derg** retained much of this structure but eliminated lower subdistrict courts and authorized selection of some subdistrict court judges. The Derg also created people's tribunals, which were under the jurisdiction of peasant associations and *kebeles*, to settle cases of land redistribution and expropriation, minor criminal and civil offenses, violation of privacy, economic sabotage, and antirevolutionary activities.

Under the **Ethiopian People's Revolutionary Democratic Front** (EPRDF), the country has a dual court system. There is a federal judiciary that includes a Supreme Court, Federal High Court, and Federal First Instance Court. Each regional state has a parallel judicial system. The Ethiopian judiciary dispenses justice between individuals and between the state and its citizens. The **constitution** contains provisions that supposedly safeguard the judiciary's independence. The **House of Peoples' Representatives** appoints federal judges while the Regional State Council appoints regional judges after consultation with the Federal Judicial Commission and the State Judicial Administration Commission. Judges hold office until they reach retirement age (60 years). Their tenure is independent of the will of the executive.

Historically, the judiciary has been marred by abuses, cronyism, **corruption**, and inefficiency. There is an enormous shortage of judges and prosecutors. People often wait for years before having their day in court. Constitutional provisions that guarantee freedom of speech and press often have been ignored by the monarchy, the Derg, and the EPRDF. Summary executions were pervasive throughout the Derg period (1974–1991), despite criticism by domestic and international **human rights** organizations.

JULIAN CALENDAR. *See* CALENDAR.

– K –

KACHAMA-GANJULE PEOPLE AND LANGUAGE. Several hundred Kachama live on the islands in Lake Abaya and in tiny communities to the west of the lake. Fewer than 100 Ganjule recently relocated from a small island in Lake Chamo to Shela-Mela on the lake's west shore. They speak an Omotic **language** in the Ometo family. Dialects include Kachama, Ganjule, and Ganta. They have 46 percent lexical similarity with **Wolaytta,** and some Kachama-Ganjule are bilingual in Wolaytta.

KACIPO-BALESI PEOPLE AND LANGUAGE. Also known as the Koe, the Kacipo-Balesi people live astride the Ethiopia-Sudan border in the Maji zone of **Southern Nations, Nationalities and People's Region.** The **Suri** reside to the south, the **Dizi** to the north, and the **Anuak** to the northeast. More than half of the 10,000 or so Kacipo-Balesi live in Sudan. They speak a Nilo-Saharan **language** of the east Sudanic family. There are numerous dialects. The language has 40 to 54 percent lexical similarity with **Murle** and 35 percent with **Mursi.** Some speakers use Suri as a second language.

KAFA. *See* KAFICHO PEOPLE AND LANGUAGE.

KAFICHO PEOPLE AND LANGUAGE. The Kaficho, previously known as the Kafa, occupy about half of Kaficho zone. In the late 14th century, Kafa became a monarchy that was ruled by a king or *tato*. Oral history has preserved the names of many of these kings. Scholars believe that people then known as the Minjo established the dynasty. The original capital was a town called Shada. In the early 16th century, King Bonkatato moved the capital to Bonga. In the 17th century, Kafa conquered the **Nayi** and **Chara** peoples. In the late 18th century, Kafa extended its empire to the **Omo River** in the southeast and nearly to the confluence of the Omo and Dincha Rivers in the south. The Kafa also withstood a number of **Oromo** attacks. Ethiopian emperor Sarsa Dengel (reigned 1563–1597) may have extended his control to the fringes of the Kafa. This may account for the introduction of Christianity into the kingdom. A monastery near Bonga dates from about 1550. The Kafa kingdom remained independent until

1897, when Emperor **Menelik II** captured it and imprisoned the last king at **Ankober**. G. W. B. Ḥuntingford's *The Galla of Ethiopia, The Kingdoms of Kafa and Janjero* offers a useful, if dated, account of the Kafa kingdom.

Bonga remains the major town for the Kaficho, who are agriculturists and number more than a half million. It is often said that the word "**coffee**" derives from Kafa, where coffee bushes grow in profusion. Most Kaficho describe themselves as Orthodox Christians, although **Catholicism**, which was introduced in the mid–19th century, and, more recently, **Protestantism**, are gaining followers. Some still believe in traditional spirits. Kaficho is an Omotic **language** with two principal dialects, Kafa and Bosho. The latter may be a separate language. Kaficho is related to **Shakacho**, the language of the people who live to the west. Kaficho is widely used and also serves as a literary language. There is an argot based on Kaficho known as Manjo. In 2000, the Kafa Shaka Peoples' Democratic Organization elected 10 persons to the **House of Peoples' Representatives**.

KAGNEW BATTALIONS. In early 1951, Ethiopia sent troops to the United Nations military action in Korea. **Haile Selassie** authorized the use of Ethiopian troops to protect the collective security principle. The emperor dubbed the battalions *Kagnew,* which had two meanings. The first meant "to bring order out of chaos" and the second "to overthrow." Brigadier General **Mulugeta Buli**, commanding General of the **Imperial Body Guard**, organized the battalions.

The first Kagnew battalion, led by Lieutenant Colonel Teshome Irgetu, saw service in Korea from 7 May 1951 to 29 March 1952. An American ship transported the first battalion from Djibouti to Pusan, Korea. The Ethiopians were attached to the U.S. seventh Division. The second Kagnew Battalion, led by Lieutenant Colonel Asfaw Andargue, was in Korea from 29 March 1952 to 5 April 1953. It also traveled on an American ship from Djibouti to Pusan. The third battalion, commanded by Lieutenant Colonel Wolde Yohannis Shitta, arrived on an American ship at Pusan on 16 April 1953 and remained until April 1954. About 5,000 Ethiopian troops, all from the Imperial Body Guard, rotated through Korea, where they fought with distinction. The Kagnew battalions suffered 120 killed in action and 536 wounded in action.

General Mark W. Clark, commander in chief of the United Nations Command, acknowledged the courageous fighting abilities of the Ethiopians and indicated they were "well known" to the enemy. Kimon Skordiles documented the history of the battalions in a book entitled *Kagnew: The Story of the Ethiopian Fighters in Korea. See also* ARMED FORCES; PEACEKEEPING OPERATIONS.

KALE HIWOT CHURCH. The Kale Hiwot Church and the Evangelical Church **Mekane Yesus** are Ethiopia's two largest **Protestant** evangelical churches. Kale Hiwot, which means "word of life," grew out of a church leadership system in which each congregation was autonomous and elected its own leaders. Initially, it had loose connections with the Baptists. Although Kale Hiwot is linked to the Society of International **Missionaries**, it is essentially independent. Today, it is a self-reliant church that maintains close contacts with grassroots congregations but is less influential at the national level. Mekane Yesus, by contrast, is trying to build a strong national church with powerful independent local centers. While Mekane Yesus is experiencing ethnic divisions, Kale Hiwot is contending with generational differences. Kale Hiwot, which has undergone rapid growth in recent years, also has a development program. In 1992, for example, the **Wolaytta** branch launched one program that earmarked $250,000 for the promotion of **environmental** awareness among residents to conserve soil, water, and forests. It also has an impressive **agricultural** cooperative outside **Debre Zeit**. Today, Kale Hiwot probably has more followers than the better-known Mekane Yesus and seems to be growing at a faster rate.

KAMBATA (KAMBATTA, KAMBAATA, KEMBATA) PEOPLE AND LANGUAGE. The Kambata people reside to the east of the **Gurage**, north of the **Gamo-Gofa-Dawro,** and west and south of the **Hadiyya**. Kambata was once an independent kingdom with a society divided into nobles, free commoners, artisans, and **slaves**. The Kambata occupy one of Ethiopia's most densely populated areas and number more than one million. As a result, there is a severe land shortage and the average holdings per household are very small. The **economy** is based on mixed cultivation with *ensete* as the staple crop. Durame is their main town. Most Kambata are Christian; some are Muslim.

They speak an east Cushitic **language** that has several dialects. The language has 81 percent lexical similarity with **Alaba**, 62 percent with **Sidamo**, 57 percent with **Libido,** and 56 percent with Hadiyya. It is an official literary language and up to one-quarter of the **population** is literate.

KARO PEOPLE AND LANGUAGE. The Karo are one of Ethiopia's smallest and most endangered ethnic groups. Numbering perhaps no more than a thousand, they live along a small portion of the east bank of the **Omo River** just north of the **Murle**. The **Hamer** and **Banna** live to their east; they have a service relationship with the Banna. Their neighbors refer to them as Kara, which means "fish" in the Karo **language**. Also known as the Kerre, they once had paramount chiefs. Their traditional religion has a Supreme Being. Formerly pastoralists, many are now **agriculturists** and rely on sorghum, maize, and beans. The Karo are masters of body painting used for a **dance**, feast, or celebration. Karo social organization is based on consolidated age groups. They speak a south Omotic language that has 81 percent lexical similarity with Hamer-Banna. Gezahegn Petros has written a brief study entitled *The Karo of the Lower Omo Valley.*

KARRAYU PEOPLE AND LANGUAGE. The Karrayu are a subgroup of the **Oromo** who inhabit the Metehara Plain and the area around Mount Fentale on the edge of East **Shoa** and near the **Afar Region** border. The Arsi-Oromo reside to the southeast, the **Afar** to the northeast, the **Amhara people** to the northwest, and the **Argobba** to the west. They number perhaps 70,000. According to tradition, the Karrayu originated in southern Ethiopia's **Boran** area. In the 16th century, pastoral Boran clans may have migrated northwards in search of better pasture. The Karrayu are pastoralists and raise cattle, camels, goats, and sheep. They also engage in small-scale irrigated and rain-fed **agriculture**. They are divided into clans and subclans; the two major divisions are Dulecha and Basso. The Basso are predominantly Muslim while the Dulecha tend to practice traditional forms of worship. They follow the *gada* age-set system. The Ittu **Oromo** and **Somalis** have migrated into territory traditionally inhabited by the Karrayu. They speak a dialect of the east Cushitic branch of Afan Oromo. The **language** is related to Afar, Somali, **Beja,** and

Saho. Ayalew Gebre has written a thorough study of the Karrayu entitled *Pastoralism under Pressure: Land Alienation and Pastoral Transformations among the Karrayu of Eastern Ethiopia, 1941 to the Present*.

KASSA HAYLU. *See* TEWODROS II.

KASSA HAYLU, LEUL-RAS (1881–1956). Governor, military commander, crown councilor, and grandson of **Sahle Selassie**. Educated at the court of **Menelik II**. Kassa began his career as governor of northern **Shoa** Province and then of **Bagemder Province**. In 1961, he joined the forces allied against **Lij Iyasu Mikael** and received the title of **ras** for his services. At **Haile Selassie**'s coronation (1930) Kassa was elevated to the status of **leul**. During the **Italian-Ethiopian War**, he remained loyal to Haile Selassie by serving as field marshal for the armies of the north. After Ethiopia's defeat, Kassa went into exile in **Jerusalem** but returned with the emperor in 1941. He was crown councilor until his death on 16 November 1956.

KEBELE. Amharic for "neighborhood." The *kebele* is the smallest government administrative unit in Ethiopia after *awarajas* and *woredas*. In 1974, the **Derg** organized some three million urban residents into urban-dwellers' associations known as kebeles. These cooperatives served as the counterparts to **peasant associations**. Each kebele normally included about 500 families or between 3,500 and 4,000 persons. The Derg initially used the kebeles to control the cities and the peasant associations to implement **land reform**. Eventually, their role expanded to include politicizing the masses, monitoring all local political activity, conscripting youths into the **People's Militia**, reeducating reactionaries, countering opposition activities, and killing antirevolutionaries during the **Red Terror**. During the Derg years, there were some 20,000 kebeles throughout Ethiopia.

The **Ethiopian People's Revolutionary Democratic Front** (EPRDF) continued the kebele system to control the population. Every effort is made to install party loyalists as kebele leaders, who are sometimes in a position to aid or withhold help from individuals. Local militias, where they have been organized, report in the first instance to the kebele leadership. The kebele has proved to be an effective, but sometimes unpopular, way to ensure EPRDF control at the local level. Currently, there are more than 30,000 kebeles in Ethiopia. *See also* ALL ETHIOPIAN SOCIALIST MOVEMENT; MENGISTU HAILE MARIAM; REVOLUTIONARY FLAME.

KEBRA NAGAST. The *Kebra Nagast* or *The Book of the Glory of Kings* contains the history of the Solomonic line of Ethiopian kings descended from the union of Solomon, king of Israel, and the Queen of Sheba. The *Kebra Nagast* has been in existence for at least a thousand years and is regarded by believers as the ultimate authority on the history of the conversion of Ethiopians from animism to followers of the Lord God of Israel. In about the mid–16th century, the *Kebra Nagast*'s existence became known in Europe. In 1528, a Spanish alchemist, Enrique Cornelio Agrippa, published the most exhaustive early translation. In 1547, Spanish editions appeared in Toledo and Barcelona. There are numerous other translations in many languages.

It is not known who compiled the original manuscript, the date of writing, nor the circumstances. Some early scholars maintained that Yishak and five other **Tigrayan** scribes compiled the *Kebra Nagast* in the early 14th century. However, most modern scholars believe that Yishak's team had translated an Arabic version of a Coptic work into **Ge'ez** and had amalgamated oral traditions with stories from the Old and New Testaments and numerous Islamic, Jewish, and patristic writings. Another interpretation is that an unknown author compiled the original manuscript after the restoration of the "Solomonic line of kings" (i.e., after the rein of Yekuno Amlak [1270–1285]).

For nearly three centuries, the best-known version was in Arabic. Most of the *Kebra Nagast* contains legends and traditions derived from sources that can be traced to the Old Testament and Chaldean writings, Syrian works, and ancient Koranic stories and commentaries. According to believers, the *Kebra Nagast* shows that the king of Ethiopia was descended from Solomon and through him from Abraham and the early patriarchs. The *Kebra Nagast* is available in a 1995 English translation by Miguel F. Brooks. *See also* ISLAM.

KEMANT PEOPLE AND LANGUAGE. The Kemant are Cushitic people who live north of **Lake Tana** and west of the **Tekeze River**.

Estimates of their **population** vary and sometimes reflect the figure for all of the **Agaw**-speaking peoples, which may be as high as a half million. The Kemant have avoided assimilation with the neighboring **Amhara people**. They continue to follow pagan religious beliefs about which they are secretive. But like Ethiopian Christians, they have a god who is said to have created man in his own image and is believed to have power over all nations. The Kemant also have a local god, Kibirwa, who apparently is the representative of the world god and who has power over the Kemant. They have their own church organization and clergy. Their **agriculture** is similar to that of the Amhara. The Kemant speak an Agaw dialect; their **language** is not written. Both their language and their religion are in decline.

KETEMA YIFRU (1929–1994). Civil servant. Born on 11 December 1929 at Gura Muleta, Hararge. After the outbreak of the **Italian-Ethiopian War**, Ketema and his family moved to British Somaliland (now Somaliland). He then was educated at the primary schools in Menchasein, British Somaliland, and in Taveta, Kenya. After Ketema graduated from the Haile Selassie Secondary School (1948), the emperor arranged for him to attend Hope College (Michigan) and Boston University.

In 1952, he returned to Ethiopia and joined the Ministry of Foreign Affairs' Italian section. The following year, Ketema became director-general of the ministry's American and Asian Department. In 1956, he received a promotion to assistant minister and then became **Haile Selassie**'s private secretary (1958–1961) and assistant minister of the pen.

In the aftermath of the **coup attempt (1960)**, the authorities imprisoned Ketema on suspicion of being involved in the plot to overthrow the emperor. However, Haile Selassie ordered his release and allowed him to resume his duties. In 1961, Ketema became minister of foreign affairs. Apart from playing a major role in creating the **Organization of African Unity**, he supported a Pan-African agenda, a nonaligned **foreign policy**, and an end to European colonialism in Africa. Ketema helped to end the Algerian-Moroccan, Biafran, Congolese, and Sudanese wars and to arrange for Nelson Mandela to receive military training in Ethiopia. He also persuaded Sudanese president Ibrahim Abboud to act as mediator during the negotiations that ended the **Ogaden War (1964)**.

Shortly after the military seized power (1974), the authorities jailed Ketema for eight years. After regaining his freedom on 11 September 1982, he worked for the United Nations World Food Programme. On 14 January 1994, Ketema died in **Addis Ababa**.

KHAT (CHAT, QAT). Khat is a mildly intoxicating and hallucinogenic stimulant (*Catha edulis*) that grows in the form of a leafy shrub several feet in height. Due to the high profit earned from the leaves, peasant farmers are increasingly planting the shrub, which grows between altitudes of 4,900 and 9,200 feet (1,500 and 2,800 meters). Traditionally used by Muslim males in Somalia, Djibouti, and Yemen, it is finding increasing receptivity throughout Ethiopia, although most Ethiopian production is still exported. As the bitter-tasting leaves must be fairly fresh, some of it moves from rural growing areas by truck and then by air. Consumers often masticate large quantities of the leaf during a session supplemented by considerable liquid (tea, soft drinks, or water). Khat chewers experience brief periods of ecstasy and euphoria followed by sleeplessness and loss of appetite. A long session goes well into the night and normally ends the next day with a hangover. Khat tends to be used by groups of people and often serves as a way to socialize. It is also expensive and results in considerable lost time from work.

Some areas of Ethiopia, **Tigray** for example, have outlawed khat, which is an illegal drug in the United States. It has been an important part of Muslim life for so many centuries, however, that it is difficult to ban or even discourage its use. The Ethiopian government has yet to announce a national policy on its production and use. A more difficult problem in outlawing production is replacing the income that it brings to farmers, many of whom have discovered they are unable to grow any other crop that results in as much revenue. Khat recently has become Ethiopia's second largest export earner after **coffee** and generates about $60 million annually. It also has become a major source of employment for persons involved in the growing, harvesting, packing, and transportation of the drug.

KIRKMAN, JOHN C. (?–1875). Scottish soldier, military adviser to Emperor **Yohannes IV**. Nothing is known of Kirkman's early life. As a young man he joined the British military and served tours of duty in Nicaragua (1855–1857), China (1863–1864), and Ethiopia (1868). Kirkman never rose above the rank of sergeant. He also worked as a steward with the British Pacific and Oriental Steamship Company.

At the end of the **Anglo-Ethiopian War**, Kirkman joined the services of the future Yohannes IV, who gave him the rank of colonel. On 11 July 1871, his troops, who had been trained by Kirkman, defeated a rival for the throne named Gobazé at **Adwa**. When Egypt threatened to invade Ethiopia (1873), Yohannes IV dispatched Kirkman to Europe with a letter asking for aid from Queen Victoria and other European monarchs. Although he failed to secure any assistance, he remained one of the emperor's close advisers.

After the **Battle of Gundet**, Kirkman supervised the return of Egyptian prisoners of war to **Massawa**. Yohannes IV then sent him on another mission to Europe, but Egyptians imprisoned him in Massawa, where he died of dysentery shortly afterwards.

KOKA DAM. *See* HYDROPOWER.

KOKA DAM DECLARATION. Ethiopia sponsored a four-day conference near the **Koka Dam** between Sudan's National Alliance for the National Salvation delegation, representing 14 political parties and 22 **labor unions**, and the insurgent Sudan People's Liberation Movement/Army. On 24 March 1986, the two sides signed the Koka Dam Declaration, which sought to create a "New Sudan" that would be free from racism, tribalism, and sectarianism. The declaration also called for a national constitutional conference preceded by lifting the state of emergency, a cease-fire, repealing the 8 September 1983 sharia laws, and the restoration of regional governments. By July 1986, it had become evident that the Koka Dam Declaration had failed to have any impact on the southern Sudanese civil war. *See also* FOREIGN POLICY.

KOMBOLCHA. See DESE.

KOMO PEOPLE AND LANGUAGE. Several thousand Komo (Koma) live in Ethiopia and more than 10,000 in Sudan between the **Baro River** and the Daka River. The Komo reportedly arrived in this area about 150 years ago after the **Oromo** drove them from the **highlands**. According to tradition, the Komo and **Murle** once lived together. The **Kwama** live to the north and east while the **Opuuo** and **Nuer** inhabit areas to the south and west. The Komo political unit is the village or small groups of villages. Elders regulate the power of chiefs and there is no supreme chief. They grow cassava, corn, **cotton**, millet, peanuts, sesame, sorghum, sweet potatoes, and tobacco. The Komo live in beehive or cylindrical huts. Different clans have different names for their Supreme Being, who is linked to the sky. They speak Nilo-Saharan **languages** of the Koman family. There are at least two dialects; Komo has 52 percent lexical similarity with Uduk. *See also* UDUK PEOPLE AND LANGUAGE.

KONSO PEOPLE AND LANGUAGE. The Konso or Komso people live in a small area of basalt hills south of Lake Chamo that ranges in altitude from about 5,000 feet (1,524 meters) to 6,000 feet (1,828 meters). In recent years, the Konso have moved in small numbers to scattered settlements beyond their core area. The Konso are now governed as a special *woreda* within **Southern Nations, Nationalities and People's Region**. They are estimated to number more than 200,000. Hostile relations with many of their neighbors, especially the **Boran** and Guji **Oromo** subgroups, prevented their expansion in every direction except to the south. They tend to have better relations with **agricultural** than pastoral peoples. Hardworking agricultural people themselves, they use fertilizer, rotate crops, and terrace the hillsides. Their crops include beans, **coffee**, **khat**, maize, millet, sorghum, and sunflower. They engage in trade with most of their neighbors. The Konso have some cultural ties to the Oromo. They have a generation-grading set known as the *kata*, which is similar to the Oromo *gada* system. The Konso probably split off many years ago from a proto-Oromo people, wandered around southern Ethiopia, and finally settled in their present land. The Konso are an amalgam of all the surrounding people.

The Konso stayed out of the Ethiopian empire until rather late. During the last expansion of modern Ethiopia, **Menelik II**'s forces passed through Konso (1897) and subdued it by promising no violence as long as the people paid tribute, but threatening to crush any resistance. Imperial troops destroyed two Konso towns that resisted and were defeated. The Italian occupation (1936–1941) had little impact on the

Konso; their relative geographical isolation tended to keep foreigners and development out of their land. Although most Konso remain pagans, **Protestant missionaries** have had some impact. The Konso speak Konsina, an East Cushitic **language** that shares 46 percent of cognates with Afan Oromo. Culturally, Konsina shares fewer cognates with the language of the **Dirasha people**, their closest neighbors. The Konso are well known for their unique carved, wooden grave markers called *waga*. The marker is traditionally erected above the grave of an important Konso man or warrior and is surrounded by smaller statues of his wives and defeated enemies. This practice is disappearing. They also are renowned for their stonework. The most thorough study of the Konso is C. R. Hallpike's *The Konso of Ethiopia*.

KONTA PEOPLE AND LANGUAGE. The Konta people reside south of **Jimma** and south of the Gojeb River in North **Omo** zone. Ameya is the most significant town. The area was long an independent kingdom; the king's title was *kawa*. Emperor Sarsa Dengel marched toward Konta and was well received by the local ruler. About 1600, the king of Konta was a vassal of the **Kafa** king to the west. In 1892, the last Konta king surrendered to **Menelik II**. The Konta are **agriculturists**; they have relatively few cattle. Most Konta converted from paganism to the **Ethiopian Orthodox Church**, although about one-third are Muslim. Their pagan beliefs included a supreme being but the people's religious life previously revolved around their belief in the spirits of the lakes. In 2000, the **Southern Nations, Nationalities and People's Region** authorized special *woreda* status for the Konta. The Konta people are part of a larger political party called the **Wolaytta, Gamo**, Gofa, Dawro, and Konta Peoples' Democratic Front, which won 27 seats in the **House of Peoples' Representatives** in the **elections (2000)**. Konta is an Omotic **language** in the Ometo family.

KOORETE PEOPLE AND LANGUAGE. The Koorete people reside in the Amaro mountains to the east of the south end of Lake Abaya and east of Lake Chamo. Administratively, they have their own Amaro special *woreda* with a capital at Kele. They number several tens of thousands. Other people in the region refer to them variously as Amaro, Badittu, and Koyra. They are **agriculturists** and practice terrace farming. Before they were conquered and became part of Ethiopia, the Koorete had an independent kingdom whose king had the title of *kate*. The Koorete believed the king had power over rainfall. They cultivate teff, corn, barley, wheat, and *ensete*. Those who have not converted to the **Ethiopian Orthodox Church** believe in a supreme being known as Tsose, and they traditionally fear left-handed **women** because they bring bad luck. The Koorete speak Koretu or Koryrigna, which is an Omotic **language** of the Ometo family. It has 54 percent lexical similarity with Dorze, 53 percent with Wolaytta, 52 percent with Gofa, and 49 percent with Gamo. *See also* DORZE PEOPLE AND LANGUAGE; GAMO-GOFA-DAWRO PEOPLES AND LANGUAGES; WOLAYTTA PEOPLE AND LANGUAGE.

KOREAN WAR. *See* KAGNEW BATTALIONS.

KRAPF, JOHANN LUDWIG (1810–1881). Missionary and explorer. Born on 11 January 1810 in Derendingen, Germany, and educated at the Basel seminary (1827–1829), where he learned **Amharic** and **Ge'ez,** and in Tübingen, where he completed his theological studies and was ordained (1834). In 1836, Krapf joined the **Church Missionary Society** (CMS).

In December 1837, Krapf arrived in **Massawa** and proceeded to **Tigray** where he tried to implement religious reforms like using Amharic rather than Ge'ez, which only priests understood, to preach the gospel. However, the prince of Tigray, Ubie, who favored the **Catholics** rather than the **Protestants**, expelled Krapf from Tigray.

In May 1839, Krapf and Carl Wilhelm Isenberg, another CMS missionary, arrived in **Shoa** Province, but their religious work also suffered because of a strong Catholic presence in the kingdom. In July 1841, Krapf, hoping to enlist British support to further his religious agenda, agreed to serve as interpreter and intermediary for **William Cornwallis Harris**, head of a recently arrived 30-man British mission. On 16 November 1841, Harris concluded a treaty of friendship and cooperation with the Shoan King, **Sahle Selassie**.

In March 1842, Krapf traveled to Massawa to receive two CMS **missionaries**, J. Mühleisen-Arnold and Johann Christian Müller.

However, Sahle Selassie, who remained under the influence of French Catholic missionaries, prevented Krapf and his colleagues from returning to Shoa. Reentry to Tigray also was barred.

As a result, in November 1843, Krapf departed for Zanzibar and the East African mainland where he helped establish a strong CMS presence. In mid-1853, he returned to Germany to regain his health. During 1867–1868, Krapf returned briefly to Ethiopia as an interpreter with the British military expedition against **Tewodros II**. In January 1868, ill health forced him to return to Germany, where he died on 26 November 1881.

KUMFEL PEOPLE AND LANGUAGE. Numbering only a few thousand, the Kumfel live in a narrow band of **Gojam** west of **Lake Tana** along the Dinder River valley. They encounter the **Gumuz people** on their western edge. Camcamba village is in the heart of Kumfel country. They belong to the **Ethiopian Orthodox Church**. The **Amhara people** who live to their north claim the Kumfel are descended from **slaves** set free by **Tewodros II**. They are cultivators and well known for bee-keeping. They speak a Cushitic **language** that is one of the **Agaw** dialects.

KUNAMA PEOPLE AND LANGUAGE. Nearly all of the Kunama reside in Eritrea in the Gash-Setit Province in the southwestern corner of the country. They tended to side with the **Derg** when it was under attack from the **Eritrean People's Liberation Front**. The Kunama constitute about 2 percent of Eritrea's population and their main town is Barentu. Small numbers of Kunama extend across the Tekeze River into Ethiopia and the famous Badme region where the **Ethiopian-Eritrean War** started.

The Kunama were entirely a pagan people when the Swedish Evangelical Mission began converting some of them in the late 19th century. There also are a small number of Muslims. However, most Kunama remain pagans who believe in a supreme being called Anna. The Kunama are Nilotic in origin and dark skinned. Their egalitarian society recognizes only the authority of the elders and village assemblies. They often farm their land cooperatively. The Kunama **language** is Nilo-Saharan and apparently has no known connection to any other language.

KWAMA PEOPLE AND LANGUAGE. The Kwama, known by many other names and probably considered by some to be **Komo** or Malo, live along the Sudan border between the Daka and Dabus (Yabus) Rivers. The **Hozo** and **Seze** live to the west, **Oromo** and **Berta** to the north, and Komo to the south. Some also reside in Gambela and Bonga towns in **Gambela Region** and there is one Kwama village in Sudan. They number more than 15,000 and are Muslims. The Kwama **language** is Nilo-Saharan in the Koman family. Many speak Afan Oromo as a second language and some know Arabic. **Amharic** is rarely spoken.

KWEGU PEOPLE AND LANGUAGE. The Kwegu number about a thousand and live in scattered settlements along the **Omo River** starting in Keficho zone and continuing south into South Omo zone. They are interspersed among the **Me'en** and **Suri**. Two closely related groups are the Idinitt and Muguji. They are hunter-gatherers and engage in flood and rain cultivation. The Me'en, Bodi (a subgroup of the Me'en), and **Mursi** look down upon them, although Mursi and Bodi men may marry Kwegu **women**. They speak an eastern Sudanic **language** that has 36 percent lexical similarity with Mursi. The Kwegu use the Bodi dialect of Me'en or Mursi as a second language.

– L –

LABOR RELATIONS BOARD. *See* LABOR UNIONS.

LABOR UNIONS. Ethiopia's 1954 **constitution** guaranteed the right to form workers' associations. However, it was not until 1962 that the imperial government issued Decree No. 40 that authorized their creation. In April 1963, the Imperial government recognized the **Confederation of Ethiopian Labor Unions** (CELU), which represented 22 industrial labor groups. By 1973, the CELU represented 167 affiliates with about 80,000 members or 30 percent of eligible industrial and service workers. The CELU never evolved into a national federation of unions but remained an association of labor groups. **Corruption**, embezzlement, election fraud, and inadequate funding plagued the CELU and its successor organizations. During 1963–1973, the

CELU sponsored several labor protests and strikes, but, as its militancy increased, the government regularly crushed labor protests, strikes, and demonstrations.

On 12 September 1974, a military junta seized power, overthrew **Haile Selassie**, and banned all strikes and unauthorized demonstrations. On 15–17 September 1974, the CELU passed a resolution that demanded the **Provisional Military Administrative Council**'s (PMAC) dissolution. On 22 September 1974, the PMAC arrested several CELU leaders and, on 19 May 1975, temporarily closed CELU headquarters for "reorganization." Such tactics failed to curtail the CELU's antigovernment activities, and, on 30 September 1975, the PMAC declared a state of emergency and arrested union officials as well as teachers and students. On 6 December 1975, the **Derg** issued a labor proclamation that abolished the CELU.

On 8 January 1977, the Derg inaugurated the All Ethiopia Trade Union (AETU) to replace the CELU. Twice as large as the CELU, the AETU initially claimed 1,341 local chapters and 287,000 members. The government intended the AETU to help build national development by increasing productivity and supporting socialism. In 1978, the Derg replaced the executive committee, charging it with abuse of authority and failure to accept the rules of democratic centralism. In 1982, the Derg issued the Trade Unions' Organization Proclamation, a Marxist-Leninist order, to enable workers to discharge their "historical responsibility" in building the national **economy** by handling with care the instruments of production and by enhancing the production and proper distribution of goods and services. In 1982, the Derg replaced the AETU leadership and subsequently renamed the organization the Ethiopia Trade Union (ETU) (1986). By this time, the government had co-opted the union and it had little impact in Ethiopian politics. After the Derg's downfall (1991), the ETU virtually disappeared.

In 1993, the **Ethiopian People's Revolutionary Democratic Front** (EPRDF) promulgated the **National Charter** and the labor law that permitted workers to form and join unions. Those barred from joining unions included employees of the civil and security services, judges, prosecutors, and those who provided "essential services." The **constitution (1994)** reaffirmed the right to form trade unions and other associations to bargain collectively, to express grievances, and to strike subject to Ethiopian law and regulations. In November 1993, the Confederation of Ethiopian Trade Unions (CETU) replaced what remained of the ETU. The leadership is elected and organized by industrial and service sector rather than by region. There is no requirement that unions belong to the CETU. The important **Ethiopian Teachers' Association** is not affiliated with the CETU.

Many restrictions on the right to strike apply equally to an employer's right to lockout. Both employers and workers must make efforts at conciliation, provide at least 10 days' notice, and give the reasons for the action. Strikes must be supported by a majority of the workers affected by the decision, and it is unlawful to strike against an order from the Labor Relations Board (LRB). If a union-management agreement cannot be reached, the LRB may arbitrate the case. The Minister of Labor and Social Affairs appoints each LRB chairman; the four-member board consists of two persons each from trade unions and employers' associations who serve three-year terms. Boards exist at the national level and in some regions.

Relations between the government and the CETU historically have been testy. In October 1994, Dawi Ibrahim, CETU chairman, criticized the government's structural adjustment program because of the negative impact it had on public sector workers. The Ethiopian **police** halted a CETU meeting and sealed off its offices, but a court later ruled against the closing of the offices. Nevertheless, the EPRDF decertified the CETU. Dawi Ibrahim, who feared for his safety, fled to the Netherlands.

In April 1997, activists loyal to the EPRDF took control of the CETU and announced that it had been recertified and that relations with the government had been normalized. Since then, the CETU has focused on workers' concerns such as job security, pay increases, and **health** and retirement benefits. In May 1998, the EPRDF licensed the Ethiopian Employers' Association, which supposedly maintains good relations and "works in harmony" with the International Labour Organisation, the CETU, and the Ministry of Labor and Social Affairs.

The government wants to be seen to support an independent trade union structure but not one that will disrupt its policies. In addition, union funding always has been a problem as some 80 percent of the workforce is engaged in subsistence farming and, therefore, is not part of the union movement. As of 2003, about 300,000 workers were unionized under nine CETU federations. Collective bargaining agreements covered approximately 90 percent of unionized workers. The CETU has been active in educational efforts related to the concerns of workers and recently received a grant from the U.S. Agency for International Development to undertake **human immunodeficiency virus/acquired immune deficiency syndrome** programs at the two major sugar factories. *See also* TAYE WOLDE SEMAYAT.

LAKE AWASA. *See* LAKES (CENTRAL AND SOUTHERN RIFT VALLEY).

LAKE RUDOLF. *See* LAKE TURKANA.

LAKES (CENTRAL AND SOUTHERN RIFT VALLEY). There is a chain of seven lakes in the central and southern **Rift Valley**. The northernmost is Lake Ziway followed by Abiata, Langano, Shala, **Awasa**, Abaya, and Chamo. Formed during a period of heavy rainfall in the Ice Age, they are slowly evaporating and now are much smaller than their original size. Their shrinkage has exposed huge areas of alluvial soil that permits productive **agriculture**. The lakes attract a variety of **bird life**. Lake Abiata-Shala **National Park** surrounds those two lakes. Nechisar National Park is located between and to the east of Lake Abaya and Lake Chamo. Lake Langano is popular with boaters and swimmers as it is free of bilharzia.

LAKES (EASTERN SALINE). Five highly saline lakes exist in the **Danakil Depression** near Djibouti. They are Gamari, Gargori, Afambo, Bario, and the Abbe, which straddles the border with Djibouti. After the **Rift Valley** opened, water from the **Red Sea** flooded much of this area. Subsequent volcanic activity raised barriers of basaltic lava. Behind the barriers the trapped inland sea began to evaporate, leaving only these scattered lakes. Huge, deep beds of natural salt also remain in the area. The **Awash River** terminates in these salt lakes, which are well known for their **bird life**.

LAKE STEPHANIE. *See* CHEW BAHIR.

LAKE TANA. Ethiopia's largest body of water, Lake Tana, is the headwaters of the **Blue Nile** and covers 1,389 square miles (3,600 square kilometers). It has an average depth of 46 feet (14 meters) but reaches depths up to 980 feet (320 meters). Lake Tana has 37 islands, about 20 of which contain churches and monasteries of historical and cultural importance. Most of the structures date from the late 16th and early 17th centuries. Many provide a sanctuary for royal treasures and tombs. Between the collapse of the **Zagwe dynasty** in the late 13th century and the establishment of **Gondar** as a capital in the early 17th century, the area around Lake Tana was the political and spiritual focus of Ethiopia's Christian empire. **Bahir Dar**, the capital of **Amhara Region**, lies at the southern end of Lake Tana. The much older but smaller town of **Gorgora** is on the north end of the lake. Much of the European exploration of Ethiopia focused on the area around Lake Tana, including that by the 18th-century Scottish traveler **James Bruce**. *See also* AMHARA PEOPLE.

LAKE TURKANA. (2,473 square miles; 3,978 square kilometers in area.) Known as Lake Rudolf until 1975; also called the Jade Sea. Rudolf refers to the Austrian crown prince Rudolf (1858–1889), who financed an expedition to the lake by Count Samuel Teleki von Szek (1845–1915) and Ludwig von Höhnel (1857–1942); Turkana is the name of the local tribe living near the lake.

The lake has existed for at least three million years and, prior to the last Ice Age, was a major tributary of the **Nile River**. Today, it is East Africa's fourth largest lake and the world's biggest permanent desert lake. Lake Turkana, which covers an area of about 2,473 square miles (6,400 square kilometers), is 10 to 20 miles (16 to 32 kilometers) wide and relatively shallow but has depths up to 250 feet (76 meters) around Central Island in the far south.

Most of Lake Turkana is in Kenya and only the northern tip extends into Ethiopia. As the lake has no outlet, some 3 meters' depth of brackish water evaporates annually. In recent years, the amount of water flowing into the lake has diminished because of several large-scale irrigation projects in southern Ethiopia. As the water level falls and the lake shrinks, a smaller and smaller part of the lake remains in Ethiopia. Between 1973 and 1989, the delta increased by about 236 square miles (380 square kilometers) due to the drop in water level.

The **Omo River**, which originates on Mount Amara in Ethiopia's western **highlands**, provides more than 80 percent of the water for

Lake Turkana. Although its water is brackish, the lake is an important source of fish, especially the Nile perch, which can weigh more than 360 pounds (800 kilograms). Other fish species include the puffer fish, tiger fish, and tilapia. Lake Turkana has a diverse **bird life** population, which includes some European species and the native African skimmer, African spoonbill, great white pelican, sacred ibis, yellow-billed stork, and countless others. The lake also is home to some of the world's most venomous reptiles, including cobras, night and puff adders, and saw-scaled vipers.

During the morning hours, strong winds blow from the east down the slopes of Mount Kulal and across the surface of the lake. The wind creates white-capped waves on the lake's surface, making navigation almost impossible. When the wind dies down in the afternoon, the lake takes on the color of green jade as the algae rise to the surface in calm water. Turkana is a desert lake surrounded by volcanic slag in the south and east and sand dunes and mudflats in the north and west. It has three islands—North, Central, and South— that confirm the volcanic origin of the lakebed and the surrounding countryside. *Quest for the Jade Sea* by Pascal James Imperato provides an excellent account of European exploration of the lake.

LALIBELA. A small town in the Lasta mountains of north-central Ethiopia, Lalibela is the location of Ethiopia's most famous monolithic **rock-hewn churches**. Previously known as Roha, which was the capital of the **Zagwe dynasty,** which ruled Ethiopia from the 10th to the 13th century. Today, Lalibela is serviced by an excellent airstrip and terminal; the 20-minute drive from the airport to Lalibela town, however, remains a trying experience. The town's current name, Lalibela, comes from the most famous of the Zagwe rulers, Lalibela, who ruled from the late 12th century to the early 13th century. Lalibela assembled craftsmen and artisans to carve the churches out of red volcanic tuff. The 11 churches are renowned for their beauty and architectural distinction as well as the fact that they are located close to each other. Each church is designed differently.

Medhane Alem (Redeemer of the World) is the world's largest rock-hewn church and stands 38 feet (11.5 meters) high and has 72 pillars. Maryam (Saint Mary) reportedly took 14 years to excavate and contains paintings depicting the star of David, and Mary and

Joseph fleeing Egypt with baby Jesus. Meskal (Cross) and Danaghel (Virgins or Martyrs) are small churches located off the square of Maryam. Two other churches, Debra Sina (Mount Sinai) and Golgotha, are found in the same complex. Debre Sina is said to be the final resting place of King Lalibela. The Selassie Chapel (Trinity Chapel), which lies within Golgotha, is the holiest place in Lalibela. The second cluster of churches consists of Emanuel, Mercurios, Abba Libanos, and Gabriel-Rufael (Gabriel and Raphael or the Archangels). Bet Lehem or the Chapel of Bethlehem is a small and simple shrine that may have been used as a monastic cell for King Lalibela's private prayers. It is connected by a tunnel to the Abba Libanos Church in the southeast cluster of churches. The most famous church in Lalibela is Bet Giorgis or Saint George. Carved from solid rock in the form of a symmetrical cruciform, Saint George is completely separate from the southeast and northwest clusters of churches.

LAMBIE, THOMAS A. (1885–1954). Medical **missionary**. Born in Pittsburgh, Pennsylvania. Lambie received his medical degree from the University of Pittsburgh (1907) and immediately sailed to Sudan to work for the American Presbyterian Mission. In 1911, he opened a new station at Nasir among the **Nuer**. On 15 January 1919, the United Presbyterian Church of North America approved his transfer to Ethiopia to help fight a flu epidemic in Sayo. He worked for the American United Presbyterian Mission (1919–1926). In 1921, **Ras** Tafari Makonnen, later **Haile Selassie**, asked Lambie to build a hospital on a 12-acre site at Gulele, outside **Addis Ababa**. In May 1923, Lambie used donations he had received during a recent trip to the United States to open the Ras Tafari Makonnen Hospital, which subsequently became the Central Medical Laboratory. He was responsible for the construction of two hospitals in Addis Ababa: one at Gulele, which subsequently became the Central Medical Laboratory, and the second at Akaki, which became home to the All-Africa Leprosy and Rehabilitation Training Center.

During his years in Addis Ababa, Lambie became increasingly concerned about the plight of communities in southern Ethiopia. In 1927, he, together with George Rhoad and Alfred Buxton, formed the Abyssinian Frontiers Mission to work with the southern **population**.

In 1927, these three men met with Rowland Bingham, founder of the Sudan Interior Mission (SIM), and agreed to join forces under the SIM's aegis to bring God's word to southern Ethiopia. Between 1927 and 1937, the SIM opened 16 centers.

During his years in Ethiopia, Lambie developed close ties with Haile Selassie and became his personal physician. To facilitate his work in Ethiopia, Lambie became an Ethiopian citizen (1934) but later lost his citizenship after falling afoul of the emperor. During the **Italian-Ethiopian War**, he acted as executive director of the **Ethiopian Red Cross Society**. On 24 March 1936, Lambie sent a telegram to *The Times* (London) that contained information about Italy's use of **chemical weapons** against Ethiopian villagers. Shortly afterwards, the Italians expelled him from the country.

During 1942–1945, Lambie was in the United States for medical treatment. In 1945, he sailed for Palestine as a member of the Independent Board for Presbyterian Foreign Missions. In 1952, Lambie opened the Berachah Tuberculosis Sanatorium in Bethlehem. He died on 14 April 1954 in Ain Arrub, Jordan. Lambie wrote several books, which are cited in the bibliography, on his experiences in Ethiopia. *See also* HEALTH.

LAND REFORM. *See* LAND TENURE.

LAND RESETTLEMENT. In 1958, the first land resettlement program in Ethiopia took place in Sidamo. Although a few more occurred after that, land resettlement only became significant after the **Derg** revolution. The number of resettlements grew rapidly after 1975. By 1982, there were 112 resettlement projects with more than 120,000 people. Many of these persons were victims of the 1973–1974 **famine** in **Wollo** who had resettled in western Wollega, Bale, and the **Ogaden**. Others were unemployed persons in **Addis Ababa**, displaced smallholders from state farms, and nomads who were redirected into agricultural pursuits. The settlements came under a Settlement Authority in the Ministry of **Agriculture** until 1979, when they were transferred to the Relief and Rehabilitation Commission (RCC). The settlements were expensive to establish, low in agricultural output, and reliant on continuing RCC assistance.

The original target was to move 1.5 million people to the resettlement areas. When the campaign ended in 1986, only about 600,000 had been relocated. About 90,000 settlers moved from **Tigray**, 107,000 from **Shoa** Province, and 370,000 from Wollo. Just over 250,000 went to western Wollega in the second phase, 150,000 settled south of **Gambela**, more than 100,000 near Pawe in what was then western **Gojam**, and 78,000 at **Kafa**. Smaller numbers went to Shoa and western **Gondar**. Some of these persons were forced to resettle and some died in the process. The program is generally considered to have been a failure, although several resettlement sites still exist and seem to be thriving.

LAND TENURE. The land tenure issue is complex and controversial, especially in a country that consists largely of peasant farmers. The early land tenure system, which dates back to the Axumite period, is not well understood, although it is known that certain churches, monasteries, bishops, and priests received land grants from the emperor. According to one account, Emperor Yekuno Amlak (reigned 1270–1285), gave the **Ethiopian Orthodox Church** (EOC) one-third of the country in exchange for its help in deposing the **Zagwe Dynasty**. There is no evidence, however, that suggests the church actually controlled all this land. Ethiopia's traditional land tenure system was so important because it determined social class; the emperor granted land on the basis of administration, **taxation**, and military service. Ethiopia's **agriculture**-based **economy** resulted in an extensive system of tribute, taxation, and rent based on the land.

The emperor often would waive his taxation rights in favor of local rulers or members of the royal family, nobility, priesthood, and religious institutions. This land was known as *gult* and allowed the holders to receive income that would otherwise have been allocated to the government. There were two types of royal land allocations. The permanent or inheritable tenure known as *rist* (also known as *rest*) had virtually no obligations for the owner. The temporary and not automatically inheritable tenure included specified conditions. Rist land could be passed on to ancestors and tended to be confined to previously unallocated land, newly acquired land, or land that had reverted to the crown. During the imperial period, therefore, there were four land tenure categories. The emperor owned the crown land

and could allocate it to the three other categories. Members of the royal family and nobility held land in perpetuity or temporarily or received the proceeds of taxation from gult land. The church or individuals associated with the church held land or received the taxes from gult land. Finally, some peasants received rist land from the crown or through inheritance or on a temporary basis for specific services rendered to the crown or to another landholder.

Prior to Ethiopia's territorial expansion of the late 19th century, most peasants worked land not held under private tenure. From this time until the 1974 revolution, most **highland** peasants worked privately held land as small-scale landholders or tenants. An estimated 35 percent of the peasant farmer **population** lived in kinship or village areas and 65 percent in private-tenure areas. The Ethiopian government created private-tenure land when it confiscated land conquered by its armies and then granted large land blocks to private individuals and institutions. Soldiers, civil servants who administered new areas, local tribes that did not resist conquest, peasants who agreed to take land at lower altitudes, the EOC, government officials, and village, clan, and tribal chiefs all benefited from these land grants. **Menelik II**'s government lacked the resources to govern these new areas; this land tenure system enhanced government control.

The EOC held a considerable amount of land, although probably less than the commonly believed one-third of the country, at the time of **Haile Selassie**'s downfall. One informed estimate placed EOC ownership at 5 percent of Ethiopia's total land area and 20 percent of its cultivated land. In some cases the EOC held the land outright. In others it belonged to individuals obligated to provide clergy for a community or by peasants who paid tribute to the EOC rather than taxes to the state. The government held an estimated 47 percent of Ethiopia's total land area but only 12 percent of its agricultural land. The government assumed that it owned all pastoral lands. Government tenure fell into several categories. Imperial representatives supervised palace land that provided agricultural produce and livestock for palace consumption. *Gebretel* land was that taken over by the government for failure by the owner to pay taxes. The government then leased or granted it to tenants. The government granted *maderia* land to government employees in lieu of salary or as a pension. The bulk of government land was called *mengist* tenure; it was either vacant land or leased to tenants for farming and grazing.

In 1975, the **Derg** instituted a series of land reforms that effectively nationalized the land so as to allocate 10 hectares to each peasant family. The new rules allowed for land transfers only in the case of inheritance. The state intervened at virtually every level of the land tenure process to impose discipline and uniformity. The Derg hoped its policies would boost agricultural development. It was common for field agents to remind the peasants that it was the Derg that gave them the land they were farming. The Derg encouraged peasants to join collectivized farms and **land resettlement** locations. During this period, rural agricultural institutions lost their decision-making power, and policy implementation and management came from government orders. There was no effort to consult peasants. After the Derg's collapse (1991), more than a half million Ethiopian peasants returned to rural areas from the army, neighboring countries, and resettlement sites.

Under the **Ethiopian People's Revolutionary Democratic Front** (EPRDF), there were heated debates about the land policy question. Ultimately, the new **constitution** decreed that "the right to ownership of rural and urban land . . . is exclusively vested in the State and in the Peoples of Ethiopia." Land is a common property of the people and cannot be sold and is not considered a market commodity. Although farmers have the right to use land and to transfer that use to their children, they cannot own it. The EPRDF encourages, however, the renting, leasing, and developing of land. Since 1991, there have been varying experiences with land distribution. In the EPRDF's early days, it was common practice to accommodate new claims through small allotments or to freeze new allocations. In densely settled areas, which continue to increase as a result of Ethiopia's high population growth rate, land is available only when someone dies without leaving an heir. In some locations, farmland has been subdivided so many times among family members that farmers no longer have enough land to grow sufficient **food** to feed the extended family. Those who lost land during the Derg are anxious to get it back but few have succeeded. Decisions on land redistribution are made at the local level and are often highly politicized with land tending to go to party loyalists. There have been a few local uprisings over land distribution decisions.

The United Nation's **Economic Commission for Africa** in its annual *Economic Report on Africa* for 2002 criticized Ethiopian land tenure policies. It noted that land tenure is one of the most pressing problems that requires institutional reform in Ethiopia. Current policies impede the development of key economic sectors and insecurity over land tenure discourages investment. The report concluded that a land title that provides ownership, whether by lease or total ownership, is an important route out of **poverty**. There is considerable research on land tenure in Ethiopia. Several especially useful studies include *Land Tenure and Land Policy in Ethiopia after the Derg* edited by Dessalegn Rahmato, *Agrarian Reform in Ethiopia* by the same author, *State and Land in Ethiopian History* by Richard Pankhurst, *Land and Society in the Christian Kingdom of Ethiopia* by Donald Crummey, *Land Tenure among the Amhara of Ethiopia* by Allan Hoben, and *Land and Peasants in Imperial Ethiopia* by John M. Cohen and Dov Weintraub.

LANGUAGES. The variety of languages in Ethiopia is as rich as its ethnic mix. In addition, it has a long history of written languages that includes **Ethiopic**, a south Semitic language grouped with south Arabian. Influenced by Cushitic elements, Ethiopic developed into **Ge'ez.** Today, **Amharic**, a Semitic language, serves as the primary language of the **Amhara people** and lingua franca for much of Ethiopia. There are an estimated 82 languages in Ethiopia, most of them described briefly in individual entries on different ethnic groups, and many more dialects. In addition to Amharic, other important Semitic languages include Tigrinya, spoken by **Tigrayans**; Harari, spoken in **Harar**; **Gurage,** spoken in an area to the southwest of **Addis Ababa**; Gafat, spoken by ethnic groups in the **Blue Nile** region of **Gojam** province; and **Argobba,** spoken northeast of Addis Ababa. The most thorough study of Semitic languages is Edward Ullendorf's *Semitic Languages of Ethiopia.*

Although Ethiopia is better known for its Semitic languages, there are actually more speakers of Cushitic languages as a first language. The most important is Afan Oromo, which is spoken by at least 40 percent of Ethiopia's population. It has an extensive oral literature, which is increasingly being committed to writing. Other important Cushitic languages are **Somali**, **Afar**, **Agau**, **Beja**, and **Saho**. Many Cushitic languages are part of the **Sidamo** group spoken by a number of tribes in southwestern Ethiopia. Between the **lakes** of southern

Ethiopia's **Rift Valley** and the **Omo River** numerous ethnic groups speak languages of the Omotic family. Among them are **Wolaytta**, **Gamo-Gofa-Dawro**, **Kaficho**, and **Shakacho**. In the far southwest and along Ethiopia's border with Sudan are several ethnic groups that speak Nilo-Saharan languages. The most numerous are the **Nuer** and **Anuak**. Perhaps 2 percent of Ethiopia's **population** speaks Nilo-Saharan languages. *See also* NATIONAL LITERACY CAMPAIGN; TIGRE-SPEAKING PEOPLES.

LEAGUE OF NATIONS. On 28 September 1923, Ethiopia gained admission to the League of Nations. **Ras** Tafari Makonnen, later **Haile Selassie**, welcomed this development as he believed that membership would protect Ethiopia from European imperialism and external threats, thereby enabling him to concentrate on the country's social and economic development. Subsequent events proved him wrong on all counts.

After the 5–7 December 1934 **Wal Wal Incident,** which involved a clash between Italian and Ethiopian troops, Haile Selassie appealed to the League of Nations on 3 January and again on 29 March 1935 to condemn Italy's aggression. However, in September 1935, the League ruled that neither country bore responsibility for the incident. Ethiopian negotiations with Italy also failed to resolve the matter, undoubtedly because Rome already had decided to attack Ethiopia. Pitman B. Potter's book *The Wal Wal Arbitration* provides the background of this incident.

On 5 October 1935, two days after the outbreak of the **Italian-Ethiopian War**, the League of Nations met and, on 7 October 1935, ruled that the Italian government had resorted to war in disregard of the League Covenant. The member states voted 50–1 (Italy against), with three abstentions (Albania, Austria, and Hungary), in favor of the resolution. On the same day, the League created a committee that recommended imposing four sanctions against Italy, including embargoes against the exportation, reexportation, or transit of arms, ammunition, and implements of war to Italy and its colonies; loans and credits to the Italian government and to public authorities, persons, or corporations in Italian territory; importation of goods grown, produced, or manufactured in Italy or its colonial possessions; and the exportation or reexportation to Italy or to its colonies of transport animals, rubber, bauxite, aluminum, iron ore, scrap iron, chromium, manganese, nickel, titanium, tungsten, anadium, their ores and ferro-alloys, tin and tin ore. On 18 November 1935, these sanctions went into effect.

On 30 June 1936, the emperor made an impassioned and unanswered plea to the League of Nations, urging its members to help Ethiopia resist "the aggressor." On 15 July 1936, the League ended its sanctions against Italy and, on 14 May 1938, voted to recognize Italy's right to remain in Ethiopia. *See also* CHEMICAL WEAPONS; EDEN, ANTHONY; HERUY WALDA SELASSIE; HOARE-LAVAL PLAN; MAKONNEN ENDAKATCHEW; SLAVERY; TEKLE-HAWARIYAT TEKLE-MARIYAM; WOLDE GIORGIS WOLDE YOHANNIS.

LEBNA DENGEL (1496–1540). Emperor of Ethiopia (1508–1540). Son of Emperor Naod (reigned 1494–1508). Also known as Dawit III and Wanag Saggad. During his minority, a regency that included his mother (Naod Mogassa) and his stepmother (Empress Eleni) administered the empire. During 1520–1526, Lebna Dengel hosted a Portuguese mission commanded by Dom Rodrigo de Lima. The emperor, who feared a Turkish occupation of **Massawa**, convinced de Lima to occupy and fortify the port. He also sought to use the Portuguese to end Ethiopia's isolation from Europe. In 1526, Lebna Dengel therefore dispatched a monk named Tsaga Zaab with de Lima to Lisbon to request that Portuguese craftsmen be sent to Ethiopia. In 1529, **Ahmad ibn Ibrahim al Ghazi** defeated the emperor's army at the Battle of Shembera Kure. As a result, Lebna Dengel lost his empire, which Gran ruled until his death (1543). On 2 September 1540, the emperor died alone and bankrupt.

LEJEAN, GUILLAUME (1828–1871). French traveler and diplomat. Born in Plouégat-Guérand in Finistère, France. Lejean spent his early career as secretary to the prefecture's council in Molaix. During 1847–1848, he traveled to Turkey, Senegal, Australia, and the Balkans. In 1860, Lejean and Orazio Antinori went to Sudan, where they toured Kordofan, the estuary of the Bahr el-Ghazal, and up the White Nile to Gondokoro. Fever forced him to return to France.

In 1862, he received an appointment as French vice-consul in **Massawa** with the mission of offsetting growing British influence by securing a commercial treaty with **Tewodros II**, protecting **Catholic missionaries** in Ethiopia, and developing a market for French goods. Despite some successes, Lejean failed to establish a strong French presence in Ethiopia largely because the emperor suspected him of being in collusion with the Egyptians. In late 1863, Tewodros II expelled Lejean.

LEUL. *See* IMPERIAL TITLES.

LIBIDO PEOPLE AND LANGUAGE. About 100,000 Libido people live west of Lake Zwai and northeast of the town of Hosaina. The **Gurage** live to their west, the **Alaba** and **Hadiyya** to the south, and the **Oromo** to the north and east. They are primarily Muslim. They speak an east Cushitic **language** that has 82 percent lexical similarity with Hadiyya, 57 percent with **Kambata**, 56 percent with Alaba, and 53 percent with **Sidamo**.

LIELT. *See* IMPERIAL TITLES.

LIJ. *See* IMPERIAL TITLES.

LIJ IYASU. *See* IYASU MIKAEL, LIJ.

LITERATURE. The first Ethiopian literature probably was a translation of the Old Testament into **Ge'ez** in the late fifth century. Translation of several works from Greek followed. The most significant contribution to Ethiopian literature is the 1,000-year-old *Kebra Nagast*. The 13th century witnessed the beginning of prolific original writing and translations from Arabic. By the late 14th century and the early 15th century, a new body of literature devoted to the lives of martyrs and saints appeared. Religious literature, both original works and translations, proliferated until a sharp decline after the **Islamic** invasions led by **Ahmad ibn Ibrahim al Ghazi** in the mid–16th century.

About the same time, the use of Ge'ez declined as a literary **language** although many significant works appeared in the 17th century. They included a theological encyclopedia, a history by Yohannes Madaber recounting the Arab conquest of Egypt, Abba Bahrey's *History of the Galla*, and a compilation of aphorisms from sources such as David, Solomon, Plato, and Aristotle.

Abu-Rumi Habessinus produced an **Amharic** translation of the Bible in Cairo, and a medical encyclopedia appeared in the early 19th century. **Tewodros II** encouraged Amharic literature as a way of developing national unity. In 1892, there was a translation of *Pilgrim's Progress*. In 1898, Afewerk Gebre Iyesus published the first Amharic novel, *Lebb Wallad Tarik* (*Imaginative Story*). Together with the *Life of Menelik II*, his work broke new ground in the use of Amharic.

Heruy Walda Selasse, considered by some to be the father of Amharic literature and a leading literary figure in the early 20th century, wrote political biography and commentary and allegorical works. **Makonnen Endalkatchew**, Kebbede Mikael, Tekle Sadek Makuria, and Germachew Tekle Hawariat followed with novels, plays, dramas in verse, histories, and biographies. **Imru Haile Selassie**, **Haddis Alemayehu**, Abbe Gubennya, Mammo Widdineh, Negash Gebre-Mariam, and Aseffa Genre-Mariam were important novelists in the 20th century. Some more recent authors write in English and Amharic. Daniachew Worku produced *The Thirteenth Sun* in English. Amare Mammo has translated several books from English into Amharic. Be'alu Girma was a renowned journalist and novelist who disappeared during the **Derg** regime. Sahle Selassie Berhane Mariam initially wrote *Shinega's Village* in the **Gurage** language. He subsequently wrote works in Amharic and English. His book called the *Warrior King* was selected as a Book of the Month. Other modern writers include Yilma Habteyes, Taddele Gebre-Hiymet, Zerihun Asfaw, and Aberra Lemma. Reidulf K. Molvaer published a useful compendium on select Ethiopian writers entitled *Black Lions*: *The Creative Lives of Modern Ethiopia's Literary Giants and Pioneers*.

Ethiopia has extensive folk literature, although much of it exists only in oral form. Amharic folk literature has most often been committed to writing. Many Amharic folk tales depict the proud patriotism and exclusiveness of the Amhara. Examples of Amharic folk literature are *The Tale of the Golden Earth*, *The Donkey Who Sinned*, and *The Goats Who Killed the Leopard*. Mahtama Sellassie Walda Masqal was one of the early compilers of folklore. There is a growing body of **Oromo** folk literature that has been translated into English by scholars like Claude Sumner. Rich Oromo literature includes humorous prose, proverbs and riddles, descriptions of magic, and prophetic statements. Ethiopian literature has received minimal attention in the outside world because until recently virtually all of it appeared in a language known only to Ethiopians. *See also* DRAMA; POETRY.

LOBO, JERONIMO (1595–1678). Jesuit **missionary** and explorer. Born in Lisbon. His father, Francisco Lobo da Gama, was governor (1596–1603) of Cape Verde. On 1 May 1609, Lobo became a Jesuit novice at Coimbra and was ordained in 1621. During 1617–1619, he taught Latin at the College of São Paulo at Braga in northern Portugal. Lobo then returned to Coimbra to study theology. Between December 1622 and January 1624, he lived in Goa, where he resumed his theological studies.

In 1624, Lobo left India en route to Ethiopia, whose emperor, **Susneyos**, had converted to Roman **Catholicism**. After arriving in Mombasa (Kenya), he unsuccessfully tried to reach his destination via the Juba River and **Oromo** country. In 1625, Lobo and eight missionaries finally arrived at the Jesuit headquarters in Fremona, **Tigray**, by way of Bailul port and the **Danakil Depression**. Apart from his religious activities, he explored the **Blue Nile** (1629). After Susneyos died (1632), the persecution of the Jesuits began. In May 1634, the Ethiopians handed Lobo and his companions over to the Turks at **Massawa**. His captors then sent Lobo to India to procure a ransom for his imprisoned fellow missionaries. He succeeded in this mission but failed to convince the Portuguese authorities to deploy a punitive expedition to Ethiopia. After spending a few years in Europe, Lobo returned to India (1640), where he became rector and subsequently provincial of the Jesuits at Goa. Lobo retired to Lisbon, where he died in Lisbon on 29 January 1678. Lobo's life and adventures are recounted in his *Itinerário of Jerónimo Lobo*.

LORING, WILLIAM WING (1818–1886). American soldier, legislator, mercenary, and businessman. Born on 4 December 1818 in Wilmington, North Carolina. Loring spent his early years in the Florida Volunteers (1835–1836). In 1842, he received a law degree from Georgetown College. Loring then served as a legislator in Florida (1843–1846) and as an officer in the U.S. Army (1846–1861). At the outbreak of the American Civil War (1861–1865), he resigned from the U.S. Army and joined the Confederate army as a brigadier general. After the war, Loring worked as a banker in New York City.

In December 1869, he joined the army of Egyptian khedive Ismail Pasha as inspector general with the rank of lewan (brigadier general). Shortly thereafter, Loring became commandant of Alexandria, with responsibility for defending the city and the coast to the mouth of the **Nile** River.

On 10 December 1875, the khedive appointed him army chief of staff and ordered him to accompany Sidar (commander in chief) Ratib Pasha on a 16,000-man military expedition to Ethiopia. Their mission was to avenge the Ethiopian victory at the **Battle of Gundet** by defeating **Yohannes IV**'s army and by restoring Egyptian prestige. The match proved to be unworkable as Ratib, who was a weak commander, ignored the counsel of the more experienced Loring. As a result, the Egyptian army suffered disastrous defeats at the Battle of Kaya Khor and the **Battle of Gura**. Nevertheless, the khedive promoted Loring to ferik (general of a division) and conferred upon him the Imperial orders of the Osmariah and Medjidie.

In 1879, he was mustered out of the army, returned to the United States, and settled in Florida before relocating to New York City, where he died on 30 December 1886. In 1874, he published an account of his time in the khedive's service entitled *A Confederate Soldier in Egypt*.

LOWLANDS. There is not a great deal of coherence to the term "lowlands" as it applies to Ethiopian politics and history. In one sense, lowland peoples tend to be non-Semitic and generally do not belong to the **Ethiopian Orthodox Church**. By definition, they live at lower altitudes and tend to have different economic systems that often depend heavily on pastoralism. During the late 19th century, many lowland peoples also were subject to conquest by highlanders. Lowland peoples are concentrated in northeastern Ethiopia, inhabited primarily by the **Afar**; and southeastern Ethiopia, inhabited by the **Somali** and by numerous ethnic groups living on the southern and western fringe of Ethiopia bordering Kenya and Sudan. Their ethnic ties frequently are linked more closely to the peoples living in neighboring countries than to **highland** Ethiopians. Lowlands normally begin below 5,000 feet (1,525 meters) altitude. *See also* AFAR REGION.

LUCY. *See* PALEOANTHROPOLOGY.

– M –

MAALE PEOPLE AND LANGUAGE. There are perhaps 20,000 Maale people living east of the **Ari** people and north of the **Hamer** and **Banna** peoples. They straddle the border between north and south **Omo**; their capital is Genda. In 1894, the Maale submitted peacefully to the forces of the Imperial Ethiopian government. Afterwards, the Maale lost considerable territory in a war with their neighbors to the north and invited the intervention of the Imperial forces to restore order. A king traditionally has led Maale society. Their concept of kingship includes a doctrine of the life-giving king, the concept of the unbroken transmission of his vital force, and the idea of politics as the orderly union of hierarchical status groups. The name of the Supreme Being of the Maale is Sosi. The Maale blame all their calamities on their sins and seek help from special sorcerers called *goji*. Maale is an Omotic **language** that belongs to the Ometo family. It has high lexical similarity with **Dorze**, Gofa, **Koorete**, and **Gamo**. Maale is spoken in the home. Donald L. Donham's *Work and Power in Maale Ethiopia* and *Marxist Modern: An Ethnographic History of the Ethiopian Revolution* are the most detailed studies of the Maale people.

MAJANGIR PEOPLE AND LANGUAGE. Also known as Masango, Masongo, Messengo, Ujang, and Tama, the Majangir may number only about 20,000 people. They populate a wide area in southwest Ethiopia from north of the Baro River near Dembi Dolo, southwards to the Gurrafarda range, the Erbu River, and other tributaries of the Akobo River. They live between Nilotic peoples such as the **Anuak** and **Nuer** to the west on the savanna of the Sudan-Ethiopia borderlands and Cushitic peoples such as the **Oromo** to their east on the **highland** plateau. Their physical appearance, **language**, and culture are different from that of their Nilotic and Cushitic neighbors. There are no written records of the Majangir before the 20th century. Most Majangir live in a tsetse-fly zone avoided by neighboring ethnic groups that depend on livestock. They hunt, fish, and raise subsistence crops. They are especially attached to honey, which they convert into an alcoholic drink called *ogol*. Drinking is a very important part of Majang society.

Although they have no permanent political leaders or chiefs, ritual experts known as *tapa* (plural) sometimes exercise chieflike functions. A *tapat* (singular) performs several tasks, including some that fulfill the role of religion. The prestige and fame of tapa, who can be male or female, tend to correspond to the size of their territories and number of followers. The Majang language belongs to the East Sudanic grouping. Variations in dialect between communities living in the northern and southern parts of their territory are relatively minor. Their literacy rate is unusually low. The most thorough study of these people is Jack Stauder's *The Majangir: Ecology and Society of a Southwest Ethiopian People.*

MAKEDA. Queen of Sheba. She maintained her capital at Dabra Makeda. According to Ethiopian traditions, Makeda and King Solomon of **Jerusalem** had a son named Menelik I who established the **Solomonic dynasty**. The story of her life and times is contained in the *Kebra Nagast*.

MAKONNEN ENDAKATCHEW (1891–1963). Shoan nobleman, civil servant and lifelong advisor to **Haile Selassie**. Born on 16 February 1890 in Tagulate, **Shoa**, and educated in various church schools and at the Menelik II Lyceum in **Addis Ababa**. Makonnen's father was one of **Menelik II**'s warriors and his mother came from a noble family. His father died in battle the year of his birth. In 1899, Makonnen moved to Menelik II's palace as a page. When the emperor became ill, he turned over the government to his grandson, **Lij Iyasu Mikael**. Makonnen supported Lij Iyasu, a move that did not advance his ambitions.

After **Ras** Tafari Makonnen, later **Haile Selassie**, became heir to the throne, Makonnen's career flourished. In 1924, he accompanied Ras Tafari to Europe. Subsequent assignments included comptroller of the **Addis Ababa–Djibouti Railway** (1924–1926), minister of commerce (1926–1931), Ethiopian envoy to the **League of Nations** and minister in London (1931–1933), mayor of Addis Ababa (1933–1934), and deputy minister of the interior and governor of **Ilubabor Province** (1935).

At the outbreak of the **Italian-Ethiopian War**, Makonnen was in charge of an army from Ilubabor that went to southeast Ethiopia to fight the Italians. He remained in exile in Palestine during the Italian occupation (1936–1941), writing two of his some 20 books during this time. He then received military training in Sudan and arrived in Addis Ababa ahead of the emperor to arrange a triumphal return on 5 May 1941. After liberation (1941), Makonnen became minister of the interior (1941–1943) and chairman of the **Council of Ministers** and then prime minister (1943–1957). In 1945, he was Ethiopia's representative at San Francisco during the signing of the United Nations Charter. Makonnen then served as president of the Senate (1957–1961) and received the highest noble title available— **ras bitwoded**. He had 16 children with his first wife, Zewditu Mengesha, and none from his second marriage to Yesheshwerq Yelma, a niece of Haile Selassie whose first husband had died during the Italian-Ethiopian War. Makonnen died on 27 February 1963 in Addis Ababa.

MAKONNEN WALDA MIKAEL, RAS (1852–1907). Soldier, diplomat, and father of **Haile Selassie**. Makonnen began his career as balambaras. In 1881, he became one of the palace treasurers and soon thereafter received the governorship of Wabari, a small district west of **Entoto**. After regaining control of **Harar**, **Menelik II** promoted Makonnen to **dajazmach** on 27 January 1887 and made him governor of Harar and commander of its 3,000-man garrison. With his well-armed military, Makonnen expanded Ethiopia's control over much **Somali**-inhabited territory and the European-occupied ports on the **Red Sea** coast. Beginning in 1888, Makonnen, along with the French, started to develop a new port at Djibouti. In May 1889, Menelik II promoted him to **ras**.

In September 1889, Makonnen went to Rome for the ratification of the **Treaty of Wichale** and to purchase weapons for the emperor. In February 1890, he returned to Ethiopia and became governor of Ittu **highlands**, west of Harar. After participating in the **Battle of Adwa**, Makonnen conquered the gold-producing regions of western Ethiopia. In October 1898, he went to **Tigray** and captured its rebellious governor, Ras **Mangasha Yohannes**. Makonnen remained in Tigray as overlord for more than a year. In mid-1900, he returned to Harar to organize an Anglo-Ethiopian punitive expedition against Mohammed Abdullah Hassan, who was also known as the Mad Mullah. In mid-1902, Makonnen went to Britain as Menelik II's representative at Edward II's coronation, and as envoy to France and Italy. He died on 22 March 1907 at the church he had built at Qulubi, 30 miles (48 kilometers) west of Harar. *See also* OGADEN, SOMALI REGION, and TIGRAY REGION.

MALO PEOPLE AND LANGUAGE. The Malo number about 50,000 in a mountainous part of the **Omo River** basin in southwest Ethiopia. The Gofa reside to the east and the **Basketo**, who were their former rivals and enemies in war, to the south. To the west are the **Dime** and to the north the Dawro. More than 90 percent of the Malo are farmers. They also raise cattle and engage in beekeeping. *Ensete* is an important part of their diet. There are four distinct social groups in Malo society associated with occupations. Two of these are related to farming and the others to crafts. Membership is ascribed at birth; Malo tend to have a caste society. The two farmer groups are the Gok'a and the Doko with the Gok'a serving as the dominant group. The Malo have their own **language,** known as Malittso, one of the Ometo dialects in the Omotic language family. In the eastern part, most Malo speak the Gofa language (Gofittso) and the culture is strongly influenced by the Gofa. In the western part, the language and culture are similar to that of the neighboring Basketo. *See also* GAMO-GOFA-DAWRO PEOPLE AND LANGUAGE.

MAMO DEGAGE WOLDE. *See* MARATHON AND DISTANCE RUNNERS.

MANGASHA JAMBARE (1892–1950). Civil servant and **patriot** commander. Born on 15 May 1892 in Gotta, **Gojam** Province. Mangasha began his career as governor in several Gojam districts. During 1937–1941, he, along with three other patriot commanders (**Negash Bezabeh**, Gessesse Belew, and Belai Zekeka), led the resistance against the Italians in Gojam until the end of the Italian occupation. Mangasha commanded a group of patriots at **Bahir Dar**, south of **Lake Tana.** He also provided guides and mules to Brigadier **Daniel Sandford**, who was commander of **Mission 101**.

After liberation (1941), Mangasha became **Haile Selassie**'s representative in Gojam. He subsequently served as governor of Bure **Damot** and **Agaw** Meder in Gojam and of **Wollega**. During 1945–1946, Mangasha was president of the Senate. On 14 April 1950, he died in **Addis Ababa**.

MANGASHA YOHANNES (1865–1906). Son of **Yohannes IV** and soldier. After his brother, Crown Prince Areaya Selasse, died in June 1888, Mangasha took command of his army with the title of **ras**. In March 1889, he fought at the **Battle of Metemma**. After Yohannes IV died on 10 March 1889, Mangasha succeeded him as commander of the Ethiopian army. However, he was no match, politically or militarily, for the man who became **Menelik II**. Rather than fight, Mangasha expressed his loyalty to the new emperor, who rewarded him with the governorship of **Tigray** (1890).

As governor, Mangasha's chief problem was how to thwart Italian plans to occupy Tigray. On 6–8 December 1891, he and several local chiefs held talks with Antonio Gandolfi, the Italian governor of Eritrea (1890–1992). They agreed to the Mareb Convention whereby both sides pledged loyalty to one another. On 2 June 1894, Mangasha arrived in **Addis Ababa** to allay Menelik II's suspicions about his dealings with the Italians. The emperor accepted his assurances of fidelity and ordered him to return to Tigray and recover all Italian-occupied territories. On 13–14 January 1895, Mangasha clashed with the Italians at the **Battle of Coatit** but had to withdraw to Senafe where, on 5 January 1895, he suffered a disastrous defeat. On 9 October 1895, the Italians again defeated his troops at Debra Aila, a setback that led to the Battle of **Amba Alage**. Despite these setbacks, he played a significant role in the **Battle of Adwa**.

Menelik II remained skeptical about Mangasha's loyalties. In 1898, Mangasha declined an imperial summons. The emperor then ordered Ras **Makonnen Walda Mikael** and Ras **Mikael Ali Abba Bula** to go to Tigray and capture Mangasha. On 10 February 1899, a contrite Mangasha submitted to Menelik II at **Dese**. The emperor subsequently imprisoned him in Addis Ababa. He was later transferred to **Ankober**, where he died on 29 December 1906.

MARATHON AND DISTANCE RUNNERS. Ethiopia has a long and proud history of producing the world's best male and, more recently, female long-distance runners. In 1956, Ethiopia first participated in the Olympic Games. The distance runners usually grow up in the Ethiopian **highlands** where the air is thin. They originate from a stock of people who tend to have slender physiques. Most of the successful runners come from modest rural backgrounds where shepherding and hard work in the fields are the norm. Many are **Oromo**. It is not unusual to see small groups of young Ethiopians streaking across the rural countryside in their free time in preparation for an upcoming long-distance event. Ethiopian men and **women** athletes won eight medals (four gold, one silver, and three bronze) in the 5,000-meter, 10,000-meter, and marathon events at the 2000 Sydney games. This placed Ethiopia 20th in the overall medal count and first among nine African countries that won medals.

One of the most significant male runners was Abebe Bikila (1932–1973). Born on 7 August 1932 in Jato, a small town near **Addis Ababa,** Abebe won the first Olympic gold medal for sub-Saharan Africa and set a world marathon record at the 1960 Rome games. Running in bare feet, he personified the natural marathon runner. Abebe won the world championships in 1960 and 1962. He also took the gold medal at the 1964 Tokyo games. This time he wore shoes but competed just weeks after having an emergency appendectomy. The circumstances of the win and his gymnastic display after the victory are still remembered by many who saw the race. Although Abebe trained for the 1968 Mexico City games, he had to withdraw from the race for health reasons. For most of his adult life, he belonged to the **Imperial Body Guard**. A March 1969 car crash paralyzed Abebe from the waist down. He died from a brain hemorrhage on 25 October 1973.

Mamo Degage Wolde (1932–2002) was another world-class runner. Born on 12 June 1932 in Dredele, near Addis Ababa, he captured the gold medal in the marathon at the 1968 Mexico City games. Mamo took the bronze medal at the 1972 Munich games. He was serving as a captain in the Imperial Body Guard when the **Derg** overthrew **Haile Selassie** (1974). Mamo was a local government official during the Derg regime. The **Ethiopian People's Revolutionary Democratic Front** accused him of involvement in the **Red Terror** and imprisoned him without trial. On 18 January 2002, the Federal High Court finally sentenced Mamo to six years' imprisonment for killing a young boy. As the sentence was retroactive and Mamo already had served nine years, he was released from prison. He died on 26 May 2002 and was buried in Addis Ababa.

Miruts Yifter (1938–) won the 5,000- and 10,000-meter races at the 1980 Moscow games. He astonished the running world by changing his pace on the last lap. Miruts took a bronze medal in the 10,000-meter race at the 1972 Munich games and was a good bet for a medal at the 1976 Montreal games. However, African countries boycotted the Olympics because of New Zealand's rugby tour of South Africa. An **Amhara**, Miruts became concerned about his political future in Ethiopia after the Derg's collapse and sought political asylum in Canada.

Ethiopia's best-known male distance runner is Haile Gebreselassie (1973–). Born on 18 April 1973 in the southern town of Assela, Haile won the 10,000-meter event in four world championships and took the gold medal at the 1996 Atlanta games and the 2000 Sydney games. He holds the world record in this event. In 2001, he announced that he would no longer run the 10,000-meter race and would move to the marathon. Haile lives modestly in Ethiopia and is active in civic affairs. His older brother, Tekeye Gebreselassie, was also a promising distance runner who sought political asylum in the Netherlands. On 25 September 2001, he became goodwill ambassador for Pathfinder International/Ethiopia, a nongovernmental organization that has worked in Ethiopia's **health** sector for more than four decades.

Other successful male runners include Million Wolde, who was born on 17 March 1979. He took a gold medal in the men's 5,000-meter race at the 2000 Sydney games. Gezahegn Abera, who was born on 17 July 1978, also won a gold medal in the marathon at the 2000 Sydney games and the 2001 world championships marathon in Edmonton. Bronze-medal winners at the 2000 Sydney games included Assefa Mezgebu, who was born on 19 June 1978 in **Sidamo**, in the 10,000 meters and Tesfaye Tola, who was born on 19 October 1974, in the marathon. Tesfaye Jifar, who was born on 23 April 1976 at Amboi, set a new record in the 2001 New York marathon.

More recently, Ethiopian women have joined the medal parade in distance running. Derartu Tulu, who was born on 21 March 1972, won the 10,000-meter gold medal at the 1992 Barcelona games and the 2000 Sydney games. She won the same event at the 2001 world championships in Edmonton. Two other Ethiopian women, Berhane Adere, who was born on 23 July 1973 in **Shoa** Province, and Gete Wami, who was born on 29 March 1974 in Debre Birhan, won respectively the silver and bronze in Edmonton. Gete Wami also won the women's marathon at the 1996 Atlanta games and captured the silver and bronze in the 10,000-meter and 5,000-meter events respectively at the 2000 Sydney games.

MARIA THERESA THALER. *See* CURRENCY.

MARTIN, CHARLES. *See* WARQNAH ISHETE.

MARXIST-LENINIST LEAGUE OF TIGRAY (MLLT). On 25 July 1985, moderate elements in the **Tigray People's Liberation Front** (TPLF), supported by **Meles Zenawi**, established the MLLT. Its first chairman was Abbay Tsefaye. The MLLT, which was the TPLF's political wing, aimed to form a united front with other national organizations to reform Ethiopia along ethnic lines. In the late 1980s, the MLLT saw itself as part of an international movement committed to struggling against U.S. and Soviet imperialism. After the **Ethiopian People's Revolutionary Democratic Front** seized power (1991), the MLLT virtually disappeared. Its views and activities remained largely a matter of speculation in the West. After the outbreak of the **Ethiopian-Eritrean War**, Asmara accused the MLLT ⊂f seeking to create a Greater **Tigray** and planning to destroy Eritrea. Currently, some opposition elements maintain that the MLLT is a shadow government while supporters argue that it is just a regional party.

MASSAIA (MASSAJA), GUGLIEMO (1809–1889). Italian **missionary**. Born Lorenzo Antonio Massaia on 8 June 1809 in Piova in the Kingdom of Piedmont. In 1825, he entered the Capuchin Franciscan order, receiving his habit on 25 September 1825. Massaia then became a theology lecturer and confessor to Prince Victor Emmanuel, afterwards the king of Italy, and Ferdinand, Duke of Genoa.

In 1846, Rome dispatched him to Ethiopia to work among the **Oromo**. As the apostolic vicar of the **Galla**, Massaia organized missions throughout southern and southwestern Ethiopia. He consecrated **Justin de Jacobis**, vicar apostolic for the Copts. This act angered the **Coptic** patriarch of Egypt who sent his own bishop, **Abba Salama**, to Ethiopia. As a result of the ensuing political agitation, the Ethiopian authorities banished Massaia from the country. In 1850, he returned to Italy and enlisted more missionaries to work in Ethiopia. On his return, he established many missions throughout Ethiopia and composed a grammar of the **Oromo language**.

In 1879, he departed Ethiopia and, the following year, convened a conference at the Convent of the Capuchin Fathers in Toulouse, France. During his presentation, Massaia asked for new missionaries to live and work among the Oromo and announced his resignation as head of the apostolic vicariate. During his 35 years as a missionary, he was exiled seven times but always returned to his work. In recognition of Massaia's many accomplishments, Pope Leo XIII (1810–1903) raised him to the archbishopric of Stauropolis and, on 10 November 1884, made him a cardinal. On 6 August 1889, Massaia died at Cremona, Italy. Interestingly, in the mid-1930s, Italian Fascists maintained that his work in Ethiopia had laid the groundwork for the Italian occupation of that country. *See also* CATHOLICISM.

MASSAWA. An ancient **Red Sea** port that has been northern Ethiopia's gateway to the sea and the terminus of one of the main trade routes from the interior. Because of its strategic importance, Massawa has attracted many foreigners who wanted to use or control the port. On 10 February 1541, 400 Portuguese soldiers, under the command of Christovãro da Gama (son of Vasco), arrived in Massawa to help repulse **Ahmad ibn Ibrahim al Ghazi** and his followers. In 1557, the Turks captured Massawa as part of a grand strategy to break Portuguese domination of the Indian Ocean. The port remained under Turkish control for more than 200 years. In the late 18th century, the sherif of Mecca governed Massawa until it passed to Mehemet Ali of Egypt. About 1850, the Turks returned Massawa to Egypt in exchange for an annual tribute. On 5 February 1885, Italy took possession of the port, which served as the capital of the Italian colony until 1900, when the administration moved to Asmara. During 1941–1952, the **British Military Administration** controlled Massawa, while from 1952 until 1991, the port was part of Ethiopia.

After the **Derg**'s downfall (1991), Ethiopia and Eritrea pledged to cooperate in developing both countries. On 27 September 1993, **Addis Ababa** and Asmara concluded a Transit and Port Service Agreement that gave the latter unhindered access to Massawa and **Asab**. However, the outbreak of the **Ethiopian-Eritrean War** nullified the agreement, thereby forcing Ethiopia to rely on the port of Djibouti for access to the sea. *See also* ETHIOPIAN-ERITREAN FEDERATION; ITALIAN-ETHIOPIAN WAR.

MATEWOS, ABUNA (1857–1926). Bishop of **Shoa** Province (1881–1889), metropolitan of Ethiopia (1889–1926), and councilor of **Menelik II**. Born and educated in Egypt. In 1881, **Yohannes IV** asked Matewos and three other clerics to come to Ethiopia. The emperor assigned Matewos to Menelik (later Menelik II), then **negus** of Shoa. After Yohannes IV died (1889), Matewos anointed Menelik II as emperor and threatened to excommunicate anyone who failed to support him. In return for his loyalty, Menelik II appointed him metropolitan of Ethiopia, a position that ranks above an archbishop but below a patriarch. Matewos accompanied the emperor on many of his travels and military campaigns and functioned as his foreign affairs adviser. In 1902, he undertook a diplomatic mission to Russia but found no common ground with the Russian church or government. In 1907–1910, Matewos served as minister of education. In 1909, he supported Menelik II's decision to proclaim **Lij Iyasu** as his heir presumptive but eventually sided with the Shoan nobles who wanted to depose him. In 1917, Matewos anointed **Zawditu Menelik** as empress. Over the next few years, he remained active in politics. In 1922, Matewos became ill and, on the advice of his physician, lived in Egypt, Djibouti, and **Dire Dawa** until his death on 4 December 1926.

MEDIA. **Menelik II** introduced mass media to Ethiopia more than a century ago. Some early newspapers included the bilingual weekly *Le Semeur d'Ethiopie* (1884) and the first **Amharic** newspaper, *Aimero* (1895). Other significant media developments included the start of radio broadcasting (1941), shortwave radio broadcasting (1963), and Ethiopian Television (1964). In 1943, the Ethiopian News Agency commenced operations.

By the late 1960s, Radio Ethiopia, Ethiopian Television, Ethiopian News Agency, and Ethiopian Press Organisation had been organized under the Ministry of Information. The imperial government was an absolute, undemocratic monarchy that granted no right to freedom of expression for the print or broadcast media.

During 1974–1991, the military ruled Ethiopia as a communist state. The country's major mass media institutions (i.e., radio, television, and press) became departments under the Ministry of Information and National Guidance. The ministry reported to the Central Committee of the **Workers' Party of Ethiopia**. The mass media concentrated on disseminating propaganda to promote the **Derg**'s political, economic, and social goals. However, the mass media also devoted time to more worthy endeavors such as promoting literacy campaigns and **health** and farming initiatives.

When the **Ethiopian People's Revolutionary Democratic Front** (EPRDF) took power (1991), the new government permitted the establishment of private mass media for the first time in Ethiopia. Numerous private daily and weekly newspapers and magazines started operations. Radio and television broadcasting, however, remained the preserve of the federal and regional states. Ethiopia's only private radio station, Radio Fana, is owned by the EPRDF through a business organization, the MegaNet Corporation. In December 1993, the Walta Information Center began operations but, like Radio Fana, is owned by the EPRDF through the MegaNet Corporation. The Walta Information Center, which has some 27 branches throughout Ethiopia, is a major domestic and international news provider. In March 1995, the Ethiopian Press Enterprise, the Ethiopian Radio and Television Enterprise, and the Ethiopian News Agency started operations. All of these institutions had the legal autonomy to generate their own finances, primarily from advertisements and sponsorships. The government also agreed to subsidize them with public funds for a maximum of five years.

Ethiopia's mass media historically have suffered from state control and censorship. Conditions under the monarchy and the Derg were particularly strict. On 12 October 1992, the Ethiopian News Agency announced that the EPRDF had adopted a new law to end four decades of press censorship. The EPRDF also took steps to allow more local **languages** to be used in broadcasting. However, critics maintain that Ethiopia still suffers from government control and government harassment of journalists. In October 1992, for example, the government issued Press Proclamation No. 34/1992. The legislation prohibited the dissemination of information that the government deemed dangerous and required the licensing of all journalists. Moreover, the law classified libel as a criminal and civil offense, demanding penalties of payment in the amount of twice the value of a publisher's assets.

According to the New York–based Committee to Protect Journalists (CPJ), Ethiopia used this legislation to imprison more than 50 journalists in 1993–1995, more than any other African country. By late 2001, the CPJ reported that there was only one journalist in jail while seven others had been freed. However, on 9 April 2002, the Paris-based Reporters sans Frontières announced that the Ethiopian authorities had jailed three journalists just weeks after Ethiopian prisons had been declared free of journalists. On 25 July 2002, the CPJ claimed that a proposed new press law would further restrict the rights of Ethiopia's private press corps.

By the early 21st century, there were several Ethiopian organizations working to improve conditions for journalists and other media workers. The Ethiopian Free Press Journalists' Association (EFPJA), founded in 1993 and registered in 2000, has sought to promote media pluralism and has criticized the EPRDF for interfering in the operations of the private print media and for its monopolistic control of the broadcast media. Another complaint is the government's practice of appointing all individuals to the boards of mass media organizations. The EFPJA also advocates the establishment of an independent Print and Broadcasting Council to protect and promote freedom of the mass media. The Ethiopian Journalists' Association represents journalists who work for government media. The Ethiopian Media Women's Association, established in 1997 and registered in 1999, works with the government and private media. See also HUMAN RIGHTS.

MEDICINE. See HEALTH.

ME'EN PEOPLE AND LANGUAGE. The Me'en number more than 50,000 in Bench-Maji zone of **Southern Nations, Nationalities, and People's Region**. Also known as the Mekan, they include the Tishena, who live in and around the town of Bachuma, and the Bodi, who live in the **lowlands** to the south near the **Omo River**. The **Dizi** and **Suri** live to the south, the **Anuak** and **Majangir** to the west, the **Sheko** and **Bench** to the north, and the **Nayi**, **Chara**, **Basketo**, and

Dime to the east. The Me'en are divided into many territorial sub-groups formed around dominant clan segments. They are predominantly agriculturists who grow sorghum, wheat, corn, teff, beans, cabbage, and peas. Most rely on digging sticks, although a few have adopted the plow. Those living in the lowlands are pastoralists. They once had close relations with the Suri; contacts today are limited. They do not have powerful chiefs; traditional leaders are clan elders, hereditary rain chiefs, and regional "deputies." In about 1898, they were incorporated into the Ethiopian Empire.

In the 1960s, the American Presbyterian Mission came to the area. However, the **Derg** expelled the mission, which dishonored Me'en leaders and tried to suppress aspects of the Me'en culture. In 1977, the Me'en retaliated by attacking **Amhara** who lived in their territory. Derg authorities put down the rebellion and executed some leaders, but the Me'en remained hostile to the revolution. Some have converted to Christianity but most follow traditional beliefs. Me'en priests communicate with the deity through the rainbow, which is believed to be the bridge that connects them with him. They also believe in the evil eye. Me'en is an eastern Sudanic **language** of the Surmic family. There are several dialects and the language is closely related to **Mursi**. It has 65 percent lexical similarity to Suri and 30 percent to **Murle**.

MEISON. *See* ALL-ETHIOPIAN SOCIALIST MOVEMENT.

MEKANE YESUS. *See* ETHIOPIAN EVANGELICAL CHURCH MEKANE YESUS.

MEKELE. (122,700, estimated 2002 **population**.) The capital of **Tigray Region,** Mekele is situated on a treeless plain 482 miles (777 kilometers) from **Addis Ababa**. Some historians believe that the town was founded in the 13th century. By the early 1870s, Mekele had reached its zenith when **Yohannes IV** was crowned emperor. In 1872, Yohannes IV chose the town as the seat of his government and built a castle as his palace. It now serves as the Yohannes IV Museum. The Abraha Castle, built in the 1890s, is similar in design to the palace and is now a hotel. Mekele is the primary transfer point for the trade in salt bars that are mined in the **Danakil Depression** and transported by camel, mule, and donkey caravans to market.

Mekele has experienced considerable development since the **Ethiopian People's Revolutionary Democratic Front** (EPRDF) took power (1991). A monument to the martyrs in the fight against the **Derg** dominates the center of town. New hotels, banks, and businesses dot the city. Mekele University College and Mekele Business College attract students from around the country. Mekele now boasts one of the country's best airports. There is a new cement plant on the outskirts. On 5 June 1998, almost simultaneously with an Ethiopian attack on Asmara airport, Eritrean planes attacked Mekele, killing at least 40 people, many of whom were children. Although located relatively close to the border with Eritrea, development projects continued uninterrupted throughout the **Ethiopian-Eritrean War.** In recent years, the town has enjoyed a high degree of economic development largely because of the actions of the **Endowment Fund for the Rehabilitation of Tigray**.

MELAKU BEYAN (1900–1940). Physician and cousin of **Haile Selassie**. Born in **Shoa** Province. In 1910, Melaku began his career as a page for **Ras** Tafari Makonnen, later Haile Selassie, who had been appointed governor of **Harar**. In 1921, he went to India for an education. Melaku then attended Muskingum College, Ohio (1922–1928), and Howard University's medical school (1930–1935).

After the outbreak of the **Italian-Ethiopian War**, he accompanied Haile Selassie into exile in Britain, where he acted as the emperor's physician, interpreter, and secretary. In September 1936, Melaku went to the United States as Haile Selassie's representative and coordinator of fund-raising activities. The following year, he established the Ethiopian World Federation as the main fund-raising organization for his country. In August 1939, Melaku suffered a nervous breakdown that caused his health to deteriorate. On 4 May 1940, he died of pneumonia.

MELES ZENAWI (1955–). Born in **Adwa** on 9 May 1955, Meles Legesse Zenawi is the third and youngest son in the family. He is the grandson of a **dajazmach**. Meles' father, Zenawi Asresu, was from the lower **Tigrayan** nobility and given the title of dajazmach during the Italian occupation. His mother was Alemash Gebreleul. He attended Queen of Sheba government school in Adwa and then graduated with honors from the prestigious General Wingate High School (1972) in **Addis Ababa**. Meles received the Haile Selassie I Prize Trust, a selective award given only to outstanding students. He studied medicine at **Addis Ababa University** for two years until he dropped out in 1974 to join the Tigrayan nationalist movement after the **Derg** had come to power.

Meles first joined the Tigray National Organization, a forerunner of the **Tigray People's Liberation Front** (TPLF). Following the TPLF's creation on 18 February 1975, Meles became one of the fighters. In fact, his name "Meles" is a *nom de guerre* in tribute to Meles Tekle, a Tigrayan nationalist student killed in 1974 by the Derg. During the first two years of the war, Meles fought in the Shembeko area in Shire District, west of **Axum**. He served as a rank-and-file member of the TPLF (1975–1979), a member of the Central Committee (1979–1983), a member of the Executive Committee (1983–1989), and chairman of the TPLF and the **Ethiopian People's Revolutionary Democratic Front** (EPRDF) (1989–1991). The 1–5 July 1991 Peace and Democracy Conference designated Meles as president of the Transitional National Government of Ethiopia and chairman of the Council of Representatives or transitional **parliament**. In the May 1995 elections, Meles was elected in **Tigray Region** to the **House of Peoples' Representatives** (HPR). On 22 August 1995, the HPR elected him as the first prime minister of the Federal Democratic Republic of Ethiopia and it reelected him to that position in 2000 for another five-year term. On 16 September 2001, Meles was reelected for the fourth time as EPRDF chairman.

In 1995, Meles received an MBA by correspondence from London's Open University. He reportedly received one of the highest scores ever given on the final examination. Well-read and in command of colloquial English, in addition to Tigrigna and **Amharic**, Meles has a particularly good understanding of economics. This is quite a change from his days in the TPLF when he espoused Marxist ideas. After the EPRDF defeated the Marxist-Leninist Derg (1991), Meles quietly dropped references to Marxism and pursued a political philosophy more acceptable to the West. Thoughtful and quiet-spoken, Meles is a formidable dialectician. Except for heavy security, he lives modestly. He enjoys reading, swimming, and tennis. Meles is married to Lemlem Mesfin (originally Azieb Mesfin) from the Wolkait area of **Gondar**. They have three children.

MENELIK II (1844–1913). Emperor (3 November 1889–12 December 1913). Born Sahle Maryam on 17 August 1844 in **Ankober**, son of Haile Melakot and grandson of **Sahle Selassie**, both of whom had been rulers of the Shoan kingdom. Educated in his grandfather's palace. After becoming emperor (1855), **Tewodros II** sought to restore the central government's authority over semi-independent territories like **Shoa** Province by mounting a series of military expeditions. During the 1855 Shoan offensive, imperial troops killed Haile Melakot and took the young prince to the emperor's capital at Magdala. On 30 June 1865, Menelik escaped and returned to Shoa, where he proclaimed himself **negus** (August 1865). As negus, he conquered the **Oromo** and annexed their land. In 1877, he recovered **Harar**, which the Egyptians had occupied in 1875.

On 3 November 1889, **Abuna Matewos**, the bishop of Shoa, crowned Menelik II the emperor of Ethiopia at the Church of Mary on Mount **Entoto**, after **Yohannes IV**'s death during the **Battle of Metemma**. Apart from an ambitious domestic agenda, the emperor sought to modernize and develop Ethiopia with the help of foreign advisers and craftsmen. By the late 19th century, he also had added much of what is now southwest Ethiopia to the empire.

Menelik II's accomplishments included the unification of the northern kingdoms of **Tigray** and **Amhara** and the establishment of a modern government. He also instituted compulsory **education** for all boys over the age of 12, suppressed **slavery**, founded **Addis Ababa**, curbed the power of the feudal nobility, and opened diplomatic relations with Britain, France, Germany, and Russia. He also achieved impressive military victories at Harar and, more importantly, at the **Battle of Adwa**. Additionally, Menelik authorized the construction of the **Addis Ababa-Djibouti Railway** and introduced postal, telegraph, and telephone services.

On 25 October 1907, Menelik announced the formation of Ethiopia's first cabinet and directed the Ministry of Justice to establish an appellate court system in the provinces. During 1908–1909, his health declined. Power gradually passed into the hands of his wife, Empress **Taytu Betul**. On 18 May 1909, Menelik II designated **Lij Iyasu** as his successor and **Ras** Resamma as regent. After suffering a stroke, Menelik II died on the night of 12–13 December 1912. *See also* FOREIGN POLICY.

MENGISTU HAILE MARIAM. Head of state and president (11 September 1987–21 May 1991); first vice-chairman of the **Provisional Military Administrative Council** (PMAC) and the **Derg**; commander in chief of the **armed forces**; and chairman of the executive and central committees of the **Commission for Organizing the Party of the Working People of Ethiopia**, **Council of Ministers**, National Economic Development Campaign, Supreme Planning Council, and National Defense and Security Council.

Despite Mengistu's notoriety, there is conflicting information about his early life and family. Various scholars have said he was born in 1936, 1937, 1939, 1940, 1941, or 1942 in **Jimma** or Holeta. Some observers maintain that he was an **Oromo** but others maintain that his mother belonged to the **Konso** and his father probably was an **Amhara**. Some believe his father was an army sergeant while others claim he was a house guard for an influential family in **Addis Ababa**. There also are reports that his father had served in both positions.

Mengistu grew up in a military environment and attended school for a few years before entering the army. The influence of Kebede Tessama, a former governor of **Gojam**, enabled him to enter Holeta (Genet) Military Academy. In 1960, he was among 40 cadets who mutinied because they had not been paid. The authorities responded by assigning all of them to the Third Division in the **Ogaden**, which was considered a hardship post. During Mengistu's tenure, a superior officer accused him of irregularities in handling spare parts, but he later received a pardon from the Third Division's commander, General Nega Tegegne. Mengistu received further military training in the United States (1963 and 1969). In 1973, he was promoted to major. Nevertheless, Mengistu became increasingly disgruntled because of **corruption** and favoritism in the army.

In June 1974, he reached a turning point in his career when he became the Third Division's representative to the Derg. Mengistu quickly embarked on a ruthless quest for political power and demonstrated an intolerance toward all who stood in his way. On 12 September 1974, he was elected as first vice-chairman of the Provisional Military Administrative Council. In August 1976, Mengistu and his colleagues established the **Revolutionary Flame**, a political party that sought to dominate the **Provisional Office for Mass Organizational Affairs**. Some of his more important appointments included chairman of the Council of Ministers (29 December 1976), chairman of the PMAC (11 February 1977), and secretary-general of the **Workers' Party of Ethiopia** (10 September 1984).

Despite Mengistu's tight control of the country's political system, his regime faced many challenges, including a **coup (1977)**, **coup attempt (1976)**, and **coup attempt (1989)**. There also was opposition from political parties such as the **Ethiopian People's Revolutionary Party,** which he sought to silence by unleashing the **Red Terror** and committing other **human rights** violations. Several rebel groups, the most important of which included the **Eritrean Liberation Front**, **Eritrean People's Liberation Front** (EPLF), **Tigray People's Liberation Front** (TPLF), and **Oromo Liberation Front** posed more serious threats to his regime. The **armed forces** also participated in a costly military campaign against Somalia during the **Ogaden War (1977–1978)**.

By the late 1980s, it had became apparent that the Mengistu regime was in its death throes. Growing military pressure against Mengistu, primarily from the EPLF and TPLF, signaled the pending demise of his regime. On 5 June 1989, Mengistu proposed to open negotiations with the EPLF and TPLF "without conditions;" the former rejected the offer while the latter accepted. However, subsequent peace talks with the TPLF failed to produce any meaningful results. On 25 June 1990, the **National Shengo** adopted a resolution that called for "nonstop recruitment" for the armed forces. On 26 July 1990, Mengistu announced that Ethiopia had abandoned communism and wanted to improve relations with the United States. On 19 April 1991, he offered to resign to preserve the country. Finally, on 21 May 1991, Mengistu fled Ethiopia without informing his closest advisers and confidants. Initially, he went to Kenya but eventually settled in Zimbabwe.

Mengistu ranked among Africa's most brutal dictators. Nevertheless, during a rare 28 December 1999 interview with the *Star*, a South African newspaper, Mengistu defended his government. Among other things, he claimed the Red Terror had been merely a fight between two social groups, one of which was seeking to overthrow his government. *See also* FOREIGN POLICY.

MENGISTU LEMMA (1928–1988). A literary giant, Mengistu was born on 8 June 1928 in **Addis Ababa** and grew up in **Harar,** where his father was the *aleqa* in the **Ethiopian Orthodox Church**. He studied religious music and classical **poetry** or *qene*. He completed his secondary education in Addis Ababa at Haile Selassie I secondary school. He then went to London where he studied at the Regent Street Polytechnic, London School of Economics, and University of London. He participated in the Ethiopian Students Society and served as the editor of its publication, *The Lion Cub*. After returning to Ethiopia, his first job was in the Ethiopian Civil Aviation Department. Mengistu moved to the Ministry of Foreign Affairs, served in New Delhi, and returned to the Ministry as director general of the division of social and economic affairs in the United Nations Department. He then became secretary general of the Amharic Language Academy in the Ministry of Education. A good socialist, he stayed on there after the **Derg** seized power (1974) and later moved to the Ministry of Culture.

Mengistu's real love was **literature**, poetry, and playwriting. Always writing in **Amharic**, he is especially known for his plays *Marriage by Abduction* and *The Marriage of Unequals*. Although his early work tended to be comedies, after the 1974 revolution he published more serious plays and poems. He died in Addis Ababa on 27 July 1988.

MENGISTU NEWAY (1919–1961). Imperial Body Guard commander and coup plotter. Born in **Addis Ababa** and attended the Holeta (Genet) Military Academy. After the outbreak of the **Italian-Ethiopian War**, Mengistu went into exile in Sudan, where he received additional military training at Sobar Academy (1940–1941). He also served as a subaltern with the commonwealth forces and with the **patriots** during the reconquest of Ethiopia. Shortly afterward, Mengistu became a confidant of **Haile Selassie**. In 1951, he suppressed a revolt against the emperor. Mengistu then served as commander with the **Kagnew Battalions** during the Korean War. In 1955, he became the Imperial Body Guard commander and, on 3 October 1956, received a promotion to brigadier general.

In collaboration with his brother, **Germane Neway**, Mengistu conspired to overthrow Haile Selassie. On 13 December 1960, the pair attempted a coup while the emperor was in Brazil. On 15–16 December 1960, loyalists suppressed the **coup attempt (1960)**, prompting Mengistu to flee into the mountains. On 24 December 1960, the authorities captured him. A court subsequently found Mengistu guilty of committing "outrages against the constitutional authorities" and sentenced him to death. On 30 March 1961, he was hanged in Addis Ababa's market.

MERCHANT MARINE. *See* TRANSPORTATION.

MEREB RIVER. The Mereb River is primarily an Eritrean river that rises near Asmara and flows south where it constitutes the border with Ethiopia for about 125 miles (200 kilometers) before turning west through Eritrea. It serves as the border for the northeast portion of Badme, the location of the Eritrean incursion in May 1998 into territory administered by Ethiopia that led to the **Ethiopian-Eritrean War**. The Mereb is known as the Gash River in western Eritrea and continues into Sudan where it joins the **Atbara River**. Although dry for much of the year, it becomes an important river in the rainy season.

MESKEL. *See* HOLIDAYS, RELIGIOUS.

MESOB. *See* HANDICRAFTS.

METEMMA. A town noted for its commercial, historic, and strategic importance. Metemma is located on Ethiopia's northern border with Sudan. Galabat town is located on the Sudanese side of the border. Historically, Galabat/Metemma has been the most important point of Ethiopian-Sudanese contact. In the late 1800s, conflict between the Mahdist or Ansar forces in Sudan and the Ethiopians reached a peak. The Mahdist movement was a combination of religious revivalism and Sudanese opposition to Egyptian rule. When Ethiopia came to the relief of beleaguered Egyptian garrisons, the Mahdists took out their wrath on Ethiopia and sacked **Gondar** (1888). In response, **Yohannes IV** led about 100,000 troops in 1889 against an estimated 60,000 to 70,000 Mahdists at the **Battle of Metemma**. An initial Ethiopian victory turned to a rout when the Mahdists killed Yohannes IV at Metemma. The Mahdists captured Yohannes IV's corpse, severed his head, and sent it back to Omdurman. The Ethiopians retreated but cattle disease and

famine complicated the situation and **Tigray** fell into disarray. These hostilities contributed to the commercial decline of Metemma and Gondar.

Coming from Sudan, British forces entered Ethiopia in 1941 to remove the Italians from Ethiopia. Although the Italians initially repulsed the British at Metemma, overwhelming force eventually defeated the Italians, and the British and Ethiopian forces moved on to **Addis Ababa**. Metemma also was an important border crossing for Ethiopian **refugees** fleeing the terrible famine of the mid-1980s. As Ethiopian-Sudanese relations worsened in the mid-1990s, Addis Ababa closed the border and Metemma became a backwater. This situation changed following the outbreak of the **Ethiopian-Eritrean War**. Eritrea closed its ports (**Asab** and **Massawa**), forcing Ethiopia to rely on the small port at Djibouti. In recent years, Ethiopia has sought other outlets to the sea, primarily Port Sudan in Sudan and Berbera in Somaliland. On 28 December 1999, the Ethiopian News Agency announced that Addis Ababa and Khartoum had concluded an agreement whereby Ethiopia could use Port Sudan on the **Red Sea** for exporting and importing goods. The Port Sudan–Gondar road passes through Metemma. Ethiopia also imports Sudanese oil through Metemma. On 30 January 2003, Ethiopia and Sudan announced the opening of a 114-mile (184-kilometer), $18.2 million road that links the two countries between Azemo and Metemma. *See also* ITALIAN-ETHIOPIAN WAR; TRANSPORTATION.

MIKAEL ALI ABBA BULA, RAS (1850–1918). Also known as Mohamed Ali. Provincial governor and father of **Iyasu Mikael**. During 1889–1891, he earned **Menelik II**'s trust by defeating numerous rebellious chiefs, one of whom was **Mangasha Yohannes**. In 1892, the emperor rewarded Mikael's loyalty by allowing him to marry his daughter, Shawaraggad Menelik. In 1894, Mikael participated in the conquest of Walamo and, in 1896, commanded an Ethiopian force at the **Battle of Adwa**. On 21 March 1910, Mikael's army supported the coup against **Taytu Betel**, which resulted in Iyasu's elevation to emperor. On 31 May 1914, Iyasu raised his father to the rank of **negus**. After Iyasu had been deposed, Mikael mobilized his army in an effort to restore his son to the throne. On 22 October 1916, a government force–led by **Fitawrari** Habte Giyorgis (1851–1926), **Kassa Halyu**, and **Ras Tafari Makonnen**—defeated Mikael at Sagle, 48 miles (80 kilometers) north of **Addis Ababa**. On 3 November 1916, Mikael marched in chains during a victory parade in Addis Ababa. A court subsequently convicted him of treason. Mikael died in captivity at Dendi on 8 September 1918.

MILITARY TITLES. Under the monarchy, the primary military titles, included ras (head), dajazmach (commander of the door, general), fitawrari (commander of the advance guard), gerazmach (commander of the left wing), kenyazmach (commander of the right wing), meridazmach (commander of the reserve), balambaras (commander of a fortress), shaleqa (commander of 1,000), metoaleqa (commander of 100), hamsaleqat (commander of 50), and asiraleqa (commander of 10). In the late 1930s, **Haile Selassie** reorganized the **armed forces** along Western norms and introduced Western military ranks (e.g., lieutenant general, major general). The titles from balambaras up became nonhereditary titles of nobility with no military status. The titles from shaleqa down became the four lowest officer ranks and were not titles of nobility. *See also* IMPERIAL TITLES.

MINING AND MINERALS. Ethiopia has reserves of gold, silver, iron, platinum, tantalum, nickel, phosphate, diatomite, copper, zinc, soda ash, and potash. Exploitation of these minerals was a priority for governments for centuries. In the mid-1300s, the area known as **Damot** Province produced considerable quantities of gold. In the 14th century, iron deposits were found in most parts of Ethiopia. In the early 17th century, silver mining flourished in Tsalamy district, near Lamalmon. On 25 December 1899, for example, **Menelik II** granted a concession to the Wollega Mining Company, owned by **Alfred Ilg**, to mine for gold, silver, and other minerals in Nedjo and the surrounding countryside. On 31 October 1953, **Haile Selassie** created the Imperial Mining Board to promote mining throughout Ethiopia.

Generally, however, the quantity and quality of the reserves are not well known and relatively few of these minerals are being exploited currently. There are an estimated 500 tons of gold reserves in Ethiopia and 25,000 tons of tantalum at just one location. In 1991, the government opened a nonalluvial gold treatment plant at Lega Dembi, located about 155 miles (250 kilometers) south of **Addis Ababa**. Sold to a private company owned by Saudi/Ethiopian magnate **Mohamed Hussein al-Amoudi**, it went back into operation in 1998 and produces 1.1 million tons of mineral ore annually. Lega Dembi has an estimated 60 to 200 tons of reserves. By 2002, due largely to Lega Dembi's privatization, gold became Ethiopia's fourth most important export after **coffee**, **khat**, and hides and skins.

In 2001, a company called Golden Prospect signed an agreement to prospect for platinum in western Ethiopia. Ethiopia produces significant quantities of limestone and marble. It exports most of the marble and uses the limestone locally for cement. Ethiopia also has huge salt deposits. Between 1984 and 1989, the mining sector contributed less than 1 percent annually of gross domestic product (GDP). By 1998, it contributed more than 6 percent of GDP.

MIRUTS YIFTER. *See* MARATHON AND DISTANCE RUNNERS.

MISSION 101. Formed in September 1939 and commanded by Colonel (later Brigadier) **Daniel Sandford** and then by Lieutenant Colonel **Orde Wingate** (later major general). Mission 101 sought to encourage the **patriots** to fight alongside the British and to prepare for **Haile Selassie**'s return to Ethiopia.

Sanford's aides included Major Robert Cheesman (1878–1962), who commanded the intelligence bureau in Khartoum, Major Arthur Bentinck, who had been in **Dese** when Italy used **chemical weapons**, Lieutenant Colonel Lawrence Athill, who previously had served as a British consul, and Arnold Wienholt (1877–1940), who had been a Red Cross transport officer during the **Italian-Ethiopian War**. On 12 August 1940, Sandford, who had devised a three-pronged strategy, crossed the frontier with one column near Gedaref en route to Mount Belaya. Shortly afterward, Major Arthur Bentinck led a column across the **Atbara River** into Ethiopia. The last column, commanded by Lieutenant Arnold Wienholt, entered Ethiopia to join Sandford but Wienholt was ambushed and killed near Matabia.

By mid-October 1940, Sandford had convinced local leaders in **Gojam**, then torn by rivalry, to sign a unity pact. The patriots provided Mission 101 with valuable intelligence and crucial military support. In January 1941, Sandford successfully attacked several Italian forts. On 8 February 1941, Wingate arrived in Gojam to assume command of all British and Ethiopian forces, including Mission 101. **Gideon Force** eventually took over the irregular operations that Mission 101 had started. *See also* WORLD WAR II.

MISSIONARIES. Since their arrival in Ethiopia in the 16th century, Christian missionaries sought to maintain good relations with the **Ethiopian Orthodox Church** (EOC) and to convert non-Christian Ethiopians. **Catholic** and **Protestant** missions started with the assumption that they might convert EOC followers through union with Rome or reformation in accordance with Protestant beliefs. The EOC accepted assistance from European missionaries so long as they did not convert the Orthodox and try to establish their own ecclesiastical jurisdiction. Ethiopian rulers sought out contact with their Christian counterparts in Europe to obtain recognition and assistance to deal with their non-Christian neighbors. There tended to be, however, a condescending attitude by European missionaries toward the EOC. Ethiopian ecclesiastical leaders understood this duplicity and insisted that Catholic and Protestant missionaries refrain from interfering with the EOC and convert only non-Christians. EOC officials feared that the missionaries had come to Ethiopia to steal their flock with offers of **health** care and **education**. As a result, the relationship between the EOC and Christian missionaries oftentimes has been acrimonious on issues of faith, worship, and Christian brotherhood.

Christians were not the only ones to seek converts in Ethiopia. Islamic penetration remained peaceful until the rise of the **Ifat Sultanate** in the 13th century. In the early 16th century, **Ahmad ibn Ibrahim al Ghazi** launched an Islamic invasion of much of Ethiopia. This had a significant effect on the rise of **Islam** in the **lowlands** but little permanent impact on the religious complexion of the **highlands**. Manoel de Almeida, a Jesuit who lived in Ethiopia from 1622 to 1633, wrote that followers of Islam were scattered throughout the empire and constituted a third of the **population**. **Fasilidas** (reigned 1632–1667), after expelling the Jesuits, sought closer links with neighboring Muslim nations and invited Yemen's ruler to send Muslim missionaries. In 1648, the first one arrived but was greeted with such opprobrium that Fasilidas sent him back. Muslim traders from Sudan and southeast Ethiopia, however, combined their trading activity with Islamic proselytization. They were particularly effective in converting the **Oromo** from traditional beliefs to Islam. **Walter Plowden**, British consul to Ethiopia, commented on the importance of Muslim traders and missionaries in converting Ethiopians to Islam. During the early 19th century, morale in the EOC was especially low as conversions to Islam in the Ethiopian highlands had been extensive. This coincided with a revival of Islamic missionary activity as a reaction to Western imperialism.

The best general account of Christian missionary activity is *The Missionary Factor in Ethiopia,* edited by Getatchew Haile, Aasulv Lande, and Samuel Rubenson. References to Muslim missionary activity appear in *Islam in Ethiopia,* by J. S. Trimingham. *See also* CATHOLICISM; CHURCH MISSIONARY SOCIETY; FLAD, JOHANN MARTIN; GOBAT, SAMUEL; KRAPF, JOHANN LUDWIG.

MULUGETA BULI (1917–1960). Born in 1917 and educated at a mission school and at Tafari Makonnen School. Mulugeta then attended the Holeta (Genet) Military Academy (1934–1936), where he was the only **Oromo** officer cadet. He spent the Italian occupation (1936–1941) in Djibouti and Kenya but returned to Ethiopia with **Haile Selassie** and the **Gideon Force** and participated in the **Battle of Maychew**. After liberation, Mulugeta served as commander of the **Imperial Body Guard** (1941–1955). During this period, he established a Public Security Department that reported to the Ministry of the Interior. In 1951, the emperor ordered Mulugeta to establish the **Kagnew battalions,** which took part in the United Nations operation in Korea (1951–1953). In 1952, some of his officers urged him to overthrow Haile Selassie but he remained loyal to the emperor. Mulugeta's subsequent assignments included chief of staff of the **armed forces** (1956–1958), private chief of staff to the emperor (1958–1959), and minister of national community development (1959–1960). In 1959, he created the Imperial Private Cabinet, which became Haile Selassie's national security staff and acted as a check on all ministers. The instigators of the **coup attempt (1960)** named Mulugeta chief of staff of the armed forces.

On 17 December 1960, loyalist forces killed him and 17 other plotters.

MUNZINGER, WERNER (1832–1875). Born in Olten, Switzerland. He was the youngest of the 10 children of Federal Counselor Josef Munzinger (1791–1855). After being a student of chemistry, geography, and physics in Solothurn and Bern, Munzinger went to Paris and Munich to study modern and oriental languages.

In 1852, he joined a trading firm based in Alexandria, Egypt. Two years later, he became the company's agent in **Massawa**. In 1855, Munzinger settled in Keren, married a local widow, and adopted her son. He became an expert in the anthropology, customs, and history of the Bogos, a Christian Coptic people who controlled much of the area's commercial activity.

During 1862–1863, Munzinger traveled with an expedition under the command of the Austrian consul general in Khartoum, Theodor von Heuglin, who wanted to explore the region between the **Nile River** and Lake Chad and to investigate the deaths of two German explorers. The expedition was a success and, in February 1863, Munzinger returned to Europe to see his family.

After returning to Africa, Munzinger settled in Mkullu near Massawa and received an appointment as French vice-consul. In October 1865, General Sir William Merewether, political resident in Aden, asked him to assume responsibility for their consulate on 15 October 1865, because the british consul, **Charles Duncan Cameron**, had been imprisoned by **Tewodros II**. During the **Anglo-Ethiopian War**, Merewether enlisted Munzinger to act as an interpreter.

In July 1871, the viceroy of Egypt appointed Munzinger as bey governor of Massawa and, in 1872, promoted him to pasha with the title governor-general of the **Red Sea** and Eastern Sudan. In June 1872, Munzinger added Keren to his domain, which included some two million people between the Red Sea and the **Nile River**. Under his administration, there was an improvement in **taxation** collection and agricultural production and an increase in exports. Additionally, Munzinger built roads, a causeway between Massawa and the mainland, irrigation channels, and a telegraph line between Massawa and Kassala, Sudan. He also suppressed several blood feuds but was unable to end **slavery**.

Despite these accomplishments, Munzinger alienated Cairo by opposing its plans to use military force to extend its influence in Ethiopia. Nevertheless, Egypt ordered him to take command of a 350-man expedition to conquer Aussa. On 14 November 1875, an **Oromo** raiding party attacked the expedition and killed Munzinger and his wife.

MURLE PEOPLE AND LANGUAGE. Most Murle live in Sudan, although several thousand inhabit Ethiopia on the west side of the **Omo River** near Sudan. Several Europeans and one American exploring **Lake Turkana** in the late 1800s encountered the Murle in the lower Omo River. The Murle once occupied territory further north and on the east side of the Omo. Even today, this area is sometimes referred to as Murle, even though Murle people no longer live there. A changing climate that lowered Lake Turkana considerably and the arrival of Ethiopian military forces in the early 1900s forced them further south and to the west of the Omo. The Murle are pastoralists and **agriculturists**. Most of them follow a traditional religion. Murle is part of the eastern Sudanic branch of the Nilo-Saharan **language** family. It is related to Didinga, which is structurally linked to Maasai. Serge Tornay has a useful chapter on the origin of the Murle in *Peoples and Cultures of the Ethio-Sudan Borderlands,* edited by M. Lionel Bender.

MURSI PEOPLE AND LANGUAGE. Although numbering perhaps no more than 5,000, the Mursi are one of Ethiopia's most famous ethnic groups because the **women** wear large lip plates. According to custom, when a Mursi woman reaches the age of about 20 a slit is cut between her lower lip and mouth. The gap is stretched until it is large enough for a small circular clay plate to be inserted between the lip and the mouth. As the lip stretches, increasingly larger plates are inserted until the woman can ideally pull the distended lip over her head. The larger the plate worn by the woman, the greater her value at time of marriage. In fact, the women often do not wear the heavy and uncomfortable lip plate, letting the distended lip hang below their jaws. A Mursi man can only marry after he has won a *Donga*, a stick fight in which two contestants painted in white chalk battle each other with heavy long poles. Fights to the death are now rare.

The Mursi live in the south Omo in an area bordered on the west by the **Omo River** and on the east by the Mago River. They are pastoralists who move between the lower Tama steppe and the Mursi Hills in Mago **National Park** depending on seasonal rains. They follow traditional religious beliefs and have a low literacy rate. They are closely related to the **Suri people**. Their language is Eastern Sudanic and a member of the Nilo-Saharan language family. Television producer Leslie Woodhead published a book on his encounters with the Mursi entitled *A Box Full of Spirits*.

MUSIC AND INSTRUMENTS. Music is a vital part of the **Ethiopian Orthodox Church** (EOC). Ethiopians chant the liturgy; the *sistra* and drums are prominent in the middle of the church's three concentric sections. In the sixth century, Ethiopia's most famous composer and musician, Saint Yared, created the chant and notation system. He invented music signs and symbols and authored religious songs and hymns. This system consists of syllabic letters, curved signs, dots, and dashes written above each line of the liturgy, hymns, and psalms. A favorite church painting depicts Yared singing in front of King Gabra Maskal (reigned 550–564). Ethiopian chronicles praise Yared for the quality of his chants. Isolated during the medieval period, Ethiopia developed unique church music. Two priests — Azaj Ghera and Azaj Regouel — introduced notation into ecclesiastical chant. The *debteras* or church musicians continue to preserve the EOC's musical culture, master the notations, and play church instruments.

Ethiopia also has a rich musical tradition outside the EOC. The instruments, songs, and melodies vary widely from one location to another. Percussion instruments in common use are the *negarit*, *kabero*, *atamo*, and *tsinatsil*. The negarit is a small kettledrum, semi-hemispheric in shape. With a body of wood or metal, it is covered at the base with a skin and played with a stick. The negarit, a ceremonial instrument, is an emblem of authority. The kabero is a small drum that accompanies Ethiopian wind and string instruments. A larger version provides accompaniment for the singing of church hymns and devotional songs. Skins cover both ends and are tied with leather thongs across the wooden instrument's body. The atamo is a small drum held in the hand or under the arm. A secular instrument usually made of wood and covered with skin or parchment, it contains a few small stones, glass beads, or seeds. It is struck with the fingers or palms of one or both hands. The tsinatsil or sistrum, which is used almost entirely in church music, consists of a small, lyre-shaped metallic frame with a wooden handle. Two or three thin bars with threaded disks run from one side to the other. When shaken, the tsinatsil produces a jingling sound.

Wind instruments include the *washint*, a simple flute made from a length of bamboo. It usually has four finger holes and accompanies other instruments on secular occasions. Other stringed instruments tune to the washint. The embilta is a larger more primitive type of flute. It has no finger holes; the mouthpiece is U-shaped. Played by groups of three, the embilta produces two tones, the fundamental and another a fourth or fifth higher. The leader produces three tones. The performers must have an excellent sense of timing. The *malakat* is a kind of trumpet about three feet (one meter) in length. Generally made of bamboo, it ends with a bugle-type cap. There are no finger holes. It was once used to herald the approach of the king or other persons of authority.

The *begana* or Ethiopian lyre is the most important of the stringed instruments. It resembles the lyre of the Greeks and Romans and is believed to replicate David's legendary harp. It has 12 strings that are plucked with fingers. Frequently used outside the EOC during Lent and festivals, it rarely accompanies a secular orchestra. The *krar* is a six-stringed instrument plucked with a plectrum or the fingers. Two arms protrude out of the instrument at an angle from each other to join a yoke. The strings attach from the yoke to the box. The only Ethiopian bowed instrument is the *masinko* or fiddle. Skin or parchment covers the diamond-shaped wooden body. The string consists of several strands of horsehair. The masinko exists throughout Ethiopia in secular settings.

There are several recent, notable Ethiopian composers. Asnakech Worku (1935–) is one of the best known musicians. She has produced an array of music in **Amharic**. Nuria Ahmed Shami Kalid (c. 1938–) was born in **Harar,** where she learned traditional vocal repertoire while making baskets and attending weddings. She has written love songs, songs about Harar, and paeans to successive governments. Erza Abate (1961–) was born in **Jimma**. A teacher, performer, and composer, he became director of the Yared Music School in 1995. He has composed many pieces for the piano. **Ashenafi**

Kebede was born in **Addis Ababa** but lived in the United States from the mid-1970s until his death (1998). He wrote several compositions for the flute, clarinet, and violin.

With so many Ethiopians living in the **diaspora**, Ethiopian music has gone commercial. Some Ethiopian performers, such as Aster Aweke, Tigist Assefa, Adaneh Teka, Malefya Teka, Asfaw Kebbede, and Admassou Abate, are popular in the diaspora and in Ethiopia. Some of those who lived outside Ethiopia for some time have added Western influences to Ethiopian music. Seleshi Demisse, who returned to Ethiopia from the United States, represents an example of this style as he narrates a story and plays the krar. Additionally, Ethiopian musicians are increasingly using Western instruments and trying innovative sounds. In 2002, a group of young Ethiopians released a hit album called *Evangadi*. It is a fusion of mideastern melody, soft reggae beat, and Western rock blended with traditional Ethiopian music.

– N –

NAPIER, SIR ROBERT CORNELIS (1810–1890). British soldier. Born on 6 December 1810 in Colombo, Ceylon (now Sri Lanka). During 1824–1826, Napier attended the British East India Company's military college at Addiscombe. On 15 December 1826, he received a commission as second lieutenant in the Bengal Engineers. For the next 41 years, Napier served in several positions in India and China, the most important of which were as a military member of the council of the governor-general of India (1861–1865) and commander of the Bombay Army (1865–1870).

In July 1867, London asked Napier how long it would take to assemble an Anglo-Indian expeditionary force for service in Ethiopia. His quick response, coupled with the duke of Cambridge's influence, led to his appointment as expedition commander. On 2 January 1868, Napier and his troops arrived at the **Red Sea** port of Zula, 30 miles (48 kilometers) southeast of **Massawa**. He built a 12-mile (19-kilometer) railway from Zula to his main camp before making a 420-mile (672-kilometer) march to **Tewodros II**'s mountain fortress at Magdala. His decisive victory over the emperor's forces ensured his reputation as one of Britain's best field commanders.

On returning to Britain, he received the title Baron Napier of Magdala (1868). He also received a pension and many other honors. Napier's subsequent appointments included commander in chief in India (1870–1876) and governor of Gibraltar (1876–1882). In December 1886, he became constable of the Tower of London. On 14 January 1890, Napier died in London. *See also* ANGLO-ETHIOPIAN WAR.

NATIONAL BANK OF ETHIOPIA. *See* BANKING.

NATIONAL CHARTER. On 22 July 1991, political groups that attended the Democratic and Peaceful Transitional Conference in Ethiopia adopted the National Charter. This document authorized the establishment of the **Transitional Government of Ethiopia** and an 87-member Council of Representatives. The National Charter also contained the interim government arrangements until the **elections (1992)** were held and a new **constitution** was adopted.

NATIONAL DEMOCRATIC REVOLUTION. On 20 April 1976, **Mengistu Haile Mariam** announced the launching of the National Democratic Revolution, which sought to facilitate the development of scientific socialism and the emergence of a people's democratic republic by ending feudalism, bureaucratic capitalism, and imperialism. On 21 April 1976, the **Provisional Military Administrative Council** (PMAC) established the People's Organizing Provisional Office (later known as the **Provisional Office for Mass Organizational Affairs**) headed by a 15-member Supreme Organizing Committee, which reported to Mengistu. This organization aimed to build a nationwide network of cadres to help establish a political party that would implement the National Democratic Revolution.

The **Ethiopian People's Revolutionary Party** (EPRP) agreed that a united front of political parties should carry out the National Democratic Revolution. However, the EPRP wanted to exclude the PMAC and include all opposition parties, some of which opposed Mengistu. This disagreement led to a split in the PMAC between hard-liners, led by Mengistu, and more moderate elements, headed by **Teferi Bante**. Eventually, Mengistu marginalized the moderates by killing Teferi and some of his associates. He then unleashed the

Red Terror against the EPRP and its supporters, thus ending any chance that the National Democratic Revolution would enjoy widespread political support. *See also* DERG.

NATIONAL LITERACY CAMPAIGN (NLC) (1979–1991). In 1974, Ethiopia's illiteracy rate was 93 percent. In May 1979, the **Derg** sought to resolve this problem by establishing the National Literacy Campaign Coordinating Committee (NLCCC) and, in July 1979, by launching the NLC, under the chairmanship of Goshu Wolde, a soldier and lawyer. The Derg initially mobilized more than 60,000 students and teachers, sending them throughout the country for two-year terms of service; eventually, the campaign involved about 1,788,000 instructors. The Derg organized the NLC into rounds that began in urban centers and then moved to rural areas. The NLC conducted its activities in 15 indigenous **languages**, beginning with **Amharic, Oromo,** Tigrinya, **Somali,** and **Wollaytta.** Subsequent languages included **Afar, Gedeo, Gurage, Hadiyya, Kafa, Kambata, Kunama, Saho, Sidamo,** and **Tigre.**

During the first two rounds (1979–1980), the government established 35,000 literacy centers and recruited 241,000 instructors. In 1980, the United Nations Educational, Scientific, and Cultural Organization (UNESCO) awarded Ethiopia its International Reading Association Literacy Prize.

By the late 12th round (1985), 16,941,075 Ethiopians had been enrolled in literacy courses, 12,037,542 of whom had passed the end-of-course examination. Postliteracy programs included 10,070,102 students. By the 20th and final round (1989), some 18.7 million Ethiopians had become literate. According to the Ministry of Education, the NLC had reduced illiteracy from 93 percent in 1974 to 25 percent in 1989.

NATIONAL PARKS. Ethiopia's **wildlife** conservation record lags behind that of other East African countries such as Kenya, Tanzania, and Uganda. Indeed, it was not until 1962 that Ethiopia asked the United Nations Educational, Scientific, and Cultural Organization (UNESCO) for help in formulating a wildlife policy. In 1963, a UNESCO mission, headed by the British conservationist Julian Huxley (1887–1975), completed a preliminary survey of Ethiopia's wildlife.

He suggested that Ethiopia establish a Wildlife Conservation Board and Department. The following year, Ian Grimwood and Leslie Brown, both of whom worked for the Kenya government service, completed a more detailed study. They proposed a three-year wildlife conservation plan and recommended the establishment of national parks at **Awash**, **Omo**, and the **Simien Mountains**.

Ethiopia eventually implemented these findings. However, development of the **tourism** sector was never a government priority. As a result, Ethiopia's national parks failed to compete with those in nearby Kenya, Tanzania, and Uganda. Since 1991, Ethiopia has sought to increase its share of the East African foreign tourism market by improving facilities at the country's national parks, but the lack of resources and the **Ethiopian-Eritrean War** have prevented any significant improvements.

As of 2002, Ethiopia had nine national parks and three wildlife sanctuaries. One of the most interesting and beautiful parks is **Bale Mountains** National Park (1,488 square miles; 2,400 square kilometers), where visitors can see the rare Simien fox and mountain nyala. Simien Mountains National Park (73 square miles; 179 square kilometers), which is on the UNESCO World Heritage List, is better known for trekking but also is the home of the rare Walia ibex and gelada baboon. Although relatively inaccessible, Omo National Park (1,570 square miles; 4,068 square kilometers) has one of the country's largest concentrations of wildlife. One of the easiest to reach from **Addis Ababa**, Awash National Park (319 square miles; 827 square kilometers), offers a nice selection of animals on a good day. Local herders, however, tend not to respect the park boundaries and scare off the animals. Other national parks include **Gambela** National Park (1,954 square miles; 5,060 square kilometers) in the far west of Ethiopia; Lake Abiata-Shala National Park (550 square miles; 887 square kilometers) to the south of Addis Ababa; Mago National Park (835 square miles; 2,161 square kilometers) in the lower Omo; Nechisar National Park (319 square miles; 514 square kilometers), near Arba Minch; Senkele, south of Addis Ababa; and Yangudi-Rassa National Park (2,933 square kilometers; 4,730 square kilometers), northeast of Addis Ababa. The three wildlife sanctuaries are Babille elephant preserve, between **Jijiga** and **Harar**; Kuni-Muktar, east of Addis Ababa near Asbe Teferi; and Yabelo, south of Addis Ababa on the road to the Kenya border.

NATIONAL SHENGO. Shengo is the **Amharic** word for assembly. On 6 April 1987, the **Derg** established a National Shengo Election Commission. On 13 June 1987, some 20 million Ethiopians voted to elect 835 members to the National Shengo. According to official results, 93.6 percent of those elected belonged to the **Workers' Party of Ethiopia**. On 9 September 1987, the National Shengo convened its first session. The legislators established the People's Democratic Republic of Ethiopia and endorsed the **constitution**, which became effective on 12 September 1987. On 10 September 1987, they also elected the president (**Mengistu Haile Mariam**), vice-president (**Fisseha Desta**), a 24-member Council of State, **Council of Ministers**, Supreme Court, procurator-general, auditor-general, and the members of the National Working People's Control Committee. *See also* PARLIAMENT.

NATIONAL WORK CAMPAIGN FOR DEVELOPMENT THROUGH CO-OPERATION. *See* ZEMACHA.

NAVY. In 1955, **Haile Selassie** authorized the establishment of the Imperial Ethiopian Navy as part of the Department of Marine. The navy's training wing included the Imperial Naval College (**Massawa**), Petty Officers' School, and the Ratings School. Norwegian officers operated these facilities. After liberation (1941), the **British Military Administration** assumed responsibility for the schools. In 1958, the navy became an autonomous branch of the **armed forces.** On 22 January 1959, the first group of naval officers graduated from the Imperial Naval College. On 26 January 1961, 50 noncommissioned officers graduated from the Petty Officers' School. By 1961, the navy's inventory included two Yugoslav torpedo boats, five American coastal patrol boats, and a reconditioned American seaplane tender. Its principal naval bases were at **Asab** and **Massawa** on the **Red Sea**. Until 1974, a small contingent of retired British naval personnel served as advisers and training supervisors.

During the **Derg** period, the navy underwent significant changes. After the outbreak of the **Ogaden War (1977–1978)**, the United States refused to deliver several "swift boats" that Ethiopia had purchased in 1976. The Derg subsequently canceled the order. In 1978, Ethiopia acquired four Soviet-built fast attack craft, including two Osa II-class armed with ship-to-ship missiles. This offensive capability allowed the

Derg to pursue its strategy of preventing the Red Sea from becoming an "Arab lake" and of coope.:ting with the Soviet Indian Ocean fleet. The navy also created a marine commando unit and a fleet air arm that included helicopters and light aircraft. By early 1991, the 3,500-man navy, which had seen little combat, had two frigates, eight missile craft, six torpedo craft, six patrol boats, two amphibious craft, and two support/training craft.

After the **Ethiopian People's Revolutionary Democratic Front** (EPRDF) seized power (1991), many of Ethiopia's naval vessels fled to Djibouti and Yemen. After Eritrea became independent on 24 May 1993, Ethiopia became landlocked. On 16 September 1996, the EPRDF put its naval vessels up for sale.

NAYI PEOPLE AND LANGUAGE. The Nayi or Nao people number more than 10,000 and reside in the border area between north Omo and Keficho zones. Most Nayi live in the villages of Goba, Gushi, Angela-Menesh, and Udadish. The **Chara** live to the south and east, the **Kaficho** to the north, and the **Me'en** to the west. Before the Kafa, today called Kaficho, conquest in the 17th century, the Nayi lived in a small independent kingdom. The king had the title of *kyas* and chiefs governed the districts. After the Kafa conquest, the king became a subking who served as a vassal to the Kafa king. The Nayi are mostly pagans who believe in a sky god and local spirits. They are **agriculturists**. They speak an Omotic **language** in the Gimira family. It is related to **Dizi** and **Sheko**. Adults speak Nayi while young people speak Kaficho, which is also the trade language.

NAZRET. (161,800, estimated 2002 **population**.) Known as Adama in the local **Oromo** language. Ethiopia's third largest city. Nazret, which is situated on a 5,320-foot (1,622-meter) plateau that divides the **Rift Valley** from the central **highlands**, is located some 62 miles (100 kilometers) southeast of **Addis Ababa** on the main truck route from the ports of Djibouti and **Asab**. Nazret is named after Christ's birthplace.

The town, which is one of the stops for the **Addis Ababa–Djibouti Railway**, is a major commercial crossroads and one of Ethiopia's largest cattle-collecting points. Nazret also provides an outlet for the produce from fruit and vegetable farms and the nearby Wonji Sugar Estate. It became the capital of **Oromia** in 2004.

With its lower elevation, warmer climate, and numerous hotels, Nazret is a retreat for residents of Addis Ababa who often frequent the nearby Sodore Spa. Nazret offers little of historical significance.

NEGASH BEZABEH (1908–1964). Government official and descendant of the royal house of Gojam's **negus Takla Hayanot**. During the **Italian-Ethiopian War**, Negash fought against the Italians with other Gojami **patriots**. However, some accused him of being a weak leader who failed to control subchiefs. Nevertheless, **Haile Selassie** and his British allies chose **Gojam** as the region to begin an offensive against the Italians. In 1940, Negash joined a united front that worked for Haile Selassie's restoration. After the emperor's return, he became vice minister in the prime minister's office and then president of the Senate (1942–1943). In 1951, Negash became involved in an unsuccessful conspiracy to assassinate Haile Selassie. The plotters had hoped to put Negash on the throne. However, some conspirators advocated the creation of a republic under **Ras Imru Haile Selassie** who, at the time, was Ethiopia's ambassador to Washington, D.C., and had nothing to do with the coup attempt. After his arrest, the emperor's Special Court tried Negash and condemned him to death. However, Haile Selassie pardoned Negash, who subsequently lived in exile in Jimma. In 1964, he died in Nehasé.

NEGASO GIDADA (1943–). Former president of Ethiopia (22 August 1995–8 October 2001). Born on 8 September 1943 in Dembi Dolo, where his father was a famous blind **Protestant** preacher. Educated in Dembi Dolo at the Nazareth Bible Academy and in **Addis Ababa** at Beta Mariam Preparatory School. Between 1962 and 1971, Negaso attended **Haile Selassie I University**, where he received a B.A. in history. Prior to graduating, he taught at Atse Zara Yakob School in Dembi Dolo. Negaso also lectured at the American Mission School in Mizan Teferi until 1974. After going into exile in 1974 to the former West Germany to avoid the **Derg**, he received an M.A. degree in ethnology and social psychology (1978) and a Ph.D. degree in ethnology (1984) from Johann Wolfgang Goethe University. His dissertation covered a history of the Sayyoo **Oromo** of southwestern **Wollega**.

After completing his education, Negaso worked as a librarian at Frankfurt University and then as director of the Third World Center. He also served as secretary and then president of the Oromo Students' Association for Germany, an organization affiliated with the **Oromo Liberation Front** (OLF). Eventually, Negaso administered the OLF's financial department. However, in 1988, he resigned his OLF membership because of an argument with Dima Neggo, another senior OLF official. After the Derg's downfall (1991), Negaso joined the Oromo People's Democratic Organization (OPDO), which was part of the **Ethiopian People's Revolutionary Democratic Front** (EPRDF).

In the **elections (1995)**, he won a seat (Oromia Region) in the **House of Peoples' Representatives**. On 23 August 1995, a joint session of the House of Peoples' Representatives and the House of the Federation designated him president of the Federal Democratic Republic of Ethiopia. His position was largely ceremonial as real power rested with Prime Minister **Meles Zenawi**. However, as president, Negaso led the government campaign against acquired immune deficiency syndrome (AIDS).

On 22 June 2001, Negaso resigned from the EPRDF after clashing with Meles during acrimonious debates in an EPRDF Central Committee meeting. The pro-government OPDO then suspended his membership. He remained president until 8 October 2001, when the Council of Peoples' Representatives elected Girma Wolde-Giorgis as president. On the same day, the council passed a bill that stipulated that former presidents who engaged in political activities would lose their pension and all other retirement benefits. As of 2003, Negaso lived in quiet retirement in Addis Ababa but remains active in the fight against **human immunodeficiency virus/acquired immune deficiency syndrome**. He also works with several local non governmental organizations and continues to speak out on important issues. Negaso is married to a German national.

NEGUS. *See* IMPERIAL TITLES.

NEGUS NAGAST. *See* IMPERIAL TITLES.

NIGISTE NAGAST. *See* IMPERIAL TITLES.

NILE RIVER. *See* BLUE NILE.

NUER. A Nilotic people, the Nuer live primarily in neighboring Sudan although they are the most numerous ethnic group in Ethiopia's **Gambela Region**. Culturally similar to the Dinka of Sudan, the Nuer are politically divided into several tribes that sometimes form loose federations. They are a seminomadic people, and cattle are their most important possession. In fact, they hold in contempt people who own few or no cattle. Nuer oral **literature**, traditional songs, and **poetry** celebrate their cattle. Nuer **women** tend to wear much ornamentation, including bright bead necklaces and bangles of ivory or bone. Most also are cicatrized: the skin is raised in patterns to decorate the face, chest, and stomach with rows of dots. Naath is the name they give to themselves.

Many Nuers, including some who live in Ethiopia, periodically support efforts to topple Sudan's government. Relations in Gambela Region between the Nuer and the **Anuak**, the next largest ethnic group, sometimes reach a flash point. The Nuer, who reside in one of the most isolated parts of Ethiopia, do not always accept easily authority from **Addis Ababa**. In 1999, the government arrested 26 Nuer political activists associated with the Gambela People's Democratic Congress. Some were arrested for inciting Nuer students to demonstrate for the use of the Nuer **language** in school while others were held on suspicion of supporting the **Oromo Liberation Front**. By late 1999, the government had released all of them. Although based on the Nuer in Sudan, the best-known study of the group is *The Nuer* by E. E. Evans-Pritchard.

NYANGATOM PEOPLE AND LANGUAGE. Also known as the Donyiro and by several other names, the Nyangatom reside in south Omo zone on the west side of the **Omo River**, west of the north end of **Lake Turkana** and astride the Ethiopian-Sudan border near the tripoint with Kenya. The several thousand Nyangatom have settlement centers near the Omo River and the Kibish River. They are seminomadic cattle herders and on a seasonal basis graze their herds inside Sudan. They are also subsistence **agriculturists**, preferring sorghum and beans. Most follow traditional religious beliefs. Nyangatom occasionally have had hostile relations with the Turkana in Kenya and the Jiye in Sudan. They speak a Nilo-Saharan **language** of the eastern Sudanic family. Their language is close to Toposa and Turkana.

– O –

OCCUPIED ENEMY TERRITORY ADMINISTRATION (OETA).
On 2 February 1941, Sir Philip Mitchell (1890–1946), the former British governor in Uganda, issued a memorandum entitled "Notes on Policy and Practice in Respect of Occupation of Italian East Africa," which sought to establish strong control over Ethiopia. Actually, Mitchell wanted to integrate Ethiopia into British East Africa. However, London was loathe to undertake a new colonial adventure. On 4 February 1941, Britain's foreign secretary, **Anthony Eden,** promised Ethiopia full restoration of its independence but under British "guidance." This policy divergence inevitably led to Anglo-Ethiopian tensions.

After British, Allied, and Ethiopian forces had liberated Ethiopia, London designated Ethiopia "occupied enemy territory" and placed the country under the Occupied Enemy Territory Administration, which Mitchell ran from Nairobi as chief political officer. Brian Kennedy-Cooke (deputy chief political officer for Eritrea) and Maurice Stanley Lush (deputy chief political officer for Ethiopia), both from the Sudan Political Service, were detailed to assist Mitchell.

These appointments coupled with the fact that **Haile Selassie** objected to the term OETA, as occupied Ethiopia had been liberated, caused concern about British motives. Other issues that bothered the emperor included Britain's confiscation of Italian weapons and equipment that he believed should have been given to Ethiopia and the decision to make **Tigray** part of Eritrea. The British also extended OETA-administered territory without consulting Haile Selassie. To thwart what he perceived as British plans to add Ethiopia to its empire, the emperor condemned the British as "plunderers" and sought to reassert his authority by appointing seven ministers on 11 May 1941 without consulting the OETA. The alarmed British eventually persuaded the emperor to regard these ministers as advisers to the appropriate OETA staff.

On 31 January 1942, London and **Addis Ababa** concluded the **Anglo-Ethiopian Agreement and Military Convention,** which ended the British Military Administration in parts of Ethiopia but allowed it to continue in the **Haud.** *See also* ITALIAN-ETHIOPIAN WAR; WORLD WAR II.

OGADEN. Comprising most of eastern Ethiopia, the Ogaden plateau is a sloping plain that stretches south of **Harar** and **Jijiga**. The Somali-Ethiopian frontier is its border on the east and the **Wabe Shebelle River** separates it from Bale region in the west. Its name comes from the Ogaden subclan of Ethiopian **Somalis**. Ogadeni Somalis belong to the Darod clan family. Other Darod subclans, such as the Marehan, straddle the Ogaden border with Somalia, and the Dulbahante, most of whom live in Somaliland, inhabit the southeast corner. Some Somalis from the Dir clan family live in the northern part of the Ogaden. The region is suitable for grazing about six months of the year and is linked closely to the Somali **economy**. Large numbers of Somalis from Ethiopia, Somaliland, and Somalia graze their animals on both sides of the border. The pastoral Somalis have no regard for the artificial frontiers of the colonial era. The existence of natural gas and possibly oil in the Ogaden adds to the potential for conflict.

In the late 19th century, **Menelik II** successfully pressed his claims for the Ogaden. In the early 1930s, the threat of an Italian invasion underscored Ethiopia's belief in the area's strategic importance. In fact, the Italian-inspired **Wal Wal Incident** in the Ogaden eventually gave rise to Benito Mussolini's call for war. Following the outbreak of the **Italian-Ethiopian War**, Somalis living in the Ogaden held no particular allegiance to Ethiopia or Italy. During the Italian occupation (1936–1941), Italy administered the Ogaden as part of Italian Somalia. After the expulsion of the Italians in 1941, the Ogaden came under the **British Military Administration** until 1948, when Britain returned it to Ethiopia.

The Ogaden has been at the center of Somalia's long-term goal of incorporating all neighboring Somali-inhabited territories under its jurisdiction as part of a **Greater Somalia** policy (the other areas sought by Somalia are Djibouti and Kenya's Northeastern Frontier Province). Throughout the early 1960s, there was regular conflict between Somalia and Ethiopia. During the **Ogaden War (1977–1978),** Somalia occupied most of the Ogaden. However, with aid and troops from Cuba and the Soviet Union, the Ethiopians defeated the Somali forces. The 1991 collapse of the Somali state ended Mogadishu's irredentist policies. As a result, Ethiopia opposes the reemergence of a hostile and unified Somalia for fear that it would renew efforts to annex the Ogaden. In any event, many Ogaden Somalis probably prefer to have more autonomy within Ethiopia rather than unite with Somalia. *See also* OGADEN NATIONAL LIBERATION FRONT; OGADEN WAR (1964); SOMALI REGION.

OGADEN NATIONAL LIBERATION FRONT (ONLF). Established on 15 August 1984 with its headquarters in Kuwait. The ONLF was a breakaway faction from the **Western Somalia Liberation Front** (WSLF), which it regarded as a puppet of Somalia's Siad Barre regime.

In 1988, ONLF elements went to the **Ogaden** but failed to initiate significant military operations. According to its political program, the ONLF seeks to defend the Ogaden and its people and resources against all internal and external enemies; restore civil, human, and religious rights; reclaim the right to national self-determination; and encourage peaceful coexistence with the international community. The ONLF rejects the view that the Ogaden problem is an Ethiopia-Somalia border dispute and maintains that it is a struggle between the Ogaden's colonized peoples and their Ethiopian colonizer.

The ONLF cooperates with other rebel groups. On 7 June 1996, for example, the ONLF and the **Oromo Liberation Front** (OLF) signed an agreement to coordinate their diplomatic, military, and political activities. On 19 September 1999, the ONLF-OLF–**Sidamo Liberation Front** joint committee met to discuss bilateral and regional issues and other matters pertaining to their common struggle. The three organizations then issued a statement that accused the **Tigray People's Liberation Front/Ethiopian People's Revolutionary Democratic Front** of causing war, **famine**, insecurity, human tragedy, and misery for the people of Ethiopia and neighboring countries. On 18 July 1991, the ONLF and the WSLF signed a merger agreement but there was no appreciable increase in military activities in the Ogaden.

The ONLF also maintains offices in various locations in Africa, Europe, the Middle East, and North America. These offices distribute literature, operate Internet Web sites, solicit support, and publicize the plight of the Ogadeni people.

Nevertheless, the ONLF has failed to mount a serious military threat against the Ethiopian government. Instead, the ONLF, which maintains bases in Kenya and Somalia, conducts infrequent, low-level cross-border raids into Ethiopia. Such strikes cause minimal damage. The lack of resources will prevent the ONLF from significantly improving its military capabilities anytime soon. *See also* SOMALI REGION.

OGADEN WAR (1964). The origins of the first Ogaden War began in 1963, when **Somali** nomads who lived in Ethiopia formed the Ogaden Liberation Front. The organization, which included an army and a provisional government, demanded that the Ethiopian government repeal **taxation** laws and grant autonomy to the Ogaden so that members would have unrestricted access to Somalia's pastures and watering holes.

On 6 February 1964, Ethiopia and the Ogaden Liberation Front, which received military and nonmilitary aid from Somalia, initiated hostilities. On 15 February 1964, Ethiopia and Somalia agreed to a cease-fire. However, the following day Somali National Army troops broke the truce by shelling the frontier town of Ferfer and unsuccessfully trying to occupy the border village of Dolo. Mogadishu declared that it had launched the attacks because Ethiopian forces had crossed the frontier in 12 places. On 30 March 1964, the **Organization of African Unity** announced that it had mediated a cease-fire. Under the terms of the settlement, Somalia agreed to halt its support of the Ogaden Liberation Front. The fighting had claimed at least 2,000 lives.

The Ethiopian government hoped to prevent future conflicts by improving **education, health** care, and water supplies for the Somali nomads. This strategy failed to mollify the Somalis. Over the next decade, there were sporadic acts of sabotage and some low-level clashes with Ethiopian security forces that eventually culminated in the outbreak of the second **Ogaden War (1977–1978)**. *See also* SOMALI REGION.

OGADEN WAR (1977–1978). The events that led to the second Ogaden war began in 1975, when the **Somali** National Army (SNA) started providing training and equipment to the **Western Somalia Liberation Front** and the Somali-Abo Liberation Front rebel groups. These two initiated military operations in Ethiopia and, by early 1977, controlled parts of the **Ogaden** and some of the Bale-Sidamo **highlands**. On 13 June 1977, Mogadishu escalated the conflict by sending 5,000 SNA soldiers, crudely disguised as guerrillas, into Hararge Province. However, Ethiopian troops thwarted the offensive by inflicting heavy casualties on the attackers. Nevertheless, by July 1977, **Addis Ababa** maintained that there were 39,450 Somali soldiers and guerrillas in Ethiopia.

Official Ethiopian documents indicate that on 13 July 1977 (most other sources use 23 July 1977), the SNA launched a conventional offensive in the Ogaden that included 70,000 troops, 40 fighter aircraft, 250 tanks, 350 armored personnel carriers, and 600 artillery pieces. With only four poorly equipped brigades in the Ogaden, Ethiopia failed to stop the offensive. Within days, the SNA had penetrated some 437 miles (700 kilometers) into Ethiopia and had seized 218,750 square miles (350,000 square kilometers) of territory. On 12 September 1977, the SNA captured **Jijiga** and, on the following day, occupied Karamara. By mid-September 1977, the SNA controlled about 90 percent of the Ogaden.

Despite these advances, several factors prevented a Somali victory. The SNA had suffered heavy tank losses during its Ogaden campaign. Moreover, the Ethiopian **Air Force** had established air superiority over the Somali Air Force while the onset of the rainy season had slowed the movement of Somali reinforcements.

The most important reason for Ethiopia's eventual victory concerned the Soviet Union (now Russia) and its Cuban and South Yemen (now Yemen) allies. At the beginning of the Ogaden War, Moscow provided arms to both sides in hopes that it could act as mediator in the conflict and could persuade Ethiopia and Somalia to join South Yemen in a federation of socialist **Red Sea** states. This strategy failed and, on 13 November 1977, Mogadishu terminated the Somali-Soviet Treaty of Friendship and Cooperation, broke diplomatic relations with Havana, and expelled all Soviet and Cuban military advisers.

On 23 November 1977, the Soviet Union launched an air- and sealift of troops, arms, and other military supplies. Within months, Moscow had delivered more than $1 billion in military aid, some 15,000 Cuban combat troops, an unknown number of South Yemeni soldiers, and a cadre of Soviet military advisers. This intervention turned the tide of the war. By early 1978, Ethiopia had liberated much of the Ogaden and, on 5 March 1978, ended the nearly six-month Somali occupation of Jijiga.

On 9 March 1978, Somalia announced the withdrawal of its forces from the Ogaden. On 15 March 1986, Somali president Siad Barre talked with **Mengistu Haile Mariam** at an Inter-Governmental Authority on Drought and Development meeting to discuss the possibility of concluding a peace agreement. On 23 March 1977, Addis Ababa announced that government forces had recaptured all military posts and administrative centers in the Ogaden. On 3 April 1988, Ethiopia and Somalia finally signed a peace agreement to end the Ogaden War.

The human cost of the Ogaden War can only be estimated. According to the Ethiopian Ministry of National Defense, at least 17,319 Ethiopian soldiers lost their lives while about 20,000 sustained injuries. Some 400 Cubans and 100 South Yemenis were killed in action. Somalia claimed to have lost approximately 8,000 soldiers. There are no reliable estimates of the number of SNA injuries. Casualties for the WSLF, the Somali-Abo Liberation Front, and the civilian **population** are unknown. Some independent observers question these estimates and suggest that the actual number of deaths and injuries is far greater. *See also* SOMALI REGION.

OLYMPIC GAMES. *See* MARATHON AND DISTANCE RUNNERS.

OMO RIVER. (620 miles; 1,000 kilometers long.) The Omo River originates in the Balbala Mountains southwest of **Addis Ababa** and terminates in **Lake Turkana**. The Omo loses about 6,000 feet (1,830 meters) in elevation from its source. During the rainy season, spectacular falls in the **highlands** contribute water to the Omo. By the time the river reaches Lake Turkana the flow becomes sluggish. The Omo is home to some of the most isolated and interesting ethnic groups such as the **Hamer, Dizi, Karo, Mursi**, and **Suri**. Ethiopia's largest and most inaccessible **national parks**—Omo on the west bank and Mago on the east bank—are part of the river system. The lower reaches of the Omo also constitute one of the least-developed parts of Ethiopia. The Omo offers popular long-distance white-water rafting trips and the opportunity to see rare **bird life** and a variety of animals.

OPERATION MOSES. *See* FALASHAS.

OPUUO PEOPLE AND LANGUAGE. The Opuuo, who live along the Sudan border in **Gambela Region** west of Jikawo, are known by many other names and probably considered by some to be **Komo**. About 5,000 Opuuo live along the **Baro River** on both sides of the border in five principal villages. They are almost surrounded by the **Nuer**. Their **language** is Nilo-Saharan in the Koman family and has 24 percent lexical similarity with Komo. The **Anuak**, who live southeast of the Opuuo, refer to them with the derogatory name "Langa." Afan Oromo is the lingua franca.

ORGANIZATION OF AFRICAN UNITY (OAU). *See* AFRICAN UNION.

OROMIA REGION. At 136,550 square miles (353,690 square kilometers), Oromia, which had a **population** of about 24 million in 2003, occupies almost one-third of Ethiopia, making it somewhat larger than Finland but a little smaller than Montana. It covers much of southern, south central, and western Ethiopia and surrounds **Addis Ababa**. Its capital moved from Addis Ababa to **Adama** (also **Nazret**) in 2004. Major towns include Assela, **Debre Zeit**, Goba, Hagere Hiywot, **Jimma**, **Nazret**, Nekempte, and Shashemene. Oromia is divided administratively into 12 zones. Topography includes high plateau, the **Bale Mountains**, the **Rift Valley,** and rolling savanna between Negele and the Kenya border. The **Awash River** winds its way primarily through Oromia. The region has an enormous variety of climates. It borders Sudan on the west and has a border with every other Ethiopian region except **Tigray Region**. The ethnic composition is 85 percent **Oromo**, 9 percent **Amhara**, just over 1 percent **Gurage,** and the remainder a variety of peoples, 90 percent of whom live in rural areas. About 85 percent of the people speak Afan Oromo as a first language although **Amharic** is also widely spoken. More than 44 percent are Muslim, about 41 percent **Ethiopian Orthodox**, 9 percent **Protestant**, and the rest followers of traditional religions or other faiths.

Agriculture is the main source of livelihood for the vast majority of **Oromos**. The main **food** crops are corn, teff, wheat, barley, peas, beans, and oil seeds. The principal cash crop is **coffee**. Oromia accounts for more than half of Ethiopia's agricultural production and about 45 percent of its livestock. Oromia has a high potential for ad-

ditional **hydropower** development. It already has major hydro generating stations at Koka, Fincha, Melka-Wakena, and Sor. It has significant reserves of gold, soda ash, platinum, limestone, gypsum, and
tantalum. Although it does not have **tourist** attractions comparable to
those found in **Tigray** and **Amhara Regions**, it is known for a huge
diversity of **bird life**, the Bale Mountains **National Park**, lakes in the
Rift Valley, hot springs, and the palace of Abba Jifar outside **Jimma**.
There are periodic security incidents in parts of Oromia perpetrated
by groups such as the **Oromo Liberation Front** that oppose the
Ethiopian People's Revolutionary Democratic Front government.

OROMO LIBERATION FRONT (OLF). Established in 1974 in
Wollega to resist domination by the ruling **Amhara**. Historically, the
OLF has been directed and financed primarily from offices outside
Ethiopia in Australia, Europe, the Middle East, and North America.
Two **Oromo** organizations, Bakalcha and Macha-Tulama Self-Help
Association, opposed the military regime that seized power in 1974.
Bakalcha became the OLF's intellectual core. Some early OLF lead-
ers had been members of the Macha-Tulama Self-Help Association.

The OLF supported Oromo self-determination for an independent
republic of **Oromia** or some kind of federal or confederal arrangement with other Ethiopian peoples. Followers were no longer willing
to accept a government controlled by non-Oromo peoples. In 1973,
the OLF began military operations in eastern Oromia, expanded activities to Bale and Arsi, and launched operations in western Oromia
(1981). Following its victory in the **Ogaden War (1977–1978)**, the
Derg turned its focus against the OLF in Bale and the Chercher
Mountains. The OLF eventually incorporated the traditional Oromo
principles of *gada* as part of its program to attract more supporters.

The OLF periodically has experienced internal schisms and policy
differences. In 1978, two OLF leaders who had been seeking to reorganize the OLF's army and political structure were assassinated. When
it became apparent the Derg would not remain in power due to its own
mismanagement and military pressure by the **Tigray People's Liberation Front** (TPLF) and **Eritrean People's Liberation Front** (EPLF),
the OLF stepped up its military activity against the Derg. In 1990, it captured several towns in western Ethiopia and expanded its operations in
Bale, Arsi, and Hararge. In 1991, the OLF joined the TPLF, EPLF, and

Derg representatives at the U.S.-organized 27 May 1991 London peace conference. Disappointed in its role as a junior partner at this conference, the OLF called for a referendum on independence for Oromia. Although unhappy with the arrangements agreed upon in London, the OLF joined the **Transitional Government of Ethiopia** for a one-year period (1991–1992), received ministerial portfolios (**Agriculture, Education**, Information, and Trade) and 21 seats in the **Council of Ministers**, and demobilized 22,200 fighters. According to an OLF-EPRDF agreement, the latter promised to release all OLF political prisoners, return all OLF property, open all closed OLF offices, and guarantee unrestricted political activity. The **Ethiopian People's Revolutionary Democratic Front** (EPRDF) failed to honor this accord and encouraged the creation of another Oromo political party, the Oromo People's Democratic Organization (OPDO), which joined the EPRDF. On 17 June 1992, the OLF therefore withdrew from the EPRDF-led government and the **elections (1992)**. On 19 June 1992, the EPRDF responded by ordering OLF government ministers to resign. Most OLF leaders then went into exile, vowing to carry on the fight against the EPRDF.

During the past 10 years, the OLF, which had been led by **Gelassa Dilbo** (1992–1999) and **Dawud Ibsa Ayana** (1999–), has conducted a low-level war against the EPRDF. The OLF occasionally has inflicted modest defeats on the Ethiopian **armed forces**. On 1 January 2003, the OLF announced that, in 2002, it had conducted 24 military operations that resulted in the deaths of 1,638 Ethiopian soldiers; some independent sources maintained that these statistics were hugely exaggerated. The government historically has responded to OLF military activities by periodically arresting OLF members and sympathizers. Several efforts to bring the OLF back into the government have failed. The EPRDF has made clear that it will not accept the OLF until it renounces violence, something it is unprepared to do on the grounds that the EPRDF would never allow it to participate equally in the competition for political power. As a result, the OLF-EPRDF standoff continues.

In 1998, the OLF sought to take advantage of the **Ethiopian-Eritrean War** by accepting Eritrean military support provided through **Somali** factions in Somalia. Beginning in 1999, the OLF temporarily and unsuccessfully operated out of Somalia against Ethiopian forces. On 22 April 1999, the OLF and the Oromo People's

Liberation Front agreed to work together against the EPRDF. The OLF also made a similar agreement with the United Oromo People's Liberation Front. The OLF continues to have close relations with Eritrea but remains aloof from cooperation with other organizations inside Ethiopia that wish to alter the current power structure.

OROMO PEOPLE AND LANGUAGE. The Oromo constitute Ethiopia's largest ethnic group. Many Oromo nationalists argue that they are a majority. A more realistic number is 40 to 45 percent of Ethiopia's **population** of about 67 million. Even then, the Oromo are much more numerous than the next largest group, the **Amhara** at about 25 percent. Even with their large numbers the Oromo never have ruled all of Ethiopia, a fact that contributes to a strong streak of Oromo nationalism that became a more organized movement in Ethiopia in the last half of the 20th century.

Conflict between the Oromo and Ethiopians from the central and northern **highlands** began in the 16th century and continued with some interruption until the end of the 19th century. The apparent goal of the Amhara and **Tigrayans** was to absorb or assimilate the Oromo in their society so that the Oromo did not pose a political threat. During much of the 20th century, that policy worked to some extent. Following the overthrow of the **Derg** regime (1991), the **Ethiopian People's Revolutionary Democratic Front** has tried to deal with Oromo and other ethnic groups by creating a federal structure of government that accords some autonomy to the regions. Although the Oromo welcome the use of their own **language** in **Oromia**, numerous other concerns remain unresolved.

The Oromo are a Cushitic-speaking people who are related to the **Konso**, **Afar**, **Somali**, and **Sidama** among others. Until fairly recently, outsiders referred to them as **Galla**, a term the Oromo never used themselves. Some say the name Oromo is derived from Oromo, son of Omer of Ghellad in Arabia, who crossed to Berbera in present-day Somaliland. Others insist that Oromo means "race" or "nation." The Oromo are divided into clans and subclans and there are three rough geographical divisions—southern, eastern, and west-central. Among the southern Oromo, for example, the principal groups are the **Boran**, Arsi, and Guji Oromo. Because they are so numerous and occupy so much of Ethiopia, the Oromo do not have a single form of

economy. Most were once pastoralists and many, especially the Boran, still are. Many have gone into **agriculture** while others live in urban areas.

Oromo society is based on an age-set system known as *gada* in which males assume different responsibilities every eight years. Before the introduction of Christianity and **Islam**, all Oromo believed in one god or Waqa who was the creator of everything, omnipresent, and the source of all life. Some Oromo continue to follow this traditional religion. It includes a person known as the *qaallu*, similar to a bishop, a religious and ritual expert who is regarded as the most senior person in his lineage and clan and the most respected in society. The place of worship is called the *galma*, usually found on a hilltop, on a hillside, or in a grove of trees. Today, mosques and **Ethiopian Orthodox** churches occupy many former galma locations. Most Oromo have converted to Islam, Ethiopian Orthodoxy, and **Protestantism**. Today, there are more Muslims than Christians.

The Oromo **language** is known as Afan Oromo or Oromiffa. It belongs to the eastern Cushitic group of languages. Somali and Afan Oromo share between 30 and 40 percent of their vocabulary. It has more than 50 percent of its vocabulary in common with Konso. The language is also related to **Afar** and **Saho**. Although there are numerous dialects, they are mutually intelligible. Over the years the language has been written in the Latin, Sabaean, and Arabic scripts. The Bible was first translated into Afan Oromo well over 100 years ago in the Sabaean script. In recent years, the Oromo concluded that the Latin script works best for their language and all materials, including those used in the school system, now appear in the Latin script. The Oromo have a rich heritage of proverbs, stories, songs, and riddles. Claude Sumner and Father George Cotter have translated some of this **literature** into English. There are also numerous published studies about the Oromo. Examples are Mohmmed Hassen's *The Oromo of Ethiopia: A History 1570–1860*, Gadaa Melbaa's *Oromia: An Introduction to the History of the Oromo People*, Asmarom Legesse's *Oromo Democracy: An Indigenous African Political System*, Asafa Jalata's *Oromo Nationalism and the Ethiopian Discourse*, G. W. B. Huntingford's *The Galla of Ethiopia: The Kingdoms of Kafa and Janjero,* and *Being and Becoming Oromo* by P. T. W. Baxter, Jan Hultin, and Alessandro Triulzi.

OYDA PEOPLE AND LANGUAGE. More than 15,000 Oyda people reside in a mountainous portion of the southwest part of north **Omo** zone. Their major village is Sawla town. The **Ari** live to the southwest and the **Maale** to the southeast. The **Gamo, Gofa, and Dawro** border the remainder of their territory. They are divided into two groups (Gamitse and Arae) based on ritual practices. Unlike most societies in southwestern Ethiopia, primogeniture is not observed in matters of property inheritance. The Oyda have a patrilineal descent system. The Oyda Nationality Democratic Organization elected one representative to the **House of Peoples' Representatives** in the **elections (2000)**. They speak an Omotic **language** in the Ometo family. It has 69 percent lexical similarity with **Wolaytta** and 61 percent with **Basketo**. Many are bilingual in Wolaytta.

– P –

PALEOANTHROPOLOGY. Eastern Africa is a possible site as the crucible of humanity. Except for a recent discovery of the Toumai fossil in Chad, the earliest hominid remains found so far have come from Ethiopia's **Rift Valley** and especially the Middle Awash region in **Afar Region**. Other teams have made important findings in the lower Omo Valley near the Kenya border. The discoveries in Ethiopia's Rift Valley are particularly exciting because they cover the range of hominid evidence beginning about 4.4 million years ago with the genus *Ardipithecus ramidus* through genus *Australopithecus afarensis, Australopithecus garhi, Australopithecus boisei, Homo habilis*, and *Homo erectus* to modern humans. The seven-million-year-old Toumai fossil suggests a combination of chimpanzee and human features but has been catalogued as a hominid. Jon Kalb's *Adventures in the Bone Trade* (2001) provides a comprehensive account of the competition to locate the origins of humankind in Ethiopia.

A team led by Tim White of the University of California at Berkeley, Gen Suwa of the University of Tokyo, and Berhane Asfaw of Ethiopia's paleoanthropology laboratory found from 1992 to 1994 at Aramis in the Central Awash teeth, jaw, and a partial skeleton. They ultimately assigned the fossils to a new genus known as *Ardipithecus* (*ardi* means "earth" in the **Afar language**) because they belong to a more primitive human ancestor than the genus *Australopithecus*. They named the species *ramidus* after the Afar word *ramid*, which means "root." Many of the findings from this important discovery have not yet been published.

In 1967, the Omo Research Expedition began in the lower Omo Valley near **Lake Turkana** (formerly called Lake Rudolf). It soon divided into three competing groups of Kenyans, Americans, and French. Richard Leakey, occasionally supported by his father, Louis, headed the Kenyan team. Richard focused most of his attention on Lake Turkana's eastern shore in Kenya. The American team, led by F. Clark Howell of the University of California at Berkeley, and the French team, led by paleontologists Camille Arambourg and Yves Coppens, worked in Ethiopia until 1974. The Plio-Pleistocene deposits in the **Omo River** have preserved a continuous record of events in the study of fossil hominid evolution. Although the quality of the findings in the Omo River was not especially high, fossils and tools indicated the presence of *Australopithecus afarensis, Australopithecus boisei* (about 2 million years old), *Homo habilis* (about 2 million years old), and *Homo erectus* (about 1.5 million years old).

On 30 November 1974, Donald Johanson, an American archaeologist then at Case Western Reserve University, and Tom Gray, an American graduate student, visited Locality 162, an archaeological site at Hadar, which is located in the Afar Region some 100 miles (161 kilometers) northwest of **Addis Ababa.** The two unearthed a 40-percent-complete skeleton of a small (three feet three inches or one meter tall), bipedal, adult female. At the time of the discovery it was the most complete skeleton of an early hominid ever found. The scientific name of the skeleton, which is locked in a safe in Addis Ababa, is *Australopithecus afarensis*. But the hominid is known to the world as Lucy, named after the Beatles' song "Lucy in the Sky with Diamonds," which was playing on a tape recorder in the camp at the time of the finding. The dating of tuffs and basalt flows where Johanson found Lucy vary between 2.9 and 3.3 million years ago. Johanson states that Lucy is nearly 3 million years old. Donald Johanson and Maitland A. Edey popularized the finding in a book entitled *Lucy: The Beginnings of Humankind* (1981).

Their discovery challenged existing views that an erect-posture hominid had evolved in tandem with an enlarged brain. However, Lucy's bones appeared too apelike to be *Homo habilis*, our closest human ancestor. They also were too old to be *Australopithecus*, a name given to the first humanlike creatures that lived in eastern and southern Africa about four million years ago. Johanson subsequently determined that Lucy had evolved from the *Australopithecines*.

In 1990, Berhane Asfaw and Tim White also led a team that found a new species of hominid remains at several locations in the Middle Awash. The most important findings occurred in 1996–1998 at Bouri and included a partial hominid skeleton. They assigned the fossils to *Australopithecus garhi*. The word *garhi* means "surprise" in the Afar language. *Garhi* was big toothed, small brained, and ape faced. They believe the species is descended from *Australopithecus afarensis* and is a candidate ancestor for early *Homo*. They dated the remains at 2.5 million years ago and believe *garhi* used tools to butcher meat from animals. In fact, the earliest known tools, dating back 2.6 million years, come from the general area where they found *garhi* fossils. On 12 July 2001, *Nature* magazine reported that a team led by Yohannes Haile-Selassie (University of California, Berkeley) had located bones of a hominid that were between 5.5 and 5.8 million years old, a finding that predated other human ancestors up to that time.

Much remains to be discovered in the Ethiopian Rift Valley. Progress has been hindered by competition among different groups seeking to identify our human ancestors. There also have been periodic political and administrative problems in dealing with the Ethiopian government. The Ethiopian Rift Valley remains a candidate, however, as the origin of hominids.

PARKYNS, MANSFIELD (1823–1894). English explorer, anthropologist, and naturalist. Born in Ruddington, Nottinghamshire, on 16 February 1823. Educated at Uppingham (1833–1835). In October 1839, Parkyns matriculated at Trinity College, Cambridge, but failed to receive a degree. In 1842, he visited Constantinople (now Istanbul), Alexandria, and Cairo.

On 5 March 1843, Parkyns departed Cairo for Ethiopia. For more than three years, he traveled throughout Ethiopia, observing daily life and the country's flora and fauna. From July 1845 to July 1846, Parkyns lived in Khartoum. He then spent 18 months in Kordofan and explored the White Nile tributaries.

After having crossed Ethiopia from **Massawa** to Khartoum, Parkyns returned to Britain in mid-1849. In 1850–1852, he served as attaché in the British embassy in Constantinople. Parkyns then returned to Britain and published his *Life in Abyssinia*, a classic travel account that is essential reading for anyone who wants to gain an understanding of conditions in mid-19th-century Ethiopia. He also considered making a trans-African crossing to Senegal but, after discussions with the Royal Geographical Society, he dropped the idea.

Parkyns turned his attention to making a career for himself in Britain. He served in the Sherwood Foresters' Militia and the Nottinghamshire Rifle Volunteers. After tours as a bankruptcy official (Exeter and London) and controller of the Court of Bankruptcy, Parkyns devoted the rest of his life to woodcarving. He died on 12 January 1894.

PARLIAMENT. Ethiopia has had three different parliaments during its constitutional history—the Parliament during the reign of **Haile Selassie**, the **National Shengo** during the last years of the **Derg,** and the Federal Parliament of Ethiopia created by the **Ethiopian People's Revolutionary Democratic Front** (EPRDF). These three parliaments have had significantly different powers and duties peculiar to the ideas of the government in power. The most important common thread through all of them has been the subservience of parliament to the executive branch.

The 1931 **constitution** led to the establishment of a bicameral system of parliament on 3 November 1931 with a Senate (Yeheg Mewesegna) and Chamber of Deputies (Yeheg Memriya) having 56 members each. Initially, the emperor appointed members of the Senate from among noblemen and prominent persons. The Chamber of Deputies was constituted by the indirect election of members drawn from the landed gentry. This arrangement continued until the outbreak of the **Italian-Ethiopian War** and resumed on 9 March 1942. During the imperial period, parliamentary power was minimal as the emperor ruled Ethiopia as an absolute monarch. There were no political parties and the constitution stipulated that state power should continue to be transferred from father to son in the framework of the **Solomonic dynasty**.

On the occasion of the silver jubilee of his coronation in 1955, Haile Selassie promulgated a new constitution. It introduced universal adult suffrage and provided for an elected Chamber of Deputies. In 1957, the first **elections** took place. The emperor continued to appoint Senate members. Parliament acted as an appendage to government institutions rather than as an independent source of state power, and there continued to be a complete absence of political parties. However, Parliament did rise above the level of a consultative organization and legislation could be passed, but only with approval of both chambers. However, the emperor had the power to dissolve Parliament and to veto legislation. Ministers were beholden to the emperor, not Parliament, although it had the power to summon ministers and approve government expenditures.

In 1974, a military junta of junior officers known as the **Derg** deposed Haile Selassie, suspended the constitution, and dissolved Parliament. **Mengistu Haile Mariam** ruled Ethiopia in the name of the Provisional Government and **Workers' Party of Ethiopia** without any legislature or parliament until it introduced a constitution in 1987. This constitution created the National Shengo (*shengo* is the **Amharic** word for "assembly") as the country's supreme organ of state power. It was modeled after legislative organizations in Marxist-Leninist countries of Eastern Europe. Regional branches of the Workers' Party of Ethiopia, mass organizations, military units, and other bodies nominated candidates to the National Shengo. The National Shengo's 835 members were elected for five-year terms from their electoral districts. The National Shengo met once annually. Its responsibilities included amending the constitution; determining foreign, defense, and security policy; establishing the boundaries and status of administrative regions; and approving economic plans. It also established the Council of State, **Council of Ministers**, and other key government organs. In fact, however, members of the now-defunct Derg continued to run the government with new titles. The National Shengo elected Mengistu to be the country's first civilian president. The Derg deputy chairman became the prime minister.

In 1991, the ERPDF overthrew the Derg and convened a national conference of coalition political parties that created the **Transitional Government of Ethiopia** (TGE). The TGE adopted a constitution on 8 December 1994 that established a federal system of government and a parliament with a House of Peoples' Representatives (lower house) and the House of Federation (upper house). The people directly elect the 548 members of the lower house from single-member districts for five-year terms. Each member represents a constituency of about 100,000 persons. State assemblies choose the members of the upper house for five-year terms. Each Ethiopian nation, nationality, and people is entitled to one representative and one additional representative for each one million of its **population**. In 2002, there were 108 members in the House of Federation.

The **elections (1995)** were the first to occur under the 1994 constitution. In the **elections (2000)**, political parties affiliated with the EPRDF won 481 seats or 88 percent of the total. Other parties that won at least three seats were the Afar National Democratic Party, Benishangul-Gumuz Peoples' Democratic Party, Gambela Peoples' Democratic Front, Council of Alternative Forces for Peace and Democracy in Ethiopia, and the Hadiyya National Democratic Organization. Members of Parliament are immune from any legal or administrative action based on an opinion expressed or vote cast. They also have partial immunity from arrest.

The House of Peoples' Representatives is the more important of the two organs. It can enact laws dealing with utilization of land, natural resources, and interstate commerce; interstate roads; postal and telecommunication services; enforcement of constitutionally established political rights; nationality, asylum, and other specified issues. The House of Federation represents Ethiopia's many different ethnic groups. Its most important function is its power to interpret the constitution. It has a mandate to promote equality among the various ethnic groups in the country and determines the amount of subsidy the federal government gives to the regional governments.

The principal law emanating from the House of Peoples' Representatives is the proclamation. The only requirement is that it not contradict the constitution. Proclamations can originate in the Council of Ministers or internally in the House. The House also publishes the official gazette of Ethiopia known as the *Negarit Gazeta*. Many observers of Ethiopian politics dismiss Parliament as a "rubber stamp" of the Council of Ministers and the EPRDF's inner circle. Although Parliament is clearly a weak organization and still in its infancy, it is too facile to conclude that it has no importance. There are some outspoken members, especially among the **Somalis**, who do not shrink from criticism of government policy. The lower house occasionally has initiated controversial investigations about **corruption** and other politically sensitive issues. It also is questionable whether an unpopular policy could be forced through Parliament. The fact remains, however, that executive branch power continues, as it always has, to reign supreme in Ethiopia. *See also* ELECTIONS (1973); ELECTIONS (1992); ELECTIONS (1994).

PATRIOTS. Term used to refer to irregular military units that fought against Rome's troops during the **Italian-Ethiopian War**. **Ras Imru Haile Selassie** commanded the patriots, who operated largely in Ethiopia's northern provinces. The area they controlled included the **Rift Valley**, northeast of **Addis Ababa** from Minjar through the **Ankober-Termaber** region to southern and western **Wollo Province**; northern **Shoa** Province; eastern **Gojam**, and eastern **Bagemder Province**.

The patriots used guerrilla tactics such as attacking convoys, remote Italian farms and settlements, police stations, small garrisons, and supply dumps and warehouses. The patriots also supported **Mission 101** and **Gideon Force**, which was commanded by **Orde Wingate**. During the last few years of the Italian occupation, the patriots became more aggressive as they had larger quantities of captured Italian weapons.

After liberation (1941), **Haile Selassie** believed that the patriots posed a potential security threat as they had operated independently of the monarchy. The emperor therefore appointed many of them to government positions in Addis Ababa or in rural areas or in the Territorial Army. The patriots still are revered throughout Ethiopia for their opposition to the Italian occupation (1936–1941). *See also* ABEBE AREGAY; AFRICA ORIENTALE ITALIANA; ARMED FORCES; BADOGLIO, PIETRO; BLACK LIONS; GRAZIANA, RODOLFO; MANGASHA JAMBARE; MENGISTU NEWAY; SANDFORD, DANIEL ARTHUR; WORLD WAR II.

PAULOS GEBRE-YOHANNES, ABUNA (1935–). Patriarch of the **Ethiopian Orthodox Church** (EOC). Born in what is now **Tigray Region** and educated at Yale University, B.A.; and Princeton University, M.A., 1972, and Ph.D., 1988. After serving a prison term (1976–1983) under the **Derg**, Paulos sought refuge in the United States, where he became patriarch of Washington, D.C.'s EOC.

In September 1991, **Abuna Matewos** resigned as patriarch after the newly established **Ethiopian People's Revolutionary Democratic Front** accused him of collaborating with the Derg. On 5 July 1992, the Holy Synod elected Paulos as the EOC's fifth patriarch. Matewos, who had taken refuge in Kenya, refused to recognize Paulos. This disagreement caused divisions within the EOC that led to some unfortunate incidents. In January 1997, a disgruntled monk supposedly tried to kill Paulos. Critics also accused Paulos of **corruption** and heresy.

Despite such problems, Paulos has had some notable accomplishments, including enhancing cooperation between the EOC and Ethiopia's Muslim communities, sponsoring meetings between Ethiopian and Eritrean religious leaders (1998, 1999, and 2000) to help seek an end to the **Ethiopian-Eritrean War**, and campaigning to alert Ethiopians to the dangers of **human immunodeficiency virus/acquired immune deficiency syndrome**.

On 3 November 2000, he received the Nansen Medal, the United Nations High Commissioner for Refugees annual award, for his work among **refugees**.

PEACEKEEPING OPERATIONS. On 6 May 1951, an Ethiopian light infantry battalion (1,158 men), commanded by Colonel Kebede Guebré, arrived in Pusan, South Korea to participate in the United Nations action against North Korea. On 18 July 1960, the UN announced that Ethiopia had agreed to contribute 460 troops to the UN operation in the Congo (July 1960–June 1964). On 25 September 1965, Major General Bruce F. McDonald (Canada) announced that Ethiopia was one of eight nations that had agreed to provide observers to the UN India-Pakistan Observation Mission (28 September 1965–22 March 1966). On 25 May 1994, Ethiopia agreed to deploy a peacekeeping force to Rwanda under the terms of UN resolution 918. During 10 April–22 July 1995, the Wugagan brigade served in Cyangugu, Rwanda, as part of the international effort to maintain peace in that Central African country. The brigade performed several duties, including promoting peace and stability, helping returnees, participating in agricultural activities, and providing health services. *See also* KAGNEW BATTALIONS.

PEARCE, NATHANIEL (1779–1820). English sailor and adventurer. Born on 14 February 1779 in East Acton, Middlesex. Educated at private schools. He joined the Royal Navy but deserted and went to China and then to Yemen, where he converted to **Islam**.

His East African adventures began on 31 December 1804, when he joined a ship en route to Ethiopia. In early 1805, Pearce joined **Henry Salt,** who was on a mission to the court of **Tigray**'s **ras** Wolde Selassie. In November 1805, Salt departed Tigray but Pearce remained behind in the service of the ras. In 1810, he escorted Salt's second Ethiopian expedition from the coast and back. In 1819, he went to Cairo and undertook a journey up the **Nile River**.

His journals, published in 1831 as the *Life and Adventures of N. Pearce*, are one of the few existing English-language sources about this period of Ethiopia's history. In June 1820, Pearce died during a voyage to Britain.

PEASANT ASSOCIATIONS. On 4 March 1975, the **Derg** issued Proclamation 31, which established peasant associations. Some of their functions included distributing land on an equitable basis; establishing judicial tribunals to settle land disputes; creating marketing and credit cooperatives; building government schools and clinics; organizing villagization programs; and preserving lands of commercial, environmental, or historical importance.

On 14 December 1975, the Derg issued the Peasant Association Organization and Consolidation Proclamation, which expanded and better defined the functions of the associations and sought to establish links between the associations and the central government. These measures aimed to make peasant associations self-governing units and responsible for raising peasant militias, which had disastrous implications during the **Red Star Campaign**. By February 1977, there were 24,707 peasant associations with approximately 6.7 million members.

The creation of peasant associations constituted one of the Derg's most revolutionary reforms. Although the competence and functioning of the associations varied greatly, they constituted a significant force for decentralization. After 1977, the Derg perceived this development as a threat and reorganized the peasant associations to ensure centralized control over them. The **Ethiopian People's Revolutionary Democratic Front** continued to downplay the political role of peasant associations. Today, they exist essentially as agricultural co-operatives.

PEOPLE'S MILITIA. In 1975, the **Derg** issued Decree No. 71, which established the People's Militia to "safeguard the revolution." In May 1976, the Derg conscripted some 30,000–40,000 peasants into the People's Militia. The recruits—who were drawn mainly from **Gojam**, **Shoa**, and **Wollo**—received only two weeks' training at a camp near the Eritrean border. Eritrean rebels, fearing that the People's Militia would be used against them, attacked the camp and killed many conscripts.

In April 1977, the Derg changed the name of the People's Militia to the Red Army. Within a year, there were about 80,000 troops in the Red Army. Each soldier received 12 weeks' basic military training at camps in Awash, Azezo, Fiche, Shashemene, and Tatek. North Korean officers often taught recruits how to operate modern weapons supplied largely by the Soviet Union. Despite this preparation, the Red Army performed poorly in Eritrea and in the **Ogaden War**. By 1980, the Red Army numbered about 150,000 troops organized into 10 divisions. Those deployed to Eritrea were called the Northern People's Divisions while those in the **Ogaden** were known as the Eastern People's Divisions. By 1984, the Red Army had been incorporated into the regular **armed forces**. In late 1989, the Derg mobilized the Red Army to halt the advance of the **Tigray People's Liberation Front** and the Ethiopian People's Democratic Movement. These and other groups had joined forces and were known as the Ethiopian People's Democratic Movement. By 1991, the Red Army, which numbered approximately 200,000 personnel, had started supporting the regular army's counterinsurgency operations in Eritrea and **Tigray**. Its efforts proved futile as the Derg had only a few months to survive.

PEOPLE'S PROTECTION BRIGADES. In 1978, the **Derg** established the 10,000-member People's Protection Brigades to act as local law enforcement agencies under the jurisdiction of each **peasant association** and *kebele*. Each brigade was subordinate to the **Commission for Organizing the Party of the Working People of Ethiopia's** Central Committee security chief. East German advisers provided up to five months' training to brigade members in **police** and military tactics.

PHILATELY. Ethiopia has a long philatelic history. In December 1867, British military authorities opened a main post office at Annesley Bay, south of **Massawa**. By the time the **Anglo-Ethiopian War** ended, there also were British military post offices in Adigrat, Antalo, Kumayli, and Senafe, at British military headquarters, and in every deployed brigade. These facilities maintained communications between Ethiopia, Britain, and India.

Other early post offices included the Egyptian facilities at Massawa (1867–1885) and the Italian facilities at **Asab** and Massawa (1883–1889). In 1892, Monseigneur Ludovic Taurin de Cahagne (1826–1899) established a regular postal service for French residents and other foreign nationals in **Addis Ababa** and **Harar**. He managed the Addis Ababa office while Casimir Mondon-Vidaillet, an adviser to **Menelik II**, handled the Harar office and the postal mule-transport system. Special couriers, called *méléktegnas*, delivered mail in Ethiopia. Such couriers were under the protection of imperial governors.

In 1892, **Alfred Ilg**, a Swiss engineer who became chancellor of state under Menelik II, convinced the emperor to establish a postal system and issue printed stamps. On 9 March 1894, Menelik II issued an edict that authorized the creation of a postal administration and the construction of the **Addis Ababa–Djibouti Railway**. A Paris-based French company, Atelier de Fabrication des Timbres-Poste, produced Ethiopia's first stamps in the same year. In 1895, stamps appeared in Addis Ababa and Harar. In November 1898 or 1899, three Swiss telegraph operators (H. Mühle, G. Spitzer, and G. Wüllscheger) and European post officers arrived from Switzerland. On 12 May 1899, Ilg started an Ethiopian postal service between Addis Ababa and Harar.

For some years, Menelik II tried to gain membership in the International Postal Union. France, Russia, and Switzerland supported Ethiopia's application but Italy persuaded other members to ignore the request because, in Rome's view, Ethiopia was a nation of tribesmen led by a barbarian. Finally, on 1 November 1908, Ethiopia succeeded in joining the Universal Postal Union. The following year, Ethiopia released a definitive set of postage stamps;

additional definitive sets appeared in 1919, 1928, and 1931. France printed most of Ethiopia's stamps, although Switzerland stepped in during **World War I**, when France was unable to do the work.

In 1928, Ethiopia inaugurated a new post office in Addis Ababa and increased the variety of its postage stamps. By 1964, there were 68 post offices in Ethiopia. A mobile postal service delivered mail to remote areas such as Assela in Arusi, Dilla in **Sidamo**, and Nekempte in **Wollega**.

The **Italian-Ethiopian War** resulted in the bombing of Addis Ababa's post office and the loss of most of Ethiopia's philatelic archives. Italian soldiers took most of what was left back to Italy. During the Italian occupation, Italy issued stamps for **Africa Orientale Italiana**. Following Italy's defeat in 1941, **Haile Selassie** resumed issuing Ethiopian stamps (1942), the first three printed in India. Increasingly, Ethiopian history, culture, flora, and fauna became the subject of Ethiopian philately.

During the **Derg** regime, political themes also became popular. In 1975, the government established the National Postal Museum in Addis Ababa that displays an Ethiopian stamp collection that dates back to 1894. Ethiopian philately today is of a high quality and tends to reflect the history, culture, and beauty of the country. Roberto Sciaky's *Ethiopia 1867–1936: History, Stamps, and Postal History* (1999) is essential for understanding Ethiopia's early philatelic history.

PIBOR RIVER. *See* SOBAT RIVER.

PLATT, WILLIAM (1885–1975). British soldier. Born on 14 June 1885 in Brooklands, Cheshire. Educated at Marlborough and the Royal Military College, Sandhurst. In 1905, Platt received a commission in the Northumberland Fusiliers. During 1907–1913, he served in India and saw action on the North-West Frontier. Platt spent most of **World War I** on the western front. In 1919, he attended Staff College and then had tours in India and Egypt. From 1927 to 1938, he held various assignments in Britain.

In 1938, Platt received a promotion to major-general and, in January 1939, arrived in Khartoum and assumed command of the Sudan Defense Force. His chief duty was to help liberate Ethiopia. Between 3 February and 27 March 1941, Platt's troops laid siege to Keren. After the British authorities established administrative control over Asmara on 2 April 1941, he advanced south and met up with General Alan Cunningham's forces at Amba Alagi. On 19 May 1941, the commander of Italian forces, **Amedeo di Savoia, Duke of Aosta,** surrendered, thereby ending the **Italian-Ethiopian War**.

On 26 August 1941, London appointed Platt commanding officer of the newly established East African Command, which included all former **Africa Orientale Italiana** territories. In September 1942, he took command of operations that completed the occupation of Madagascar. Platt subsequently trained African troops required for the Burma campaign.

After **World War II**, he joined the family engineering firm and became a member of the Arts Council. Platt died in London on 28 September 1975.

PLOWDEN, WALTER CHICHELE (1820–1860). First British consul general to Ethiopia, based in **Massawa**. Born on 8 August 1820 and educated at Dr. Evans's School, Hampstead. In 1839–1843, Plowden worked for the firm of Carr, Tagore, and Company in Calcutta, India. After resigning, he wanted to return to Britain. However, at Suez, Plowden met John T. Bell, who eventually became the grand chamberlain to **Tewodros**, and the two decided to go to Ethiopia to discover the source of the White Nile. They failed to achieve this goal but Plowden remained in Ethiopia until 1847, when he returned to Britain after being shipwrecked in the **Red Sea**.

In 1848, Plowden received an appointment as consul general to Ethiopia. On 2 November 1849, Plowden and **Ras Alula Qubi** signed a Treaty of Friendship and Commerce. On 18 January 1860, the Foreign Office ordered Plowden to leave Ethiopia and return to Massawa because there was no "special advantage" to his repeated trips to the interior. On the return journey, 400 rebels, led by Garred, who was the nephew of Tewodros, attacked his caravan outside **Gondar**. Plowden sustained a serious chest wound. Gondar merchants ransomed him for 1,000 **Maria Theresa thalers**. However, he died of his wounds in Gondar town on 13 March 1860. Friends dispatched his manuscripts to his brother, Trevor Chichele Plowden, who published them under the title *Travels in Abyssinia and the Galla Country*.

POETRY. Traditionally, Ethiopian poetry was intended to be sung. The ancient Greeks and Ethiopians regarded poetry as a branch of **music**.

Poetry, song, and music are virtually inseparable. Poetry and rhymed verse are common features in religious and secular occasions. A poetic reference may help a litigant win a point while verse is often sung at weddings and funerals. Minstrels offer poetic songs and ballads.

There are three main poetic categories. These include poems written in **Ge'ez,** historic popular poems in **Amharic**, Tigrinya, and **Tigre**, and modern religious and secular Amharic verse. Rhyme is the dominant feature of all three types. Lines end in the same sets of consonants and vowels. A rhyme normally persists for several lines and then another begins with a different consonant and vowel.

Ethiopian poetry emphasizes meaning and understanding of metaphor and allusion. The religious allusions of Ge'ez poetry require, for example, a thorough knowledge of religious legends and the Bible. The first important Ge'ez verses appeared in the sixth century in the form of religious poetry known as the *malka,* which presented 55-line rhymed stanzas referring to the moral and physical attributes of the saints. Malka poems began to appear frequently by the time of **Zara Yacob**. This form continues to be used by ecclesiastics and laymen.

In the 18th century, Ge'ez *qene* (poetic compositions) became popular as part of the **Ethiopian Orthodox Church** liturgy. Produced in monasteries, qene has strict meter and uniform rhyme that follow the substance of the psalms. Qene meter depends primarily on accent or stress. Qene is an original type of poetry that, upon recitation, becomes a dramatized musical performance. Two actors—the whispering poet and the singing reciter—aided by a chorus of church musicians, take the poem sung through its musical stages in a growing crescendo culminating in a climax. Well-known Ethiopian playwright and poet **Mengistu Lemma** has published and explained qene poetry for the public. Tseggaye Gebre-Medhin, who writes in Amharic and English, is one of Ethiopia's most famous playwrights and poets.

Since the 14th century, minstrels have composed verse in various **languages**. This verse often relies on puns and plays on words and occurs most often at weddings and funerals. Popular poetry in Amharic dates from the 20th century when individual poetic expression became prominent for the first time. Poems initially tended to be long and instructive, stressing morality and the value of patriotism. Modern verse **drama** has become rich in creativity and variety.

POLICE. Historically, civil police played no role in traditional Ethiopian society, as provincial armies enforced the law and punished criminals. In 1916, Emperor **Lij Iyasu Mikael** established a civilian municipal guard to maintain law and order in **Addis Ababa**. The municipal guard also collected taxes, escorted distinguished foreign visitors, and served as body guards for local officials. However, this unit enjoyed little public support because of its inefficiency. By the early 1930s, the police force numbered approximately 3,000 personnel, some of whom had seen service with the King's African Rifles or the Italian army.

In April 1933, a four-man Belgian team arrived in Addis Ababa to reorganize the police force. In 1935, **Haile Selassie** authorized the establishment of British-trained police units in Addis Ababa, **Dire Dawa**, and along the **Addis Ababa–Djibouti Railway**. The **Anglo-Ethiopian Agreement and Military Convention (1942)** provided for the appointment of a British commissioner of police and the recruitment of British police officers and inspectors. Britain also helped to create the Imperial Ethiopian Police (IEP), under the Ministry of the Interior, as a centralized national force with paramilitary and constabulary units. IEP personnel received training at Kolfe Police Constable Training School, which started operations in 1942, or the Aba Dina Police Academy, which opened in 1946. In 1956, Haile Selassie ordered the amalgamation of the separate city police forces with the IEP and appointed the first Ethiopian (Brigadier General Tsique Dibou) as commissioner of police. By 1960, the IEP had some 23,000 members. After its federation with Ethiopia (1952), Eritrea had a separate 3,000-member police force. In 1962, the government created the Emergency Police to deal with security threats beyond the capabilities of the regular police. By the early 1970s, the IEP had become an independent agency commanded by the commissioner of police, who reported directly to the emperor. In early 1974, the police force had grown to approximately 28,000 personnel in all branches, including 6,800 in the mobile emergency force, 1,200 frontier guards, and a 3,200-member rapid-reaction commando unit.

After Haile Selassie's downfall, the **Derg** significantly reduced the power of the national police because it believed that many of its members supported the "rightist opposition." The Derg viewed the police with suspicion because of their association with the ruling class under the emperor. Under the Derg, the police commissioner reported to the Ministry of the Interior and the police force confined its activities to suppressing political dissent. In July 1975, the Ethiopian **armed forces** took over all police functions in Eritrea because local units were suspected of being sympathetic to the **Eritrean People's Liberation Front**. In 1977, **Mengistu Haile Mariam** reorganized the police by appointing a loyal commissioner of police and establishing a security committee that reported to the Ministry of the Interior, and accorded the army a larger role in criminal investigations and in maintaining public order. The **People's Protection Brigades** enforced law at the local level. By 1982, these changes had reduced the number of police personnel to about 17,000.

After it seized power (1991), the **Ethiopian People's Revolutionary Democratic Front** (EPRDF) dissolved the police force and assumed responsibility for internal security duties throughout the country. In mid-1994, the EPRDF reestablished the police force, which included some demobilized soldiers. In August 1995, the government transferred responsibility for the federal police and prisons from the Ministry of Internal Affairs, which was abolished, to the Ministry of Justice.

Ethiopia has relied on governments such as those of Britain and Germany to improve police efficiency. On 2 November 2002, Ethiopia and Sudan concluded an agreement whereby Khartoum would offer student grants and training classes to Ethiopian police officers to fight terrorism and criminality. The EPRDF claimed that such training helped to curb police excesses and that it disciplined policemen who abused their authority or accepted bribes or kickbacks. However, opposition groups and **human rights** organizations continued to report irregularities throughout the police force.

PONCET, CHARLES-JACQUES (c. 1655–1710). French surgeon and traveler. Born in Franche-Comté. Apart from a brief tour in the French military, Poncet spent his early career in Cairo as an apothecary and medical practitioner. In early 1868, Haji Ali, an emissary from **Iyasu I**, arrived in Cairo and implored Poncet to accompany him to Ethiopia to attend to the emperor's skin disease. Shortly thereafter, Poncet, Haji Ali, and Father Charles Xaverius de Brevedent departed Cairo. In mid-1699, Brevedent died at Barko. A few days later, Poncet arrived in **Gondar** and successfully treated Iyasu

I and one of his children. Apart from his medical duties, Poncet explored Gondar town and **Lake Tana**. In mid-1700, he departed Gondar for Cairo via **Axum** and **Massawa**. Poncet's *Voyage to Ethiopia in the Years 1698, 1699 and 1700* is the only European source for the history of this period. He eventually left Cairo for Isfahan, where he died in 1710.

POPULATION. Ethiopia's long history but limited record keeping does not lend itself to accurate population estimates. In addition, the boundaries of the territory under Ethiopian control have fluctuated over the years. One foreign traveler observed in the late 15th century that most parts of Ethiopia had no stone houses or permanent buildings. **Axum** may have been the only significant urban center at that time. On the other hand, foreigners reported areas of dense population as early as the 15th century. Eighteenth-century visitors commented on numerous small villages and rural areas with relatively dense populations. **William Cornwallis Harris** suggested that **Shoa**'s population in the early 19th century was 1 million Christians while Muslims and pagans numbered 1.5 million. Henry Dufton thought that **Tewodros II** ruled over fewer than 4 million subjects. Writing in the late 19th century, G. Simon put the Ethiopian population at 4 or 5 million. After **Menelik II**'s Imperial expansion, one of his foreign advisers said the population by 1900 had reached about 10 million. Prior to the 20th century, Ethiopia's birth rate appears to have been relatively low and the average life span was not very long.

During the 1920s and 1930s, population estimates by foreigners fluctuated between 8 and 14 million people. Italian authorities during the occupation of Ethiopia put the population estimate at a low 7.5 million in 1938. There may have been a political agenda for this number as Italy had been encouraging the settlement of poor Italians from overpopulated regions to Ethiopia. A 1957 partial **census** put the population at just over 22 million. In 1965, an Ethiopian geographer estimated the population at between 25 and 30 million. The 1984 census placed the population at more than 42 million. The annual population growth rate averaged 2.2 percent between 1950 and 1970 and 2.7 percent from 1970 to 1984. The **World Bank** put the growth rate at 2.4 percent in 1999, down from 2.9 percent in 1995. On the other hand, the CIA *World Fact Book* suggested the 2001 growth rate was 2.7 percent. In 2003, Ethiopian authorities estimated the population at more than 70 million. This makes Ethiopia Africa's third most populous country after Nigeria and Egypt. If worldwide population growth patterns continue unchanged (an unlikely event) until 2050, Ethiopia would become the world's ninth most populous country by midcentury. One factor that will affect population growth rates is **human immunodeficiency virus/acquired immune deficiency syndrome**.

There are about 130 persons per square mile (50 per square kilometer) in Ethiopia and the urban population constitutes about 17 percent of the total. Urban population growth rates are increasing at about 6 percent annually. **Famine** and **food** shortages in rural areas in 2002–2003 have contributed to this high rate of urbanization. About 46 percent of the population is under the age of 14 years, 51 percent from 15–64 years, and 3 percent over 65 years. The **Oromo** comprise approximately 40 to 45 percent of the population, **Amhara** 25 percent, **Sidama** and related peoples 9 percent, **Tigrayan** 7 percent, **Somali** 6 percent, **Afar** 4 percent, **Gurage** 2 percent, and numerous other peoples 7 percent.

PORTAL, GERALD HERBERT (1858–1894). British diplomat. Born on 13 March 1858 in Laverstoke. After graduating from Eton, Portal entered the Foreign Office and served in Rome (1880–1884) and Cairo (1884–1891). During his time in Egypt, he undertook several temporary-duty assignments. On 17 October 1887, for example, Portal received orders for Ethiopia, with instructions to heal the rift between **Yohannes IV** and Italy that had developed over the ownership of **Massawa**. **Ras Alula Qubi**, who loathed the Italians, sought to thwart Portal's mission by trying to convince the emperor that London and Rome were working together to wrest this important port from Ethiopia. Nevertheless, on 4 December 1887, Portal was well received when he arrived at Yohannes IV's camp at Wafala. However, the emperor told Portal that he would not cede an inch of territory to Italy. On 31 December 1887, he returned to Cairo. Although Portal had failed to accomplish his mission, his professionalism in Ethiopia had earned the respect of his colleagues and superiors.

His subsequent service included tours at Zanzibar (consul general) and an 1892–1893 mission to Uganda that eventually resulted in the declaration of a British protectorate over that country. Portal died in London on 25 January 1894 from a fever that was associated with his African travels. His account of his time in Ethiopia is entitled *My Mission to Abyssinia*.

POSTAL SYSTEM. *See* PHILATELY.

POTTERY. *See* HANDICRAFTS.

POVERTY. By any index, Ethiopia is one of the world's poorest countries. At the same time, the government attaches a high priority to poverty reduction. This is an especially difficult challenge in a country with a high **population** growth rate and one where 85 percent of the inhabitants live in rural areas. The **World Bank** issued a study in 1992 that suggested about 50 percent of Ethiopians live below the poverty line. In the mid-1990s, there was some improvement. Between 1994 and 1997, 16 percent of urban dwellers moved out of poverty while 14 percent dropped back in. Severe **food** shortages and drought in the late 1990s and again in 2002–2003 have undoubtedly worsened the situation, especially for peasant farmers.

Studies show that rural households with higher **education**, access to more resources such as land and oxen, and access to road infrastructure and those closer to towns had lower levels of poverty. In urban Ethiopia, fewer households (36 percent) headed by males were under the poverty line than households (48 percent) headed by females. Urban poverty is especially high among families affected by divorce and separation, persons above the age of 40, those who never attended school (42 percent), and casual laborers (100 percent). Public sector employees and those working in the civil service had the lowest rate of poverty.

On 15 August 2002, Ethiopia delivered its 250-page poverty strategy reduction paper to the World Bank. It proposed creating a free-market **economy**, reducing poverty, and reducing dependence on food aid. It set a goal of a 7 percent annual growth rate based on **agricultural**-development-led **industrialization**, judicial and civil service reform, decentralization, and capacity building. It also stressed **educational** reform from primary to university level as a key to poverty reduction and growth. *See also* INTERNATIONAL MONETARY FUND.

POVERTY REDUCTION AND GROWTH FACILITY (PRGF). *See* INTERNATIONAL MONETARY FUND.

PRESTER JOHN. Mythical Christian priest-king. Beginning in the 12th century, rumors about Prester John and his lost Christian kingdom started circulating throughout Europe. About 1165, Prester John supposedly sent a letter to the Byzantine emperor, Manuel I Comnenus (c. 1122–1180), and other Christian kings. This letter described a kingdom in India where riches abounded and poverty was unknown. This news excited the imagination of medieval Europe. Marco Polo (1254–1324) and other travelers unsuccessfully searched for Prester John during their trip to Asia.

In the 14th century, European scholars and theologians argued that Prester John lived in Ethiopia, which was then considered part of India. The prospect of finding the elusive priest-king generated considerable activity throughout Europe. In 1400, England's king Henry IV (1367–1413) sent a letter to the king of **Abyssinia**, Prester John. When Portugal's prince Henry (1394–1460), known as the Navigator, embarked on his program of maritime discovery, he hoped to find Prester John and persuade him to join in a war against **Islam**. After Prince Henry's death, Lisbon launched a two-pronged expedition to open a route to the Indies and to locate Prester John. Bartolomeu Dias (c. 1450–1500) sailed south around Africa to the East while Pero da Colvilhão set out for Ethiopia via Egypt and the **Red Sea**. The latter reached Ethiopia but was barred from leaving. After these two missions, Europe's interest in Prester John gradually faded.

PRIME MINISTER. *See* COUNCIL OF MINISTERS.

PROTESTANTISM. Peter Heyling (c. 1607–1652), a German Lutheran trained as a physician and lawyer, probably was the first Protestant **missionary** to visit Ethiopia. In 1634, he arrived in **Gondar** to infuse the churches of the Orient with new evangelical life. Heyling also practiced medicine and taught Hebrew and Greek to the clergy. He lived under the protection of Emperor **Fasilidas** (reigned 1632–1667) and remained highly regarded by Ethiopian clergy long after his death. However, Heyling apparently did not leave behind any Protestant followers.

The **Church Missionary Society (CMS)** and the Bible Society in Britain published an **Amharic** version of the Gospels (1824), the New Testament (1829), and then the entire Bible (1840). An Ethiopian monk from Gondar known as Abraham or Abu Rumi translated these materials. In 1830, the CMS sent the Reverend **Samuel Gobat**, a Swiss, and the Reverend Christian Kugler, a German, to Ethiopia. Kugler died the same year in a hunting accident in **Adwa** while Gobat continued to Gondar, where he distributed Amharic translations of the four Gospels. On a return visit to Europe in 1833, Gobat recruited the Reverend Carl Wilhelm Isenberg (1806–1864), a Prussian, to join him in Ethiopia. Shortly after his return to Ethiopia, Gobat fell ill in Adwa. Gobat and Isenberg, both of whom remained in Adwa, disagreed on the most effective way to reach Ethiopians. In 1836, ill health forced Gobat to give up his missionary career. His account is contained in *Journal of Three Years' Residence in Abyssinia*.

In 1837, two Württemberg residents, the Reverend Carl Heinrich Blumhardt, an Anglican, and the Reverend **Johann Ludwig Krapf**, brought up in the pietistic tradition of uniting Lutherans and Calvinists, joined Isenberg in 1837. After they had irritated local officials, Adwa's governor asked all three to leave in 1838, thereby ending the CMS mission. Isenberg then went to **Ankober** but eventually left Ethiopia for Malta (1839). Krapf learned Afan Oromo while living in **Shoa** Province but failed to get permission to work among the **Oromo**. In 1842, Krapf left Ethiopia, but the following year he and Isenberg tried to return to **Tigray**. In 1843, local authorities closed the CMS mission. The CMS failed to reform the **Ethiopian Orthodox Church** and preach to the Oromo, but it distributed some 8,000 copies of the Holy Scriptures in **Amharic** and **Ge'ez**. Isenberg and Krapf published their *Journals of the Rev. Messrs. Isenberg and Krapf*. In addition, *Travels, Researches, and Missionary Labours during an Eighteen Years' Residence in Eastern Africa* documented Krapf's missionary activities.

Johann Martin Flad, a Pilgrim Brethren missionary, joined Krapf, who returned to Ethiopia in 1855. Krapf fell ill the same year and retired to Europe. Emperor **Tewodros II** was more interested in artisans than missionaries. Nevertheless, Flad persevered at **Debre Tabor** until 1868, when events leading to the **Anglo-Ethiopian War** complicated matters for the missionaries and the Pilgrim Brethren came to an end. In the meantime, however, the London Society for Promoting Christianity Amongst the Jews sent the Reverend **Henry Aaron Stern** to Ethiopia (1860) to work among the **Falashas** in the Gondar area. In 1863, officials arrested and imprisoned him for five years until he was evacuated by British forces. Despite his incarceration Stern had considerable success among the Falashas. Indigenous evangelists carried on the society's work. E. C. Dawson recounts Stern's life in *Henry A. Stern: Missionary Traveller and Abyssinian Captive*.

Two Lutheran undertakings, the German Hermannsburg Mission and the Swedish Evangelical Mission (SEM) laid the foundation for evangelical Christianity in Ethiopia. In 1866, an SEM group settled among the **Kunama** and expanded their activities along the **Red Sea** coast by 1872. The SEM's goal was to preach among the Oromo but local officials prevented its missionaries from leaving the coastal area. In 1877, the Swedes finally set out for Oromo country and, after many setbacks, reached **Jimma** in 1883, where Sultan Abba Jifar II gave them a warm welcome. They established a headquarters at Imkullu and became an indigenous and self-supporting society. The leader of this effort was the Reverend Bengt Peter Lundahl, who died of smallpox in 1885. Anders Svensson replaced Lundahl and led the SEM effort until 1913. By 1889, the number of communicants had reached only 84.

In 1903, the SEM established a new station in northern Kunama. After early successes, **World War I** intervened and interrupted the SEM's efforts among the Kunama, who lived in Eritrea and Ethiopia. In the 1920s, the SEM resumed its work. In the meantime, the SEM pressed forward among the Oromo. The Reverend Karl Cederqvist joined the effort in 1893 and carried out a pioneering ministry until his death in **Addis Ababa** in 1919. Two Ethiopian evangelists, Niguse Tashu and Gebre Ewostateos, were critical to the SEM's success. They introduced several reforms, including the use of Afan Oromo in services. In 1899, Onesimos Nesib published the Bible in Afan Oromo. Evangelical Christianity took root in western Ethiopia and led ultimately to the creation of the **Evangelical Church Mekane Yesus**.

In the 20th century, missionary activity in Ethiopia increased dramatically with the arrival of North American missionaries. In 1919,

Dr. **Thomas Lambie** of the United Presbyterian Church in North America arrived at Sayo in western Ethiopia. By 1940, his work had resulted in the establishment of the Evangelical Church Bethel as a national church under indigenous leadership. In 1921, Bibeltrogna Vanner arrived and the German Hermannsburg Mission and the Sudan Interior Mission came in 1927. These new arrivals also adopted the policy of establishing congregations in Ethiopian Orthodox areas. By 1935, 10 Protestant missionary societies were active in Ethiopia: SEM, Swedish Bible Friends' Mission, United Presbyterian Mission of North America, Seventh-Day Adventist Mission, Church Mission to Jews, Bible Churchman's Missionary Society, British and Foreign Bible Society, Society for the Propagation of the Gospel in Foreign Parts, Sudan Interior Mission, and German Hermannsburg Mission. Except for the Swedish parishes in Eritrea and the Church Mission to Jews, the congregations of each society numbered only about 150. Several of them operated schools and hospitals; they were particularly active in western and southwestern Ethiopia. Following the outbreak of the **Italian-Ethiopian War**, the number of foreign missionaries decreased and Rome soon closed most of the societies. When British troops arrived in 1941, only the German missionaries, six Seventh-Day Adventists, and two Presbyterians remained in Addis Ababa.

In the late 1960s, there were an estimated 250,000 Protestants in Ethiopia. By the late 1970s, Ethiopian Evangelical Church Mekane Yesus claimed some 400,000 members, while the Bethel Evangelical Church had about 5,000 followers and the Seventh-Day Adventists approximately 15,000. Despite severe repression of missionaries during the **Derg** regime, the Protestants continued to grow and have stepped up their expansion after the **Ethiopian People's Revolutionary Democratic Front** (EPRDF) came to power (1991).

Foreign missionaries are still active in Ethiopia but play a smaller role while many indigenous Protestant groups, including Pentecostals, have taken root. Although the Protestants claim higher numbers, they could constitute up to 5 percent of Ethiopia's **population** of 70 million. The most comprehensive account of Protestant missionary activity in Ethiopia is *Evangelical Pioneers in Ethiopia* by Gustav Aren. Other useful sources are *Priests and Politicians* by Donald Crummey, *The Missionary Factor in Ethiopia* edited by

Getatchew Haile, Aasulv Lande, and Samuel Rubenson, and *The Survival of Ethiopian Independence* by Sven Rubenson. There are dozens of memoirs by 20th-century missionaries in Ethiopia. Thomas Lambie alone has published four books on his experiences in the country. *See also* CATHOLICISM.

PROVISIONAL MILITARY ADMINISTRATIVE COUNCIL (PMAC). On 15 September 1974, the **Armed Forces Coordination Committee** transformed itself into the PMAC under the chairmanship of Lieutenant General **Aman Mikael Andom**. The PMAC, with a membership of 126 military men, included representatives from each branch of the **armed forces**, military academies, and major units within each service. Twelve groups of 8–10 each comprised the PMAC's main council. An inner core of 8–10 men, in which **Mengistu Haile Mariam** played a key role, emerged as the real force behind the PMAC. On 9 September 1987, the **National Shengo** dissolved the PMAC. *See also* NATIONAL DEMOCRATIC REVOLUTION.

PROVISIONAL OFFICE FOR MASS ORGANIZATIONAL AFFAIRS (POMOA). In December 1975, the **Derg** established the People's Organizing Provisional Office to implement the **National Democratic Revolution**. On 20 April 1976, the Derg renamed this organization the POMOA, which insiders usually called the "political bureau." Haile Fida, who belonged to the **All Ethiopian Socialist Movement** (AESM), served as its chairman. The POMOA's 15-member Central Committee was divided into four subcommittees (philosophy dissemination and information; political education; current affairs; and organizational matters). The POMOA had branch offices at the provincial, regional, and district levels. The Central Committee also operated the Yekatit '66 Political School to spread Marxist ideology and to train party cadres. On 21 April 1976, the POMOA helped to implement the National Democratic Revolutionary Program, which sought to move the country toward "scientific socialism."

Apart from the AESM, other organizations that belonged to the POMOA included the **Workers' League**, **Revolutionary Flame**, **Ethiopian Oppressed People's Revolutionary Struggle**, and

Ethiopian Marxist-Leninist Revolutionary Organization. All five parties espoused a Marxist-Leninist agenda. The differences between them concerned their attitudes toward military rule and government personalities. In February 1977, the five parties formed the United Front of Ethiopian Marxist-Leninist Organizations. This coalition adopted an ambitious program that included politicizing the population, building a people's army, improving the quantity and quality of party cadres, and including oppressed nationalities in the party and government.

However, chronic clashes between the AESM and the Revolutionary Flame over the POMOA and government appointments prevented any significant progress toward achieving these goals. Nevertheless, the POMOA continued to grow by establishing cells throughout Ethiopia and enlisting some 4,000 cadres. The Revolutionary Flame's increasing power and influence gradually transformed the POMOA into a military organization dominated by **Mengistu Haile Mariam.**

PUBLIC HEALTH. *See* HEALTH.

– Q –

QAT. *See* KHAT.

QENE. *See* POETRY.

QUEEN OF SHEBA. *See* MAKEDA.

– R –

RAS. *See* IMPERIAL TITLES; MILITARY TITLES.

RAS DASHEN. *See* SIMIEN MOUNTAINS.

RASSAM, HORMUZD (1826–1910). Born in Mosul, Mesopotamia, (now Iraq) and attended Magdalen College, Oxford. In the late 1840s and early 1850s, Rassam undertook archaeological excavations in Assyria and Babylonia. In 1854, he accepted an Indian government position as political interpreter at Aden. In 1861, the Indian government sent him to Zanzibar to represent British interests. In 1864, Rassam arrived in the region to deliver a letter to **Tewodros II** that expressed London's displeasure about the emperor's decision to imprison European **missionaries** and the British consul, **Charles Duncan Cameron**. However, he had to wait at **Massawa** nearly a year before receiving permission to enter Ethiopia. Initially, Tewodros II responded positively to Rassam's mission by freeing the captives. However, the emperor subsequently rearrested them and jailed Rassam and his two aides, Henry Blanc and W. F. Frideaux. Tewodros II took all of them to his mountain stronghold at Magdala. On 2 December 1867, Tewodros II learned that an Anglo-Indian military expedition had landed at Annesley Bay. To avoid a confrontation, the emperor released the three diplomats. Nevertheless, on 14 April 1868, Anglo-Indian units, under the command of General Sir **Robert Napier**, stormed Magdala, defeated Tewodros II's army, and freed all captives. On 15 April 1868, Tewodros committed suicide rather than surrender. Rassam recounted his exploits in a two-volume study entitled the *British Mission to Theodore, King of Abyssinia* (1869). After leaving Ethiopia, Rassam spent the rest of his life researching and exploring in Assyria and Babylonia. He died on 16 November 1910 in Brighton, England.

RASTAFARIANS. The roots of the Rastafarians go back to slave rebellions in the Caribbean beginning in the late 1700s. There are subsequent links to Revivalism, the back-to-Africa movement of Marcus Garvey, and a reaction to European subjugation and domination. Rastafarians take their name from **Ras** Tafari Makonnen, who ascended to the throne of Ethiopia in 1930 as **Haile Selassie**. The descendants of African slaves in Jamaica interpreted this development as confirmation that the day of deliverance had arrived. The Rastafarian movement began to grow in the 1930s. The Rastafarians regard Ethiopia as their ancestral home and view Ethiopia as Zion. In a broader sense, the movement is an example of Ethiopianism as reflected in biblical references to Ethiopia covering a much larger part of Africa than present-day Ethiopia. At its peak the movement in

Ethiopia counted thousands of followers from the Caribbean, the United States, and the United Kingdom residing on 500 acres of land granted by Haile Selassie near Shashemene, located about 130 miles (209 kilometers) south of **Addis Ababa.**

Today, Rastafarians residing in Ethiopia occupy only about 11 acres of land outside Shashemene and number perhaps 500 followers. The Marxist-Leninist government of **Mengistu Haile Mariam** reduced the land available to them. They do not integrate easily with Ethiopians; the current government politely tolerates the movement. To some Ethiopians, they are guests who have overstayed their welcome. The Rastafarian movement might have faded into history were it not for the music of Bob Marley, the king of reggae and the most famous Rastafarian. Reggae music has been a powerful way of communicating the message and spirit of Rastafari in North America but has not attracted a significant number of followers in Ethiopia. The small Rastafarian community outside Shashemene is tired of being treated as a **tourist** attraction and a source of marijuana, which is illegal in Ethiopia in any event.

RED ARMY. *See* PEOPLE'S MILITIA.

RED CROSS. *See* ETHIOPIAN RED CROSS SOCIETY.

RED SEA. Known in ancient times as Sinus Arabicus or Erythraean Sea. The Red Sea covers an area of approximately 170,000 square miles (440,300 square kilometers) and is about 1,450 miles (2,330 kilometers) long and approximately 225 miles (362 kilometers) wide. The Red Sea is located between Africa (Egypt, Eritrea, and Sudan) and the Arabian Peninsula (Saudi Arabia and Yemen) and forms part of the **Rift Valley.** The Bab-el-Mandeb strait links the Red Sea with the Gulf of Aden and the Arabian Sea. The Dahlak Archipelago is the largest group of islands in the Red Sea.

Although Ethiopia is now a landlocked country, the Red Sea has played a vital role in its history. Most scholars believe that the persons who colonized what is today Eritrea and northern Ethiopia came in the pre-Christian period from the southwest coast of Arabia. Millions of years earlier Ethiopia's Rift Valley may have been the origin of humankind. Hence, these same South Arabians may have had their origin in Ethiopia. Nevertheless, the South Arabians introduced into Ethiopia the camel, incense, many nutritive plants, better arms, and improved building techniques. The South Arabians also contributed to the development of Ethiopia's first **language**, **Ge'ez**.

Trade has been the most important component of the Red Sea's relationship with Ethiopia. Trade with Punt, possibly today's eastern **Tigray**, may have occurred with the First or Second Dynasties (3546–3190 BC) of the Egyptian pharaohs. Through the 20th Dynasty (1198–1167 BC), there is evidence of continuing contact with Punt. There appear to have been contacts between Ethiopia and ancient Israel during King Solomon's reign (c. 974–932 BC). In the early fourth century BC, Egypt resumed ties with Ethiopia under the Egyptian Ptolemies. The first Ptolemy dispatched an expedition to the Red Sea coast to capture elephants for military purposes. In the third century BC, elephant exploitation continued with Ptolemy II and Ptolemy III. An important pre-Axumite civilization at **Yeha** in present-day Tigray Region existed in the millennium before Christ. It had connections across the Red Sea with the Sabaeans of South Arabia. Archaeologists have identified nearly 100 Sabaean sites on the route to the Red Sea. Beginning in the first century AD, the success of the Axumite empire depended heavily on its Red Sea trade.

By the late 13th century, information about Ethiopia had reached Europe. In the early 14th century, a Dominican monk, Guillaume Adam, visited Socotra Island near the entry to the Red Sea. Although he failed to reach Ethiopia, he wrote of its importance to the king of France. Subsequently, a host of European visitors came to Ethiopia, most via the Red Sea, which also served as a way for foreigners to attack Ethiopia. In 1557, a 3,000-man Turkish force captured the port of **Massawa**. The Egyptians later acquired control of Massawa from the Ottomans. By the mid–19th century, Britain and France started deploying their warships to the Red Sea. In 1875, Egypt seized several **Somali** ports and occupied **Harar** town. In 1875–1876, Egyptian troops from Massawa invaded Tigray. he defeated Egyptian forces at the **Battle of Gundet** (1875) and at the Battle of Gura (1976). However, he failed to drive the Egyptians from Massawa.

The **Suez Canal**'s opening on 17 November 1869 enhanced the Red Sea's importance, especially for Italy, which wanted a colonial empire in Africa. In November 1869, **Giuseppe Sapeto** purchased the port of

Asab on behalf of the Italian shipping company Società Raffaele Rubattino. In March 1870, he purchased two additional parcels of land. In September 1880, he concluded an agreement with the sultan of Raheita, who placed his territory that was 30 miles (48 kilometers) southeast of Asab under Italian protection. On 5 February 1885, the Italians occupied Massawa. **Menelik II** recognized Italian sovereignty over its Red Sea colony in the **Treaty of Wichale**. In 1890, Italy named its colony Eritrea, after the Latin term *Erythraeum Mare* or Red Sea.

In 1896, the Italians, supplied via the Red Sea and operating out of Eritrea, invaded Ethiopia but suffered a humiliating defeat by Menelik II's forces at the **Battle of Adwa**. Rome also used the Red Sea in preparation for the **Italian-Ethiopian War**. Although Ethiopia regained control of Eritrea and the Red Sea coastline as a result of the **Ethiopian-Eritrean Federation** (1952), it immediately became embroiled in a struggle against groups like the **Eritrean Liberation Front** and the **Eritrean People's Liberation Front,** which wanted Eritrean independence. This chapter ended in 1991, when the **Ethiopian People's Revolutionary Democratic Front** accepted Eritrea's demand for independence. At that point, Ethiopia became a landlocked state but had access to the Eritrean ports of Massawa and Asab until the outbreak of the **Ethiopian-Eritrean War**. *See also* ADULIS; AXUM.

RED STAR CAMPAIGN. The **Derg**'s largest military offensive, which marked a turning point in the war with Eritrea. On 25 January 1982, **Mengistu Haile Mariam** unveiled the Red Star Campaign in a speech in Asmara to eliminate the "secessionist bandits" in Eritrea (**Eritrean People's Liberation Front** [EPLF]), Tigray (**Tigray People's Liberation Front**), and **Gondar** (**Ethiopian People's Revolutionary Party** and **Ethiopian Democratic Union**) and to stimulate reconstruction in those areas. The dual campaign included a plan to organize the peasants by providing them with political and technical education, military training, and arms to defend Eritrea and an economic development strategy. Mengistu maintained that the Red Star's success depended on defeating the EPLF. The **Commission for Organizing the Party of the Working People of Ethiopia**—assisted by the government, army, and peasantry—was responsible for implementing the Red Star Campaign.

By March 1982, the Derg had drafted and deployed 136,540 troops (5,681 officers, 82,444 other ranks, and 48,415 militia members) to the Second Revolutionary Army for the Red Star Campaign. They joined the 30,000–40,000 troops already stationed in Eritrea. Between January and February 1982, nearly all government departments, including the president's office, supported the Red Star Campaign by relocating to Asmara from **Addis Ababa**. Soviet military advisers helped to plan the campaign.

For the campaigns in Eritrea, Tigray, and Gondar, the **armed forces** had mobilized 14 divisions (63 brigades, of which 53 were infantry, six mechanized, and four para-commandos). The Derg also had assigned 55 aircraft, 131 tanks, 162 armored cars, 102 infantry vehicles, 499 artillery pieces, 48 rocket launchers, 873 mortars, 691 antiaircraft guns, 1,349 antitank guns, 7,174 machine guns, and one **navy** warship.

In January 1982, the Derg launched the Red Star Campaign. Ethiopian operations in Eritrea were limited primarily to Sahel district and focused on Nakfa, a town located about midway between Keren and Alghena. The EPLF, which may have suffered up to 15,000 casualties, rebuffed the Ethiopian offensive in Sahel district that resulted in 37,176 government casualties. By September 1982, the EPLF had started a largely successful counteroffensive behind enemy lines. Significant government operations in Tigray and Gondar never materialized. Beginning in late October 1982, there was increasing unrest in the Ethiopian army, especially among peasant conscripts. By early 1983, it had become apparent that the Red Star Campaign had been a failure. *See also* AIR FORCE; PEOPLE'S MILITIA.

RED TERROR (1977–1978). On 4 February 1977, the **Derg** launched the Red Terror campaign, which crippled the **Ethiopian People's Revolutionary Party**, the **Ethiopian Democratic Union**, and the **All-Ethiopia Socialist Movement**. Those involved in the Red Terror jailed or tortured untold thousands of Ethiopians and killed up to 100,000 of the Derg's political opponents.

After the **Ethiopian People's Revolutionary Democratic Front** seized power (1991), the authorities detained thousands of individuals suspected of participating in the Red Terror campaign. By 1997, the special prosecutor's office had identified 5,198 alleged perpetrators. On 15 January 1997, the Federal High Court indicted 2,246 of them and charged in absentia 2,952 others. On 28 December 1999, **Mengistu Haile Mariam** defended the Red Terror, saying it was a fight between two different social groups for control of the country. He also maintained that the Red Terror helped to preserve the "revolution." By 2003, Ethiopia's **judiciary** had yet to complete court proceedings against all those accused of participating in the Red Terror. *See also* HUMAN RIGHTS.

REFUGEES. Ethiopian law provides for the granting of refugee and asylum status in accordance with the 1951 United Nations Convention Relating to the Status of Refugees and its subsequent protocol. Ethiopia, a country that both receives and generates refugees, has a history of cooperating with the UN High Commissioner for Refugees (UNHCR) and other humanitarian agencies in assisting refugees. On 21 January 2003, the UNHCR reported that Ethiopia hosted 148,737 refugees (50,906 **Somalis** who lived in six camps, 93,500 Sudanese who lived in five camps near **Gambela** and Asosa, 3,871 Eritreans, and 460 urban refugees). Since 1997, more than 200,000 Somali refugees have been repatriated. There were approximately 10,000 Ethiopian refugees (5,000 in Kenya, some 2,000 in Sudan, more than 2,000 in Djibouti, about 1,000 in Yemen). There also were nearly 3,000 Ethiopian asylum seekers in Europe and the United States.

RELIEF AND REHABILITATION COMMISSION. *See* DISASTER PREVENTION AND PREPAREDNESS COMMISSION; FAMINE.

RELIEF SOCIETY OF TIGRAY (REST). In 1978, the **Tigray People's Liberation Front** (TPLF) established REST as a humanitarian organization to coordinate relief, rehabilitation, and development programs in **Tigray Region** and among Tigrayan **refugees** in Sudan. REST's establishment reflected the TPLF's recognition of the importance of international assistance and the fact that nongovernmental agencies (NGOs) and foreign governments found it politically more acceptable to work with a relief agency than a liberation movement. Initially funded largely by NGOs in the United States, Canada, Australia, and Europe, REST also received assistance from support committees in the **diaspora**. REST always has been an arm of the TPLF and its personnel moved between the two organizations. The TPLF largely determines REST policy.

REST was especially active during the Ethiopian **famine** of the mid-1980s and led large numbers of famine victims from liberated parts of Tigray to refugee camps in neighboring Sudan. It also pressured NGOs, the United Nations, and foreign donors to assist the refugees, many of whom died en route to Sudan. As a result of this effort, however, REST gained considerable legitimacy with international NGOs. After the defeat of the **Derg** (1991) and the establishment of the **Ethiopian People's Revolutionary Democratic Front**, REST continued to function as the humanitarian arm of the TPLF. It played a major role in relieving famines in Tigray and assisted displaced Tigrayans during the **Ethiopian-Eritrean War**. In recent years, foreign governments increasingly have provided assistance to REST.

RESERVED AREAS. *See* HAUD.

REVOLUTIONARY FLAME. In August 1976, **Mengistu Haile Mariam** and 15 **Derg** members formed this political party in the hope of dominating the **Ethiopian People's Revolutionary Party**, an influential member of the **Provisional Office for Mass Organizational Affairs** (POMOA). Mengistu served as titular chairman but Master Sergeant Legesse Asfaw, a member of the **Provisional Military Administrative Council**'s standing committee, acted as executive officer. After its admission to the POMOA, the Revolutionary Flame marginalized the **All-Ethiopian Socialist Movement** (AESM) and the **Ethiopian Oppressed Peoples Revolutionary Struggle**, two influential parties that posed a challenge to Mengistu's leadership. By 1977, the Revolutionary Flame also had challenged the AESM for control of the *kebeles*. By late 1977, thousands of military personnel, who had received training in the Soviet Union, Bulgaria, Cuba, Czechoslovakia, East Germany, and Yugoslavia, had joined the Revolutionary Flame, thereby ensuring its dominance in the political arena. The Revolutionary Flame also enjoyed support among senior government officials and professionals who feared the AESM's program. After Mengistu decided to transform the POMOA into the **Workers' Party of Ethiopia**, the Revolutionary Flame's influence waned.

RIFT VALLEY. The faulting that led to the Rift Valley's formation some 40 million years ago occurred during the Eocene epoch of the Tertiary period. Its northerly section lies in Asia, where it runs up the Gulf of Aqaba, into Israel, the Dead Sea, and the Jordan Valley. Northward through Lebanon and into Turkey it becomes less and less distinctive. Southward from Aqaba, it continues along the **Red Sea**. Near Aden, one rift system travels beneath the Indian Ocean while the Great Rift enters Ethiopia at the **Afar Depression**. It divides the mountainous **highlands** in central Ethiopia and then enters Kenya with the **Omo River**. A chain of lakes marks the Great Rift's passage southward through Kenya and northern Tanzania where it meets the Western Rift Valley.

The Rift Valley is rich in volcanoes. All significant volcanic activity occurred 20 million to 40 million years ago, leaving great lava plateaus now dissected by numerous rivers. Today, most volcanoes are extinct but some remain dormant. In 1960 and 1970–1971, the Erta Ale vent erupted in the Afar Depression. Geologists calculate that in the Kenyan and Ethiopian portions of the Rift Valley more than 250,000 cubic miles (400,000 cubic kilometers) of lava and ash covers the land. This is equivalent to almost two miles (three kilometers) of depth over all of Britain.

The Ethiopian Rift Valley consists of three principal subdivisions: the Afar or Danakil Plains, the Awash valley, and the central and southern lakes. The Rift Valley is broad at its northern extremity but narrows sharply as it continues southwest toward Kenya. A series of lakes dots the Ethiopian Rift Valley. Starting on the northern border with Djibouti is Lake Abbe. Moving southwest is Lake Yardi, followed by the **Awash River** to the artificially created lake behind the **Koka Dam**. Continuing southwest, a string of lakes beginning with Zwai and including Langano, Abiata, Shala, and **Awasa** divides the highlands on each side. Further south are Lakes Abaya and Chamo. The Ethiopian Rift Valley ends at the Kenyan border near the seasonal Lake **Chew Bahir** and **Lake Turkana**, most of which is in Kenya. *See also* AFAR REGION; LAKES (CENTRAL AND SOUTHERN RIFT VALLEY); LAKES (EASTERN SALINE).

RIMBAUD, ARTHUR (1854–1891). Traveler, trader, poet, and arms dealer. Born on 20 October 1854 in Charleville-Mézières, France.

During 1861–1865, Rimbaud attended the Institut Rossat, where he won 13 academic prizes and 11 merits; and the Collège de Charleville (1865–1870), where he continued to win awards for his academic performance. After the declaration of the Franco-Prussian War on 19 July 1870, Rimbaud traveled to Paris, where he was imprisoned on suspicion of being a spy. In the early 1870s, Rimbaud established a literary reputation.

During 1880–1891, he sought to make a fortune in Africa. In November 1878, Rimbaud went to Alexandria, Egypt. In 1880, he spent a short time in Aden as a trader before going to Ethiopia, where he worked as a **coffee** merchant. His home remains a **tourist** attraction in **Harar**. Rimbaud died on 10 November 1891. Alain Borer provides an account of his time in Ethiopia in a book entitled *Rimbaud in Abyssinia*.

RIST. *See* LAND TENURE.

ROADS. *See* TRANSPORTATION.

ROCK-HEWN CHURCHES. Although the best-known rock-hewn churches are in **Lalibela**, numerous others are found throughout Ethiopia, especially in **Tigray Region**. Some churches in northern Ethiopia date back to the sixth century and possibly earlier. The design of these churches follows the Christian basilica pattern. They are unique in design and artwork and were most probably cut with simple chisels. Ethiopians probably are responsible for building them as there is no evidence that foreign labor helped in their construction. Tigray's churches are of greater historical importance than those in Lalibela because they span a longer period of time and cover a wider area. There are rock-hewn churches in other parts of Ethiopia such as Bale region south of **Addis Ababa**. The Adadi Mariam (Mother Mary) rock-hewn church is west of Addis Ababa. Believed to have been constructed between the 13th and 16th century, Adadi Mariam was covered over in the 16th century and rediscovered in the late 19th century.

Lalibela's churches, excavated from solid rock, are a major **tourist** attraction. In addition, there are more than 150 ancient, rock-hewn churches in Tigray Region. There also are a few others scattered throughout Ethiopia. The builders of these churches employed construction methods that are no longer used. There are examples of completely rock-hewn interiors where the churches were built into a cliff face or free-standing outcrop of rock. There are cave churches where the church has a facade across the mouth of the cave and varying degrees of architectural detail excavated from the cave walls and roof. The architecture generally follows the Christian basilica pattern. Although the architecture is uniquely Ethiopian, there are influences from Egypt and Greece. It is often impossible to visit the interior of the churches because local church officials refuse access or the most architecturally interesting areas are in that part of the church where only priests are allowed.

According to oral tradition, Tigray's earliest churches were built in the mid-fourth century and were the work of kings whose names are in dispute. Other churches are believed to have been hewn in the reign of King Kaleb of **Axum** during the first part of the sixth century and King Gabra Masqal (reigned c. 550–564). Following a long gap, additional churches appeared in other parts of Tigray in the mid-10th century, during the reign of Yekuno Amlak (reigned 1270–1285), **Dawit I** (reigned 1380–1412), **Zara Yakob** (reigned 1434–1468). The association of these kings with certain churches suggests that they were responsible for their construction. There was no additional construction after the **Islamic** invasion by **Ahmad ibn Ibrahim al Ghazi** in the 16th century. Most historians believe that Ethiopians built the rock-hewn churches and that foreign workmen played no role in the construction. The painted murals in the rock-hewn churches appear to date from the 13th century to the late 17th century. Some churches are elaborately decorated and painted from the floor to the ceiling. Their artwork reflects a strong Byzantine influence.

Most churches continue to be used for Christian worship. The churches outside Lalibela may have greater historical importance because they cover a longer period of time and are found over a wider area of Ethiopia. Especially useful accounts of these churches include *Churches in Rock* by Georg Gerster, *Rock-Hewn Churches of Eastern Tigray* by the Oxford University Expedition to Ethiopia, and *Antiquities of North Ethiopia* by Otto A. Jager and Ivy Pearce.

RODD MISSION (1897). In early 1897, Sir J. Rennell Rodd, Lord Cromer's chief aide in Cairo, received instructions to negotiate an agreement with **Menelik II** that would address outstanding border issues between Ethiopia and surrounding British territories and to improve British commercial prospects in Ethiopia. On 10 March 1897, Rodd departed Egypt for Ethiopia. Other members of his mission included Lieutenant-Colonel Reginald Wingate, director of military intelligence in the Egyptian army; Captain Count Gleichen, member of the War Office's intelligence section; Captain Harald George Carlos Swayne, an officer with extensive **Somali** experience; and Charles S. T. Speedy, an **Amharic**-speaking officer who had served in the **Anglo-Ethiopian War**.

On 28 April 1897, Menelik II welcomed to **Addis Ababa** the Rodd mission, which had traveled via Zeila and **Harar**. On 14 May 1897, Menelik II and Rodd finally concluded a treaty. Its major provisions included agreeing to allow subjects of both countries to do business together (Article I), fix the border between Ethiopia and British Somaliland (now Somaliland) (Article II), keep the Zeila-Harar route open to traders of both countries (Article III), permit British goods destined for Ethiopia to transit Zeila duty free (Article IV), approve Ethiopia's importation of arms and ammunition across British Somaliland (Article V), and secure Menelik II's promise to prevent the movement of arms and munitions across Ethiopia to Mahdist forces in the Sudan.

ROME AGREEMENTS (1935). On 7 January 1935, Italian dictator Benito Mussolini and French foreign minister Pierre Laval concluded eight protocols known as the Rome Agreements. Those that pertained to Ethiopia included protocols that protected the status quo at the mouth of the **Red Sea**, French recognition of Italy's economic primacy in Ethiopia, and Rome's commitment to participate in the financing of the **Addis Ababa–Djibouti Railway**. Supposedly, Mussolini also received a verbal commitment that France would not oppose an Italian attack against Ethiopia. Although Laval denied the existence of such a bargain, the Rome Agreements laid the diplomatic groundwork for Italy's military offensive against Ethiopia. *See also* HOARE-LAVAL PLAN; ITALIAN-ETHIOPIAN WAR.

– S –

SAHLE MARYAM. *See* MENELIK II.

SAHLE SELASSIE (1795–1847). Ras and then **negus** of **Shoa** (1813–1847). Son of Wassan Saggar, ras of Shoa (1780–1813). Born as Haylu Walda-Kiros. On 7 June 1813, he became ras, after his father's death. The **Oromo**, who had conquered much of Shoa in the 16th and 18th centuries but had been pacified by Sahle's father and grandfather, sought to regain their independence. Sahle thwarted this threat by using military force and divide-and-rule tactics against the various Oromo tribes. As a result, he established his authority and nearly doubled the size of the Shoa empire during his reign. In 1830, Sahle built a camp outside Debre Berhan that eventually developed into a town called Angolala. However, his capital remained **Ankober**, a town with a **population** of about 25,000. In the 1830s, Sahle adopted the title of negus without the emperor's consent and declared Shoa's independence. He proved to be a benevolent despot who ensured peace, stability, and good government but faced continuing Oromo revolts and persistent unrest in Awash and territories inhabited by the Arsi and **Gurage**. To improve his army capabilities, Sahle acquired modern military equipment from Britain and France. He also welcomed a British mission headed by **William Cornwallis Harris** (1841–1843) and a French mission commanded by Rochet d'Héricourt (1841–1844). During the closing years of his reign, Sahle named his son, Haile Malekot, as heir. He then convened a council of Oromo chiefs in Angolala and made them swear loyalty to his successor. Shortly before his death on 12 October 1847 in Debre Berhan, Sahle relinquished his throne to his son. *See also* TEWODROS II.

SAHO PEOPLE AND LANGUAGE. Saho is more properly a **language** group than an ethnic designation. Most Saho-speaking peoples live in Eritrea, but some extend across the central part of the Ethiopian-Eritrean border until they reach the **Tigrayan** and **Afar** peoples. The total number of Saho-speaking peoples in both countries is estimated at about 150,000. They never have been politically unified and are subdivided into clans or factions. Most Saho are pastoralists, although some are turning to **agriculture. Islam** has had a deep impact on most Saho and some have learned how to read and write Arabic. The Irob live near a section of the Ethiopian-Eritrean border that was at the center of the **Ethiopian-Eritrean War**. They are a Saho-speaking Christian group who live in Ethiopia and migrate on the plateau as far as **Debre Damo**. There also are several small groups of Saho-speaking Afars. Saho is an eastern Cushitic language that is close to Afar. Irob is a separate dialect.

SALT, HENRY (1780–1827). British artist, collector of antiquities, Egyptologist, government official, and traveler. Born on 14 June 1780 in Lichfield. Educated at the free school in Lichfield and then at a boarding school in Market Bosworth, Leicestershire. Salt then returned to Lichfield to study art before going to London to enhance his artistic skills.

In 1802, Salt received an appointment as secretary to George Annesley, earl of Mountmorris, Viscount Valentia. He accompanied Valentia on two journeys (1802–1806) to the Indies, Ceylon (now Sri Lanka), Ethiopia, and Egypt. Salt's 1805 visit to Ethiopia included a trip to the Dahlak Archipelago that proved **James Bruce**'s account of his visit had contained so many factual errors that it seemed likely that he had never gone to the archipelago. He then called on **Ras Wolde Selassie** in **Tigray,** who approved his request to visit **Axum** and **Adwa**. As Salt prepared to leave Ethiopia, the ras produced letters for George III, purportedly from the emperor but actually from himself. On 26 October 1806, Salt landed at Portsmouth.

On 26 December 1808, he attended a meeting of the African Association (also known as the Society for Promoting the Discovery of the Interior Parts of Africa) and convinced its committee to finance another journey to Ethiopia to procure "useful and curious information." On 2 March 1809, he departed Britain and arrived in **Massawa** on 10 February 1810, with a letter and presents from George III for the emperor. **Nathaniel Pearce**, who had helped arrange Salt's 1805 visit to Ethiopia, again rendered service to his mission. Political unrest prevented Salt from visiting **Gondar** but he, along with Pearce, again spent time with Ras Wolde Selassie and made a tour of the **Tekeze River**. On 11 January 1811, Salt arrived back in Britain and, in 1814, published *A Voyage to Abyssinia and Travels into the Interior of That Country*, which remains an essential study for understanding the early British presence in Ethiopia.

After his Ethiopian travels, Salt served in the diplomatic service as consul general to Egypt. He subsequently sold a significant number of antiquities to the British Museum. On 30 October 1827, Salt died from a disease of the spleen in Dessuke, a village near Alexandria, Egypt.

SANDFORD, DANIEL ARTHUR (1882–1972). British soldier, farmer, and adviser to **Haile Selassie**. Born on 18 June 1882 at Landkey, North Devon. Educated at Saint Paul's School. In 1900, Sandford entered Woolwich, eventually received a Royal Artillery commission, and then served in Bombay and Karachi. In 1906, he was posted to Aden. The following year, Sandford returned to Britain for a gunnery course. In 1909, he went back to Aden.

Sandford's association with Ethiopia and East Africa began in 1910, when he joined the Sudan Civil Service and received a posting to the British legation in **Addis Ababa** as Sudan government liaison officer. After serving on the western front during **World War I**, he returned to Ethiopia, where he was general manager for the Abyssinian Corporation (1919–1921). In 1922, Sandford retired from the military and leased a farm at Mulu, north of Addis Ababa. He then was adviser to the governor of Maji Province (1935).

After the outbreak of the **Italian-Ethiopian War**, Sandford returned to Britain. In 1939, he joined the Middle East Intelligence Center, Cairo. He subsequently assumed command of **Mission 101,** which aimed to help Ethiopian resistance fighters, known as **patriots**, to fight the Italians and prepare the way for **Haile Selassie**'s return to Ethiopia. On 12 August 1940, Mission 101 crossed into **Gojam** and initiated military operations.

After liberation, Sandford served as the emperor's principal military and political adviser (1941), principal adviser to the Ministry of the Interior (1942), personal adviser to the emperor (1944), and director general of Addis Ababa Municipality (1945–1948). In 1951, he retired but continued to work on his farm. On 22 January 1972, Sandford died near Addis Ababa.

SAPETO, GIUSEPPE (1811–1895). Italian author, linguist, **missionary**, and imperialist. Born at Carcare, Genoa. In 1829, Sapeto became a Lazarist missionary. His early travels took him to Lebanon and Egypt. In 1837, he sailed to **Massawa** with Arnaud-Michel d'Abbadie and **Antoine d'Abbadie**. Sapeto then proceeded inland to **Adwa** and **Gondar** and eventually joined the Italian Lazarist Monsignor **Justin de Jacobis**. Illness forced Sapeto to leave Ethiopia. After recuperating, he returned to Massawa and explored the **Danakil Depression**. In 1851, Sapeto visited the country of the Bogos, Mensa, and Habab in northwest Ethiopia and collected **Ge'ez**, **Tigray**, and Bilan vocabularies.

In 1858, he served as an interpreter for a mission that Agaw Negussé, a rebel who opposed **Tewodros II**, sent to Europe to garner support from the pope and Emperor Napoleon III (1808–1873). Sapeto returned to Ethiopia with Count Russell, who was to secure economic concessions and a port for France. The mission failed after Tewodros II killed Agaw Negussé and defeated his forces. The emperor also briefly imprisoned Sapeto. After his release, he went to Paris, where he became curator of Oriental manuscripts at the Bibliothèque Nationale. Later, Sapeto became a professor of Arabic at Florence and Genoa.

After the opening of the **Suez Canal** (1869), the Italian government asked Sapeto to return to the **Horn of Africa** and obtain a **Red Sea** port. On 15 November 1869, he purchased the port of **Asab** for 6,000 **Maria Theresa thalers** from two sultans, the brothers Hassan ibn Ahmad and Ibrahim ibn Ahmad, on behalf of the Italian shipping company Società Raffaele Rubattino of Genoa. When Sapeto returned to Asab to finalize the deal, the two brothers and another sultan, Abd Allah Sahim, raised the price to 8,350 Maria Theresa thalers. On 11 March 1870, Sapeto concluded a new agreement with the trio that included the Bay of Buya. In September 1880, he concluded an agreement with the sultan of Raheita, who placed his territory that was 30 miles (48 kilometers) southeast of Asab under Italian protection.

The following year, Sapeto returned to Italy and devoted the remainder of his life to scholarly pursuits. In 1895, he died in Genoa.

SENATE. *See* PARLIAMENT.

SEYOUM MESFIN (1949–). Ethiopian foreign minister (1991–). Born on 25 January 1949 in **Adigrat**. Educated at **Bahir Dar** Polytechnic Institute (1968–1971) and **Haile Selassie I University** (1972–1974). After the **armed forces** seized power (1974), Seyoum dropped out of the university and joined the **Tigray People's Liberation Front** (TPLF). In 1976, he became a member of the TPLF's Central Committee in charge of diplomacy. During the 1979 TPLF congress at Shire, the delegates elected Seyoum, then known as Seyoum Hassan, as head of the Foreign Relations Office, which was based in Sudan.

In 1989, he became an Executive Committee member of the **Ethiopian People's Revolutionary Democratic Front** (EPRDF) and received the foreign affairs portfolio. After participating in the London Peace Conference (1991), Seyoum returned to **Addis Ababa** and assumed responsibility for foreign affairs in the Transitional National Government. In the **elections (1995),** he won a seat in the **House of People's Representatives (Tigray Region).**

In the late 1990s, Seyoum participated in numerous important regional diplomatic efforts that sought to preserve the **Horn of Africa**'s fragile stability. These included an unsuccessful attempt to restore peace to Somalia by facilitating the signing of the **Sodere** agreement between 26 **Somali** factions (1997) and to mediate an end to the Eritrea-Yemen border dispute (November–December 1995) over the Hanish Islands archipelago. He also worked tirelessly to reach a peace agreement during the **Ethiopian-Eritrean War.** As of 2004, Seyoum maintained his foreign affairs portfolio and remained one of the most powerful members of the Ethiopian government and a strong ally of Prime Minister **Meles Zenawi.** *See also* OGADEN; SOMALI REGION.

SEZE PEOPLE AND LANGUAGE. The Seze live in a small enclave near Begi (Beigi) in **Benishangul/Gumuz Region.** Numbering about 3,000 they reside north of the **Hozo,** east of the **Kwama,** and south and west of the **Oromo.** The Seze speak an Omotic **language** of the Mao family that is related to but separate from **Bambassi.** Their lingua franca is Afan Oromo, a language that evokes some negative attitudes. Very few Seze speak **Amharic** or Arabic.

SHABO PEOPLE AND LANGUAGE. The Shabo straddle the western border of **Southern Nations, Nationalities and People's Region** and **Gambela Region.** The **Majangir** live to their west and the **Shakacho** are their neighbors in all other directions. The 1,000 or so Shabo are known by some as Shako but are not to be confused with the Sheko, who also are known as Shako. Outsiders call them "Mekeyer," a term they do not like. They are hunter-gatherers and beekeepers and live in family units rather than villages. They speak a distinct Nilo-Saharan **language** that is apparently a hybrid. It has 30 percent lexical similarity with Majang. They are bilingual in Majang or Shakacho.

SHAKACHO PEOPLE AND LANGUAGE. Sometimes called the Mocha, Shakacho (also spelled Shekacho) is the name the people use themselves. They number well over 100,000 and live in the Sheka Zone of **Southern Nations, Nationalities and People's Region** and **Gambela Region**. The **Oromo** reside to the north, **Majangir** to the west, **Sheko** to the south, and **Kaficho** to the east. During the 16th century, the Shakacho established a kingdom that the Oromo conquered in the 18th century. In the late 19th century, **Menelik II** incorporated the territory into the Ethiopian empire. In the 16th century, many Shakacho converted to Christianity but many held to traditional beliefs that included possession cults. In recent years, **Protestant** churches have made significant inroads into the Shakacho community. The **economy** is based on the production of *ensete*, cereals, and vegetables. Livestock, honey, **coffee**, and spices also are important parts of the economy. Their principal town is Masha. They speak a north Omotic **language** that is closely related to Kaficho.

SHANKALA (SHANKELLA, SHANQELLA). Shankala, an **Amharic** term meaning "black," often is used to refer to Ethiopia's dark-skinned peoples, especially those who live along the Sudan border and the lower reaches of the **Blue Nile**. The word implies inferiority and sometimes is associated with **slavery**. **Highland** Ethiopians once considered the Shankala impure and primitive and enslaved many of them before the government outlawed the practice. Others were taken into the Arab slave trade. Contact between the **Axumite** empire and the Shankala dates to at least the fourth century. Emperor **Susneyos** conducted a series of raids against the Shankala who lived in the **lowlands** northwest of **Lake Tana**. Like Emperor Sarsa Dengel, Susneyos took many slaves during these expeditions. Joachim Abbé Le Grand's 1628 map and Hiob Ludolf's 1683 map of **Abyssinia** show an area listed as Shankala near the present-day border with Sudan. Over the centuries, there was considerable concubinage between the Shankala and the highlanders. The **Oromo** in western Ethiopia also enslaved certain Shankala peoples, especially those living in the **Janjero kingdom** and **Kafa**. Disdain by the **Amhara**, **Tigrayan**, and some Oromos toward the Shankala continued until fairly recently.

SHEKO PEOPLE AND LANGUAGE. More than 20,000 Sheko or Shako people reside in the western part of Bench zone. The **Bench people** live to the east, the **Majangir** and **Shakacho** to the north, the **Anuak** to the east, and the **Me'en** to the south. Known as the Dan or Danir to the neighboring Majangir, the Sheko have a mixed pastoral and **agricultural** economy in the **highlands** of the Gurrafarda Mountains. There has been considerable contact—both friendly and hostile—over the years between the Majangir and the Sheko. Despite racial and cultural differences, there also has been a fair amount of intermarriage between the two peoples. The Sheko periodically raided the Majangir for **women** and **slaves**. The last raid occurred after the Italian occupation (1936–1941) and before the Ethiopians reestablished full control. The Majangir responded with a counterraid and razed a Sheko village before the Ethiopian government intervened. Most Sheko are pagan and believe in a sky god and spirits. Some have converted to Christianity. They speak an Omotic **language** in the **Gimira** family. Sheko is the primary language in the home and in public and for their religion.

SHELTER. Because of the enormous differences in altitude and wide variety of ethnic groups, Ethiopian housing or shelter varies widely from one part of the country to the other. Construction materials for shelter in towns usually consist of cinder block for walls and a tin roof. The style does not vary widely in urban areas. Construction materials and style in rural areas are another matter. In some cases, it is possible to determine the ethnic background of a village by the housing type. Most houses or huts in the **highlands** use a conical frame of many sticks with thick thatch for a roof. A mixture of mud and grass fills in the gaps between the stick foundation in order to keep out the cold and insects. Most of these huts are not partitioned inside. Windows are rare and made by leaving a small area of the frame uncovered by mud. A piece of inverted pottery often caps the apex of the thatched roof to seal it from the rain.

The conical house with a thatched roof is also common in parts of **Tigray**, northern **Bagemder,** and Lasta, although the walls are often constructed of stone and the house may be two stories. Access to the second floor is by a flight of stone steps built along the wall either on the outside or on the inside. Stone houses are usually partitioned into at least two rooms per floor. They may also have wood-framed doors and windows. Stone houses with flat roofs are also common in Tigray. Rectangular in plan, they have thick, heavy roofs of stone and mud that keep the interiors cool. Rectangular house plans are common in **Harar** town. Built with stone and mortar, the houses have two stories, the upper one normally reserved for **women** and the lower one serving as a living area with stone benches built into the walls. The front doors and window frames may be richly carved.

Gurage huts are circular in plan; the walls are constructed of attractively woven wattle. The Gurage build the cone-shaped roof as a separate unit of stick frame and thatch. The roof rests on top of the round wall and is supported at the apex by a strong center pole. In the hot **lowlands** inhabited by pastoral people, much less elaborate shelters constructed from grass are common. They have the advantage of being cheap and easy to move or even leave behind as their inhabitants seek new pastures. They are low to the ground and built of stick frames covered by matting. The **Afars** prefer to carry their shelter with them. Each one can be neatly stacked and bound and placed on the back of a camel. Settled inhabitants in the **Danakil** and the **Ogaden** favor a rectangular building with a sturdy frame and light wall lining covered by a heavy mud and stone roof. There are numerous additional housing styles in other parts of Ethiopia.

SHIFTA. Amharic term (*wenbedye*) that refers to an outlaw, brigand, or rebel. Ethiopians often use this derogatory term to describe **Somali** dissidents who live in the **Ogaden**. During Ethiopia's war against Eritrean secessionists, government troops used the term to describe Eritrean rebels.

SHOA (SHAWA, SHEWA). Shoa was the southern of the three principal provinces of the **Abyssinian** empire. From the mid–10th century to the late 13th century, Shoa was the residence of the Abyssinian sovereigns, who had been driven out of **Axum**, their former capital. **Amda Tseyon** established Ethiopian control over Shoa. About 1528, **Islamic** invaders, led by **Ahmad ibn Ibrahim al Ghazi**, conquered Shoa, which subsequently fell prey to **Oromo** raiders for more than a century. In 1682, an Abyssinian chief reconquered Shoa, but the region remained independent of northern Abyssinia until 1855, when **Tewodros II** reduced it to submission. After **Yohannes IV**'s death on 10 March 1889, **Menelik II**, **negus** of Shoa, became emperor of Ethiopia. The capital, **Addis Ababa**, became the empire's seat of government. On 1 January 1939, Italian authorities united Addis Ababa and parts of **Amhara** and Oromo-Sidama into a new Shoa Province. During the **Haile Selassie** government and the **Derg** period, Shoa extended nearly to **Dese** in the north and Lake Shala in the south, to the **Awash River** in the east and the **Blue Nile** in the northeast.

Today, what had been Shoa is approximately three zones in **Oromia Region** (i.e., east Shoa, west Shoa, and northwest Shoa) and two zones in **Amhara Region** (i.e., north Shoa and Oromia). Although many believe that the Amhara are Shoa's principal inhabitants, the Oromo are actually the majority.

SIDAMA PEOPLE AND LANGUAGE. The Sidama people live in south central Ethiopia in the area between **Lake Awasa** in the north, the towns of Agere Selam and Dilla in the south, the Bilate River in the west, and the Bale **highlands** in the east. A densely populated part of **Awasa**, the capital of **Southern Nations, Nationalities and People's Region**, is multiethnic and the major city in Sidama territory. There is considerable confusion among non-Sidama people as to which groups are properly called Sidama.

Before the 16th-century **Oromo** invasions, Cushitic-speaking people resided in much of southern Ethiopia. The Oromo and **Amharas** referred to all of them as Sidama, although some of the groups do not even speak a **language** that belongs to the Sidama language family. There may be 2.5 million Sidama, but because but loosely related people are sometimes included, it is not unusual to see a **population** figure of 5 or 6 million. Until **Menelik II** conquered them at the end of the 19th century, the Sidama are believed to have had kingships.

The Sidama have a mixed **economy**. Cattle are important to them but they also keep sheep and goats. *Ensete* or the false banana is a significant part of their diet. They also grow wheat, barley, corn, and cabbage. **Coffee** is an important cash crop and the Sidama variety is now marketed in Europe and North America. In recent years, **khat** has become an important cash crop. The Sidama have a highly developed system of **agriculture** that includes terraced fields, plowing with oxen, and use of animal manure for fertilizer. The Sidama consist of clusters of clans and lineages that occupy a definite area. People of each territorial segment claim descent from one common forefather and may be described as a subtribe. There are three primordial ancestors and 13 subtribes. An unwritten legal system called *sera* governs Sidama community relationships and sets local cultural norms. The Sidama have retained their traditional religious systems although **Protestant missionaries** have had a major impact in recent years. Some Sidama continue to revere spirits and believe that pythons are reincarnations of ancestors. The Sidama social organization is based on an age-group system like the Oromo *gada* system.

The Sidama speak an east Cushitic **language**. Sidama is used to describe a language group and, in fact, has contributed many loan words to **Gurage** and Afan Oromo, which are not part of the Sidama language family. The confusion on who is a Sidama carries over to the language. Sidama has a 64 percent lexical similarity with **Alaba**, 62 percent with **Kambata**, and 53 percent with **Hadiyya**, all languages spoken by Cushitic-speaking peoples who live to the north and west of the Sidama. These and other languages are usually included in the Sidama language family. *See also* SIDAMO LIBERATION FRONT.

SIDAMO LIBERATION FRONT (SLF). Established in 1978; until July 1999, it was known as the Sidamo Liberation Movement. The SLF launched an offensive against the **Derg** shortly after it received **Somali** recognition and support. In 1978, Wolde Amanuel Dubale, who had been chief administrator of Sidamo region, became leader of the SLF. In late 1982, Ethiopian forces launched a major campaign against the SLF that curbed the group's military activities. It has not been an important movement in recent years. *See also* SIDAMA PEOPLE AND LANGUAGE.

SILTI PEOPLE AND LANGUAGE. The Silti live at the foot of the **Rift Valley**'s escarpment southwest of **Addis Ababa** and south of the town of Butajira. The **Gurage people** live all around them and they are often considered to be Gurage. They are estimated to number 150,000. Their economy is based on the *ensete* plant supplemented by cash crops like red pepper. Most Silti are Muslim although there are some in the northern part of their territory who belong to the **Ethiopian Orthodox Church**. They speak a distinct Semitic language that is generally classified as belonging to eastern Gurage. It is not mutually intelligible with either north or west Gurage. Silti is an official literary language. *See also* AGRICULTURE; LANGUAGE.

SIMIEN MOUNTAINS. Known as the Roof of Africa. Ras Dashen is the fourth highest mountain in Africa (14,901 feet; 4,543 meters). The Simien Mountains lie north of **Gondar** and south of **Axum**. They consist of several plateaus separated by river valleys and date back to massive seismic activity some 40 million years ago. Molten lava from the earth's core reached a thickness of 9,840 feet (3,000 meters). The mountains are now largely devoid of trees, and subsequent erosion has created a jagged landscape of gorges, chasms, and precipices. The Simien Mountains have many summits above 13,000 feet (3,962 meters). Most of Ethiopia's endemic animals, including the Walia ibex, Simien fox, and gelada baboon, live in the Simien Mountain **National Park**. Temperatures drop below freezing at higher elevations from October to December. Trekking is a popular activity in the Simien Mountains. *See also* RIFT VALLEY.

SKINNER, ROBERT PEET (1866–1960). American diplomat. Born in Massillon, Ohio, on 24 February 1866. Robert Skinner is largely responsible for the establishment of official relations between the United States and Ethiopia. While serving as the American consul in Marseilles, France, he led a December 1903 mission to **Addis Ababa** to negotiate a commercial treaty between Ethiopia and the United States. Emperor **Menelik II** enthusiastically received the Skinner mission. After nine days of discussions, they agreed upon language for a treaty that the U.S. Senate ratified on 12 March 1904. Skinner commented that relations between the two countries were based solely on commerce and had no political motive. He recounted his mission in a book entitled *Abyssinia of To-Day*.

Skinner's subsequent diplomatic posts included Hamburg (1908–1913), Berlin (1913–1914), London (1914–1924), Paris (1924–1926), Greece (1926–1931), Latvia, Estonia, and Lithuania

(1931–1933), and Turkey (1933–1936). In 1936, he retired to Belfast, Maine, where he died on 1 July 1960.

SLAVERY. From time immemorial, slavery existed in Ethiopia. In 1875 and 1889, Ethiopia issued edicts to end slavery but lacked the political will and capabilities to enforce them. On 23 September 1923, Ethiopia promised to end slavery and the slave trade as a condition of joining the **League of Nations**. However, the country moved slowly toward honoring this pledge. On 15 September 1923, Empress **Zawditu Menelik** and the regent, **Ras** Tafari Makonnen, later **Haile Selassie**, issued a decree that outlawed the export of slaves to foreign countries. On 21 March 1924, another law prevented the buying and selling of slaves and ordered that slaves be freed after their master's death. Despite these actions, a 1927 League of Nations report indicated there were only 1,109 freed slaves in Ethiopia. On 8 April 1932, Britain's Anti-Slavery and Aborigines Protection Society reported that there were at least two million slaves in Ethiopia, an enormous number given that Ethiopia's total **population** was between seven and eight million. Haile Selassie accepted a British Anti-Slavery Society suggestion to establish a Department of Slavery under Frank De Halpert to supervise the abolition of slavery.

On 19 October 1935, **Emilio De Bono** sought to legitimize Italy's presence in Ethiopia by issuing a proclamation that abolished slavery in Italian-occupied territories. On 12 April 1936, another decree outlawed slavery throughout Ethiopia. After liberation (1941), the imperial government issued Proclamation No. 22 of 1942, which abolished the legal status of slavery throughout Ethiopia. Despite this action, slavery continued to exist in remote parts of the country for several decades.

SOBAT RIVER. Three important rivers—the Akobo, the Baro, and the Gilo—in southwest Ethiopia join at the Sudan-Ethiopia border to form the Sobat River, which flows into the White Nile south of Malakal in Sudan. Several Sudanese rivers, including the Pibor, contribute modest amounts of water to the flow at this point. The Sobat provides 14 percent of the water reaching the Aswan Dam in Egypt. The Akobo River rises in the hill country near Mizan Teferi, and flows west and then northwest to form the border with Sudan until it joins the Pibor and then the Sobat. The Baro rises east of Metu and flows due west until it forms for a short distance the border with Sudan and joins the Sobat.

The Sobat/Baro once had active shipping activity between Sudan and Ethiopia. In 1902, **Menelik II** granted Britain the right to establish a port and customs station at Itang. On 15 May 1902, Britain and Italy signed the **Addis Ababa** agreement that concerned the **Blue Nile**, **Lake Tana**, and the Sobat River and demarcated the borders between Sudan on the one hand and Ethiopia and Eritrea on the other. In 1907, the station moved to **Gambela**, now the regional capital. Steamers began transporting **coffee**, salt, beeswax, skins, and **cotton** along the Sobat/Baro to Malakal on the White Nile and then to Khartoum. The long-running civil war in southern Sudan and silting of the river ended the transport business several decades ago. The Baro is about 175 miles (280 kilometers) in length. The Baro, Pibor, and Akobo serve as the border between Sudan and Ethiopia for about 250 miles (400 kilometers). The Gilo River rises in the hills near the town of Mizan Teferi and flows due west, passing through Gambela **National Park** and a major swamp before linking up with the Pibor River and then the Sobat River.

SODERE. Located 78 miles (125 kilometers) southeast of **Addis Ababa**, Sodere is best known for its hot springs and resort hotel. Particularly popular with Ethiopians, the hotel has a large and naturally heated swimming pool. The forest that grows along the nearby **Awash River** is an excellent location for viewing **bird life** and vervet monkeys. Crocodiles and hippopotamuses inhabit the river and adjacent areas. The government occasionally uses Sodere for official conferences. In December 1996, 26 **Somali** factions held talks in Sodere under the auspices of the Ethiopian government and the Intergovernmental Authority on Development. In early January 1997, the talks concluded with the formation of a 41-member National Salvation Council that was charged with drafting a transitional charter and holding a national reconciliation conference. Unfortunately, the Sodere talks failed to restore stability to Somalia.

SOMALI PEOPLE AND LANGUAGE. There are more than 12 million Somalis residing in the **Horn of Africa**. About 7.5 million live in Somalia and Somaliland while another 4 million reside in Ethiopia, most of them in southeastern Ethiopia's **Somali Region**.

Another 300,000 Somalis inhabit Djibouti, and several hundred thousand live in Kenya. Ethnic Somalis are united by a common language, culture, and acceptance of **Islam**. Most Somalis trace their genealogical origin to the mythical founding father known as Samaale or Samaal. There is still not total agreement on the origin of the Somalis. Some scholars argue that they came from the **Red Sea**'s western coast or southern Arabia. More recent information suggests that they originated in southern Ethiopia's **highlands**. The Somalis belong to the Omo-Tana subgroup of the eastern Cushites. The original home of this subgroup seems to have been on the **Omo River** and the **Tana River** and covered an area from **Lake Turkana** to the Indian Ocean coast. They apparently split from the main branch of the Cushite peoples during the first half of the first millennium BC. Other large Cushitic tribes in the Horn of Africa are the **Oromo** and the **Afar**. Between the 11th and 13th centuries, many Somalis converted to Islam.

Somalis organize themselves along clan lines. There are six clans known as the Digil, Rahanweyn, Hawiye, Dir, Isaq, and Darod. These clan families divide into subgroups, sub-subgroups, and extended families. Primarily a pastoral people and fiercely independent, Somalis move in significant numbers across the border between Ethiopia and Somalia and Somaliland. Much of Ethiopia's Somali Region is known as the **Ogaden**, which is also the name for one of the Somali subgroups. The Somali folk hero, Seyyid Mohamed Abdille Hassan, the so-called Mad Mullah who waged a holy war (1899–1920) against Ethiopia, belonged to this subgroup. In the 20th century, there was sporadic conflict along the Ethiopian-Somali border. At the outbreak of the **Italian-Ethiopian War**, Italian troops invaded Ethiopia from Somalia. In 1960, the newly independent Somali Republic announced a policy of incorporating into a **Greater Somalia** all Somalis in the Horn of Africa, including those living in Ethiopia. Somalia invaded and briefly controlled most of southeastern Ethiopia during the **Ogaden War (1977–1978)**.

Somalis are polygamous; men have up to four wives according to Islamic code. They tend to have large families to sustain their pastoral way of life. **Women** take charge of the sheep and goats while the men deal with the camels. Women seldom wear veils and enjoy considerable freedom of movement and independence. Somali women also can be very forceful. Somalis attach considerable importance to oratory and **poetry**. Some Somalis are virtually walking encyclopedias. There was no written Somali script until 1973. The Somali Region uses Somali in the educational system. It is almost impossible to penetrate Somali society without having fluency in spoken Somali. In this oral society, there is considerable conversation during the long **khat**-chewing sessions. The most widely spoken dialect is Common Somali, which also is used for broadcasting purposes. Common Somali applies to several dialects, all of which are mutually intelligible. Ethiopian Somalis speak Common Somali. *See also* ADAL SULTANATE; OGADEN WAR (1964).

SOMALI REGION. The Somali National Regional State, also known as Region 5, occupies all of southeast Ethiopia and includes the entire border with Somalia and part of the border with Djibouti and Kenya. The region is divided into nine zones and **Jijiga** is the capital. Virtually all residents, who number about 3.5 million, are **Somali**. In recent decades, the region has experienced significant conflict. The **Ogaden War (1964)** and the **Ogaden War (1977–1978)** between Somalia and Ethiopia resulted in a significant flow of Ethiopian **refugees** from the Somali ethnic group into Somalia. In the late 1980s and early 1990s, the Somali civil war led to a reverse refugee flow of Somalis from Somalia into Ethiopia. Some of these refugees remained as of 2003.

After the **Ethiopian People's Revolutionary Democratic Front** came to power (1991), it reorganized Ethiopia's regions and created Somali Region. Government presence in much of the area remains weak and services are limited. There are occasional security incidents attributed to the militant wing of the indigenous **Ogaden National Liberation Front** and the Somalia-based fundamentalist al-Ittihad al-Islami (Unity of **Islam**). The region's inhabitants are pastoralists and agropastoralists who herd cattle, camels, sheep, and goats. There is considerable movement by these people across the Somalia-Ethiopia border. The most common crop grown by agropastoralists is sorghum. The 2002–2003 drought and **famine** severely affected Somali Region.

SOUTHERN NATIONS, NATIONALITIES AND PEOPLE'S RE-GION (SNNPR). Covering 43,367 square miles (112,323 square kilometers), SNNPR, which has a **population** of about 11 million, lies in the southern part of Ethiopia and borders Sudan and Kenya to the south, **Gambela Region** to the west, and **Oromia Region** to the north and east. Geographically, it comprises 10 percent of Ethiopia and is divided into nine zones, 72 *woredas* (districts) and five special woredas. The capital is located in **Awasa**; other major towns include Arba Minch, Dilla, Hosaina, and Soddo. The **Omo River** dissects the region. Altitude varies from just over 1,200 feet (375 meters) at **Lake Turkana** to 13,800 feet (4,200 meters) at Mount Goge in North Omo. Numerous rivers flow through the SNNPR and **Lakes Awasa**, Chamo, and Abaya are found there. The SNNPR is ethnically the most complex region in Ethiopia and consists of more than 45 different groups, some of them very small in number. More than 90 percent of the residents live in rural areas. Persons speaking one of the **Sidama languages** number about 18 percent, one of the **Gurage** languages 15 percent, and **Wolaytta** 12 percent. Residents speak numerous other languages; **Amharic** is the working language of the people in the region.

Coffee is the most important cash crop. Important **food** crops include corn, teff (used in making *injera*), *ensete*, potatoes, and wheat. Cattle, sheep, goats, and chickens as well as beekeeping are also important to the **economy**. There are limited deposits of gold, coal, clay, diatomite, limestone, nickel, iron, and asbestos in the region. Forests and shrubs cover about 18 percent of the SNNPR. Although isolated and difficult to reach, the **Omo River** area is ethnically one of the most fascinating locations in Africa. There are also a few tropical forests in Keficho, Shekicho, and Omo zones. Although poorly developed, Nechisar, Mago, and Omo **National Parks** have considerable **tourist** potential.

Organized political parties in the SNNPR have actively opposed the **Ethiopian People's Revolutionary Democratic Front** (EPRDF) during the past 10 years. During elections, there have often been unfortunate incidents where supporters of the EPRDF used unfair and/or illegal tactics to ensure victory at the polls.

STERN, HENRY AARON (1820–1885). German **missionary** and explorer. Born on 11 April 1820 near Gelnhausen. Educated at a school in Frankfurt. In 1839, Stern accepted a position with a London commercial firm that quickly went out of business. On 15 March 1840, he converted from Judaism to Christianity. Stern then entered the Operative Jewish Converts' Institution, where he learned the printing trade. In August 1842, he enrolled in the Hebrew College of London Jews' Society. On 14 July 1844, the bishop of **Jerusalem** ordained Stern as an Anglican deacon.

In 1860, the London Society for Promoting Christianity among the Jews sent him to Ethiopia to establish a mission among the **Falashas**. However, **Tewodros II** insisted that the Falashas be baptized into the **Ethiopian Orthodox Church**. Despite this setback, Stern built a mission station at Jenda near **Gondar** and convinced **Johann Martin Flad** and his wife to become its managers. He returned to London and published his *Wanderings among the Falashas in Abyssinia* (1862) and then returned to Ethiopia. In 1863, Stern again clashed with Tewodros II because a passage in the book referred to the low social status of the emperor's mother. Tewodros II jailed Stern. After the **Anglo-Ethiopian War**, he regained his freedom and returned to Britain, where he became head of the Home Missions of the London Jews' Society until he died.

STRUCTURAL ADJUSTMENT FACILITY (SAF). *See* INTERNATIONAL MONETARY FUND.

SUEZ CANAL. On 17 November 1869, the Suez Canal, which is 101 miles (163 kilometers) long from Suez to Port Said, connected the **Red Sea** with the Mediterranean. Its opening changed Ethiopia's economic and political history. European maritime nations immediately began searching for fueling stations to service their ships en route to India and the Far East. For example, Società Raffaele Rubattino, a Genoese shipping company, purchased **Asab** (1869). There also were disagreements between Ethiopia and Italy about the ownership of **Massawa**. *See also* SAPETO, GIUSEPPE.

SURI PEOPLE AND LANGUAGE. The Suri people call themselves Suri, although they are widely known as Surma in European writings and have been given other names by nearby peoples. More than 40,000 Suri live on the Boma plateau on both sides of the southwestern Sudan-Ethiopia border, although most of them live in Ethiopia.

The **Mursi** live to the east, the **Murle** to the southeast, and the **Anuak** to the northwest. Some believe the Suri migrated from the banks of the **Nile River** where the Dinka now live, following the Akobo River eastward. In about 1850, Suri chiefs worked out an accommodation with their neighbors to the east. Traditionally, they have had poor relations with the Anuak; they have a reputation for being fierce warriors. Previously nomadic pastoralists, today they are mainly **agriculturists** although they keep sheep and goats. Cattle are highly prized but difficult to raise because of the presence of the tsetse fly. The Suri engage in trade and make **pottery** for neighboring tribes. They have six exogamous clans and a system of chiefs and subchiefs. Men and boys are divided into 10-year age-sets. They live in beehive-shaped huts similar to the Mursi pattern. The **women** wear heavy iron bracelets and anklets while the men wear ivory, wire, and brass bracelets, and ear rings and iron bells on the legs and arms. They follow traditional religious beliefs similar to the Murle and call their Supreme Being Tuma. They speak an eastern Sudanic **language** that has numerous dialects. Suri has 81 percent lexical similarity with Mursi.

SUSNEYOS (SAGAD, SELTAN, SELTAN SEGUED, MALAK SAGAD) (c. 1571–1632). Emperor (1607–1632). Son of Prince Fasilidas and great-grandson of **Lebna Dengel**. When Susneyos was nine years old, **Oromo** warriors captured him and killed his father. He remained in captivity for more than a year. **Dajazmach** Asbo released Susneyos, who was put under the care of the Empress Dowager Adems-Mogassa.

After the death of Sarsa Dengel (reigned 1563–1597), Susneyos became a possible claimant to the throne, thus becoming a threat to powerful nobles who hoped to manipulate Sarsa Dengel's young, illegitimate son who had succeeded him. Susneyos therefore sought refuge in **Gojam**, where he lived the life of a *shifta*. On 10 March 1607, he scored a decisive victory at the Battle of Gol in Gojam against Emperor Yacob (reigned 1597–1603, 1604–1607), who died during the fighting.

As emperor, Susneyos experienced many troubles. To establish his authority, he replaced governors and other senior officials with his own relatives and supporters. For years, the emperor faced revolts and intrigues from some of those who had lost their positions. Difficulties with non-Christian Ethiopians also led to battles, particularly against the

Agaw of **Gojam**, the **Falashas** of Semen, and the Oromo. Additionally, Susneyos conducted campaigns near the **Atbara River**, Taka River, **Danakil Depression**, **Enarya**, and Sarki in the Sennar kingdom.

Religious squabbling also posed a major threat to the monarchy. The **Ethiopian Orthodox Church** (EOC) bitterly opposed encroaching Portuguese **Catholicism** in the country. The emperor, on the other hand, supported the Portuguese, in part because he hoped to secure military aid from Lisbon to repel the restive Oromo and recruit artisans and craftsmen to help develop Ethiopia. In 1622, Susneyos further alienated the EOC by recognizing Roman Catholicism as Ethiopia's official religion. The arrival in Ethiopia of the Roman Catholic patriarch Affonso Mendez provoked widespread and sustained unrest. On 24 June 1662, the embattled emperor proclaimed the restoration of Ethiopian Orthodoxy. Susneyos died a few months later, at Danqaz, on 16 September 1632.

– T –

TAFARI MAKONNEN. *See* HAILE SELASSIE.

TAKLA GIYORGIS (1826–1872). Emperor (1868–1871). Born Wagshum Gobaze in Lasta. After **Tewodros II** hanged Gobaze's father (1858), Gobaze went into hiding. In 1864, he rebelled against the emperor but avoided a direct confrontation with his forces. In 1865, he returned to Lasta and assumed command of an army his mother and stepfather had assembled. Gobaze then moved into **Tigray** and defeated Tewodros II's deputy, Tiso Gobaze. During the **Anglo-Ethiopian War (1867–1868)**, he and his 60,000-man army remained neutral.

After Tewodros II committed suicide on 13 April 1868, Gobaze proclaimed himself Emperor Takla Giyorgis. He was the last monarch to reside in **Gondar**. Menelik (later **Menelik II**) coveted his throne. Takla Giyorgis avoided a conflict with Menelik by concluding an agreement that kept **Shoa** outside Menelik's sphere of influence. On 11 July 1871, Menelik's army scored a decisive victory over the emperor's forces at the Battle of Asem. During the fighting, Menelik's soldiers captured Takla Giyorgis, who was imprisoned and subsequently dethroned. He died the following year.

TAKLA HAYMANOT (1847–1901). Negus of **Gojam** and **Kafa.**
Born as Adal Tessemma. His father, **Dajazmach** Tessemma Goshu,
died during his minority. Consequently, a rival named Dajazmach
Dasta Guala assumed control of Gojam and imprisoned Adal, who
eventually escaped to the **lowlands** where he raised an army that defeated Dasta's troops. In exchange for Adal's submission, Emperor
Takla Giyorgis confirmed him as Gojam's governor, appointed him
as dajazmach, and allowed him to marry his paternal sister Laqetch
Gebre Medhin. On 11 July 1871, the future **Yohannes IV** defeated
the emperor's forces at **Adwa** and reinstated Dasta. After becoming
emperor on 21 January 1872, Yohannes IV left Gojam; Adal returned
and killed Dasta. On 20 January 1881, Yohannes IV crowned Adal as
Negus Takla Haymanot of Gojam and **Kafa.**

Takla then pursued a strategy of extending his domain to the southwest and to the **Oromo** tribes that lived in the Gibe River vicinity.
This conflict of interest eventually led to Takla's defeat and capture
at the **Battle of Embabo.** In August 1882, Yohannes IV met Takla
and Menelik (later **Menelik II**) at Warayelu, **Wollo.** The emperor
freed Takla but took some of his conquered territories and gave the
rest to Menelik. After his defeat, Takla focused on civic projects such
as building bridges and churches.

In the late 1880s, Mahdist raiders from Sudan encroached on his
territory. On 18 January 1888, a large Mahdist army defeated Takla's
soldiers at Sarweha in Dembea. Shortly afterward, Yohannes IV suspected Takla and Menelik of plotting against him. To destroy Takla's
power, Yohannes IV's army laid waste to much of Gojam, thus ending any possibility that Takla would become emperor. After becoming emperor (1889), Menelik II named Takla governor of Gojam and
appointed him as one of his advisers. Takla participated in the **Battle
of Adwa** and some other minor military expeditions. He died on 10
January 1901. *See also* GOBANA DACHI; NEGASH BEZABEH.

TAXATION. Modern taxation dates from 1934, when **Haile Selassie**
levied the first direct tax upon all Ethiopians. All adults had to pay a
modest tax and a 20 percent tax on all salaries and feudal dues. However, collection capabilities were poor and some parts of the northern
provinces resisted paying the tax collector. In 1956, the emperor revised the taxation system in favor of a direct tax on personal and

business income, land, **education**, **health**, and cattle. There also were transaction taxes, stamp duties, and an indirect tax on alcohol, perfume, yarns, textiles, salt, motor fuel, and tobacco. In November 1967, additional legislation affected taxes paid by corporations, wealthy Ethiopians, and **agricultural** landlords.

The **Derg** expanded the economy's state sector and discouraged the private sector. It instituted an income tax on the economically active population that included a marginal tax rate that reached 85 percent. This led to pervasive **corruption**. After seizing power in 1991, the **Ethiopian People's Revolutionary Democratic Front** (EPRDF) changed the policy on personal income tax, corporate tax, and sales and excise taxes. It also introduced new **mining** income, capital gains, and rental taxes that aimed to rationalize the tax structure, broaden the tax base, and reduce the marginal tax rate. The goal was to stimulate economic growth, end fiscal imbalance, and avoid economic inefficiencies. The EPRDF began a policy of sharing tax receipts with regional governments as part of its decentralization effort. The central government collects certain taxes, especially the important tax on the import and export of goods. Regions collect other taxes such as rural land use fees, agricultural income tax, and fees for services rendered by regional governments. Several taxes, such as royalty and rent for large mining and gas operations, are collected jointly.

In 2002, the government introduced major changes to the tax laws. The principal one was the creation a value-added tax (VAT) that took effect in January 2003. Prior to the VAT, the 15 percent sales tax was imposed on every taxable sale and a business purchaser was not entitled to claim credit for sales tax paid on its purchases. The VAT, which the EPRDF says is a more efficient way to collect tax, ends this situation. The Federal Inland Revenue Authority administers the VAT. The government created a separate Ministry of Revenue and a tax reform program office to oversee the six new tax programs. In addition to the VAT, they include the tax policy and legislation project, the taxpayer identification number project, the presumptive taxation project, the large taxpayer office project, and operational programs, systems, and procedures.

Most government revenue comes from tax collection. On average, taxes contribute 70 percent of all domestic revenue. Tax revenue averages more than 12 percent of gross national product. About 39 percent is direct tax, 30 percent indirect tax, and 31 percent foreign trade tax. Tax revenues more than tripled between 1982–1983 and 1997–1998. The increase in collections was due mainly to new taxes from urban land lease, mining income tax, rental income tax, and several other sources. Increased economic activity and improved tax collection also contributed to the additional revenue. *See also* ECONOMY.

TAYE WOLDE SEMAYAT (1949–). Professor at **Addis Ababa University** and president of the **Ethiopian Teachers' Association** (ETA). Born in Nazret, a town 62 miles (100 kilometers) south of **Addis Ababa**. After graduating from high school, Taye went to the United States where he eventually received a Ph.D. from the University of Missouri. He then returned to Ethiopia and joined the political science faculty at Addis Ababa University. In 1992, Taye was elected president of ETA, the country's second largest **labor union** with some 120,000 members. In June 1996, the authorities arrested him for belonging to an underground political organization called the Ethiopian National Patriots Front and for conspiring against the state. Taye's supporters claimed the charges had been fabricated to silence his criticism of the government's educational policies. In June 1999, a court, whose proceedings breached international standards for a fair trial according to Amnesty International, sentenced Taye to 15 years' imprisonment. During his incarceration, Amnesty International repeatedly urged his release as a prisoner of conscience. On 14 May 2002, he was released. *See also* HUMAN RIGHTS; JUDICIARY.

TAYTU BETUL (c. 1850–1918). Empress (1889–1918). Born near **Gondar**. Her family was from Yejjo in **Oromo** country north of **Shoa** Province. Educated in **Amharic**, international affairs, law, politics, and religion. As a young woman, she had many husbands, including a general who served under **Tewodros II** and a governor of one of **Yohannes IV**'s provinces.

On 29 April 1883, Taytu married **Menelik II**, thus becoming queen of Shoa. On 5 November 1883, she was crowned empress of Ethiopia. Taytu opposed Menelik II's open-door and modernization policies. She correctly believed that Italy coveted Ethiopia while other European nations sought commercial and political ties with the monarchy to advance their own interests. In support of her anti-European agenda, Taytu was largely responsible for abrogating the **Treaty of Wichale** and played a role in the **Battle of Adwa**. Domestically, she sought to ensure northern domination of Ethiopian politics by uniting key families in marriage alliances. This policy created many enemies who opposed or feared northern control of Ethiopia. Some of her other accomplishments include naming Menelik II's capital **Addis Ababa**, financing its first hotel, and ensuring that **women** had access to **education**.

During the emperor's debilitating illness (1906–1910), Taytu assumed control of the monarchy largely by making government appointments and land grants. On 21 March 1910, her enemies, who included Tasamma Nadaw, Habta-Giyorgis Dinagde, Dames Nasibu, Gebre-Sellase Barya-Gabr, Warsane Terfe, and **Mikael Ali Abba Bula,** supported a successful coup against Taytu. **Abuna Matewos** passed an injunction that barred the empress from conducting government affairs and restricted her to caring for the ailing emperor. On 22 March 1910, Taytu accepted these terms. After Menelik II's death (1913), the empress retired to Entoto Maryam, a church she had built and had endowed on a hill above Addis Ababa. Taytu died on 11 February 1918. *See also* ENTOTO.

TEFERI BANTE (1921–1977). Soldier and chairman of the **Provisional Military Administration Council** (PMAC) (28 November 1974–3 February 1977). Born in **Addis Ababa**. In 1941, Teferi joined the army and subsequently graduated from Holeta (Genet) Military Academy. He then served in various posts in the second, third, and fourth divisions as well as in army headquarters. On 29 November 1974, the PMAC elected Teferi as its chairman to replace Brigadier General **Aman Michael Andom,** who had been executed on **Bloody Saturday**. **Mengistu Haile Mariam** had hoped that he could dominate the lackluster Teferi. However, Mengistu's opponents gradually made Teferi one of the **Derg**'s most influential leaders who opposed the **National Democratic Revolution**. On 3 February 1977, Colonel Daniel Asfaw and a security contingent arrested Teferi and six other Derg officials during a Central Committee meeting in **Menelik II**'s old palace. A firing squad then executed all of them. The Derg subsequently accused Teferi of failing to denounce the **Ethiopia People's Revolutionary Party** for opposing the National Democratic Revolution during his nationwide speeches on 29 and 30 January 1977. *See also* ARMED FORCES.

TEKEZE RIVER. (378 miles; 608 kilometers long.) The Tekeze River rises in Ethiopia's central tableland east of **Lalibela**. It courses west, takes a sharp turn to the north just west of Lalibela, and follows a trench along the east side of the **Simien Mountains** until it again turns northwest. The Tekeze forms the northwest border with Eritrea near the tripoint with Sudan. After entering Sudan, the Tekeze is known as the Setit River until it merges at Tomat village with the **Atbara River**, which joins the **Nile** north of Khartoum at Atbara town. During the rainy season, the Tekeze rises about 16 feet (5 meters) above normal, making passage impossible except at the few locations where there are bridges.

TEKLE-HAWARIYAT TEKLE-MARIYAM (1884–1977). Born in June 1884 in **Shoa** Province. Educated at a church school in **Addis Ababa**, and subsequently studied in **Harar**, where he became close to the family of **Ras Makonnen Walda Mikael**, the father of the future **Haile Selassie**. Tekle-Hawariyat participated in the **Battle of Adwa**. He then went to Russia and eventually enrolled in the Saint Petersburg Military School and, after being commissioned in 1905, attended the Michael Artillery School. He received a commission (1906–1908) and became a Russian army officer. Before returning to Ethiopia in 1908, he toured Britain, France, and Italy.

Tekle-Hawariyat served initially as head of the **Addis Ababa** municipality. He then briefly accompanied a British exploration team to **Lake Tana** and subsequently became comptroller of the **Addis Ababa–Djibouti Railway** (1915). In 1917, Tekle-Hawariyat became governor of **Jijiga,** where he earned a reputation as a reformer for transforming the garrison town into a more modern urban center. His next assignment was governor of western **Harar**'s Chercher Province, a position he held for seven years. Tekle-Hawariyat again made numerous reforms, established a capital at Asabe Teferi, and encouraged economic development. In 1928, **Ras** Tafari Makonnen, later **Haile Selassie**, briefly imprisoned him in Addis Ababa. In 1930, Haile Selassie asked him to draft Ethiopia's 1934 **constitution**, which remained in force until 1955.

Tekle-Hawariyat next served in several positions, including minister of finance; minister or ambassador to France, Britain, and Switzerland; and delegate to the **League of Nations,** although he was recalled before Ethiopia joined the League. During the **Italian-Ethiopian War,** Tekle-Hawariyat commanded Ethiopian units. He eventually fled to Djibouti, where he organized relief for Ethiopian **refugees.** Italian pressure and disagreements with Haile Selassie about the course of the war persuaded Tekle-Hawariyat to move to Madagascar, where he lived as an unsuccessful farmer until 1952. In 1955, he reconciled with Haile Selassie and returned to his farm at Hirna in Hararge, where he emphasized the modernization of **agriculture.** Tekle-Hawariyat died in April 1977 and was buried in **Dire Dawa.**

TEKLE HAYMANOT, SAINT. *See* DEBRE LIBANOS.

TELECOMMUNICATIONS. Ethiopia's telecommunications history began in 1894, when **Alfred Ilg** and Léon Chefneux (1853–1927) built the country's first long-distance telephone line between **Addis Ababa** and **Harar.** By 1897, telephone service had been extended to Baltchi, Fantale, Gara Muleta, Kulubi, Kuni, Lgdar din, and Tchoba. During 1902–1905, engineers built a line between Addis Ababa and Adikuala, **Adwa,** Asmara, **Ankober, Dese,** Korem, Marto, **Mekele,** and Woreilu. During 1905–1913, Addis Ababa opened telephone connections to **Gambela, Gondar,** Nekempte, and Sidamo. A telegraph linked Addis Ababa, **Dire Dawa,** and Djibouti to service the **Addis Ababa–Djibouti Railway.** In 1909, Ethiopia joined the International Postal, Telegraph, and Telephone Service and, in 1932, the International Telecommunications Union. In 1933, Ethiopia introduced radio-telephone communications. By 1935, 170 towns had telephone service, and international links had been established with Aden, Cairo, and Djibouti. The **Italian-Ethiopian War** destroyed much of Ethiopia's telecommunications network. However, during the Italian occupation of Ethiopia (1936–1941), Italian engineers built Addis Ababa's first automatic telephone exchange.

After **World War II, Haile Selassie** gave priority to the restoration of the country's telephone and telegraphic infrastructure. On 15 October 1952, he created the Imperial Board of Telecommunications

(IBT) to fulfill this mission. During 1953–1963, the IBT repaired war damage, established manual exchanges in 12 towns, and expanded Addis Ababa's automatic telephone exchange. Between 1962 and 1973, the IBT expanded existing automatic exchanges between Addis Ababa, Asmara, and **Debre Zeit**; installed new exchanges in **Asab**, Asmara, Dese, Harar, **Jimma**, Keren, **Massawa**, and **Nazret**; and built manual exchanges in 83 towns. Telex services also opened in Addis Ababa and some rural areas.

After Haile Selassie's downfall, Ethiopia received international aid to build the country's first Earth satellite station and a network of microwave facilities. In 1979, international communications were accelerated by the construction of an international satellite Earth station in Sululta that replaced the aging high-frequency radio communications facility. By 1994, the new system had some 345 satellite connections to 23 countries in Asia, Europe, the Far East, the Indian Ocean, the Middle East, and North America. In 1981, the **Derg** created the Ethiopian Telecommunications Authority (ETA), which performed the same role as the defunct ITB.

During the 1984–1994 development program, the Ethiopian Telecommunications Corporation (ETC) expanded and modernized the telecommunications sector by building another international Earth satellite station at Sululta and domestic satellite stations at Asmara, Gode, Humera, Mekele, and Sululta. A new development program, initiated in 1994, seeks to develop new rural connections, improve existing infrastructure, and introduce modern telecommunications. In 2002, the ETC, which operated 351,000 customer connections, invited interested companies to bid for a 30 percent share in the state-owned corporation.

TERZIAN, SARKIS (1868–1915). Armenian trader, gunrunner, and diplomat. Born in Arakpir in what is now Turkey. In 1882, Terzian traveled to Egyptian-occupied **Harar**. In 1887, he helped **Menelik II**, at the time the **negus** of **Shoa**, occupy the city. In recognition of his service, Menelik II appointed him governor of Gildessa and Biokobbo, both in Harar Province. Apart from his official duties, Terzian played a significant role in opening trade relations between Shoa and the outside world and establishing an oxcart transport system between **Addis Ababa** and **Dire Dawa**. Additionally, he supplied Menelik II with large quantities of firearms and imported Ethiopia's first ammunition factory. Terzian also undertook several diplomatic missions (e.g., Paris, London, Berlin, Vienna, Rome, Brussels, and Washington, D.C.) at the request of Menelik II. He also recruited several Armenians to provide technical support to the emperor's various development projects.

TESFAYE GEBRE KIDAN (c. 1939–). Soldier and **Derg** member. Born in Gursum in Hararge and educated at an elementary school in Gursum and at Medahene Alem High School in **Harar**. During 1959–1960, Tesfaye attended the Holeta (Genet) Military Academy, where he met **Mengistu Haile Mariam**. Upon graduation, he received a posting to the Third Division's tank battalion. Over the next several years, he underwent additional military training in the United States (1962) and served in the **Ogaden** (1963–1965), **Addis Ababa** (1965–1967), **Gojam** (1967–1968), and Eritrea.

In June 1974, he joined the Derg as the representative of the Third Division's tank battalion. In December 1974, Tesfaye received a promotion to lieutenant colonel. During 1974–1976, he served as chairman of the Derg's defense committee. In 1976, Tesfaye joined the **Revolutionary Flame**. After the Derg's December 1976 reorganization, he became the defense committee's cochairman with Lieutenant Colonel Haddis Tedla. During the **Ogaden War (1977–1978)**, Tesfaye served as commander in chief of the eastern front and then assumed command of military operations in Eritrea (1978–1979). In December 1978, Tesfaye was promoted to brigadier. On 2 January 1980, he became minister of defense primarily to improve morale in the **armed forces**.

After receiving a promotion to lieutenant general on 2 March 1982, Tesfaye became a politburo member of the **Workers' Party of Ethiopia** on 17 September 1984. On 16 March 1987, Major General Haile Georgis Habte Mariam replaced him as minister of defense. On 11 September 1987, the Peoples Democratic Republic of Ethiopia held its founding congress and elected Tefaye to its politburo. He presided over the court-martial of 13 generals who had participated in the **coup attempt (1989)**. However, Tesfaye resigned this position after Mengistu overruled his recommendation for long prison sentences for the plotters and ordered the execution of the generals.

From 21 to 28 May 1991, he served as acting head of state. However, after the **Ethiopian People's Revolutionary Democratic Front** seized power (1991), Tesfaye took refuge in the Italian embassy. After regaining his freedom, he became secretary general of the Ethiopian National Democratic Party that was created on 2 April 1994. *See also* OGADEN WAR (1964).

TEWODROS II (THEODORE) (1818–1868). Emperor of Ethiopia (1855–1868). Known officially as the Elect of God, the Slave of Christ, the King of Kings, and Emperor of **Abyssinia**. Born as Kassa Haylu and educated at several monasteries. His father was Haylu Walda Giyorgis, a governor of Qwara Province. However, Kassa lived with his mother, Wayzaro Ategati, in the **Gondar** area. He gained military experience by participating in the campaigns of his half brother, **Dajazmach** Kenfu. After Kenfu's death (1839), his lands and governorship fell into the hands of Empress Manan Liben-Andie, mother of **Ras Alula Qubi**. This impoverished Kassa, who spent the early 1840s as a *shifta* in the Tana region.

About 1845, there was a reconciliation between Kassa and Ali. As a result, Kassa married Ali's daughter, Tawabach, and became governor of Qwara Province. However, relations between Kassa and Manan remained tense. In June 1847, the empress and her army moved against Kassa. After defeating her, Kassa became governor of the regions north and west of **Lake Tana**.

In 1852, he launched a military campaign to gain control of Ethiopia. On 27 November 1852, Kassa defeated Dajazmach Goshu of **Gojam** at the Battle of Gur Amba. He scored additional victories over Ras Ali at the **Battle of Ayshal** and over Dajazmach **Webe Hayla Maryam** at the Battle of Derasge (9 February 1855). With his main rivals eliminated, Kassa, taking the name Tewodros II, was crowned emperor on 11 February 1855.

To strengthen his position, he deprived many local kings and princes of their power and appointed loyal administrators in their place. Next, Tewodros II created a disciplined, professional army for the first time in the country's history. Such tactics enabled him to reunify Ethiopia and to modernize the country. He also made judicial reforms such as limiting the collective responsibility for crimes and encouraged his subjects to abandon polygamy and **slavery**.

Despite his achievements, Tewodros II faced considerable unrest and rebellions in all provinces. He responded to these problems by launching military campaigns against his enemies. However, this strategy failed to stabilize the empire. Tewodros II also clashed with the **Ethiopian Orthodox Church** after he reduced its landholdings to finance his central government. Seeking submission by burning 41 churches in **Gondar** only widened the gulf between the emperor and the church.

Amidst these problems, Ethiopia's relations with Britain started to deteriorate. In 1862, Tewodros II wrote a letter to Queen Victoria (1837–1901) that proposed the creation of an Anglo-Ethiopian alliance. Queen Victoria's failure to answer this letter angered the emperor, who, in 1864, imprisoned some European **missionaries** and **Charles Duncan Cameron**, the British consul. Tewodros II also jailed **Hormuzd Rassam**, a British envoy, and his two aides, who had come to Ethiopia to secure the captives' release.

Britain retaliated by deploying a military expedition from India to Ethiopia. The ensuing **Anglo-Ethiopian War** resulted in the defeat of Tewodros II's army on 10 April 1868. On 13 April 1868, he committed suicide by shooting himself in the mouth rather than surrender to the British. *See also* FOREIGN POLICY; NAPIER, SIR ROBERT CORNELIS.

TEWOFLOS (THEOPHILOS), ABUNA (1910–1974?). Patriarch of the **Ethiopian Orthodox Church** (EOC). Born on 24 April 1910 at the Debre Elias monastery in **Gojam**. Educated locally and in **Addis Ababa** under the guidance of **Abuna** Yohannes. Tewoflos then entered a monastery in **Debre Libanos** (1930). After the **Italian-Ethiopian War**, **Haile Selassie** named him as one of 20 religious scholars to have a modern **education** at the imperial palace under Professor Betre Tsadik Kassa. After graduation, Tewoflos received an appointment as head of the Holy Trinity theological college. In 1942, he became administrator of Trinity Cathedral. On 25 July 1948, the patriarch of Alexandria consecrated Tewoflos as bishop of Hararge.

On 18 February 1950, he became deputy patriarch of the EOC and archbishop. In this position, Tewoflos created an evangelical mission and a youth branch to bring Ethiopians closer to the church, improved church training and education, and established the EOC in the United States, Trinidad, and Guyana.

On 7 April 1961, Tewoflos became patriarch of the EOC. He represented the church at meetings throughout the world and presided over a World Council of Churches conference in Addis Ababa (1971). Tewoflos twice served as president of the All-African Council of Churches. His stormy relationship with the **Derg** proved to be his undoing. On 18 August 1974, Tewoflos attacked a government proposal that sought to separate church and state and remove the emperor as head of the EOC. On 17 October 1974, the Derg retaliated by accusing him and the EOC of tax evasion and warned if both failed to pay, they would face nationalization of their buildings and land upon which taxes were due. On 18 February 1976, Addis Ababa radio announced that the Derg had removed Tewoflos from office and placed him under arrest. According to the Derg, he arranged the murder of several priests, misappropriated relief funds, and accumulated a private fortune worth millions of dollars. On 18 February 1997, Catholic World News reported that it had received information that, after his arrest, armed guards had taken Tewoflos away and executed him. *See also* TAXATION.

TIGRAY LIBERATION FRONT. *See* TIGRAY PEOPLE'S LIBERATION FRONT.

TIGRAY PEOPLE AND LANGUAGE. There are more than four million Tigrayans in Ethiopia and nearly two million in Eritrea (Tigrayans are distinct from the Tigre people, most of whom live in Eritrea). Tigrayans comprise about 7 percent of Ethiopia's **population**. In the fourth century, the Tigrayans, a Semitic people, adopted Christianity and today almost all belong to the **Ethiopian Orthodox Church** (EOC). Most live in **Tigray Region** but there are many Tigray communities scattered throughout Ethiopia. The Tigrayans have the reputation of being fiercely independent, tough fighters, and good administrators. Most are involved in **agriculture**. The land where they live has a thin cover of soil that they make the best of by terracing and constructing minidams. Using plows, the Tigrayans grow teff, barley, wheat, millet, and a variety of vegetables. They also raise cattle, fat-tail sheep, and goats. The Tigrayans reside in the original kingdom of **Axum**, which continues to influence how they see their role in society. Along with the **Amhara people**, they have long been considered Ethiopia's "chosen" people. Some Tigrayans undoubtedly see themselves as of purer racial stock than the Amhara, who mixed more with other peoples. Traditionally more isolated than the Amhara, the Tigrayans historically have opposed centralized rule by the more numerous Amhara. During the **Italian-Ethiopian War**, some Tigrayans collaborated with the Italians, probably as part of an effort to have more influence in the affairs of the **Africa Orientale Italiana** government.

Although there are some differences among the Tigrinya-speaking peoples of Ethiopia and Eritrea, they are basically ethnically homogeneous. They share a similar history, have the same physical characteristics, speak the same **language**, and adhere to the EOC's teachings. They also have the same social structure and **land tenure** system. Over the years, there has been substantial intermarriage between Tigrinya-speaking peoples in Tigray Region and Eritrea. For these reasons, the **Ethiopian-Eritrean War** surprised most outsiders.

The Tigrayans have a long history of resisting foreign invasion. In 1534, the **Islamic** army of **Ahmad ibn Ibrahim al Ghazi** encountered strong opposition when it reached Tigray. The Tigrayans also scored a significant victory over the Italians at the **Battle of Adwa** in Tigray's heartland. The **Tigray People's Liberation Front** was in large part responsible for the defeat of the **Derg** (1991). Useful background information on the Tigrayans is found in *The Central Ethiopians: Amhara, Tigrinya, and Related Peoples* by William A. Shack.

Tigrayans speak Tigrinya, which derives from **Ge'ez**. Linguists continue to argue whether Tigrinya or **Tigre** is closer to Ge'ez. To further confuse matters, the name Tigrinya comes from the name of the province, previously called Tigre but known today as Tigray. Tigre and Tigrinya are two distinct languages and are as different as Spanish and Italian. The morphology of Tigrinya does not deviate significantly from Ge'ez, and the phonetics are similar. The syntax deviates from the Semitic type in much the same way that **Amharic** does. Tigrinya vocabulary is predominantly Semitic but contains Cushitic and **Agaw** elements. There are few dialectal differences, although several minor regional distinctions exist. Tigrinya **literature** developed slowly and late because Ge'ez dominated as a literary language long after it ceased to be used as a vernacular. The greater use of Amharic for literary purposes also interfered with Tigrinya's development for literature. The **Ethiopian-Eritrean Federation** significantly encouraged the production of works in Tigrinya. One of the most useful sources on Tigrinya is Edward Ullendorff's *Semitic Languages of Ethiopia*.

TIGRAY PEOPLE'S LIBERATION FRONT (TPLF). On 18 February 1975, a small group of university students from **Tigray Region** who opposed the **Derg** established the TPLF at Dedebit, some 40 miles (65 kilometers) from the town of Sheraro. The three most important TPLF leaders (Aregowie Berhe, Sebhat Nega, and **Meles Zenawi**) came from **Adwa** and attended that town's government school. Shortly after its formation, the TPLF sought to create a united front by merging with the Tigray Liberation Front, which recently had started operations under the command of a teacher named Tecle Haimanot and a pharmacist called Gebre Kidane.

For the next 16 years, the TPLF, which developed into one of Africa's most disciplined and committed liberation groups, fought against an array of enemies. From 1975 to 1978, it spent much of its time fighting other groups in Tigray that also opposed the Derg. By 1978, the TPLF had prevailed over the **Ethiopian Democratic Union** and the **Ethiopian People's Revolutionary Party**. During 1978–1985, a **famine** distracted the TPLF, thereby hampering efforts to resolve internal ideological problems and those with allied organizations like the EPLF. In 1979, Sebhat Nega, a former school director in Adwa, became TPLF chairman. He and other rebel leaders expanded the TPLF's popular support by relying on Maoist doctrine that embraced the political and social issues of the masses, emphasized self-reliance, extolled Tigrayan nationalism, and conducted a protracted conflict.

The 1985–1991 period witnessed the final stage of the war against the Derg. By this time, the peasantry was generally unified behind the TPLF, which could focus on military confrontation with the Derg forces. In 1989, the TPLF occupied Tigray and built alliances with other anti-Derg parties. On 17 January 1991, it created an umbrella organization of like-minded groups called the **Ethiopian People's Revolutionary Democratic Front** (EPRDF) and convened its first congress. On 23 February 1991, the EPRDF, in cooperation with the **Eritrean People's Liberation Front**, launched Operation Tewodros and, within a month, had expelled government forces from **Gondar** and **Gojam**. On 21 May 1991, **Mengistu Haile Mariam** fled for Zimbabwe. On 28 May 1991, a joint TPLF-EPLF force ended the war by occupying **Addis Ababa**.

After its victory, the EPRDF approved the EPLF's plan to create an independent state in Eritrea and established the **Transitional Government of Ethiopia**. The TPLF has been the core of the EPRDF ever since and, in 2000, Meles Zenawi was elected to his second five-year term as prime minister. In 2001, internal political divisions and disagreements about the handling of the **Ethiopian-Eritrean War** plagued the TPLF. As of 2004, some of these problems continued to exist. Although many Ethiopians resent the control that Tigrayans continue to exercise in the government and military, there is grudging understanding that the TPLF was largely responsible for getting rid of the Derg, and for that, they deserve time to sort out Ethiopia's problems. The question is how much time the other ethnic groups and opposition parties will give the Tigrayans.

TIGRAY REGION. Covering an area of 31,000 square miles (80,000 square kilometers), Tigray is Ethiopia's most northerly region. Together with **Amhara Region**, it forms the core of ancient **Abyssinia**. It has a **population** of about 3.5 million, of whom 94.8 percent are Tigrayan. The **Amhara people** number about 2.5 percent, Eritreans less than 1 percent, and there are small numbers of **Saho**, **Agaw**, and other peoples. Followers of the **Ethiopian Orthodox Church** constitute 95.5 percent of the population, Muslims 4.1 percent, and **Catholics** most of the remainder. Tigray's capital and largest city is **Mekele**. Other sizable towns include Adigrat, **Axum**, **Adwa**, Alamata, and Enda Selassie. It is divided administratively into four zones. Most of Tigray is a high plateau and includes a spectacular range of mountains near Adwa between Axum and Adigrat. The region slopes off to the west where it borders Sudan and drops off sharply to the east where it encounters the **Danakil Depression**.

Most Tigrayans are peasant farmers although many are organized into cooperatives. Over the years, there has been considerable terracing of steep hillsides to obtain maximum advantage of the thin layer of soil. The Tigrayans also have implemented a major effort to build minidams to make better use of limited water resources. Tigray tends to be drier than other parts of **highland** Ethiopia. The **Ethiopian-Er-itrean War (1998–2000)** began at Badme in Tigray and fighting was concentrated along the Tigrayan-Eritrean border. The conflict forced many Tigrayan farmers out of the border area.

The Axumite empire was centered in Tigray; the city of Axum and associated archaeological sites are favorites with **tourists**. There also are some 120 **rock-hewn churches** scattered throughout the eastern part of the region. At the **Battle of Adwa** (1896), the Ethiopians over-whelmed the Italians, the first defeat of a European military force in sub-Saharan Africa. *See also* ENDOWMENT FUND FOR THE RE-HABILITATION OF TIGRAY; RELIEF SOCIETY OF TIGRAY.

TIGRE-SPEAKING PEOPLES. There is considerable confusion among foreigners between the Tigre-speaking peoples, nearly all of whom live in Eritrea, and the more numerous Tigrinya-speaking **Tigrayans** who live in Ethiopia. Tigrinya-speakers also reside in Er-itrea. Tigre is a linguistic designation for several subgroups concen-trated in the northern part of Eritrea that speak a **language** known as Tigre. Some believe that Tigre is a direct linguistic descendent of **Ge'ez**. Until the late 19th century, Europeans often mistakenly claimed that Tigrayans living in Ethiopia's **Tigray Region** spoke Tigre. Tigrinya and Tigre are two distinct and mutually unintelligible **languages**. There is no federation of tribes who call themselves Tigre; in local usage Tigre refers to the serf class of the Beni Amer, Mensa, Beit Asgade, and other people found among all Tigre-speaking peoples. They are descended from the main body of Islamized **Beja** people who reside between the **Red Sea** and the **Nile River** in neigh-boring Sudan. Small groups of Tigre-speaking peoples have migrated to Sudan and Ethiopia.

TIMKAT. *See* HOLIDAYS, RELIGIOUS.

TIS ISAT FALLS. *See* BLUE NILE.

TOURISM. Ethiopia is potentially a center for tourism in Africa. A country of enormous diversity and spectacular beauty, it has so far at-tracted primarily the "adventure tourist." Historically, one of the most interesting countries in Africa, it offers the **Axumite** ruins dating back to the first century, ancient **rock-hewn churches** in **Tigray**, the 12th-century churches cut from stone at **Lalibela,** and the 17th-century capital at **Gondar**. There also are the **Blue Nile** Falls, some of the world's most diverse **bird life**, rafting trips on the **Omo** and **Awash Rivers**, unique fauna species such as the walia ibex and Simien fox, and a diversity of ethnic groups. **Ethiopian Airlines** offers regular air service to virtually all the tourist locations and, in 2002, Ethiopia began allowing nationals from 33 countries to obtain tourist visas upon arrival in the country. The United States, Canada, Japan, and most European countries are included on the list. Internal travel in Ethiopia is relatively inexpensive but sometimes slow and unpredictable.

Several factors have contributed to Ethiopia's relatively underdeveloped tourism sector. Tourism has never been a government priority. Periodic internal conflict, most recently the **Ethiopian-Eritrean War**, has discouraged potential tourists from visiting the country. The tourist infrastructure outside **Addis Ababa** is still largely government run and is generally inferior as there are no first-class hotels in the interior. It is difficult to use credit cards and vehicle rentals are neither plentiful nor especially reliable. The cost of internal flights is twice as high for foreigners as it is for Ethiopian nationals. Although Ethiopia has numerous **national parks,** they have been poorly maintained and cannot compete with those in Kenya, Uganda, and Tanzania. Ethiopia is poor and upscale tourists are sometimes depressed by the **poverty** that they encounter when traveling around the country.

Approximately 140,000 tourists visited Ethiopia in 1997. By 1999, when Ethiopia was at war with Eritrea, the number dropped to about 92,000 but had climbed back to 109,000 in 2000. Tourism earned Ethiopia about $16 million in 2000. Following the end of conflict with Eritrea, the number of tourists jumped to 146,000 in 2001 and earnings increased to an estimated $77 million. The Ethiopian government is beginning to appreciate tourism's potential and hoped to attract 320,000 tourists in 2002. The best and most current tourist guides are *Ethiopia: The Bradt Travel Guide* by Philip Briggs (2002) and *Lonely Planet Ethiopia, Eritrea, and Djibouti* (2000). Another useful guide is John Graham's *Ethiopia: Off the Beaten Trail* (2002).

TRADE. *See* ECONOMY.

TRADE UNIONS. *See* LABOR UNIONS.

TRANSITIONAL GOVERNMENT OF ETHIOPIA (TGE). On 1–5 July 1991, the **Ethiopian People's Revolutionary Democratic Front** (EPRDF) convened the Peace and Democracy Conference. In attendance were 83 delegates who represented 28 organizations and liberation groups and discussed Ethiopia's future political structure. On 22 July 1991, the EPRDF, **Oromo Liberation Front** (OLF), **Afar Liberation Front**, and several Somali groups like the **Western Somali Liberation Front** and the **Ogaden National Liberation Front** adopted a Transitional Charter that established the TGE. The new government included an 87-member Council of Representatives and a **National Charter** that functioned as a transitional **constitution**. There were 32 political groups represented on the Council of Representatives, but EPRDF-allied groups held 32 of the 87 seats. The TGE included a 17-member, ethnically mixed **Council of Ministers**. The OLF held four of the ministerial positions. The Council of Representatives elected **Meles Zenawi** as chairman of the Council of Representatives and president of Ethiopia. The TGE sought to build the institutions and infrastructure necessary to help Ethiopia establish a democracy and market-oriented **economy**. The TGE decentralized power, demobilized the army, and established independent courts.

Despite the participation of various political and ethnic groups in the TGE, violent clashes occurred throughout many parts of Ethiopia. Critics maintained that this instability had resulted from the dominance of the EPRDF and its allies in the TGE. As a result, in June 1992, the OLF withdrew from the government. In March 1993, the TGE expelled members of the Southern Ethiopia Peoples' Democratic Coalition. Despite these developments, President Meles pledged to oversee the formation of a multiparty democracy. In June 1994, there were **elections** for a 547-member Constituent Assembly that adopted the constitution of the Federal Democratic Republic of Ethiopia. In May and June 1995, there were elections for Ethiopia's national **Parliament** and regional legislatures. Although most opposition parties boycotted these elections, international and nongovernmental observers concluded that the elections were generally free and fair. After these elections and the establishment of the Federal Democratic Republic of Ethiopia, the transition period was completed.

TRANSITIONAL SECURITY ZONE (TSZ). On 31 July 2000, the United Nations Security Council (UNSC) adopted Resolution 1312, which established the **United Nations Mission in Ethiopia and Eritrea** (UNMEE) that, among other things, would supervise the TSZ. On 12 February 2001, the TSZ, a 15-mile (25-kilometer)-deep demobilized strip that runs the entire length of the Eritrean side of the border, came into existence. The TSZ allowed for the disengagement of Ethiopian and Eritrean forces, the UN-monitored restoration of Eritrean civil administration, and the return of **refugees** to those areas occupied by Ethiopia after the battles of May 2000.

During 2000–2003, numerous problems plagued the TSZ, including a clash between Ethiopian militiamen and UNMEE (4–5 October 2002) and Eritrean accusations that UNMEE personnel had tortured villagers and looted their property (9 October 2002). There also have been mutual accusations between Ethiopia and Eritrea about various TSZ violations.

TRANSPORTATION. Ethiopia presents an enormous challenge to surface transport due to the extremes in its topography and the fact that it is landlocked. Divided by the **Rift Valley** with high plateaus on each side, bisected by numerous rivers, and several major mountain ranges, the terrain has presented builders of roads and railroads with huge obstacles. A severe rainy season in parts of Ethiopia adds to the construction and maintenance woes. There is only one railroad in the country—the narrow-gauge **Addis Ababa–Djibouti Railway**. More than 90 percent of all freight and passengers move by road. Ethiopia has large fleets of trucks and buses owned by both the government and private entrepreneurs. There are about 2,550 miles (4,100 kilometers) of paved road and 13,000 miles (21,000 kilometers) of all-weather, unpaved road. There are many additional seasonal tracks that can be navigated during parts of the year by trucks, four-wheel-drive vehicles, and even sturdy sedans. For a country the size of Texas and California combined, this still leaves a lot of territory without all-weather roads. The road system tends to radiate in all directions from **Addis Ababa** like the spokes of a wheel.

One of the positive contributions of the Italian occupation of Ethiopia from 1936–1941 was road construction. Although their construction was undertaken to consolidate Italy's rule over the country, many of these roads, some of them spectacular feats of engineering, remain in use to the present day. By 1941, there were about 4,350 miles (7,000 kilometers) of all-weather roads in Ethiopia. Road construction then stagnated due to lack of funds until 1951, when the government established the Imperial Highway Authority. Initially, the **World Bank** and the U.S. Bureau of Public Roads helped significantly to increase road infrastructure. The **Derg** restructured the Imperial Highway Authority as the Ethiopian Road Authority and Rural Roads Task Force. The latter developed rural roads outside the main system and extended feeder roads. In recent years, the **Ethiopian People's Revolutionary Democratic Front** has given a high priority to road improvement and new construction. The World Bank, the European Union, Italy, and Japan provide much of the financing. The government gave special attention to paving or repaving the road from Addis Ababa to the port of **Asab** in Eritrea and from Addis Ababa to **Awasa**. Following the outbreak of conflict with Eritrea in 1998, Eritrea put **Asab** off limits and Ethiopia began discussions with Sudan to use the **Red Sea** port of Port Sudan and to improve the road from **Gondar** to Port Sudan.

Except for brief stretches on a few slow-moving rivers where small craft can operate, there is effectively no transport by waterway. During the first half of the 20th century, there was important barge and river traffic on the Baro/**Sobat River** between **Gambela** in Ethiopia and the point where the Sobat connects with the White Nile in Sudan. Silting and security problems along the river ended this traffic. Surprisingly, Ethiopia still has a merchant marine fleet from the time that it had access to Red Sea ports. When Eritrea broke away in 1991, Ethiopia became landlocked. Until the conflict with Eritrea, these vessels used the ports of Asab and **Massawa** in Eritrea. Now they focus on Djibouti and will probably become more active in Port Sudan. Ethiopia's merchant marine has 11 vessels of at least 1,000 gross registered tons (GRT) for a total of 85,382 GRT. The fleet includes six cargo ships, one container vessel, one petroleum tanker, and three roll-on/roll-off ships. In 2002, Ethiopian Shipping Lines S. C. employed 283 seagoing staff and 142 shore-based personnel. *See also* AVIATION.

TREATY OF WICHALE (UCCIALLI, WACHALE). On 2 May 1889, Menelik (later **Menelik II**) and **Pietro Antonelli** concluded this treaty. Some of its more important articles pledged both countries to maintain perpetual "peace and friendship" (Article I), appoint diplomatic and consular officers (Article II), establish a special commission to define the border between Ethiopia and Italian-occupied Eritrea (Article III), allow Menelik to import arms and ammunition through **Massawa** (Article VI), and prohibit **slavery** (Article XIV). The Italian version of Article XVII required Ethiopia to conduct its **foreign policy** through Rome. However, the **Amharic** version indicated that the emperor could use Italy if he so desired. On 12 October 1889, Italy notified Britain, France, Germany, and Russia that, according to this article, it had responsibility for Ethiopia's foreign policy. In 1890, Menelik II learned of the mistranslation but failed to resolve the matter after protracted negotiations with Italy. In February 1893, he denounced the Treaty of Wichale.

TRIPARTITE TREATY. Two factors contributed to the adoption of this treaty on 13 December 1906. Britain, France, and Italy had been working at cross-purposes in Ethiopia by competing for influence at the court of **Menelik II**. These three countries also feared that Ethiopia would experience considerable instability after the emperor's death as he had not named a successor.

To resolve these problems, Britain, France, and Italy signed the Tripartite Treaty in London. Accordingly, they promised to cooperate in maintaining Ethiopia's political and territorial integrity. The treaty's other important articles included a pledge to refrain from agricultural, commercial, and industrial concessions that would be in the interests of one state but injurious to the other two and to build the **Addis Ababa–Djibouti Railway**. Despite the determination of their respective governments to cooperate, the British, French, and Italian legations in **Addis Ababa** continued to compete with one another to dominate Ethiopian affairs. *See also* FOREIGN POLICY.

TSADKAN GEBRE TENSAE (1954–). Born on 12 September 1954. Chief of General Staff of the **Ethiopian National Defense Forces** (ENDF) and commander of ground forces (1991–2001). Born in a village near Adigrat, **Tigray Region**, where he attended elementary and secondary school (1960–1971). Tsadkan then studied at the **Haile Selassie I University** (1972–1975) but left before graduating to join the **Tigray People's Liberation Front** (TPLF). He rose quickly through the ranks and became an aide to TPLF commander Seye Abraha (1980) and a member of the Central Committee (1983–1991). Tsadkan also served as operational commander for the final assault on **Addis Ababa**. He then became chief of staff of the Ethiopian **Armed Forces** (1991–1995) and chief of staff of the ENDF. In 1995, Tsadkan received a M.A. in business administration from Britain's Open University.

As ENDF chief of staff and commander of ground forces, he worked tirelessly to improve its military capabilities and to professionalize the officer corps. Tsadkan also enjoyed a good reputation among the rank and file. More importantly, he was responsible for the ENDF's decisive military victory during the **Ethiopian-Eritrean War (1998–2000).**

After a TPLF Central Committee meeting on 15–18 March 2001, Prime Minister **Meles Zenawi** purged many of its members because of ideological differences. On 26 May 2001, Meles then sacked Tsadkan after he refused to order the armed forces to come to his aid. For more than a year, Tsadkan lived quietly in Addis Ababa while his family took refuge in the United States. In late 2002, Tsadkan undertook a United Nations **Economic Commission for Africa** mission to South Africa to help examine the impact of **human immunodeficiency virus/ acquired immune deficiency syndrome** on Africa's military capabilities. He then joined his family in the United States and enrolled in George Washington University's graduate program.

TSAMAI PEOPLE AND LANGUAGE. Some 10,000 Tsamai, who are known by numerous other names, reside in the **lowlands** west of Lake Chamo and west of the **Dirasha** and **Konso peoples**. They live along the banks of the Weyito River, where they are mixed subsistence farmers and practice flood irrigation. They eat honey, wild game, and fish but eat beef and mutton only on special occasions. The Tsamai traditionally relied on rainmakers and they consulted black stones for omens before engaging in any important activity and to explain unusual events. Their society is structured around an age-set system. They speak an east Cushitic **language** that has high lexical similarity with **Gawwada** dialects, 61 percent with **Bussa,** and 31 percent with Konso. They use Konso for trade.

– U –

UDUK PEOPLE AND LANGUAGE. The Uduk originate in neighboring Sudan. Most now in Ethiopia live in **refugee** camps, especially at Bonga east of **Gambela** town on the main road to Gore. Uduk is a term that came into use during colonial times; the people are not known locally by that name. Neighboring tribes refer to them in several ways. The northern Uduk call themselves *'kwanim pa* and the southern Uduk prefer *Kamus.* The term means "people of the homeland." They number more than 20,000 in Sudan and Ethiopia. The Uduk **language**, *'twam pa* or "speech of the homeland," is Nilo-Saharan and is related to Koman. It is, however, not mutually intelligible with any other language. The sound of the spoken language is crisp, rhythmic, and musical with sharp monosyllables, precisely contrasted tones, implosives, and explosives. Wendy James produced a thorough study entitled *'Kwanim Pa: The Making of the Uduk People.*

UNITED NATIONS ECONOMIC COMMISSION FOR AFRICA. *See* ECONOMIC COMMISSION FOR AFRICA.

UNITED NATIONS MISSION IN ETHIOPIA AND ERITREA (UNMEE). The **Ethiopian-Eritrean War** ended on 18 June 2000, when both nations signed a **Cessation of Hostilities Agreement** or the Algiers Agreement. On 31 July 2000, the United Nations Security Council (UNSC) approved the deployment of UNMEE observers, plus civilian support staff, to the cease-fire line until 31 January 2001. On 15 September 2000, the UNSC adopted Resolution 1320, which further defined the UNMEE's size and role. Mission strength was set at 4,200 troops. The UNMEE's mission was to monitor the peace accord's implementation, confirm the withdrawal of Ethiopian forces to positions occupied on 6 May 1998, ensure that Eritrean units remained 25 kilometers away from redeployed Ethiopian troops, supervise the **Transitional Security Zone** (TSZ), and coordinate and provide technical assistance for land-mine clearance. On 15 September 2000, a 40-man team of unarmed UNMEE observers arrived in **Addis Ababa** and Asmara. On 23 March 2001, Ethiopia and the UN concluded a status of forces agreement that clarified the legal status of UNMEE civilian and military personnel in Ethiopia.

The UNMEE has been subjected to a constant barrage of criticism from Ethiopia and Eritrea involving violations of the TSZ and mistreatment of villagers in the TSZ. Both countries accuse the UNMEE of showing favoritism toward the other. For example, in April 2002, Ethiopia declared Major General Patrick Cammaert (Netherlands), who had been appointed UNMEE commander on 1 November 2000, persona non grata for his "political bias" toward Eritrea and for taking a group of journalists via Eritrea to the disputed town of Badme. On 10 October 2002, the UN named Britain's Major General Robert Gordon as his replacement.

UNIVERSITY COLLEGE OF ADDIS ABABA. *See* EDUCATION, UNIVERSITY.

URBINO, GIUSTO DA (1814–1856). Italian Capuchin **missionary**. Born as Jacopo Curtopassi on 30 August 1814 in Matraia, Lucca. In 1831, he joined the Capuchin order and received the religious name of Giusto da Urbino. In December 1846, he landed at **Massawa** as a member of a religious mission led by **Gugliemo Massaia**. Shortly thereafter, he settled in **Bagemder**. Apart from his religious duties, Urbino studied many of Ethiopia's **languages** and compiled a **Ge'ez**-Latin dictionary (1845). In May 1855, **Abuna Abba Salama**, who was anti-Catholic, expelled Urbino and other Roman **Catholic** missionaries. In April 1856, he intended to return to Ethiopia via Sudan, but died in Khartoum.

– V –

VILLAGIZATION PROGRAM. **Mengistu Haile Mariam**'s 1978 revolution-day speech endorsed a commitment to collectivization and set the scene for the villagization program. This scheme aimed to increase the number of peasant households participating in **agricultural** producers' cooperatives. In 1985, villagization or the concentration of scattered homesteads into centralized villages began. During its first year in Hararge, the **Derg** reportedly constructed 150,000 houses in some 2,000 villages. It quickly became accepted as national policy and a major national goal. The Derg established a National Coordinating

Committee for Villagization and the program spread to **Shoa**, Arsi, **Kafa**, **Wollega**, and **Ilubabor** in the first year. Officials laid out houses in precise geometrical grids and the houses tended to look alike.

By September 1987, the Derg claimed that eight million people had moved to 1.3 million houses. This represented 22 percent of the rural **population** at the time. The campaign envisaged villagizing the entire rural population of about 40 million. As a result of security problems, the Derg excluded **Tigray** and Eritrea. Many persons moved reluctantly and some areas such as **Gojam** and western Shoa resisted. Some critics said the villages were little more than strategic hamlets in places like Bale and parts of Hararge. Other areas such as Arsi and parts of Shoa were better suited to the program. In the end, villagization involved an enormous amount of work and disruption for very uncertain future benefits. The government usually failed to provide the promised social services and many villagers returned to their original homes after the Derg's fall.

– W –

WABE SHEBELLE RIVER. (about 700 miles; 1,340 kilometers long.) The Wabe Shebelle originates in a deep valley north of the **Bale Mountains** and receives tributaries from the southeastern slopes of the Chercher Mountains of Hararge. It also receives drainage from the **Harar-Jijiga** area. The lower part of the river's banks contains some significant irrigation projects. The river is one of the main sources of water in the dry **Ogaden** region. The principal towns along the lower reaches of the Wabe Shebelle are Gode, Kelafo, and Mustahil. The Wabe Shebelle crosses into Somalia and the river disappears in the sand before it reaches the Indian Ocean. The **Oromo** inhabit the upper reaches of the river and the **Somali** the lower section.

WAG. Wag is an ancient **Agaw** principality that converted to Christianity in the sixth century. It is located in **Amhara Region** north of **Lalibela**. Scholars believe that Wag had been an important center of political power during the period following the collapse of the **Axumite** empire during the ninth century and before the rise at Lalibela of the **Zagwe dynasty**. Wag's major town is Sekota, which is architecturally significant for its two-story stone houses. Wag is arid and densely populated. Today, most inhabitants subsist on cultivation from overused and degraded soil that has low production yields. Wag was at the center of the terrible **famine** that struck Ethiopia in the mid-1980s.

WAGSHUM GOBAZE. *See* TAKLA GIYORGIS.

WALAMO KINGDOM. *See* WOLAYTTA PEOPLE AND LANGUAGE.

WAL WAL INCIDENT (UAL UAL). On 23 November 1934, an Anglo-Ethiopian boundary commission, which was surveying the boundary between British Somaliland (now Somaliland) and Ethiopia, arrived in Wal Wal, a settlement in southeast Ethiopia about 62 miles (100 kilometers) from the border. An Italian force, which had earlier deployed from Italian Somalia, confronted the commission. The British protested the Italian presence but withdrew to avoid an incident.

However, the Ethiopians refused to depart. On 5–7 December 1934, there was a clash between the Ethiopian and Italian troops. The Italian commander sent an ultimatum to **Addis Ababa**, demanding reparations, an apology, a salute to the Italian flag, and the punishment of the Ethiopian soldiers involved in the incident. **Haile Selassie** refused to accede to these demands and sought to resolve the problem through arbitration in accordance with the 1928 Ethiopian-Italian treaty of friendship. Italian dictator Benito Mussolini rejected this proposal. On 3 January 1935, Haile Selassie took the matter to the **League of Nations**. On 29 January 1935, another incident occurred at Afdub, near Wal Wal, in which Ethiopian troops killed five **askaris** who belonged to an Italian unit. On 10 February 1935, Mussolini mobilized two army divisions and subsequently announced that Italy was prepared to spend $850 million in a two-year campaign to gain "complete satisfaction." Meanwhile, the League continued its search for a solution to the crisis. On 4 September 1935, the League announced that neither Ethiopia nor Italy was responsible for the Wal Wal incident. Less than a month later, Italy invaded Ethiopia. *See also* ITALIAN-ETHIOPIAN WAR (1935–1936).

WAR CRIMES. *See* CHEMICAL WEAPONS.

WARQNAH ISHETE (1865–1952). Physician, educator, and diplomat. Born on 21 October 1865 in **Gondar**. In 1867, Emperor **Tewodros II** took Warqnah's family and other prominent people of Gondar to his mountain fortress of Magdala. The family eventually abandoned Warqnah. Shortly after **Robert Napier**'s expedition arrived in Ethiopia (1867), Colonel Charles Chamberlain, a British officer attached to the 23rd Indian Pioneer Regiment, adopted Warqnah and took him back to India. After Chamberlain died (1871), Warqnah entered a mission school in Amritsar. The **missionaries** changed his name to Charles W. Martin. In 1882, he graduated from Lahore Medical College. In 1887, Warqnah received an appointment as assistant surgeon in the British medical service in India. Two years later, he resigned his position and went to Scotland to continue his medical studies at Edinburgh University. In 1890, Warqnah returned to India and became a district medical officer and civil surgeon in Burma.

During 1898–1901, he was in the service of **Menelik II**. Warqnah then served as medical officer in a British military expedition against the Mad Mullah (Muhammad Abdile Hassan) in Somaliland. In February 1902, he returned to Burma. The following year, Warqnah participated in another expedition against the Mad Mullah. In 1908–1915, he was medical officer at the British legation in **Addis Ababa**. In 1919, Warqnah returned to Burma, retired after 29 years' service with the British government, and went back to Ethiopia.

The second phase of his career encompassed an array of economic, educational, diplomatic, medical, and social activities. Among other things, Warqnah operated farms and flour mills, headed a school for freed **slaves** (1925), served as director for the Tafari Makonnen School (1925–1930), and received an appointment as governor of Chercher (1930) and later of Danakil (1933). In 1927, he went to New York and negotiated a $20 million contract with the J. G. White Engineering Company to build the **Lake Tana** dam. In 1935–1937, Warqnah was Ethiopian minister in Britain but eventually moved to India. In 1941, he returned to Ethiopia and continued to serve **Haile Selassie** until his death. *See also* HEALTH.

WAVELL, ARCHIBALD PERCIVAL (1883–1950). British soldier. Born on 5 May 1883 in Colchester and educated at Winchester and the Royal Military College, Sandhurst (1900). Over the next 40 years, Wavell served in South Africa, India, Russia, Ypres, Palestine, and Transjordan. He also held several positions in the War Office.

In August 1939, Wavell became general officer commander in chief Middle East, which included Ethiopia. He immediately sent for **Daniel Sandford**, who arrived in Cairo on 1 September 1939 and assumed command of the Ethiopian section of the Middle East intelligence bureau. Sandford also started planning for a rebellion in Ethiopia. Wavell approved Sandford's plan to create **Mission 101** despite objections by Stewart Symes, governor general of Sudan, and Major General **William Platt**.

In October 1939, Wavell and **Anthony Eden** arrived in Khartoum to find out why so little had been done to liberate Ethiopia. The two concluded that **patriot** resistance had been growing but poor British leadership had failed to plan for an offensive. After arriving back in Cairo, Wavell ordered **Orde Wingate** to Khartoum to organize an invasion force that eventually became known as **Gideon Force**. He also facilitated **Haile Selassie**'s return to Ethiopia despite opposition from Symes and Platt. Wavell's strong leadership undoubtedly played a large role in the quick Allied victory in Ethiopia.

During 1943–1947, Wavell served as viceroy of India. After retirement, he became president of the Royal Society of Literature and the Kipling, Browning, Poetry, and Virgil Societies. Wavell died on 24 May 1950 in London.

WEAVING. *See* HANDICRAFTS.

WEBE HAYLA MARYAM (1799–1867). Ruler of **Tigray** and Semen (1831–1855). Born in Semen, a place ruled by his father. During his youth, Webe helped his father to expand his domain toward Walqayet and Woggara west of Tigray. After his father's death (1826), the elders selected Webe over his half brother **Dajazmach** Marso Hayla Maryam, who was supposed to have succeeded his father, to be their chief.

During 1826–1831, Webe engaged in a series of conspiracies and military campaigns to solidify his position, eliminate his enemies, and expand his domain. Finally, in February 1831, Webe and an ally named **Ras** Mareye launched a successful attack against Dajazmach Sibagadis, who ruled Tigray (1818–1831). This campaign left Webe in control of Tigray. He unsuccessfully sought to acquire foreign aid and technicians by making overtures to Britain, France, and the Vatican.

In 1842, Webe and Beru Goshu of **Gojam** attacked Ras **Alula Qubi**, who controlled most of central and northern Ethiopia. Eventually, however, he had to withdraw because of a successful counteroffensive by Beru Aligaz, an ally of Ras Alula. A short while later, Webe repaired relations with Alula and the two of them launched an unsuccessful campaign against Kassa Haylu (later **Tewodros II**). In 1854, Webe agreed to pay tribute to Kassa, who rejected the offering. On 9 February 1855, Kassa defeated Webe's forces at the Battle of Derasge and imprisoned his enemy. Webe gained his freedom after Kassa married his daughter. A subsequent jail term hastened Webe's death.

WELDE-GIYORGIS WELDE-YOHANNIS (c. 1894–1981). Born at Gubela in **Shoa** Province of peasant farmers and educated at various church schools. Welde-Giyorgis was a master of *qene* **poetry**. In 1920, Tafari Makonnen, later **Haile Selassie**, summoned him to **Addis Ababa** to help translate religious books from **Ge'ez** to **Amharic**. He subsequently became one of Ethiopia's first journalists. During the Italian occupation of Ethiopia (1936–1941), the authorities arrested Welde-Giyorgis and forced him to work on a Fascist newspaper in Addis Ababa. After Italy's defeat (1941), Welde-Giyorgis helped start the *Addis Zemen* (New Era) newspaper. In 1966, the Ministry of Information accorded him the title of "Father of Ethiopian Newspapers." He became an adviser to several ministers of information. He was author of some 24 books, of which the most famous was the novel *Agazi,* which was used as a secondary-school textbook for teaching Amharic for many years prior to the 1974 revolution. Welde-Giyorgis died on 19 December 1981.

WELLBY, MONTAGU SINCLAIR (1866–1900). British soldier and explorer. Born on 10 October 1866 in London. Educated at the University College School, Rugby, and Royal Military College, Sandhurst. In August 1886, Wellby received a commission as lieutenant in the 18th Hussars. In 1894, he obtained a promotion to captain and then served as regimental adjutant (1897–1898). Wellby began his career as an explorer by making two trips to northern Somalia to map the area inhabited by the Dulbahante people (1894–1895) and a journey to China and the Central Asian countries of Mongolia and Tibet (1896).

In August 1898, the War Office's Intelligence Division asked Wellby to accompany John Lane Harrington, the British agent in **Addis Ababa**, to Ethiopia. On 7 September 1898, Wellby arrived at Harrington's camp near the **Somali** port of Zeila and informed Harrington that he planned to explore **Lake Rudolf** before proceeding to the **Nile River**. Since Harrington doubted that **Menelik II** would approve such an expedition, Wellby proceeded to Berbera in hopes of continuing his journey. However, local British officials refused to sanction his trip because it would violate boundary treaties. On 25 October 1898, he rejoined Harrington and went to Addis Ababa. Shortly afterwards, Menelik II allowed him to travel to Lake Rudolf under Ethiopian escort.

On 18 December 1898, Wellby, in command of a 44-man column (30 Ethiopians, 9 Somalis, and 5 Sudanese), departed Addis Ababa. In mid-March 1899, he arrived at Lake Rudolf's northern shore. After exploring Lake Rudolf and the **Omo River**, Wellby proceeded westward toward Omdurman, Sudan. On 15 July 1899, he informed the Royal Geographical Society that he had succeeded in mapping the area between Lake Rudolf and the Nile. In late 1899, Wellby returned to Britain before joining his unit in South Africa. On 5 August 1900, he died at Paardekop of wounds received in action against a Boer unit at Mertzicht.

WESTERN SOMALIA LIBERATION FRONT (WSLF). Since the late 1960s, this movement had an erratic existence. In 1975, it "reestablished" itself as the WSLF with the objective of recovering the **Ogaden**. Its 15-man committee, located in the Ogaden, was under joint **Somali-Oromo** leadership. On 15 January 1976, the WSLF held a conference near **Harar** and decided to form another wing called the Somali-Abo Liberation Front to represent Arusi, Bale, and Sidamo provinces and the Oromos who wanted separation from Ethiopia and inclusion in a **Greater Somalia**.

During the early months of the **Ogaden War (1977–1978)**, the WSLF succeeded in driving many Ethiopian troops out of the

Ogaden. By mid-November 1977, the 6,000-man WSLF, supported by the Somali National Army, had occupied all the Somali-speaking areas of the Ogaden and had laid siege to **Harar**. After the Ethiopian **armed forces** scored a decisive victory over the Somali National Army, the WSLF weakened largely because Somali military support had waned. Nevertheless, the WSLF continued to launch some periodic, low-level operations. On 22 January 1984, for example, the WSLF attacked the **Addis Ababa–Djibouti Railway**. Shortly afterward, however, it announced a temporary halt in military operations against Ethiopia because of an internal dispute within the organization. Many of its leaders maintained that Somalia had used the WSLF to support its expansionist policies and now argued for autonomy within a federal Ethiopian union. On 15 August 1984, these dissidents broke away from the WSLF and established the **Ogaden National Liberation Front**. Afterwards, the WSLF virtually disappeared. However, some pro-Somali WSLF elements continued to receive modest support from Mogadishu for a decade after the Ogaden War. After the **Derg's** downfall (1991), the remnants of the WSLF adopted a pro-**Ethiopian People's Revolutionary Democratic Front** (EPRDF) policy while on 18 July 1991, anti-EPRDF elements signed a merger agreement with the ONLF. The pro-government WSLF faction was the only western Somali political organization that signed the Ethiopian Transitional Charter for Peace and Stability (1991). *See also* OGADEN WAR (1964); SOMALI REGION.

WHITE TERROR. *See* ALL-ETHIOPIAN SOCIALIST MOVEMENT; ETHIOPIAN PEOPLE'S REVOLUTIONARY PARTY; RED TERROR.

WICHALE. *See* TREATY OF WICHALE.

WILDLIFE. Although Ethiopia is larger than Texas and California combined, its high **population** growth rate and current population of more than 70 million has put considerable pressure on the land and significantly reduced the amount of wildlife in the past century. Poaching, civil war, **deforestation**, burning of land, overgrazing, and periodic drought have contributed to the decrease in wildlife. It takes a real effort to see most of the species remaining in Ethiopia. Some are confined to small, isolated parts of the country. The following wildlife can still be seen in Ethiopia: baboon, black rhinoceros, buffalo, bushpig, cheetah, civet cat, crocodile, dik-dik, duiker, eland, elephant, forest hog, gazelle, gerenuk, giraffe, greater and lesser kudu, guereza or colobus monkey, hartebeest, hippopotamus, hyena, impala, jackal, klipspringer, leopard, lion, Menelik's bushbuck, mountain nyala, Nile lechwe, oryx, reedbuck, Simien fox, tiang, vervet monkey, Walia ibex, warthog, waterbuck, white-eared kob, and zebra. *See also* ETHIOPIAN WILDLIFE AND NATURAL HISTORY SOCIETY; NATIONAL PARKS.

WINGATE, ORDE (1903–1944). British soldier. Liberator of **Addis Ababa**. Born on 26 February 1903 in Naini Tal, India. Educated at Hill Side, a private preparatory school, and Charterhouse School. On 3 February 1921, Wingate entered the Royal Military Academy, Woolwich. On 11 July 1923, he passed out of Woolwich and was gazetted to the Royal Garrison Artillery. In January 1926, Wingate received a place at the prestigious Army School of Equitation, Weedon. On 5 October 1926, he enrolled at the School of Oriental Studies in London to study Arabic. Wingate began his African career by serving in the Sudan Defense Force (1928–1933). He then explored the Libyan desert (1933). After serving with various artillery units in Britain (1933–1936), he received a posting to Palestine and Transjordan (1936–1939).

After the outbreak of **World War II**, Wingate played a significant role in the Allied campaign in the **Horn of Africa**. On 6 November 1940, he arrived in Khartoum with orders to work with **Haile Selassie** to organize resistance in preparation for an invasion of Italian-occupied Ethiopia. On 20 January 1941, the unit—known as **Gideon Force**—crossed into Ethiopia at Um Idla, where the emperor joined Wingate. There was little resistance to Gideon Force and, on 5 May 1941, he and Haile Selassie entered Addis Ababa. Despite Wingate's impressive victory, some influential British officials resented his intense loyalty to the emperor. As a result, he departed Ethiopia prematurely and returned to Britain and received a minor posting to the British Home Guard.

However, on 24 February 1942, Wingate received a promotion to brigadier and a mission to organize a guerrilla force comprised of

British, Indian, and Burmese soldiers to fight against the Japanese in Burma. His efforts led to a promotion to major-general (1943). On 24 March 1944, he died in a plane crash over the Naga jungles in north Assam before completing his mission. Wingate remains a hero in Britain and Ethiopia. *See also* SANDFORD, DANIEL ARTHUR; ITALIAN-ETHIOPIAN WAR; MISSION 101.

WOLAYTTA PEOPLE AND LANGUAGE. The Wolaytta, often spelled Wolaita, number about two million and are known by a number of other names, including Walamo, Ualamo, Uba, and Ometo. Located to the west and north of Lake Abaya, the **Gamo-Gofa-Dawro** live to their west and south, the **Sidama** to the east, and the **Hadiyya** and **Kambata** to the north. The Wolaytta reportedly paid tribute to Emperor **Amda Seyon** (1312–1344). Three successive dynasties ruled the people. The **Damot** kingdom was the first dynasty. The second dynasty was based in Kuca and lasted until about 1550. Islamic invasions briefly overran the Wolaytta in the 1530s, but they never came under Muslim control. A third dynasty arose about 1550–1570 that had a line of 14 kings. By the late 18th century, there was a kingdom of Walamo that included Konta, Kullo, Kuca, Tambaro, and Gamo. It became tributary to the **Kafa** kingdom until the last king, T'ona, was conquered by **Menelik II** in 1894 and taken prisoner to **Shoa** Province. Before its conquest by Menelik II, there was a local feudal hierarchy and the highest office was commander of the cavalry.

The Wolaytta are a homogeneous people and live in one of Ethiopia's most densely populated rural areas. They are **agriculturists**; corn and *ensete* are staple crops. Cash crops include **coffee**, fruit, ginger, **cotton**, and tobacco. They live in large beehive-shaped huts built in the middle of gardens. The roofs have a pole on which one or more ostrich eggs are impaled. Although most Wolaytta are **Ethiopian Orthodox** and **Protestants**, some are Muslims and their pagan religion survives in a few areas. The supreme being, called Tosa, resides in the sky. The most popular deity is the spirit of the **Omo River**, to whom they sacrifice goats and chickens. The spirit of Lake Abaya is especially important to **women**. Wolaytta is a north Omotic **language**. It has more than 80 percent lexical similarity with Gamo, Gofa, and Dorze and more than 40 percent lexical similarity with Maale and Koorete. Wolaytta is an official literary language.

WOLDE GIORGIS WOLDE YOHANNES (c. 1902–1976). Government official and confidant of **Haile Selassie.** Born in Bulga, **Shoa** Province, of humble parents. Educated at the Ecole Impériale Menelik II in **Addis Ababa.** Wolde Giorgis began his career as a clerk and interpreter in an Addis Ababa hospital. In 1926, he went to Geneva where he served in the Ethiopian mission to the **League of Nations.** In the 1930s, Wolde Giorgis became private secretary to Haile Selassie. After the outbreak of the **Italian-Ethiopian War,** he accompanied the emperor into exile in Britain.

On 10 May 1941, Haile Selassie appointed Wolde Giorgis minister of the pen, an influential position that enabled him to become one of the most powerful men in Ethiopia. He also managed the Society for the Unification of Ethiopia and Eritrea, which subsidized Eritrea's Unionist Party. In 1943, Wolde Giorgis became minister of the interior, a position that enabled him to tighten his control over the provincial administration. In 1949, Wolde Giorgis relinquished this portfolio and then became minister of justice. On 25 April 1955, Wolde Giorgis's opponents, led by Tafere Worq Kidane Wold, persuaded Haile Selassie to sack him. Haile Selassie then appointed Wolde Giorgis as governor of the remote Arusi Province (1955–1960). He subsequently served as governor of Gema Goffa Province (1960–1961). In 1961, Wolde Giorgis eventually went into exile and died in Britain on 29 July 1976.

WOLLEGA PROVINCE. Wollega was one of the administrative divisions during the **Haile Selassie** government and **Derg** period. It reached the Sudan border; Nekempte was its principal town. After the **Ethiopian People's Revolutionary Democratic Front** (EPRDF) reorganized the regions, Wollega became west Wollega and east Wollega zones of **Oromia Region** and Asosa and Kemashi zones and Bebieg special *woreda* of **Benishangul/Gumuz Region.**

In the late 1880s, **Ras Gobana Dachi** defended western Wollega against Mahdist incursions from the Sudan. In 1886, Emperor **Menelik II** annexed Wollega. The **Oromo Liberation Front,** which developed after the 1974 revolution, drew most of its early support from western Wollega.

WOLLO PROVINCE (WELO, WELLO). Wollo was one of the administrative divisions during the **Haile Selassie** government and the

Derg period. **Dese** and Woldia were two of Wollo's major towns. After the **Ethiopian People's Revolutionary Democratic Front** (EPRDF) rearranged the regions, Wollo ceased to exist. Today, it corresponds roughly to north and south Wollo zones of **Amhara Region** and zones one and four of **Afar Region**. **Lalibela**'s rock churches are in Wollo Province as is the mountain fortress of Magdala where Emperor **Tewodros II** died (1868). The **Zagwe dynasty** ruled from Wollo Province from about 1137 until 1270. In 1909, the incapacitated Emperor **Menelik II** designated his grandson, **Lij Iyasu Mikael**, who was the son of Menelik II's daughter and **Ras Mikael**, the **Oromo** and former Muslim ruler of Wollo, as his successor. Empress **Taytu Betul** quickly usurped power and, on 27 September 1916, **Amhara** nobles deposed Lij Iyasu. The town of Dese in Wollo served as Haile Selassie's last headquarters before he went into exile after the outbreak of the **Italian-Ethiopian War**.

WOMEN. As Ethiopia is a traditional society, it is not surprising that efforts to improve and modernize the status of women have encountered considerable resistance. The 1994 **constitution** takes note of "the historical legacy of inequality and discrimination suffered by women in Ethiopia" and guarantees them "equal rights with men." This guarantee is often not applied in practice and the constitution remains in conflict with the 1960 civil code and the 1957 penal code, both of which are still in force. The 1960 civil code, for example, recognizes the husband as the legal head of the family and designates him as the sole guardian of children over five years of age. Revisions to the civil and penal codes are under review and a draft family law has the goal of ending discriminatory elements of the 1960 civil code.

There is limited juridical recognition of common law marriage irrespective of the number of years the couple has been married, the number of children produced, and common property accumulated. Should the relationship end, the woman is entitled to only three months' financial support. In practice, a husband has no obligation to provide financial assistance to his family. The traditional custom of abduction of women and girls for marriage is illegal under the penal code but still widely practiced in some parts of Ethiopia. The constitution defines the age of consent for marriage as 15 for females and l8 for males. Early-childhood marriage is common in rural areas, where 85 percent of Ethiopians live. Girls as young as nine are sometimes forced into arranged marriages.

In 1997, the government adopted a National Program of Action to enhance the status of women. The program seeks to expand **educational** and work opportunities for women, improve women's access to **health** care, and educate women about certain unhealthy traditional practices such as early marriage and **female circumcision**. Girls now attend school in larger percentages in some regions and there has been a decline in early marriages and marriages by abduction. Due in large part to Ethiopia's overwhelming **poverty**, there has been little progress in the areas of health care or wage employment.

Wife beating and marital rape are common social problems. While women have recourse to the **police** and the court system, societal norms and limited police and **judicial** infrastructure prevent most women from seeking redress, especially in rural areas. In many cases, women are unaware of their legal rights. Child prostitution remains fairly common, especially in resort towns and at truck stops. Clients prize young girls because they believe that they are free of sexually transmitted diseases. Pervasive poverty, migration to urban areas, and limited educational and job opportunities increase the incidence of child prostitution. Child labor is also widespread and enhances the possibilities for sexual abuse and rape.

WONDO GENET. The Wondo Genet hot springs resort is located south of **Addis Ababa** and about 9 miles (15 kilometers) southeast of Shashemene. Surrounded by a dense forest and populated by many birds and colobus and vervet monkeys, Wondo Genet is a favorite getaway for Ethiopians and foreigners alike. The swimming pools are fed by water from the hot springs. Hiking trails from the resort allow visitors to see bushbucks, hyenas, and baboons.

WOODWORK. *See* HANDICRAFTS.

WOREDA (WEREDA). **Amharic** term for an administrative unit roughly equivalent to a district. Several *kebeles* comprise a *woreda* and several woredas constitute an *awaraja* or zone. There are some 600 woredas in Ethiopia. **Oromia Region** has the largest number at 180.

WORKERS' LEAGUE. Political party during the **Derg** period. Senaye Likke, an **Oromo** academic who had been leader of the Ethiopian Students' Union in North America, was the driving force behind the Workers' League. Other important party personalities included **Fikre Selassie Wogderes** who eventually became secretary general of the Derg, and Colonel Daniel Asfaw, who was chief of the Derg's Security Department. In 1972, he returned to Ethiopia and started working for the Pasteur Institute in **Addis Ababa**. Senaye also took a part-time teaching position in **Debre Zeit**, where he met many **air force** personnel from the local air base. The military acquaintances he made during this period eventually formed the core supporters of the Workers' League.

In late 1975, Senaye started a newspaper called *Workers*. In July 1976, he formed the Workers' League, which supported the notion of a peasant rebellion in Bale, part of the Oromo heartland. By September 1976, 313 party members, most of whom belonged to the **armed forces**, had received training in East European countries.

During the **coup (1977)**, Senaye and Colonel Daniel were killed during a shoot-out between supporters of **Mengistu Haile Mariam** and **Teferi Bante**. Other fatalities included Teferi and several of his colleagues. Senaye's death contributed to the decline of the Workers' League. Nevertheless, on 26 February 1977, the Workers' League along with the **All-Ethiopian Socialist Movement**, **Ethiopian Oppressed People's Revolutionary Struggle**, Ethiopian Marxist-Leninist Revolutionary Organization, and **Revolutionary Flame** announced the formation of the Joint Front of Ethiopian Marxist-Leninist Organizations. This coalition sought to provide a platform to bring about the creation of the **Workers' Party of Ethiopia**.

In mid-1978, the **Revolutionary Flame**, supported by the Derg's Security Department and Intelligence Department, started purging the Workers' League. In September 1978, the Derg finally eliminated the Workers' League, ostensibly because it had been plotting to overthrow Mengistu Haile Mariam.

WORKERS' PARTY OF ETHIOPIA (WPE). Established on 12 September 1984. On 6–11 September 1984, the WPE held its founding congress, which included 1,742 delegates and observers from some

75 foreign countries. On 8 September 1984, the congress adopted the WPE's draft constitution and authorized the establishment of central and regional party bodies. On 10 September 1984, the congress elected **Mengistu Haile Mariam** as the WPE's secretary-general, a 135-member Central Committee, and an 11-member Political Bureau with six alternate members. The congress also dissolved the **Commission for Organizing the Party of the Working People of Ethiopia**.

The WPE instituted a democratic centralist structure and made its Central Committee an expanded version of the **Derg**. Most WPE members came from the **armed forces**. The WPE's Political Bureau was the Derg's most important decision-making body. It operated in a fashion similar to that of the Communist Party of the Soviet Union; Secretary-General Mengistu's position generally prevailed. The 1987 **constitution** decreed that the WPE should be the "formulator" of the country's development process and the "leading force" of the state and in society. On 5 March 1990, Mengistu sought to mollify the opposition by replacing the WPE with the Ethiopian Democratic Unity Party. On 18 June 1991, the **Ethiopian People's Revolutionary Democratic Front** formally abolished the WPE. *See also* WORKERS' LEAGUE.

WORLD BANK. Ethiopia has long been one of the World Bank's largest recipients of loans. In fact, the World Bank's first loan to an African country, a highway project, went to Ethiopia (1950). Currently, Ethiopia is the largest African beneficiary of World Bank aid with about $667 million committed in the fiscal year ending in 2001. The World Bank's Ethiopian portfolio consists of 18 projects valued at $1.8 billion in several sectors. Recently approved projects include assistance for a **demobilization campaign** and reintegration of soldiers following the conflict with Eritrea, **human immunodeficiency virus/acquired immune deficiency syndrome**, postwar emergency recovery and rehabilitation, **women**'s development, and conservation of medicinal plants.

Ethiopia has agreed with the World Bank and the **International Monetary Fund** to accept a medium-term macroeconomic framework package and a $150 million Economic Rehabilitation Support Credit from the International Development Association (IDA) to help the government stabilize the **economy**. The World Bank Institute is helping to train a large number of Ethiopians in areas such as anti-**corruption** strategy, safety nets and social funds, economic growth and **poverty** reduction, girls' **education**, and macroeconomic management. *See also* DEBT; TRANSPORTATION.

WORLD WAR I. Ethiopia played no direct role in World War I. However, during 1915–1916, Germany unsuccessfully sought to involve Ethiopia in the conflict. One plan focused on persuading **Addis Ababa** and the Somali rebel Muhammad Abdile Hassan, who was known by his European enemies as the Mad Mullah, to attack British-, French-, and Italian-ruled territories in eastern Africa. Berlin believed that such operations would facilitate a Turkish campaign against Egypt and bolster its military operations in the colony of British East Africa (now Kenya) and German East Africa (later Tanganyika and now Tanzania) by forcing London to redeploy some of its forces from those operational theaters to the **Horn of Africa**. In exchange, Germany promised to recognize any territorial conquests made by Ethiopia or the Mad Mullah. As a goodwill gesture, Berlin and Constantinople (now Istanbul) restored some monastic properties in **Jerusalem** to Ethiopia.

Another scheme involved Leo Frobenius, a noted German Africanist. On 17 November 1914, the German General Staff approved his request to undertake a mission to the Horn of Africa. Frobenius, a personal friend of Emperor Wilhelm II (1859–1941), proposed to deliver secret diplomatic mail to the German consulate in Addis Ababa as Ethiopia, a landlocked country, had been cut off from Germany. More importantly, he wanted to travel to Sudan to organize an uprising of Mahdiya partisans against the British. On 15 February 1915, Frobenius arrived at **Massawa** via Istanbul, Aleppo, Damascus, and the **Red Sea** port of Al-Wajh. The party traveled under the cover of the Fourth German Inner-African Research Expedition. Initially, the Italian authorities allowed the group freedom of movement but, on 23 March 1915, ordered them to leave the colony, thus ensuring the mission's failure.

On 12 April 1916, Major Freiherr Othmar von Stotzingen, who belonged to the 27th Division of the 13th Army Corps (Württemberg), arrived in Damascus and confided in Faisal, the sharif of Mecca's third son, that he was on his way to Yemen to build a telegraph line from southern Arabia to Ethiopia across the Red Sea. Stotzingen also claimed that he wanted to ship arms and ammunition to German East Africa via Ethiopia. He failed to complete either project. *See also* FOREIGN POLICY.

WORLD WAR II. By 1 June 1940, the Italian army in Ethiopia numbered 255,950 troops, 182,000 of whom were **askaris** organized into colonial divisions, brigades, battalions, or Bandi Armatedi Confini groups of irregulars commanded by Italian officers. Eritreans constituted the bulk of askaris but there also were Ethiopians and Somalis who joined askari units.

On 10 June 1941, Italy declared war on Britain and France. This action brought Ethiopia into World War II and boosted the morale of Ethiopians, who had been fighting the Italians since the outbreak of the **Italian-Ethiopian War**. Britain, which had been reluctant to support what many perceived as a "native insurrection" against a European colonial power, quickly devised a strategy to liberate Ethiopia.

On 25 July 1940, London approved **Haile Selassie**'s decision to depart Britain for Sudan to help organize an Allied force to invade Ethiopia. On 12 August 1940, Britain authorized the deployment of **Mission 101**, under the command of Brigadier **Daniel Sandford**, to **Gojam**. On 28 October 1940, **Sir Anthony Eden** chaired a meeting in Khartoum that authorized weapons shipments to Ethiopian forces, which henceforth would be known as "**patriots**." On 20 November 1940, **Orde Wingate** arrived in Gojam to help organize **Gideon Force** and to liberate Ethiopia.

On 19 January 1941, an imperial army numbering some 60,000 British, Indian, and South African troops launched a four-front offensive against **Africa Orientale Italiana** (AOI). On 2 February 1941, a British column, under Lieutenant General **William Platt**'s command, invaded Eritrea and captured Agordat. On 28 March 1941, British troops overcame Italian resistance and occupied Keren. This victory enabled the British to divide their forces. One group moved north and captured **Massawa** (8 April) and **Asab** (12 June) while the other went south into Ethiopia to rendezvous with other Allied units.

On 31 January 1941, elements from the 1st South African Division entered Ethiopia from Moyale, Kenya, and overran Mega (20 February) and Neghelli (23 March). Another force, under General **Alan Gordon Cunningham**'s command invaded Italian Somalia from Kenya, crossed the Juba River, entered Mogadishu (26 February), and captured more than 10,000 prisoners. Cunningham's troops then went into Ethiopia and captured Gabredarre (9 March) and **Jijiga** (19 March). On 30 March 1941, Cunningham occupied **Dire Dawa**, thereby cutting the strategically important **Addis Ababa–Djibouti Railway**. The fourth column deployed to Ethiopia from Sudan and captured Bure (6 March). Four days later, another Allied army went into southern Ethiopia from Kenya. By April 1941, Italian forces were in disarray. On 6 April 1941, South African units occupied Addis Ababa. However, British authorities prevented Haile Selassie from returning to his capital for fear that his presence would cause the general populace to seek revenge against the city's Italian community. Nevertheless, on 5 May 1941, the emperor entered Addis Ababa without British consent. **Amedeo di Savoia,** Duke of Aosta and a 38,000-man army made its last stand at Ambi Alagi. On 19 May 1941, the exhausted Italians surrendered. Although scattered Italian and colonial units continued fighting in **Gondar** until 29 November 1941, the conquest of the AOI was complete. During the course of the AOI campaign, the Italian army lost some 290,000 troops while the Allies suffered only 1,154 casualties. *See also* ABYE ABABA; ARMED FORCES; BADOGLIO, PIETRO; BLACK LIONS; FOREIGN POLICY; GRAZIANI, RODOLFO; IMRU HAILE SELASSIE; MANGASHA JAMBARE; MENGISTU NEWAY.

– X –

XAMIR PEOPLE AND LANGUAGE. Some 80,000 Xamir people live northeast of **Lake Tana** in North Wollo zone of **Amhara Region** and north of Weldiya. The population, which belongs to the **Ethiopian Orthodox Church**, grows wheat and sorghum. The area suffered considerable disruption during the war against the **Derg**. The **Amhara people** surround the Xamir. They speak a Cushitic **language** called Xamtanga that has 45 percent lexical similarity with **Kemant** and is a distinct language from **Agaw**. The Xamir use **Amharic** as a second language although most **women** and older people speak only Xamtanga. There is a desire to develop Xamtanga **literature** and there is an association of Xamtanga-speakers in Weldiya.

– Y –

YARED, SAINT. *See* MUSIC AND INSTRUMENTS.

YEHA. Ethiopia's oldest known capital, Yeha, is believed to date back to the fifth century B.C. and may have been a major center of the Di'amat kingdom, which probably had close ties to the Saba kingdom in Yemen. Located off the main road between **Adwa** and the current zonal capital of Adigrat in **Tigray Region**. Yeha is the site of the Temple of the Moo, a pre-Christian temple that consists of a single walled oblong chamber measuring 66 feet by 50 feet. The roof and second floor of the windowless structure collapsed many years ago. The remaining walls are built of smoothly polished stones, placed on top of each other without the use of mortar, defying earthquakes and the forces of nature for at least 2,500 years. The religion practiced in the temple is not known with certainty but may be linked to the pagan faith of the Sabaen civilization of South Arabia.

For many years, scholars believed that Yeha predated the much more famous Ethiopian capital at **Axum**. Recent research suggests, however, that the two cities existed contemporaneously. It is not known whether Yeha and Axum were separate political centers or whether one ruled over the other. By the time the Axumite empire reached the height of its influence, Yeha had become a town of minimal importance. Europeans have known about Yeha since the 16th century when the famous Portuguese traveler Father **Francisco Alvares** described the temple after spending the night nearby in 1520. Scottish explorer **James Bruce** visited Yeha during his 1769–1772 visit to Ethiopia and British traveler **Henry Salt** wrote about it after returning from an 1809–1810 journey to Ethiopia.

YEM PEOPLE AND LANGUAGE. An estimated 70,000 Yem, Yemsu, or Yemma people constitute a special *woreda* in **Southern Nations, Nationalities and People's Region** (SNNPR) and otherwise live among the **Oromo**, **Gurage**, and **Hadiyya**. Located east of

Jimma, the Yem were once a special district in **Oromia**. The Hadiyya and Gurage peoples live to their east and the Oromo to the west. The Oromo referred to them as *Janjero*, meaning "baboon," a highly derogatory term. In 1894, **Menelik II**'s forces conquered their kingdom, which had an elaborate political administration. Until this time, the kingdom was isolated and had little contact with its neighbors. They are reputedly southwest Ethiopia's most ancient people. In 1420, the Yem were first mentioned by the name Janjero in the victory songs of King Yeshaq. Like many of the peoples in SNNPR, the Yem have formed their own political party known as the Yem Peoples' Democratic Unity Party and they won one seat in the **House of Peoples' Representatives** in the **elections (2000)**. They practice hoe cultivation and are part of the *ensete* culture. Christianity has spread widely among the Yem. They speak an Omotic **language** known as Yemsa, which has 24 percent lexical similarity with Mocha. Young people tend to be bilingual in **Amharic** while older ones are likely to be bilingual in Afan Oromo. *See also* JANJERO KINGDOM.

YOHANNES I (16?–1682). Emperor of Ethiopia (1667–1682). Son of **Fasilidas**. His throne name was Aelaf Saggad. Shortly after becoming emperor, Yohannes I issued an amnesty for all those imprisoned during his father's reign and abolished the cattle tax. One of his first major crises emerged when the clergy of Lasta Province started preaching a doctrine that violated conventional wisdom about the nature of the Trinity. The clergy also threatened to terminate their allegiance to the monarchy unless their views were accepted. In 1668, Yohannes I went to **Gojam** and organized its defenses against the **Oromo**. In 1677, the emperor deployed an expedition against the clergy. The ensuing fighting devastated Lasta Province. During the same year, he convened an **Ethiopian Orthodox Church** (EOC) council that, among other things, passed laws to segregate Muslims, Turks, and Europeans. Yohannes I also informed all Europeans that they would be expelled unless they joined the EOC. In 1669, his troops escorted those Europeans who refused to join the EOC to Sennar. In 1679, Yohannes I convened another EOC council to discuss another letter sent by the Lasta clergy in which they claimed that the Father was incarnate in the Virgin Mary. The emperor responded by sending another expedition to Lasta that ravaged the region. In June 1681,

Yohannes I made his last public appearance at an EOC council at **Gondar** that excommunicated Akala Krestos, who was a follower of **Ewostatewos**. After falling ill at Aringo, near **Debre Tabor**, Yohannes I went to Gondar, where he died on 19 July 1682.

YOHANNES IV (1831–1889). Emperor (21 January 1872–10 March 1889). Last emperor to be referred to as king of Zion. Born as Kassa Abba Bezbez. In 1864, **Tewodros II** appointed him as balambaras and then as **ras** of **Tigray**. After Tewodros II imprisoned **Abuna Abba Salama** after a dispute over the **Ethiopian Orthodox Church**'s land holdings, Kassa rebelled against the emperor. In 1867, he declared Tigray independent and sent a delegation to Egypt to get its own bishop. In 1868, Kassa allied himself with **Robert Cornelis Napier** in exchange for 12 artillery pieces and 750 rifles. After Tewodros II committed suicide on 12 April 1868 rather than surrender to the British, **Takla Giyorgis** crowned himself emperor. Shortly thereafter, he demanded that he take custody of Kassa's bishop. This dispute led to a war that resulted in Takla's imprisonment.

On 21 January 1872, Abuna Atnatyos crowned Kassa as Emperor Yohannes IV. He proved to be a progressive ruler who spent most of his time unifying Ethiopia and thwarting military threats from Egypt, Italy, and the Mahdists of the Sudan. By 1874, Yohannes IV had unified **Bagemder**, **Gojam**, Lasta, and Semen. Defending Ethiopia against foreign encroachment proved to be a more daunting undertaking. Egypt already had blockaded the routes to and from Ethiopia by occupying the primary **Red Sea** ports and Galabat, a Sudanese transshipment point on the border with Ethiopia. In 1873, the emperor sent an unsuccessful diplomatic mission to Europe seeking aid and diplomatic support against Egypt. He subsequently thwarted Cairo's territorial ambitions by scoring impressive victories at the **Battle of Gundet** and the **Battle of Gura**.

Yohannes IV then continued his efforts to reunify Ethiopia. In 1878, he secured Menelik's (later **Menelik II**) submission and subsequently crowned him **negus** of **Shoa**. In 1880, the emperor also crowned **Ras Adal Tessemma** as negus of **Gojam** and **Kafa**. He urged both monarchs to reunify the adjoining regions. However, on 6 June 1882, Menelik and **Takla Haymanot** clashed at the **Battle of**

Embabo. Yohannes IV rebuked both of them. To ensure Shoa's future allegiance, the emperor arranged a marriage between his son, **Ras** Areaya Selasse, and Menelik's daughter, **Zawditu Menelik**.The rise of the Mahdist movement in the Sudan led to **William Hewett**'s arrival in Ethiopia and to the subsequent signing of the **Hewett Treaty** between Britain, Egypt, and Ethiopia. After diplomatic overtures to the Mahdi and his successor, Khalifa Abdullah Muhammed, failed, Yohannes IV's troops clashed with Mahdist forces at Galabat, al-Jirra, and Kufit. On 5 February 1885, Italy, with British approval, took possession of **Massawa** and eventually moved into the interior, thus wrecking the Hewett Treaty. **Ras Alula Qubi,** one of the emperor's most trusted generals, defeated the Italians at the **Battle of Dogali**. As subsequent attacks against the Italians failed, Yohannes IV concluded a truce with them and refocused his attention on the Mahdists, who again rejected his diplomatic overtures. His army therefore engaged them at the **Battle of Metemma**. On 9 March 1889, Yohannes IV was mortally wounded and died the following day. The Ethiopian offensive collapsed, thus enabling the Mahdists to score a victory and to behead the emperor and many senior officials and parade them around the Sudan. *See also* ANGLO-ETHIOPIAN WAR; BATTLE OF KUFIT; FOREIGN POLICY; METEMMA; SHOA.

– Z –

ZAGWE DYNASTY. One of the most obscure periods of Ethiopian history, the Zagwe dynasty lasted from about 1117 until 1270. Following **Axum**'s decline, there was a southward shift in political power from **Tigray** to Lasta in the early 12th century. **Agaw** speakers lived in Lasta's mountains. A chief known as Marara, Marari, or Mara founded the Zagwe dynasty. The capital was located at Adafa in the mountains not far from **Lalibela**. The Zagwe dynasty produced no coinage, inscriptions, or apparently even chronicles. Subsequent writings about the Zagwe rulers often refer to them as usurpers. The Zagwe dynasty is best known for the excavation of spectacular **rock-hewn churches**. The Zagwe rulers took a keen interest in Christianity.

Marara ruled approximately from 1117–1133. His grandson, Yemrehana Krestos (reigned 1133–1172), succeeded him and built one of Lasta's finest cave churches. Located outside Lalibela, it followed the tradition of **Axum**'s churches. His cousin, Harbe, succeeded him. Harbe failed to obtain independence for the **Ethiopian Orthodox Church** from the Coptic Church of Egypt. The best known of the Zagwe rulers and Harbe's brother, Gebra Maskal Lalibela, was the next in line. He is believed to have remained in power until 1212 or 1225. King Lalibela is responsible for the excavation of the rock-hewn churches bearing his name. Lalibela later moved his capital to Roha near the new churches. Lalibela's nephew, Na'akeuto La'ab, succeeded him and built a beautiful church in a cave outside Lalibela. He abdicated in favor of Lalibela's son, Yitbarek. Increasing regional opposition to Zagwe rule coincided with problems in the ruling family. In 1270, the Zagwe dynasty collapsed and power shifted to **Shoa** and the rise of Yekuno Amlak (1270–1285).

ZAMANA MASAFENT. *See* ERA OF THE PRINCES.

ZARA YAKOB (c. 1399–1468). Emperor (1434–1468). Born in Telq. Zara, whose throne name was Constantine, was one of Ethiopia's greatest emperors. Scholars often compare him to **Ezana**, **Menelik II**, and **Haile Selassie**. During his first years on the throne, Zara Yakob launched a campaign to eliminate paganism and unholy practices in the **Ethiopian Orthodox Church**. He also strengthened the monarchy and centralized the country's administration by bringing remote regions under imperial control and by replacing local warlords with government administrators. Zara Yakob's campaigns against the **Falashas** and the Muslims ensured his reputation as a military commander. In the late 1440s, he established military colonies in Eritrea and placed parts of **Tigray** under his control.

The emperor was a fearless diplomat, admonishing Egypt for persecuting the Copts and warning Cairo that he would divert the waters of the **Blue Nile** if such practices continued. In 1445, problems with Egypt continued as Zara Yakob's troops scored a victory over Badlay-ad-Din, ruler of the **Adal sultanate**, at the Battle of Gomit in **Dawaro**. The sultan of Egypt retaliated by ordering the beating of the patriarch of Alexandria and by threatening to execute him. The emperor defused the situation by freeing an imprisoned Egyptian envoy. In 1450, he sent a diplomatic mission to Europe headed by Pietro Rombulo of Messina, Italy. Among other things, Zara Yakob's envoy visited Pope Nicholas V and the king of Naples and Sicily, Alfonso Aragon. Rombulo returned to Ethiopia with a small group of artisans.

In 1450, the emperor presided over a council of the clergy that ended decades of strife with the **Ewostathians** and with the clergy by agreeing that both Saturday and Sunday could be observed as holy days. *See also* COPTIC ORTHODOX CHURCH OF ALEXANDRIA.

ZAWDITU MENELIK (1876–1901). Second daughter of **Menelik II**, empress of Ethiopia (11 February 1917–1 April 1930) and first reigning female monarch of Ethiopia since the **Queen of Sheba**; she announced that after herself only men should rule the country. In September 1883, Zawditu married **Yohannes IV**'s son, **Ras** Areaya Selasse, as part of a political settlement between her father, who was then **negus** of **Shoa**, and the emperor. After her husband died on 10 June 1888, she married **Dajazmach** Gwangul Zege, whose family had lost territory to her father. However, this marriage also failed to effect a lasting reconciliation between the two families. Zawditu's fourth marriage, to Gugsa Wale (1877–1930), was successful.

On 11 February 1917, **Abuna Matewos** crowned her empress in Saint George's Cathedral, **Addis Ababa** while Ras Tafari Makonnen, later **Haile Selassie**, became regent and heir to the throne. As empress, she opposed modernization and close ties to Europe because of her belief that such innovations would increase Ras Tafari's influence. Despite Zawditu's maneuvering, the regent gradually became more powerful largely because of his determination to improve the lives of Ethiopians and to enhance Ethiopia's international reputation. Frustrated with her growing isolation, the empress became a mystic during the last two years of her reign. After her husband died in a battle with Imperial forces on 31 March 1930, Zawditu apparently had a nervous and physical breakdown. She died, childless, of pneumonia and complications from diabetes on 1 April 1930.

ZAY PEOPLE AND LANGUAGE. About 5,000 Zay live on the shores of Lake Zwai and the lake's eastern islands. They are **agriculturists** and fishermen. They speak a Semitic **language** that has no dialect

414 • ZAYSE-ZERGULLA PEOPLE AND LANGUAGE

variations. It has 61 percent lexical similarity with Harari and 70 percent with East **Gurage**. They use **Amharic** or Afan Oromo as a second language. The **Oromo** refer to the Zay as "Lak'i" or "Laqi." *See also* HARAR.

ZAYSE-ZERGULLA PEOPLE AND LANGUAGE. More than 20,000 Zayse-Zergulla reside to the west of Lake Chamo. The **Bussa** live to the west, the **Dirasha** to the south, and the **Gofa** to the north and east. The men work terraced fields. They speak an Omotic **language** in the Ometo family. There are separate Zayse and Zergulla dialects, both of which are close to the Gidicho dialect of **Koorete**.

ZEMACHA. Amharic term that Ethiopians traditionally used to describe a large military campaign. In October 1974, the **Derg** sought to quell student discontent by announcing that it would close senior secondary schools, colleges and universities and assign students and teachers to rural areas to work on state programs. Publicly, however, the Derg maintained that Zemacha enabled students and teachers to instruct peasants about the revolution's goals, help local communities plan and implement development programs, and improve **health** standards in rural areas.

On 12 December 1974, the Derg launched Zemacha, otherwise known as the Development and Literacy through Cooperation Campaign. The authorities mobilized some 60,000 students and teachers between the ages of 18 and 40 for Zemacha. This initiative was an immediate failure as students and teachers used Zemacha as a platform to denounce the Derg's refusal to accelerate **land reform** and to demand the formation of a people's government. The Derg responded to this challenge by jailing some 1,000 students. To demonstrate solidarity with the students, Zemacha personnel went on strike.

On 23 August 1975, the Derg, seeking to punish the students, extended Zemacha for another year. On 19 October 1975, the Derg announced that it had appointed Major Kiros Alemayehu as Zemacha chairman and four program coordinators for **agriculture**, **education**, engineering, and **health**. Despite these appointments, student protests and desertions escalated. On 18 December 1975, the Derg offered an amnesty to all those who returned to their posts. This gesture accomplished nothing. On 17 July 1976, the Derg dissolved Zemacha.

ZERIHUN YETMGETA (1941–). Artist. Born in **Addis Ababa** and educated at a boarding school. In 1956, Zerihun won first prize in a national art competition. After completing high school, he enrolled in the Empress Menen **Handicraft** School. Zerihun then studied at the School of Fine Art in Addis Ababa (1963–1968) where he eventually became a faculty member. During the **Derg** period (1974–1991), Zerihun, like all artists, suffered as a result of harsh government policies against artistic expression. After the **Ethiopian People's Revolutionary Democratic Front** seized power (1991), his career again flourished and he reestablished his international reputation. Zerihun's paintings have been exhibited in Cuba, Switzerland, and many other countries and museums. In 1992, he was awarded the Prix de la Biennale at DAK-ART 92 in Senegal.

ZERVOS, JACOVOS G. (1883–1956). Greek physician. Born on the island of Cephalonia. In 1909, Zervos arrived in **Harar**. During 1912–1913, he participated in the Balkan War as a member of the Hellenic Army Medical Corps. In 1914, Zervos arrived in **Dire Dawa**, where he befriended **Ras** Tafari Makonnen, later **Haile Selassie**, and became his personal physician. He accompanied Ras Tafari on his 1924 tour of Europe. Zervos also went into exile with Haile Selassie and returned to Ethiopia with him after liberation (1941). In 1933, he received the rank of Greek honorary minister and envoy extraordinary to Ethiopia. In 1947, the University of Greece appointed him honorary professor of pathology. In 1952, the emperor conferred on him the title of **Bitwoded** and decorated him with the Grand Cross of the Order of Menelik. Zervos died of a heart attack on 10 June 1956.

Appendix

HEADS OF STATE

Imperial Period (?–1974)

Menelik I
Ezana I
Aphilas
Uzana
Wazeba
Ella Amida I, II, III?
Ezana II
Shizana
Ella Abreha
Ella Asfeha
Ella Shahel
Agabe
Levi
Ella Amida IV?
Yakor (Jacob)   486–489
Dawit (David)   486–489
Armah I   489–503
Zitana   504–505
Yakor (Jacob) II   505–514
Ella Asbeha (Caleb)   514–542
Beta Israel   542–c. 550
Gabra Masqal   c. 550–564
Anaeb
Alamiris
Joel
Israel

Gersem I
Ella Gabaz
Ella Saham
Armah II
Iathlia
Hataz I
Wazena
Za Ya'abiyo
Armah III
Unknown
Hataz II
Gersem II
Hataz III
Marari   1117–1133
Yemrehana Krestos   1133–1172
Gebra Maskal Lalibela   1172–1212 or c. 1185–1225
Na'akeuto La'ab   1212–1260
Yitbarek (Yetbarak)   1260–1268
Yekuno Amlak (Tasfa Iyasus)   1270–1285? or 1268–1283?
Yaqeb'a Seyon (Solomon) I   1285–1294
Hezba Asgad   1294–1297
Senfa Asgad   1294–1297
Kedma (Qedma) Asgad   1297–1299
Djin Asgad   1297–1299
Sab'a Asgad   1297–1299
Wedem Arad   1299–1314
Amda Seyon I   1312–1342? or 1314–1344?
Newaya Kresto   1344–1372
Newaya Maryam   1372–1382
Dawit (David) I   1382–1411
Tewodros (Theodore) I   1411–1414
Yeshak (Isaac) I   1414–1429
Endreyas (Andrew)   1429–1430
Takla Maryam   1430–1433
Sarwe Iyasus   1433
Amda Iyasus   1433–1434
Zara Yakob (Constantine I)   1434–1468
Baeda Mariam I   1468–1478

Constantine (Eskender; Alexander) II   1478–1484
Amda Seyon II   1494
Na'od   1494–1508
Lebna Dengel (David II)   1508–1540
Galawedos (Claudius)   1540–1559
Menas   1560–1564
Sarsa Dengel   1564–1597
Yacob (Jacob)   1597–1603, 1604–1607
Za Dengel   1603–1604
Susneyos (Sissinios)   1607–1632
Fasilidas (Basilides)   1632–1667
Yohannes (John) I   1667–1682
Iyasu (Jesus) I   1682–1706
Takla Haymanot I   1706–1708
Tewoflos (Theophilus)   1708–1711
Yostos (Justus)   1711–1716
Dawit (David) III   1716–1721
BeKafa   1721–1730
Iyasu II   1730–1755
Iyoas (Joas) I   1755–1769
Yohannes II   1769
Takla Haymanot II   1769–1777
Solomon II   1777–1779
Tekle Giorgis (George) I   1779–1784
1788–1789, 1794–1795, 1795–1796, 1797–1799, 1800
Jesus III   1784–1788
Ba'eda Maryam   1788
Hezekiah Ba'eda Maryam II   1789–1795, 1795
Solomon III   1796–1797, 1799
Demetrius   1799–1800, 1800–1801
Egwala Seyon   1801–1818
Joas II   1818–1821
Gigar   1821–1826, 1826–1830
Ba'eda Maryam III   1826
Jesus IV   1830–1832
Gabra Krestos   1832
Sahla Dengel   1832–1840, 1841–1855
Yohannes III   1840–1841

Tewodros (Theodore) II   1855–1868
Tekle Giorgis II   1868–1872
Yohannes IV   1872–1889
Menelik II   1889–1913
Lij Iyasu (Joshua)   Regent, 1909–1913, 1913–1916
Empress Zawditu   1916–1930
Haile Selassie[1]   Regent   1916–1930, 1930–1936, 1941–1974
Victor Emmanuel III (proclaimed emperor of Ethiopia by the Italian government)   1936–1941

Italian Period (1936–1941); Administered by a Governor General with the Title of Viceroy

Pietro Badoglio   9 May 1936–22 May 1936[2]
Rodolfo Graziani   22 May 1936–21 December 1937[3]
Amedeo Di Savoia   21 December 1937–19 May 1941
Pietro Gazzera   23 May 1941–6 July 1941
Guglielmo Nasi   July 1941–27 November 1941[4]

CHAIRMEN OF THE PROVISIONAL MILITARY ADMINISTRATION COUNCIL

Aman Mikael Andom   12 September 1974–17 November 1974
Mengistu Haile Mariam   17 November 1974–28 November 1974
Tafari Benti   28 November 1974–3 February 1977
Mengistu Haile Mariam   11 February 1977–10 September 1987

PRESIDENTS OF THE REPUBLIC

Mengistu Haile Mariam   10 September 1987–21 May 1991
Tesfaye Gabre Kidan   21 May 1991–27 May 1991

PRESIDENT OF THE PROVISIONAL GOVERNMENT

Meles Zenawi   27 May 1991–22 August 1995[5]

PRESIDENTS OF THE REPUBLIC

Negasso Gidada   22 August 1995–8 October 2001
Girma Wolde-Giyorgis Lucha   8 October 2001–present

PRIME MINISTERS

Makonnen Endelkahew   1943–1 November 1957
Abebe Aragai   27 November 1957–15 December 1960
Aklilu Habte-Wold   17 April 1961–27 February 1974
Endelkahew Makonnen   28 February 1974–22 July 1974
Mikael Imru   22 July 1974–11 September 1974
Fikre Selassie Wogderess   11 September 1987–8 November 1989
Haile Yimenu   8 November 1989–26 April 1991
Tamrat Layne   6 June 1991–22 August 1995
Meles Zenawi   22 August 1995–present

NOTES

1. In exile during the Italian occupation, from May 1936 to January 1941.
2. Badoglio departed Addis Ababa on 22 May 1936 but did not officially relinquish his office until 11 June 1936.
3. Graziani officially assumed office on 11 June 1936.
4. Nasi served as vice–governor general.
5. Acting as interim president. Until 23 July 1991, served as chairman of the Supreme Council of the Ethiopian People's Revolutionary Democratic Front (EPRDF).

Bibliography

The following bibliography provides readers with a general introduction to the field of Ethiopian studies. Much of the available literature is in English, although useful material appears in other languages such as French, German, and Italian. Scholars who desire more comprehensive surveys of writings should refer to the "Ethiopia Bibliography, Library Science, and Reference Materials" section of this bibliography, which contains references to the more significant compilations of sources on Ethiopia.

Over the past few decades, there has been an impressive array of scholarly publications on most aspects of Ethiopia's history. However, additional work still is needed on Ethiopian military affairs, especially during the postindependence period; the careers of some colonial governors and officials and many of Ethiopia's African political leaders; opposition movements; environmental problems; transportation infrastructure; the judiciary; and the political, economic, social, and medical impact of the acquired immune deficiency syndrome (AIDS).

Concerning the Italian colonial period, books and articles normally fall into two categories. Many of those written before independence usually extol the virtues of Italian colonial rule, while those produced after independence are often highly critical of Italian colonialism. More-balanced future assessments of the political, military, economic, and social implications of the colonial experience undoubtedly will result in greater understanding of Ethiopia's historical development.

Apart from books and articles, archival data is essential to Ethiopian scholars. The most important repository for such materials in the Institute for Ethiopian Studies in Addis Ababa. Other useful collections are located in the Abdine Archives (Cairo), Archives des Capucins (Toulouse), Archives Nationales, Section Outre-Mer, Ministère de la Marine et des Colonies (Paris), Archivo Storico della Società Geografica Italiana (Rome), Archivo Storico del soppresso Ministero dell'Africa Italiana (Rome), Bibliothèque Nationale (Paris), British Museum (London), Ministero degli Affari Esteri (Rome), Ministère des Affaires Etrangères (Paris), Ministero della Guerra (Rome), and the Public Record Office (Kew).

Apart from the items contained in this bibliography, readers interested in recent Ethiopian affairs also should consult contemporary periodicals such as *Africa Analysis, Africa Confidential, Africa Research Bulletin, Focus on Africa, Horn of Africa Bulletin,* and *New African.* The *Economist* Intelligence Unit's quarterly and annual country reports on Ethiopia also are useful, especially with regard to economic matters. Lastly, annuals such as *Africa Contemporary Record* and *Africa South of the Sahara* provide valuable sources of more current information.

There are numerous scholarly periodicals and newspapers that are devoted entirely to Ethiopia. Other specialized journals that regularly publish articles about Ethiopia include the *Bulletin of the School of Oriental and African Studies, Geographical Journal, Journal of African History, Journal of Modern African Studies,* and *Northeast African Studies.* Journals published in Ethiopia normally can be found only in major public or university libraries. The same can be said of Ethiopian newspapers although several of them are on the Internet. The following list, which is by no means comprehensive, provides the reader with a summary of some of the more important publications.

Addis Tribune (weekly newspaper), 1992–present
Aethiopica: International Journal of Ethiopian Studies, 1998–present
Agazen
Annales d'Ethiopie, 1955–1990, 2000–present
Bulletin of Public Health
Bulletin of the University College of Addis Ababa Ethnological Society
The Business Review (weekly newspaper), 2001–present
Capital, (weekly newspaper), 1998–present
Eritrean Studies Review, 1996–present
Ethiopia Observer, 1956–1974
Ethiopia: Seven Days Update, (weekly newspaper)
Ethiopian Economic Review, 1959–present
Ethiopian Geographical Journal, 1963–present
The Ethiopian Herald (daily newspaper), 1943–present
Ethiopian Journal of African Studies, 1981–1988
Ethiopian Journal of Agricultural Sciences, 1990–present
Ethiopian Journal of Development Research, 1974–present
Ethiopian Journal of Economics, 1992–present
Ethiopian Journal of Education, 1967–present
Ethiopian Journal of Health Development, 1984–present
Ethiopian Journal of Health Sciences
Ethiopian Medical Journal, 1963–present
Ethiopian Review, 1991–present
Ethiopian Science and Technology Newsletter

Ethiopian Statistical Association Newsletter
Ethiopian Trade Journal, 1960–1970, 1980–present
Ethiopianist Notes (East Lansing), 1977–1979, became *Northeast African Studies*
Fortune (weekly newspaper), 2000–present
Journal of Eritrean Studies, 1986–1991
Journal of Ethiopian Law, 1964–present
Journal of Ethiopian Statistical Association, 1990?–present
Journal of Ethiopian Studies, 1963–present
Journal of Modern African Studies, 1963–present
Journal of Oromo Studies, 1993–present
The Monitor (newspaper), 1993–present
Negarit Gazeta, 1942–present
Nubica et Aethiopica, 1990–present
Oromo Commentary, 1991–present
Rassegna di Studi Etiopici, 1941–present
The Reporter (weekly newspaper), 1995–present
SEBIL Journal, 1988–present
SINET: Ethiopian Journal of Science, 1977–present
The Scope (newspaper), 2002–present
The Sub-Saharan Informer (daily newspaper), ?–present
The Sun (daily newspaper), 1996–present

Lastly, it should be noted that the romanization of Amharic is characterized by numerous diacritical marks that account for any discrepancies in the names included in the bibliography. To simplify matters, the authors have refrained from using any diacritical marks in the bibliography or the dictionary.

ABBREVIATIONS

AA	*African Affairs*
AAU	Addis Ababa University
AAUP	Addis Ababa University Press
AHS	*African Historical Studies*
AI	Amnesty International
APP	Artistic Printing Press
AQ	*Africa Quarterly*
AR	*Africa Report*
AS	*African Studies*
ASR	*African Studies Review*

AT	*Africa Today*
CEA	*Cahiers d'Études Africaines*
CH	Current History
CJAS	*Canadian Journal of African Studies*
CP	Clarendon Press
CR	*Contemporary Review*
CUP	Cambridge University Press
EGJ	*Ethiopian Geographical Journal*
EJAS	*Ethiopian Journal of African Studies*
EJE	*Ethiopian Journal of Education*
EN	*Ethiopianist Notes*
EO	*Ethiopia Observer*
ESR	*Eritrean Studies Review*
FA	*Foreign Affairs*
FS	Franz Steiner Verlag
GJ	*Geographical Journal*
GP	Government Printer
HA	*Horn of Africa*
HMSO	Her/His Majesty's Stationery Office
HS	The Hakluyt Society
HSU	Haile Selassie I University
HT	*History Today*
IA	International Affairs
IAI	International African Institute
IDA	International Development Association
IJAHS	*International Journal of African Historical Studies*
JAH	*Journal of African History*
JAL	*Journal of African Law*
JAS	*Journal of African Studies*
JC	James Currey
JDA	*Journal of Developing Areas*
JEL	*Journal of Ethiopian Law*
JES	*Journal of Ethiopian Studies*
JICH	*Journal of Imperial and Commonwealth History*
JMAS	*Journal of Modern African Studies*
JOS	*Journal of Oromo Studies*
JRAS	*Journal of the African Society*
JRGS	*Journal of the Royal Geographical Society*
JRUSI	*Journal of the Royal United Service Institution*
JSS	*Journal of Semitic Studies*
LR	Lynne Rienner Publishers
NAS	*Northeast African Studies*

NC	*The Nineteenth Century and After*
NGM	*National Geographic Magazine*
NS	New Series
OUP	Oxford University Press
PRGS	*Proceedings of the Royal Geographical Society*
RA	*Rural Africana*
ROAPE	*Review of African Political Economy*
RSP	Red Sea Press
RT	The Round Table
SIAS	Scandinavian Institute of African Studies
SSM	*Social Science and Medicine*
TJH	*Transafrican Journal of History*
TWQ	*Third World Quarterly*
USGPO	United States Government Printing Office
USM	*United Service Magazine*
WD	*World Development*
WP	Westview Press
WT	*World Today*
YUP	Yale University Press
ZB	Zed Books

BIBLIOGRAPHY

Contents

Ethiopia Bibliography, Library Science, and Reference Materials	428
Antiquities and History to 1855	440
History from 1855 to Present	446
Military and Security Affairs	451
Italian Invasion and World War II	467
Economic Affairs	493
Regional Affairs (Horn of Africa) and the African Union	502
Agriculture, Famine, Land, and Rural Affairs	513
Religion, Missions, and Missionaries	526
Foreign Affairs	537
Eritrea	547
Law and Human Rights	554
Government and Politics	560
Anthropology, Ethnology, Local History, and Paleoanthropology	570
Architecture, Arts, Language, Literature, and Music	579

Health, Medicine, and Welfare   586
Education   591
Environment, Fauna, Flora, Geography, Nile Waters, Population,
    and Tourism   597
General and Collected Works   608
Communications, Media, Post, Press, and Transport   613
Cities and Urban Affairs   616
Women   619
Travel and Exploration   621

Ethiopia Bibliography, Library Science, and Reference Materials

Abbink, Jon G. "A Bibliography of the Ethiopian Jews, 1958–1984." *Studies in Bibliography and Booklore*, 16 (1986): 37–48.

——. *Ethiopian Society and History. A Bibliography on Ethiopian Studies 1957–1990*. Leiden: African Studies Center, 1991.

——. *A Preliminary Ethnographic Bibliography of Ethiopia, 1959–1962*. Nijmegen: Katholieke Universiteit, Institut voor Culturele en Sociale Anthropologie, 1985.

——. "A Select Ethnographic Bibliography of Ethiopia, 1958–1982." *Behaviour Science Research*, 19 (1/4) (1984/1985): 58–111.

——. *A Supplementary Bibliography: Eritreo-Ethiopian Studies in Society and History: 1960–1995*. Leiden: African Studies Center, 1996.

Abdullahi Hassen, Tesfayesus Mahary, and Jelaludin Ahmed. *Annotated Bibliography of the Population of Ethiopia*. Addis Ababa: UNECA, Population Division, 1990.

Abstracts of Social Science Theses and Dissertations Submitted to Eastern African Universities. 2 vols. Addis Ababa: Organization for Social Science Research in Eastern Africa, 1989–1990.

Addis Ababa. Institute of Ethiopian Studies. *Publications by Researchers of the Institute of Ethiopian Studies (1963–1975)*. Addis Ababa: Research and Publications Department, 1976.

——. *List of IES Publications (1963–1975)*. Addis Ababa: Research and Publications Department, 1976.

Aescoly, Aaron Zeev. "The Falashas: A Bibliography." *Kirjath Sepher*, 12 (1935/1936): 254–65, 370–83, 498–505 and 13 (1936/1937): 250–65, 383–93, 506–12.

African Section. Library of Congress. *Africa South of the Sahara: Index to Periodical Literature, 1900–1970*. 4 vols. Boston: G. K. Hall, 1971– , supplements.

Ahmed, Hussein. "The Historiography of Islam in Ethiopia." *Journal of Islamic Studies*, 3 (1) (1992): 15–46.

Alasebu Gebre Selassie. *Select Bibliography: Women in Agricultural and Rural Development*. Addis Ababa: National Workshop on Women in Agricultural Development, 1983.

———. *Women and Development in Ethiopia: An Annotated Bibliography*. Addis Ababa: St. George Printing Press, 1981.

Alem Habtu. "Books on the Ethiopian Revolution: A Review Essay." *Socialism and Democracy*, (3) (1986): 27–60.

Allen, Christopher (ed.). *Africa Bibliography*. Manchester: Manchester University Press, 1991–1996 (annual).

Alula Hidaru and Dessalegn Rahmato (eds.). *A Short Guide to the Study of Ethiopia: A General Bibliography*. Westport, Conn., and London: Greenwood Press, 1976.

Anderson, Gerald H. (ed.). *Biographical Dictionary of Christian Missions*. Grand Rapids, Mich.: William B. Eerdmans, 1999.

Andrzejewski, B. W. "A Survey of Cushitic Literatures, 1940–1975." *EN*, 2 (1) (1978): 1–27.

Aynor, H. S. *Guide to Selected Documents on the Relations between Israel and Ethiopia*. Jerusalem: Hebrew University, 1985.

Bahru Zewde. "Bibliography of the Works of Richard Alan Caulk." *JES*, 17 (1984): 35–36.

Bairu Tafla. "Production of Historical Works in Ethiopia and Eritrea. Some Notes on the State of Recent Publications." *Aethiopica: International Journal of Ethiopian Studies*, 1 (1998): 176–206.

———. "Register of International Scholars in Ethiopian and Eritrean Studies." *Aethiopica: International Journal of Ethiopian Studies*, 3 (2000): 166–87.

———. "Some Documents on Nineteenth-Century Ethiopia from the Nachlass of Gerhard Rohlfs." *Rassegna di Studi*, 29 (1982/1983): 175–235.

Barringer, T. A. (ed.). *Africa Bibliography*. Manchester: Manchester University Press, 1997–present (annual).

Basic Documents of the Ethiopian Revolution. Addis Ababa: Provisional Office for Mass Organizational Affairs, Agitation, Propaganda and Education Committee, 1977.

Baylor, Jim. *Ethiopia: A List of Works in English*. Berkeley: University of California, Institute for International Studies, 1968.

Beckingham, Charles Fraser. "European Sources for Ethiopian History before 1634." *Paideuma*, (33) (1987): 167–78.

Beer, David F. "Ethiopian Literature and Literary Criticism in English: An Annotated Bibliography." *Research in African Literature*, 6 (1) (1975): 44–57.

Belaynesh, Mikael, Stanislaw Chojnacki, and Richard Pankhurst. (eds.). *The Dictionary of Ethiopian Biography. Volume I: From Early Times to the End of the Zagwé Dynasty c. 1270 A.D.* Addis Ababa: Institute of Ethiopian Studies, 1975.

Bell, Pamela M. *British Information Office. Addis Ababa. Catalogue of Books.* Addis Ababa: British Information Office, 1968.

——. *Land Tenure in Ethiopia: A Bibliography.* Addis Ababa: HSU, 1968.

Black, George F. *Ethiopica and Amharica: A List of Works in the New York Public Library.* New York: New York Public Library, 1928.

Blackhurst, Hector (ed.). *Africa Bibliography.* Manchester: Manchester University Press, 1984–1990 (annual).

——. *East and Northeast Africa Bibliography.* Lanham, Md.: Scarecrow Press, 1996.

Bondestam, Lars. *Ethiopia: A Selected Bibliography Regarding Agriculture, Economy, Demography, Health, and Statistics.* Uppsala: SIAS, 1973.

Bonk, Jonathan James. *An Annotated and Classified Bibliography of English Literature Pertaining to the Ethiopian Orthodox Church.* Metuchen, N.J., and London: The American Theological Association and Scarecrow Press, 1984.

Brown, Clifton Fleming. *Ethiopian Perspectives: A Bibliographical Guide to the History of Ethiopia.* Westport, Conn., and London: Greenwood Press, 1978.

Bulletin of Ethiopian Manuscripts. Addis Ababa: Ethiopian Manuscript Microfilm Library, Ministry of Culture and Sports, 1986.

Cannistraro, Philip V. (ed.). *Historical Dictionary of Fascist Italy.* Westport, Conn., and London: Greenwood Press, 1982.

Casada, James Allen. "British Exploration in East Africa: A Bibliography with Commentary." *Africana Journal* (1974): 195–239.

——. *Sir Richard F. Burton: A Biobibliographical Study.* Boston: G. K. Hall, 1990.

Chaine, M. *Catalogue des Manuscrits Éthiopiens de la Collection Antoine d'Abbadie à la Bibliothèque Nationale.* Paris: Ernest Leroux, 1912.

——. *Catalogue des Manuscrits Éthiopiens de la Collection Mondon-Vidailhet à la Bibliothèque Nationale.* Paris: Ernest Leroux, 1913.

Chojnacki, Stanislaw, and Mergia Diro. *Ethiopian Publications in 1961 Ethiopian and 1969 Gregorian Calendar.* Addis Ababa: Institute of Ethiopian Studies, 1970.

Chojnacki, Stanislaw, Mergia Diro, and Richard Pankhurst (eds.). *Register of Current Research on Ethiopia and the Horn of Africa.* Addis Ababa: Institute of Ethiopian Studies, 1969.

Conover, Helen F. *North and Northeast Africa: A Selected Annotated List of Writings, 1951–1957.* Washington, D.C.: Library of Congress, 1957.

Conti Rossini, Carlo. *Bibliografia Etiopica (1927–Guino 1936).* Rome: A cura del Ministero delle Colonie, Sindicato Italiano Arti Grafiche, 1936.

——. *Notice sur les Manuscrits Ethiopiens de la Collection d'Abbadie.* Paris: Imprimerie Nationale, 1914.

———. "Pubblicazioni Etiopica dal 1936 al 1945." *Rassegna di Studi Etiopici*, 4 (1944): 1–133.

Danton, J. P. "Libraries in the Land of the Lion of Judah." *Library Journal*, 87 (1962): 1732–36.

Darch, Colin (ed.). *Africa Index to Current Periodical Literature*. Munich: K. G. Saur Verlag (Hans Zell), 1977 (annual).

———. *The Library of the Public Health College at Gondar: A Report and Evaluation*. Addis Ababa: HSU, 1972.

———. *A Soviet View of Africa: An Annotated Bibliography on Ethiopia, Somalia, and Djibouti*. Boston: G. K. Hall, 1980.

———. "Status of Professional Librarians at Haile Selassie I University." *Ethiopian Library Association Bulletin*, 3 (2) (1975): 33–41.

De Contenson, Henri. "Compte-Rendu Bibliographique des Annales d'Éthiopie." *Syria*, 46 (1969): 161–67.

Delaney, Annette. *Ethiopian Survey: A Selected Bibliography*. Washington, D.C.: African Bibliographic Center, [1964].

Devens, Monica S. "An Annotated Bibliography of the Works of Wolf Leslau." In Stanislav Sergert and Andras J. E. Bodrogligeti (eds.). *Ethiopian Studies*. Wiesbaden: Otto Harrassowitz, 1983: 1–37.

Duignan, Peter and S. Wright. *Catalogue of Ethiopian Manuscript Collections in the Cambridge University Library*. Cambridge: CUP, 1961.

Eldon, Rita. "The National Library of Ethiopia." *EO*, 1 (1957): 369–70.

Ethiopia. Ministry of Foreign Affairs. *Bibliography of Ethiopia*. Addis Ababa: Ministry of Foreign Affairs, 1968.

Ethiopia. National Library. *A Guide for Readers*. Addis Ababa: APP, 1976.

Ethiopia, 1950–1962: A Select Bibliography. Washington, D.C.: Africa House, 1963.

Ethiopia: The Top 100 People. Paris: Indigo Publications, 2002.

Ewing, William H. "Current Status of Legal Research in Ethiopia: A Bibliographical Essay." *RA*, (11) (1970): 97–106.

Falivene, M. Rosaria (comp.) and Alan F. Jesson (ed.). *Historical Catalogue of the Manuscripts of Bible House Library*. London: The British and Foreign Bible Society, 1982.

Fekade Azeze. "Ethiopian Creative Writing and Criticism in English: A Review and Bibliography." *JES*, 18 (1985): 34–50.

Fumagalli, Giuseppe. *Bibliografia Etiopica: Catalogo Descrittivo e Ragionato Degli Scritti Pubblicati dalla Invenzione della Stampa Fino a Tutto il 1891, Intorno alla Etiopia e Regioni Limitrofe*. Milan: U. Hoepli, 1893.

Garretson, Peter P. "Some Amharic Sources for Modern Ethiopian History, 1889–1935." *Bulletin of the School of Oriental and African Studies*, 41 (2) (1978): 283–96.

Geda Worku. *Bibliography of Educational Publications on Ethiopia*. Addis Ababa: National University, Faculty of Education, Research Center Library, 1975.

Germa Makonnen. *A Bibliography of Ethiopia Bibliographies, 1933–1972*. Addis Ababa: AAU Libraries, 1976.

Getachew Gebrewold. *Books, Documents and Pamphlets on Ethiopian Economy in the National Bank of Ethiopia Library*. Addis Ababa: Economic Research and Planning Division, 1976.

——. "Ethiopia-Economic Developments since February 1974: A Bibliography." *Africana Journal*, 12 (1) (1981): 53–71 and 12 (2) (1981): 99–104.

Getatchew Haile. "Documents on the History of Ase Dawit (1382–1413)." *JES*, 16 (1983): 25–35.

——. "Who Is Who in Ethiopia's Past. Part I: At the Court of Ase Lebna Dangel (1508–1540)." *NAS*, 6 (3) (1984): 47–52.

——. "Who Is Who in Ethiopia's Past. Part II: The Zagwe Royal Family after Zagwe." *NAS*, 7 (3) (1984): 41–48.

Getahun Dilebo. "Historical Origins and Development of the Eritrean Problem, 1889–1962." *Current Bibliography on African Affairs*, 7 (3) (1974): 221–44.

Girma Makonnen. *A Bibliography of Ethiopian Bibliographies, 1932–1972*. Addis Ababa: AAU, University Libraries, 1976.

——. *Ethio-Somalia Boundary Dispute: A Bibliography*. Addis Ababa: HSU, 1974.

Goldschmidt, Lazarus. *Bibliotheca Aethiopica*. Leipzig: E. Pfeiffer, 1893.

——. *Die Abessinischen Handschriften der Stadtbibliothek zu Frankfurt am Main*. Berlin: Calvary, 1897.

Grébaut, Sylvain. *Catalogue des Manuscrits Ethiopiens de la Collection Griaule*. Paris: Institut d'Ethnologie, 1938.

Grey, Robert Daniel. "Ethiopian Politics, Imperial and Revolutionary: A Bibliography." *Africana Journal*, 12 (1) (1981): 3–51.

Gupta, Sushma. "A Cumulative Index of the *JES*, Volumes I–XXVX, 1963–1992 (Revised and edited by Shiferaw Bekele)." *JES*, 27 (1) (1994): 143–87.

——. "Development of Libraries, Documentation and Information Centres in Ethiopia in the Twentieth Century." *International Information and Library Review*, 27 (4) (1995): 317–31.

Gupta, Sushma, and Taddesse Tamrat. "The International Conference of Ethiopian Studies 1959–1991. Bibliography and Index, I–IX and XI (Revised and Edited by Taddesse Tamrat)." *JES*, 27 (1) (1994): 29–142.

Hacque, I. Desta Beyene, and Marcos Sahlu. *Bibliography on Soils, Fertilizers, Plant Nutrition, and General Agronomy in Ethiopia*. Addis Ababa: International Livestock Center for Africa, 1985.

Haile Gabriel Dagne. *A Bibliography of Educational Publications on Ethiopia*. Addis Ababa: HSU, Faculty of Education, Research Centre, 1969.

Haile Mäsqäl Gäbre Wold. *The Ethiopian Nationalities: A Bibliography*. 2 vols. Addis Ababa: Institute of Ethiopian Studies, 1991.

Haskell, Daniel Carl. *Ethiopia and the Italo-Ethiopian Conflict, 1936: A Selected List of References*. New York: New York Public Library, 1936.

——. "Ethiopia and the Italo-Ethiopian Conflict, 1928–1935." *Bulletin of the New York Public Library*, 40 (1936): 13–20.

Heldman, Marilyn E., and Getatchew Haile. "Who is Who in Ethiopia's Past, Part III: Founders of Ethiopia's Solomonic Dynasty." *NAS*, 9 (1) (1987): 1–12.

Hess, Robert L., and Dalvan M. Coger. *Bibliography of Primary Sources for Nineteenth-Century Tropical Africa*. Stanford: Hoover Institution Press, 1972.

Höjer, Christiane. *Ethiopian Publications: Books, Pamphlets, Annuals, and Periodical Articles Published in Ethiopia in Foreign Languages from 1942 Till 1962*. Addis Ababa: HSU, Institute of Ethiopian Studies, 1974.

Hopkins, Simon. "Bibliography of the Writings of Professor Edward Ullendorff." *JSS*, 34 (2) (1989): 253–89.

Hussein Ahmed. "Recent Islamic Periodicals in Ethiopia (1996–1998)." *NAS*, 5 (2) (1998): 7–21.

Institute of Ethiopian Studies. *A Catalogue of Clandestine Literature on Ethiopia*. Addis Ababa: Institute of Ethiopian Studies, AAU, 1995.

Italy. Ministerio degli Affari Esteri. Direzione Centrale Degli Affari Coloniali. *Raccolta di Pubblicazioni Coloniali Italiane: Primo Indice Bibliografico*. Rome: Tipografia della Camera dei Deputati, 1911.

Kafelew Zanebu. *EO Index, Vol. I–XVI, 1956–1974*. Addis Ababa: Institute of Ethiopian Studies, AAU, 1986.

Kamil, Murad. *Catalogue of all Manuscripts in the Monastery of St. Catherine on Mount Sinai*. Wiesbaden: Harrassowitz, 1970.

Kaplan, Steven, and Ben Dor. *Ethiopian Jewry: An Annotated Bibliography*. Jerusalem: Ben Zvi Institute, 1988.

Karnik, Sharmila S. "Conflict Situation in the Horn of Africa: Select Annotated Bibliography." *African Currents*, 10/11 (19/22) (1995): 111–33.

Kassahun Checole. "Eritrea: A Preliminary Bibliography." *Africana Journal*, 6 (4) (1975): 303–14.

Kebbede Gessesse. *Index to the JES*. Addis Ababa: HSU, 1973.

Kebbede Gessesse, Kebbede Abba Ire, and Rosa Araya. "Theses on Ethiopia by Ethiopians or Others Accepted for B.A. or B.Sc. Degrees by the Haile Selassie I University, 1960–1972." *Quaderni di Studi Etiopici*, 6/7 (1986): 215–310.

Kesete Belay. *Ethiopia: A Bibliography of Science*. Gabarone: National Institute of Development Research and Documentation, University of Botswana, 1982.

Kinefe-Rigb Zelleke. "Bibliography of the Ethiopic Hagiographical Traditions." *JES*, 13 (2) (1975): 57–102.

Kloos, Helmut, and Zein Ahmed Zein. *Health and Disease in Ethiopia: A Guide to the Literature, 1940–1985*. Addis Ababa: Ministry of Health, 1988.

——. *Health, Disease, Medicine, and Famine in Ethiopia: A Bibliography*. Westport, Conn., and London: Greenwood Press, 1991.

Koehn, Peter Harold. "Selected Bibliography: The Municipality of Addis Ababa, Ethiopia." *African Urban Studies*, (1975): 133–60.

Kornegay, Francis A. "The Speculative Geopolitics of Conflict and Intervention in Northeast Africa: A Review Essay." *Current Bibliography on African Affairs*, 14 (1) (1981/82): 3–12.

Legum, Colin (ed.). *Africa Contemporary Record: Annual Survey and Documents*. New York and London: Africana Publishing Company, 1968/69 (annual).

Leslau, Wolf. *An Annotated Bibliography of the Semitic Languages of Ethiopia*. The Hague: Mouton, 1965.

——. *Bibliography of the Semitic Languages of Ethiopia*. New York: New York Public Library, 1946.

——. "A Supplementary Falasha Bibliography." *Studies in Bibliography and Booklore*, 3 (1957/1958): 9–27.

——. "Ten Years of Ethiopic Linguistics (1946–1956)." *Annales d'Éthiopie*, 2 (1957): 277–313.

Library of Congress. *Accessions List for East Africa*. Nairobi: Library of Congress Office, (1968; six times per year).

——. *The Italo-Ethiopian Dispute: A List of Books and Pamphlets*. Washington, D.C.: Library of Congress, 1935.

——. *List of United States Documents on Abyssinia*. Washington, D.C.: Library of Congress, Division of Bibliography, 1919.

——. *Quarterly Index to Periodical Literature, Eastern and Southern Africa*. Nairobi: Library of Congress Office, (1991; four times per year).

Littmann, Euno. *Publications of the Princeton Expedition to Abyssinia*. 4 vols. Leiden: Brill, 1910–1915.

Lockot, Donald Merrit. "Father Jeronymo Lobo's Writings Covering Ethiopia, Including Hitherto Unpublished Manuscripts in the Palmella Library." Ph.D. diss., Harvard University, 1959.

Lockot, Hans Wilhelm. *Bibliographia Äthiopica: Die Äthiopienkundliche Literatur des Deutsch-sprachigen Raums*. Wiesbaden: FS, 1982.

——. "German Literature on Ethiopia in the Libraries of Addis Ababa." *EO*, 11 (1) (1967): 68–71.

Macomber, William F., and Getatchew Haile. *A Catalogue of Ethiopian Manuscripts Microfilmed for the Ethiopian Manuscript Microfilm Library, Addis Ababa, and for the Monastic Manuscript Microfilm Library, Collegeville*. 9 vols. Collegeville: Monastic Manuscript Microfilm Library, 1975–1987.

Mahadevan, Vijitha. *Contemporary African Politics and Development: A Comprehensive Bibliography, 1981–1990*. Boulder: LR, 1994.

Marcus, Harold Golden. *The Modern History of Ethiopia and the Horn of Africa: A Select and Annotated Bibliography*. Stanford: Hoover Institution Press, 1972.

Matthews, Daniel G. *A Current Bibliography on Ethiopian Affairs: A Select Bibliography from 1950–1964*. Washington, D.C.: African Bibliographic Center, 1965.

———. *Ethiopian Outline: A Bibliographical Research Guide*. Washington, D.C.: African Bibliographic Center, 1966.

McCann, James Craig. "The Ethiopian Chronicles: An African Documentary Tradition." *NAS*, 1 (2) (1979): 47–61.

McClure, Bryan. "Religion and Nationalism in Southern Ethiopia." Current Bibliography on African Affairs, 5 (5/6) (1972): 497–508.

Munro-Hay, Stuart C., and Richard Pankhurst. *Ethiopia*. Oxford and Santa Barbara: ABC-Clio, 1995.

Ofcansky, Thomas P. "Ethiopia: A Selected Military Bibliography." *African Research and Documentation*, (87) (2001): 29–65.

———. "The Italian-Ethiopian War: A Selected Bibliography Part I." *African Research and Documentation*, (88) (2001): 65–81.

———. "The Italian-Ethiopian War: A Selected Bibliography Part II." *African Research and Documentation*, (89) (2002): 19–47.

Ofosu-Appiah, L. H., and Keith Irvine (eds.). *The Encyclopedia Africana Dictionary of African Biography: Ethiopia-Ghana*. New York: Reference Publications, 1977.

Pankhurst, Richard. "The Foundation of Education, Printing, Newspapers, Book Production, Libraries, and Literacy in Ethiopia." *EO*, 6 (3) (1962): 241–90.

———. "The Library of Emperor Tewodros at Magdala." *Bulletin of the School of Oriental and African Studies*, 36 (1) (1973): 17–42.

———. "Menghestu Lemma: A Bibliography." *JES*, 21 (1988): 206–13.

———. *Provisional Bibliography on the Italian Invasion and Occupation and Liberation of Ethiopia (1935–1941)*. Addis Ababa: HSU, Institute of Ethiopian Studies, 1972.

———. "Secular Themes in Ethiopian Ecclesiastical Manuscripts: VI. A Catalogue of Illustrations of Historical and Ethnographic Interest in the Bayerischen Staatsbibliothek and Staatliches Museum für Volkerkunde, in Munich." *JES*, 32 (2) (1999): 1–14.

Pankhurst, Rita. "Bibliography of Publications Written, Edited, or Annotated by Richard Pankhurst." *Aethiopica: International Journal of Ethiopian Studies*, 5 (2002): 15–41.

———. "Libraries in Post-Revolutionary Ethiopia." *Information Development Papers*, 4 (4) (1988): 239–45.

Pankhurst, Rita, and Richard Pankhurst. "A Select Annotated Bibliography of Travel Books on Ethiopia." *Africana Journal*, 9 (1) (1978): 113–32 and 9 (3) (1978): 101–33.

Pastorett, Tomma N. *Ethiopia: Selected Unclassified References*. Maxwell Air Force Base, Ala.: Air University Library, 1977.

Paulos Milkias. *Ethiopia: A Comprehensive Bibliography*. Boston: G. K. Hall and Company, 1989.

Pearson, James Douglas. "Bibliography of Charles Fraser Beckingham." *JSS*, 29 (1984): 179–88.

——. *Guide to Manuscripts and Documents in the British Isles Relating to Africa*. 2 vols. London: Mansell, 1993, 1994.

Penzer, Norman M. *Annotated Bibliography of Sir Richard Burton, K.C.M.G.* London: A. M. Philpot, Ltd., 1923.

Platt, Thomas Pell. *A Catalogue of the Ethiopic Biblical Mss. in the Royal Library of Paris and in the British and Foreign Bible Society*. London: Richard Watts, 1823.

Prabhu, P. M. "Select Bibliography [on Ethiopia, Eritrea, Somalia, and Djibouti]." *AQ*, 34 (2) (1994): 237–87.

Prunier, Gérard A. "La Corne d'Afrique: Éléments Bibliographiques Récents." *Arabica*, 40 (1) (1993): 32–61.

Raineri, Osvaldo. *Catalogo dei Totoli Protettori Etiopici della Collezione Sandro Angelini*. Rome: Edizioni Pia Unione Preziosissimo Sangue, 1990.

Rainero, Romain H. "Les Études Italiennes sur l'Afrique de la fin de la Deuxième Guerre Mondiale à nos Jours." *Afrique Contemporaine*, 19 (109) (1980): 16–21.

Reilly, P. M. *Ethiopia: Land Resources Bibliography*. Surrey: Ministry of Overseas Development, Land Research Division, 1978.

Research and Information Centre on Eritrea. *Bibliography on Eritrea*. Rome: Research and Information Centre on Eritrea, 1982.

Resoum S. Kidane. *The Great Horn of Africa: A Directory of Resources on the World Wide Web*. London: Institute for African Alternatives, 2000.

Rheker, J. R. et al. *Bibliography of East African Mountains, Compiled on the Occasion of the "Workshop on Economy and Socio-Economy of Mount Kenya Area" in Nanyuki, Kenya, March 5–12th, 1989*. Berne: University of Berne, Institute of Geography, 1989.

Roberts, Ursala, and Solomon Amde. *Medicine in Ethiopia: A Bibliography*. Addis Ababa: HSU, Central Medical Library, 1970.

Rosenfeld, Chris Prouty. "Index to the First Ten Years of *EO*." *EO*, 10 (4) (1966): 326–51.

——. "Subject and Author Index, *EO* (1967–1974) and *JES* (1963–1975)." *NAS*, 2 (1) (1980): 81–112.

Rosenfeld, Eugene, and Chris Prouty Rosenfeld. *Historical Dictionary of Ethiopia*. Metuchen, N.J., and London: Scarecrow Press, 1981.

Sbacchi, Alberto. "The Archives of the Consolata Mission and the Formation of the Italian Empire 1913–1943." *History in Africa*, 25 (1998): 319–40.

Scarcia Amoretti, Biancamaria (ed.). *Islam in East Africa: New Sources (Archives, Manuscripts, and Written Historical Sources. Oral History, Archaeology); International Colloquium, Rome, 2–4 December 1999*. Rome: Herder, 2001.

Schever, Yvette. *Bibliographies for African Studies 1979–1986*. London: Hans Zell Publishers, 1988.

Schwab, Peter. "Bibliography on Ethiopia." *Genève-Afrique*, 12 (2) (1973): 122–29.

——. "Selected Bibliography on Ethiopia: Politics and Economics." *East Africa Journal*, 6 (10) (1969): 41–44.

Sergew Haile Salassie. *Bibliography of Ancient and Medieval Ethiopian History*. Addis Ababa: Star Printing Press, 1969.

——. *Source Material for Ancient and Medieval History of Ethiopia*. Addis Ababa: HSU, 1967.

Sheffield, England. City Libraries. *Abyssinia, Italy, the League of Nations*. Sheffield: City Libraries, 1935.

Shiferaw Bekele. "Bibliography of Senior Essays of the Department of History, Addis Ababa University, on Ethno-History and Related Topics." *Sociology-Ethnology Bulletin*, 1 (2) (1992): 102–10.

Shiller, A. A. "Customary Law Tenure among the Highland Peoples of Northern Ethiopia: A Bibliographical Essay." *African Law Studies*, 1 (1969): 1–22.

Simon, Jean. "Bibliographie Éthiopienne, 1946–1951." *Orientalia*, 21 (1952): 47–66, 209–30.

Solomon Gebre Christos. *A Decade of Ethiopian Language Publication*. Addis Ababa: HSU Library, 1970.

Sommer, John. *A Study Guide for Ethiopia and the Horn of Africa*. Boston: African Studies Centre, Boston University, 1969.

Steffanson, Borg G., and Ronald K. Starrett (eds.). *Documents on Ethiopian Politics*. 4 vols. Salisbury, N.C.: Documentary Publications, 1976.

Stella, Gian Carlo. *Adwa: A Bibliography*. Addis Ababa: Institute of Ethiopian Studies, AAU, 1996.

——. *Africa Orientale (Etiopia-Eritrea-Somalia): Colonialismo Italiano Bibliografia*. Ravenna: G. C. Stella, 1983.

——. *Bibliografia Politico-Militaire del Conflitto Italo-Abissino, 1935–36*. Ravenna: G. C. Stella, 1988.

——. "Carlo Conti Rossini e i suoi Scritti Circa l'Etiopia e l'Eritrea (Saggio Bibliografico)." *Quaderni di Studi Etiopici*, 3/4 (1984): 106–28.

——. *Pellegrino Matteucci. Bibliografia*. Ravenna: G. C. Stella, 1983.
Strelcyn, Stefan. *Catalogue des Manucsrits Éthiopiens de l'Accademia Nazionale dei Lincei*. Rome: Accademia Nazionale dei Lincei, 1976.
——. *Catalogue of Ethiopian Manuscripts in the British Library Acquired since the Year 1877*. London: British Museum Publications, 1978.
——. *Catalogue of Ethiopic Manuscripts in the John Rylands University Library of Manchester*. Manchester: Manchester University Press, 1974.
Taye Gulilat. *A Preliminary Bibliography on Ethiopian Economy*. Addis Ababa: HSU, 1969.
Thomas, T. H. "Modern Abyssinia: A Selected Geographical Bibliography." *Geographical Review*, 27 (1) (1937): 120–28.
Tirmizi, Sayyid Akbarali Ibrahimali. *Indian Sources for African History: Guide to the Sources of the History of Africa and of the Indian Diaspora in the Basin of the Indian Ocean in the National Archives of India*. 2 vols. Delhi: International Writers' Emporium [with UNESCO], 1988–1989.
Trudnos, A. *Oromo Documentation, Bibliography and Maps*. Warsaw: Department of African Languages and Culture, Institute of Oriental Studies, 1984.
Tvedt, Terje. *The River Nile and Its Economic, Political and Cultural Role: An Annotated Bibliography*. Bergen: Centre for Development Studies, 2002.
Ullendorff, Edward. "The African Semitic Languages (a Selected Bibliography)." In A. N. Tucker and M. A. Bryan. *The Non-Bantu Languages of North-Eastern Africa*. Oxford: Oxford University Press, 1956: 207–10.
——. *Catalogue of Ethiopian Manuscripts in the Bodleian Library*. Vol. 2. Oxford: CP, 1952.
——. "The Ethiopic Manuscripts in the Royal Library, Windsor Castle." *Rassegna di Studi Etiopici*, 12 (1953): 71–79.
Ullendorff, Edward, and Anne Kelly. "Index of C. Conti Rossini's 'Storia d'Etiopia'." *Rassegna di Studi Etiopici*, 18 (1962): 97–141.
Ullendorff, Edward, and Stephen G. Wright. *Catalogue of Ethiopian Manuscripts in the Cambridge University Library*. Cambridge: Cambridge University Press, 1961.
University of London. School of Oriental and African Studies. *Bibliography of Africa*. Boston: G. K. Hall, 1963–1984.
Unseth, Peter. *Linguistic Bibliography of the Non-Semitic Languages of Ethiopia*. East Lansing: Michigan State University, 1990.
Urban, Emil Karl. *Bibliography of the Avifauna of Ethiopia*. Addis Ababa: APP, 1970.
Varley, Douglas Harold. *Bibliography of Italian Colonization in Africa with a Section on Abyssinia*. New York: Humanities Press, 1970.
Verdier, Isabelle. *Ethiopia: The Top 100 People*. Paris: Indigo Publications, 1997.

Vitale, C. S. *Bibliography on the Climate of Ethiopia: Including the Province of Eritrea.* Silver Spring, Md.: U.S. Department of Commerce, 1968.

Volpe, Michael L. "An Annotated Bibliography of Ethiopian Literature in Russian." *Rassegna di Studi Etiopici*, 32 (1988): 171–93.

——. "New Works by Soviet Experts on Ethiopia." *Africa in Soviet Studies Annual*, (1985): 253–61.

——. "New Works of Soviet Ethiopiologists." *Peoples and Asia and Africa*, (1) (1982): 169–72.

Woolbert, Robert Gale. "Bibliographical Article: Italian Colonial Expansion in Africa." *Journal of Modern History*, 4 (1) (1932): 430–45.

Worku Geda. *Bibliography of Educational Publications on Ethiopia.* Addis Ababa: HSU, Faculty of Education, 1975.

——. *Index of the Ethiopian Journal of Education (1967–1975).* Addis Ababa: HSU, Faculty of Education, 1975.

Wright, Stephen G. "Book and Manuscript Collections in Ethiopia." *JES*, 2 (1) (1964): 11–24.

——. *Ethiopian Incunabula [A Bibliography of Pre-1936 Printed Material Produced in Ethiopia].* Addis Ababa: Commercial Printing Press, 1967.

——. "National Libraries in Ethiopia." *University College Review*, 1 (1) (1961): 41–46.

Wright, William. *Catalogue of the Ethiopic Manuscripts in the British Museum Acquired since the Year 1847.* London: Gilbert and Rivington, 1877.

——. (ed.). *Facsimiles of Manuscripts and Inscriptions.* 5 vols. London: William Cloves and Sons, 1875–83.

——. "List of the Magdala Collection of Ethiopic Manuscripts in the British Museum." *Zeitschrift der Deutschen Morgenländischen Gesellschaft*, 24 (1870): 599–616.

Yarley, D. H. *A Bibliography of Italian Colonisation in Africa with a Section on Abyssinia.* Folkestone: Dawsons, 1970.

Yonas, T. *The Organization and Management of Libraries in Addis Ababa, with Special Emphasis on Public Libraries, 1985–1986.* Addis Ababa: Department of National Libraries and Archives, 1987.

Zanutto, S. "Bibliografica dell'Africa Orientale Italiana." *Gil Annali de Africa Italiana*, 4 (1941): 1335–1405.

——. *Bibliografia Etiopica, in Continuazione alla "Bibliografia Etiopica" die G. Fumagalli.* 2 vols. Roma: Published for the Ministry of Colonies by the Sindicato Italiano Arti Grafiche, 1929.

Zelleke, Kinefe-Rigb. "Bibliography of the Ethiopic Hagiographical Traditions." *JES*, 13 (2) (1975): 57–102.

Zewde Kumlachew. *A Bibliography of Ethiopian Materials Published in the USSR.* Addis Ababa: HSU Libraries, 1975.

——. *Some Bibliographical Materials on the Drought in Ethiopia*. Addis Ababa: AAU Libraries, 1975.

Zotenberg, H. *Catalogue des Manuscrits Ethiopiens (Gheez et Amharique) de la Bibliotheque Nationale*. Paris: Imprimerie Nationale, 1877.

Antiquities and History to 1855

Abdussamad H. Ahmad. "Ethiopian Slave Exports at Matamma, Massawa, and Talura c. 1930–1885." *Slavery and Abolition*, 9 (3) (1988): 93–102.

Abir, Mordechai. "The Emergence and Consolidation of the Monarchies of Enarea and Jimma in the First Half of the Nineteenth Century." *JAH*, 6 (2) (1965): 205–19.

——. *Ethiopia: The Era of Princes; The Challenge of Islam and the Reunification of the Christian Empire 1769–1855*. New York: Frederick A. Praeger, 1968.

——. *Ethiopia and the Red Sea: The Rise and Decline of the Solomonic Dynasty and Muslim-European Rivalry in the Region*. London: FC, 1980.

——. "Trade and Politics in the Ethiopian Region, 1830–1855." Ph.D. diss., School of Oriental and African Studies, 1964.

Andersen, Knud Tage. "The Queen of the Habasha in Ethiopian History, Tradition, and Chronology." *Bulletin of the School of Oriental and African Studies*, 63 (1) (2000): 31–63.

Anfray, Francis. "L'Archéologie d'Axoum en 1972." *Paideuma*, 18 (1972: 50–78.

——. "Aspects de l'Archéologie Éthiopienne." *JAH*, 9 (3) (1968): 345–66.

——. "Chronique Archéologique 1960–64." *Annales d'Ethiopie*, 6 (1965): 3–48.

——. "The Civilization of Aksum from the First to the Seventh Century." In G. Mokhtar (ed.). *General History of Africa II: Ancient Civilizations of Africa*. Berkeley: University of California Press, 1981: 362–78.

——. "Les Fouilles de Yeha (Mai–Juin 1972)." *Travaux de la Recherche Coordonnée sur Programme RCP*, 230 (1) (1972): 57–64.

——. "Matara." *Annales d'Éthiopie*, 7 (1967): 33–97.

——. *Today's Ethiopian Archaeology*. Addis Ababa: HSU, Faculty of Arts, 1965.

Appleyard, David L., et al. *Letters from Ethiopian Rulers (Early and Mid-Nineteenth Century)*. London: OUP, 1985.

The Archaeological Expedition in Ethiopia (Aksum) of the Instituto Universitario Oriental and Boston University. Naples: Institute Universitario Orientale, 1998.

Azaïs, R. P., and R. Chambard. *Cinq Années de Recherches Archéologiques en Éthiopie, Province du Harar et Éthiopie Méridionale*. Paris: Librairie Orientaliste Paul Geuthner, 1931.

Baldet, Henri. *Some Aspects of the Pre-History of Ethiopia: Melka Kontoure and the Omo Valley*. Addis Ababa: General Wingate School, 1972.

Bard, Kathryn et al. "Archaeological Investigations at Bieta Giyorgis, Ethiopia: 1993–1995 Field Seasons." *Journal of Field Archaeology*, 24 (4) (1997): 387–403.

Basset, René. "Études sur l'Histoire d'Éthiopie." *Journal Asiatique*, 17 (1881): 315–434 and 18 (1881): 93–183, 285–389.

Bates, Darrell. "The Abyssinian Boy." *History Today*, 29 (12) (1979): 816–23.

Beardsley, Grace Hadley. "The Ethiopian in Greek and Roman Civilization." Ph.D. diss., Johns Hopkins University, 1922.

Beauregard, Erving E. "Menelik II: Another Look." *TJH*, 5 (2) (1976): 21–31.

Beckingham, Charles Fraser, and George Wynn Brereton Huntingford. *Some Records of Ethiopia, 1593–1646*. London: HS, 1954.

Beke, Charles Tilstone. "A Description of the Ruins of the Church of Martula Mariam in Abissinia." *Archaeologia*, 32 (1847): 38–57.

Belai Giday. *Ethiopian Civilization*. Addis Ababa: Belai Giday, 1992.

Berry, LaVerle. "The Solomonic Monarchy at Gondar, 1630–1755: An Institutional Analysis of Kingship in the Christian Kingdom of Ethiopia." Ph.D. diss., Boston University, 1976.

Brown, Clifton Fleming. *The Conversion Experience in Axum during the Fourth and Fifth Centuries*. Washington, D.C.: Howard University Press, 1973. Also in Lorraine A. Williams (ed.). *Africa and the Afro-American Experience*. Washington: Howard University Press, 1071: 33–58.

——. "A Study of the Evolution of the Theocratic Kingship in Medieval Ethiopia." Ph.D. diss., Howard University, 1979.

Budge, Ernest Alfred Thompson Wallis. *The Queen of Sheba and Her Only Son Menyelek, Being the Book of the Glory of Kings*. London: Medici Society, 1922.

Burette, Henry A. *A Visit to King Theodore*. London: J. C. Hotten, 1868.

Burstein, Stanley (ed.). *Ancient African Civilizations: Kush and Axum*. Princeton, N.J.: Markus Wiener Publishers, 1998.

Butzer, Karl W. "Rise and Fall of Aksum, Ethiopia: A Geo-Archaeology Interpretation." *American Antiquities*, 46 (3) 91981): 471–95.

Chernetsov, S. B. *The Ethiopian Feudalist Monarchy since the 17th Century*. Moscow: Nauka, 1990. [In Russian.]

Chittick, H. Neville. "Excavations at Aksum 1973–74: A Preliminary Report." *Azania*, 9 (1974): 159–205.

——. "Radio Carbon Dates from Aksum." *Azania*, 11 (1976): 179–81.

Contenson, H. de. "Pre-Aksumite Culture." In G. Mokhtar (ed.). *General History of Africa II: Ancient Civilizations of Africa*. Berkeley: University of California Press, 1981: 341–61.

Coutinho, J. Siqueira. *Os Portuguese na Ethiopia*. Lisbon: Congresso da Historia, 1938.

Crummey, Donald. "Imperial Legitimacy and the Creation of Neo-Solomonic Ideology in 19th Century Ethiopia." *CEA*, 28 (1) (1988): 13–43.

De Contenson, Henri. "Les Monuments d'Art Sud-Arabes Découverts sur le Site Haoulti (Ethiopie) en 1959." *Syria*, 39 (1962): 68–83.

——. "Pre-Aksumite Culture." In G. Mokhtar (ed.). *General History of Africa II: Ancient Civilizations of Africa*. Berkeley: University of California Press, 1981: 341–59.

——. "Les Fouilles à Axoum en 1958." *Annales d'Éthiopie*, 5 (1963): 3–39.

——. "Les Fouilles de Haoulti en 1959: Rapport Préliminaire." *Annales d'Éthiopie*, 5 (1963): 41–86.

——. "Les Premiers Rois d'Axoum d'Aprés les Découvertes Récentes." *Journal Asiatique*, 248 (1960): 78–96.

——. "Les Principes Étapes de l'Ethiopie Antique." *CEA*, 2 (5) (1961): 12–23.

——. "Les Subdivisions de l'Archéologie Éthiopienne. Etat de la Question." *Revue Archéologique*, (1962): 189–91.

Doresse, Jean. *L'Empire Prêtre-Jean: L'Ethiopie Antique et Mediévale*. 2 vols. Paris: Plon, 1957.

——. *Ethiopia: Ancient Cities and Temples*. London: Elek Books, 1959.

Ege, S. *Class, State, and Power in Africa: A Case Study of the Kingdom of Shawa (Ethiopia) about 1840*. Wiesbaden: Harrassowitz, 1996.

Fattovich, Rodolfo. *Aksum and the Habashat: State and Ethnicity in Ancient Northern Ethiopia and Eritrea*. Boston: Boston University, African Studies Center, 2000.

——. "Archaeology and Historical Dynamics: The Case of Bieta Giyorgis (Aksum), Ethiopia." *Annali* (Vol. 57). Naples: Instituto Universitario Orientale, 1997.

——. "Remarks on the Peopling of the Northern Ethiopian-Sudanese Borderland in Ancient Historical Times." *Rivista degli Studi Orientali*, 58 (1/4) (1984): 85–106.

——. "Remarks on the Pre-Aksumite Period in Northern Ethiopia." *JES*, 23 (1990): 1–33.

——. "Some Remarks on the Origins of the Aksumite Stelae." *Annales d'Ethiopie*, 14 (1987): 43–69.

Fattovich, Rodolfo, and Kathryn A. Bard. "The I.U.O./B.U. Excavations at Beta Giyorgis (Aksum) in Tigray (Northern Ethiopia)."*JES*, 30 (1) (1997): 1–29.

Fernyhough, Timothy. "Slavery and the Slave Trade in Southern Ethiopia in the Nineteenth Century." *Slavery and Abolition*, 9 (3) (1988): 103–30.

Forbes, Rosita. "The Queen of Sheba." *The Mentor*, 14 (5) (1926): 3–11.

Foster, William (ed.). *The Red Sea and Adjacent Countries at the Close of the Seventeenth Century*. London: HS, 1949.

Garstang, John. *Meroë: The City of the Ethiopians*. Oxford: Oxford University Press, 1911.

Getatchew Haile. "A Note on Writing History From Forgotten Documents." *NAS*, 2 (1) (1980): 73–77.

———. "A Page From the History of Emperor Tewodros II, EMML 1558, f. 27r." *EN*, 2 (2) (1978): 31–34.

———. "Power Struggle in the Medieval Court of Ethiopia: The Case of Batargela-Maryam." *JES*, 15 (1982): 37–56.

———. "A Preliminary Investigation of the Tomara Tasbe't of Emperor Zar'a Ya'eqob of Ethiopia." *Bulletin of the School of Oriental and African Studies*, 43 (2) (1980): 207–34.

Hardy, J. P. (ed.). *Johnson: The History of Rasselas Prince of Abyssinia*. London: OUP, 1968.

Hirsch, Bertrand and François-Xavier Fauvelle-Aymar. "L'Éthiopie Médiévale. État des Lieux Nouveaux Éclairages." *CEA*, 42 (2) (2002): 315–35.

Hotten, John Camden (ed.). *Abyssinia and Its People: or, Life in the Land of Prester John*. London: J. C. Hotton, 1868.

Huntingford, George Wynn Brereton (ed. and trans.). *The Glorious Victories of Amda Seyon, King of Ethiopia*. Oxford: CP, 1965.

Hussein Ahmed. "Aksum in Muslim Historical Traditions." *JES*, 29 (2) (1996): 47–66.

Jackson, John G. *Ethiopia and the Origin of Civilization*. New York: The Blyden Society, 1939.

Jäger, Otto A. and Ivy Pearce. *Antiquities of North Ethiopia: A Guide*. Stuttgart: Brockhaus, 1974.

Kaplan, Stephen. "Notes towards a History of Ase Dawit I (1382–1413)." *Aethiopica: International Journal of Ethiopian Studies*, 5 (2002): 71–88.

Kirwan, L. P. "The Christian Topography and the Kingdom of Axum." *GJ*, 138 (2) (1972): 166–77.

Kobishanov, Yuri M. *Aksum*. State College, Pa.: Pennsylvania State University Press, 1966.

———. "Aksum: Political System, Economics, and Culture, First to Fourth Century." In G. Mokhtar (ed.). *General History of Africa II: Ancient Civilizations of Africa*. Berkeley: University of California Press, 1981: 381–99.

Lamb, Alaistair. "Prester John." *HT*, 7 (5) (1957): 312–21.

Littmann, Euno. *The Chronicle of King Theodore of Abyssinia*. New York: Charles Scribner's Sons, 1902.

Ludolphus, Job. *A New History of Ethiopia*. London: Smith, Elder, 1682.

Marrassini, Paolo. "Some Considerations on the Problem of the 'Syriac Influences' on Aksumite Ethiopia." *JES*, (23) (1990): 35–46.

McCrindle, John W. "Arabia and Abyssinia in Ancient Times." *SGM*, 12 (1896): 139–47.

——. *The Commerce and Navigation of the Erythraean Sea*. Amsterdam: Philo Press, 1982.

Merid Wolde Aregay. "Southern Ethiopia and the Christian Kingdom, 1508–1708, With Special Reference to the Galla Migrations and Their Consequences." Ph.D. diss., University of London, 1971.

——. *Two Unedited Letters of Galawdewos, Emperor of Ethiopia, 1540–1559*. Lisbon: Centro des Estudos Historicos Ultramarinos, 1964.

Munro-Hay, Stuart C. *Aksum: An African Civilisation of Late Antiquity*. Edinburgh: Edinburgh University Press, 1991.

——. "Aksumite Overseas Interests." *NAS*, 13 (2/3) (1991): 127–40.

——. "The Chronology of Aksum: A Reappraisal of the History and Development of the Aksumite State from Numismatic and Archaeological Evidence." Ph.D. diss., University of London, 1978.

——. *Excavations at Aksum: An Account of Research in the Ancient Ethiopian Capital Directed in 1972–74 by the Late Dr. Neville Chittick*. Nairobi: British Institute in Eastern Africa, 1989.

——. "The Rise and Fall of Aksum: Chronological Considerations." *JES*, (23) (1990): 47–53.

——. "A Tyranny of Sources: The History of Aksum from its Coinage." *NAS*, 3 (3) (1981/1982): 1–16.

Natsoulas, Theodore. "The Greeks in Ethiopia: Economic, Political, and Social Life c. 1740–1936." Ph.D. diss., Syracuse University, 1975.

——. "Greeks in Tegre and Shoa during the First Half of the Nineteenth Century." *JES*, 29 (1) (1996): 9–34.

——. "Prologue to Modern Ties between Greece and Ethiopia. The Efforts of Ioannis Kotzikas, 1845–1868." *NAS*, 6 (1/2) (1984): 147–70.

Pankhurst, Estelle Sylvia. "Archaeological Discoveries in Ethiopia." *EO*, 4 (3) (1960): 66–73.

Pankhurst, Richard. "Ethiopia and Somalia." In J. F. Ade Ajayi (ed.). *General History of Africa VI: Africa in the Nineteenth Century Until the 1880s*. Berkeley: University of California Press, 1989: 376–411.

——. *The Ethiopian Borderlands: Essays in Regional History from Ancient Times to the End of the 18th Century*. Lawrenceville, N.J.: RSP, 1997.

——. "Ethiopian Slave Reminiscences of the 19th Century." *TJH*, 5 (1) (1976): 98–110.

——. A Social History of Ethiopia: *The Northern and Central Highlands from Early Medieval Times to the Rise of Emperor Tewodros II*. Trenton, N.J.: RSP, 1992.

Petrides, S. Pierre. *Le Livre d'Or de la Dynastie Salomonienne d'Ethiopie*. Paris: Plon, 1964.

Phillips, Jacke. "Punt and Aksum: Egypt and the Horn of Africa." *JAH*, 38 (3) (1997): 423–57.

Phillips, Wendell. *Qataban and Sheba*. Baltimore: Johns Hopkins University, 1969.

Phillipson, David W. "Aksum in Africa." *JES*, (23) (1990): 55–65.

———. *Ancient Ethiopia: Aksum, Its Antecedents and Successors*. London: British Museum Press, 1998.

———. "The Excavation of Gobedra Reckshelter, Axum." *Azania*, 12 (1977): 53–82.

———. "Excavations at Aksum, Ethiopia, 1993–4." *Antiquaries Journal*, 75 (1995): 1–41.

———. *The Monuments of Aksum*. Addis Ababa and London: AAU Press and The British Institute in Eastern Africa, 1997.

———. "The Significance and Symbolism of Aksumite Stelae." *Cambridge Archaeological Journal*, 4 1994): 189–210.

Phillipson, David W., and Jacke Phillips. "Excavations at Aksum, 1993–96: A Preliminary Report." *JES*, 31 (2) (1998): 1–128.

Rey, C. F. *The Romance of the Portuguese in Abyssinia*. London: H. F. and G. Witherby, 1929.

Russell, Michael. *Nubia and Abyssinia*. London: Darf Publishers, 1833.

Samia Dafa'alla. "Succession in the Kingdom of Napata, 900–300 B.C." *IJAHS*, 26 (1) (1993): 167–74.

Sergew Hable-Selassie. *Ancient and Medieval Ethiopian History to 1270*. Addis Ababa: United Printers, 1972.

Schuster, Angela M. H. "Hidden Sanctuaries of Ethiopia." *Archaeology*, 47 (1) (1994): 28–35.

Shiferaw Bekele. "Yohannes II." *Aethiopica: International Journal of Ethiopian Studies*, 5 (2002): 89–111.

Snowden, Frank M. *Blacks in Antiquity: Ethiopians in the Greco-Roman Experience*. Cambridge, Mass.: Harvard University Press, 1970.

Taddesse Tamrat. "The Horn of Africa: The Solomonids in Ethiopia and the States of the Horn of Africa." In D. T. Niane (ed.). *General History of Africa IV: Africa from the Twelfth to the Sixteenth Century*. Berkeley: University of California Press, 1984: 423–54.

Tedros Kiros. *The Meditations of Zara Yaqoub, a 17th-Century Ethiopian Philosopher*. Boston: Boston University, African Studies Center, 1994.

Tekle Tsadik Mekouria. "Christian Aksum." In G. Mokhtar (ed.). *General History of Africa II: Ancient Civilizations of Africa*. Berkeley: University of California Press, 1981: 401–20.

Weld-Blundell, Herbert (trans.). *The Royal Chronicles of Ethiopia, 1769–1840*. Cambridge: Cambridge University Press, 1922.

Wosene Yefru. "The Pre-Axumite Period: Historiographical Inquiry of Classical Ethiopia in Antiquity." *Henok*, 2 (1991): 1–18.

Zewde Gabre-Selassie. "The Process of Reunification of the Ethiopian Empire 1868–89." 2 vols. D.Phil. diss., Oxford University, 1971.

History from 1855 to Present

Abbink, Jon G. "Breaking and Making the State: The Dynamics of Ethnic Democracy in Ethiopia." *Journal of Contemporary African Studies*, 13 (2) (1995): 149–63.

——. "Ethnicité et 'Démocratisation': Le Dilemme Éthiopien." *Politique Africaine*, (57) (1995): 135–41.

Abebe Hailemelekot. *The Victory of Adowa and What We Owe to Our Heroes: The First Victory of Africa over Colonialists.* Addis Ababa: Abebe Hailemelekot, 1998.

Addis Hiwet. *Ethiopia: From Autocracy to Revolution.* London: Review of African Political Economy, 1975.

Akpan, M. B. "Liberia and Ethiopia, 1880–1914: The Survival of Two African States." In A. Adu Boahen (ed.). *General History of Africa VII: Africa under Colonial Domination 1880–1935.* Berkeley: University of California Press, 1985: 249–82.

——. "Liberia and Ethiopia, 1914–35: Two Independent African States in the Colonial Era." In A. Adu Boahen (ed.). *General History of Africa VII: Africa under Colonial Domination 1880–1935.* Berkeley: University of California Press, 1985: 712–45.

Alemseged Abbay. "The Trans-Mareb Past in the Present." *JMAS*, 35 (2) (1997): 321–34.

Andargachew Tiruneh. *The Ethiopian Revolution 1974–1987.* Cambridge: CUP, 1993.

Anderson, Ruth Thompson. "A Study of the Career of Theodore II, Emperor of Ethiopia, 1855–1868." Ph.D. diss., Ohio State University, 1966.

Asfa Yilma. *Haile Selassie, Emperor of Ethiopia.* New York: D. Appleton-Century Company, 1936.

Assefa Endeshaw. *The February 1974 Ethiopian Revolution.* London: Centre of Ethiopian Studies, 1994.

Bahru Zewde. *A History of Modern Ethiopia 1855–1974.* London: JC, 2001.

——. *Pioneers of Change in Ethiopia: The Reformist Intellectuals of the Early Twentieth Century.* London: JC, 2002.

Bairu Tafla. *A Chronicle of Emperor Yohannes IV (1872–89).* Stuttgart: FS, 1977.

——. "Four Ethiopian Biographies: Dajjazmac Garmame, Dajjazmac Gabra-Egzi'abeher Moroda, Dajjazmac Balca, and Kantiba Gabru Dasta." *JES*, 7 (2) (1969): 1–31.

——. *Pioneers of Change in Ethiopia: The Reformist Intellectuals of the Early Twentieth Century.* Oxford: JC, 2002.

Balsvik, R. *Haile Selassie's Students: The Intellectuals and Social Background to a Revolution 1952–1977*. East Lansing: African Studies Center, Michigan State University, 1985.

Bentwich, Norman. "Ethiopia: Twenty-Five Years after the Emperor's Restoration." *Quarterly Review*, 304 (650) (1966): 379–84.

Biles, Peter. "Living on the Edge." *AR*, 37 (2) (1992): 22–24.

Cassiers, Anne and Jean-Michael Bessette. *Memoires Ethiopiennes*. Paris: L'Harmattan, 2001.

Caulk, Richard Alan. *"Between the Jaws of Hyenas": A Diplomatic History of Ethiopia (1876–1896)*. Wiesbaden: Harrassowitz Verlag, 2002.

——. "Yohannes IV, the Mahdists, and the Colonial Partition of North-East Africa." *TJH*, 1 (2) (1971): 22–42.

Clapham, Christopher. "Ethiopia." In René Lemarchand (ed.). *African Kingships in Perspective*. London: FC, 1977: 35–63.

Colaable, J. "Ethiopia: End of the Reign of Haile Selassie I." *Revista de Politica International*, (135) (1974): 10–34 and (136) (1974): 103–22.

Combes, Paul. *L'Abyssinie en 1896*. Paris: A. André et Cie, 1896.

Conti Rossini, Carlo. *Etiopia e Genti di Etiopia*. Firenze: R. Bemporad, 1937.

——. *Storia d'Etiopia*. Bergamo: Istituto Italiano d'Arti Grafiche, 1928.

Crummey, Donald. "The Violence of Tewodros." *JES*, 9 (2) (1971): 107–25.

Darkwah, Rexford Henry Kofi. "Emperor Theodore II and the Kingdom of Shoa 1855–1865." *JAH*, 10 (1) (1969): 105–15.

——. "The Rise of the Kingdom of Shoa 1813–1889." Ph.D. diss., University of London, 1966.

——. *Shewa, Menelik and the Ethiopian Empire 1813–1889*. London: Heinemann, 1978.

Dawit Wolde Giorgis. *Red Tears: War, Famine and Revolution in Ethiopia*. Trenton, N.J.: RSP, 1989.

Donham, Donald L. *Marxist Modern: An Ethnographic History of the Ethiopian Revolution*. Oxford: JC, 1999.

——. and Wendy James. *The Southern Marches of Imperial Ethiopia*. Cambridge: Cambridge University Press, 1986.

Erlich, Haggai. *Ethiopia and the Challenge of Independence*. Boulder: LR, 1986.

——. "A Political Biography of Ras Alula, 1875–1897." Ph.D. diss., University of London, 1973.

——. *Ras Alula and the Scramble for Africa: A Political Biography: Ethiopia and Eritrea 1875–1897*. Lawrenceville, N.J.: RSP, 1996.

Fernyhough, Timothy Derek. "Serfs, Slaves and Shefta: Modes of Production in Southern Ethiopia from the Late Nineteenth Century to 1941." Ph.D. diss., University of Illinois Urbana-Champaign, 1986.

Firebrace, James, and Gayle Smith. *The Hidden Revolution: An Analysis of Social Change in Tigray (Northern Ethiopia) Based on Eyewitness Accounts.* London: War on Want, 1982.

Germany, Elizabeth. *Ethiopia My Home: The Life of John Moraitis.* Addis Ababa: Shama Books, 2001.

Getahun Dilebo. "Emperor Menelik's Ethiopia, 1865–1916: National Unification or Amhara Communal Domination." Ph.D. diss., Howard University, 1974.

Getatchew Haile. "The Unity and Territorial Integrity of Ethiopia." *JMAS,* 24 (3) (1986): 465–87.

Ghanotakis, Anestis John. "The Greeks of Ethiopia, 1889–1970." Ph.D. diss., Boston University, 1979.

Gilkes, Patrick. "The Coming Struggle for Ethiopia." *AR,* 20 (3) (1974): 33–35, 43.

——. *The Dying Lion: Feudalism and Modernization in Ethiopia.* London: Julian Friedmann, 1974.

——. "Ethiopia: The Beginning of Change?" *CR,* 255 (1302) (1974): 1–7.

Gorham, Charles. *The Lion of Judah: A Life of Haile Selassie I, Emperor of Ethiopia.* New York: Farrar, Straus and Giroux, 1966.

Guèbrè Sellassié. *Chronique du Règne de Ménélik II, Roi des Rois d'Éthiopie.* 2 vols. Paris: Librairie Orientale et Américaine, 1930/1931.

Guluma Gemeda. "Subsistence, Slavery, and Violence in the Lower Omo Valley, Ca. 1898–1940's." *NAS,* 12 (1) (1990): 5–19.

Haile Selassie I (ed. Edward Ullendorff). *My Life and Ethiopia's Progress: 1892–1937.* Oxford: Oxford University Press, 1987.

——. (ed. Harold Marcus, trans. Ezekiel Gebisssa). *My Life and Ethiopia's Progress: Haile Selassie I King of Kings of Ethiopia, Vol. II.* Chicago: Research Associates School Times Publications, 1997.

Hailu Lemma. "The Political Economy of Ethiopia, 1875–1974: Agricultural, Educational, and International Antecedents to the Revolution." Ph.D. diss., University of Notre Dame, 1979.

Hammond, Jenny. *Fire from the Ashes: A Chronicle of the Revolution in Tigray, Ethiopia, 1975–1991.* Lawrenceville, N.J.: RSP, 1999.

Hansberry, William Leo. *Pillars in Ethiopian History.* Washington, D.C.: Howard University Press, 1974.

Holcomb, B. K. and S. Ibssa. *The Invention of Ethiopia: The Making of a Dependent Colonial State in Northeast Africa.* Trenton, N.J.: RSP, 1990.

Holden, David. "Ethiopia—Forty Years On." *Encounter,* 40 (2) (1973): 76–87.

Indrias Getachew. *Beyond the Throne: The Enduring Legacy of Emperor Haile Selassie I.* Addis Ababa: Shama Books, 2001.

Irma Taddia. "Ethiopian Source Material and Colonial Rule in the Nineteenth Century: The Letter to Menilek (1899) by Blatta Gabra Egzi'abeher." *JAH,* 35 (3) (1994): 493–514.

James, Wendy, et al. (eds.). *Remapping Ethiopia: Socialism and After*. Athens: Ohio University Press, 2002.

Kapuscinski, Ryszard. *The Emperor: Downfall of an Autocrat*. New York: Vintage, 1984.

Kinfe Abraham. *Ethiopia from Empire to Federation*. Addis Ababa: Ethiopian International Institute for Peace and Development Press, 2001.

Lockot, Hans Wilhelm. *The Mission: The Life, Reign, and Character of Haile Selassie I*. London: Hurst, 1989.

Luther, Ernest W. *Ethiopia Today*. Stanford: Stanford University Press, 1958.

Manna Gebre Medhin. "The New Policy and Philosophy of Theodore II, King of Kings of Ethiopia: The Reaction of Abuna Salama, Head of the Ethiopian Coptic Orthodox Church." *EJAS*, 3 (2/4/1): 5–34.

Marcus, Harold Golden. "The End of the Reign of Menelik II." *JAH*, 11 (4) (1970): 571–89.

——. *Haile Selassie I: The Formative Years, 1892–1936*. Berkeley: University of California Press, 1987.

——. "A History of the Negotiations Concerning the Border between Ethiopia and British East Africa, 1897–1914." In Jeffrey Butler (ed.). *Boston University Papers on Africa*. Vol. II, *African History*, Boston: Boston University Press, 1966: 237–65.

——. "The Last Years of the Reign of the Emperor Menelik 1906–1913." *Journal of Semitic Studies*, 9 (1964): 229–34.

——. *The Life and Times of Menelik II: Ethiopia 1844–1913*. Lawrenceville, N.J.: RSP, 1995.

——. "Menelik II." In Norman R. Bennett (ed.). *Leadership in Eastern Africa*. Boston: Boston University Press, 1968: 3–62.

McCann, James Craig. "'Children of the House': Slavery and Its Suppression in Lasta, Northern Ethiopia, 1916–1935." In Suzanne Miers and Richard Roberts (eds.). *The End of Slavery in Africa*. Madison: University of Wisconsin Press, 1988: 332–61.

Merie-Hazen Wolde-Qirqos. *History of the Last Ten Years of Emperor Menelik's Reign, 1903–1913*. Addis Ababa: Berhanena Selam, 1957.

Molvaer, Reidulf Knut. "About the Abortive Coup Attempt in Addis Abeba from 5 Tahsas to 8 Tahsas 1953 (14–17 December 1960)." *NAS*, 3 (2) (1996): 97–125.

Mosley, Leonard. *Haile Selassie: The Conquering Lion*. Englewood Cliffs, N.J.: Prentice Hall, 1965.

Mustoe, N. E. "Modern Ethiopia." *AA*, 61 (244) (1962): 216–22.

Pankhurst, Estelle Sylvia. *Ethiopia: A Cultural History*. Woodford Green, UK: Lalibela House, 1955.

Pankhurst, Richard. "Captain Speedy's 'Entertainment': The Reminiscences of a Nineteenth-Century British Traveller to Ethiopia." *Africa*, 38 (3) (1983): 428–48.

——. "Decolonization of Ethiopia, 1940–1955." *HA*, 1 (4) (1978): 10–16.

——. "The Emperor Theodore and the Question of Foreign Artisans in Ethiopia." In Jeffrey Butler (ed.). *Boston University Papers on Africa, Vol. II, African History*. Boston: Boston University Press, 1966: 215–235.

——. "Menilek and the Utilisation of Foreign Skills in Ethiopia." *JES*, 5 (1) (1967): 29–86.

——. "The Role of Foreigners in Nineteenth-Century Ethiopia, Prior to the Rise of Menilek." In Jeffrey Butler (ed.). *Boston University Papers on Africa, Vol. II, African History*. Boston: Boston University Press, 1966: 181–214.

Prather, Ray. *The King of Kings of Ethiopia, Menelik II*. Nairobi: Kenya Literature Bureau, 1981.

Prouty, Chris. *Chronology of "Menelik" II of Ethiopia*. East Lansing: Michigan State University, 1976.

——. *Empress Taytu and Menelek II: Ethiopia 1883–1910*. Trenton, N.J.: RSP, 1986.

Quaranta di San Severino, Ferdinando. *Ethiopia: An Empire in the Making*. London: P.S. King and Son, 1939.

Raphaeli, Nimrod. "Ethiopia: Emperor, Elites, and Modernization." *Civilisations*, 17 (4) (1967): 422–31.

Rémond, Georges. "L'Agonie de L'Empereur Ménélik." *Le Correspondent*, (244) (1911): 335–59.

Rubenson, Sven. *King of Kings: Tewodros of Ethiopia*. Oxford: Oxford University Press, 1966.

——. *The Survival of Ethiopian Independence*. London: Heinemann, 1976.

——. et al (eds.). *Tewodros and His Contemporaries, 1855–1868*. Addis Ababa: AAUP; and Lund: Lund University Press, 1994.

Sandford, Christine. *Ethiopia under Haile Selassie*. London: Dent, 1946.

——. *The Lion of Judah Hath Prevailed: Being the Biography of His Imperial Majesty Haile Selassie I*. London: Dent, 1955.

Schwab, Peter. *Ethiopia and Haile Selassie*. New York: Facts on File, 1972.

——. "Haile Selassie: Leadership in Africa." *Plural Societies*, 6 (2) (1975): 19–30.

——. *Haile Selassie I: Ethiopia's Lion of Judah*. Chicago: Nelson-Hall, 1979.

Skinner, Elizabeth and James Skinner. *Haile Selassie*. London: Thomas Nelson and Sons, 1967.

Smith, Mason McCann. *When the Emperor Dies*. New York: Random House, 1981.

Spencer, John Hathaway. "Haile Selassie: Leadership and Statesmanship." *EN*, 2 (1) (1978): 1–28.

——. "Haile Selassie: Triumph and Tragedy." *Orbis*, 18 (4) (1975): 1129–52.

Tadesse Beyene et al. (eds.). *Kasa and Kasa: Papers on Lives, Times, and Images of Tewodros II and Yohannes IV (1855–1889)*. Addis Ababa: Institute of Ethiopian Studies, 1990.

Talbot, David Abner. *Contemporary Ethiopia*. New York: Philosophical Library, 1952.

——. *Haile Selassie I: Silver Jubilee*. The Hague: Van Stockum, 1955.

Taylor, Richard Bingham. *Menelik of Ethiopia*. London: Longman, 1978.

Terrefe Woldetsadik. "The Unification of Ethiopia (1880–1935): Wallaga." *JES*, 6 (1) (1968): 73–86.

Teshale Tibebu. *The Making of Modern Ethiopia, 1896–1974*. Lawrenceville, N.J.: RSP, 1995.

Tibebe Eshete. "Towards a History of the Incorporation of the Ogaden 1887–1935." *JES*, 27 (2) (1994): 69–87.

Triulzi, Alessandro. "Prelude to the History of a No-Man's Land: Bela Shangul, Wallagga, Ethiopia, (c. 1800–1898)." Ph.D. diss., Northwestern University, 1980.

Ullendorff, Edward. The Two Zions: Reminiscences of Jerusalem and Ethiopia. Oxford: Oxford University Press, 1988.

Vestal, Theodore M. *Ethiopia: A Post-Cold War African State*. Westport, Conn.: Praeger Publishers, 1999.

——. *Freedom of Association in the Federal Democratic Republic of Ethiopia*. Boston: Boston University, African Studies Center, 1998.

Walker, Craven Howell. *The Abyssinian at Home*. London: Sheldon Press, 1933.

Wylde, Augustus Blandy. *Modern Abyssinia*. London: Methuen and Company, 1901.

Yaltasamma. *Les Amis de Ménélik II*. Paris: Librairie Orientale et Américaine, 1899.

Zervos, Adrien. *L'Empire d'Ethiopie: Le Miroir de l'Ethiopie Moderne 1906–1935*. Alexandria: L'Ecole Professionnelle des Freres, 1936.

Zwede Gabre-Selassie. *Yohannes IV Ethiopia: A Political Biography*. Oxford: CP, 1975.

Military and Security Affairs

Abbink, Jon G. "Briefing: The Eritrean-Ethiopian Border Dispute." *AA*, 97 (389) (1998): 551–65.

——. "Ethnic Conflict in the 'Tribal Zone': The Dizi and Suri in Southern Ethiopia." *JMAS*, 31 (4) (1993): 675–82.

——. "Ritual and Political Forms of Violent Practice among the Suri of Southern Ethiopia." *CEA*, 38 (150/152) (1998): 271–95.

Abdussamad H. Ahmad. "Emperor Yohannis' Campaign in Gojjam, August 1888 to February 1889." *NAS*, 13 (1) (1991): 1–7.

Abélès, Marc. "La Guerre vue d'Ochollo Éthiopie Méridionale." *CJAS*, 11 (3) (1977): 455–70.

"The Abyssinian Expedition." *Colburn's United Service Magazine*, (470) (1868): 81–90; (472) (1868): 409–13; and (473) (1868): 565–70.

Acton, Roger. *The Abyssinian Expedition and the Life and Reign of King Theodore*. London: The Illustrated London News, 1868.

Afeworki Wolde Michael. "A Brief Study on the Military History of Ethiopia, 1868–1936." B.A. Thesis. University College of Addis Ababa, 1964.

Africa Watch. *Evil Days: Thirty Years of War and Famine in Ethiopia*. New York: Human Rights Watch, 1991.

——. *Mengistu Has Decided to Burn Us Like Wood: Bombing of Civilians and Civilian Targets by the Air Force*. London: Human Rights Watch, 1990.

Amare Tekle. "Military Rule in Ethiopia (1974–87): The Balance Sheet." *HA*, 13/14 (3/4) (1990/1991): 38–58.

Aronson, Jack M. "The Imperial Ethiopian Navy." *U.S. Naval Institute Proceedings*, 92 (4) (1966): 165–67.

Assam, Hormuzd. *Narrative of the British Mission to Theodore, King of Abyssinia*. 2 vols. London: John Murray, 1969.

Auf, C., et al. "Von der Hand in den Mund: Ex-Soldaten in Äthiopien Erfahrung aus der Evaluierung von Reintegrationsprogrammen." *Afrika Spectrum*, 30 (2) (1995): 163–76.

Babile Tola. *To Kill a Generation: The Red Terror in Ethiopia*. Washington, D.C.: Free Ethiopia Press, 1989.

Baffour Agyeman-Duah. *The United States and Ethiopia: Military Assistance and the Quest for Security 1953–1993*. Lanham, Md.: University Press of America, 1994.

——. "The U.S. and Ethiopia: The Politics of Military Assistance." *Armed Forces and Society*, 12 (2) (1986): 287–306.

Bahru Zewde. "The Military and Militarism in Africa: The Case of Ethiopia." In Eboe Hutchful and Abdoulaye Bathily (eds.). *The Military and Militarism in Africa*. Dakar: Council for the Development of Economic and Social Research in Africa, 1998: 257–289.

Baker, Ross K. "The Ethiopian Army and Political Stability: Prospects and Potentials." *Middle East Studies*, 6 (3) (1970): 331–39.

Bandini, F. *Gli Italiani in Africa: Storia delle Guerre Coloniali (1882–1943)*. Milan: Longanesi, 1971.

Baratieri, Oreste. *Memorie d'Africa (1892–1896)*. Paris: Ch. Delagrave, 1899.

Bates, Darrell. *The Abyssinian Difficulty: The Emperor Theodorus and the Magdala Campaign, 1867–68*. London: Oxford University Press, 1979.

"La Bataille d'Adowa d'Après un Récit Abyssin." *Revue Française de l'Étranger et des Colonies et Exploration*, 21 (1896): 656–58.

Battaglia, Roberto. *La Prima Guerra d'Africa*. Torino: G. Einaudi, 1958.

Baynham, Simon, and Richard Snailham, "Ethiopia." In John Keegan (ed.). *World Armies*. New York: Facts on File, 1979: 206–11.

Beckingham, Charles Fraser. "A Note on the Topography of Ahmed Gran's Campaigns in 1542." *JSS*, 4 (4) (1959): 362–73.

Beke, Charles Tilstone. *The British Captives in Abyssinia*. London: Longmans, Green and Company, 1867.

Bellavita, Emilio. *Adua, i Precedenti: La Battaglia, le Consequence (1881–1931)*. Genoa: Revista di Roma, 1931.

Berhane Woldemichael. "Ethiopian Military in Disarray." *ROAPE*, (44) (1989): 60–63.

Beri, H. M. L. "Ogaden War and the Arms Flux into the Horn of Africa." *Strategic Analysis*, 1 (11) (1978): 14–20.

Berkeley, George Fitz Hardinge. "The Abyssinian Question and Its History." *Nineteenth Century*, 53 (311) (1903): 79–97.

——. *The Campaign of Adowa and the Rise of Menelik*. London: Constable and Company Ltd., 1935.

Biles, Peter. "Bitter Foes." *WT*, 56 (7) (2000): 11–13.

——. "Too Great a Burden." *WT*, 56 (5) (2000): 4–6.

Bizzoni, Achille. "The Battle of Adowa, 1896: A Contemporary Italian View." *EO*, 14 (2) (1971): 115–39.

Blake, Greg. "Ethiopia's Decisive Victory at Adowa." *Military History*, 14 (4) (1997): 62–68.

Blanc, Henry. *A Narrative of Captivity in Abyssinia; with Some Account of the Late Emperor Theodore, His Country and People*. London: FC, 1970.

——. *The Story of the Captives*. London: Longmans, Green, Reader and Dyer, 1868.

Bloch, George. "No Compromise for Eritrea and Ethiopia." *Jane's Intelligence Review*, 12 (1) (2000): 40–44.

Boyce, Frank. "The Internationalizing of Internal War: Ethiopia, the Arabs, and the Case of Eritrea." *Journal of International and Comparative Studies*, 5 (3) (1972): 51–73.

Bronzuoli, A. *Adua*. Rome: Istituto Poligrafico dello Stato, 1935.

Brown, D. J. Latham. "The Ethiopian-Somaliland Frontier Dispute." *International Law and Comparative Law Quarterly*, 5 (1956): 245–64.

——. "Recent Developments in the Ethiopia-Somaliland Frontier Dispute." *International Law and Comparative Law Quarterly*, 10 (2) (1961): 167–78.

Caulk, Richard Alan. "Armies as Predators: Soldiers and Peasants in Ethiopia c. 1850–1935." *IJAHS*, 1 (3) (1978): 475–93.

——. "The Army and Society in Ethiopia." *EN*, 1 (3) (1978): 17–24.

——. "Firearms and Princely Power in Ethiopia in the Nineteenth Century." *JAH*, 13 (4) (1972): 609–30.

——. "Menelik II and the Ethio-Egyptian War of 1875–1876: A Reconsideration of Source Material." *RA*, (11) (1970): 63–69.

——. "Notes on the Conquest of Harar and the Eastward Movement." Addis Ababa: HSU, [mimeogr.], 1967.

——. "The Occupation of Harar: January 1887." *JES*, 9 (2) (1971): 1–19.

——. "The Significance of the Battle of Adua." *History Journal*, 1 (1) (1967): 13–16.

——. "Territorial Competition and the Battle of Embabo, 1882." *JES*, 13 (1) (1975): 65–88.

Chandler, David G. "The Expedition to Abyssinia, 1867–8." In Brian Bond (ed.). *Victorian Military Campaigns*. London: Hutchinson and Company, 1967: 107–59.

Cheek, James. "Ethiopia: A Successful Insurgency." In Edwin G. Corr and Stephen Sloan (eds.). *Low-Intensity Conflict: On Threats in a New World*. Boulder: WP, 1992: 125–49.

Christides, Vassilios. "The Himyarite-Ethiopian War and the Ethiopian Occupation of South Arabia in the Acts of Gregentius (c. 530 A.D.)." *Annales d'Ethiopie*, 9 (2) (1972): 115–46.

Chronology of the Ethio-Eritrean War and Basic Documents. Addis Ababa: Walta Information Center, 2001.

Clapham, Christopher. "Ethiopia: The Institutionalisation of a Marxist Regime." In Christopher Clapham and George Philip (eds.). *The Political Dilemmas of Military Regimes*. Ottawa: Barnes and Noble Books, 1985: 255–76.

——. "Ethiopia and Eritrea: Insecurity and Intervention in the Horn." In Oliver Furley and Roy May (eds.). *African Interventionist States*. Aldershot: Ashgate Publishers, 2001: 119–37.

——. "Ethiopia and Somalia." In *Conflicts in Africa*. London: International Institute of Strategic Studies, 1972: 1–23.

——. "The Ethiopian Coup d'Etat of December 1960." *JMAS*, 6 (4) (1968): 495–507.

——. "The Structure of Regional Conflict in Northern Ethiopia." *Disasters*, 15 (3) (1991): 244–54.

——. *Transformation and Continuity in Revolutionary Ethiopia*. Cambridge: Cambridge University Press, 1988.

Clark, Kimberly M. "The Demobilization and Reintegration of Soldiers: Perspective from USAID." *AT*, 42 (1/2) (1995): 49–60.

Clarke, Walter S. "The 'Esayi Dream: A Footnote to the Ogaden War." *NAS*, 13 (1) (1991): 29–38.

Cohen, John Michael. "Traditional Politics and the Military Coup in Ethiopia." *AA*, 74 (295) (1975): 222–48.

Cole, Ernest. *Ethiopia: Political Power and the Military*. Paris: The Indian Ocean Newsletter, 1985.

Colletta, Nat J., et al. *Case Studies of War-to-Peace Transition: The Demobilization and Reintegration of Ex-Combatants in Ethiopia, Namibia, and Uganda*. Washington, D.C.: World Bank, 1996.

Connell, Dan. "From Alliance to the Brink of All-Out War: Explaining the Eritrea-Ethiopia Border Crisis." *Middle East Report*, 28 (3) (1998): 40–43.

———. "New Ethiopian Offensive in the Ogaden." *HA*, 3 (4) (1980/1981): 51–54.

Conti Rossini, Carlo. *Italia ed Etiopia: Dal tratto d'Uccialli alla Battagli di Adua*. Rome: Istituto per l'Oriente, 1935.

Corselli, Rodolfo. *La Battaglia di Adua Secondo gli Ultimi Accertamenti*. Rome: Carlo Voghera, 1930.

Crispi, Francesco. *La Prima Guerra d'Africa: Documenti e Memorie*. Milano: G. Garzanti, 1939.

Currie, C. B. "Medical History of the Abyssinian Expedition." *Army Medical Department Report*, 9 (1867): 277–99.

Defense Intelligence Agency. Directorate for Intelligence Research. *Ethiopia Embattled: A Chronology of Events in the Horn of Africa, 1 July 1977–30 March 1978*. Washington, D.C.: Defense Intelligence Agency, 1978.

Del Bono, Giulio. *Da Assab ad Adua*. Rome: Unione Editoriale d'Italia, n.d.

DeMars, William Emile. "Helping a People in a People's War: Humanitarian Organizations and the Ethiopian Conflict, 1980–1988." Ph.D. diss., University of Notre Dame, 1993.

Dercon, Stefan, and Daniel Ayalew. "Where Have All the Soldiers Gone: Demobilization and Reintegration in Ethiopia." *WD*, 26 (9) (1998): 1661–75.

D'Hendecourt, Louis. *L'Expedition d'Abyssinie en 1868*. Paris: J. Claye, 1869.

Diamond, Robert A., and David Fouquet. "American Military Aid to Ethiopia and Eritrean Insurgency." *AT*, 19 (1) (1972): 37–43.

Dispatches from the Electronic Front: Internet Responses to the Ethio-Eritrean Conflict. Addis Ababa: Walta Information Center, c. 2000.

Dunn, J. "For God, Emperor, Country! The Evolution of Ethiopia's Nineteenth-Century Army." *War in History*, 7 (3) (1994): 278–99.

Dye, William McE. *Moslem Egypt and Christian Abyssinia; Or, Military Service under the Khedive*. New York: Atkin and Prout Printers, 1880.

Eavis, Paul. "SALW in the Horn of Africa and the Great Lakes Region: Challenges and Ways Forward." *Brown Journal of World Affairs*, 9 (1) (2002): 251–60.

"The Egyptian Campaign in Abyssinia." *Littell's Living Age*, 134 (1877): 278–87.

El-Khawas, Mohamed A. "Arab Involvement in the Horn of Africa: The Ogaden War." *Journal for Arab and Islamic Studies*, 2 (3/4) (1981): 567–82.

Enahoro, Peter. "Ethiopia: Army Tightens Grip." *Africa*, (68) (1977): 16–18.

——. "Ethiopia-Sudan-Somalia: War of Nerves." *Africa*, (66) (1977): 16–17.

Erickson, E. "Sociology of a Company Town under United States Army Sponsorship." Ph.D. diss., University of Chicago, 1952.

Erlich, Haggai. "The Ethiopian Army and the 1974 Revolution." *Armed Forces and Society*, 9 (3) (1983): 455–81.

Esterhuysen, Pieter. "Eritrea-Ethiopia: Family Feud." *Africa Insight*, 28 (1/2) (1998): 90–92.

Ethiopia. Ministry of Foreign Affairs. *Memorandum: War Drums on the Horn of Africa March of Somalia's Expansionism.* Addis Ababa: Berhanena Selam Printing Press, 1977.

"Ethiopia." In George Thomas Kurian (ed.). *World Encyclopedia of Police Forces and Penal Systems.* New York and Oxford: Facts on File, 1989: 109–12.

"Ethiopia: Conquest and Terror." *HA*, 4 (1) (1981): 8–19.

Ethiopia Ministry of Information. *National Defence in Ethiopia.* Addis Ababa: Publications and Foreign Languages Press Department, 1968.

"Ethiopia-Somalia: Battle of Marda Pass." *Africa*, (73) (1977): 31–33.

"Ethiopia-Somalia: Gains and Loses in the Ogaden War." *Africa*, (72) (1977): 41–44.

"Ethiopia's Hidden War: The Oromo Liberation Struggle." *HA*, 5 (1) (1982): 62–67.

"Ethiopia's Young Navy." *EO*, 3 (9) (1959): 281–91.

Fanton, A. *L'Abyssinie: Lors de l'Expédition Anglaise (1867–1868).* Paris: Librairie Orientaliste Paul Geuthner, 1936.

Festing, E. G. "Britain's Little Wars: The Abyssinian Expedition Thirty Years Ago. *USM*, 15 (824) (1897): 429–33.

Fourrière, Sylvain. "Erythrée-Ethiopie: Un An de Guerre." *Afrique Contemporaine*, (190) (1999): 55–61.

Gaibi, Agostino. *La Guerra d'Africa (1895–1896).* Rome: Tiber, 1930.

Galaydh, Ali K. *Intergovernmental Negotiation: Soviet-Somali Relations and the Ogaden War, 1978–1979.* Washington, D.C.: Georgetown University, 1993.

Gebru Tareke. *Ethiopia: Power and Protest. Peasant Revolts in the Twentieth Century.* Cambridge: Cambridge University Press, 1991.

——. "The Ethiopia-Somalia War Revisited." *IJAHS*, 33 (3) (2000): 615–34.

——. "From Lash to Red Star: The Pitfalls of Counter-Insurgency in Ethiopia, 1980–82." *JMAS*, 40 (3) (2002): 465–98.

——. "Preliminary History of Resistance in Tigrai (Ethiopia)." *Africa*, 39 (2) (1984): 201–26.

Ghebresillash Girman. *Kalter Krieg am Horn von Afrika. Regional Konflikte: Äthiopien und Somalia im Spannungsfeld der Supermächte 1945–1991.* (Baden-Baden: Nomos Verlagsgesellschaft, 1999).

Gilkes, Patrick. "The Battle of Af Abet and Eritrean Independence." *NAS,* Vol. 2 No. 3 (1995): 39–52.

——. "The Ethiopian Army; Ideology and Morale and Myth and Reality." *Proceedings of the Second International Conference on the Horn of Africa.* New York: New School for Social Research, 1987: 136–44.

Gilkes, Patrick, and Martin Plaut. *War in the Horn: The Conflict between Eritrea and Ethiopia.* London: The Royal Institute of International Affairs, 1999.

Githongo, John. "Trouble in the Horn: The Threat of War between Eritrea and Ethiopia." *East African Alternatives,* September/October 1998: 4–7.

Gleichen, Count A. E. *With the Mission to Menelik, 1897.* London: Edward Arnold, 1898.

Great Britain. *Abyssinian Raids into British Territory.* London: HMSO, 1925.

Great Britain. Foreign Office. *Correspondence Relating to the Murder of Mr. Jenner, and the Ogaden Punitive Expedition.* London: HMSO, 1901.

——. *Correspondence Respecting Abyssinian Raids and Incursions into British Territory.* London: HMSO, 1925.

——. *Papers Concerning Raids from Ethiopian Territory into the Anglo-Egyptian Sudan.* London: HMSO, 1932.

——. *Treaty Regulating the Importation into Ethiopia of Arms, Ammunition, and Implements of War, 21 August 1930.* London: HMSO, 1932.

Great Britain. India Office. *Abyssinian Expedition: Papers Connected with the Abyssinia Expedition.* 4 parts. London: HMSO, 1867–68.

Great Britain. Parliament. *Papers Connected with the Abyssinian Expedition.* London: HMSO, 1876.

Great Britain. War Office. *The Abyssinian Campaigns: The Official Story of the Conquest of Italian East Africa.* London: HMSO, 1942.

Griaule, M. "Un Camp Militaire Abyssin." *Journal de la Société des Africanistes,* 4 (1934): 117–22.

Grilz, Almerigo. "Ethiopia Fights a War of Confusion." *Jane's Defense Weekly,* 7 (16) (25 April 1987): 762–64.

Haile Semere. "The Roots of the Ethiopian-Eritrean Conflict." *Issue,* 15 (1987): 9–17.

——. "The Roots of the Ethiopia-Eritrea Conflict: The Erosion of the Federal Act." *Journal of Eritrean Studies,* 1 (1) (1996): 1–18.

Hailu Tsegaye. "The Ethiopia-Somalia Conflict." Ph.D. diss., University of Manchester, 1983.

Hall, Marilyn Ann. "The Ethiopian Revolution: Group Interaction and Civil-Military Relations." Ph.D. diss., George Washington University, 1977.

Haly, George Thomas. *The Abyssinian Expedition and the Management of Troops in Unhealthy Localities*. London: Smith, Elder and Son, 1867.

Hamilton, Kevin. "Beyond the Border War: The Ethio-Eritrean Conflict and International Mediation Efforts."*Journal of Public and International Affairs*, 11 (2000): 113–36.

Hendrie, Barbara. "Assisting Refugees in the Context of Warfare." In Tim Allen (ed.). *In Search of Cool Ground: War, Flight, and Homecoming in Northeast Africa*. London: JC, 1996: 35–43.

——. *The Impact of the War in Tigray*. Addis Ababa: Inter-Africa Group, 1991.

——. "The Impact of War in Tigray Province, Ethiopia." In Terje Tvedt (ed.). *Conflicts in the Horn of Africa: Human and Ecological Consequences of Warfare*. Uppsala: Department of Social and Economic Geography, Uppsala University, 1993: 85–98.

Henty, George Alfred. *The March to Magdala: Letters Reprinted from the "Standard" Newspaper*. London: Tinsley Brothers, 1868.

Henze, Paul Bernard. "Eritrea: The Endless War." *Washington Quarterly*, 9 (2) (1986): 23–36.

——. *Eritrea's War*. Addis Ababa: Shama Books, 2001.

——. *Rebels and Separatists in Ethiopia: Regional Resistance to a Marxist Regime*. Santa Monica: The Rand Corporation, 1985.

Hernon, Ian. "The Magdala Campaign, 1867–8." In Ian Hernon. *Massacre and Retribution: Forgotten Wars in the Nineteenth Century*. Stroud: Sutton Publishing, 1998: 99–129.

Holland, Trevenen James, and Henry Montague Hozier. *Record of the Expedition to Abyssinia*. 3 vols. London: HMSO, 1870.

Hooker, J. R. "The Foreign Office and the 'Abyssinian Captives.'" *JAH*, 11 (2) (1961): 245–58.

Hozier, Henry Montague. *The British Expedition to Abyssinia*. London: Macmillan and Company, 1869.

Iyob, Ruth. "The Ethiopian-Eritrean Conflict: Diasporic vs. Hegemonic States in the Horn of Africa." *JMAS*, 38 (4) (2000): 659–82.

Jacobs, M., and C. Schloeder. *Impacts of Conflict on Biodiversity and Protected Areas in Ethiopia*. Washington, D.C.: Biodiversity Support Program, 2001.

Jadout, Jacques. "Les Missions Militaires Belges en Ethiopie, Janvier 1930–Octobre 1935: La Collaboration Officielle, Aspects Technique, Economique et Diplomatique." *Revue Belge d' Histoire Militaire*, 27 (1) (1987): 23–48.

Jaenen, Cornelius J. "Theodore II and British Intervention in Ethiopia." *Canadian Journal of History*, 1 (2) (1996): 27–56.

Jésman, Czeslaw. "Egyptian Invasion of Ethiopia." *AA*, 58 (230) (1959): 75–81.

——. "The Tragedy of Magdala: An Historical Study." *EO*, 10 (2) (1966), 94–151.

Kaplan, Robert D. "The Loneliest War." *Atlantic*, 262 (1) (1988): 58–67.

Khadiagala, Gilbert M. "Reflections on the Ethiopia-Eritrea Border Conflict." *The Fletcher Forum of World Affairs*, 23 (2) (1999): 39–56.

Kidane Mengisteab. "Some Latent Factors in the Ethio-Eritrea Conflict." *ESR*, 3 (2) (1999): 89–106.

Koehn, Peter. "Ethiopian Politics: Military Intervention and Prospects for Further Change." *AT*, 22 (2) (1975): 7–21.

Korn, David A. "Ethiopia on the Verge of Disaster." *Journal of Third World Studies*, 7 (1) (1990): 20–40.

Le Houerou, Fabienne. *Ethiopie-Erythree: Freres Ennemis de la Corne de l'Afrique*. Paris: L'Harmattan, 2000.

Laitin, David Dennis. "The War in the Ogaden: Implications for Siyaad's Role in Somali History." *JMAS*, 17 (1) (1979): 95–115.

Laitin, David Dennis, and D. A. Harker. "Military Rule and National Secession: Nigeria and Ethiopia." In Morris Janowitz (ed.). *Civil Military Relations: Regional Perspectives*. (Beverly Hills, Sage Publications, 1981): 258–86.

Lefebvre, Jeffrey Alan. *Arms for the Horn: U.S. Security Policy in Ethiopia and Somalia, 1953–1991*. Pittsburgh: University of Pittsburgh Press, 1992.

——. "Donor Dependency and American Arms Transfers to the Horn of Africa: The F-5 Legacy." *JMAS*, 25 (3) (1987): 465–88.

——. "The United States, Ethiopia, and the 1963 Somali-Soviet Arms Deal: Containment and the Balance of Power Dilemma in the Horn of Africa." *JMAS*, 36 (4) (1998): 611–43.

Lefever, Ernest W. *Spear and Scepter: Army, Police, and Politics in Tropical Africa*. (Chapters 4 and 5 on Ethiopia). Washington: Brookings Institutions, 1970.

Lemmu Baissa. "The Oromo and the Quest for Peace in Ethiopia." *Transafrica Forum*, 9 (1) (1992): 57–68.

——. "U.S. Military Assistance to Ethiopia, 1953–1974: A Reappraisal of a Difficult Patron-Client Relationship." *NAS*, 11 (3) (1989): 51–70.

Levine, Donald Nathan. "The Military in Ethiopian Politics: Capabilities and Constraints." In Henry Bienen (ed.). *The Military Intervenes: Case Studies in Political Development*. New York: Russell Sage Foundation, 1968: 5–34.

——. "Politics and the Military in Ethiopia." In American Institute for Research. *The Military and Politics in Five Developing Nations*. Kensington, Md.: Center for Research in Social Systems, 1970: 16–34.

Lewis, Ioan Myrddin. "The Ogaden War and the Fragility of Somali Segmentary Nationalism." *AA*, 88 (353) (1989): 573–79.

Lewis, William H. "Ethiopia-Somalia (1977–1978)." In Robert E. Harkavy and Stephanie G. Neuman (eds.). *The Lessons of Recent Wars in the Third World, Volume I: Approaches and Case Studies.* Vol. I. Lexington, Mass.: Lexington Books, 1985: 99–116.

Lukanty, Jadwiga. "Armed Conflicts in Ethiopia and the Superpowers." *Hemispheres*, 6 (1989): 101–20.

Lyons, Terrence. "The International Context of Internal War: Ethiopia/Eritrea." In Edmond J. Keller and Donald Rothchild (eds.). *Africa in the New International Order.* Boulder: LR, 1996: 85–99.

MacDougall, Patrick Leonard. "The Egyptian Campaign in Abyssinia, From the Notes of a Staff Officer." *Blackwood's Edinburgh Magazine*, 122 (1877): 26–39.

MacMunn, George. "The British Expedition to Abyssinia, 1867–68." *Nineteenth Century*, 118 (705) (1935): 569–79.

Manaye, T. *Ethio-Eritrean Conflict and Its Impact on the Region.* Nairobi: Junior Graphics, 1999.

Marcus, Harold Golden. "The Embargo on Arms Sales to Ethiopia, 1916–1930." *IJAHS*, 16 (2) (1983): 263–79.

Markakis, John. "The Military State of Ethiopia's Path to Socialism." *ROAPE*, (21) (1981): 7–25.

Markakis, John. "The 1963 Rebellion in the Ogaden." In T. Labahn (ed.). *Proceedings of the Second International Congress of Somali Studies, University of Hamburg, August 1–6 1983.* vol. 2 Hamburg: Helmut Buske, 1984: 291–310.

Markakis, John, and Nega Ayele. *Class and Revolution in Ethiopia.* Trenton, NJ: RSP, 1986.

Markham, Clements Robert. "The Abyssinian Expedition." *Macmillan's Magazine*, 17 (1868): 435–46 and 18 (1868): 193–208, 289–96, 879–96

——. *A History of the Abyssinian Expedition.* London: Macmillan and Company, 1869.

Matthies, Volker. "Der Ogadenkrieg zwischen Somalia und Äthiopien von 1977/78." *Afrika Spectrum*, 22 (3) (1987): 237–53.

Maurice, F. "The Dongola Campaign." *USM*, 13 (810) (1896): 113–23.

Mayall, John. "The Battle for the Horn: Somali Irredentism and International Diplomacy." *WT*, 34 (9) (1978): 336–43.

Mburu, Nene. "Patriots or Bandits? Britain's Strategy for Policing Eritrea, 1941–1952." *Nordic Journal of African Studies*, 9 (2) (2000): 85–104.

McCann, James Craig. "The Political Economy of Rural Rebellion in Ethiopia: Northern Resistance to Imperial Expansion, 1928–1935." *IJAHS*, 18 (4) (1985): 601–23.

McMunigle, Francis M. "Ethiopia: Its Significance to the Defense Posture of the United States." Thesis. Air University, Air War College, 1964.

McVay, William D. "The Role of the Imperial Ethiopian Air Force as an Instrument of National Power." Thesis. Air University, Air War College, 1965.

Menarini, G. *La Brigata Dabormida alla Battaglia d'Adua*. Naples: Detken, 1898.

Merid Wolde Aregay. "A Reappraisal of the Impact of Firearms in the History of Warfare in Ethiopia (c. 1500–1800)." *JES*, 14 (1)(1980): 98–121.

Merriam, John G. "Military Rule in Ethiopia." *CH*, 71 (421) (1976): 170–73, 183–84.

Mesfin Wolde Mariam. *The Background of the Ethio-Somalia Boundary Dispute*. Addis Ababa: Berhanena Selam, 1964.

Michaelson, Marc. "Peace Fails, War Resumes—Why?" *Institute of Current World Affairs Letters*, (February 1999): 1–11.

Mohammed Hassen Ali. "The Militarization of the Ethiopian State and its Impact on the Oromo." In *Proceedings: Fifth International Conference on the Horn of Africa*. New York: Center for the Study of the Horn of Africa, 1991: pp. 91–102.

Morelli, Anthony. *The Role of U.S. Military Assistance in Ethiopia*. Montgomery, Ala.: Air University, 1970.

Mrázkova, Jana. "The Colonial War in Ethiopia, 1885–1986." *Archiv Orientalni*, 48 (1980): 195–216.

Muffin, Tom. "Ethiopia and Eritrea: A War of Attrition." *Air Forces Monthly*, (149) (2000): 66–71.

Murray, Roger. "The Role of the Military in Ethiopia." *Challenge*, 7 (1) (1967): 33–34.

Myatt, Frederick. *The March to Magdala: The Abyssinian War of 1868*. London: Leo Cooper, 1970.

Napier, Robert Cornelius. "The Abyssinian Expedition." *Blackwood's Magazine*, 123 (1867): 510–33.

Napper, Larry C. "The Ogaden War: Some Implications for Crisis Prevention." In Alexander L. George (eds.). *Managing U.S.-Soviet Rivalry: Problems of Crisis Prevention*. Boulder, Colo.: WP, 1983: 225–54.

Nicholas, Gildas E. F. "Peasant Rebellions in the Socio-Political Context of Today's Ethiopia." *Pan African Journal*, 7 (3) (1974): 235–62.

Norme Pratiche per la Guerra Italo-Abissinia. Napoli: A. Marano, 1887.

Nzo-Nguty, Bernard. "Impact and Contradictions of United States Military Assistance to Ethiopia." *African Studies Association Papers*, 25 (71) (1982): 1–33.

"Ogaden: The Scourge of War." *Africa*, (81) (1978): 27–29.

Onyango, P. Godfrey. "Territorial Claim as the Model Determinant of Inter-State Conflicts between Ethiopia and Somalia, 1960–1991." In P. Godfrey Okoth and Bethwell A. Ogot (eds.). *Conflict in Contemporary Africa*. Nairobi: Jomo Kenyatta Foundation, 2000: 82–93.

Pankhurst, Estelle Sylvia. "The Haile Selassie Military Academy." *EO*, 4 (10) (1960): 331–32.

——. "The Haile Selassie Military Academy (Harar)." *EO*, 2 (2) (1958): 79–80.

Pankhurst, Richard. "The Battle of Adwa." *Quarterly Yekatit*, 7 (3) (1984): 11–16 and 10 (3) (1987): 15, 18–20

——. "The Battle of Adwa as Depicted in Traditional Ethiopian Art: Changing Perceptions." *Bulletin des Seances de l'Academie Royale des Sciences d'Outre-Mer*, 33 (2) (1987): 199–233.

——. "The Battle of Adwa: The View by 'The Times.'" *Quarterly Yekatit*, 8 (3) (1985): 17–21.

——. "The Battle of Dogali." *Quarterly Yekatit*, 10 (2) (1986): 19–21.

——. "The Battle of Maqdala." *Quarterly Yekatit*, 11 (3) (1988): 22–26.

——. "The Effects of War in Ethiopian History." *EO*, 7 (2) (1963): 143–64.

——. "The Ethiopian Army of Former Times." *EO*, 7 (2) (1963): 118–43.

——. "Fire-Arms in Ethiopian History (1800–1935)." *EO*, 6 (2) (1962): 135–80.

——. "Guns in Ethiopia." *Transition*, 20 (1965): 26–33.

——. "The Historic Battle of Adowa." *Archiv Orientalni*, 2 (4) (1970): 20–24.

——. *A History of the Ethiopian Army*. Addis Ababa: Artistic Printers, 1967.

——. "The History of the Battle of Adowa." *EO*, 2 (4) (1970): 20–24.

——. "The History of Fire-Arms in Ethiopia Prior to the Nineteenth Century." *EO*, 11 (3) (1967): 202–25.

——. "Indian Reactions to the Anglo-Indian Intervention against Emperor Tewodros of Ethiopia." *Quarterly Review of Historical Studies, Calcutta*, 19 (3) (1979/1980): 7–38.

——. "Indian Reactions to the Anglo-Indian Intervention against Emperor Téwodros of Ethiopia: The Magdala Campaign of 1867–8." *Africa*, 36 (3/4) (1981): 390–418.

——. "An Inquiry into the Penetration of Fire-Arms into Southern Ethiopia in the 19th Century Prior to the Reign of Menelik." *EO*, 12 (2) (1968): 128–36.

——. *An Introduction to the History of the Ethiopian Army*. Genbot, Ethiopia: Imperial Ethiopian Air Force 101st Training Centre, 1959.

——. "Linguistic and Cultural Data on the Penetration of Fire-Arms into Ethiopia." *JES*, 9 (1) (1971): 47–82.

——. "Menelik's Proclamation on Mobilizing His Forces for the Battle of Adua." *EO*, 1 (11) (1957): 347–48.

——. "The Napier Expedition and the Loot from Maqdala." *Présence Africaine*, (133/134) (1985): 233–40.

——. "Popular Opposition in Britain to British Intervention against Emperor Tewodros of Ethiopia." *EO*, 16 (3) (1973): 141–203.

——. "The Role of Fire-Arms in Ethiopian Culture (16th to 20th Centuries)." *Journal des Africanistes*, 48 (2) (1971): 131–44.

——. "Sir Robert Napier's Comments on Clement Markham's History of the Abyssinian Expedition." *EO*, 12 (1) (1968): 58–60.

Papp, Daniel S. "The Soviet Union and Cuba in Ethiopia." *CH*, 76 (445) (1979): 110–14, 129–30.

Pateman, Roy. "The Eritrean War." *Armed Forces and Society*, 17 (1) (1990): 81–98.

——. "Soviet Arms Transfers to Ethiopia." *TransAfrica Forum*, 8 (1) (1991): 43–57.

Paulos Milkias. "Ethiopia and Eritrea at War: Saga of Triumph and Tragedy at the Dawn of the Millennium." *HA*, 17 (1–4) (1999): 33–71.

Payton, Gary D. "The Soviet-Ethiopian Liaison: Airlift and Beyond." *Air University Review*, 31 (1) (1979): 66–73.

Péninou, Jean-Louis. "The Ethiopian-Eritrean Border Conflict." *Boundary and Security Bulletin*, 6 (2) (1998): 46–50.

——. "Guerre Absurde entre l'Ethiopie et l'Erythrée." *ROAPE*, 25 (77) (1998): 504–8.

Pétridès, Stephanos Pierre. *Les Héroes d'Adowa: Ras Makonnen Prince d'Éthiopie*. Paris: Plon, 1963.

Plaut, Martin. "On the Map." *WT*, 54 (7) (1998): 191–92.

——. "Towards a Cold Peace? The Outcome of the Ethiopia-Eritrea War of 1988–2000." *ROAPE*, 87 (28) (2001): 125–29.

Porter, Bruce D. "The Ogaden War." In Bruce D. Porter (ed.). *The USSR in Third World Conflicts: Soviet Arms and Diplomacy in Local Wars 1945–1980*. Cambridge: CUP, 1984: 182–215.

Pritchard, H. B. "Photography in Connection with the Abyssinian Expedition." *British Journal of Photography*, 5 (1868): 601–3.

Raineri, Osvaldo. "La Battaglia di Adua Secondo Cerulli Ethiopico." *Aethiopica: International Journal of Ethiopian Studies*, 1 (1998): 85–100.

Rainero, Romain H. "The Battle of Adowa on 1 March 1896: A Reappraisal." In J. A. de Moor and H. L. Wesseling (eds.). *Imperialism and War*. Leiden: E. J. Brill and Universitaire pers Leiden, 1989: 189–200.

Rennell, Francis James. *British Military Administration in Occupied Territories in Africa during the Years 1941–1947*. London: HMSO, 1948.

Robinson, Arthur E. "The Egyptian-Abyssinian War of 1874–1876." *JRAS*, 26 (103) (1927): 263–80.

Rodgers, Nini. "The Abyssinian Expedition of 1867–1868: Disraeli's Imperialism or Jane's Murray's War?" *Historical Journal*, 27 (1) (1984): 129–49.

——. "The Antecedents of the Anglo-Abyssinian Campaign of 1867–1868." Ph.D. diss., Queen's University, Belfast, 1979.

Romero Garcia, Eladi. "1896: El Desastre Italiano de Adua." *Historia y Vida*, 22 (252) (1989): 92–99.

Rovaud, Alaui. "La Guerre d'Ethiopie et l'Opinion Mondiale." *L'Afrique et l'Asie*, 156 (1988): 56–61.

Rubenson, Sven. "Adwa 1896: The Resounding Protest." In Robert I. Rotberg and Ali Mazrui (eds.). *Protest and Power in Black Africa*. New York: OUP, 1970: 113–42.

S. W. F. "The War Department, Abyssinia, and Army Supply." *Colburn's United Service Magazine*, (472) (1868): 317–23.

Schwab, Peter. "Rebellion in Ethiopia: A Study of Gojam Province." *East Africa Journal*, 6 (11) (1969): 29–33.

——. "Rebellion in Gojam Province, Ethiopia." *CJAS*, 4 (2) (1970): 240–56.

Shehim, Kassim. "Ethiopia, Revolution, and the Question of Nationalities: The Case of the Afar." *JMAS*, 23 (2) (1985): 331–48.

Shepard, A. F. *The Campaign in Abyssinia*. Bombay: Times of India, 1868.

Shindo, Eiichi. "Hunger and Weapons: The Entropy of Militarisation." *ROAPE*, (33) (1985): 6–22.

Silkin, Trish, and Barbara Hendrie. "Research in the War Zones of Eritrea and Northern Ethiopia." *Disasters*, 21 (2) (1997): 166–76.

Simonds, Charles R. "External Military Involvement in the Provision of Humanitarian Relief in Ethiopia." In Thomas G. Weiss (ed.). *Humanitarian Emergencies and Military Help in Africa*. Basingstoke: Macmillan, 1990: 61–73.

Simone, Edward C. *The Southwestern Military Campaigns of Sahla Selassie: A Reappraisal*. Addis Ababa: Historical Society of Ethiopia, 1971.

Skordiles, Kimon. *Kagnew: The Story of the Ethiopian Fighters in Korea*. Tokyo: Radio Press, 1954.

Skutsch, Carl. "Ethiopia: Civil War, 1978–1991." In James Ciment (ed.). *Encyclopedia of Conflicts Since World War II. Vol. II Cambodia through Haiti*. Armonk, N.Y.: Sharpe Reference, 1999; pp. 608–14.

——. "Ethiopia: War with Somalia, 1977–1978." In James Ciment (ed.). *Encyclopedia of Conflicts Since World War II. Vol. II Cambodia through Haiti*. Armonk, N.Y.: Sharpe Reference, 1999; pp. 603–7.

Somali Democratic Republic. The Ministry of Foreign Affairs. *Background to the Liberation Struggle of the Western Somalis*. Mogadishu: The Ministry of Foreign Affairs, 1978.

——. *Ethiopia's Invasion of Somalia 1982–83*. Mogadishu: The Ministry of Foreign Affairs, 1983.

Somali Democratic Republic. Ministry of Information and National Guidance. *The Disastrous Damages of Ethiopian Aggression*. Mogadishu: Ministry of Information and National Guidance, 1978.

——. *Horn of Africa Conflict*. Mogadishu: Ministry of Information and National Guidance, 1982.

Somali Democratic Republic. Ministry of Information. Public Relations Service. *Somalia: A Divided Nation Seeking Reunification*. Mogadishu: Public Relations Service, 1965.

"The Somalian-Ethiopian-Kenyan Conflict: 1960–1964." In Massachusetts Institute of Technology. Center for International Studies. *The Control of Local Conflict: A Design Study on Arms Control and Limited War in Developing Areas*. Cambridge, Mass.: Massachusetts Institute of Technology, 1967: 457–505.

Sorenson, John S. "'An African Nightmare': Discourse on War and Famine in the Horn of Africa (Ethiopia)." Ph.D. diss., York University, 1978.

Spencer, John Hathaway. "A Reassessment of Ethiopian-Somali Conflict." *HA*, 1 (3) (1978): 23–30.

Stanley, Henry Morton. *Coomassie and Magdala: The Story of Two British Campaigns in Africa*. New York: Harper and Brothers, 1874.

Styan, D. "Chroniques de la Guerre Érythéo-Éthiopienne." *Politique Africaine*, 77 (2000): 183–92.

Swancara, John W. *Project 19: A Mission Most Secret*. Spartanburg, S.C.: Honoribus, 1996.

Tavenna, E. "Un Detail des Expéditions Coloniales: Le Service du Train dans la Campagne des Anglais en Abyssinie (1967–1868)." *Journal des Sciences Militaries*, 63 (1896): 185–210.

Teferi Teklehaimanot. "The Ethiopian Feudal Army and Its Wars, 1868–1936." Ph.D. diss., Kansas State University, 1971.

Tekeste Negash and Kjetil Tronvoll. *Brothers at War: Making Sense of the Eritrean-Ethiopian War*. Oxford: JC, 2000.

Thomas, George. *The Abyssinian Expedition and the Management of Troops in Unhealthy Localities*. London: Smith, Elder and Son, 1867.

Touval, Saadia. "The Shifta Warfare." *East Africa Journal*, Vol. 3, No. 2 (1966), pp. 7–10.

Trivelli, Richard M. "Divided Histories, Opportunistic Alliances: Background Notes on the Ethiopian-Eritrean War." *Afrika Spectrum*, 33 (3) (1998): 257–89.

Tsegaye Tegenu. *The Evolution of Ethiopian Absolutism: The Genesis and the Making of the Fiscal Military State, 1696–1913*. Stockholm: Almqvist and Wiksell, 1996.

Tsehai Berhane Selassie. "Political and Military Traditions of Ethiopian Peasantry, 1800–1941." D.Phil. diss., Oxford University, 1981.

Turton, David. "Warfare, Vulnerability, and Survival: A Case from South-Western Ethiopia." *Disasters*, 15 (3) (1991): 254–64.

Tweedie, William. "Letters from a Staff Officer with the Abyssinian Expedition." *Blackwood's Magazine*, 103 (1868): 349–66, 728–47 and 104 (1868): 202–25, 350–68.

United States. Army. Army Intelligence and Security Command. Intelligence and Threat Analysis Center. *Ethiopia-Somalia Ground Forces Comparison Study*. Arlington, VA: Army Intelligence and Security Command, 1977.

United States. Congress. Senate Subcommittee on United States Security Agreements and Commitments Abroad of the Committee on Foreign Relations. *United States Security Agreements and Commitments Abroad: Ethiopia*. Washington, D.C.: USGPO, 1970.

United States. House of Representatives. Report of a Staff Survey Mission to Ethiopia, Iran and the Arabian Peninsula. *United States Arms Policies in the Persian Gulf and Red Sea Areas: Past, Present, and Future*. Washington, D.C.: USGPO, 1977.

Urquhart, David. *The Abyssinian War: The Contingency of Failure*. London: Diplomatic Review Office, 1868.

Valdés, Nelson P. "Cuba's Involvement in the Horn of Africa: The Ethiopian-Somali War and the Eritrean Conflict." In Carmelo Mesa-Lago and June S. Belkin (eds.). *Cuba in Africa*. Pittsburgh: Center for Latin American Studies, University of Pittsburgh, 1982: 65–103.

Veltze, Alois. *Die Schlacht bei Adua am 1 März 1896*. Berlin: Junker und Dünnhaupt, 1935.

Viaud, Pierre. "Ethiopie: La Guerre Oubliée des Trois Fronts." *Afrique Contemporaine*, (135) (1985): 46–52.

Vivo, Raul Valdes. *Ethiopia: The Unknown Revolution*. Havana: Social Sciences Publishers, 1978.

Waters, Monk. "The Battle of Amba Aradam." *EO*, 10 (3) (1966): 222–27.

Weiss, Kenneth G. *The Soviet Involvement in the Ogaden War*. Alexandria, Va.: Institute of Naval Studies, Center for Naval Analysis, 1980.

Welch, Claude E. "The Military and Social Integration in Ethiopia." In H. Dietz (ed.). *Ethnicity, Integration and the Military*. Boulder, Colo.: WP, 1991: 151–78.

"Why? The Eritrean-Ethiopian Conflict." *ROAPE*, 25 (77) (1998): 508–26.

Wilkins, H. St. Clair. *Reconnoitering in Abyssinia: A Narrative of the Proceedings of the Reconnoitering Party, Prior to the Arrival of the Main Body of the Expeditionary Force*. London: Smith, Elder and Company, 1870.

Wingate, Ronald. "Two African Battles: 2. The Battle of Galabat, 8th–11th March, 1889." *JRUSI*, 109 (634) (1964): 149–54.

Wolffsohn, Lily. "The Battle of Adowa." *USM*, 13 (811) (1896): 225–33.

———. "An Italian Doctor in Abyssinia." *USM*, 13 (813) (1896): 556–60.

———. "The Italian Losses in the War." *USM*, 15 (821) (1897): 39–45.

———. "A Prisoner in Abyssinia." *USM*, 13 (814) (1896): 612–14.

Woodward, Peter. "Ethiopia and the Sudan: The Inter-State Outcome of Domestic Conflict." *CR*, 230 (1336) (1977): 231–34.

———. *War—or Peace—in North-East Africa?* London: The Centre for Security and Conflict Studies, 1989.

Woolbert, Robert Gale. "Feudal Ethiopia and Her Army." *FA*, 14 (1) (1935): 71–81.

Wright, Patricia. "Italy's African Dream: Part I, The Adowa Nightmare." *HT*, 23 (3) (1973): 153–160.

Wylly, H. C. "Italy's Last War in Africa." *USM*, 44 (997) (1911): 252–360.

Yohannis Abate. "Civil-Military Relations in Ethiopia." *Armed Forces and Society*, 10 (3) (1984): 380–400.

——. "Ethiopia: The Origins of Military Intervention." *NAS*, 3 (1) (1981): 1–14.

——. "The Legacy of Imperial Rule: Military Intervention and the Struggle for Leadership in Ethiopia, 1974–78." *Middle Eastern Studies*, 19 (1) (1983): 28–42.

Young, John. *Peasant Revolution in Ethiopia: The Tigray People's Liberation Front, 1975–1991*. Cambridge: Cambridge University Press, 1997.

——. "The Tigray and Eritrean Peoples Liberation Fronts: A History of Tensions and Pragmatism." *JMAS*, 34 (1) (1996): 105–20.

——. "The Tigray People's Liberation Front." In Christopher Clapham (ed.). *African Guerrillas*. (Bloomington and Indianapolis: Indiana University Press, 1998): 36–52.

Yusuf, Abdulqawi. "The Anglo-Ethiopian Treaty of 1897 and the Somali-Ethiopian Dispute." *HA*, 3 (1) (1980): 38–42.

Zeleke Banjaw. "The Role of the Military in Development." B.A. Thesis. Haile Selassie University, 1971.

Zoll, Donald Atwell. "The British Hostage Rescue in Ethiopia 1867–68." *Military Review*, 68 (6) (1988): 54–63.

Italian Invasion and World War II

Abbati, Alfred Henry. *Italy and the Abyssinian War*. London: General Press, 1936.

Abraham, Emmanuel. "Abyssinia and Italy—The Case for Ethiopia." *JRAS*, 37 (137) (1935): 374–77.

Abyssinia Association. *Abyssinia Unconquered*. London: Abyssinia Association, 1938.

——. *Treaties Broken by Italy in the Abyssinian War*. London: Abyssinia Association, 1935.

"The Abyssinian Dispute: The Background of the Conflict." *New Statesman and Nation*, (7 September 1935): 321–26.

Adamson, Carol Alice. "Sweden and the Ethiopia Crisis 1934–1938." Ph.D. diss., University of Wisconsin, 1987.

"The Aftermath of the Italian Conquest of Abyssinia." *JRUSI*, 81 (523) (1936): 632–35.

Agbi, S. O. "The Japanese and the Italo–Ethiopian Crisis, 1935–1936." *Journal of the Historical Society of Nigeria*, 11 (1983): 130–41.

Ahmed Hassen Omer. "Italian Politics in Northern Shawa and Its Consequences 1936–1941." *JES*, 28 (2) (1995): 1–13.

Aldrick, J. "An Ethiopian Escapade." *Africa*, 50 (3) (1995): 387–98.

Allen, William Edward David. *Guerrilla War in Abyssinia*. London: Penguin Books, 1943.

Appelius, Mario. *Il Crollo dell'Impero Dei Negus*. Milan: A. Mondadori, 1937.

"L'Armée Éthiopienne." *Revue Militaire Français*, (170) (1935): 259–63.

Arnold, A. C. "The Italo–Abyssinian Campaign, 1935–36." *JRUSI*, 82 (525) (1937): 71–88.

Artieri, G. *La Guerre Dimenticate di Mussolini: Etiopia e Spagna*. Milan: A. Mondadori, 1995.

Asante, S. K. B. "The Afro-American and the Italo-Ethiopian Crisis, 1934–1936." *Race*, 15 (2) (1973): 167–84.

———. "The Catholic Missions, British West African Nationalists, and the Italian Invasion of Ethiopia, 1935–36." *AA*, 73 (291) (1974): 204–16.

———. "I. T. A. Wallace Johnson and the Italo–Ethiopian Crisis." *Journal of the Historical Society of Nigeria*, 7 (4) (1975): 631–46.

———. "The Impact of the Italo-Ethiopian Crisis of 1935–36 on the Pan-African Movement in Britain." *Transactions of the Historical Society of Ghana*, 13 (2) (1972): 217–77.

———. "The Italo-Ethiopian Conflict: A Case Study in British West African Response to Crisis Diplomacy in the 1930's." *JAH*, 15 (2) (1974): 291–302.

———. *Pan-African Protest: West Africa and the Italo-Ethiopian Crisis, 1934–1941*. London: Longman, 1977.

———. South Africa and the Italo-Ethiopian Crisis, 1935–36." *Ghana Social Sciences Journal*, 3 (1) (1970): 47–53.

———. "The West African Response to the Italo-Ethiopian Crisis, 1934–1942." Ph.D. diss., University of London, 1972.

Askew, William C. "The Secret Agreement between France and Italy on Ethiopia, January 1935." *Journal of Modern History*, 25 (1) (1953): 47–48.

Auer, Paul de. "The Lesson of the Italo-Abyssinian Conflict." *New Commonwealth Quarterly*, 1 (1936): 1–19.

Australia. Parliament. *Italo-Abyssinian Dispute: Statement by the Minister for External Affairs Regarding the Position of Australia in Relation to the Dispute*. Canberra: Government Printer, 1935.

Badoglio, Pietro. *La Guerra d'Etiopia*. Milan: A. Mondadori, 1936.

———. *The War in Abyssinia*. London: Methuen, 1937.

Baer, George W. *The Coming of the Italian-Ethiopian War*. Cambridge, Mass.: Harvard University Press, 1967.

——. "Haile Sellassie's Protectorate Appeal to King Edward VIII." *CEA*, 9 (2) (1969): 306–12.

——. "Sanctions and Security: The League of Nations and the Italian-Ethiopian War, 1935–1936." *International Organization*, 27 (2) (1973): 165–79.

——. *Test Case: Italy, Ethiopia, and the League of Nations*. Stanford, Conn.: Hoover Institution, 1976.

Bahru Zewde. "The Ethiopian Intelligentsia and the Italo-Ethiopian War, 1935–1941." *IJAHS*, 26 (2) (1993): 271–95.

Baker, Robert L. "The Fighting in Ethiopia." *CH*, 43 (1936): 622–24.

——. "Italian Army Troubles in Ethiopia." *CH*, 43 (1936): 512–13.

——. "With the Armies in Ethiopia." *CH*, 44 (1936): 65–66.

Baravelli, G. C. *The Last Stronghold of Slavery: What Abyssinia Is*. Rome: Società Editrice di "Novissima," 1935.

Barker, Arthur J. *The Civilizing Mission: A History of the Italo-Ethiopian War of 1935–1936*. New York: The Dial Press, Inc., 1968.

——. *Eritrea 1941*. London: Faber and Faber Ltd., 1966.

——. *The Italo-Ethiopian War 1935–36*. London: Cassell and Company Ltd., 1968.

——. *The Rape of Ethiopia*. New York: Ballantine Books, 1971.

Barker, Francis Fisk. "Anglo-French Relations during the Ethiopian Crisis." M.A. thesis, University of California, Berkeley, 1942.

Barnes, James Strachey. *Half a Life Left*. London: Eyre and Spottiswoode, 1937.

Barros, James. *Britain, Greece, and the Politics of Sanctions: Ethiopia 1935–1936*. London: Royal Historical Society, 1982.

Barton, Sidney. "Abyssinia: The Bridge between Africa and Asia." *Journal of the Royal Central Asian Society*, 40 (1941): 436–40.

Baskerville, Beatrice C. *What Next, O Duce?* London: Longmans, Green and Company, 1937.

Basler, Werner. "Der Aggressionskrieg Italiens Gegen Athiopien 1935/36." *Militargeschichte*, 21 (6) (1982): 688–98.

Bastin, Jean. *L'Affaire d'Ethiopie et les Diplomates (1934–1937)*. Brussels: L'Édition Universelle, 1938.

Battaglini, Guido. *Con S. E. de Bono: Nel Turbinio di una Preparazione*. Intra: Airoldi, 1938.

Baudendistel, Rainer. "Force Versus Law: The International Committee of the Red Cross and Chemical Warfare in the Italo-Ethiopian War 1935–1936." *International Review of the Red Cross*, 38 (322) (1998): 81–104.

Bell, Stephen. "The Liberation of Addis Ababa." *After the Battle*, 71 (1991): 36–41.

Benedetti, Achille. *La Guerra Equatoriale con l'Armata del Maresciallo Graziani*. Milan: Zucchi, 1936.

Bentwich, Norman. *Ethiopia at the Paris Peace Conference*. London: Abyssinian Association, 1946.

——. "Ethiopia Today." *IA*, 20 (4) (1944): 509–18.

——. *Wanderer in War (1939–45)*. London: Victor Gollancz Ltd., 1946.

Beonio-Brocchieri, Vittorio. *Cieli d'Etiopia: Adventure di un Pilota di Guerra*. Milan: A. Mondadori, 1936.

Berkeley, George Fitz Hardinge. "The Abyssinian Soldier." *NC*, 124 (1941): 456–64.

Bernasconi, G. *Le Guerre e la Politica dell'Italia nell'Africa Orientale*. Milan: Prora, 1935.

Bianchi, Gianfranco. *Rivelazioni sul Conflitto Italo-Etiopico*. Milan: Centro Editoriale Insegnanti e Scrittori, 1967.

Bidou, Henry. "La Conquête de l'Ethiopie." *Revue des Deux Mondes*, 8 (33) (1936): 880–913.

Birkby, Carel. *It's a Long Way to Addis*. London: Frederick Muller, Ltd., 1942.

——. *The Saga of the Transvaal Scottish Regiment*. Cape Town: Howard Timmins for Hodder and Stoughton Ltd., 1950.

——. *Springbok Victory: The South African Press Association's First War Correspondent with the Forces of East Africa*. Johannesburg: Libertas Publications, 1941.

Bollati, Ambrogio. *La Campagne Italo-Etiopica nella Stampa Militare Estera*. Rome: Istituto Poligrafico dello Stato, 1938.

Bonardi, Pierre. *Servizio Stampa Africa Orientale*. Florence: Beltrami, 1936.

Bongiovanni, Alberto. *La Fine dell'Impero. Africa Orientale 1940–1941*. Milan: Mursia, 1974.

Borruso, P. "Le Missioni Cattoliche Italiane nella Politica Imperiale del Fascismo, 1936–40." *Africa*, 44 (1) (1989): 50–78.

Bosca, Quirino. *Cronistoria della Campagna Italo-Etiopica dal 2 Ottobre 1935 al 18 Maggio 1936*. Rome: Guanella, 1937.

Boulemmine, E. "Les Difficultés Italo-Éthiopiennes: L'Incident de Walwal." *Afrique Française*, 45 (1935): 23–31.

Braddick, Henderson B. "A New Look at American Policy during the Italo-Ethiopian Crisis, 1935–36." *Journal of Modern History*, 34 (1) (1962): 64–73.

Brett-James, Anthony. *Ball of Fire: The Fifth Indian Division in the Second World War*. Aldershot: Gale and Polden Ltd., 1951.

Britalicus (pseud.). *This Abyssinia Business*. Glasgow: n.p., 1939.

Brocchieri, V. Beonio. *Cieli d'Etiopia*. Milan: A. Mondadori, 1936.

Brogle, Werner. *Krieg in Abessinien und Flucht durch den Sudan*. Zurich: Rascher, 1937.

Bruls, J. *Vers les Hauts Plateaux d'Abyssinie: Avec les Congolais en Guerre.* Louvain: Éditions SAM, 1946.

Burns, Emile. *Abyssinia and Italy.* London: Victor Gollancz, 1935.

Cabiati, Aldo. *La Conquista dell'Impero. Cronaca Ragionata della Guerra Italo-Abissina 1935–1936.* Milan: Sonsogno, 1936.

Canada. Secretary of State for External Affairs. *Documents Relating to the Italo-Ethiopian Conflict.* Ottawa: J. O. Patenaude, I.S.O., 1936.

Candlin, A. H. S. "War in Ethiopia (1941): Coordinated Irregular and Regular Campaigns." *The Army Quarterly and Defence Journal,* 104 (1) (1974): 580–89.

Cape, Norman. *Ethiopia Booklet no. VIII: Italian Occupation and WW II Period 1936–1943.* Newbury: Philip Cockrill, 1982.

Caravaglios, Maria Genoino. "La Santa Sede e L'Inghilterra in Etiopia Durante il Secondo Conflitto Mondiale." *Africa,* 35 (2) (1980): 217–54.

Cargnelutti, Federico. *Africa Orientale Scacchiere Nord: Contributo alla Storia della Campagna di Guerra, 1940–1941.* Udine: Del Bianco, 1962.

Carlton, David. "The Dominions and British Policy in the Abyssinian Crisis." *JICH,* 1 (1) (1972): 59–77.

Carnimeo, Nicolangelo. *Cheren: 1 Febbraio–27 Marzo 1941.* Naples: Casella, 1950.

Carter, Boake. *Black Shirt, Black Skin.* Harrisburg, Pa.: Telegraph Press, 1935.

Castellani, Sir Aldo. "Hygienic Measures and Hospital Organization of the Italian Expeditionary Forces during the Ethiopian War." *Journal of the Royal Society of the Arts,* 86 (1938): 675–89.

——. "The Medical Care of an Expeditionary Force in the Tropics." *JRUSI,* 84 (533) (1939): 105–16.

Catalano, Franco. *L'Economia Italiana di Guerra: La Politica Economico-Finanziaria del Fascismo dalla Guerra d'Etiopia alla Caduta del Regime, 1935–1943.* Milan: Istituto Nazionale per la Storia del Movimento di Liberazione, 1969.

——. *L'Impresa Etiopica e Altri Saggi.* Milan: La Goliardica, 1965.

Chaplin, William Watts. *Blood and Ink: An Italian-Ethiopian War Diary.* New York: Telegraph Press, 1936.

Charteris, J. "The Italian Reverses." *NC,* 124 (1941): 360–64.

Chiavarelli, Emilia. *L'Opera della Marina Italiana nella Guerra Italo-Etiopica.* Milan: Giuffrè, 1969.

Chimiel, J. "Czechoslovak Armaments Industry and the Italo–Ethiopian Conflict." *Asian and African Studies,* 1 (2) (1992): 170–89.

Chukumba, Stephen Uneze. *The Big Powers against Ethiopia: Anglo-Franco-American Diplomatic Maneuvers during the Italo-Ethiopian Dispute, 1934–1938.* Washington, D.C.: University of America Press, 1979.

——. "The League of Nations Powers, the United States, and the Italo-Ethiopian Dispute: A Comparative Study, 1934–1938." Ph.D. diss., Georgetown University, 1975.

Ciano, Galeazzo. *Diary 1939–43*. London: W. Heinemann, 1947.

Cimmaruta, Roberto. *Ual-Ual*. Milan: A. Mondadori, 1936.

Coffey, Thomas M. *Lion by the Tail: The Story of the Italian-Ethiopian War*. New York: The Viking Press, 1974.

Cohen, Armand. *La Société des Nations Devant le Conflit Italo-Éthiopien (Décembre 1934–Octobre 1935), Politique et Procedure*. Geneva: Droz, 1960.

Collombet, E. *L'Ethiopie Moderne et son Avènement à la Communauté Internationale*. Dijon: Belvet, 1935.

Communist Party of the United States of America. Harlem Section. *War on Ethiopia: An Interview with Tecle Hawariate, Ethiopian Ambassador*. New York: The Harlem Division of the Communist Party, 1936.

Comyn-Platt, Thomas. *The Abyssinian Storm*. London: Jarrolds Publishers Ltd., 1935.

"Le Conflit Italo-Éthiopien." *La Revue de Paris*, 42 (4) (1935): 721–37.

Contemporary Problems: The Negus and the Negro Problem. Calcutta: E. Benasaglio, 1936.

Conti Rossini, Carlo. "Pubblicazioni Etiopica dal 1936 al 1945." *Rassegna di Studi Etiopici*, (1944): 1–132.

Cooksey, Joseph James. *A Serious Aspect of the Abyssinian Situation*. London: New Mildmay Press, 1935.

Cooper, Avery J. "The War in Ethiopia." *CH*, 43 (1935): 168–73.

Corazzi, Paolo. *Etiopia, 1938–1946: Guerriglia e Filo Spinato*. Milan: Mursia, 1983.

Cormack, R. P. "Some Medical Aspects of the Campaign in Somaliland and Ethiopia 1941." *East African Medical Journal*, 20 (11) (1943): 357–75.

Costi, Robert Leland. "To Stop a War: Efforts by the League of Nations and the United States to Place Economic Restrictions on Italy during the Italo-Ethiopian War, 1935–1936." Ph.D. diss., University of Idaho, 1973.

Crosskill, W. E. *The Two-Thousand Mile War*. London: Robert Hale Ltd., 1980.

Cunningham, A. *First Report on East Africa Force Operations Covering the Period from 1st November, 1940 to the Fall of Addis Ababa on 5 April, 1941*. London: HMSO, 1946.

——. *Second Report on East Africa Force Operations Covering the Period from Occupation of Addis Ababa on 6th April, 1941, to the Cessation of Hostilities in the Area for Which East Africa Force Was Responsible on 11th July, 1941*. London: HMSO, 1946.

Curie, Eve. *Journey among Warriors*. New York: Doubleday Doran, 1943.

Currey, Muriel Innes. "On the Tigre Front." *NC*, 119 (709) (1936): 341–49.

——. *A Woman at the Abyssinian War*. London: Hutchinson and Company Ltd., 1936.

D. P. E. "Italian Possessions in Africa II: Italian East Africa." *The Bulletin of International News*, (24 August 1940): 1065–74.

Daney, Pierre. "Questions d'Éthiopie et d'Afrique Orientale." *Revue Politique et Parlementaire*, 164 (1935): 427–68.

D'Annunzio, Ugo V. *Italy, Britain, and the League in the Italo-Ethiopian Conflict: A Collection of Speeches*. New York: Unione Italiana d'America, 1935.

Dascalu, Nicolae. "Opinia Publica din Statele Unite ale Americii si Razboiul Italo-Etiopian (1935–1936)." *Revista de Istorie*, 36 (2) (1983): 273–90.

Dascalu, Nicolae, and P. Eggleston. "The Ethiopian War, 1935–1936, in World Historiography." *Revista de Istorie*, 31 (10) (1978): 1793–811.

Davies, Baron D. *Nearing the Abyss: The Lesson of Ethiopia*. London: Constable and Company Ltd., 1936.

Dean, Vera Micheles. "The League and the Italian-Ethiopian Dispute." *Geneva Special Studies*, Geneva: Geneva Research Council, 1935.

——. "The League and the Italo-Ethiopian Crisis." *Foreign Policy Report*, 11 (18) (1935): 213–24.

——. "The Quest for Ethiopian Peace." *Foreign Policy Report*, 11 (26) (1936): 317–32.

——. "The Quest for Ethiopian Peace." *Geneva Special Studies*, Geneva: Geneva Research Council, 1936.

——. "Saving the League at Ethiopia's Expense?" New York: Foreign Policy Association, 1935.

Deakin, F. W. *The Brutal Friendship*. London: Weidenfeld and Nicolson, 1962.

De Bono, Emilio. *Anno XIIII: The Conquest of an Empire*. London: The Crescent Press, Ltd., 1937.

——. "Planning the Ethiopian Campaign." *Harper's Monthly Magazine*, 175 (1937): 260–69.

DeFelice, Renzo. "La Santa Sede e il Conflitto Italo-Etiopiano nel Diario di Bernadino Nogara." *Storia Contemporanea*, 8 (4) (1977): 823–34.

Del Boca, Angelo. *The Ethiopian War 1935–1941*. Chicago: University of Chicago Press, 1969.

——. *Gli Italiani in Africa Orientale: La Caduta dell'Impero*. Rome: Laterza, 1976.

——. *La Preparazione e le Prime Operazioni*. Rome: Istituto Nazionale Fascista di Cultura, 1937.

Del Canuto, Francesco. "I Falascia fra Politica Antisemita e Politica Razziale." *Storia Contemporanea*, 19 (6) (1988): 1267–85.

Delhougne, G. *La Guerre dans les Hautes Herbes: Reportage sur la Campagne Belge d'Abyssinie*. Liège: Soledi, 1945.

Dodds-Parker, Douglas. *Setting Europe Ablaze*. Windlesham: Springwood Books, 1983.

Doody, John. *The Burning Coast*. London: Michael Joseph, 1955.

Dore, Gianni. "Etnologia e Storia nella Ricerca di Giovanni Ellero." *Africa*, 48 (1) (1993): 35–46.

———. "Guerra d'Etiopia e Ideologia Coloniale nella Testimonianza Orale di Reduci Sardi." *Movimento Operaio e Socialista*, 5 (3) (1982): 475–87.

Dore, Gianni, and Irma Taddia. "I Documenti Inediti di Giovanni Ellero sull' Etiopia." *Africa*, 48 (1) (1993): 21–23.

Dower, Kenneth Cecil Gandar. *Abyssinian Patchwork*. London: Frederick Muller, Ltd., 1949.

———. *Askaris at War in Abyssinia*. Nairobi: The East African Standard Ltd., c. 1943.

Driberg, J. H. "Conditions of Warfare in Ethiopia." *New Statesman*, (31 August 1935): 268–69.

DuBois, W. E. B. "Inter-Racial Implications of the Ethiopian Crisis." *FA*, 14 (1) (1935): 82–92.

Duff, A. C. "'Q' in the East African Campaign, 1941." *The Royal Engineers Journal*, 56 (1942): 265–74 and 57 (1943): 161–69.

Dugan, James, and Laurence Lafore. *Days of Emperor and Clown: The Italo-Ethiopian War, 1935–1936*. Garden City, N.J.: Doubleday, 1973.

Duprey, A. Gingold. *De l'Invasion à la Libération de l'Ethiopie*. Paris: Paul Dupont, 1955.

Durand, Mortimer Henry Marion. "A Correspondent in Abyssinia." *Journal of the Royal Central Asian Society*, 23 (1936): 263–70.

———. *Crazy Campaign: A Personal Narrative of the Italo-Abyssinian War*. London: George Routledge and Sons, 1936.

Edwards, Charles P. "The Western League Powers and the Italo-Ethiopian Affair." Ph.D. diss., Fletcher School of Law and Diplomacy, 1955.

Elkins, H. R. "Meet the Ethiopians." *CH*, 44 (1936): 71–78.

Ellsberg, Edward. *Under the Red Sea Sun*. New York: Dodd, Mead, 1946.

Endalkachew Makonnen. *Why Was the Lion of Judah Defeated?* Jerusalem: Living Waters Press, 1939.

England, Italy, and Abyssinia: An Englishman's Impartial Survey. London: British-Italian Council for Peace and Friendship, 1936.

Erlich, Haggai. "Haile Sellassie and the Arabs, 1935–1936." *NAS*, (New Series) 1 (1) (1994): 47–61.

———. "Tigrean Nationalism, British Involvement, and Haile Sellassie's Emerging Absolutism: Northern Ethiopia 1941–1943." *Asian and African Studies*, 15 (2) (1981): 191–227.

———. "The West African Response to the Italo-Ethiopian Crisis, 1934–1942." Ph.D. diss., University of London, 1972.

Eshetu Tabaya. "The Ethiopian Patriots as Seen at the Time." *EO*, 3 (1959): 388–95 and 4 (1) (1959): 30–32.

——. "Tactics and Strategy of the Ethiopian Patriotic Struggle, 1935–1941." B.A. thesis. AAU, 1982.

Ethiopia. Directorate of the Army. *British Military Legislation*. Addis Ababa: Directorate of Printing and Stationery Services, 1941.

Ethiopia. Ministry of Information. *The Italo–Ethiopian War, 1935–41: Genesis, Ordeal, Victory*. Addis Ababa: Ministry of Information, 1975.

Ethiopia. Ministry of Justice. *Documents on Italian War Crimes*. 2 vols. Addis Ababa: Ministry of Justice, 1949, 1950.

Ethiopia. Press and Information Service. *La Civilisation de l'Italie Fasciste*. 2 vols. Addis Ababa: Press and Information Department, 1946.

"The Ethiopian Patriots: Their Valiant Struggle against Italian Fascist Aggression in the Years 1934–1941." *EO*, 3 (10) (1959): 302–8.

Etschmann, Wolfgang. "Ostafrika in Zweiten Weltkrieg. Der Britisch-Italienische Konflikt am Horn von Afrika." *Österreichische Militärische*, 32 (3) (1994): 265–70.

"L'Europe Devant le Conflit Italo-Éthiopien." *Le Mois*, (57) (1935): 25–46.

Evans, Geoffrey. "The Battle of Keren." *HT*, 16 (4) (1966): 260–68.

——. *The Desert and the Jungle*. London: William Kimber, 1959.

Evans-Pritchard, Edward. "Operations on the Akobo and Gila Rivers 1940–41." *The Army Quarterly and Defence Journal*, 103 (4) (1973): 70–479.

Fair, Stanley D. "Mussolini's Chemical War." *Army*, 35 (1) (1985): 44–53.

Farago, Ladislas. *Abyssinia on the Eve*. New York: G. P. Putnam's Sons, 1935.

——. (ed.). *Abyssinian Stop Press*. London: Robert Hale Ltd., 1936.

"The Fascist Italian Invasion and the Ethiopian People's Struggle for Liberation." *Meskerem*, (1981): 68–89.

Fikru Gebrekidan. "In Defense of Ethiopia: A Comparative Assessment of Caribbean and African-American Anti-Fascist Protests 1936–1941." *NAS*, (New Series), 2 (1) (1995): 145–74.

Fitzgerald, Paul. "American Neutrality and the Italo-Ethiopian Conflict." Ph.D. diss., Georgetown University, 1953.

Ford, James W. *The Communists and the Struggle for Negro Liberation: Their Position on Problems of Africa, of the West Indies, of War, of Ethiopian Independence*. New York: The Harlem Division of the Communist Party, 1936.

——. *War in Africa: Italian Fascism Prepares to Enslave Ethiopia*. New York: Workers Library Publishers, 1935.

Franchini, Mario. *Ogadèn*. Bologna: Cappelli, 1937.

Friedlander, Robert A. "New Light on the Anglo-American Reaction to the Ethiopian War, 1935–1936." *Mid-America*, 45 (2) (1963): 115–25.

Fromow, George H. *The Italo-Abyssinian Crisis and the Revival of the Roman Empire*. London: Sovereign Grace Advent Testimony, 1935.

Fuller, John Frederick Charles. *The First of the League Wars: Its Lessons and Omens*. London: Eyre and Spottiswoode Ltd., 1936.

Fuller, Mia. "Wherever You Go, There You Are: Fascist Plans for the Colonial City of Addis Ababa and the Colonizing Suburb of Eur' 42." *Journal of Contemporary History*, 31 (2) (1996): 397–418.

Gallo, Max. *L'Affaire d'Éthiopie: Aux Origines de la Guerre Mondiale*. Paris: Éditions du Centurion, 1967.

Gardner, John W. *Ethiopia: 1942–1945*. London: Anglo-Ethiopian Society, 1998.

Garrat, G. T. "Abyssinia." *JRAS*, 36 (1937): 36–50.

Gat, Moshe. "Britain's Position Regarding the Issue of the Oil Embargo in the Italo-Ethiopian Crisis, November 1935–March 1936." In Pinhas Artzi (ed.). *Bar-Ilan Studies in History*. Ramat-Gan: Bar-Ilan University Press, 1978: 255–74.

Gebru Tareke. "Peasant Resistance in Ethiopia: The Case of Weyane (Uprising in Eastern Tigrai 1943)." *JAH*, 25 (1) (1984): 77–92.

Gentizon, Paul. *La Conquête de l'Éthiopie*. Paris: Berger-Levrault, 1936.

——. *La Revanche d'Adoua*. Paris: Berger-Levrault, 1936.

Giovani, Mario. *L'Avventura Facista in Etiopia*. Milan: Teeti, 1976.

Glover, Michael. *An Improvised War: The Abyssinian Campaign of 1940–1941*. London: Leo Cooper, 1987.

Goglia, Luigi. "Un Aspetto dell'Azione Politica Italiana Durante la Campagna d'Etiopia 1935–1936: La Missione del Senatore Jacopo Gasparini nell' Amhara." *Storia Contemporanea*, 8 (4) (1977): 791–822.

——. *Storia Fotografica dell'Impero Fascista, 1935–1941*. Rome-Bari: Edizioni Laterza, 1985.

Graziani, Rudolfo. *Il Fronte Sud*. Milan: A. Mondadori, 1938.

Great Britain. *Agreement and Military Convention between the United Kingdom and Ethiopia*. London: HMSO, 1942.

——. *Le Campagne d'Etiopia*. London: HMSO, 1945.

——. *Documents on British Foreign Policy: Italo-Ethiopian Dispute, March 1934 to October 1935*. London: HMSO, 1976.

——. *Documents on British Foreign Policy: Italo-Ethiopian War and German Affairs, October 1935 to February 1936*. London: HMSO, 1976.

Great Britain. Foreign Office. *Dispute between Ethiopia and Italy: Documents and Proceedings of the League of Nations, October 7, 1935, to January 22, 1936*. London: HMSO, 1936.

——. *Documents Relating to the Dispute between Ethiopia and Italy*. London: HMSO, 1935.

——. General Staff (Intelligence). Headquarters Troops in Sudan. *Handbook of Western Italian East Africa*. 2 vols. Khartoum: GP, 1941.

——. War Office. *The Abyssinian Campaigns: The Official Story of the Conquest of Italian East Africa*. London: HMSO, 1942.

Great Britain. War Office. General Staff. Intelligence Division. *A Handbook of Ethiopia*. Khartoum: GP, 1941.

Greenfield, Richard. "Remembering the Struggle." *Makerere Journal*, 9 (1964): 7–32.

Grigg, Edward. "The Hour of Decision: 1. Italy, Abyssinia, and Europe." *Fortnightly Review*, 146 (1936): 1–10.

——. "The League and Abyssinia." *Fortnightly Review*, 144 (1935): 129–40.

Gruhl, Max. *Abyssinia at Bay*. London: Hurst and Blackett Ltd., 1935.

Guicheteau, Gerard. "Il y a Cinquante Ans: Mussolini Chasse le Négus." *Historama*, (28) (1986): 80–85.

Gwynn, Charles William. "The War with Italy." *Fortnightly Review*, 157 (1941): 154–58.

Halden, Leon G. "The Diplomacy of the Ethiopian Crisis." *Journal of Negro History*, 22 (2) (1937): 163–99.

——. "Italy and Abyssinia." *The Bulletin of International News*, (27 July 1935): 35–40.

——. "The League Council and the Italian Case against Abyssinia." *The Bulletin of International News*, (12 October 1935): 215–20.

——. "The Next Meeting of the League Council and the Abyssinian Problem." *The Bulletin of International News*, (6 October 1936): 915–22.

Hamilton, Edward. *The War in Abyssinia: A Brief Military History*. London: The Unicorn Press, 1936.

Hardie, Frank. *The Abyssinian Crisis*. Hamden, Conn.: Archon Books, 1974.

Harmsworth, Geoffrey. *Abyssinia Marches On*. London: Hutchinson and Company Ltd., 1941.

——. *Abyssinian Adventure*. London: Hutchinson and Company Ltd., 1935.

Harris, Brice. *The United States and the Italo-Ethiopian Crisis*. Stanford: Stanford University Press, 1964.

Harris, Sir John. "Italy and Abyssinia." *CR*, 148 (836) (1935): 148–55.

Harris, Joseph E. *African-American Reactions to War in Ethiopia 1936–1941*. Baton Rouge: Louisiana State University Press, 1994.

Henson, Herbert Hensley. *Abyssinia: Reflections of an Onlooker*. London: Hugh Rees, 1936.

Hérelle, S. "Les Négociations Franco-Italiennes et l'Éthiopie." *L'Afrique Française*, 44 (1934): 628–31.

Herrman, Gerhard. *Abessinien: Raum als Schicksal*. Leipzig and Berlin: Teubner, 1935.

Hiett, Helen. "The American Negro and the Italo-Ethiopian Crisis, 1934–1936." M.A. thesis, Howard University, 1966.

——. "Public Opinion and the Italo-Ethiopian Dispute: The Activities of Private Organizations in the Crisis." *Geneva (Special) Studies*, 7 (1) (1936): 3–28.

Hingston, W. R. *The Tiger Strikes (The Indian Divisions)*. Calcutta: Thacker's Press and Directories, 1943.

Hoare, Samuel. *Italy and Ethiopia, Collective Action for Security Demanded.* New York: Carnegie Endowment for International Peace, 1935.

Hodson, H. V. "The Economic Aspects of the Italo-Abyssinian Conflict." In Arnold J. Toynbee. *Survey of International Affairs, 1935.* Vol. II. London: OUP, 1936: 414–42.

——. "The Problem of Raw Materials." In Arnold J. Toynbee. *Survey of International Affairs, 1935.* Vol. I. London: Oxford University Press, 1936: 340–88.

Hollis, M. Christopher. *Italy in Africa.* London: Hamish Hamilton Ltd., 1941.

Houérou, F. *L'Epopée des Soldats de Mussolini en Abyssinie 1936–1938.* Paris: L'Harmattan, 1994.

——. "Des Oubliés d'Histoire: Les 'Ensables' en Ethiopie." *Revue d'Histoire Moderne et Contemporaine*, 36 (1) (1989): 152–65.

Hubbard, Wynant Davis. *Fiasco in Ethiopia: The Story of a So-Called War by a Reporter on the Ground.* New York: Harper and Brothers, 1936.

Iadarola, Antoinette. "The Anglo-Italian Agreement of 1925: Mussolini's 'Carte Blanche' for War against Ethiopia." *NAS*, 1 (1) (1979): 45–56.

——. "Prolegomena to the Ethiopian Crisis: Anglo-Italian Relations towards Ethiopia, 1923–1934." Ph.D. diss., Georgetown University, 1975.

Imperiali, A. "Appunti di un Antifascista nell'Ethiopia di Mussolini." *Studi Piacentini*, 12 (1992): 201–12.

"Indian Forces in Ethiopia during the Second World War." *EO*, 4 (10) (1960): 332–33.

Italian Community of Toronto. *What Do You Know about Ethiopia?* Toronto: Italian Publishing Company, 1935.

Italian Historical Society. *The Italo-Ethiopian Controversy.* New York: Italian Historical Society, 1935.

"The Italo-Abyssinian War." *JRUSI*, 81 (521) (1936): 173–75; and 81 (522) (1936): 410–14.

The Italo-Ethiopian Dispute: Abstracts from the Memorandum of the Italian Government to the League of Nations. Rome: Società Editrice di 'Novissima,' 1935.

Italy. Istituto Agronomo per l'Africa Italiana. *Main Features of Italy's Action in Ethiopia 1936–1941.* Florence: Istituto Agronomo per l'Africa Italiana, 1946.

Italy. Istituto per gli Studi di Politica Internazionale. *Il Conflitto Italo-Etiopico: Documenti.* 2 Vols. Milan: Istituto per gli Studi di Politica Internazionale. 1936.

Italy. Esercito. Comando delle Forze Armate della Somalia. Officio Storico. *La Guerra Italo-Ethiopica: Fronte Sud.* 4 vols. Addis Ababa: Ufficio Superiore Topocartografico del Governo Generale dell' A.O.I., 1937.

"Italy and Abyssinia." *JRUSI*, 80 (517) (1935): 164; 80 (518) (1935): 411–12; and 80 (519) (1935): 629–33.

Italy and Abyssinia. Rome: Società Editrice di Novissima, 1936.

Italy and the Treaties. Rome: Pallotta, 1936.

Italy's Failure in Abyssinia. London: The Abyssinia Association, [1937].

Italy's War-Crimes in Ethiopia: Evidence for the War Crimes Commission. Woolford Green: New Times and Ethiopia News, 1945.

Jacobs, F. J. "4 Field Regiment in East Africa, 1939–1941." *Militaria*, 4 (4) (1974): 48–57.

Jevons, Herbert Stanley. *Italian Military Secrets: Three Years' Preparation for the Abyssinian War*. London: H. S. Jevons, 1937.

——. "New Era in Ethiopia." *CR*, 161 (1942): 213–19.

Johnson, A. G. "Return to Magdala." *The Army Quarterly and Defence Journal*, 84 (1) (1962): 90–97.

Jorre, F. M. Della, and F. Santagata. *Da Ual-Ual alla Vittoria dell' Endertà*. Genoa: Pagano, 1936.

Junod, Marcel. *Warrior without Weapons*. London: Jonathan Cape, 1951.

Kacza, Thomas. *Äthiopiens Kampf gegen die Italienischer Kolonialisten, 1935–41*. Pfaffenweiler: Centaurus, 1993.

Kent, Peter C. "Between Rome and London: Pius XI, the Catholic Church, and the Abyssinian Crisis of 1935–1936." *International History Review*, 11 (1989): 252–71.

Konovaloff, Thomas. *Con le Armate del Negus (Un Bianco fra i Neri): Diari e Memoire Col. Thomas Konovaloff*. Bologna: Zanichelli, 1938.

Koren, William. "Imperialist Rivalries in Ethiopia." *Foreign Policy Report*, 11 (14) (1935): 169–80.

——. "The Italian-Ethiopian Dispute." *Geneva Special Studies*, Geneva: Geneva Research Council, 1935.

Laderchi, Ruggeri. "Tactical and Administrative Lessons of the War in Abyssinia." *JRUSI*, 83 (530) (1938): 233–46.

Lammas, J. R. *Campaigning in Abyssinia*. Brentford: St. George's Press, 1944.

Lapradelle, Albert de. *Le Conflit Italo-Éthiopien*. Paris: Éditions Internationales, 1936.

Large, David Clay. "Mussolini's 'Civilizing Mission.'" *Military History Quarterly*, 5 (2) (1993): 44–53.

Lass-Westphal, Ingeborg. "Protestant Missions during and after the Italo-Ethiopian War 1935–1937." *JES*, 10 (1) (1972): 89–101.

"The Last Partition of Africa?" *RT*, (99) (1935): 507–23.

Laurens, Franklin Davenport. *France and the Italo-Ethiopian Crisis, 1935–1936*. The Hague: Mouton, 1967.

Laveleye, Victor de. "La Belgique et le Conflit Italo-Éthiopien." *La Revue Belge*, 12 (3) (1935): 97–101.

——. "L'Opinion Belge et le Conflit Italo-Éthiopien." *La Revue Belge*, 12 (3) (1935): 509–14.

League of Nations. League Against Imperialism and for National Independence. International Secretariat. *The War Danger over Abyssinia*. London: The Nation, 1935.

League of Nations Union. *The Abyssinian Dispute*. London: Pelican Press, 1935.

"The League of Nations and the Italo-Abyssinian Affair." *JRUSI*, 81 (521) (1936): 165–73.

Lechenberg, Harold C. "With the Italians in Eritrea." *NGM*, 68 (3) (1935): 265–96.

Lee, M. P. "The Geneva Treatment of the Manchurian and Abyssinian Crises." Ph.D. diss., London School of Economics and Political Sciences, 1946.

Legionarius [pseud.]. *The Grounds of Serious Charges Brought by Italy against Abyssinia*. Rome: Ardita Publishers, 1935.

Lenzi, Giulio. *Diari Africani*. Pisa: Giardini, 1973.

Leroux, Eugène-Louis. *Le Conflit Italo-Éthiopien devant la S.D.N.* Paris: Librairie Technique et Economique, 1937.

Lessing, Pieter. "The Fall of Mussolini's East African Empire." *History of the Second World War*, 14 (1973): 365–73.

Lingelback, William E. "Italy: A Nation in Arms." *CH*, 42 (1935): 205–6.

——. "Italy in the Grip of Sanctions." *CH*, 43 (1936): 395–96.

——. "Italy Mobilizes for War." *CH*, 42 (1935): 91–93.

——. "Italy on the Eve of War." *CH*, 42 (1935): 539–40.

——. "Italy's Fight against Sanctions. *CH*, 43 (1936): 620–22.

——. "Italy's Growing Military Costs." *CH*, 42 (1935): 316–18.

——. "The Strain on Italian Finance." *CH*, 42 (1935): 635–55.

——. "War Strained Italy." *CH*, 44 (1936): 63–65.

——. "Wartime Italy." *CH*, 43 (1935): 281–83.

"L'Inquiétant Développement du Conflit Italo-Éthiopien." *Le Mois*, (55) (1935): 23–28.

Lloyd, H. P. "The Italian-Abyssinian War, 1935–36: The Operations; Massawa–Addis Ababa." *The Royal Air Force Quarterly*, 8 (1937): 357–67.

Loffredo, Renato. *Cheren: 31 Gennaio–27 Marzo 1941*. Milan: Longanesi, 1973.

Lorence, W. E. "The Italian Campaign in Northern Ethiopia." *Military Engineer*, (July 1937): 267–77.

Lowell, A. Lawrence. "Alternatives before the League." *FA*, 15 (1) (1936): 102–11.

Lucchini, Carlo. *Ali Italiane in Africa Orientale 1935–1940*. Parma: Storia Militare, 1997.

Luconi, Stefano. "The Influence of the Italo-Ethiopian Conflict and the Second World War on Italian-American Voters: The Case of Philadelphia." *Immigrants and Minorities*, 16 (3) (1997): 1–18.

Lupold, Harry Forest. "Italo-Ethiopia War, 1935–1936." *Social Studies*, 61 (5) (1970): 213–15.

Lupu, N. Z. "Conflictul Italo-Etiopian si Unele Schimbari in Raportul de Forte pe Plan International." *Revista de Istorie*, 30 (5) (1977): 883–99.

——. "The Italo-Ethiopian Conflict and Changes in the Balance of Power at the International Level." *Revue de Istori*, 30 (5) (1977): 883–99.

MacCallum, Elizabeth Pauline. *Rivalries in Ethiopia*. Boston and New York: World Peace Foundation, 1935.

MacCreagh, Gordon. *The Last of Free Africa*. New York: The Century Company, 1928.

MacDonald, John Forrest. *Abyssinian Adventure*. London: Cassell and Company Ltd., 1957.

Macfie, John William Scott. *An Ethiopian Diary: A Record of the British Ambulance Service in Ethiopia*. London: University Press of Liverpool, 1936.

MacLean, Robinson. *John Hoy of Ethiopia*. New York: Farrar and Rinehart, 1936.

Makin, William James. *War over Ethiopia*. London: Jarrolds Publishers Ltd., 1935.

Mandelstam, André N. *Le Conflit Italo-Éthiopien devant la Société des Nations*. Paris: Librairie du Recueil Sirey, 1937.

Maraventano, Saverio. *Diario della Colonna Maraventano: A.O.I. 1941*. Domodossola: La Cartografica C. Antonioli, 1963.

Marcus, Harold Golden. "The Anglo-Ethiopian Campaign against the Italians, 1941–1942." In Jay Spaulding and Stephanie Beswick (eds.). *White Nile, Black Blood: War, Leadership, and Ethnicity from Khartoum to Kampala*. Lawrenceville, N.J.: RSP, 2000: 113–32.

——. "Disease, Hospitals, and Italian Colonial Aspirations in Ethiopia, 1930–1935." *NAS*, 1 (1) 1 (1979): 21–26.

——. "Ethiopia (1937–1941)." In American University. *Challenge and Response in Internal Conflict*. Vol. 3, *The Experience in Africa and Latin America*. Washington, D.C.: American University, 1968: 1–31.

Marder, Arthur J. "The Royal Navy and the Ethiopian Crisis of 1935–36." *American Historical Review*, 85 (5) (1970): 1327–56.

Marès, Roland de. "La Crise Italo-Éthiopienne." *La Revue de Paris*, 42 (5) 5 (1935): 203–13.

Martelli, George. *Italy against the World*. London: Chatto and Windus, 1937.

Masotti, Pier Marcello. *Ricordi d'Etiopia di un Funzionario Coloniale*. Milan: Pan, 1981.

——. "Il Rimpatrio di Donne, Bambini, Vecchi ed Invalidi Italiani dall' Etiopia nel 1942–43." *Storia Contemporanea*, 15 (3) (1984): 463–73.

Matthews, Herbert Lionel. *Eyewitness in Abyssinia: With Marshal Badoglio's Forces to Addis Ababa*. London: Secker and Warburg, 1937.

——. *Two Wars and More to Come*. New York: Carrick and Evans, Inc., 1938.

Mattioli, Guido. *L'Aviazione Fascista e la Conquista dell'Impero*. Rome: L'Aviazione, 1939.

Mazengia, Dina. "British Foreign Policy in the Italo-Ethiopian Conflict, December 1934–July 1936: A Study in Appeasement." Ph.D. diss., University of New York at Albany, 1979.

McClellan, Charles. "Observations on the Ethiopian Nation, Its Nationalism, and the Italo-Ethiopian War." *NAS*, 3 (1) (1996): 57–86.

——. "The Tales of Yoseph and Woransa: Gedeo Experiences in the Era of the Italo-Ethiopian War." In Melvin Page et al. (eds.). *Personality and Political Culture in Modern Africa*. Boston: African Studies Center, Boston University, 1998: 181–94.

Medlicott, W. N., D. Dakin, and M. E. Lambert (eds.). *The Italo-Ethiopian Dispute, March 21, 1954–October 3, 1935*. London: HMSO, 1976.

Melly, John M. "Ethiopia and the War from the Ethiopian Point of View." *IA*, 15 (1) (1936): 103–21.

Mennevée, Roger. *Les Origines du Conflit Italo-Éthiopien et la Société des Nations, des Incidents Oual-Oual à l'Aggression Italienne*. Paris: Les Documents Politiques, 1936.

Merglen, Albert. "Der Feldzug in Äthiopien 1940–1941: Subversiver Kampf und Konventioneller Krieg." *Wehrewissenschaft Rundschau*, 10 (1960): 132–38.

——. "Guerre Subversive et Conflit Conventionnel: La Campagne d'Éthiopie 1940–1941." *Revue Historique de l'Armée*, 1 (1959): 45–53.

Meriwether, Lee. *Italy's Seizure of Ethiopia: Does It Merit Censure or Approval?* St. Louis: Domus Italica, 1935.

Michael, Alazar Tesfa. *Eritrea To-Day: Fascist Oppression under Nose of British Military*. Woolford: New Times Book Department, 1945.

Migliorini, Elio. *L'Italia in Africa*. Rome: Istituto Poligrafico dello Stato, 1935.

Mikre Sellassie Gabre Ammanuel. "Church and Missions in Ethiopia in Relation to the Italian War and Occupation and the Second World War." Ph.D. diss., University of Aberdeen, 1976.

Minardi, Salvatore. *Alle Origini dell'Incidente Ual Ual*. Caltanissetta: Sciascia, 1990.

Mockler, Anthony. *Haile Selassie's War: The Italian-Ethiopian Campaign, 1935–1941*. Oxford: OUP, 1984.

Monfried, Henry de. "The Drama of Ethiopia." *NC*, 188 (702) (1935): 177–85.

——. *Le Drame Éthiopien*. Paris: Bernard Grasset, 1935.

——. *Les Guerriers de L'Ogaden*. Paris: Gallimard, 1936.

Montanelli, Indro. *XX Battaglione Eritreo*. Milan: Panorama, 1936.

Moran, Herbert Michael. *Letters from Rome: An Australian's View of the Italo-Abyssinian Question*. Sydney: Angus and Robertson Ltd., 1936.

Mori, Renato. *Mussolini e la Conquista dell'Ethiopia*. Florence: Le Monnier, 1978.

Mosley, Leonard Oswald. *Gideon Goes to War: The Story of Major-General Orde C. Wingate*. London: Arthur Barker, 1955.

Munro, Anna Marie. "The Role of France in the Italo-Ethiopian Conflict." M.A. thesis. University of California, Berkeley, 1949.

Naish, Reginald T. *1934—and After! Abyssinia and Italy*. London: Thynne, 1936.

Naylor, Richard Harold. *Abyssinia: What the Stars Foretell*. London: Hutchinson and Company, Ltd., 1935.

Nelson, Elizabeth Jean. "To Ethiopia and Beyond: The Primacy of Struggle in Mussolini's Public Discourse." Ph.D. diss., University of Iowa, 1988.

Nelson, Kathleen, and Alan Sullivan. *John Melly of Ethiopia*. London: Faber and Faber Ltd., 1937.

Nevins, Allan. "The Ethiopian Crisis." *CH*, 48 (1935): 168–73.

——. "Ethiopia's Peril." *CH*, 42 (1935): 510–12.

——. "The Hoare-Laval Mystery." *CH*, 43 (1935): 502–7.

——. "Italy and Abyssinia." *CH*, 41 (1935): 717–18.

——. "Italy Mobilizes against Abyssinia." *CH*, 41 (1935): 583–84.

——. "Italy's Gamble for Ethiopia." *CH*, 42 (1935): 577–90.

——. "The League Acts against Italy." *CH*, 43 (1935): 274–80.

——. "Oil Embargo Delays." *CH*, 43 (1936): 616–18.

——. "A Way Out for Italy." *CH*, 43 (1936): 390–95.

Newman, Edward William Polson. "Abyssinia and the War." *CR*, 159 (1941): 38–45.

——. *Ethiopian Realities*. London: G. Allen and Unwin Ltd., 1936.

——. *Italian Campaign in Abyssinia*. London: T. Butterworth, [1937].

——. "Italienisch Ostafrika." *Auslese*, 11 (1937): 789–92.

——. "The Italo-Abyssinian War." *JRUSI*, 80 (520) (1935): 842–49; 81 (521) (1936): 173–75; and 81 (522) (1936): 410–14.

——. *Italy's Conquest of Abyssinia*. London: Thornton Butterworth, 1937.

——. *New Abyssinia*. London: Rich and Cowan, Ltd., 1938.

Nickell, James Merle. "The British Press and the Ethiopian Crisis, 1935–1936." Ph.D. diss., University of Kentucky, 1977.

Nicolle, David, and Raffaele Ruggeri. *The Italian Invasion of Abyssinia 1935–36*. London: Osprey, 1997.

Niessel, A. "Les Opérations en Éthiopie." *Revue des Deux Mondes*, 30 (1935): 416–25.

484 • BIBLIOGRAPHY

9.

Noel-Buxton, Lord. "Abyssinia Rediviva." *CR*, 159 (1941): 610–15.
Nolan, William A. *Russia's Role in the Ethiopian War*. Chicago: H. Regency Company, 1951.
Nugent, John Peer. *The Black Eagle*. New York: Stein and Day, 1971.
Ormesson, Wladimir d' (ed.). *La Sécurité Collective à la Lumière du Conflit Italo-Éthiopien*. Geneva: Entr'aide Universitaire Internationale, 1936.
Orpen, Neil. *South African Forces in World War II*. Vol. I, *East African and Abyssinian Campaigns*. Cape Town: Purnell and Sons, 1968.
Ortega y Gasset, Eduardo. *Etiopia: El Conflicto Italo-Abisinio*. Madrid: Pueyo, 1935.
"Ostafrika im Zweiten Weltkrieg: Der Britisch-Italienische Konflikt am Horn von Afrika." *Österreichische Militärische Zeitschrift*, 32 (3) (1994): 265–70.
"The Outlook for Ethiopia." *RT*, (124) (1941): 709–22.
Padoan, Luigi. *Italia e Abissinia*. Milan: Il Mondo Geografico, 1935.
Pankhurst, Estelle Sylvia. *British Policy in Eastern Ethiopia, the Ogaden, and the Reserved Area*. Woodford Green: Lalibela House, 1946.
——. *British Policy in Eritrea and Northern Ethiopia*. Woodford Green: Lalibela House, 1946.
——. "Ethiopia, Africa, and the League." *EO*, 3 (11) (1959): 334–43.
——. "Fascist Foreign Policy and the Italo-Ethiopian War." *EO*, 3 (11) (1959): 334–43.
——. "The Genesis of the Italo-Ethiopian War (1935–41)." *EO*, 3 (12) (1959): 377–88; and 4 (1) (1960): 7–29.
——. *Italy's War Crimes in Ethiopia (1935–1941)*. Chicago: The Ethiopian Holocaust Remembrance Committee, 2001.
Pankhurst, Richard. "A Brief Note on the Fascist Murder of the Monks and Deacons of Däbrä Lobanos in May 1937." *Sociology-Ethnology Bulletin*, 1 (3) (1994): 12–13.
——. "A Chapter in Ethiopia's Commercial History: Developments during the Fascist Occupation of 1936–41." *EO*, 14 (1) (1971): 46–67.
——. "The Development of Racism in Fascist Italy's Colonial Empire (1935–1941)." *EJAS*, 4 (2) (1987): 31–51.
——. "Economic Verdict on the Italian Occupation of Ethiopia (1936–1941)." *EO*, 14 (1) (1971): 68–82
——. "Emperor Haile Sellassie's Litigation in England to Reassert the Independence of Ethiopia during the Italian Occupation in 1937 and 1938." *EO*, 14 (1) (1971): 3–10.
——. "The Ethiopian National Anthem in 1941: A Chapter in Anglo-Ethiopian Wartime Relations." *EO*, 5 (1) (1972): 63–66.
——. "The Ethiopian Patriots and the Collapse of Italian Rule in East Africa, 1940–1941." *EO*, 12 (2) (1968): 92–127.

——. "The Ethiopian Patriots: The Lone Struggle 1936–1940." *EO*, 13 (1) (1970): 40–56.

——. "La Fine dell'Africa Italiana nel Libelle di Arconovaldo Bonaccorsi." *Studi Piacentini*, (11) (1992): 10–19.

——. "Italian and 'Native' Labour during the Italian Fascist Occupation of Ethiopia, 1935–41." *Ghana Social Science Journal*, 2 (2) (1972): 42–73.

——. "Italian Fascist Claims to the Port of Jibuti, 1935–1941." *EO*, 14 (1) (1971): 26–30.

——. "The Italo-Ethiopian War and League of Nations Sanctions, 1935–1936." *Genève Afrique*, 13 (2) (1974): 5–29.

——. "Italy and Ethiopia: The First Four Years of the Resistance Movement (1936–1941)." *AQ*, 9 (4) (1970): 338–73.

——. "The Legal Question of Racism in Eritrea during the British Military Administration: A Study of Colonial Attitudes and Responses, 1941–1945." *NAS*, (New Series) 2 (2) (1995): 25–70.

——. "Massawa 1935–1941." *EJAS*, 2 (1/2) (1982): 1–39.

——. "The Medical History of Ethiopia during the Italian Fascist Invasion and Occupation (1935–1941)." *EO*, 16 (2) (1973): 108–17.

——. "'Old Stones': The Loot of Ethiopian Antiquities during the Fascist Invasion of 1935–36." *Dialogue*, 3 (1) (1970): 33–41.

——. "A Page of Ethiopian History: Italian Settlement Plans during the Fascist Occupation of 1936–1941." *EO*, 8 (2) (1970): 145–56.

——. "Plans for Mass Jewish Settlement in Ethiopia (1936–1943)." *EO*, 15 (4) (1972): 235–45.

——. "Post–World War II Ethiopia: British Military Policy and Action for the Dismantling and Acquisition of Italian Factories and Other Assets." *JES*, 29 (1) (1996): 35–77.

——. "Road-Building during the Italian Fascist Occupation of Ethiopia (1936–1941)." *AQ*, 15 (3) (1976): 21–63.

——. "Sanctions and Ethiopia 1935–36." *Addis Reporter*, 1 (33) (1969): 17–20.

——. "The Secret History of the Italian Fascist Occupation of Ethiopia, 1935–41." *AQ*, 16 (4) (1977): 35–86.

——. "Sviluppo dello Razzismo nell'Impero Facisto Italiano." *Studi Piacentini*, 3 (1988): 175–97.

Parker, R. A. C. "Great Britain, France, and the Ethiopian Crisis, 1935–1936." *The English Historical Review*, 89 (351) (1974): 293–332.

Paturzo, Michele. *La Marina Mercantile e il Suo Contributo alla Conquista dell'Impero*. Rome: Cremonese, 1937.

Pernot, Maurice. "Le Conflit Italo-Éthiopien et la Politique Africaine de l'Italie." *L'Europe Nouvelle*, 18 (1935): 183–84.

Persichelli, Siro. *Eroismo Eritreo nella Storia d'Italia*. Rome: Edizioni Ricordi d'Africa, 1968.

Pesenti, Gustavo. *La Prima Divisone Eritrea alla Battaglia d'Ascianghi*. Milan: L'Eroica, 1937.

———. *Storia della Prima Divisione Eritrea, 8 Aprile 1935–XIII–lx Maggio XIV*. Milan: L'Eroica, 1937.

Phayre, Ignatius (pseud. [W. G. Fitzgerald]). "Italy's Military Problems in Abyssinia." *English Review*, 61 (1935): 270–81.

———. "Mussolini's African Adventure." *CH*, 42 (1935): 365–71.

———. "Mussolini's 'Master-Work' in Africa." *Quarterly Review*, (525) (1935): 75–91.

———. "The Rape of Abyssinia." *NC*, 117 (700) (1935): 646–58.

Pieroni, Piero. *L'Italia in Africa*. Florence: Vallecchi, 1974).

Pierotti, Francesco. *Vita in Etiopia, 1940–41*. Bologna: Cappelli, 1959.

Pigli, M. *Italian Civilization in Ethiopia*. London: Dante Aligheiri Society, c. 1936.

Pignatelli, Luigi. *La Guerra dei sette Mesi*. Naples: Mezzogiorno, 1961.

Platt, William. *The Abyssinian Storm*. London: Jarrolds Publishers Ltd., 1935.

———. *The Campaign against Italian East Africa 1940–41*. London: Ministry of Defence, 1952.

———. *Report on the Operations in Eritrea and Abyssinia*. London: HMSO, 1946.

Pomilio, Mario. *Con i Dubat, Fronte Sud*. Florence: Vallecchi, 1937.

Post, Gaines. "The Machinery of British Policy in the Ethiopian Crisis." *The International History Review*, 1 (4) (1979): 522–41.

Potter, Marguerite. "British Policy during the Italo-Ethiopian Crisis." Ph.D. diss., University of Texas, Austin, 1956.

Potter, Pitman B. "The Wal Wal Arbitration." *American Journal of International Law*, 30 (1) (1936): 27–44.

———. *The Wal Wal Arbitration*. Washington, D.C.: Carnegie Endowment for International Peace, 1938.

"The Powers and Abyssinia." *JRUSI*, 80 (519) (1935): 633–35.

Pradelle, Albert de la. *Le Conflit Italo-Éthiopien*. Paris: Éditions Internationales, 1936.

Procacci, Giuliano. "Le Internazionali e l'Aggressione Fascista all'Etiopia." *Annali dell'Istituto Giangiacomo Feltrinelli*, 18 (1977): 7–170.

Prochaazka, Roman von. *Abyssinia: The Powder Barrel*. London: British International News Agency, 1935.

Raugh, Harold E. "General Wavell and the Italian East African Campaign." *Military Review*, 63 (7) (1983): 54–66.

Rava, Maurizio. "Il Programma dell' Ethiopia e la Guerra Contro l'Italia." *Nuova Antologia*, (1 August 1935): 339–47.

——. "L'Inghilterra e l'Ethiopia, Date e Fatti." *Nuova Antologia*, (1 September 1935): 74–90.

——. *Parole ai Coloniali*. Milan: A. Mondadori, 1935.

"Report of the League of Nations." *American Journal of International Law*, 30 (1, Supplement) (1936): 1–26.

Rice, Esmé Ritchie. *Eclipse in Ethiopia*. London: Marshall, Morgan and Scott Ltd., 1938.

Richardson, Charles O. "The Rome Accords of January 1935 and the Coming of the Italian-Ethiopian War." *The Historian*, 41 (1) (1978): 41–58.

Ridley, C. W. "Amba Alagi 1941." *Journal for the Society of Army Historical Research*, 67 (270) (1989): 75–79

Ridley, Francis A. *Mussolini over Africa*. London: Wishart Books Ltd., 1935.

Ritter, Rudolf, and Elder von Xylander. *Die Eroberung Abessiniens*. Berlin: Mittler, 1937.

Robertson, J. C. *The Ethiopian Crisis*. Salisbury: Central Africa Historical Association, 1978.

Robertson, James C. "The Hoare-Laval Plan." *Journal of Contemporary History*, 10 (3) (1975): 433–64.

——. "The Origins of British Opposition to Mussolini over Ethiopia." *Journal of British Studies*, 9 (1969): 122–42.

Robinson, Cedric J. "The African Diaspora and the Italo-Ethiopian Crisis." *Race*, 27 (2) (1985): 51–65.

Rochat, Giorgio. *Guerre Italiane in Libia e Etiopia: Studi Militari 1921–1939*. Paese: Pagus, 1991.

——. *Il Colonalismo Italiano: Documenti*. Torino: Loescher, 1973.

——. *Militari e Politici nella Preparazione della Campagna d'Etiopia: Studio e Documenti 1932–1936*. Milan: Franco Angeli, 1971.

Roghi, Bruno. *Tessere Verde in Africa Orientale*. Milan: Ed. Elettra, 1936.

Roi, M. L. "From the Stresa Front to the Triple Entente: Sir Robert Vansittart, the Abyssinian Crisis, and the Containment of Germany." *Diplomacy and Statecraft*, 6 (1) (1995): 61–90.

Rosenthal, Eric. *The Fall of Italian East Africa*. London: Hutchinson and Company Ltd., 1941.

Ross, Rod. "Black Americans and Italo-Ethiopian Relief, 1935–1936." *EO*, 15 (2) (1972): 122–31.

Rossetti, M. Carlo. *Le Conflit Italo-Ethiopien: Ses Origines et ses Conséquences*. Rome: Corriere Diplomatico e Consolare, 1936.

——. *On Ne Nous Aura Pas*. Rome: Tipografia ditta L. Cecchina, 1936.

Rosso, Augusto. *Italy's Conflict with Ethiopia: The Facts of the Case*. New York: American League for Italy, 1935.

Rouaud, Alain. "La Guerre d'Ethiopie et l'Opinion Mondiale." *Afrique et l'Asie Modernes*, (156) (1988): 56–61.

Rousseau, Charles. *Le Conflit Italo-Éthiopien devant le Droit International.* Paris: Éditions A. Pedone, 1938.

Rowan-Robinson, Henry. *England, Italy, Abyssinia: The First Complete Study of the Previous Relations of England and Italy to Abyssinia and of the Existing Military and Political Situation in That Country.* London: William Clowes and Sons, 1935.

Rubens, M. L. "Non-White Reaction to the Italo-Ethiopian Crisis, 1934–1936." B.Litt. thesis. University of Oxford, 1978.

Russell, Dudley. "Lighter Africa: Stories from the Eritrean-Abyssinia Campaign 1940–41." *The Journal of the United Service Institution of India,* 84 (354) (1954): 37–51.

Salmon, E. Marling. *Beyond the Call of Duty: African Deeds of Bravery in Wartime.* London: Macmillan and Company Ltd., 1952.

Salvemini, Gaetano. "Can Italy Live at Home?" *FA,* 14 (2) (1936): 243–58.

——. "Mussolini, the Foreign Office, and Abyssinia." *CR,* 148 (837) (1935): 268–77.

——. "The Vatican and the Ethiopian War." In F. Keene (ed.). *Neither Liberty nor Bread.* New York: Harper, 1940: 191–200.

"Sanctions in the Italo-Ethiopian Conflict." *International Conciliation,* (315) (1935): 539–44.

Sava, L. *Ethiopia under Mussolini's Rule.* Woolford Green: New Times and Ethiopia News, 1940.

Sbacchi, Alberto. *Ethiopia under Mussolini: Fascism and the Colonial Experience.* London: ZB, 1985.

——. "I Governatori Coloniale Italiani in Ethiopia: Gelosie e Rivalta nel Periodo 1936–1940." *Studia Contemporanea,* 8 (1977): 835–77.

——. "Italian Colonization in Ethiopia: Plans and Projects, 1936–1940." *Africa,* 32 (4) (1977): 501–16.

——. "The Italians and the Italo-Ethiopian War 1935–1936." *TJH,* 5 (2) (1976): 123–38.

——. "Italy and Ethiopia: The Colonial Interlude Revisited." *HA,* 17 (1/2/3/4) (December, 1999): 88–110.

——. "Italy and the Treatment of the Ethiopian Aristocracy, 1937–1940." *IJAHS,* 10 (2) (1977): 209–41.

——. *Legacy of Bitterness: Ethiopia and Fascist Italy, 1935–1941.* Lawrenceville, N.J.: RSP, 1977.

——. "Legacy of Bitterness: Poison Gas and Atrocities in the Italo-Ethiopian War." *Genève-Afrique,* 13 (2) (1974): 30–53.

——. "The Price of Empire: Towards an Enumeration of Italian Casualties in Ethiopia 1935–1940." *EN,* 2 (2) (1978): 35–46.

——. "In Search of Legitimacy: The United States and the Recognition of the Italian Empire, 1936–1940." *HA,* 16 (1, 2, 3 ,4) (1998): 96–110.

———. "Secret Talks for the Submission of Haile Selassie and Prince Asfaw Wassen, 1936–1939." *IJAHS*, 7 (4) (1974): 668–80.

Scaetta, H. "Geography, Ethiopia's Ally." *FA*, 14 (1) (1935): 62–70.

Schaefer, Charles. "Serendipitous Resistance in Fascist-Occupied Ethiopia, 1936–1941." *NAS*, 3 (1) (1996): 87–115.

Schaefer, Ludwig Frederick. (ed.). *The Ethiopian Crisis: Touchstone of Appeasement?* Boston: D. C. Heath, 1961.

Scott, James Brown. "Neutrality of the United States." *American Journal of International Law*, 29 (4) (1935): 644–52.

Scott, William Randolph. "The American Negro and the Italo-Ethiopian Crisis 1934–1936: A Study of Some Negro Reactions." M.A. thesis, Howard University, 1966.

———. "Black Nationalism and the Italo-Ethiopian Conflict, 1934–1936." *Journal of Negro History*, 63 (2) (1978): 118–34.

———. "Colonel John C. Robinson: The Brown Condor of Ethiopia." *Pan African Journal*, 5 (1) (1972): 59–69.

———. "Hubert F. Julian and the Italo-Ethiopian War: A Dark Episode in Pan-African Relations." *Umoja*, 2 (2) (1978): 77–93.

———. "Malaku E. Bayen: Ethiopian Emissary to Black America, 1936–1941." *EO*, 15 (2) (1972): 132–38.

———. *The Sons of Sheba's Race: African-Americans and the Italo-Ethiopian War, 1935–1941*. Bloomington: Indiana University Press, 1993.

Scroggs, William O. *A Short History of the Abyssinia Question*. London: British-Italian Bulletin, 1936.

"The Secret Laval-Mussolini Agreement of 1935 on Ethiopia." *Middle East Journal*, 15 (1) (1961): 69–78.

Serra, Enrico. *Carristi dell'"Ariete" (Fogli di Diario 1941–1942)*. Rome: privately printed, 1979.

———. "Mussolini, l'Etiopia e un Segreto di Sir Samuel Hoare." *Nuova Antologia*, (477) (1960): 481–88.

———. "La Questione Italo-Etiopica alla Conferenza di Stresa." *Affari Esteri*, 9 (34) (1977): 313–39.

Serra, Fabrizio. *La Conquista Integrale dell'Impero*. Rome: Unione Editoriale d'Italia, 1938.

Shirreff, David. *Bare Feet and Bandoliers: Wingate, Sandford, the Patriots, and the Part They Played in the Liberation of Ethiopia*. London and New York: The Radcliffe Press, 1995.

A Short History of the Abyssinian Question. London: British-Italian Bulletin, 1935.

Sillani, Tomaso (ed.). *L'Africa Orientale Italiana e il Conflitto Italo-Etiopico*. Rome: La Rassegna Italiana, 1936.

Simmons, Thomas E. *The Brown Condor: The True Adventures of John C. Robinson*. Silver Spring, Md.: Bartley Press, 1988.

Simon, Yves. *La Campagne d'Étiopie et la Pensée Politique Française*. Brussels: Desclée, 1937.

Smith, Alan. "The Open Market: The Economy of Kenya's Northern Frontier Province and the Italo-Abyssinian War." *East Africa Journal*, 6 (11) (1969): 34–42.

Smith, Louis John. "Great Britain and the Abyssinian Crisis, 1935–1936." Ph.D. diss., Michigan State University, 1977.

Spencer, John Hathaway. "The Italo-Ethiopian Dispute and the League of Nations." *The American Journal of International Law*, 31 (4) (1937): 614–41.

Starace, Achille. *La Marcia su Gondar della Colonna Celere A.O. e le Successive Operazioni nella Etiopia Occidentale*. Milan: A. Mondadori, 1936.

Steer, George Lowther. *Caesar in Abyssinia*. London: Hodder and Stoughton Ltd., 1936.

——. *Sealed and Delivered: A Book on the Abyssinian Campaign*. London: Hodder and Stoughton Ltd., 1942.

Stella, Gain Carlo. *Bibliografia Politico-Militare del Conflitto Italo-Abissino, 1935–36*. Ravenna: G. C. Stella, 1988.

Stephenson, Jeanne. "The American Attitude toward the Ethiopian Crisis." Ph.D. diss., Vanderbilt University, 1941.

Stern, W. B. "The Treaty Background of the Italo-Ethiopian Dispute." *The American Journal of International Law*, 30 (2) (1936): 189–203.

Stevens, J. D. "A Black Correspondent Covers the Ethiopian War 1935–1936." *Journalism Quarterly*, 49 (2) (1972): 349–51.

"The Strategy of the War: Twilight in Italian East Africa." *RT*, (123) (1941): 464–71.

Sullivan, Brian R. "The Italian-Ethiopian War, October 1935–November 1941: Causes, Conduct, and Consequences." In A. Hamish Ion and E. J. Errington (eds.). *Great Powers and Little Wars: The Limits of Power*. Westport, Conn. and London: Praeger, 1993: 167–201.

Surtees, G. "A 'Q' War: An Administrative Account of the Eritrean and Abyssinian Campaign, 1941." *JRUSI*, 108 (631) (1963): 256–69.

Sykes, Christopher. *Orde Wingate*. London: Collins, 1959.

Taddia, Irma. "Un Funzionario tra Ricerca Scientifica e Colonialismo: Giovanni Ellero." *Africa*, 48 (1) (1993): 24–34.

Tanghe, Raymond. *Le Conflit Italo-Ethiopien*. Montreal: Éditions Albert Levesque, 1939.

Temperly, A. C. "The War in Abyssinia." *Journal of the Royal Asiatic Society of Great Britain and Ireland*, 23 (1926): 251–62.

Terlinden, Vicomte Charles. *Le Conflit Italo-Éthiopien et la Société des Nations*. Liège: Desoer, 1936.

Thompson, Robert Norman. *Liberation: The First to Be Freed*. Vancouver, B.C.: Battleine Books, 1987.

Thwaite, Daniel. *The Seething African Pot*. London: Constable and Company Ltd., 1936.

Tillett, Lowell R. "The Soviet Role in League Sanctions against Italy, 1935–1936." *American Slavic and East European Review*, 15 (1956): 11–16.

Toscano, Mario. "Eden's Mission to Rome on the Eve of the Italo-Ethiopian Conflict." In A. O. Sarkassian (ed.). *Studies in Diplomatic History*. New York: Barnes and Noble, 1961: 126–52.

Tosti, Amedeo. *The Greatest Colonial Enterprise in the World*. Rome: Novissima Roma, c. 1936.

——. *Vita Eroica di Amedeo Duca d'Aosta*. Milan: A. Mondadori, 1952.

Toynbee, Arnold J. *Abyssinia and Italy*. London: Published for the Royal Institute of International Affairs by Oxford University Press, 1936.

——. *Treaties Broken by Italy in the Abyssinian War*. London: The Abyssinian Association, 1937.

Trofimov, V. A. "Agressiia Italii v Efiopii i ee Posledstviia." *Voprosy Istorii*, (8) (1976): 63–74.

Tsehai, B. "Anglo-Ethiopian Relations, 1934–1942." Ph.D. diss., University of Bristol, 1980.

Valle, Pedron A. del. *Roman Eagles over Ethiopia*. Harrisburg, Pa.: Military Service Publishing Company, 1940.

Varanini, V. "Le Forze Armate dell'Abissinia." *Gerarchia*, 15 (1935): 349–54.

Vaucher, Paul, and Paul-Henri Siriex. *L'Opinion Britannique: La Société des Nations, et la Guerre Italo-Éthiopienne*. Paris: Publication du Centre d' Études de Politique Étrangère, 1936.

Vecchi, B. V. *Sei Mesi sul Fronte Nord-Etiopico*. Milan: Biehi, 1936.

Verich, Thomas Michael. "The European Powers and the Italo-Ethiopian War 1935–1936: A Diplomatic History." Ph.D. diss., Duke University, 1973.

——. *The European Powers and the Italo-Ethiopian War, 1935–1936: A Diplomatic Study*. Salisbury, N.C.: Documentary Publications, 1980.

Viljoen, C. van R. "The War in Abyssinia." *Assegai*, 18 (9) (1979): 9, 11, 13–15.

Villari, Luigi. "Abyssinia and Italy: The Italian Case." *JRAS*, 34 (137) 137 (1935): 366–73.

——. *Italy, Abyssinia and the League*. Rome: Dante Alighieri Society, 1936.

——. "Italy and Abyssinia: The Italian Case." *The English Review*, 61 (1935): 143–49.

——. *Storia Diplomatica del Conflitto Italo-Etiopico*. Bologna: N. Zanichelli, 1943.

Villari, Luigi, and E. Abraham. "Abyssinia and Italy: The Case for Ethiopia." *JRAS*, 34 (1935): 374–77.

Virgin, Eric. *The Abyssinia I Knew*. London: Macmillan Company, 1936.

Vitali, Giovanni. *Le Guerre Italiane in Africa*. Milan: Sonzogno, 1936.

Volta, S. *Graziani a Neghelli*. Florence: Vallecchi, 1936.

Waley, Daniel. *British Public Opinion and the Abyssinian War 1935–6*. London: Maurice Temple Smith, 1975.

Walker, Craven Howell. "The Emperor of Abyssinia and His Army." *Africa Observer*, 4 (1935): 14–19.

——. *The War Danger over Abyssinia*. London: League Against Imperialism and for National Independence, [1935].

Waterhouse, Francis A. *Gun Running in the Red Sea*. London: Sampson Low, Marston and Company Ltd., c1936.

Watt, D. C. "The Secret Laval-Mussolini Agreement of 1935 on Ethiopia." *The Middle East Journal*, 15 (1) (1961): 69–78.

Watteville, H. de. "Italy and Abyssinia." *The Army Quarterly*, 31 (1) (1936): 76–83; and 32 (2) (1936): 251–61.

——. "The Italo-Abyssinian War." *NC*, 120 (714) (1936): 138–52.

Webb, G. S. R. "Wheels over Eritrea." *The Journal of the United Service Institution of India*, 71 (306) (1941): 224–32.

Weerts, Maurice Louis. "The Late M. A. Antonin and Ethiopian Resistance during the Years 1935 to 1940." *JES*, 8 (2) (1970): 171–80.

Weisbord, Robert G. "Black Americans and the Italian–Ethiopian Crisis: An Episode in Pan-Negroism." *The Historian*, 34 (2) (1972): 230–41.

——. "British West Indian Reaction to the Italian-Ethiopian War: An Episode in Pan-Africanism." *Caribbean Studies*, 10 (1) (1970): 34–41.

Weller, George Anthony. *The Belgian Campaign in Ethiopia: A Trek of 2,500 Miles through Jungle Swamps and Desert Wastes*. New York: Belgian Information Center, 1942.

Wencker-Wildberg, Friedrich. *Abessinien: Das Pulverass Afrikas*. Düsseldorf: Bagel, 1935.

Werbrouck, R. *La Campagne des Troupes Coloniales Belges en Abyssinie*. Léopoldville: Courrier d'Afrique, c. 1945.

Wesley, Charles Harris. "The Significance of the Italo-Ethiopian Question." *Crisis*, 18 (5) (1935): 148–51.

White, Freda. *The Abyssinian Dispute*. London: League of Nations Union Publications, 1935.

——. "Peace Terms for Abyssinia." *CR*, 149 (1936): 540–47.

Wienholt, Arnold. *The Africans' Last Stronghold*. London: John Long, 1938.

Wilcox, Francis O. "The Use of Atrocity Stories in War." *The American Political Science Review*, 34 (6) (1940): 1167–78.

Wilson, Hugh Robert. *For Want of a Nail: The Failure of the League of Nations in Ethiopia*. New York: Vantage Press, 1959.

Wingate, Orde Charles. "An Appreciation of the Ethiopian Campaign (1941)." *EO*, 15 (4) (1972): 204–26.

Woiserit Salome Gabre Egziabker. "The Ethiopian Patriots: 1936–1941." *EO*, 12 (2) (1968): 63–91.

Woolbert, Robert Gale. "Ethiopia: Silent Partner." *Asia*, (1942): 429–31.

——. "Feudal Ethiopia and Her Army." *FA*, 14 (1) (1935): 71–81.

——. "The Future of Ethiopia." *FA*, 20 (3) (1942): 535–51.

——. "Italy in Abyssinia." *FA*, 13 (3) (1935): 499–508.

——. "The Rise and Fall of Abyssinian Imperialism." *FA*, 14 (4) (1936): 692–97.

Woolf, Leonard Sydney. *The League and Abyssinia*. London: Hogarth Press, 1936.

Work, Frank Ernest. *Ethiopia: A Pawn in European Diplomacy*. New Concord, Ohio: Ernest Work, 1935.

——. "Italo-Ethiopian Relations." *Journal of Negro History*, 20 (4) (1935): 438–47.

Worker, J. C. "With the Fourth (Uganda) K.A.R. in Abyssinia and Burma." *The Uganda Journal*, 12 (1) (1948): 52–56.

Wright, Patricia. "Italy's African Dream: Part II, Fatal Victory, 1935–6." *History Today*, 23 (4) (1973): 256–65.

——. "Italy's African Dream: Part III, Nemesis in 1941." *History Today*, 23 (5) (1973): 336–44.

Wright, Quincy. "The British Courts and Ethiopian Recognition." *The American Journal of International Law*, 31 (4) (1937): 683–88.

——. "The Test of Aggression in the Italo-Ethiopian War." *The American Journal of International Law*, 30 (1) (1936): 45–56.

Xylander, Rudolf. *La Conquista dell'Abissinia*. Milan: Treves, 1937.

Zappa, Paolo. *L'Intelligence Service el'Etiopia*. Milan: Corbaccio, 1936.

Zilliacus, Konni. *Abyssinia*. London: New Statesman and Nation, 1935.

Zimmern, Alfred Eckhard. "The Crucial Test of the League." *CR*, 148 (839) (1935): 513–20.

——. "The League's Handling of the Italo-Abyssinian Dispute." *IA*, 14 (6) (1935): 751–68.

——. "The Testing of the League." *FA*, 14 (3) (1936): 373–86.

Zoli, Corrado. *La Conquista dell'Impero*. Bologna: Zanichelli, 1937.

——. "The Organization of Italy's East African Empire." *FA*, 16 (1) (1937): 80–90.

Economic Affairs

Abdussamad H. Ahmad. "Gojjam: Trade, Early Merchant Capital, and the World Economy 1901–1935." Ph.D. diss., University of Illinois, 1986.

——. "Trade and Islam in the Towns of Bagemdir 1900–1935." *JES*, 29 (2) (1996): 5–21.

Abir, Mordechai. "Salt Trade and Politics in Ethiopia and in the Zämänä Mäsafent." *JES*, 4 (2) (1966): 1–10.

——. "Southern Ethiopia." In Richard Gray and David Birmingham (eds.). *Pre-Colonial African Trade: Essays on Trade in Central and Eastern Africa before 1900*. London: Oxford University Press, 1970: 119–37.

——. "Trade and Politics in the Ethiopian Region, 1830–1855." Ph.D. diss., University of London, 1964.

Addis Ababa Chamber of Commerce. *Making the Most of Ethiopia's Economic Environment: Proceedings of a Symposium Held at the United Nations Economic Commission for Africa, Addis Ababa, Ethiopia Nov. 10–11, 1997*. Addis Ababa: Addis Ababa Chamber of Commerce, 1998.

Admassu Bezabeh. "Balance of Payments Constraint and Economic Development of Ethiopia: 1960–1974." Ph.D. diss., University of California Berkeley, 1978.

Admit Zerihun. "Total Factor Productivity in the Ethiopian Manufacturing Sector: Extent and Trend." *Ethiopian Journal of Economics*, 7 (1) (1998): 1–25.

Agricultural and Industrial Bank. *Survey of Production and Manufacturing*. Addis Ababa: Agricultural and Industrial Bank, 1975.

Ahmed Zekaria. "Harari Coins: A Preliminary Survey." *JES*, 24 (1991): 23–46.

Asmerom Kidane. "The Demand and Price Structure for Selected Food Products in Ethiopia." Ph.D. diss., Pennsylvania State University, 1973.

Assefa Bequele. "The Banking Proclamation of 1963." *EO*, 8 (4) (1965): 281–92.

——. "Industrialization and Labour Absorption: Projections for Ethiopia, 1968–1983." Ph.D. diss., Indiana University, 1973.

Assefa Bequele, and Eshetu Chole. *A Profile of the European Economy*. London: Oxford University Press, 1969.

Bahru Zewde. "Economic Origins of the Absolutist State in Ethiopia." *JES*, 17 (1984): 1–29.

——. "An Overview and Assessment of Gambella Trade (1904–1935)." *International Journal of African Historical Studies*, 20 (1) (1987): 75–94.

Befekadu Degefe. "Ethiopia." In Adebayo Adedeji (ed.). *The Indigenisation of African Economies*. London: Hutchinson and Company, 1981: 238–77.

——. *Indigenisation of Ethiopian Economy*. Addis Ababa: Institute of Development Research, 1976.

——. "The Making of the Ethiopian National Currency, 1941–45." *JES*, 26 (2) (1993): 23–51.

Befekadu Degefe, and Berhanu Nega (eds.). *Annual Report on the Ethiopian Economy: Vol. I 1999/2000*. Addis Ababa: Ethiopian Economic Association, 2000.

Belai Giday. *Currency and Banking Ethiopia*. Addis Ababa: Belai Giday, 1987.

Bent, J. Theodore. "The Ancient Trade route across Ethiopia." *Geographical Journal*, 2 (1893): 140–46.

Bereket Kebede and Mekonen Taddesse (eds.). *The Ethiopian Economy: Poverty and Poverty Alleviation*. Addis Ababa: Addis Ababa University, 1996.

Berhanu Abegaz (ed.). *Essays on Ethiopian Economic Development*. Aldershot: Avebury, 1994.

———. "Ethiopia." In Shantayanan Devarajan, David R. Dollar, and Torgny Holmgren (eds.). *Aid and Reform in Africa*. Washington, D.C.: The World Bank, 2001: 166–226.

Blaug, Mark. "Employment and Unemployment in Ethiopia." *International Labour Review*, 110 (2) (1974): 117–43.

Bondestam, Lars. "Notes on Foreign Investment in Ethiopia." In Carl Widstrand (ed.). *Multinational Firms in Africa*. New York: Africana Publishing Company, 1975: 125–42.

———. "Notes on Multinational Corporations in Ethiopia." *African Review*, 5 (4) (1975): 535–49.

———. "People and Capitalism in the North-Eastern Lowlands of Ethiopia." *JMAS*, 12 (3) (1974): 423–39.

———. "Underdevelopment and Economic Growth in Ethiopia." *Kronick van Afrika*, 1 (1974): 20–35.

Brown, S. L. *Foreign Investments in Ethiopia*. New York: School of Business and Civil Administration, College of the City of New York, 1953.

Cabal, Carol R. "Household Food Energy Intake of Semi-Subsistent Households in Integrated Crop-Livestock Agricultural Systems in the Central Highlands of Ethiopia." Ph.D. diss., University of Hawaii, 2000.

Cherian, K. A. *Ethiopia Today: An Up-to-Date, Illustrated Review of Economic Development*. Addis Ababa: Central Printing Press, 1969.

Daniel Teferra. "The Phenomenon of Underdevelopment in Ethiopia." Ph.D. diss., University of Wisconsin Madison, 1979.

Debebbe Habte-Yohannes. "The Addis Ababa Bank." *EO*, 8 (4) (1965): 339–44.

Dercon, Stefan. "On Market Integration and Liberalisation: Method and Application to Ethiopia." *Journal of Development Studies*, 32 (1) (1995): 112–42.

Dercon, Stefan, and Lulseged Ayalew. "Coffee Prices and Smuggling in Ethiopia." *Ethiopian Journal of Economics*, 3 (2) (1994): 49–82.

Duggar, J. W. "Monetary Development in Ethiopia since 1931." *EO*, 10 (3) (1966): 206–14.

Duri Mohammed. "Private Foreign Investment in Ethiopia (1950–1968)." *JES*, 7 (2) (1969): 53–78.

Edwards, Jon R. "Slavery, the Slave Trade, and the Economic Reorganization of Ethiopia 1916–1935." *African Economic History*, 11 (1982): 3–14.

Ege, S. (ed.). *Ethiopia: Problems of Sustainable Development*. Trondheim: Trondheim University, College of Arts and Science, 1990.

Eshetu Chole. "Constraints to Industrial Development in Ethiopia." In Eshete Chole et al. (eds.). *The Crisis of Development Strategies in Eastern Africa.* Addis Ababa: Organization for Social Science Research in Eastern Africa, 1990: 236–60.

——. "The Dismal Economy: Current Issues of Economic Reform and Development in Ethiopia." *Ethiopian Journal of Economics*, 2 (1) (1993): 37–72.

——. "Ethiopia's Balance of Payments 1975–1985." *JES*, 22 (1989): 1–11.

——. (ed.). *Fiscal Decentralization in Ethiopia.* Addis Ababa: Department of Economics, AAU, 1994.

——. "The Impact of War on the Ethiopian Economy." In *Proceedings: Fourth International Conference on the Horn of Africa.* New York: Center for the Study of the Horn of Africa, 1990: 93–9.

——. "Issues of Vertical Imbalance in Ethiopia's Emerging System of Fiscal Decentralization." *Ethiopian Journal of Economics*, 3 (2) (1994): 25–48.

——. "Opening Pandora's Box: Preliminary Notes on Fiscal Decentralization in Contemporary Ethiopia." *NAS*, (NS) 1 (1) (1994): 7–30.

——. "Privatization and Deregulation in Ethiopian Industry: Problems, Prospects, and Impact on Economy." *JES*, 26 (1) (1993): 33–58.

——. "Towards a History of the Fiscal Policy of the Pre-Revolutionary Ethiopian State, 1941–74." *JES*, 17 (1984): 88–106.

Etherington, D. M., and A. Yainshet. "The Impact of Income Terms of Trade for Coffee on Capital Goods Imports and Investment in Ethiopia." *Eastern Africa Economic Review*, 4 (1) (1988): 48–52.

Ethiopia. Ministry of Commerce. *Economic Handbook.* Addis Ababa: Berhanenna Selam Printing Press, 1958.

Ethiopia. Ministry of Commerce and Industry. *Economic Progress of Ethiopia.* Addis Ababa: East African Standard, for the Ministry, 1955.

Ezekiel B. Gebissa. "Consumption, Contraband, and Commodification: A History of Khat in Harerge, Ethiopia, c. 1930–1991." Ph.D. diss., Michigan State University, 1997.

Ezra Kristian Ghebrat. "Foreign Trade and Economic Development: The Ethiopian Experience. 1961–1971." Ph.D. diss., New School for Social Research, 1982.

Fraser, Ian S. "The Abyssinian Framework for Economic Development in Ethiopia." *JEL*, 3 (1) (1966): 113–50.

Gabrahiwot Baykadagn. *The State and the Economy of Early 20th Century Ethiopia: Prefiguring Political Economy Circa 1910.* London: Kamak House, 1995.

Gamby, Raymond R. "The Effect of Government Policies on Economic Development in Ethiopia." *Ethiopian Business Journal*, 4 (1) (1967): 25–32.

Gashaw Dagnew. "Exchange Rate Policy in Ethiopia: An Agenda for Action." *Ethiopian Journal of Economics*, 1 (1) (1992): 71–98.

Getachew Yoseph (ed.). *The Ethiopian Economy: Problems and Prospects of Private Sector Development.* Addis Ababa: University Printing Press, 1994.

Getachew Yoseph and Abdulhamid Bedri Kello (eds.). *Proceedings of the Third Annual Conference on the Ethiopian Economy: Problems and Prospects of Private Sector Development in Ethiopia.* Addis Ababa: AAU, 1994.

Getaneh Assefa. "The Mineral Resources Potential of Ethiopia." *Dialogue: Journal of Addis Ababa University Teachers Association,* 1 (2) (1992): 99–130.

Gill, Gerard J. (ed.). *Readings on the Ethiopian Economy.* Addis Ababa: HSU, Institute of Development Research: 1974.

Ginzberg, Eli, and Herbert A. Smith. *Manpower Strategy for Developing Countries: Lessons from Ethiopia.* New York: Columbia University Press, 1967.

Girma Kebbede. "State Capitalism and Development: The Case of Ethiopia." *JDA*, 22 (1) (1987): 1–23.

Graham, Richard C. *Economic Development in Ethiopia 1960.* Washington, D.C.: USGPO, 1961.

Great Britain. Department of Overseas Trade. *Economic Conditions in Ethiopia 1929–1931.* London: HMSO, 1932.

Griffin, Keith B. (ed.). "The Economic Crisis in Ethiopia." In W. L. Hollist and F. L. Tullis (eds.). *Pursuing Food Security: Strategies and Obstacles in Africa, Asia, Latin America, and the Middle East.* Boulder, Colo.: LR, 1987: 121–36.

——. *The Economy of Ethiopia.* Basingstoke: Macmillan, 1992.

Gryziewicz, S. "Main Determinants of Ethiopian Economic Development Policy." *EO*, 7 (3) (1964): 192–201.

——. "An Outline of the Fiscal System in Ethiopia." *EO*, 8 (4) (1965): 293–324.

Gyenge, Zoltán. *Ethiopia on the Road of Non-Capitalist Development.* Budapest: Institute for World Economics, Hungarian Academy of Sciences, 1976.

Haar, Stephen George. "Long Distance Trade, Political Economy and National Reunification in the Christian Kingdoms of Ethiopia, c. 1800–1900." Ph.D. diss., UCLA, 1990.

Haile Kebret Taye. "A Macroeconometric Model of a Subsistence Economy: The Case of Ethiopia." Ph.D. diss., University of Ottawa, 1996.

Hansson, G. *Ethiopia 1994: Economic Achievements and Reform Problems.* Stockholm: Swedish International Development Authority, 1995.

Harvey, C. *Banking Reform in Ethiopia.* Brighton: Institute of Development Studies, 1996.

Hayter, Frank E. *Gold of Ethiopia*. London: Stanley Paul and Company, 1936.

Henock Kifle. "The Determinants of the Economic Politics of States in the Third World: The Agrarian Policies of the Ethiopian State, 1941–1973." Ph.D. diss., University of Massachusetts, 1987.

——. "Ethiopian Economic Development: An Alternative." *Challenge*, 9 (2) (1969): 10–18.

Henze, Paul Bernard. *Contrasts in African Development: The Economies of Kenya and Ethiopia*. Santa Monica, Calif.: Rand Corporation, 1989.

——. *Ethiopia Crisis of a Marxist Economy: Analysis and Text of a Soviet Report*. Santa Monica, Calif.: Rand Corporation, 1989.

——. *Ethiopia's Economic Progress for the 1990s*. Santa Monica, Calif.: Rand Corporation, 1989.

International Monetary Fund. *Ethiopia: Recent Economic Developments*. Washington, D.C.: IMF Staff Country Reports, 1999.

Joireman, Sandra Fullerton. "Contracting for Land: Lessons from Litigation in a Communal Tenure Area of Ethiopia." *CJAS*, 30 (2) (1996): 214–32 and 30 (3) (1996): 424–42.

——. *Property Rights and Political Development in Ethiopia and Eritrea 1941–74*. Oxford: JC, 2000.

Kidane Mariam G. Egziabher. "Structural Adjustment, Its Economic and Social Impact: The Experience of Ethiopia." M.A. thesis, American University, 1999.

Kinfe Abraham. *Ethiopia: The Dynamics of Economic Reforms*. Addis Ababa: Ethiopian International Institute for Peace and Development Press, 2001.

Kohl, Melvin J. *Ethiopia—Treasure House of Africa: A Review of Ethiopian Currency and Related History*. Santa Monica, Calif.: The Society for International Numismatics, 1969.

Kurimoto, Eisei. "Trade Relations between Western Ethiopia and the Nile Valley during the Nineteenth Century." *JES*, 28 (1) (1995): 53–68.

Leaman, John Harold. "The Spatial Role of Commercial Banking in Economic Development: The Example of Ethiopia." Ph.D. diss., University of New York, Buffalo, 1976.

LeBel, Phillip. "Economic and Social Predicators of the Ethiopian Revolution." *HA*, 1 (2) (1978): 53–59.

Love, Robert S. "Economic Change in Pre–Revolutionary Ethiopia." *AA*, 78 (312) (1979): 339–55.

——. "Funding the Ethiopian State: Who Pays?" *ROAPE*, (44) (1989): 18–26.

——. "A Note on Financing the Ethiopian Revolution." *NAS*, 10 (1) (1988): 39–45.

Love, Robert S., and Richard Disney. "The Lomé Convention: A Study of its Benefits with Special Reference to Ethiopia." *JES*, 3 (2) (1976): 95–116.

Maxwell, S., and A. Lirenso. "Linking Relief and Development: An Ethiopian Case Study." *IDS Bulletin*, 25 (4) (1994): 65–76.

McBain, Norman S., and James Pickett. "Footwear Production in Ethiopia: A Case Study of Appropriate Technology." *JMAS*, 13 (3) (1975): 415–27.

McCann, James Craig. *Household Economy, Demography, and the "Push" Factor in Northern Ethiopian History, 1916–1935.* Boston: Boston University, African Studies Center, 1984.

——. "Households, Peasants, and Rural History in Lasta, Northern Ethiopia 1900–35." Ph.D. diss., Michigan State University, 1984.

Mekonnen Tadesse and Abdulhamid Bedri Kello (eds.). *The Ethiopian Economy: Problems of Adjustment.* Addis Ababa: Department of Economics, AAU, 1994.

Melady, Thomas Patrick. *The Economic Future of Ethiopia.* Pittsburgh: Duquesne University Press, 1959.

Merid Wolde Aregay. "The Early History of Ethiopian Coffee Trade and the Rise of Shawa." *JAH*, 29 (1) (1988): 19–25.

——. "Society and Technology in Ethiopia 1500–1800." *JES*, 17 (1984): 127–47.

Mulatu Wubneh. "Foreign Technical Assistance and Development in Ethiopia: A Case Study of the Glass and Bottle Plant." *NAS*, 13 (2/3 (1991): 19–36.

——. "State Control and Manufacturing Labor Productivity in Ethiopia." *JDA*, 24 (3) (1990): 311–26.

Naude, Willem A. "On the Persistence of Shocks to Ethiopia's Terms of Trade: A Time Series Analysis." *Eastern Africa Social Science Research Review*, 11 (1) (1995): 59–72.

Pankhurst, Richard. "The Advent of the Maria Theresa Dollar in Ethiopia: Its Effect on Taxation and Wealth Accumulation, and Other Economic, Political, and Cultural Implications." *NAS*, 1 (3) (1978/1980): 19–48.

——. *Economic History of Ethiopia 1800–1935.* Addis Ababa: HSU, 1968.

——. "Ethiopian Monetary and Banking Innovations in the Nineteenth and Early Twentieth Centuries." *JES*, 1 (2) (1963): 64–120.

——. "Ethiopian Tax Collection Prior to the Time of Menelik: A Collation and Analysis of Estimates." *NAS*, 5 (3) (1983/1984): 59–81 and *NAS*, 7 (1) (1985): 23–47.

——. "Ethiopian Tax Documents of the Early Twentieth Century." *JES*, 11 (2) (1973): 157–66.

——. "The History of Currency and Banking in Ethiopia From the Middle Ages to 1935." *EO*, 8 (4) (1965): 358–407.

——. "The History of Taxation in Northern Ethiopia." *HA*, 4 (2) (1981): 26–31.

——. "Indian Trade with Ethiopia, the Gulf of Aden, and the Horn of Africa in the Nineteenth and Twentieth Centuries." *CEA*, 14 (3) (1974): 453–97.

——. *An Introduction to the Economic History of Ethiopia from Early Times to 1800*. London: Sidgwick and Jackson, 1961.

——. "The Perpetuation of the Maria Theresa Dollar and Currency Problems in Italian-Occupied Ethiopia." *JES*, 8 (2) (1970): 89–117.

——. "The Trade of Central Ethiopia in the Nineteenth and Early Twentieth Centuries." *JES*, 2 (2) (1964): 41–91.

——. "The Trade of the Gulf of Aden Ports of Africa in the Nineteenth and Early Twentieth Centuries." *JES*, 3 (1) (1965): 36–81.

——. "The Trade of Northern Ethiopia in the Nineteenth and Early Twentieth Centuries." *JES*, 2 (1) (1964): 49–159.

——. "The Trade of Southern and Western Ethiopia and the Indian Ocean Ports in the Nineteenth and Early Twentieth Centuries." *JES*, 3 (2) (1965): 37–74.

Peterson, Stephen B. "Financial Reforms in a Devolved African Country: Lessons from Ethiopia." *Public Administration and Development*, 21 (2001): 131–48.

Roman Habtu. "The Political Economy of Import Substitution Industrialization in Ethiopia: Capitalist and Socialist Variants." Ph.D. diss., University of Massachusetts, 1988.

Savoyat, E., et al. "Petroleum Exploration in the Ethiopian Red Sea." *Journal of Petroleum Geology*, 12 (2) (1989): 187–204.

Schaefer, Charles. "Competitors Yet Partners: The Bank of Ethiopia and Indian Informal Bankers, 1931–1936." *JES*, 27 (2) (1994): 45–68.

——. "Enclavistic Capitalism in Ethiopia, 1906–1936: A Study of Currency, Banking, and Informal Credit Networks." Ph.D. diss., University of Chicago, 1990.

——. "The Politics of Banking: The Bank of Abyssinia, 1905–1931." *IJAHS*, 25 (2) (1992): 361–89.

Schwab, Peter. "The Tax System of Ethiopia." *The American Journal of Economics and Sociology*, 29 (1) (1970): 77–88.

Shibeshi Ghebre. "Fiscal Deficits and the Monetary Sector in Ethiopia." *Ethiopian Journal of Economics*, 3 (1) (1994): 47–68.

Shiferaw Bekele (ed.). *An Economic History of Ethiopia. Volume I: The Imperial Era, 1941–74*. Dakar: Council for the Development of Economic and Social Research in Africa, 1995.

Shimekit Lemma. "State Agrarian Policies and Periodic Markets in Ethiopia." *JES*, 29 (1) (1996): 78–105.

Simoons, Frederick J. *Northwest Ethiopia: Peoples and Economy*. Madison: University of Wisconsin Press, 1960.

——. "Some Questions on the Economic Prehistory of Ethiopia." *JAH*, 6 (1) (1965): 1–13.

Sisay Asefa. "Socioeconomic Studies of Ethiopia, 1974–1982." *NAS*, 6 (1/2) (1984): 95–104.

Takashi, Yamano. "Food Aid's effects on Household Behavior in Rural Ethiopia." Ph.D. diss., Michigan State University, 2000.

Taye Mengistae. "Skill Formation and Job Matching Effects in Wage Growth in Ethiopia." *Journal of African Economics*, 10 (1) (2001): 1–36.

Tegegne Gebre Egziabher, et al. (eds.). *Aspects of Developments in Ethiopia. Proceedings of a Workshop on the Twenty-Fifth Anniversary of IRD, 26–28, November 1999, Addis Ababa, Ethiopia*. Addis Ababa: AAUP, 1999.

Tekeste Negash. *A Brief Assessment of the Iron and Steel Industry in Ethiopia*. Addis Ababa: United Nations Industrial Development Organization, 1977.

Teketel Haile-Mariam. "The Production, Marketing, and Economic Impact of Coffee in Ethiopia." Ph.D. diss., Stanford University, 1973.

Teodros Wolde Medhin. "The Financial Sector in a Low-Income Economy: The Case of Ethiopia." Ph.D. diss., University of Wisconsin–Milwaukee, 1994.

Tirfe Mammo. *The Paradox of Africa's Poverty: The Role of Indigenous Knowledge, Traditional Practices and Local Institutions—The Case of Ethiopia*. Lawrenceville, NJ: RSP, 1999.

Troxel, Oliver L. *Basic Data on the Economy of Ethiopia*. Washington, D.C.: USGPO, 1958.

United States. Department of Commerce. *Foreign Economic Trends: Ethiopia*. Washington, D.C.: Bureau of International Commerce, 1968.

——. *Foreign Economic Trends: Ethiopia*. Washington, D.C.: Bureau of International Commerce, 1969.

Von Baudissin, Georg Graf. "An Introduction to Labour Developments in Ethiopia." *JEL*, 2 (1) (1965): 101–10.

——. "Labour Policy in Ethiopia." *International Labour Review*, 89 (6) (1964): 551–69.

Wasserman, Max J. "The New Ethiopian Monetary System." *The Journal of Political Economy*, 54 (4) (1946): 358–62.

Wolday Amha. "Maize Marketing in Ethiopia: Liberalization and Price Integration Issues." *Ethiopian Journal of Development Research*, 21 (1) (1999): 79–120.

World Bank. *Economic Memorandum on Ethiopia*. Washington, D.C.: World Bank, 1981.

——. *Economic Memorandum on Ethiopia*. Washington, D.C.: World Bank, 1977.

——. *Ethiopia*. Washington, D.C.: International Bank for Reconstruction and Development, 1951.

——. *Ethiopia: An Export Action Program*. Washington, D.C.: World Bank, 1986.

——. "Ethiopia: Anti-Corruption Report." Washington, D.C.: World Bank, 1998.

——. *Ethiopia: Industrial Sector Review*. Washington, D.C.: World Bank, 1985.

——. *Ethiopia: Policy Agenda for Economic Revival*. Washington, D.C.: World Bank, 1989.

——. *Ethiopia: Recent Economic Developments and Prospects for Recovery and Growth*. Washington, D.C.: World Bank, 1987.

——. "Ethiopia: Regionalization Study." Washington, D.C.: World Bank, 1999.

——. *Ethiopia: Review of Public Finances*. 2 vols. Washington, D.C.: World Bank, 1998.

——. *Ethiopia's Economy in the 1980s and Framework for Accelerated Growth*. Washington, D.C.: World Bank, 1990.

Wuhib Muluneh. "Land-Lockedness and Dependency on Coastal Countries: The Case of Ethiopia." *Geopolitics and International Boundaries*, 2 (1) (1997): 56–68.

Yishak Mengesha. "Prospects for a Securities Market in Ethiopia." *Ethiopian Journal of Economics*, 7 (1) (1998): 81–119.

Young, Maurice de. "An African Emporium: The Addis Markato." *JES*, 5 (2) (1967): 103–22.

Regional Affairs (Horn of Africa) and the African Union

Abir, Mordechai. "Ethiopia and the Horn of Africa." In Richard Gray (ed.). *The Cambridge History of Africa* Vol. 4 *From c. 1600 to c. 1790*. Cambridge: Cambridge University Press, 1975: 537–77.

Aboagye, Festus. "Towards New Peacekeeping Partnerships in Africa? The OAU Liaison Mission in Ethiopia-Eritrea." *African Security Review*, 10 (2) (2001): 19–33.

Agyeman-Duah, B. "The Horn of Africa: Conflict, Demilitarization, and Reconstruction." *Journal of Conflict Studies*, 16 (2) (1996): 44–63.

Allen, Tim (ed.) *In Search of Cool Ground: War, Flight, and Homecoming in Northeast Africa*. Geneva: United Nations Research Institute for Social Development, 1996.

Amare Tekle. "The Horn of Africa: Myths, Misconceptions, and Reality." *Ufahamu*, 17 (3) (1988/1989): 78–89.

——. "Peace and Stability in the Horn of Africa: Problems and Prospects." *NAS*, 11 (1) (1989): 75–108.

Assefaw Bariagaber. "Political Violence and the Uprooted in the Horn of Africa: A Study of Refugee Flows from Ethiopia." *Journal of Black Studies*, 28 (1) (1997): 26–42.

Ayoob, M. *The Horn of Africa: Regional Conflict and Super-Power Involvement*. Canberra: Strategic Defence Studies Centre, Australia National University, 1978.

Azad, A. "The Horn of Africa: Defeat for Imperialism." *African Communist*, (74) (1978): 37–50.

Bell, J. Bowyer. *The Horn of Africa*. New York: Crane, Russak, 1973.

Bereket Habte Selassie. "The American Dilemma on the Horn." *JMAS*, 22 (2) (1984): 249–72.

——. *Conflict and Intervention in the Horn of Africa*. New York: Monthly Review Press, 1980.

——. "The OAU and Regional Conflicts: Focus on the Eritrean War." *AT*, 35 (3/4) (1988): 61–67.

Bhardwaj, Raman G. "Conflict in the Horn of Africa." *Journal of the Institute for Defence Studies and Analyses*, 10 (4) (1978): 369–82.

——. *The Dilemma of the Horn of Africa*. New Delhi: Sterling Publishers Ltd., 1979.

Bhattacharya, S. S. B. "The Horn of Africa and the Indian Ocean: Security and Strategic Impact." *AQ*, 34 (2) (1994): 61–79.

Bowman, Larry W., and Jeffrey A. Lefebvre. "U.S. Strategic Policy in Northeast Africa and the Indian Ocean." *AR*, 28 (6) (1983): 4–9.

Brind, Harry. "Soviet Policy in the Horn of Africa." *IA*, 60 (1) (1983/1984): 75–95.

Castagno, Alphonso Anthony. "Conflicts in the Horn of Africa." *Orbis*, 4 (2)(1960): 204–15.

Caulk, Richard Alan. "Ethiopia and the Horn." In Andrew D. Roberts (ed.). *The Cambridge History of Africa*. Vol. 7, *From 1905 to 1940*. Cambridge: CUP, 1986: 702–41.

Chaliand, Gérard. "The Horn of Africa's Dilemma." *Foreign Policy*, (10) (1978): 116–31.

Clapham, Christopher. "Boundary and Territory in the Horn of Africa." In Paul Nugent and A. I. Asiwaju (eds.). *African Boundaries: Barriers, Conduits, and Opportunities*. London: Pinter, 1996: 237–50.

——. "The Horn of Africa." In Michael Crowder (ed.). *The Cambridge History of Africa*. Vol. 8, *From c. 1940 to c. 1975*. Cambridge: Cambridge University Press, 1984: 458–501.

——. "The Horn of Africa: A Conflict Zone." In Oliver Furley (ed.). *Conflict in Africa*. London and New York: Tauris Academic Studies, 1995: 72–91.

——. "The Horn of Africa: Consequences of Insurgency." *Africa Insight*, 23 (4) (1993): 184–89.

——. "The Political Economy of Conflict in the Horn of Africa." *Survival*, 32 (5) (1990): 403–20.

Clark, Desmond J. *Prehistoric Cultures of the Horn of Africa*. Cambridge: CUP, 1954.

Cliffe, Lionel. "Regional Dimensions of Conflict in the Horn of Africa." *TWQ*, 20 (1) (1999): 89–111.

Clifford, E. H. M. "The British Somaliland-Ethiopia Boundary." *GJ*, 87 (4) (1936): 289–307.

Commonwealth of Australia. *Regional Conflict and Superpower Rivalry in the Horn of Africa*. Canberra: Australian Government Publishing Service, 1984.

"Conflict on the Horn of Africa." *Bulletin of the Africa Institute of South Africa*, 15 (5) (1977): 100–19.

Creative Associates International. *Preventing and Mitigating Conflicts: A Revised Guide for Practitioners Prepared for the Greater Horn of Africa Initiative*. Washington, D.C.: Creative Associates International, 1997.

Creed, John and Kenneth Menkhaus. "The Rise of Saudi Regional Power and the Foreign Policies of Northeast African States." *NAS*, 8 (2/3) (1986): 1–22.

Crocker, Chester A. "U.S. and Soviet Interests in the Horn of Africa." *Department of State Bulletin*, 86 (2106) (1986): 29–32.

Dalal, K. L. "India and the Horn of Africa: Foreign Policy Perspectives." *AQ*, 34 (2) (1994): 3–11.

Danfulani, S. A. "Regional Security and Conflict Resolution in the Horn of Africa: Somalian Reconstruction after the Cold War." *International Studies*, 36 (1) (1999): 35–61.

David, Steven Roy. "Realignment in the Horn: The Soviet Advantage." *International Security*, 4 (2) (1979): 69–90.

——. "The Realignment of Third World Regimes from One Superpower to the Other: Ethiopia's Mengistu, Somalia's Siad, and Egypt's Sadat." Ph.D. diss., Harvard University, 1980.

Doornbos, Martin, et al. (eds.). *Beyond Conflict in the Horn: Prospects for Peace, Recovery, and Development in Ethiopia, Somalia and the Sudan*. Trenton, N.J.: RSP, 1992.

Doresse, Jean. *Histoire Sommaire de la Corne Orientale de l'Afrique*. Paris: Librairie Orientaliste Paul Geuthner, 1971.

Dougherty, James E. *The Horn of Africa: A Map of Political-Strategic Conflict*. Cambridge: Institute for Foreign Policy Analysis, 1982.

Duffield, Mark, and John Prendergast. *Without Troops and Tanks: Humanitarian Intervention in Ethiopia and Eritrea*. Lawrenceville, NJ: RSP, 1994.

Erlich, Haggai. *The Cross and the River: Ethiopia, Egypt, and the Nile*. Boulder: LR, 2002.

Farer, Tom J. "Dilemmas on the Horn." *AR*, 22 (2) (1977): 2–6.

——. *War Clouds on the Horn of Africa: A Crisis for Detente*. Washington, D.C.: Carnegie Endowment for International Peace, 1976.

——. *War Clouds on the Horn of Africa: The Widening Storm*. New York: Carnegie Endowment for International Peace, 1979.

Farid, Abdel Majid (ed.). *The Red Sea: Prospects for Stability*. New York: St. Martin's Press, 1984.

Felgas, Hélio. "As Guerras do 'Corno de Africa.'" *Revista Militar*, 42 (4) (1990): 221–42.

Francis, Samuel T. "Conflict in the Horn of Africa." *Journal of Social and Political Studies*, 2 (3) (1978): 155–68.

Fukui, Katsuyoshi, and John Markakis (eds.). *Ethnicity and Conflict in the Horn of Africa*. London: JC, 1994.

Gamst, F. C. "Conflict in the Horn of Africa." In M. L. Foster and R. A. Rubinstein (eds.). *Peace and War: Cross-Cultural Perspective*. New Brunswick, N.J.: Transaction Books, 1986: 133–51.

Gascon, Alain. "Les Mouvements Armées dans la Corne de L'Afrique et au Sudan: L'Eclatement des Etats Centraux." *Études Polemologiques*, (51) (1989): 61–77.

Getachew Metaferia. "The Ethiopian Connection to the Pan-African Movement." *Journal of Third World Studies*, 12 (2) (1995): 300–25.

Gorman, Robert F. *Conflict in the Horn of Africa*. New York: Praeger, 1981.

——. "Prospects for Reconciliation in the Horn of Africa." *HA*, 4 (4) (1983): 3–14.

Greenfield, Richard David. "Refugees in North-Eastern Africa: The Situation in 1979." *RT*, (277) (1980): 39–52.

——. *Wretched of the Horn: Forgotten Refugees in Black Africa*. New York: Lilian Barber Press, 1987.

Grottanelli, Vinigi L. "The Peopling of the Horn of Africa." In H. Neville Chittick and Robert I. Rotberg (eds.). *East Africa and the Orient: Cultural Syntheses in Pre-Colonial Times*. New York and London: Africana Publishing Company, 1975: 44–75.

Gurdon, Charles. (ed.). *The Horn of Africa*. London: UCL Press, 1994.

Gusarov, V. "OAU and the Problems of Settling Conflicts in Chad and on the Horn of Africa." In Round Table on Problems of Contemporary Africa. *Problems of Contemporary Africa: Proceedings of the Round Table held in Rome, 28–30 November, 1983*. Rome: Instituto Italo Africano, 1984: 55–65.

Haberland, Eike. "The Horn of Africa." In Bethwell A. Ogot (ed.). *General History of Africa*. Vol. 5, *Africa from the Sixteenth to the Eighteenth Century*. Berkeley: University of California Press, 1992: 703–49.

Haile Selassie I. "Towards African Unity." *JMAS*, 1 (3) (1963): 281–91.

Halliday, Fred. "US Policy in the Horn of Africa: 'Aboulia' or Proxy Intervention." *ROAPE*, 4 (10) (1977): 8–32.

Harbeson, John Willis. "The Horn of Africa: From Chaos, Political Renewal?" *CH*, 90 (556) (1991): 221–24.

——. "The International Politics of Identity in the Horn of Africa." In John Willis Harbeson and Donald Rothchild (eds.). *Africa in World Politics*. Boulder, Colo.: WP, 1991: 119–43.

——. "Post Cold War Politics in the Horn of Africa: The Quest for Political Identity Intensified." In John Willis Harbeson and Donald Rothchild (eds.). *Africa in World Politics: Post Cold War Challenges.* Boulder, Colo.: WP, 1995: 127–46.

Harris, Cobie. "Fire in the Horn: Prolonged War in Ethiopia and Eritrea." In Karl P. Magyar and Constantine Danopoulos (eds.). *Prolonged War: A Post-Nuclear Challenge.* Maxwell AFB, Ala.: Air University Press, 1994: 131–55.

Harris, Gordon. *The Organization of African Unity.* New Brunswick, N.J.: Transaction Publishers, 1994.

Henze, Paul Bernard. *Arming the Horn, 1960–1980.* Washington, D.C.: Wilson Center, 1982.

——. "Flexible Persistence over Four Decades: The Soviet Union and the Horn of Africa." In Milos Martic. *Insurrection: Five Schools of Revolutionary Thought.* New York and London: Dunellen, 1975: 361–74.

——. *The Horn of Africa: From War to Peace.* London: MacMillan Press, 1991.

——. *Russians and the Horn: Opportunism and the Long View.* Marina del Rey, Calif.: European American Institute, 1983.

——. "Three Decades of Arms for the Horn of Africa: A Statistical Analysis." *Conflict,* 10 (2) (1990): 135–72.

——. *The United States and the Horn of Africa: History and Current Challenge.* Santa Monica: The Rand Corporation, 1990.

Hilletework Mathias. "Superpowers' Involvement in the Horn of Africa: The Ethiopian-Somali Border Conflict." Ph.D. diss., Howard University, 1985.

Hizkias Assefa. "An Interest Approach to Resolution of Civil Wars in the Horn of Africa: Lessons from the Negotiations on the Eritrean Conflict." In Kumar Rupesinghe (ed.). *Internal Conflict Governance.* New York: St. Martin's Press, 1992: 169–85.

——. "Conflict Resolution Perspectives on Civil Wars in the Horn of Africa." *Negotiation Journal,* 5 (2) (1990): 73–83.

Hoskyns, Catherine. *Case Studies in African Diplomacy: The Ethiopia-Somali-Kenya Dispute, 1960–1967.* Dar-es-Salaam: Oxford University Press, 1969.

Hughes, Anthony J. "Reagan and Africa: Policy Options in the Horn." *HA,* 4 (2) (1981):3–10.

Hutchison, R. A. (ed.). *Fighting for Survival: Insecurity, People, and the Environment in the Horn of Africa.* Geneva: International Union for the Conservation of Nature and Natural Resources, 1991.

Iyob, Ruth. "The Foreign Policies of the Horn: The Clash between the Old and the New." In Gilbert M. Khadiagala and Terrence Lyons (eds.). *African Foreign Policies: Power and Process.* Boulder, Colo.: LR, 2001: 107–29.

——. "Regional Hegemony: Domination and Resistance in the Horn of Africa." *JMAS,* 31 (2) (1993): 257–76.

Jama, Abdi Awaleh. *Basis of the Conflict in the Horn of Africa*. Mogadishu: State Printing Agency, 1978.

James, Frank Linsly. *The Unknown Horn of Africa: An Exploration from Berbera to the Leopard River*. London: George Philip, 1888.

Janke, Peter. "The Horn of Africa." In Robert Thompson (ed.). *War In Peace: Conventional and Guerrilla War since 1945*. New York: Harmony Books, 1981: 248–53.

Johnson, Douglas. "The Structure of a Legacy: Military Slavery in Northeast Africa." *Ethnohistory*, 36 (1) (1989): 72–88.

Joireman, Sandra Fullerton. "Property Rights and the Role of the State: Evidence from the Horn of Africa." *Journal of Development Studies*, 38 (1) (2001): 1–28.

Keller, Edmond J. "The OAU and the Ogaden Dispute." In Georges Nzongola-Ntalaja (ed.). *Conflict in the Horn of Africa*. Atlanta: African Studies Association Press, 1991: 97–116.

———. "United States Foreign Policy on the Horn of Africa: Policymaking with Blinders On." In Gerald J. Bender, James S. Coleman, and Richard L. Sklar (eds.). *African Crisis Areas and U.S. Foreign Policy*. Berkeley: University of California Press, 1985: 178–93.

Kurimoto, Eisei, and Simon Simonse (eds.). *Conflict, Age, and Power in North East Africa*. London: JC, 1998.

Lancaster, Carol J. "The Horn of Africa." In A. Lake et al. (eds.) *After the Wars*. New Brunswick, N.J.: Transaction, 1990: 168–90.

Lefebvre, Jeffrey A. *Arms for the Horn: U.S. Security Policy in Ethiopia and Somalia, 1953–1991*. Pittsburgh, Pa.: University of Pittsburgh Press, 1991.

———. "The United States and Egypt: Confrontation and Accommodation in Northeast Africa, 1956–60." *Middle Eastern Studies*, 29 (2) (1993): 321–38.

Legum, Colin. *The Horn of Africa: Prospects for Political Transformation*. London: Research Institute for the Study of Conflict and Terrorism, 1992.

———. "The Red Sea and the Horn of Africa in International Perspective." In William L. Dowdy and Russell B. Trood (eds.). *The Indian Ocean: Perspectives on a Strategic Arena*. Durham: Duke University Press, 1985: 193–208.

———. "The Troubled Horn of Africa." *Current Affairs Bulletin*, 52 (4) (1975): 12–22.

Legum, Colin, and Bill Lee. *Conflict in the Horn of Africa*. New York and London: Africana Publishing Company, 1979

———. "Crisis in the Horn of Africa: International Dimensions of the Somali-Ethiopian Conflict." In Colin Legum (ed.). *Africa Contemporary Record: Annual Survey and Documents 1977–1978*. New York and London: Africana Publishing Company, 1979: A33–A46.

———. *The Horn of Africa in Continuing Crisis*. New York: Africana, 1979.

——. "The Horn of Africa: The Widening Conflict." In Colin Legum (ed.). *Africa Contemporary Record: Annual Survey and Documents 1979–1980*. New York and London: Africana Publishing Company, 1981: A46–A57.

Lewis, Ioan Myrddin. *Nationalism and Self-Determination in the Horn of Africa*. London: Ithaca, 1983.

——. *Peoples of the Horn of Africa: Somali, Afar, and Saho*. London: IAI, 1955.

Liang Gencheng. "U.S. Policy toward the Horn of Africa." *NAS*, 6 (1/2) (1984): 41–59.

Luckham, Robin, and D. Bekele. "Foreign Powers and Militarism in the Horn." *ROAPE*, (30) (1984): 8–20; and (31) (1984): 7–28.

Lyons, Ron. "The USSR, China, and the Horn of Africa." *ROAPE*, (12) (1978): 5–29.

Lyons, Terrence. "The Horn of Africa Regional Politics: A Hobbesian World." In W. Howard Wriggins (ed.). *Dynamics of Regional Politics: Four Systems on the Indian Ocean Rim*. New York: Columbia University Press, 1992: 158–64.

——. "The International Context of Internal War: Ethiopia/Eritrea." In Edmond J. Keller and Donald Rothchild. *Africa in the New International Order: Rethinking State Sovereignty and Regional Security*. Boulder, Colo.: LR, 1996: 85–99.

Lytton, Earl of. *The Stolen Desert: A Study of Uhuru in North East Africa*. London: MacDonald and Company, 1966.

Makinda, Samuel M. "Conflict and Accommodation in the Horn of Africa: Kenya's Role in the Somali-Ethiopian Dispute." *Australian Outlook*, 37 (1) (1983): 34–39.

——. "Conflict and the Superpowers in the Horn of Africa." *TWQ*, 4 (1) (1982): 93–103.

——. "The Horn of Africa in the Changing World Climate." In R. H. Bruce (ed.). *Prospects for Peace: Changes in the Indian Ocean Region*. Perth: Indian Ocean Centre for Peace Studies, 1992: 235–51.

——. *Security in the Horn of Africa*. London: International Institute for Strategic Studies, 1992.

——. "Shifting Alliances in the Horn of Africa." *Survival*, 27 (1) (1978): 11–19.

——. *Superpower Diplomacy in the Horn of Africa*. New York: St. Martin's Press, 1987.

——. "United States Policy in the Horn of Africa since 1974." *Australian Journal of Politics and History*, 30 (3) (1984): 363–77.

Markakis, John. "Group Conflict and Human Rights in the Horn of Africa." *Issue*, 22 (2) (1994): 5–8.

——. *National and Class Conflict in the Horn of Africa*. Cambridge: CUP, 1987.

——. "The Organisation of African Unity: A Progress Report." *JMAS*, 4 (2) (1966): 135–53.

——. "Radical Military Regimes in the Horn of Africa." *Journal of Communist Studies*, 1 (3/4) (1985): 14–38.

——. *Resource Conflict in the Horn of Africa*. London: Sage, 1998.

Mayall, James. "The Battle for the Horn: Somali Irredentism and International Diplomacy." *WT*, 34 (9) (1978): 336–45.

——. "The National Question in the Horn of Africa." *WT*, 39 (9) (1983): 336–43.

Medhane Tadesse. *The Eritrean-Ethiopian War: Retrospect and Prospects: Reflections on the Making of Conflicts in the Horn of Africa, 1991–1998*. Addis Ababa: Mega Printing Enterprise, 1999.

Menkhaus, Ken, and John Prendergast. "Conflict and Crisis in the Horn of Africa." *CH*, 98 (628) (1999): 213–17.

Mesfin Wolde-Mariam. *The Horn of Africa Conflict and Poverty*. Addis Ababa: Walta Information Center, 1999.

Middle East Research and Information Project. *Upheaval in the Horn: Somalia, Eritrea, Ethiopia*. Washington, D.C.: Middle East Research and Information Project, 1977.

Miller, Dawn M. "'Raising the Tribes': British Policy in Italian East Africa, 1938–41." *Journal of Strategic Studies*, 22 (1) (1999): 96–123.

Mottern, Nicholas. *Suffering Strong: The Journal of a Westerner in Ethiopia, The Sudan, Eritrea, and Chad*. Trenton, N.J.: RSP, 1988.

Negussay Ayele. "A Brief Profile of the Wars in the Horn of Africa." *NAS*, 6 (1/2) (1984): 1–12.

——. "The Horn of Africa: Revolutionary Developments and Western Reactions." *NAS*, 3 (1) (1981): 15–29.

Novati, Giampaolo Calchi. "Italy in the Triangle of the Horn: Too Many Corners for a Half Power." *JMAS*, 32 (3) (1994): 369–85.

Nyong'o, Peter Anyang (ed.). "Crises and Conflicts in the Horn of Africa: Problems and Challenges for Africa." *Genéve-Afrique*, 27 (2) (1989): 59–70.

Nzongola-Ntalaja, Georges (ed.). *Conflict in the Horn of Africa*. Atlanta: African Studies Association Press, 1991.

Okbazghi Yohannes. *The United States and the Horn of Africa: An Analytical Study of Pattern and Process*. Boulder, Colo.: WP, 1997.

Olsen, Gorm Rye. "Domestic and International Causes of Instability in the Horn of Africa, with Special Emphasis on Ethiopia." *Cooperation and Conflict*, 26 (1) (1991): 21–31.

Ottaway, Marina. "Nationalism Unbound: The Horn of Africa Revisited." *SAIS Review*, 12 (2) (1992): 111–28.

——. *Soviet and American Influence in the Horn of Africa*. New York: Praeger, 1982.

——. "Superpower Competition and Regional Conflicts in the Horn of Africa." In R. Craig Nation and Mark V. Kauppi (eds.). *The Soviet Impact in Africa.* Lexington, Mass.: Lexington, 1984: 165–93.

Patman, Robert G. "The Horn of Africa: Prospects for the Resolution of Conflict." *NAS*, 12 (2/3) (1993): 91–106.

——. *The Soviet Union in the Horn of Africa: The Diplomacy of Intervention and Disengagement.* Cambridge: Cambridge University Press, 1990.

Prunier, Gérard. "Les Mouvements Armés dans la Corne de L'Afrique et la Valée du Nil: Particularités et Interactions." *Études Polemologiques*, (46) (1988): 169–76.

Prendergast, John. "Building for Peace in the Horn of Africa: Diplomacy and Beyond." United States Institute of Peace Special Report (June 28, 1999): 1–11.

Ratliff, William E. *Follow the Leader in the Horn: The Soviet-Cuban Presence in East Africa.* Washington, D.C.: Cuban American National Foundation, 1986.

Reece, Gerald. "The Horn of Africa." *IA*, 30 (4) (1954): 440–49.

Reese, Cynthia M. "U.S.-Soviet Competition for Influence in the Horn of Africa." M.A. thesis, American University, 1987.

Remnek, Richard. "The Horn of Africa Retrospect and Prospect." *Strategic Review*, 18 (4) (1990): 39–50.

Ruiz, Hiram A. *Beyond the Headlines: Refugees in the Horn of Africa.* Washington, D.C.: United States Committee for Refugees, 1988.

Sadr, Karim. *The Development of Nomadism in Ancient Northeast Africa.* Philadelphia: University of Pennsylvania Press, 1991.

Samuels, Michael A., et al (eds.). *White Paper: The Horn of Africa.* Washington, D.C.: Center for Strategic and International Studies, 1978.

Sanderson, George N. "The Nile Basin and the Eastern Horn, 1870–1908." In Roland Oliver and G. N. Sanderson (eds.). *The Cambridge History of Africa Vol. 6 From 1870 to 1905.* Cambridge: Cambridge Univeristy Press, 1985: 592–679.

Sauldie, Madan M. *Superpower in the Horn of Africa.* London: Oriental University Press/Apt Books, 1987.

Schraeder, Peter J. "The End of the Cold War and U.S. Foreign Policy toward the Horn of Africa in the Immediate Post-Siyaad and Post-Mengistu Eras." *NAS*, 1 (1) (1994): 91–119.

——. "The Horn of Africa: U.S. Foreign Policy in an Altered Cold War Environment." *Middle East Journal*, 46 (4) (1992): 571–93.

——. "U.S. Intervention in the Horn of Africa amidst the End of the Cold War." *AT*, 40 (2) (1993): 7–27.

Schwab, Peter. "Cold War on the Horn of Africa." *AA*, 77 (306) (1978): 6–20.

Shams, B. Feraidoon. "Conflict in the African Horn." *CH*, 73 (432) (1977): 199–204, 225–26.

Sharma, J. P. "The Horn of Africa: An Arab-Maghreb Perspective." *AQ*, 34 (2) (1994): 109–20.

Shelton, L. G. "The Sino-Soviet Split: The Horn of Africa, November 1977 to February 1979." *Naval War College Review*, 32 (3) (1979): 78–87.

Shepherd, George W. "Dominance and Conflict on the Horn: Notes of United States–Soviet Rivalry." *AT*, 32 (3) (1985): 7–21.

Sherman, Richard F. "Marxism on the Horn of Africa." *Problems of Communism*, 29 (5) (1980): 61–64.

Sheth, V. S. "Changing International Relations and Conflict Resolution in the Horn." *African Currents*, 11 (1990): 48–57.

——. "OAU and the Ethiopia-Somalia Boundary Dispute." *AQ*, 30 (1/2) (1990): 27–33.

Shinnie, Peter L. "The Nilotic Sudan and Ethiopia." In J. D. Fage (ed.). *The Cambridge History of Africa*. Vol. 2, *From ca. 500 B.C. to ca. A.D. 1050*. Cambridge: Cambridge University Press, 1978: 210–71.

Silberman, Leo. "Change and Conflict in the Horn of Africa." *FA*, 37 (4) (1959): 649–59.

Sinclair, Michael R. *The Strategic Significance of the Horn of Africa*. Pretoria: Institute for Strategic Studies, University of Pretoria, 1980.

Sirage, B. K. "Exchange Rate Policy and Export Performance: A Case Study of Ethiopia." Ph.D. diss., University of Lancaster, 1995.

Skurnik, W. A. E. "Continuing Problems in the Horn of Africa." *CH*, 82 (482) (1983): 120–23, 137.

Slikkerveer, Leendert J. *Plural Medical Systems in the Horn of Africa: The Legacy of "Sheikh" Hippocrates*. London and New York: Kegan Paul International, 1990.

Sorenson, John (ed.). *Disaster and Development in the Horn of Africa*. New York: St. Martin's Press, 1995.

——. *Imaging Ethiopia: Struggles for History and Identity in the Horn of Africa*. New Brunswick, N.J.: Rutgers University Press, 1993.

Spencer, John Hathaway. *Ethiopia: The Horn of Africa and U.S. Policy*. Cambridge, Mass.: Institute for Foreign Policy Analysis, 1977.

Stairs, Edward. "The Horn of Africa." In The Royal United Services Institute for Defence Studies (ed.). *Defence Yearbook 1978/70*. London: Brassey's Publishers, 1978: 128–39.

Taddesse Tamrat. "Ethiopia, the Red Sea, and the Horn." In Roland Oliver (ed.). *The Cambridge History of Africa*. Vol. 3, *From c. 1050 to c. 1600*. Cambridge: Cambridge University Press, 1977: 98–182.

——. "The Horn of Africa: The Solomonids in Ethiopia and the State of the Horn of Africa." In D. T. Niane (ed.). *General History of Africa*. Vol. 4, *Africa from the Twelfth to the Sixteenth Century*. London: Heinemann Educational Books Ltd., 1984: 423–54.

Thurston, Raymond L. "The United States, Somalia and the Crisis in the Horn." *HA*, 1 (2) (1978): 11–20.

Toggia, Pietro, Pat Lauderdale, and Abebe Zegeye (eds.). *Crisis and Terror in the Horn of Africa: Autopsy of Democracy, Human Rights, and Freedom.* Aldershot: Ashgate Publishing Ltd., 2000.

Turton, David. "War and Ethnicity: Global Connections and Local Violence in North East Africa and Former Yugoslavia." *Oxford Development Studies*, 25 (1) (1997): 77–94.

United States House of Representatives. Committee on Foreign Affairs. Subcommittee on Africa and Select Committee on Hunger, International Task Force. *Conflict and Famine in the Horn of Africa.* Washington, D.C.: USGPO, 1991.

United States House of Representatives. Committee on Foreign Affairs. Subcommittees on Africa and International Operations. *An Assessment of Recent Developments in the Horn of Africa.* Washington, D.C.: USGPO, 1992.

United States Senate. Committee on Foreign Relations. Subcommittee on African Affairs. *Current Situation in the Horn of Africa.* Washington, D.C.: USGPO, 1991.

——. *Ethiopia and the Horn of Africa.* Washington, D.C.: USGPO, 1976.

——. *The Horn of Africa: Changing Realities and U.S. Response.* Washington, D.C.: USGPO, 1992.

Urban, Mark. "Soviet Intervention in the Ogaden Counter-Offensive of 1978." *Journal of the Royal United Service Institute for Defence*, 128 (2) (1983): 42–53.

Valdés, Nelson P. "Cuba's Involvement in the Horn of Africa: The Ethiopian-Somali War and the Eritrean Conflict." *Cuban Studies*, 10 (1) (1980): 49–79.

Valenta, Jiri. "Soviet-Cuban Intervention in the Horn of Africa: Impact and Lessons." *Journal of International Affairs*, 34 (2) (1980/1981): 353–68.

Watson, Paul. "Arms and Aggression in the Horn of Africa." *Journal of International Affairs*, 40 (1) (1986): 159–76.

Wiberg, Hakan. "Focus on the Horn of Africa." *Journal of Peace Research*, 16 (3) (1979): 189–95.

Woodward, Peter. "A New Map of Africa? Reflections on the Horn." *Africa Insight*, 23 (1) (1993): 6–15.

——. *The Horn of Africa: Politics and International Relations.* London and New York: I. B. Tauris Publishers, 1996.

——. *War—or Peace—in North-East Africa?.* London: Centre for Security and Conflict Studies, 1989.

Yodfat, Aryeh Y. "The Soviet Union and the Horn of Africa." *NAS*, 1 (3) (1979/1980): 1–17; 2 (1) (1980): 31–57 and 2 (2) (1980): 65–81.

Youssuf, R. A. "The Situation in the Horn of Africa." *Nigerian Forum*, 2 (5) (1983): 1097–1109.

Zelniker, Shimshon. *The Superpowers and the Horn of Africa*. Tel Aviv: Tel Aviv University, 1982.

Agriculture, Famine, Land, and Rural Affairs

Abay Asfaw and Assefa Admassie. "The Impact of Education on Allocative and Technical Efficiency of Farmers: The Case of Ethiopian Small Holders." *Ethiopian Journal of Economics*, 5 (1) (1996): 1–26.

Abbink, Jon G. "Me'en Means of Subsistence: Notes on Crops, Tools, and Ethnic Change." *Anthropos*, 83 (1/3) (1988): 187–93.

Abdussamad H. Ahmad. "Peasant Conditions in Gojam during the Great Famine 1888–1892." *JES*, 20 (1987): 1–18.

Abrar Suleiman. "Evaluating the Efficiency of Farmers in Ethiopia." *Ethiopian Journal of Economics*, 4 (2) (1995): 47–66.

Adhana Haile. "Peasant Responses to Famine in Ethiopia." *JES*, 21 (1988): 1–56.

Alemayehu Gebrehiwot. "Agricultural Research and Extension Linkages in the Central Province of Ethiopia: An Inter-Organisational Analysis." Ph.D. diss., University of Reading (UK), 1988.

Alemayehu Lirenso. "Ethiopia's Experience with Rural Cooperatives: 1975–90." *Ethiopian Journal of Development Research*, 15 (1) (1993): 1–28.

——. "Rural Service Cooperatives in Ethiopia: Tasks and Performance." *NAS*, 7 (2) (1985): 51–8.

Alemneh Dejene. *Environment, Famines, and Politics in Ethiopia: A View from the Village*. Boulder, Colo., and London: LR, 1990.

——. *Peasants, Agrarian Socialism, and Rural Development in Ethiopia*. Boulder, Colo.: WP, 1987.

——. "The Training and Visit Agricultural Extension in Rainfed Agriculture: Lessons from Ethiopia." *World Development*, 17 (10) (1989): 1647–59.

Almagor, Uri. *Pastoral Partners: Affinity and Bond Partnerships among the Dassenetch of Southwest Ethiopia*. Manchester: Manchester University Press, 1978.

Almaz Zewde. "The Chilalo Agricultural Development Unit as a Strategy of Rural Transformation." Ph.D. diss., Michigan State University, 1991.

——. "Defining Rural Development Constraints in Ethiopia." *NAS*, 13 (2/3) (1991): 37–49.

Amare Abebe Shenqit. "Evaluation of Methods for Screening Drought Tolerant Dry Bean Lines in the Rift Valley of Ethiopia." Ph.D. diss., Colorado State University, 1995.

Asmerom Kidane. "Demographic Consequences of the 1984-1985 Ethiopian Famine." *Demography*, 26 (3) (1989): 515–22.

Ayalew Gebre. *Pastoralism under Pressure: Land Alienation and Pastoral Transformation among the Karrayu of Eastern Ethiopia, 1941 to the Present.* Maastricht: Shaker Publishing, 2001.

Aynalem Adugna and Helmut Kloos. "Two Population Distribution Maps for Ethiopia Based on the 1984 Census." *NAS*, 9 (1) (1987): 89–96.

Babiker, Mustafa (ed.). *Resource Alienation, Militarisation, and Development: Case Studies from East African Drylands.* Addis Ababa: Organization for Social Science in Eastern and Southern Africa, 2002.

Baker, Jonathan. "Migration in Ethiopia and the Role of the State." In Jonathan Baker and Tade Akin Aina (eds). *The Migration Experience in Africa.* Uppsala: Nordiska Afrikainstitutet, 1995: 234–54.

Baulch, Bob. "Entitlements and the Wollo Famine of 1982–1985." *Disasters*, 11 (3) (1987): 195–204.

Bekele Ambaye Shiferaw. "Peasant Agriculture and Sustainable Land Use in Ethiopia: Economic Analysis of Constraints and Incentives for Soil Conversation." S.D. diss., Norges Landbrukshogskole (Norway), 1998.

Bekele Ambaye Shiferaw, and Stein T. Holden. "Peasant Agriculture and Land Degradation in Ethiopia: Reflections on Constraints and Incentives for Soil Conservation and Food Security." *Forum for Development Studies*, 1 (1997): 277–306.

——. "Soil Erosion and Smallholders' Conservation Decisions in the Highlands of Ethiopia." *WD*, 27 (4) (1999): 739–52.

Berhanu Gebremedhin. "The Economics of Soil Conservation Investments in the Tigray Region of Ethiopia." Ph.D. diss., Michigan State University, 1998.

Berhane Hailu. *An Overview of Agricultural Development of Tigray: Existing Efforts and Future Prospects.* Mekelle: Tigray Bureau of Agriculture and Natural Resources Development, 1995.

Bondestam, Lars. "People and Capitalism in the North-Eastern Lowlands of Ethiopia." *JMAS*, 12 (3) (1974): 423–39.

Brandt, S. A. "New Perspectives on the Origins of Food Production in Ethiopia." In J. D. Clark and S. A. Brandt (eds.). *From Hunters to Farmers: The Causes and Consequences of Food Production in Africa.* Berkeley: University of California Press, 1984: 173–90.

Brietzke, Paul H. "Land Reform in Revolutionary Ethiopia." *JMAS*, 14 (4) (1976): 637–60.

Brown, Judith Reynolds. *Faranji: A Venture into Ethiopia.* Santa Barbara, CA: Fithian Press, 1994.

Brown, Leslie H. "Coffee Production and Its Problems." *EO*, 4 (6) (1960): 182–212.

Campbell, David J. "Strategies for Coping with Severe Food Deficits in North-eastern Africa." *NAS*, 9 (2) (1987): 43–54.

Campbell, John. "Land or Peasants? The Dilemma Confronting Ethiopian Resource Conservation." *African Affairs*, 90 (358) (1991): 5–21.

Carr, Claudia J. *Pastoralism in Crisis: The Dasanetch and Their Ethiopian Lands*. Chicago: University of Chicago, Department of Geography, 1977.

Clarke, John. *Ethiopia's Campaign against Famine: Resettlement and Rehabilitation*. London: Harney and Jones, n.d.

Clay, Jason W., Sandra Steingraber, and Peter Niggli. *The Spoils of Famine: Ethiopian Famine Policy and Peasant Agriculture*. Cambridge: Cultural Survival, 1988.

Clay, Jason W., Sandra Steingraber, Peter Niggli, and B. K. Holcomb. *Politics and the Ethiopian Famine 1984–1985*. Cambridge, Mass.: Cultural Survival, 1986.

Cohen, John Michael. "Effects of Green Revolution Strategies on Tenants and Small Scale Landowners in the Chilalo Region of Ethiopia." *JDA*, 9 (3) (1975): 335–58.

——. "Ethiopia: A Survey on the Existence of a Feudal Peasantry." *JMAS*, 12 (4) (1974): 665–72.

——. "Ethiopia after Haile Selassie: The Government Land Factor." *AA*, 72 (289) (1973): 365–82.

——. "Foreign Involvement in the Formulation of Ethiopia's Land Tenure Policies." *NAS*, 7 (2) (1985): 23–50 and 7 (3) (1985): 1–20.

——. *Integrated Rural Development: The Ethiopian Experience and the Debate*. Uppsala: SIAS, 1987.

——. "Peasants and Feudalism in Africa: The Case of Ethiopia." *CJAS*, 8 (1) (1974): 155–57.

——. "Rural Change in Ethiopia: A Study of Land, Elites, Power, and Values in Chilalo Awraja." Ph.D. diss., University of Colorado at Boulder, 1973.

——. *Rural Development: The Ethiopian Experience and the Debate*. Uppsala: SIAS, 1987.

Cohen, John Michael, and Nils-Ivar Isaksson. "Food Production Strategy Debates in Revolutionary Ethiopia." *WD*, 16 (3) (1988): 323–48.

——. "The Size of Peasant Holdings and Government Policies: Questions Raised by Recent Research in Arsi Region, Ethiopia." *NAS*, 9 (1) (1987): 97–103.

——. "Villagisation in Ethiopia's Arsi Region." *JMAS*, 25 (3) (1987): 435–64.

——. *Villagization in the Arsi Region of Ethiopia*. Uppsala: Swedish University of Agricultural Sciences, 1987.

Cohen, John Michael, Nils-Ivar Isaksson, Arthur A. Goldsmith, and John W. Mellor. "Rural Development Issues Following Ethiopian Land Reform." *AT*, 23 (2) (1976): 7–28.

Coppock, D. L. *The Borana Plateau of Southern Ethiopia: Synthesis of Pastoral Research, Development, and Change, 1980–91*. Addis Ababa: International Livestock Centre, 1994.

Croppenstedt, A. and Mulat Demeke. *Determinants of Adoption and Level of Demands for Fertiliser for Cereal-Growing Farmers in Ethiopia*. Oxford: Centre for the Study of African Economies, 1996.

Crummey, Donald E. "Abyssinian Feudalism." *Past and Present*, (89) (1980): 115–38.

——. *Ethiopian Plow Agriculture in the Nineteenth Century*. Urbana: University of Illinois, 1981.

——. "Ethiopian Plow Agriculture in the Nineteenth Century." *JES*, 16 (1983): 1–23.

——. *Land and Society in the Christian Kingdom of Ethiopia*. Urbana: University of Illinois Press, 2000.

Crummey, Donald E., and Shumet Sishagne. "Land Tenure and the Social Accumulation of Wealth in Eighteenth-Century Ethiopia: Evidence from the Qwesqwam Land Register." *IJAHS*, 24 (2) (1991): 241–58.

Cutler, Peter. "Famine Forecasting: Prices and Peasant Behavior in Northern Ethiopia." *Disasters*, 8 (1) (1984): 48–56.

Daniel Teferra. "Subsistence Production Behavior and Famine in Ethiopia." *NAS*, 9 (2) (1987): 23–41.

Dejene Aredo. "Developmental Aid and Agricultural Policies in Ethiopia, 1957–1987." *Africa Development*, 17 (3) (1992): 209–37.

——. "The Regional Dimension of Agricultural Planning and Policies in Ethiopia, 1960–1991: A Review and Implications for Today." *Ethiopian Journal of Development Research*, 18 (2) (1996): 31–78.

Dercon, Stephan and Lulseged Ayalew. "Income Portfolios in Rural Ethiopia and Tanzania: Choices and Constraints." Journal of Development Studies, 36 (2) (1996): 850–75.

——. *Smuggling and Supply Response: Coffee in Ethiopia*. Oxford: Centre for the Study of African Economies, University of Oxford, 1995.

Dessalegn Rahmato. "Agrarian Change and Agrarian Crisis: State and Peasantry in Post-Revolution Ethiopia." *Africa*, 63 (1) (1993): 36–55.

——. *Agrarian Reform in Ethiopia*. Trenton, N.J.: RSP, 1985.

——. "Food Aid and Food Dependency in Ethiopia" In Eshetu Chole et al. (eds.). *The Crisis of Development Strategies in Eastern Africa*. Addis Ababa: Organization for Social Science Research in Eastern Africa, 1990: 54–67.

——. *Land and Agrarian Unrest in Wollo, Northeast Ethiopia, Pre- and Post-Revolution*. Addis Ababa: AAUP, 1996.

——. (ed.). *Land Tenure and Land Policy in Ethiopia after the Derg: Proceedings of the Second Workshop of the Land Tenure Project*. Addis Ababa: Land Tenure Project, Institute of Development Research, 1994.

——. "Resilience and Vulnerability: Enset Agriculture in Southern Ethiopia." *JES*, 28 (1) (1995): 23–51.

Dieci, Paolo, and Claudio Viezzoli. *Resettlement and Rural Development in Ethiopia: Social and Economic Research, Training, and Technical Assistance in the Beles Valley*. Milan: Franco Angeli, 1992.

Disney, Richard. "Some Measures of Rural Income Distribution in Ethiopia." *Development and Change*, 7 (1) (1976): 35–44.

Dunning, Harrison C. "Land Reform in Ethiopia: A Case Study in Non-Development." *U.C.L.A. Law Review*, 18 (2) (1970): 271–307.

Ehret, Christopher. "On the Antiquity of Agriculture in Ethiopia." *JAH*, 20 (2) (1979): 161–77.

Ellis, Gene. "The Feudal Paradigm as a Hindrance to Understanding Ethiopia." *JMAS*, 14 (2) (1976): 275–95.

——. "Feudalism in Ethiopia: A Further Comment on Paradigms and Their Use." *NAS*, 1 (3) (1979/1980): 91–97.

——. "Land Tenancy Reform in Ethiopia: A Retrospective Analysis." *Economic Development and Cultural Change*, 28 (3) (1980): 523–46.

Fafchamps, Marcel, and Agnes R. Quisumbing. "Control and Ownership within Rural Ethiopian Households." *Journal of Development Studies*, 38 (6) (2002): 47–82.

Fassil G. Kiros. "Food and Development in Ethiopia: Retrospect and Prospect." *JES*, 21 (1988): 83–110.

For Their Own Good: Ethiopia's Villagisation Programme. London: Survival International, 1988.

Gebre-Wold-Ingida Worq. "Ethiopia's Traditional System of Land Tenure and Taxation." *EO*, 5 (4) (1962): 302–39.

Gebru Tareke. "Rural Protest in Ethiopia, 1941–1970: A Study of Three Rebellions." Ph.D. diss., Syracuse University, 1977.

Getachew Diriba. *Economy at the Cross Roads: Famine and Food Security in Rural Ethiopia*. Addis Ababa: CARE International, 1995.

Getachew Gebru. "Land Tenure and Access to and Use of Feed Resources in the Mixed Farming System of the Ethiopian Highlands." Ph.D. diss., University of Wisconsin–Madison, 2000.

Getachew Mequanent. "Community Development and the Role of Community Organizations: A Study in Northern Ethiopia." *CJAS*, 32 (3) (1998): 494–520.

Getachew Olana et al. *Farmers' Response to New Technologies in Coffee Production: The Case of Small Farmers in Ghimbi CIPA, Wollega*. Hanover: University of Hanover, Institute of Horticultural Economics, 1995.

Getachew Woldemeskel. "The Consequences of Resettlement in Ethiopia." *AA*, 88 (352) (1989): 359–74.

Grepperud, Sverre. "Population Pressure and Land Degradation: The Case of Ethiopia." *Journal of Environmental Economics and Management*, 30 (1) (1996): 18–33.

Haile M. Larebo. *Building an Empire: Italian Land Policy and Practice in Ethiopia 1935–1941*. Oxford: Oxford University Press, 1994.

——. "The Italian Background of Capitalist Farming in Ethiopia: The Case of Cotton." *NAS*, (NS) 2 (1) (1995): 31–60.

——. *The Myth and Reality of Empire-Building: Italian Land Policy and Practice 1935–1941*. Ph.D. diss., University of London, 1990.

Hailu Abatena. "Grass Root Participation in the Development Process: An Empirical Study of the Problems of Rural Development in Ethiopia." Ph.D. diss., Syracuse University, 1978.

Hailu Lemma. "The Politics of Famine in Ethiopia." *ROAPE*, (33) (1985): 44–58.

Hallpike, Christopher Robert. "Konso Agriculture." *JES*, 8 (1) (1970): 31–43.

Hammond, L. *Lessons Learned Study: Ethiopia Drought Emergency 1999–2000*. Addis Ababa: USAID-Ethiopia, 2001.

Hammond, L., and Daniel Maxwell. "The Ethiopian Crisis of 1999–2000: Lessons Learned, Questions Unanswered." *Disasters*, 26 (3) (2002): 262–79.

Hancock, Graham. *Ethiopia: The Challenge of Hunger*. London: Victor Gollancz, 1985.

Harbeson, John Willis. "Afar Pastoralists and Ethiopian Rural Development." *RA*, (28) (1975): 71–86.

——. "Revolution and Rural Development in Ethiopia." *RA*, (28) (1975): 1–5.

Helland, John. *Development Interventions and Pastoral Dynamics in Southern Ethiopia: A Discussion of Natural Resources Management in Borana Pastoralism*. Boston: Boston University, African Studies Center, 1992.

Hendrie, Barbara. "Managing Famine Disaster: Popular Participation in Tigray." *ESR*, 2 (1) (1997): 111–27.

Hoben, Allan. *Land Tenure among the Amhara of Ethiopia: The Dynamics of Cognatic Descent*. Chicago: University of Chicago Press, 1973.

——. "Perspectives on Land Reform in Ethiopia: The Political Role of the Peasantry." *RA*, (28) (1975): 55–69.

——. "Social Anthropology and Development Planning: A Case Study in Ethiopian Land Reform Policy." *JMAS*, 10 (4) (1972): 561–82.

Hogg, Richard. "Changing Land Use and Resource Conflict among Somali Pastoralists in the Haud of Ethiopia." *Ethiopian Journal of Development Research*, 17 (1) (1995): 43–62.

——. *Pastoralists, Ethnicity and the State in Ethiopia*. London: Haan, 1997.

Holmberg, J. *Grain Marketing and Land Reform in Ethiopia*. Uppsala: SIAS, 1977.

Howell, Philippa. "Crop Failure in Dalocha, Ethiopia: A Participatory Emergency Response." *Disasters*, 22 (1) (1998): 57–75.

Huffnagel, H. P. (ed.). *Agriculture in Ethiopia*. Rome: Food and Agricultural Organization, 1961.

Hultin, J. *Man and Land in Wollega, Ethiopia*. Gothenburg: Gothenburg University, Department of Social Anthropology, 1977.

Hunri, Hans. *Ecological Issues in the Creation of Famines in Ethiopia*. Berne: University of Berne, 1988.

Hussein, Abdel Mejuid (ed.). *Rehab: Drought and Famine in Ethiopia*. London: IAI, 1976.

Jacobs, Michael John. "Influence of Grazing, Fire, and Rainfall Regime on Plant Species Dynamics in an Ethiopian Perennial Grassland." Ph.D. diss., Utah State University, 1999.

Jansson, Kurt, Michael Harris, and Angela Penrose. *The Ethiopian Famine*. London: ZB, 1987.

Jayne, Thomas S., John Strauss, and Takashi Yamano. "Giving to the Poor? Targeting of Food Aid in Rural Ethiopia." *WD*, 29 (5) (2001): 887–910.

Jayne, Thomas S., et al. "Targeting of Food Aid in Rural Ethiopia: Chronic Need or Inertia?" *Journal of Development Economics*, 68 (2) (2002): 247–88.

Kassa Negussie Getachew. *Among the Pastoral Afar in Ethiopia*. Utrecht: International Books, 2001.

Kelemen, Paul. *The Politics of Famine in Ethiopia and Eritrea*. Manchester: Manchester University Press, 1985.

Keller, Edmond J. "Drought, War, and the Politics of Famine in Ethiopia and Eritrea." *JMAS*, 30 (4) (1992): 609–24.

Kidane Mengisteab. *Ethiopia: Failure of Land Reform and Agricultural Crisis*. Westport, Conn., and London: Greenwood Press, 1990.

——. "The Nature of the State and Agricultural Crisis in Post-1975 Ethiopia." *Studies in Comparative International Development*, 24 (1) (1989): 20–38.

——. "The Political Economy of Land Reform: An Exploratory Study of Structural Changes in Ethiopia's Agriculture, 1975–1981." Ph.D. diss., University of Denver, 1984.

King, Preston. *An African Winter*. Harmondsworth, UK: Penguin Books Ltd., 1986.

Kissi, Edward. "The Politics of Famine in U.S. Relations with Ethiopia, 1950–1970." *IJAHS*, 33 (1) (2000): 113–31.

——. "Famine and the Politics of Food Relief in the United States Relations with Ethiopia: 1950–1991." Ph.D. diss., Concordia University, 1998.

Kloos, Helmut. "Development, Drought, and Famine in the Awash Valley of Ethiopia." *ASR*, 25 (1) (1982): 2–48.

——. "Peasant Irrigation Development and Food Production in Ethiopia." *GJ*, 157 (3) (1991): 295–306.

——. and Bernt Lindtjorn. "Malnutrition during Recent Famines in Ethiopia." *NAS*, (NS) 1 (1) (1994): 121–36.

Land Tenure Surveys of the Provinces of Arussi, Gamu Gofa, Shoa, Sidamo, Wollega, Wello, Eritrea. Addis Ababa: Ministry of Land Reform and Administration, 1967–1970.

Love, Roy. "The Ethiopian Coffee *Filiere* and Its Institution: *Cui Bono*." *ROAPE*, 28 (88) (2001): 225–40.

McCann, James Craig. *Frontier Agriculture, Food Supply, and Conjuncture: A Revolution in Dura on Ethiopia's Mazega 1898–1930*. Boston: Boston University, African Studies Center, 1989.

——. *A Great Agrarian Cycle? A History of Agricultural Productivity and Demographic Change in Highland Ethiopia, 1900–1987*. Boston: Boston University, African Studies Center, 1988.

——. *Plows, Oxen, and Household Managers: A Reconsideration of the Land Paradigm and the Production Equation in Northeast Ethiopia*. Boston: Boston University, African Studies Center, 1984.

Mann, H. S. *Land Tenure in Chore (Shoa): A Pilot Study*. Addis Ababa: HSU, 1965.

Mann, H. S., and J. C. D. Lawrance. *Land Taxation in Ethiopia: Summary*. Addis Ababa: Ministry of Finance, 1964.

Markos Ezra and Gebre-Egziabher Kiros. "Rural Out-Migration in the Drought-Prone Areas of Ethiopia: A Multilevel Analysis." *International Migration Review*, 25 (3) (2001): 749–71.

Masfield, A. *Food Security in Ethiopia: An Update*. Brighton: Institute of Development Studies, 1997.

Maxwell, Daniel. "Why Do Famines Persist? A Brief Review of Ethiopia 1999–2000." *IDS Bulletin*, 33 (4) (2002): 48–54/

McCann, James Craig. "A Dura Revolution and Frontier Agriculture in Northwest Ethiopia: 1898–1920." *JAH*, 31 (1) (1990): 121–34.

——. "A Great Agrarian Cycle? Productivity in Highland Ethiopia, 1900 to 1987." *Journal of Interdisciplinary History*, 20 (3) (1990): 389–416.

——. *From Poverty to Famine in Northeast Ethiopia: A Rural History, 1900–1935*. Philadelphia: University of Pennsylvania Press, 1987.

——. *People of the Plow: An Agricultural History of Ethiopia, 1800–1990*. Madison: University of Wisconsin Press, 1995.

——. "The Social Impact of Drought in Ethiopia: Oxen, Households, and Some Implications for Rehabilitation." In Michael Glantz (ed.). *Drought and Hunger in Africa: Denying a Famine a Future*. Cambridge: CUP, 1987: 245–67.

——. "Toward a History of Modern Highland Agriculture in Ethiopia: The Sources." *Henok*, 2 (1991): 97–107.

McClellan, Charles W. "Land, Labor, and Coffee: The South's Role in Ethiopian Self-Reliance, 1889–1935." *African Economic History*, 9 (1980): 69–83.

Mehari Gebre-Medhin and B. Vahlquist. "Famine in Ethiopia: The Period 1973–75." *Nutrition Reviews*, 35 (1977): 194–202.

Merid Wolde Aregay. "The Early History of Ethiopia's Coffee Trade and the Rise of Shawa." *JAH*, 29 (1) (1988): 19–25.

Mesfin Bezuneh and Carl C. Mabbs-Zeno. "The Contribution of the Green Revolution to Social Change in Ethiopia." *NAS*, 6 (3) (1984): 9–17.

Mesfin Mirotchie. "Productivity Analysis of Private and Socialized Agriculture in Ethiopia." Ph.D. diss., Virginia Polytechnic Institute, 1989.

Mesfin Wolde Mariam. *Rural Vulnerability to Famine in Ethiopia, 1958–1977.* Delhi: Vikas Publishing House, 1984.

Miller, Clarence John, et al. *Production of Grains and Pulses in Ethiopia.* Menlo Park, Calif.: Stanford Research Institute, 1969.

Moser, Patrick. "On Famine's Brink." *AR*, 33 (1) (1988): 40–43.

Muhereza, Frank Emmanuel. "Cross-Border Grazing and the Challenges for Development in the Dryland Areas of Eastern Africa: The Case of Karamoja." *Ethiopian Institute for Peace and Development Occasional Papers*, 4 (11) (1999): 3–26.

Mulugetta Mekuria. "Agricultural Technology Development and Transfer in Ethiopia: Challenges and Experiences." *African Rural and Urban Studies*, 1 (3) (1994): 39–64.

——. "An Economic Analysis of Smallholder Wheat Production and Technology adoption in the Southeastern Highlands of Ethiopia." Ph.D. diss., Michigan State University, 1994.

Nicholson, G. Edward. *Cotton in Ethiopia.* Addis Ababa: Ministry of Agriculture, Imperial Ethiopian Government, 1956.

Olmstead, Judith. "The Versatile Ensete Plant: Its Use in the Gamu Highland." *JES*, 12 (2) (1974): 147–58.

Omiti, John M., et al. "Some Policy Implications of the Restructuring of Rural Factor Markets Following Agrarian De-Collectivization in Ethiopia." *Human Ecology*, 28 (4) (2000): 585–603.

Ottaway, Marina. "Land Reform and Peasant Associations: A Preliminary Analysis." *RA*, (28) (1975): 39–54.

——. "Land Reform in Ethiopia 1974–1977." *ASR*, 20 (3) (1977): 79–90.

Pankhurst, Alula. *Resettlement and Famine in Ethiopia: The Villagers' Experience.* Manchester: Manchester University Press, 1992.

Pankhurst, Estelle Sylvia. "Coffee Cultivation and Processing." EO, 1 (10) (1957): 324–29.

Pankhurst, Richard. "The Great Ethiopian Famine of 1888–1892: A New Assessment." *Journal of the History of Medicine and Allied Sciences*, 21 (1) (1966): 95–124 and 21 (2) (1966): 271–94.

——. "The History of Famine and Pestilence in Ethiopia Prior to the Founding of Gondar." *JES*, 10 (2) (1972): 37–64.

——. "Notes for a History of Ethiopian Agriculture." *EO*, 7 (3) (1964): 210–41.

——. "Some Factors Depressing the Standard of Living of Peasants in Traditional Ethiopia." *JES*, 4 (2) (1966): 45–98.

——. *State and Land in Ethiopian History*. Addis Ababa: HSU, 1966.

Parker, Ben. *Ethiopia: Breaking New Ground*. Oxford: Oxfam, 1995.

Pausewang, Siegfried. "History of Land Tenure and Social Personality Development in Ethiopia." *RA*, (11) (1970): 82–9.

——. *Methods and Concepts of Social Research in a Rural Developing Society: A Critical Appraisal Based on Experience in Ethiopia*. Munich: Weltforum, 1973.

——. "Participation in Social Research in Rural Ethiopia." *JMAS*, 26 (2) (1988): 253–76.

——. "Peasant Society and Development in Ethiopia." *Sociologia Ruralis*, 13 (2) (1973): 172–91.

——. *Peasants, Land and Society: A Social History of Land Reform in Ethiopia*. Munich: Weltforum Verlag, 1983.

——. et al. (eds.). *Ethiopia: Options for Rural Development*. London: ZB, 1990.

Penrose, Angela (ed.). *Beyond the Famine: An Examination of the Issues Behind the Famine in Ethiopia*. Geneva: International Institution for Relief and Development and Food for the Hungry International, 1988.

Phillipson, David W. "The Antiquity of Cultivation and Herding in Ethiopia." In T. Shaw et al (eds.). *The Archaeology of Africa: Food, Metals, and Towns*. London: Routledge, 1993: 344–57.

Pickett, J. *Economic Development in Ethiopia: Agriculture, Market, and the State*. Paris: OECD, 1991.

Prose, Angela (ed.). *Beyond the Famine: An Examination of Issues behind Famine in Ethiopia*. Geneva: Food for the Hungry International, 1988.

Provisional Military Government of Socialist Ethiopia. *Ethiopia: Agrarian Revolution and Rural Development*. Addis Ababa: The Provisional Military Government, 1979.

Rainero, Romain H. *I Primi Tentativi di Colonizzazione Agricola e di Popolamento dell'Eritrea, 1890–95*. Milan: Marzorati, 1960.

Ramachandran, Mahadevan. "Food Security: Economics of Famine, Food Aid, and Market Integration in Ethiopia." Ph.D. diss., Clark University, 1997.

Relief and Rehabilitation Committee. *The Challenges of Drought, Ethiopian Decade of Struggle*. Addis Ababa: Relief and Rehabilitation Committee, 1985.

——. *Settlement Policy*. Addis Ababa: Relief and Rehabilitation Committee, 1981.

Robinson, Harry Joseph and Mammo Bahta. *An Agricultural Credit Programme for Ethiopia*. Menlo Park: Stanford Research Institute, 1969.

Rock, M. J. "The Politics of Famine in Ethiopia." Ph.D. diss., University of Leeds, 1994.

Schwab, Peter. "The Agricultural Income Tax and the Changing Role of Parliament in Ethiopia." *Genève-Afrique*, 8 (1) (1969): 34–45.

Shepherd, Jack. *The Politics of Starvation*. New York: Carnegie Endowment for International Peace, 1975.

Shields, Todd J. "Ethiopia: The War on Relief." *AR*, 33 (4) (1988): 17–22.

Sileshi Wolde-Tsadik. "Impacts of Land Tenure and Taxation on Agricultural Development in Ethiopia." Ph.D. diss., University of Maryland, 1977.

Simoons, Frederick. "The Agricultural Implements and Cutting Tools of Begemder and Semyen, Ethiopia." *Southwestern Journal of Anthropology*, 14 (1958): 386–406.

Singh, Harjinder. *Agricultural Problems in Ethiopia*. Delhi: Gian Publishing House, 1987.

Sisay Asefa. "Economic Development and Agricultural Policy in Ethiopia: The Haile Selassie Years." *African Studies Association Papers*, 27 (4) (1984): 1–40.

———. "Food Crisis in Northeast Africa." *NAS*, 9 (2) (1987): 13–21.

Sivini, Giordano. "Famine and the Resettlement Program in Ethiopia." *Africa*, 41 (2) (1986): 211–42.

Smeds, Helmer. "The Ensete Planting Culture of Eastern Sidamo. Ethiopia." *Acta Geographica*, 13 (4) (1955): 1–39.

Snell, Marilyn Berlin. "Against the Grain: Why Pool Nations Would Lose in a Biotech War on Hunger." *Sierra*, July/August 2001: 30–33.

Solomon Bellete. "An Economic Analysis of Small-Holders Agriculture in the Central Highlands of Ethiopia: A System Simulation Approach." Ph.D. diss., Oregon State University, 1979.

Solomon Gashaw. "Agrarian Reform, Peasantry, and the State in the Showa Region of Ethiopia, 1975–1982." Ph.D. diss., University of Wisconsin Madison, 1987.

Solomon Inquai. "Famine and Population Manipulation in Ethiopia." *Anthropology Today*, 3 (1) (1987): 12–14.

Southard, Addison E. "The Story of Abyssinia's Coffees." *Tea and Coffee Trade Journal*, 34 (1918): 212–15, 324–29.

Ståhl, Michael. "Capturing the Peasants through Cooperatives: The Case of Ethiopia." *NAS*, 12 (1) (1990): 95–122.

———. *Contradictions in Agricultural Development: A Study of Three Minimum Package Projects in Southern Ethiopia*. Uppsala: SIAS, 1973.

———. *Ethiopia: Political Contradictions in Agricultural Development*. Stockholm: Raben and Sjogren, 1974.

Stanley, S. "Ensete in the Ethiopian Economy." *Ethiopian Geographical Journal*, 4 (1) (1966): 30–37.

Stepanek, Julia Caley. "Lessons from Ethiopia's High-Input Technology Promotion Program: How the Organization of the Fertilizer Subsector Affects Maize Production." Ph.D. diss., Michigan State University, 1999.

Survival International. *For Their Own Good: Ethiopia's Villagisation Programme*. London: Survival International, 1988.

Sutcliffe, J. P. "Soil Conservation and Land Tenure in Highland Ethiopia." *Ethiopian Journal of Development Research*, 17 (1) (1995): 63–88.

Sylvain, Pierre G. "Ethiopian Coffee: Its Significance to World Coffee Problems." *Economic Botany*, 12 (1958): 111–39.

Teferi Abate. "Land Redistribution and Intra-Household Relations: The Case of Two Communities in Northern Ethiopia." *Ethiopian Journal of Development Research*, 17 (1) (1995): 23–42.

Tekalign Wolde-Mariam. "A City and Its Hinterland: The Political Economy of Land Tenure, Agriculture, and Food Supply for Addis Ababa, Ethiopia (1887–1974)." Ph.D. diss., Boston University, 1995.

Tesfai Tecle. "An Approach to Rural Development: A Case Study of the Ethiopian Package Projects." *RA*, (28) (1975): 87–105.

———. "An Economic Evaluation of Agricultural Package Programs in Ethiopia." Ph.D. diss., Cornell University, 1974.

Tewelde B. Zerom. "Agricultural Development Policy in Ethiopia: A Retrospective and Prospective Analysis." Ph.D. diss., University of Pittsburgh, 1984.

Tsegay Wolde-Georgis. "Land, Peasants, and the State in Ethiopia: Past and Present." *Scandinavian Journal of Development Alternatives and Area Studies*, 16 (1997): 171–86.

Tsighe Zemenfes. "Patterns of Crop Association in the Peasant Sector of Ethiopia." *Ethiopian Journal of Development Research*. 14 (1) (1992): 70–103.

———. "The Political Economy of Land Degradation in Ethiopia." *NAS*, 2 (2) (1995): 71–98.

Turton, David. "Mursi Response to Drought: Some Lessons for Relief and Rehabilitation." *AA*, 84 (336) (1985): 331–46.

———. "Non-Planned Resettlement after Drought, an Ethiopian Example." *Disasters*, 8 (3) (1984): 22–27.

———. "Response to Drought: The Mursi of Southwestern Ethiopia." *Disasters*, 1 (4) (1977): 275–87.

Turton, David, and P. Turton. "Spontaneous Resettlement after Drought: An Ethiopian Example." *Disasters*, 8 (3) (1984): 178–89.

United States. Agency for International Development. Food and Agricultural Division. *A Review of the Agricultural Sector*. Washington, D.C.: USGPO, 1970.

United States. Department of Agriculture. *A Survey of Agriculture in Ethiopia*. Washington, D.C.: USGPO, 1969.

United States. House of Representatives. Committee on Foreign Affairs. Subcommittee on Africa and the International Task Force of the Select Committee on Hunger. *Famine in Ethiopia*. Washington, D.C.: USGPO, 1990.

United States. House of Representatives. Committee on Foreign Affairs. Subcommittees on Human Rights and International Organizations and on Africa. *Update on Recent Developments in Ethiopia: The Famine Crisis*. Washington, D.C.: USGPO, 1988.

United States. House of Representatives. International Task Force of the Select Committee on Hunger. *Famine Relief in Ethiopia: An Update*. Washington, D.C.: USGPO, 1990.

——. *Renewed Challenge in Ethiopia*. Washington, D.C.: USGPO, 1987.

United States. House of Representatives. Select Committee on Hunger and the Committee of Foreign Affairs. *U.S. Response to Relief Efforts in Sudan, Ethiopia, Angola, and Mozambique*. Washington, D.C.: USGPO, 1988.

United States. House of Representatives. Subcommittee on Africa of the Committee on Foreign Affairs. *Emergency Famine Relief Needs in Ethiopia and Sudan*. Washington, D.C.: USGPO, 1986.

United States. House of Representatives. Subcommittee on Human Rights and International Organizations and the Subcommittee of Africa of the Committee on Foreign Affairs. *Human Rights and Food Aid in Ethiopia*. Washington, D.C.: USGPO, 1986.

Vestal, Theodore M. "Ethiopia's Famine: A Many-Dimensioned Crisis." *WT*, 41 (7) (1985): 125–28.

——. "Famine in Ethiopia: Crisis of Many Dimensions." *AT*, 32 (4) (1985): 7–28.

Watson, E. "Ground Truths: Land and Power in Konso, Ethiopia." Ph.D. diss., Cambridge University, 1999.

Webb, P. and J. von Braun. *Famine and Food Security in Ethiopia: Lessons for Africa*. Chichester, UK: Wiley, 1994.

Westphal, E. *Agricultural Systems in Ethiopia*. Wageningen: Centre for Agricultural Publishing and Documentation, 1974.

Wilding, R. *The History of Pastoralism and the Emergence of the Borana Oromo: A Review of Issues*. Addis Ababa: International Livestock Centre for Africa, 1985.

Winer, N. "Agriculture and Food Security in Ethiopia." *Disasters*, 13 (1) (1989): 1–8.

Wolday Amha. "The Performance of Maize and Teff Marketing in Southern Ethiopia." *Ethiopian Journal of Economics*, 4 (1) (1995): 101–31.

Wood, A. "Resettlement in Illubabor Province, Ethiopia." Ph.D. diss., University of Liverpool, 1977.

Wood, A. P. "Rural Development and National Integration in Ethiopia." *AA*, 82 (329) (1983): 509–39.

Workneh Negatu, Yared Amare, and Yigremew Adal (eds.). *Current Issues on Land Tenure in Ethiopia: Access, Food Production, and Natural Resources Management*. Addis Ababa: AAUP, 2002.

Wosene Yefru. "The Agricultural Performance of the Ethiopian Peasant Associations a Decade After: 1975–1985." *Henok*, 2 (1991): 109–22.

Yared Amare. "Land Redistribution and Its Implications for Peasant Differentiation in Wogda, Northern Shewa." *Ethiopian Journal of Development Research*, 17 (1) (1995): 1–22.

——— . *Land Redistribution and Socioeconomic Change in Ethiopia: The Case of Wogda, Northern Shewa*. Boston University, African Studies Program, 1994.

——— . *Seasonal Patterns of Household and Child Food Consumption among Amhara Peasants: The Case of Wogda, Central Ethiopia*. Boston University, African Studies Program, 1998.

Yeraswork Admassie. *Twenty Years to Nowhere: Property Rights, Land Management, and Conservation in Ethiopia*. Lawrenceville, N.J.: RSP, 2000.

Yigremew Adal. "Rural Land Holding Readjustment in West Gojjam, Amhara Region." *Ethiopian Journal of Development Research*, 19 (2) (1997): 57–89.

Yohannis Kebede. "Household Decision-Making: The Adoption of Agricultural Technologies in Ethiopia." Ph.D. diss., McGill University, 1993.

Zeiler, Jean A. "Genocide Convention—Intentional Starvation—Ethiopian Famine in the Eritrean War for Independence: The Applicability of the Genocide Convention to Government Imposed Famine in Eritrea." *Georgia Journal of International and Comparative Law*, 19 (1989): 589–612.

Zemenfes Tsighe. "The Political Economy of Land Degradation in Ethiopia." *NAS*, (NS) 2 (2) (1995): 71–98.

Religion, Missions, and Missionaries

Abba Ayele Teklehaymanot. *Miscellanea Aethiopica*. Addis Ababa: Capuchin Franciscan Institute of Philosophy and Theology

Abbas Haji Gnamo. "Islam, the Orthodox Church, and Oromo Nationalism (Ethiopia)." *CEA*, 42 (1) (2002): 99–120.

Abbink, Jon G. "An Historical-Anthropological Approach to Islam in Ethiopia: Issues of Identity and Politics." *Journal of African Cultural Studies*, 11 (2) (1998): 109–24.

——— . "Seged Celebration in Ethiopia and Israel: Continuity and Change of a Falasha Religious Holiday." *Anthropos*, 78 (5/6) (1983): 789–810.

——— . "Reading the Entrails: Analysis of an African Divination Discourse." *Man*, 28 (4) (1993): 705–26.

——— . "Ritual and Environment: The Mosit Ceremony of the Ethiopian Me'en People." *Journal of Religion in Africa*, 25 (2) (1995): 163–90.

Abdussamad H. Ahmad. "The Gondar Muslim Minority in Ethiopia: The Story up to 1935." *Journal of the Institute of Muslim Minority Affairs*, 9 (1) (1988): 76–85.
——. "Popular Islam in Twentieth Century Africa: The Muslims of Gondar, 1900–1935." In Said S. Samatar (ed.). *In the Shadow of Conquest: Islam in Colonial Northeast Africa*. Trenton, N.J.: RSP, 1992: 102–16.
——. "Priest Planters and Slavers of Zage (Ethiopia)." *IJAHS*, 29 (3) (1996): 543–56.
——. "Trade and Islam in the Towns of Bagemdir, 1900–1935." *JES*, 29 (2) (1996): 5–21.
Abiy Tsesgaye. "Ethiopia and Social Change: A Philosophical Assessment." Ph.D. diss., Howard University, 1999.
"The Abyssinian Schism." *The Dublin Review*, 53 (1863): 33–65.
Alberto, Abba Antonios. *The Apostolic Vicariate of Galla, A Capuchin Mission in Ethiopia (1846–1942): Antecedents, Evolution, and Problematics*. Addis Ababa: Capuchin Franciscan Institute of Philosophy and Theology, 1998.
Alemayehu Mekonnen. "Effects of Culture Change on Leadership in the Pentecostal/Charismatic Churches in Addis Ababa, Ethiopia." Ph.D. diss., Fuller Theological Seminary, 1995.
Al-Hashimi, M. A. *Oppressed Muslims in Ethiopia*. London: E-Shabazz Press, 1987.
Anderson, William B. *Ambassadors by the Nile: The Church in North East Africa*. London: Lutterworth Press, 1963.
Arén, Gustav. *The Envoys of the Gospel in Ethiopia: In the Steps of the Evangelical Pioneers*. Stockholm: Verbum Publishers, 1999.
——. *Evangelical Pioneers in Ethiopia: Origins of the Evangelical Church Mekane Yesus*. Stockholm: EFS Forlaget, 1978.
Attwater, Donald. *A Short Introduction to the Ethiopian Orthodox Church*. Addis Ababa: Ethiopian Orthodox Church, 1965.
Aymro Wondmagegnehu and Joachim Motovu. *The Ethiopian Orthodox Church*. Addis Ababa: The Ethiopian Orthodox Mission, 1970.
Bairu Tafla. "The Establishment of the Ethiopian Church." *Tarikh*, 2 (1) (1967): 28–42.
Bakke, Johnny Erik. "Christian Ministry: Patterns and Functions within the Ethiopian Evangelical Church Mekane Yesus." Th.D. diss., Uppsala Universitet, 1986.
Balisky, Paul E. "Wolaitta Evangelists: A Study of Religious Innovation in Southern Ethiopia, 1937–1957." Ph.D. diss., University of Aberdeen, 1997.
Beatty, David. "The Hidden Churches of Tigre." *Geographical Magazine*, 69 (12) (1997): 8–15.
Bebela Birri. "History of the Evangelical Church Bethel, 1919 to 1947." Th.D. diss., Lutheran School of Theology, 1995.
Beke, Charles Tilstone. *Christianity among the Gallas*. London: T. C. Savill, 1848.

——. *A Description of the Ruins of the Church of Martula Maryam in Abessinia*. London: J. B. Nichols and Son, 1847.

Belay Guta Olam. "Muslim Evangelism in Ethiopia." M.A. thesis, Fuller Theological Seminary, 1997.

Bent, James Theodore. *The Sacred City of the Ethiopians*. London: Longmans, Green and Company, 1893.

Bergsma, Stuart. *Rainbow Empire: Ethiopia Stretches Out Her Hands*. Grand Rapids: Eerdmans Publishing, 1932.

——. *Sons of Sheba*. Grand Rapids, Mich.: Eerdmans Publishing, 1933.

Bernoville, Gaëton. *L'Épopée Missionaire d'Éthiopie, Monseigneur Jarosseau et la Mission des Gallas*. Paris: Éditions Albin Michel, 1950.

Berry, LaVerle and R. Smith. "Churches and Monasteries of Lake Tana, Ethiopia, 1972." *Africa*, 34 (1/2) (1972): 1–34.

Bidder, Irmgard. *Lalibela: The Monolithic Churches of Ethiopia*. Cologne: M. DuMont Schauberg, 1958.

Brant, Albert E. *In the Wake of Martyrs: A Modern Saga in Ancient Ethiopia*. Langley, Canada: Omega Publishers, 1992.

Braukämper, Ulrich. "Aspects of Religious Syncretism in Southern Ethiopia." *Journal of Religion in Africa*, 22 (3) (1992): 194–207.

——. "Islamic Principalities in Southeast Ethiopia between the Thirteenth and Sixteenth Centuries: Part 1." *EN*, 1 (1) (1977): 17–56.

——. "Islamic Principalities in Southeast Ethiopia between the Thirteenth and Sixteenth Centuries: Part 2." *EN*, 1 (2) (1977): 1–43.

Brooks, Miguel F. (ed.). *A Modern Translation of Kebra Nagast (The Glory of Kings)*. Lawrenceville, N.J.: RSP, 1996.

Budge, Ernest Alfred Thompson Wallis. *The Alexander Book of Ethiopia*. Oxford: Oxford University Press, 1933.

——. *The Book of Saints of the Ethiopian Church*. 4 vols. Cambridge: Cambridge University Press, 1928.

Buxton, David Roden. "The Christian Antiquities of Northern Ethiopia." *Archaeologia*, 92 (1947): 1–42.

——. "The Rock-Hewn and Other Medieval Churches of Tigré Province, Ethiopia." *Archaeologia*, 103 (1971): 33–100.

Caraman, Philip. *The Lost Empire: The Story of the Jesuits in Ethiopia 1555–1634*. London: Sidgwick and Jackson, 1985.

Carmichael, T. "Contemporary Ethiopian Discourse on Islamic History: The Politics of Historical Representation." *Islam et Sociétés au Sud du Sahara*, 10 (1996): 169–86.

Caulk, Richard Alan. "Religion and State in Nineteenth Century Ethiopia." *JES*, 10 (1) (1972): 23–41.

Chaillot, Christine. *The Ethiopian Orthodox Tewahedo Church Tradition*. Paris: Inter-Orthodox Dialogue, 2002.

Chojnacki, Stanislaw. "Day Giyorgis." *JES*, 7 (2) (1969): 43–52.

———. "The Iconography of Saint George in Ethiopia, Part 1." *JES*, 11 (1) (1973): 57–73.

———. "The Iconography of Saint George in Ethiopia, Part 2." *JES*, 11 (2) (1973): 51–92.

———. "The Iconography of Saint George in Ethiopia. Part 3 (Saint George the Martyr)." *JES*, 12 (1) (1974): 71–132.

———. "The Nativity in Ethiopian Art." *JES*, 12 (2) (1974): 11–56.

———. "Note on the Early Iconography of Saint George and Related Equestrian Saints in Ethiopia." *JES*, 13 (2) (1975): 39–55.

The Church of Ethiopia: An Introduction to the Contemporary Church. Addis Ababa: Ethiopian Orthodox Church, 1973.

Cotterell, F. Peter. *Born at Midnight*. Chicago: Moody Press, 1998.

Coulbeaux, Jean Baptiste. *Histoire Politique et Religieuse de l'Abyssinie*. 3 vols. Paris: Geuthner, 1929.

Cowley, Roger Wenman. *Ethiopian Biblical Interpretation: A Study in Exegetical Tradition and Hermeneutics*. Cambridge: Cambridge University Press, 1988.

———. "Old Testament Introduction in the Andemta Commentary Tradition." *JES*, 12 (1) (1974): 133–75.

Crippa, Giovanni. "Consolata Missionaries in Ethiopia before and during the Italian Colonisation (1913–1942)." Ph.D. diss., Pontificia Universitas Gregoriana (Vatican), 1996.

Crummey, Donald E. "European Religious Missions in Ethiopia, 1830–1868." Ph.D. diss., University of London, 1967.

———. "Missionaries and Their Contributions to Our Understanding of Ethiopian History." *RA*, (11) (1970): 38–47.

———. *Priests and Politicians: Protestant and Catholic Missions in Orthodox Ethiopia, 1830–1868*. Oxford: CP, 1972.

———. "Shaikh Zakaryas: An Ethiopian Prophet." *JES*, 10 (1) (1972): 55–66.

———. "Society and Ethnicity in the Politics of Christian Ethiopia during the Zamana Masafent." *IJAHS*, 8 (2) (1975): 266–78.

Crummey, Donald E., and Shumet Sishagne. "The Lands of the Church of Dabra S'ahay Qwesqwam, Gondar." *JES*, 26 (2) (1993): 53–62.

Cumbers, John. *Living with the Red Terror: Missionary Experiences in Communist Ethiopia*. Kearney, Neb.: Morris Publishing, 1996.

Daoud, Marcos. *Liturgy of the Ethiopian Church*. Addis Ababa: Berhanena Selam, 1954.

Davis, Raymond J. *Fire on the Mountains: The Story of a Miracle—The Church in Ethiopia*. Toronto: Sudan Interior Mission, 1966.

———. *The Winds of God*. Scarborough, Ont.: SIM International, 1984.

Devine, Alexander. *Abyssinia: Her History and Claims to the Holy Places of Jerusalem*. London: Burlington Publishing Company, 1926.

Dawson, E. C. *Henry A. Stern: Missionary Traveller and Abyssinian Captive.* London: The Sunday School Union, n.d.

Dempsey, James. *Mission on the Nile.* London: Burns and Oates, 1955.

Donham, Donald L. *Marxist Modern: An Ethnographic History of the Ethiopian Revolution.* Berkeley: University of California Press, 1999.

Donne, R. D. "'A Place in Which to Feel at Home': An Exploration of the Rastafari as an Embodiment of an Alternative Spatial Paradigm." *Journal for the Study of Religion*, 13 (1/2) (2000): 99–122.

Dowling, Theodore Edward. *The Abyssinian Church.* London: Cape and Fenwick, 1909.

Duff, Clarance W. *Cords of Love: A Pioneer Mission to Ethiopia.* Phillipsburg, N.J.: Presbyterian and Reformed Publishing Company, 1980.

Edele, Blaine Alan. "A Critical Edition of Genesis in Ethiopic." Ph.D. diss., Duke University, 1995.

Eide, Øyvind M. *Revolution and Religion in Ethiopia: The Ethiopian Evangelical Church Mekane Yesus under the DERG 1974–85.* Oxford: JC, 2000.

——. "The Swedish Evangelical Mission in Ethiopia: An Analysis of the Dynamics between Mission, Church, and Society from 1866 to 1991." *Svensk Missions Tidskrift*, 85 (3/4) (1997): 325–48.

Emmanuel Abraham. *Reminiscences of My Life.* Oslo: Lunde Forlag, 1995.

Ephraim Isaac. *The Ethiopian Church.* Boston: H. N. Sawyer Company, 1968.

——. "Social Structure of the Ethiopian Church." *EO*, 14 (4) (1971): 240–88.

——. "A Study of Mashafa Berhan and the Question of Hebraic-Jewish Molding of Ethiopian Culture." Ph.D. diss., Harvard University, 1969.

Erlich, Haggai. "Ethiopia and Islam in Postrevolution Perspective." *EN*, 1 (1) (1977): 9–16.

——. "Identity and Church: Ethiopian-Egyptian Dialogue, 1924–59." *International Journal of Middle East Studies*, 32 (1) (2000): 23–46.

Ethiopia. Ministry of Information. *Religious Freedom in Ethiopia.* Addis Ababa: Publications of Foreign Languages Press Department, Ministry of Information, 1965.

Ezer, Gadi Ben. *The Ethiopian Jewish Exodus: Narratives of the Migration to Israel 1977–1985.* London and New York: Routledge, 2002.

Fairman, Maron and Edwin. *The Tumbling Walls.* Philadelphia: United Presbyterian Board of Foreign Missions, 1957.

"Faith and Culture in Ethiopia: Towards a Pastoral Approach to Culture." *Ethiopian Review of Cultures, Special Issue, Vol. VI–VII.* 1997.

Fargher, Brian L. *Ethiopian Revivalist: Autobiography of Evangelist Mehari Choramo.* Edmonton, Alta.: Enterprise Publications, 1997.

——. *The Origins of the New Churches Movement in Southern Ethiopia, 1927–1944.* Leiden: E. J. Brill, 1996.

Findlay, Louis. *The Monolithic Churches of Lalibela in Ethiopia.* Cairo: Société d'Archéologie Copte, 1944.

Flad, Johann Martin. *The Falashas (Jews) of Abyssinia.* London: W. Macintosh, 1869.

——. (edited by W. D. Veitch). *Notes from the Journal of F. [i.e. J.] M. Flad, one of Bishop Gobat's Pilgrim Missionaries in Abyssinia.* London: Nisbet and Company, 1860.

——. *A Short Description of the Falasha and Kamants in Abyssinia.* n.p.? [St.] Chrischona Missions Press, 1866.

——. *60 Jahre in der Mission unter den Falschas in Abessinien.* Basel: Brunnen Verlag, 1922.

Forsberg, Malcolm. *Land Beyond the Nile.* New York: Harper and Brothers, 1958.

Freeman, Nona. *Unseen Hands: The Story of Revival in Ethiopia.* Hazelwood, N.D.: Word Aflame Press, 1987.

Geddes, Michael. *The Church History of Abyssinia.* London: R. Chilwell, 1696.

Gerster, Georg. *Churches in Rock: Early Christian Art in Ethiopia.* London: Phaidon, 1970.

Getatchew Haile. "The Forty-Nine-Hour Sabbath of the Ethiopian Church." *JSS*, 33 (2) (1988): 233–54.

——. et al (eds.). *The Missionary Factor in Ethiopia: Papers from a Symposium on the Impact of European Missions on Ethiopian Society, Lund University, August 1996.* Frankfurt: Peter Lang, 1998.

Gibb, Christine. "Sharing the Faith: Religion and Ethnicity in the City of Harar." *HA*, 16 (1–4) (1998): 144–62.

Gidada Solon. *The Other Side of Darkness.* New York: Friendship Press, 1972.

Girma Beshah and Merid Wolde Aregay. *The Question of the Union of the Churches in Luso-Ethiopian Relations (1500–1632).* Lisbon: Junta de Investigaçoes do Ultramar, 1964.

Gobat, Samuel. *Journal of a Three Years' Residence in Abyssinia, in Furtherance of the Objects of the Church Missionary Society.* London: Hatchard and Son and Seeley and Sons, 1834.

Guluma Gemeda. "The Islamization of the Gibe Region, Southwestern Ethiopia from c. 1830s to the Early Twentieth Century." *JES*, 26 (2) (1993): 63–79.

Haberland, Eike. "The Influence of the Christian Ethiopian Empire on Southern Ethiopia." *JSS*, 9 (1) (1964): 235–38.

Haile Gabriel Dagne. "The Gebzenna Charter 1894." *JES*, 10 (1) (1972): 67–80.

Haile Mariam Larebo. "The Ethiopian Orthodox Church." In P. Ramet (ed.). *Eastern Christianity and Politics in the Twentieth Century.* Durham, N.C.: Duke University Press, 1988: 375–99, 450–52.

——. "The Ethiopian Orthodox Church and Politics in the Twentieth Century." *NAS*, 9 (3) (1987): 1–17 and 10 (1) (1988): 1–23.

Hammerschmidt, Ernst. "Jewish Elements in the Cult of the Ethiopian Church." *JES*, 3 (2) (1965): 1–12.

Hancock, Graham. *The Sign and the Seal: The Quest for the Lost Ark of the Covenant*. New York: Simon and Schuster, 1992.

Hanson, Herbert M. and Della. *For God and Emperor*. Mountain View, Calif.: Pacific Press Publishing, 1958.

Heffner, Edna S. *Ethiopia: Land beyond the Rift*. Privately Published, 1957.

Hege, Nathan B. *Beyond our Prayers: Anabaptist Church Growth in Ethiopia, 1948–1998*. Scottsdale, Pa.: Herald Press, 1998.

Heldman, Marilyn E. "Architectural Symbolism, Sacred Geography, and the Ethiopian Church." *Journal of Religion in Africa*, 22 (3) (1992): 222–41.

——. "Creating Religious Art: The Status of Artisans in Highland Christian Ethiopia." *Aethiopica: International Journal of Ethiopian Studies*, 1 (1998): 131–47.

——. "The Sacred Art of Ethiopia." *Historian*, 57 (1) (1994): 35–42.

Heyer, Friedrich. "Some Aspects of Dependence and Independence of the Orthodox Church on the Feudal Class of Ethiopia." *NAS*, 4 (1) (1982): 33–8.

Huntingford, George Wynn Brereton. "Saints of Medieval Ethiopia." *Abba Salama*, 10 (1979): 257–326.

Hussein Ahmed. "The Historiography of Islam in Ethiopia." *Journal of Islamic Studies*, 3 (1) (1992): 15–46.

——. "Islamic Literature and Religious Revival in Ethiopia (1991–1994)." *Islam et Sociétés au sud du Sahara*, 12 (1998): 89–108.

——. "The Life and Career of Shaykh Talha B. Jafar (c. 1853–1936)." *JES*, 22 (1989): 13–30.

——. "Trends and Issues in the History of Islam in Ethiopia." In N. Alkali et al. (eds.). *Islam in Africa*. Ibadan: Spectrum Books, 1993: 205–20.

Hyatt, Harry Middleton. *The Church of Abyssinia*. London: Luzac and Company, 1928.

Isenberg, Carl Wilhelm, and Johann Ludwig Krapf. *Journals of the Rev. Messrs. Isenberg and Krapf, Missionaries of the Church Missionary Society, Detailing Their Proceedings in the Kingdom of Shoa, and Journeys in Other Parts of Abyssinia, in the Years 1839, 1840, 1841, and 1842*. London: Seeley, Burnside and Seeley, 1842.

Iwarson, Jonas. "Islam in Eritrea and Abyssinia." *Moslem World*, 18 (1928): 356–64.

Jaenen, Cornelius J. "The Galla or Oromo of East Africa: Religion." *Southwestern Journal of Anthropology*, 12 (2) (1956): 171–90.

Kane, Thomas L. "An Amharic Version of the Origin of the Cross." *Bulletin of the School of Oriental and African Studies*, 44 (2) (1981): 273–89.

Kaplan, Steven. "Can the Ethiopian Change His Skin? The Beta Israel (Ethiopian Jews) and Racial Discourse." *AA*, 98 (393) (1999): 535–50.

——. "Court and Periphery in Ethiopian Christianity." *Asian and African Studies*, 20 (1) (1986): 141–52.

——. "The Ethiopian Holy Man as Outsider and Angel." *Religion*, 15 (3) (1985): 235–49.

——. "The Falasha and the Stephanite: An Episode from 'Gadld Gabrd Masih." *Bulletin of the School of Oriental and African Studies*, 48 (2) (1985): 278–82.

——. "Falasha' Religion: Ancient Judaism or Evolving Ethiopian Tradition." *Jewish Quarterly Review*, 79 (1) (1988): 49–65.

——. "Indigenous Categories and the Study of World Religions in Ethiopia: The Case of the Beta Israel (Falasha)." *Journal of Religion in Africa*, 22 (3) (1992): 208–21.

——. "The Invention of the Ethiopian Jews: Three Models." *CEA*, 14 (3) (1993): 645–58.

Kassim Shehim. "The Influence of Islam on the Afar." Ph.D. diss., University of Washington, 1982.

Kessis Kefyalew Merahi. *The Contribution of the Orthodox Tewahedo Church to the Ethiopian Civilization*. Addis Ababa: Kessis Kefyalew Merahi, 1999.

Krapf, Johann Ludwig. *Travels, Researches, and Missionary Labours during an Eighteen Years' Residence in Eastern Africa*. London: Trubner, 1860.

Krylov, A. "Islam and Nationalism: Two Trends of the Separatist Movement in Ethiopia." *NAS*, 12 (2/3) (1990): 171–76.

Lambie, Thomas A. *Boot and Saddle in Africa*. Philadelphia: Blakiston Company, 1943.

——. *A Doctor Carries On*. New York: Fleming H. Revell Company, 1942.

——. *A Doctor without a Country*. New York: Fleming H. Revell Company, 1939.

——. *A Doctor's Great Commission*. Wheaton, Ill.: Van Kampen Press, 1954.

Lass-Westphal, Ingeborg. "Protestant Missions during and after the Italian–Ethiopian War 1935–1937." *JES*, 10 (1) (1972): 89–101.

Leslau, Wolf (trans.). *Falasha Anthology*. New Haven, Conn.: Yale University Press, 1951.

Letters from the Captive Missionaries in Abyssinia. London: Abyssinian Captives Liberation Fund, 1865.

Mara, Yolande. *The Church of Ethiopia: The National Church in the Making*. Asmara: Il Poligrafico, 1972.

Matthew, A. F. "The Monolithic Church on Yekka." *JES*, 7 (2) (1969): 89–98.

McClure, Bryan. "Religion and Nationalism in Southern Ethiopia." *Current Bibliography on African Affairs*, 5 (1972): 497–508.

McClure, W. Don. *Red-Headed, Rash, and Religious: Letters from a Pioneer Missionary*. Pittsburgh, Pa.: Pickwick Press, Inc., 1954.

534 • BIBLIOGRAPHY

McLeish, Alexander (ed.). *Light and Darkness in East Africa: A Missionary Survey of Uganda, Anglo-Egyptian Sudan, Abyssinia, Eritrea, and the Three Somalilands*. London: World Dominion Press, 1927.

Meinardus, Otto F. A. "Ecclesiastica Aethiopica in Aegypto." *JES*, 3 (1) (1965): 23–35.

Millard, Candice S. "Keepers of the Faith: The Living Legacy of Aksum." *NGM*, 200 (1) (2001):110–25.

Mohammed Hassan Ali. "Islam as a Resistance Ideology among the Oromo of Ethiopia: The Wallo Case, 1700–1900." In Said S. Samatar (ed.). *In the Shadow of Conquest: Islam in Colonial Northeast Africa*. Trenton, N.J.: RSP, 1992: 75–101.

Molnar, Enrico C. Selley. *The Ethiopian Orthodox Church: A Contribution to the Ecumenical Study of Less Known Eastern Churches*. Pasadena, Calif.: Bloy House Theological School, 1969.

Moore, Dale H. "Christianity in Ethiopia." *Church History*, 5 (3) (1936): 271–84.

Munro-Hay, Stuart C. *Ethiopia and Alexandria: The Metropolitan Episcopacy of Ethiopia*. (Wiesbaden: Pan, 1997).

Munro-Hay, Stuart C., and Roderick Grierson. *The Ark of the Covenant*. London: Weidenfeld and Nicholson, 1999.

[Murphy, Dominick]. "The Christians of Abyssinia." *The Dublin Review*, 17 (1844): 105–33.

Musie Ghebreghiorghis. "Franciscan Missionaries to Ethiopia during the Early Renaissance." *Quaderni di Studi Etiopici*, (3/4) (1984): 34–62.

Negaso Gidada and Donald Crummey. "The Introduction and Expansion of Orthodox Christianity in Qelem Awarja, Western Wallaga, from about 1886 to 1941." *JES*, 10 (1) (1972): 103–12.

Nicholas, Archbishop of Axum. *Church's Revival: Emancipation from 1600 Years Guardianship: Free Church in Free State Achieved by His Majesty Haile Selassie 1st, Emperor of Ethiopia*. Cairo: Costa Tsouma and Company, 1955.

O'Mahoney, Kevin. *The Ebullient Phoenix: A History of the Vicariate of Abyssinia. Book I: 1839–1860*. Asmara: Ethiopian Studies Centre, 1982.

——. *The Ebullient Phoenix: A History of the Vicariate of Abyssinia. Book II: 1860–1881*. Asmara: Ethiopian Studies Centre, 1987.

Oriental Orthodox Conference, Interim Secretariat (ed.). *The Oriental Orthodox Churches Addis Ababa Conference, January 1965*. Addis Ababa: Artistic Printers, 1965.

Otto, Dale. "The Rock-Hewn Churches of Tigre." *EO*, 11 (2) (1967): 121–57.

Parfitt, Tudor, and E. T. Semi (eds.). *The Beta Israel in Ethiopia and Israel: Studies on the Ethiopian Jews*. Richmond: Curzon Press, 1998.

Partee, Charles. *The Story of Don McClure: Adventure in Africa*. Grand Rapids, Mich.: Zondervan Publishing House, 1990.

Paulos Yohannes. "Filsata: The Feast of the Assumption of the Virgin Mary and the Mariological Tradition of the Ethiopian Orthodox Tewahedo Church." Ph.D. diss., Princeton Theological Seminary, 1988.

Quirin, James. "Caste and Class in Historical North-West Ethiopia: The Beta Israel and Kemant, 1300–1900." *JAH*, 39 (2) (1998): 195–220.

Rice, Esmee Ritchie (ed.). *Eclipse in Ethiopia and Its Corona Glory*. London: Marshall, Morgan and Scott, 1937.

Ruud, Lee Gordon. "Effectiveness of Radio Voice of the Gospel as a Form of Christian Mission, with Special Attention to Its Mission in Ethiopia." Th.D. diss., School of Theology Claremont, 1977.

Saeverãs, O. *On Church-Mission Relations in Ethiopia, 1944–69, with Special Reference to Evangelical Church Mekane Yesus and the Lutheran Missions*. Lunde: Forlag og Bokhandel, 1974.

Salamon, Hagar. *The Hyena People: Ethiopian Jews in Christian Ethiopia*. Berkeley.: University of California Press, 1999.

Sergew Haile Selassie. *The Church of Ethiopia: A Panorama of History and Spiritual Life*. Addis Ababa: Ethiopian Orthodox Church, 1970.

Seyoum Welde-Yohannes. *Ras Ali and Tewodros: The Position of Islam in Central Ethiopia*. Addis Ababa: HSU, Faculty of Arts, 1968.

Shack, William. "The Masqal–Pole: Religious Conflict and Social Change in Gurageland." *Africa*, 38 (4) (1968): 457–68.

Shelemay, Kay Kaufman, and Peter Jeffrey (eds.). *Ethiopian Christian Liturgical Chant: An Anthology*. 3 vols. Madison: A-R Editions, 1993, 1994, and 1997.

Shenk, Calvin Earl. *The Development of the Ethiopian Orthodox Church and Its Relationship with the Ethiopian Government from 1930 to 1970*. New York: New York University Press, 1972.

——. "The Ethiopian Orthodox Church: A Study in Indigenization." *Missiology*, 16 (3) (1988): 259–78.

——. "The Italian Attempt to Reconcile the Ethiopian Orthodox Church: The Use of Religious Celebrations and Assistance to Churches and Monasteries." *JES*, 10 (1) (1972): 125–35.

Simpson, William. *Abyssinian Church Architecture*. London: The Royal Institute of British Architecture, 1869.

——. *Ancient Coptic Churches of Egypt and Abyssinia*. London: The Royal Institute of British Architecture, 1897.

Spencer, Diana. "In Search of St. Luke Ikons in Ethiopia." *JES*, 10 (2) (1972): 67–95.

Stern, Henry Aaron. *The Captive Missionary: Being an Account of the Country and People of Abyssinia*. London: Cassell, Peter and Galpin, [1868].

Stitz, Volker. "Distribution and Foundation of Churches in Ethiopia." *JES*, 13 (1) (1975): 11–36.

Stjärne, Per. "Missionary Work in Ethiopia." *EO*, 4 (3) (1960): 77–82.

Sumner, Claude. "The Ethiopic Liturgy: An Analysis." In Elliott P. Skinner. *Peoples and Cultures of Africa: An Anthropological Reader*. Garden City, N.J.: Doubleday/Natural History Press, 1973: 689–99. Also, in *JES*, 1 (1) (1963): 40–6.

Symons, R. *What Christianity Has Done for Abyssinia*. London: Watts and Company, 1928.

Taddesse Tamrat. "The Abbots of Däbrä-Hayq, 1248–1535." *JES*, 8 (1) (1970): 87–117.

——. *Church and State in Ethiopia, 1270–1527*. London: Oxford University Press, 1972.

——. "A Short Note on the Traditions of Pagan Resistance to the Ethiopian Church (14th and 15th Centuries)." *JES*, 10 (1) (1972): 137–50.

Tito Lipisa, Abba. *The Cult of Saints in the Ethiopian Church*. Rome: Typis Pontificiae Universitatis Gregorianae, 1963.

Trimingham, John Spencer. *The Christian Church and Missions in Ethiopia (Including Eritrea and the Somalilands)*. London and New York: World Dominion Press, 1950.

——. *Islam in Ethiopia*. London: Oxford University Press, 1952.

Ullendorff, Edward. *Ethiopia and the Bible*. London: Oxford University Press, 1968.

——. "Hebraic-Jewish Elements in Abyssinian (Monophysite) Christianity." *JSS*, 1 (1956): 216–56.

Vaisanen, Seppo Sakari. "The Challenge of Marxism to Evangelical Christianity with Special Reference to Ethiopia." Th.D. diss., Fuller Theological Seminary, 1981.

Waldmeier, Theophilus. *The Autobiography of Theophilus Waldmeier, Missionary: Being an Account of Ten Years' Life in Abyssinia, and Sixteen Years in Syria*. London: S. W. Partridge and Company, 1886.

Willmott, Helen M. *The Doors Were Opened: The Remarkable Advance of the Gospel in Ethiopia*. London: Sudan Interior Mission, no date.

Wise, E. F. "Christianity in Abyssinia." *The Dublin Review*, (450) (1951): 53–66.

Witakowski, Witold. "The Magi in Ethiopic Tradition [of the Gospels]." *Aethiopica: International Journal of Ethiopian Studies*, 2 (1999): 69–89.

Wolff, Joseph. *Journal of the Rev. Joseph Wolff*. London: James Burns, 1839.

Yassim M. Aberra. "Muslim Institutions in Ethiopia: The Asmara Awqaf." *Journal of the Institute of Muslim Minority Affairs*, 5 (1) (1984): 203–23.

Foreign Affairs

Aberra Jembere. "Treaty-Making Power and Supremacy of Treaty in Ethiopia." *JEL*, 7 (2) (1970): 409–34.

Abir, Mordechai. "The Origins of the Ethiopian-Egyptian Border Problem in the Nineteenth Century." *JAH*, 8 (3) (1967): 443–61.

Abraham Demoz. "Emperor Menelik's Phonograph Message to Queen Victoria." *Bulletin of the School of Oriental and African Studies*, 32 (2) (1969): 251–56.

Afeworki Paulos. "Superpower—Small State Interaction: The Case of U.S.-Ethiopian Relations, 1945–1986." Ph.D. diss., George Washington University, 1987.

Agyeman-Duah, Baffour. "United States Military Assistance Relationship with Ethiopia, 1953–77: Historical and Theoretical Analysis." Ph.D. diss., University of Denver, 1984.

Albright, David E. "U.S. Strategy in the Event of a Somali Military Regime Inclined toward Rapprochement with Ethiopia and the USSR." In W. J. Taylor et al. (eds.). *Strategic Responses to Conflict in the 1980s*. Lexington, Mass.: D. C. Heath, 1984: 377–84.

Aleme Eshete. "Ethiopia and the Bolshevik Revolution, 1917–1935." *Africa*, 32 (1) (1977): 1–27.

———. "European Political Adventures in Ethiopia at the Turn of the 20th Century." *JES*, 12 (1) (1974): 1–17.

Alvares, Alfonso. *The Portuguese Embassy to Abyssinia*. London: HS, 1964.

Alvares, González Francisco. *Narratives of the Portuguese Embassy to Abyssinia During the Years 1520–1527*. London: HS, 1881.

Amare Tekle. "The Determinants of the Foreign Policy of Revolutionary Ethiopia." *JMAS*, 27 (3) (1989): 479–502.

Arnold, Percy. *Prelude to Magdala: Emperor Theodore of Ethiopia and British Diplomacy*. London: Bellew Publishing, 1991.

Asafa Jalata. "The Impact of Racist U.S. Foreign Policy on the Oromo National Struggle." *JOS*, 6 (1/2) (1999): 49–90.

Asgede Hagos. "Arabism: Ethiopia's Wartime Bogeyman in Eritrea." *ESR*, 1 (1) (1996): 119–41.

Bahru Zewde. "Relations between Ethiopia and the Sudan on the Western Ethiopian Frontier, 1898–1935." Ph.D. diss., University of London, 1976.

———. "Twixt Sirdar and Emperor: The Anuak in Ethio-Sudanese Relations 1902–1935." *NAS*, 12 (1) (1990): 79–93.

Bairu Tafla. *Ethiopia and Germany: Cultural, Political, and Economic Relations, 1871–1936*. Wiesbaden: FS, 1981.

——. *Ethiopia and Austria: A History of Their Relations*. Wiesbaden: Harrassowitz, 1994.

——. "The Impact of Dogali on International Policy of the Central European Powers." *Aethiopica: International Journal of Ethiopian Studies*, 5 (2002): 112–124.

Beke, Charles Tilstone. *The British Captives in Abyssinia*. London: Longmans, Green, Reader and Dyer, 1867.

——. "British Embassy to Shoa." *Westminster Review*, 41 (1844): 183–218.

——. *The French and English in the Red Sea*. London: Taylor, 1962.

Bishku, Michael B. "Israel and Ethiopia: From a Special to a Pragmatic Relationship." *Conflict Quarterly*, 14 (2) (1994): 39–62.

Borer, Alain. *Rimbaud in Abyssinia*. New York: William Morrow and Company, 1984.

Boulvin, Fritz. *Une Mission Belge en Ethiopie*. Bruxelles: Société Belge Études Coloniales, 1906.

Bowring, Walter. "Great Britain, the United States, and the Disposition of Italian East Africa." *Journal of Imperial and Commonwealth History*, 20 (1) (1992): 88–107.

Brown, D. J. Latham. "The Ethiopian-Somaliland Frontier Dispute." *International and Comparative Law Quarterly*, 10 (1961): 167–78.

Burgess, Joseph Guy. "Ethiopia's Diplomacy and the Struggle to Preserve its Independence, 1855–1900." Ph.D. diss., Columbia University, 1980.

Capenny, S. H. F. "The Proposed Anglo-Abyssinian Boundary in East Africa." *Scottish Geographical Magazine*, 21 (1905): 260–63.

Caplin, A. S. "British Policy towards Ethiopia 1909–1919." Ph.D. diss., University of London, 1971.

Caulk, Richard Alan. "Menelik II and the Diplomacy of Commerce: Prelude to an Imperial Foreign Policy." *JES*, 17 (1984): 62–87.

——. "The Origins and Development of the Foreign Policy of Menelik II, 1865–1896." Ph.D. diss., University of London, 1966.

Cerulli, Enrico. "Ethiopia's Relations with the Muslim World." In Ivan Hrbek (ed.). *General History of Africa, 3: Africa from the Seventh to the Eleventh Century*. Berkeley: University of California Press, 1988: 575–85.

Charlin, T. "A Propos des Conflits de Frontière Entre la Somalie, L'Éthiopie et le Kenya." *Revue Française des Sciences Politiques*, 16 (2) (1966): 310–19.

Chatterji, Suniti Kumar. *India and Ethiopia from the 7th Century B.C.* Calcutta: Asiatic Society, 1968.

Chhabra, Hari Sharan. "Ancient Indo-Ethiopian Relations." *EO*, 4 (10) (1960): 343–46.

Clapham, Christopher. "Ethiopia." In Timothy M. Shaw and Olajide Aluko (eds.). *The Political Economy of African Foreign Policy: Comparative Analysis*. New York: St. Martin's Press, 1984: 79–93.

——. "The Foreign Policies of Ethiopia and Eritrea." In Stephen Wright (ed.). *African Foreign Policies*. Boulder, Colo.: WP, 1999: 84–99.

Clifford, E. H. M. "The British Somaliland–Ethiopia Boundary." *GJ*, 87 (4) (1936): 289–307.

"Consul Skinner's Mission to Abyssinia." *NGM*, 15 (4) (1904): 164–66.

Conti Rossini, Carlo. *Italia ed Etiopia. Dal Trattato d'Ucciali alla Battaglia di Adua*. Roma: Pubblicazioni dell'Instituto per l'Oriente, 1935.

Crummey, Donald. "Initiatives and Objectives in Ethio-European Relations, 1827–1862." *JAH*, 15 (3) (1974): 433–44.

Davydov, L. "The USSR and Ethiopia: Close Friendship and Cooperation." *International Affairs*, (2) (1979): 90–94.

Diplomatic Relations between Portugal and Ethiopia. Lisbon: S. N. I., 1963.

"Diplomatic Relations with Europe." *EO*, 1 (11) (1957): 343–48.

Donzel, Emery Johannes van. (ed.). *Foreign Relations of Ethiopia, 1642–1700: Documents Relating to the Journeys of Khodja Murad*. Leiden: Nederlands Historisch-Archaeologisch Instituut te Istanbul, 1979.

Ehret, Christopher. *Ethiopians and East Africans: The Problem of Contacts*. Nairobi: East African Publishing House, 1974.

Erlich, Haggai. "Ethiopia and Egypt: Ras Tafari in Cairo, 1924." *Aethiopica: International Journal of Ethiopian Studies*, 1 (1998): 64–84.

——. *Ethiopia and the Middle East*. Boulder: LR, 1994.

——. "Haile Selassie and the Arabs, 1935–1936." *NAS*, 1 (1) (1994): 47–61.

Ethiopia. Ministry of Foreign Affairs. *Foreign Policy of the Federal Democratic Republic of Ethiopia*. Addis Ababa: Ministry of Foreign Affairs, 1996.

——. *Memorandum: War Drums on the Horn of Africa—March of Somalia's Expansionism*. Addis Ababa: Berhanena Selam Printing Press, 1977.

——. *Western Somalia and Abyssinian Colonialism*. Addis Ababa: Ministry of Foreign Affairs, 1975.

Ethiopia. Ministry of Information. *Ethio-Somalia Relations*. Addis Ababa: Ministry of Information, 1962.

Fries, Felix T. "Anglo-Italian Relations 1884–1885, and the Italian Occupation of Massawah." Ph.D. diss., Cambridge University, 1940.

——. "The Hewitt Mission to Abyssinia." *JRAS*, 35 (140) (1936): 268–89 and 35 (141) (1936): 397–412.

Gaudio, Attilio. *L'Ethiopie et la Somalie: L'Afrique de 1945 à 1970*. Paris: Marchés Tropicaux et Méditarranéens, 1971.

Getachew Belayneh. "The Role of United States Economic Assistance in Ethiopia." Ph.D. diss., University of Utah, 1971.

Giglio, Carlo. "Article 17 of the Treaty of Uccialli." *JAH*, 6 (2) (1965): 221–31.

Germany, Elizabeth. *Ethiopia My Home: The Story of John Moraitis*. Addis Ababa: Shama Books, 2001.

Gleichen, Albert Edward Wilfred. *With the Mission to Menelik, 1897*. London: Edward Arnold, 1898.

Gotlieb, M. J. "The United States and Ethiopia through Dictatorship and Revolution." M.Phil. thesis. Oxford: Oxford University, 1979.

Great Britain. *Correspondence Respecting Abyssinia. 1846–1868*. London: HMSO, 1868.

———. *Further Correspondence Respecting British Captives in Abyssinia*. London: HMSO, 1866.

Greenfield, Richard David. "The Emperor's East African State Visits." *EO*, 8 (1964): 106–34.

Gross, Ernest A., D. P. de Villers, Endalkatchew Makonnen, and Richard A. Falk. *Ethiopia and Liberia vs. South Africa: The South West Africa Case*. Los Angeles: African Studies Center, University of California, 1968.

Gruber, Ruth. *Rescue: The Exodus of the Ethiopian Jews*. New York: Atheneum, 1987.

Gwynn, Charles William. "Surveys of the Proposed Sudan-Abyssinian Frontier." *GJ*, 18 (6) (1901): 562–73.

Hagos Mehary. *The Strained U.S.-Ethiopian Relations*. Stockholm: Almqvist and Wiksell International, 1989.

Hamilton, David. "Ethiopia's Frontiers: The Boundary Agreements and Their Demarcation, 1896–1956." D.Phil. diss., Oxford University, 1974.

———. "Schedule of International Agreements Relating to the Boundaries of Ethiopia." *EO*, 16 (2) (1973): 58–69.

Hansberry, Leo. "Ethiopian Ambassadors to Latin Courts and Latin Emissaries to Prester John." EO, 9 (2) (1965): 90–99.

Harris, Joseph E. "Race and Misperception in the Origins of United States–Ethiopian Relations." *TransAfrica Forum*, 3 (2) (1986): 9–23.

Hess, Robert Lee. "Germany and the Anglo-Italian Colonial Entente." In Prosser Gifford and William Roger Louis (eds.). *Britain and Germany in Africa*. New Haven: Yale University Press, 1967: 153–78.

———. "Italian Imperialism in Its Ethiopian Context." *IJAHS*, 6 (1) (1973): 94–109.

Hickey, Dennis. "Ethiopia and Great Britain: Political Conflict in the Southern Borderlands, 1916–1935." Ph.D. diss., Evanston, Ill.: Northwestern University, 1984.

Hohler, Thomas Beaumont. *Diplomat Petrel*. London: John Murray, 1942.

Hoskyns, Catherine (ed.), *Case Studies in African Diplomacy: The Ethiopia-Somali-Kenya Dispute 1960–67*. Nairobi: Oxford University Press, 1969.

Hussein, A. M. "The Ethiopian-Sudanese Boundary: A Study in Historical and Political Geography." Ph.D. diss., University of London, 1981.

Hussein, S.A. "Islam, Christianity, and Ethiopia's Foreign Policy." *Journal of Muslim Minority Affairs*, 17 (1) (1997): 129–39.

Iadarola, Antoinette. "Ethiopia's Admission to the League of Nations: Assessment of Motives." *IJAHS*, 8 (4) (1975): 601–22.

Jacoby, Catherine Murray. *On Special Mission to Abyssinia*. New York: Privately Published, 1933.

Jaenen, Cornelius J. "Blondeel: The Belgian Attempt to Colonize Ethiopia." *AA*, 55 (220) (1956): 214–18.

——. *Ethiopia before the Congo: A Proposed Belgian Colony in Ethiopia 1838–1856*. Ottawa: Institute for International Cooperation, University of Ottawa, 1975.

——. "Theodore II and British Intervention in Ethiopia." *CJAS*, 1 (1) (1966): 117–22.

Jesman, Czeslaw. *The Russians in Ethiopia*. London: Chatto and Windus, 1958.

Kapil, Ravi Laxminarayan. "Territorial Issues in the Horn of Africa with Special Reference to the Ethiopia-Somalia Boundary." Ph.D. diss., University of Wisconsin, 1961.

Karadawi, Ahmed. "The Smuggling of Ethiopian Falasha to Israel through Sudan." *AA*, 90 (358) (1991): 23–49.

Kassim Shehim. "Israel-Ethiopian Relations: Change and Continuity." *NAS*, 10 (1) (1988): 25–37.

Keefer, Edward C. "The Career of Sir Joseph L. Harrington: Empire and Ethiopia, 1884–1918." Ph.D. diss., Michigan State University, 1974.

——. "Great Britain and Ethiopia, 1897–1910: Competition for Empire." *IJAHS*, 6 (3) (1973): 468–74.

——. "Great Britain, France, and the Ethiopian Tripartite Treaty of 1906." *Albion*, 13 (4) (1981): 364–79.

Keller, Edmond J. "The Politics of State Survival: Continuity and Change in Ethiopian Foreign Policy." *The Annals*, 489 (1987): 76–87.

Kilhefner, Donald W. "The United States and Ethiopia, 1903–1915." M.A. thesis, Howard University, 1968.

Kirk, John Miller. "An Analysis of the Ethiopian, Iranian, and Nicaraguan Revolutions from the Perspective of United States Involvement." Ph.D. diss., University of Texas Austin, 1985.

Kirwan, L. P. "An Ethiopian-Sudanese Frontier Zone in Ancient History." *GJ*, 138 (4) (1972): 457–65.

Korn, David A. "Ethiopia: Dilemma for the West." *WT*, 42 (1) (1986): 4–7.

——. *Ethiopia, the United States and the Soviet Union*. Carbondale: Southern Illinois University Press, 1986.

Lemmu Baissa. "Foreign Policy Decision-Making: The Case of Ethiopia, 1959–1981." Ph.D. diss., Syracuse University, 1988.

Le Roux, Cornelius Johannes Brink. "The Origin and Historical Development of the Ethiopia–Somalian Boundary Dispute." *Journal for Contemporary History*, 7 (2) (1982): 47–75.

Lindahl, Ulf J. "An Historic Letter from the United States' Mission to Mene-lik." *Menelik's Journal*, 12 (3) (1996): 924–35.

Lyons, Terrence. "Internal Vulnerability and Inter-State Conflict: Ethiopia's Regional Foreign Policy." In Marina Ottaway (ed.). *The Political Economy of Ethiopia*. New York: Praeger, 1990: 157–73.

——. "Reaction to Revolution: United States-Ethiopian Relations, 1974–1977." Ph.D. diss., Johns Hopkins University, 1994.

——. "The United States and Ethiopia: The Politics of a Patron-Client Rela-tionship." *NAS*, 8 (2/3) (1986): 53–75.

Mackenzie, Barbara Jean. "The Politics of Famine Relief: A Study of United States and Canadian Relations with Ethiopia, 1984–1986." MA thesis, Simon Fraser University (Canada): 1991.

Makeev, D. A. "Sovetsko-Efiopskie Otnosheniia v 20–30e Gody." *Narody Azii i Afriki*, (5) (1975): 139–45.

Malecot, Georges R. "La Politique Étrangère de l'Ethiopie." *Revue Française d'Études Politiques Africaines*, (79) (1972): 39–57.

Manheim, Frank J. "The United States and Ethiopia: A Study in American Im-perialism." *Journal of Negro History*, 17 (2) (1932): 141–55.

Marcus, Harold Golden. "A Background to Direct British Diplomatic Involve-ment in Ethiopia, 1894–1896." *JES*, 1 (2) (1963): 121–32.

——. "Britain and Ethiopia, 1896 to 1914: A Study of Diplomatic Relations." Ph.D. diss., Boston University, 1964.

——. "Ethio–British Negotiations Concerning the Western Border with Sudan, 1896–1902." *JAH*, 4 (1) (1963): 81–94.

——. *Ethiopia, Great Britain, and the United States 1941–1974: The Politics of Empire*. Berkeley: University of California Press, 1983.

——. "The Foreign Policy of the Emperor Menelik 1896–1898: A Rejoinder." *JAH*, 7 (1) (1966): 117–22.

——. "A History of the Negotiations Concerning the Border between Ethiopia and British East Africa, 1897–1914." In Jeffrey Butler (ed.). *Boston Univer-sity Papers on Africa*. Vol. II. Boston: Boston University Press, 1966: 237–65.

——. "Imperialism and Expansionism in Ethiopia from 1865 to 1900." In Lewis Gann and Peter Duignan (eds.). *Colonialism in Africa*. Vol. I. Cam-bridge: Cambridge University Press, 1969: 420–61.

——. "A Note on the First United States Diplomatic Mission to Ethiopia in 1903." *EO*, 8 (2) (1963): 162–68.

——. "A Preliminary History of the Tripartite Treaty of December 13, 1906." *JES*, 2 (2) (1964): 21–40.

——. "The Rodd Mission of 1897." *JES*, 3 (2) (1965): 25–35.

Markakis, John. "The Somali in Ethiopia." *ROAPE*, 23 (70) (1996): 576–70.

——. "The Somali in the New Political Order of Ethiopia." *ROAPE*, (59) (1994): 71–79.

——. "The United States and the Ethiopian Discovery of the Ogaden in 1948." In Hussein M. Adam and Charles L. Geshekter (eds.). *Proceedings of the First International Congress of Somali Studies*. Atlanta: Scholars Press, 1992: 206–13.

Mazrui, Ali A. "Liberia and Ethiopia as Pan-African Symbols: Rise, Decline, and Change." *Liberian Studies Journal*, 22 (2) (1997): 192–98.

McCann, James Craig. "Ethiopia, Britain, and Negotiations for the Lake Tana Dam, 1922–1935." *IJAHS*, 14 (4) (1981): 667–99.

Mekuria Bulcha. *Flight and Integration: Causes of Mass Exodus from Ethiopia and Problems of Integration in the Sudan*. Uppsala: Nordic Institute of African Studies, 1988.

Merivale, Herman. "British Mission to Shoa." *Edinburgh Review*, 80 (1844): 43–67.

Mesfin Wolde Mariam. "The Background of the Ethio-Somalian Boundary Dispute." *JMAS*, 2 (2) (1964): 189–219.

——. *The Background to the Ethio-Somalian Boundary Dispute*. Addis Ababa: Berhanenna Selam, 1964.

Mesfin Yimam. "Growing Ethio-Japanese Relations." *Ethioscope*, 2 (2) (1996): 10–18.

Miers, Suzanne. "Britain and the Suppression of Slavery in Ethiopia." *Slavery and Abolition*, 18 (3) (1997): 257–88.

Muthanna, I. M. *Indo-Ethiopian Relations for Centuries*. Addis Ababa: APP, 1961.

Nalty, Bernard C. *The Diplomatic Mission to Abyssinia, 1903*. Washington, D.C.: U.S. Marine Corps, 1961.

——. *Guests of the Conquering Lion: The Diplomatic Mission to Abyssinia, 1903*. Washington, D.C.: U.S. Marine Corps, 1959.

Natsoulas, Theodore. "The Hellenic Presence in Ethiopia: A Study of a European Minority in Africa (1740–1936)." *Abba Salama*, 8 (1977): 5–239.

——. "Prologue to Modern Ties Between Greece and Ethiopia: The Efforts of Ioannis Kotzikas during the Era of Tewodoros, 1845–1868." *NAS*, 6 (1/2) (1984): 147–70.

——. "Yohannes's Greek Advisers." *NAS*, 7 (3) (1985): 21–40.

Negussay Ayele. "The Foreign Policy of Ethiopia." In Olajide Aluko (ed.). *The Foreign Policies of African States*. London: Hodder and Stoughton, 1977: 46–71.

——. "The 1952–1959 Ethio-Italian Boundary Negotiations: An Exercise in Diplomatic Futility." *JES*, 9 (2) (1971): 127–47.

——. "The Politics of the Somalia–Ethiopia Boundary Problem, 1960–1967." Ph.D. diss., University of California, Los Angeles, 1969.

——. "Rhetoric and Reality in the Making of Boundaries on the Horn of Africa in 1897." *EO*, 13 (1) (1970): 16–30.

Norberg, Viveca Halldin. *Swedes in Haile Selassie's Ethiopia, 1924–1952: A Study in Early Development Co-Operation*. New York: Africana Publishing Company, 1977.

Novati, Giampaolo Calchi. "Re-Establishing Italo-Ethiopian Relations after the War: Old Prejudices and New Policies." *NAS*, 3 (1) (1996): 27–49.

Nuri, Maqsud Ulhasan. "Cuban Policy in Africa: The Limits of the Proxy Model." Ph.D. diss., University of South Carolina, 1990.

Ohlbaum, Diana L. "Ethiopia and the Construction of Soviet Identity, 1974–1991." *NAS*, (NS) 1 (1) (1994): 63–89.

——. "Identity and Interests in Soviet Foreign Policy: The Case of Ethiopia, 1974–1991." Ph.D. diss., Johns Hopkins University, 1998.

Ojo, Olusola. "Ethiopia's Foreign Policy Since the 1974 Revolution." *HA*, 3 (4) (1980/1981): 3–12.

Pankhurst, Estelle Sylvia. *British Policy in Eastern Ethiopia: The Ogaden and the Reserved Area*. Woodford Green: Sylvia Pankhurst, 1946.

——. *British Policy in Eritrea and Northern Ethiopia*. Woodford Green: Sylvia Pankhurst, c. 1945.

Pankhurst, Richard. "The Aksum Obelisk in Rome." *Ethioscope*, 3 (1) (1997): 18–26.

——. *Britain in Ethiopia: The Centenary 1896–1996*. London: Foreign and Commonwealth Office, 1996.

——. "Ethiopia, Europe: Ancient Links." *Ethioscope*, 2 (2) (1996)" 32–44.

——. "A History of the Axum Obelisk Return Struggle by Someone Who Participated in It." *HA*, 16 (1–4) (1998): 127–43.

——. "Italian Settlement in Eritrea and Its Repercussions, 1889–1896." In *Boston University Papers on Africa*. vol. I Boston: Boston University Press, 1964: 119–56.

——. "Robert Skinner's Unpublished Account of the First American Diplomatic Expedition to Ethiopia." *EO*, 1 (1) (1970): 31–36.

——. "Yohannes Kotzika, the Greeks, and British Intervention against Emperor Tewodros of Ethiopia (1867–1868)." *EO*, 14 (1973): 141–203.

Papp, Daniel S. "The Soviet Union and Cuba in Ethiopia." *CH*, 76 (445) (1979): 110–14, 129–30.

Parfitt, Tudor. *Operation Moses: The Untold Story of the Secret Exodus of the Falasha Jews from Ethiopia*. New York: Stein and Day, 1985.

Pateman, Roy G. "Soviet-Ethiopian Relations: The Horns of Dilemma." In M. Light (ed.). *Troubled Friendships: Moscow's Third World Ventures*. London: British Academic Press, 1993: 110–39.

Pétridès, Stephanos Pierre. *The Boundary Question between Ethiopia and Somalia: A Legal and Diplomatic Survey*. New Delhi: People's Publishing House, 1983.

Petterson, Donald K. "Ethiopia Abandoned? An American Perspective." *IA*, 62 (4) (1986): 627–45.

Plante, Julian G. "The Ethiopian Embassy to Cairo of 1443." *JES*, 13 (2) (1975): 133–40.

Portal, Gerald Herbert. *My Mission to Abyssinia*. London: Edward Arnold, 1892.

Ram, K. V. *The Barren Relationship, Britain and Ethiopia, 1805–1868: A Study of British Policy*. New Delhi: Concept, 1985.

——. "Diplomatic Practices of Ethiopia in the 19th Century." *TJH*, 15 (1986): 127–43.

Rapoport, Louis. *Redemption Song: The Story of Operation Moses*. San Diego: Harcourt Brace Jovanovich, 1986.

Rassam, Hormuzd. *Narrative of the British Mission to Theodore, King of Abyssinia*. 2 vols. London: John Murray, 1869.

Robinson, William I. "Global Capitalism and the Oromo Liberation Struggle: Theoretical Notes on U.S. Policy towards the Ethiopian Empire." *JOS*, 4 (1/2) (1997): 1–46.

Rodd, Sir James Rennell. *Social and Diplomatic Memories, 1884–1901*. 2nd Series. London: Edward Arnold, 1923.

Rollins, Patrick Joseph. "Russia's Ethiopian Adventure, 1888–1905." Ph.D. diss., Syracuse University, 1967.

Rossetti, Carlo. *Storia Diplomatica Durante il Regno di Menelik II*. Turin: Societa Tipografica–Editrice Nazionale, 1910.

Rubenson, Sven. "The Protectorate Paragraph of the Wichale Treaty." *JAH*, 5 (2) (1964): 243–83.

——. *Wichale XVII the Attempt to Establish a Protectorate over Ethiopia*. Addis Ababa: APP, 1964.

——. et al. *Correspondence and Treaties 1800–1854*. Evanston: Northwestern University Press, 1987.

Sanderson, George N. "Contributions from African Sources to the History of European Competition in the Upper Valley of the Nile." *JAH*, 3 (1) (1962): 69–90.

——. "The Foreign Policy of the Negus Menelik, 1896–1898." *JAH*, 5 (1) (1964): 96–97.

Sbacchi, Alberto. "In Search of Legitimacy: The United States and the Recognition of the Italian Empire, 1936–1940." *HA*, 16 (1/4) (1998): 96–110.

Schraeder, Peter J. "U.S. Foreign Policy toward Ethiopia and Somalia." In Peter J. Schraeder. *United States Foreign Policy toward Africa: Incrementalism, Crisis, and Change*. New York: Cambridge University Press, 1994: 114–88.

Seleshi Sisaye. "Swedish Aid to Ethiopia, 1954–1967." *JAS*, 8 (2) (1981): 85–90.

Shepherd, Jack. "Food Aid As an Instrument of U.S. Foreign Policy: The Case of Ethiopia 1982–1984." Ph.D. diss., Boston University, 1989.

Shiferaw Bekele. "Some Notes on the Genesis and Interpretation of the Tripartite Treaty." *JES*, 18 (1985): 63–79.

Shinn, David H. "A Survey of American-Ethiopian Relations Prior to the Italian Occupation of Ethiopia." *EO*, 14 (4) (1971): 297–311.

Silberman, Leo. "Why the Haud Was Ceded." *CEA*, 2 (5) (1961): 37–82.

Skinner, Robert Peet. *Abyssinia of To-Day: An Account of the First Mission Sent by the American Government to the Court of the King of Kings, 1903–1904*. New York: Longmans, Green and Company, 1906.

———. "Making a Treaty with Menelik." *World's Work*, 9 (1905): 5795–812.

———. *Our Mission to Abyssinia*. Washington, D.C.: USGPO, 1904.

Sorenson, Manuel James. "A Study of Anglo-Ethiopian Relations, 1800 to 1936." Ph.D. diss., University of Nebraska, 1950.

Southard, Addison. *Abyssinia: Present Commercial Status of the Country with Special Reference to the Possibilities for American Trade*. Washington, D.C.: USGPO, 1918.

Spears, Iain Sinclair. "Intervention and Conflict in Ethiopia: The Impact of the United States and the Soviet Union." M.A. thesis, Queen's University, Kingston, 1991.

Stauffer, Robert B., and Mulford J. Colebrook. "Economic Assistance and Ethiopia's Foreign Policy." *Orbis*, 5 (3) (1961): 320–41.

Stevens, Richard P. "The 1972 Addis Ababa Agreement and the Sudan's Afro-Arab Policy." *JMAS*, 14 (2) (1976): 247–74.

Szajkowski, B. "Ethiopia: A Weakening Soviet Connection?" *WT*, 45 (8/9) (1989): 153–56.

Taha, Faisal Abdel Rahman Ali. *The Settlement of the Sudan-Ethiopia Boundary Dispute*. Khartoum: Khartoum University Press, 1975.

Talbot, David Abner. "Ethiopia in World Politics." *Pan African Journal*, 1 (7) (1947): 7–11.

Tegegnework Gettu. "Conflict and Accommodation in Ethio-Sudanese Relations, 1956–1986." Ph.D. diss., Columbia University, 1987.

Tekeda Alemu. "The Unmaking of Ethio-American Military Relations: U.S. Foreign Policy toward the Ethiopian Revolution." Ph.D. diss., Claremont Graduate University, 1983.

Teshome G. Wagaw. "The International Political Ramifications of Falasha Emigration." *JMAS*, 29 (4) (1991): 557–82.

Trueman, Trevor. "Western Foreign Policy, Profits, and Human Rights: The Case of Ethiopia." *JOS*, 6 (1/2) (1999): 91–108.

Ullendorff, Edward. "The Anglo-Ethiopian Treaty of 1902." *Bulletin of the School of Oriental and African Studies*, 30 (3) (1967): 283–3127.

United States. Department of State. Bureau of Intelligence and Research. *Ethiopia–French Territory of the Afars and Issas Boundary*. Washington, D.C.: USGPO, 1976.

———. *Ethiopia-Kenya Boundary*. Washington, D.C.: USGPO, 1976.

——. *Ethiopia–Somalia Boundary*. Washington, D.C.: USGPO, 1975.

United States. House of Representatives. Committee on Foreign Affairs. Subcommittee on Africa. *Ethiopia: The Challenges Ahead*. Washington, D.C.: USGPO, 1995.

——. *The Political Crisis in Ethiopia and the Role of the United States*. Washington, D.C.: USGPO, 1991.

United States. House of Representatives. Select Committee on Hunger. *Ethiopia and Sudan: Warfare, Politics and Famine*. Washington, D.C.: USGPO, 1988.

Varnis, Steven L. *Reluctant Aid or Aiding the Reluctant? U.S. Food Aid Policy and Ethiopian Famine Relief*. New Brunswick, N.J.: Transaction Publishers, 1990.

Venkataram, Krishnamurthy. "British Policy in Ethiopia, 1899–1907." Ph.D. diss., Dalhousie University (Canada), 1971.

——. "Foreign Policy of Theodore II of Ethiopia: An Interpretation." *TJH*, 3 (1/2) (1973): 129–45.

Vestal, Theodore M. "Peace Corps in Ethiopia: An Overall View." *EO*, 9 (1) (1965): 11–24.

Vignéras, Sylvain. *Une Mission Française en Abyssinie*. Paris: Armand Colin et Cie, 1897.

Weaver, Jerry L. "Sojourners Along the Nile: Ethiopian Refugees in Khartoum." *JMAS*, 23 (1) (1985): 147–56.

Wondimneh Tilahun. *Egypt's Imperial Aspirations over Lake Tana and the Blue Nile*. Addis Ababa: United Printers Ltd., 1979.

Woodward, Peter. "Ethiopia and the Sudan: The Inter-State Outcome of Domestic Conflict." *CR*, 230 (1336) (1977): 231–34.

Yagya, V. S. "Ethiopia and Its Neighbors: An Evolution of Relations, 1974–1989." *NAS*, 12 (2/3) (1990): 107–16.

Yakobson, Sergius. *The Soviet Union and Ethiopia: A Case of Traditional Behavior*. Notre Dame: University of Notre Dame Press, 1965.

——. "The Soviet Union and Ethiopia: A Case of Traditional Behavior." *The Review of Politics*, 25 (3) (1963): 329–42.

Yusuf, Abdulqawi A. "The Anglo-Ethiopian Treaty of 1897 and the Somali-Ethiopian Dispute." *HA*, 3 (1) (1980): 38–42.

Zewde Gabre-Sallassie. *Continuity and Discontinuity in Menelik's Foreign Relations 1865–1896*. (Monograph). March 1996.

Eritrea

Abeba Tesfagiorgis. *A Painful Season and a Stubborn Hope: The Odyssey of an Eritrean Mother*. Lawrenceville, N.J.: RSP, 1992.

Abuetan, Baird. "Eritrea: United Nations Problem and Solution." *Middle Eastern Affairs*, 2 (2) (1951): 35–51.

Addis Birhan (pseud.). *Eritrea a Problem Child of Ethiopia: Causes, Consequences, and Strategic Implications of the Conflict*. [Addis Ababa]: Marran Books, 1998.

Aliboni, Roberto. "Eritrean Independence in an International Perspective." *Lo Spettatore Internazionale*, 14 (3) (1979): 163–72.

Amare Tekle. *Eritrea and Ethiopia from Conflict to Cooperation*. Lawrenceville, N.J.: RSP, 1994.

——. "The Creation of the Ethio-Eritrean Federation: A Case Study in Postwar International Relations." Ph.D. diss., University of Denver, 1964.

Andargachew Tirineh. "Eritrea, Ethiopia, and the Federation 1941–1952." *NAS*, 3 (1) (1980/1981): 99–119.

Araia Tseggai. "Ethiopian Economic Policy in Eritrea: The Federation Era." *NAS*, 6 (1/2) (1984): 81–93.

Assefaw Bariagaber. "Liberalization and Democratization in Ethiopia: Domestic Consequences of the Conflict in Eritrea." *ERS*, 1 (1) (1996): 69–90.

"Behind the U.N. Sponsored Federal Act: Secret Deals amongst the Interested Parties (Part 1)." *Journal of Eritrean Studies*, 2 (1) (1987): 37–52 and 2 (2) (1988): 25–41.

Bell, J. Bowyer. "Endemic Insurgency and International Order: The Eritrean Experience." *Orbis*, 18 (2) (1974): 427–50.

Bereket Habte Selassie. *Eritrea and the United Nations and Other Essays*. Trenton, N.J.: RSP, 1989.

——. "The Evolution of the Principle of Self-Determination." *HA*, 1 (4) (1978): 3–9.

——. *Reflections on the Future Political System of Eritrea*. Washington, D.C.: Eritreans for Peace and Democracy, 1990.

Berhane Woldegabriel. "Demobilising Eritrea's Army." *ROAPE*, (58) (1993): 134–35.

Bhardwaj, Raman G. "Eritrea Secessionism." *India Quarterly*, 35 (1) (1979): 83–92.

Campbell, John Franklin. "Rumblings along the Red Sea: The Eritrean Question." *FA*, 48 (3) (1970): 537–48.

Cervenka, Zdenek. "Eritrea: Struggle for Self-Determination or Secession?" *Afrika Spektrum*, 12 (1) (1977): 37–48.

Cesari, Cesare. *Contributo alla storia delle Truppe Indigene della Colonia Eritrea e della Somalia Italiana*. Città di Castello: Tipografia dell'Unione arti Grafiche, 1913.

Clemens, Peter. "The United States and Humanitarian Demining in Eritrea: Training the Trainer, 1995–97." *Contemporary Security Policy*, 21 (1) (2000): 68–98.

Cliffe, Lionel. "Dramatic Shift in the Military Balance in the Horn: The 1984 Eritrea Offensive." *ROAPE*, (30) (1984): 93–96.

——. *Eritrea—25 Years of Struggle for Independence: A Critical Appraisal.* Nottingham: Spokesman, 1987.

——. "The Impact of War and the Response to It in Different Agrarian Systems in Eritrea." *Development and Change*, 30 (3) (1989): 373–400.

Cliffe, Lionel, and Basil Davidson (eds.). *The Long Struggle of Eritrea for Independence and Constructive Peace.* Trenton, NJ: RSP, 1988.

Cliffe, Lionel, Basil Davidson, and Bereket Habte Selassie (eds.). *Behind the War in Eritrea.* Nottingham: Spokesman, 1980.

Connell, Dan. *Against All Odds: A Chronicle of the Eritrean Revolution.* Lawrenceville, N.J.: RSP, 1993.

——. "The Birth of the Eritrean Nation." *HA*, 3 (1) (1980): 14–24.

——. "Eritrea: The Politics of Refugees." *HA*, 2 (4) (1979): 4–7.

——. "Inside the EPLF: The Origins of the 'People's Party' and Its Role in the Liberation of Eritrea." *ROAPE*, 28 (89) (2001): 345–64.

Cubbit, G. "Eritrea: Land without Peace." *Africa Institute Bulletin*, 15 (5) (1977): 111–19.

Cumming, Duncan Cameron. "The Disposal of Eritrea." *The Middle East Journal*, 7 (1) (1952/1953): 18–32.

——. "The UN Disposal of Eritrea." *AA*, 52 (207) (1953): 127–36.

Ellingson, Lloyd. "The Emergence of Political Parties in Eritrea, 1941–1950." *JAH*, 18 (2) (1977): 261–81.

——. "Eritrea: Separatism and Irredentism, 1941–1985." Ph.D. diss., Michigan State University, 1986.

"Eritrea: War and Drought." *HA*, 4 (1) (1981), 20–28.

Eritrean Liberation Front. *ELF: The National Revolutionary Vanguard of the Eritrean People.* n.p.?: Eritrean Liberation Front, 1978.

——. *The Eritrean Revolution: Sixteen Years of Armed Struggle.* Beirut: ELF Foreign Information Center, 1977.

——. *The National Democratic Revolution versus Ethiopian Expansion.* Beirut: ELF Foreign Information Center, 1979.

——. *Political Programme.* Beirut: ELF Foreign Information Center, 1975.

——. *The Struggle of Eritrea.* Damascus: Eritrean Liberation Front, n.d..

Eritrean Liberation Front. Foreign Information Centre. *The Eritrean Revolution: 16 Years of Armed Struggle September 1, 1961–September 1, 1977.* Beirut: ELF Information Centre, 1977.

Eritrean People's Liberation Front. "Eritrea: Intervention and Self-Reliance." *ROAPE*, (10) (1978): 104–14.

Eritrean Relief Association. *Health Service Delivery in Eritrea.* Khartoum: Eritrean Relief Association, 1983.

"Eritrea's Borders: Selected Treaties." *Journal of Eritrean Studies*, 3 (1) (1988): 65–72.

Erlich, Haggai. *The Struggle over Eritrea, 1962–1978.* Stanford: Hoover Institute, 1982.

"Ethio-Italian Treaty of 1928 on the Use of the Port of Assab by Ethiopia." *Journal of Eritrean Studies*, 3 (1) (1988): 60–4.

Ethiopia. Department of Press and Information. *The Recovery of Ethiopia.* Addis Ababa: Berhanena Selam Printing Press, 1951.

Evans, Alona E. "Federation of Ethiopia and Eritrea Case Note." *American Journal of International Law*, 62 (1) (1968): 202–4.

Eyassu Gayim. *The Eritrean Question: The Conflict between the Right of Self-Determination and the Interests of States.* Uppsala, Sweden: Iustus Forlag, 1993.

Firebrace, James, with Stuart Holland. *Never Kneel Down.* Trenton, N.J.: RSP, 1985.

Fouad Makki. "Nationalism, State Formation, and the Public Sphere: Eritrea 1991–96." *ROAPE*, 23 (70) (1996): 475–97.

Gebre Hiwet Tesfagiorgis. *Eritrea: A Case of Self-Determination.* Washington, D.C.: Eritreans for Peace and Democracy, 1990.

Great Britain. British Military Administration. *Eritrea and Her Neighbors.* Asmara: British Military Administration, 1944.

——. *Races and Tribes of Eritrea.* Asmara: British Military Administration, 1943.

——. *Handbook of Eritrea.* Vol. 2, *Communications.* Khartoum: Government Printer, 1943.

——. Ministry of Information. *Handbook for Eritrea.* Asmara: British Military Administration, n.d.?

Habtu Ghebre-Ab. *Ethiopia and Eritrea: A Documentary Study.* Trenton, N.J.: RSP, 1993.

Hambly, D. M. "Railway Improvisation in Eritrea." *The Journal of the United Service Institution of India*, 78 (330) (1948): 68–73.

Heiden, Lynda. "The Eritrean Struggle." *Monthly Review*, 30 (2) (1978): 13–29.

Henze, Paul Bernard. *Eritrea: The Dilemmas of Marxism.* Philadelphia: Foreign Policy Research Institute, 1988.

——. "Eritrea: The Endless War." *The Washington Quarterly*, 9 (2) (1986): 23–36.

——. "Eritrean Options and Ethiopia's Future." *Henok*, 1 (1990): 117–40.

——. *Ethiopia and Eritrea in Transition: The Impact of Ethnicity on Politics and Development.* Santa Monica, Calif.: Rand Corporation, 1995.

Hizkias Assefa. "An Interest Approach to the Resolution of Civil Wars in the Horn of Africa: Lessons from the Negotiations on the Eritrean Conflict." In Kumar Rupesinghe (ed.). *Internal Conflict and Governance.* Basingstoke: Macmillan, 1992: 169–186.

——. "The Challenge of Mediation in Internal Wars: Reflections on the INN Experience in the Ethiopian-Eritrean Conflict." *Security Dialogue*, 23 (3) (1992): 101–6.

Hussey, E. R. J. "Eritrea Self-Governing." *AA*, 53 (213) (1954): 320–28.

Irma Taddia. "Modern Ethiopia and Colonial Eritrea." *Aethiopica: International Journal of Ethiopian Studies*, 5 (2002): 125–38.

Iyob, Ruth. "The Eritrean Experiment: A Cautious Pragmatism?" *JMAS*, 35 (4) (1997): 647–73.

——. *The Eritrean Struggle for Independence: Domination, Resistance, Nationalism 1941–93*. Cambridge: Cambridge University Press, 1995.

Johnson, Michael and Trish Johnson. "Eritrea: The National Question and the Logic of Protracted Struggle." *AA*, 80 (319) (1981): 181–95.

Jordan Gebre-Medhin. "The EPLF and Peasant Power in Eritrea." *HA*, 5 (4) (1982/1983): 46–50.

——. "Nationalism, Peasant Politics and the Emergence of a Vanguard Front in Eritrea." *ROAPE*, (30) (1984): 48–57.

——. *Peasants and Nationalism in Eritrea*. Trenton, N.J.: RSP, 1989.

Kaplan, Robert D. *Surrender or Starve: The Wars behind the Famine*. Boulder, Colo., and London: WP, 1988.

Kinnock, Glenys. *Eritrea: Images of War and Peace*. London: Chatto and Windus, 1988.

Kramer, Jack. "Africa's Hidden War." *Evergreen Review*, 15 (94) (1971): 25–29, 61–63.

——. "Hidden War in Eritrea." *Venture*, 21 (5): (1969): 18–9.

Lobban, Richard. *Eritrean Liberation Front: A Close-Up View*. Pasadena, Calif.: Munger Africana Library Notes, 1972.

——. "The Eritrean War: Issues and Implications." *CJAS*, 10 (2) (1976): 335–46.

Longrigg, Stephen Hemsley. *A Short History of Eritrea*. Oxford: CP, 1945.

Machida, Robert. *Eritrea: The Struggle for Independence*. Trenton, N.J.: RSP, 1987.

Markakis, John. "Nationalist Revolution in Eritrea." *JMAS*, 26 (1) (1988): 51–70.

Martini, F. *Il Diario Eritreo*. 4 vols. Firenze: Vallechi, 1946.

Mesfin Araya. "Eritrea, 1941–1952, the Failure of the Emergence of the Nation-State: Towards a Clarification of the Eritrean Question in Ethiopia." Ph.D. diss., City University of New York, 1988.

——. "The Eritrean Question: An Alternative Explanation." *JMAS*, 28 (1) (1990): 79–100.

Morgan, Edward. "A Geographic Evaluation of the Ethiopian-Eritrea Conflict." *JMAS*, 14 (4) (1977): 667–74.

Morison, Geoffrey. *Eritrea and the Southern Sudan: Aspects of Some Wider African Problems*. London: Minority Rights Group, 1976.

Mustafa, Zubeida. "The Eritrean Problem: Its International Implications." *Pakistan Horizon*, 28 (2) (1975): 67–70.

Negussay Ayele. "The Eritrean Problem Revisited." *JES*, 22 (1989): 137–55.

Nene Mburu. "Patriots or Bandits? Britain's Strategy for Policing Eritrea, 1941–1952." *Nordic Journal of African Studies*, 9 (2) (2000): 85–104.

Okbazghi Yohannes. *Eritrea: A Pawn in World Politics*. Gainesville: University of Florida Press, 1991.

——. "The Eritrean Question: A Colonial Case?" *JMAS*, 25 (4) (1987): 643–68.

Ottaway, Marina. "Mediation in a Transitional Conflict: Eritrea." *The Annals*, 518 (1991): 69–81.

Pankhurst, Estelle Sylvia. *Eritrea on the Eve*. Woodford Green: New Times and Ethiopia News Books, 1952.

Pankhurst, Estelle Sylvia, and Richard Pankhurst. *Ethiopia and Eritrea: The Last Phase of the Reunion Struggle, 1941–1952*. Essex: Lalibela House, 1953.

Papstein, Robert. *Eritrea: Revolution at Dusk*. Trenton, N.J.: RSP, 1991.

Pateman, Roy. "Eritrea and Ethiopia: Strategies for Reconciliation in the Horn of Africa." *AT*, 38 (2) (1991): 43–55.

——. "Eritrea, Ethiopia, and the Middle Eastern Powers: Image and Reality." *NAS*, 8 (2/3) (1986): 23–39.

——. *Eritrea: Even the Stones Are Burning*. Lawrenceville, N.J.: RSP, 1990.

——. "Eritrean Resistance during the Italian Occupation." *Journal of Eritrean Studies*, 3 (2) (1989): 13–24.

——. "The Eritrean War." *Armed Forces and Society*, 17 (1) (1990): 82–99.

——. "Eritrea's Struggle for Independence." *Current Affairs Bulletin*, 60 (11) (1984): 25–31.

——. "Liberte, Egalite, Franternite: Aspects of the Eritrean Revolution." *JMAS*, 28 (3) (1990): 457–72.

——. "The War in Eritrea: Drawing to an End?" *The Horn Review*, 1 (1) (1991): 1–13.

Peninou, Jean Louis. *Eritrea: The Guerrillas of the Red Sea*. New York: Eritreans for Liberation in North America, 1975.

Pool, David. *Eritrea: Africa's Longest War*. London: Anti-Slavery Society, 1980.

Rasmuson, John R. *A History of Kagnew Station and American Forces in Eritrea*. Alexandria, Va.: Information Division IACS–I. Headquarters, United States Army Security Agency, 1973.

Research and Information Centre on Eritrea. *Revolution in Eritrea: Eyewitness Reports*. Rome: Research and Information Centre on Eritrea, 1979.

Revolution in Eritrea: The Ethiopian Military Dictatorship and Imperialism. New York: Eritreans for Liberation in North America, 1975.

Sherman, Richard F. "Eritrea: Survey of Social and Economic Change." *HA*, 1 (3) (1978): 31–37.

——. *Eritrea: The Unfinished Revolution*. New York: Praeger Publishers, 1980.

Sheth, V. S. "Eritrean Struggle for Independence: Internal and External Dimensions." *International Studies*, 24 (1) (1987): 53–64.

Shields, Todd J. "Ethiopia: The War on Relief." *AR*, 33 (4) (1988): 17–22.

Shumet Sishagne. "Discord and Fragmentation in Eritrean Politics, 1941–1981." Ph.D. diss., University of Illinois Urbana–Champaign, 1992.

Silkin, Trish. "Women in Struggle: Eritrea." *TWQ*, 5 (4) (1983): 909–13.

Smock, David R. "Eritrean Refugees in the Sudan." *JMAS*, 20 (3) (1982): 451–65.

Suau, Anthony. *Region in Rebellion: Eritrea*. Washington, D.C.: National Geographic Society, 1985.

Taylor, Richard Bingham. "Amhara Cloud over Eritrea." *Geographical Magazine*, (46) (1974): 196–201.

Teame Tewolde-Berham. "The Eritrea-Ethiopia Conflict: An Eritrean View." *WT*, 44 (7) (1988): 110–12.

Tekeste Negash. *Eritrea and Ethiopia: The Federal Experience*. Uppsala: Nordiska Afrikainstitutet, 1997.

——. *Italian Colonialism in Eritrea, 1882–1941: Policies, Praxis, and Impact*. Uppsala: Almqvist and Wiksell International, 1987.

——. *No Medicine for the Bite of a White Snake: Notes on Nationalism and Resistance in Eritrea 1890–1940*. Uppsala: University Press, 1987.

Tekie Fessehatzion. "A Brief Encounter with Democracy: From Acquiescence to Resistance During Eritrea's Early Federation Years." *ERS*, 2 (2) (1998): 19–64.

——. "The Eritrean Struggle for Independence and National Liberation." *HA*, 1 (2) (1978): 29–34.

——. "The International Dimensions of the Eritrean Question." *HA*, 6 (2) (1983): 7–24.

Tesfatsion Medhanie. *Eritrea: Dynamics of a National Question*. Amsterdam: B. R. Gruner, 1986.

——. *Peace Dialogue on Eritrea: Prospects and Problems Today*. Amsterdam: B. R. Gruner, 1989.

Trevaskis, Gerald Kennedy Nicholas. *Eritrea: A Colony in Transition, 1941–1952*. London: Oxford University Press, 1960.

Tronvill, Kjetil. "Borders of Violence—Boundaries of Identity: Demarcating the Eritrean Nation-State." *Ethnic and Racial Studies*, 22 (6) (1999): 1037–61.

United Nations. *The United Nations and the Independence of Eritrea*. New York: United Nations Department of Public Information, 1996.

Warren, Herrick and Anita Warren. "The U.S. Role in the Eritrean Conflict." *AT*, 23 (2) (1976): 39–53.

White, Philip. "The Eritrea-Ethiopia Border Arbitration." *ROAPE*, 29 (92) (2002): 345–56.

With, Peter. *Politics and Liberation: The Eritrea Struggle, 1961–1986*. Aarhus, Denmark: University of Aarhus, 1987.

Law and Human Rights

Abbink, Jon G. "Ethnicity and Constitutionalism in Contemporary Ethiopia." *JAL*, 41 (2) (1997): 159–74.

Abdussamad H. Ahmad. "Border Conflict and Chiefly Power: Trading in Slaves in Bela-Shangul and Gumuz, Ethiopia—Border Enclaves in History, 1897–1938." *JAH*, 40 (3) (1999): 433–46.

Aberra Jembere. *An Introduction to the Legal History of Ethiopia 1434–1974*. Münster: Lit Verlag, 2000.

Aberra W. Meshesha. *Democratic Constitution for Ethiopia*. Virginia Beach, Va.: Conerstone Publishing Inc., 1996.

Africa Watch. *Ethiopia: Conscription: Abuses of Human Rights during Recruitment to the Armed Forces*. New York: Human Rights Watch, 1990.

———. *Ethiopia: The Curtailment of Rights*. New York: Human Rights Watch, 1997.

Ahooja, Krishna. "Law and Development in Ethiopia: A Report." *EO*, 10 (2) (1966): 152–63.

Amare Tekle. "The New Constitution of Ethiopia." *JAS*, 15 (3/4) (1988): 80–93.

Amnesty International. *End of an Era of Brutal Repression: A New Chance for Human Rights*. London: AI, 1991.

———. *Ethiopia: Accountability Past and Present—Human Rights in Transition*. London: AI, 1995.

———. *Ethiopia and Eritrea: Human Rights Issues in a Year of Armed Conflict*. London: AI, 1999.

———. *Ethiopia: The Human Rights Situation*. London: AI, 1977.

———. "Ethiopia: Political Imprisonment, and Torture Reports—Report 1." *Journal of Eritrean Studies*, 3 (2) (1989): 41–55.

———. "Ethiopia: Political Imprisonment and Torture Reports—Report 2." *Journal of Eritrean Studies*, 3 (2) (1989): 56–59.

———. *Human Rights Violations in Ethiopia*. London: AI, 1977.

———. *Political Imprisonment in Ethiopia*. London: AI, 1989.

———. *Update on Political Imprisonment*. London: AI, 1991.

———. *Violation of Rights of Man in Ethiopia*. London: AI, 1978.

Andargatchew Tesfaye. "Ethiopia." In Dae H. Chang (ed.). *Criminology: A Cross Cultural Perspective*. Vol. 1 Durham: Carolina Academic Press, 1976: 388–62.

Andreas Eshete. "Implementing Human Rights and a Democratic Constitution in Ethiopia." *Issue*, 21 (1/2) (1993): 8–13.

Beckstrom, John H. "Adoption in Ethiopia Ten Years after the Civil Code." *JAL*, 16 (2) (1972): 145–68.

——. "Divorce in Urban Ethiopia, Ten Years after the Civil Code." *JEL*, 6 (2) (1969): 283–304.

——. "Transplantation of Legal Systems: Early Report on the Reception of Western Laws in Ethiopia." *Journal of Comparative Law*, (1973): 557–83.

Bekele Mesfin. "Prison Conditions in Ethiopia." *HA*, 2 (2) (1979): 4–11.

Bereket Habte Selassie. "Constitutional Development in Ethiopia." *JAL*, 10 (2) (1966): 74–91.

——. "The Eritrean Question in International Law. *HA*, 6 (2) (1983): 25–30.

Brietzke, Paul H. "Ethiopia's 'Leap in the Dark': Federalism and Self-Determination in the New Constitution." *JAL*, 39 (1) (1995): 19–38.

——. *Law, Development, and the Ethiopian Revolution*. Lewisburg, Pa.: Bucknell University Press, 1982.

——. "Private Law in Ethiopia." *JAL*, 18 (2) (1974): 148–67.

Buhagiar, W. "Marriage under the Civil Code of Ethiopia." *JEL*, 1 (2) (1964): 730–99.

Calhoun, Craig. "Ethiopia's Ethnic Cleansing." *Dissent*, 46 (1) (1999): 47–50.

Consolidated Laws of Ethiopia. Addis Ababa: HSU, 1972.

Conte, Carmelo, and Guglielmo Gobbi. *Ethiopia: Introduzione alla Etnologia del Diritto*. Milan: Giuffrè, 1976.

Conti Rossini, Carlo. *Principi di Diritto Consuetudinario della Colonia Eritrea*. Rome: Tipografia dell'Unione Editrice, 1916.

David, René. "A Civil Code for Ethiopia: Considerations on the Codification of the Civil Law in African Countries." *Tulane Law Review*, 37 (2) (1963):187–204.

——. "Ethiopia: L'Enseignement du Droit en Ethiopie." *JAL*, 6 (2) (1962): 96–100.

——. "Les Sources du Code Civil Éthiopien." *Révue Internationale de Droit Comparé*, 3 (1962): 498–506.

Ethiopian Human Rights Council. *Democracy, Rule of Law, and Human Rights in Ethiopia: Rhetoric and Practice*. Addis Ababa: Ethiopian Human Rights Council, 1995.

——. *The Human Rights Situation in Ethiopia*. Addis Ababa: Ethiopian Human Rights Council, 1994.

Ewing, W. (ed.). *The Consolidated Laws of Ethiopia*. 2 vols. Addis Ababa: HSU Press, 1971.

Fasil Nahum. *Constitution for a Nation of Nations: The Ethiopian Prospect*. Lawrenceville, N.J.: RSP, 1997.

Fisher, Stanley Z. "Criminal Procedure for Juvenile Offenders in Ethiopia." *JEL*, 7 (1) (1970): 115–37.

——. *Ethiopian Criminal Procedure*. Addis Ababa: HSU and OUP, 1969.

——. "Some Aspects of Ethiopian Arrest Law: The Electric Approach to Codification." *JEL*, 3 (2) (1966): 463–90.

——. "The Traditional Criminal Procedure in Ethiopia." *American Journal of Comparative Law*, 19 (4) (1971): 709–46.

Fisseha-Tsion Menghistu. "The Process of Making the New Constitution; Its Historical Significance and Practical Application: The Case of Human and Civil Rights within Due Process of Law." *Henok*, 2 (1991): 161–81.

Gaim Kibreab. "Mass Expulsion from Ethiopia of Eritreans and Ethiopians of Eritrean Origin from Ethiopia and Human Rights Violations." *ESR*, 3 (2) (1999): 107–37.

Geraghty, T. F. "Field Research in Ethiopian Law." *African Law Studies*, 3 (1970): 17–22.

——. "People, Practice, Attitudes, and Problems in the Lower Courts in Ethiopia." *JEL*, 6 (2) (1969): 427–512.

Goldberg, Everett F. "An Introduction to the Law of Business Organizations." *JEL*, 8 (2) (1972): 495–523.

——. "Protection of Trademarks in Ethiopia." *JEL*, 8 (1) (1972): 130–47.

Graven, Philippe. *An Introduction to Ethiopian Penal Law*. Addis Ababa: HSU, Faculty of Law and Oxford University Press, 1965.

——. "Joinder of Criminal and Civil Proceedings." *JEL*, 1 (1) (1964): 135–50.

——. "The Penal Code of the Empire of Ethiopia." *JEL*, 1 (2) (1964): 267–98.

Guadagni, Marco. *Ethiopian Labour Law Handbook*. Asmara: Il Poliografico, 1972.

Haile, Daniel. *Law and the Status of Women in Ethiopia*. Addis Ababa: African Training and Research Centre for Women, Economic Commission for Africa, 1980.

Ibrahim Idris. "Ethiopian Immigration Law on the Exclusion and Deportation of Foreign Nationals." *African Journal of International and Comparative Law*, 2 (1) (1990): 117–30.

Inter-Africa Group. *Constitutionalism: Reflections and Recommendations: The Symposium on the Making of the New Ethiopian Constitution, 17–21 May 1993*. Addis Ababa: Center for Dialogue on Humanitarian Peace and Development Issues in the Horn of Africa, 1994.

International Commission of Jurists. "The Rebellion Trials in Ethiopia: Comments by an Observer." *Bulletin of the International Commission of Jurists*, 12 (1961): 29–37.

International Human Rights Law Group. *Ethiopia in Transition: A Report on the Judiciary and the Legal Profession*. Washington, D.C.: International Human Rights Law Group, 1994.

International Transparency Commission on Africa. *Federal Ethiopia at Cross-Roads*. London: ITCO-Africa, 1995.

Khalif, Mohamud H. and Martin Doornbos. "The Somali Region in Ethiopia: A Neglected Human Rights Tragedy." *ROAPE*, 29 (91) (2002): 73–94.

Krzeczunowicz, Jerzy. "The Ethiopian Civil Code: Its Usefulness, Relation to Custom, and Applicability." *JAL*, 7 (3) (1963): 172–77.

——. *The Ethiopian Law of Extra Contractual Liability*. Addis Ababa: HSU, Faculty of Law, 1970.

——. "Ethiopian Legal Education." *JES*, 1 (1) (1963): 68–74.

——. *Formation and Effects of Contracts in Ethiopian Law. The Ethiopian Law of Extra-Contractual Liability, and the Ethiopian Law of Compensation for Damages*. Addis Ababa: Central Printing Press, 1970.

——. "Hierarchy of Laws in Ethiopia." *JEL*, 1 (1) (1964): 111–17.

——. "The Present Role of Equity in Ethiopian Civil Law." *JAL*, 13 (3) (1969): 145–57.

——. "Statutory Interpretation in Ethiopia." *JEL*, 1 (2) (1964): 315–25.

Lechenperg, H. P. "Open-Air Law Courts of Ethiopia." *NGM*, 68 (11) (1935): 633–46.

Levine, Donald Nathan. "Is Ethiopia Cutting off Its Head Again?" *Ethiopian Review*, (1993): 25–31.

Lewis, William. "Ethiopia's Revised Constitution." *Middle East Journal*, 10 (2) (1956): 194–99.

Mantel-Niecko, Joanna. "Law That Generates Instability: The Case of the Ethiopian Proclamations of September 1987." *NAS*, 12 (2/3) (1990): 83–89.

Marein, Nathan. *The Ethiopian Empire: Federation and Laws*. Rotterdam: Royal Netherlands Printing and Lithographing Company, 1954.

McCarthy, Paul. "'De Facto' and Customary Partnerships in Ethiopian Law." *JEL*, 5 (1) (1968): 105–22.

Mesfin Bekele. "Prison Conditions in Ethiopia." HA, 2 (2) (1979): 4–11.

Miers, Suzanne. "Britain and the Suppression of the Slave Trade in Ethiopia." *Slavery and Abolition*, 18 (3) (1997): 257–88.

Minasse Haile. "The New Ethiopian Constitution: Its Impact upon Unity, Human Rights, and Development." *Suffolk Transnational Law Review*, 20 (1) (1996): 1–84.

Moore–Harell, Alice. "Economic and Political Aspects of the Slave Trade in Ethiopia and the Sudan in the Second Half of the Nineteenth Century." *IJAHS*, 32 (2/3) (1999): 407–21.

Niggli, Peter. *Doubtful Methods in the Struggle Against Famine: Ethiopia, Deportations and Forced-Labour Camps . . . Ten Months Later*. Washington, D.C.: Union of Oromo in North America, 1986.

"The 1931 Constitution of Ethiopia." *EO*, 5 (4) (1962): 362–65.

Packer, George. "Ethiopia's Prisoners of Blood." *Dissent*, 43 (3) (1996): 117–28.

Pankhurst, Estelle Sylvia. "The New Ethiopian Penal Code: A Survey." *EO*, 2 (8) (1958): 259–87.

Paul, James C. N. "Ethnicity and the New Constitutional Orders of Ethiopia and Eritrea." In Yash Ghai (ed.). *Autonomy and Ethnicity: Negotiating Competing Claims in Multi-Ethnic States*. London: Cambridge University Press, 2000: 173–96.

——. "Human Rights and the Structure of Security Forces in Constitutional Orders: The Case of Ethiopia." *Review of International Commission of Jurists*, 60 (1998): 135–66.

Paul, James C. N., and Christopher Clapham (eds.). *Ethiopian Constitutional Development: A Sourcebook*. 2 vols. Addis Ababa: APP, 1967, 1971.

"The Rebellion Trials in Ethiopia." *Bulletin of the International Commission of Jurists*, 12 (1961): 29–37.

Redden, Kenneth R. *The Legal System of Ethiopia*. Charlottesville, Va.: The Mitchie Company, 1968.

Rossi, M. *Matrimonio e Divorzio nel Diritto Abissino*. Milan: Edizioni Unicopli, 1982.

Russell, Franklin F. "Eritrean Customary Law." *JAL*, 3 (2) (1959): 99–104.

——. "The New Ethiopian Civil Code." *Brooklyn Law Review*, 29 (1963): 236–41.

——. "The New Ethiopian Penal Code." *American Journal of Comparative Law*, 10 (1961): 265–77.

——. "The New Ethiopian Penal Code." *EO*, 2 (8) (1958): 258–86.

Ryle, John. "An African Nuremberg." *The New Yorker*, 2 October 1995, 50–2, 57–61.

Sand, Peter H. "Roman Origins of the Ethiopian 'Law of the Kings.'" *JEL*, 11 (1980): 71–81.

Scholler, Heinrich. *The Special Court of Ethiopia, 1920–1935*. Stuttgart: FS, 1985.

——. and Paul H. Brietzke. *Ethiopia: Revolution, Law and Politics*. Stuttgart: FS, 1985.

Schwab, Peter. "Human Rights in Ethiopia." *JMAS*, 14 (1) (1976): 155–60.

Sedler, Robert Allen. "The Chilot Jurisdiction of the Emperor of Ethiopia." *JAL*, 8 (2) (1959): 59–76.

——. *The Conflict of Laws in Ethiopia*. New York: OUP, 1966.

——. "The Development of Legal Systems: The Ethiopian Experience." *Iowa Law Review*, 53 (3) (1967): 562–635.

——. "Nationality, Domicile and Personal Law in Ethiopia." *JEL*, 2 (1) (1965): 161–79.

Selamu Bekele and J. Vanderlinden. "Introducing the Ethiopian Law Archives: Some Documents on the First Ethiopian Cabinet." *JEL*, 4 (2) (1967): 411–31.

Serapiao, Luis. "International Law and Self-Determination: The Case of Eritrea." *Issue: A Journal of Opinion*, 15 (1987): 3–8.

Singer, Norman Joseph. "The Ethiopian Civil Code and the Recognition of Customary Law." *Houston Law Review*, 9 (3) (1972): 460–94.

——. "Islamic Law and the Development of the Ethiopian Legal Code." *Howard Law Journal*, 17 (1) (1971): 130–68.

——. "Legal Development in Post-Revolutionary Ethiopia." *HA*, 1 (2) (1978): 21–27.

——. "From Tradition to Tradition: Legal Modernization in Ethiopia." SJD diss., Harvard University, 1975.

——. "A Traditional Legal Institution in a Modern Legal Setting: The Atbia Dagnia of Ethiopia." *UCLA Law Review*, 18 (2) (1970): 308–34.

Sisaye Seleshi. "Human Rights and U.S. Aid to Ethiopia: A Policy Dilemma." *AQ*, 18 (4) (1979): 17–30.

Steen, William M. *The Ethiopian Constitution*. Washington, D.C.: Ethiopian Research Council, 1936.

Syoum Gebregziabher. *Collection of Labour Laws of Ethiopia*. Addis Ababa: The Federation of Employers of Ethiopia, [1967].

United States. Department of Labor. *Labor Law and Practices in the Empire of Ethiopia*. Washington, D.C.: Bureau of Labor Statistics, 1966.

United States. House of Representatives. Committee on Foreign Affairs. Subcommittees on Human Rights and International Organizations, International Economic Policy and Trade, and on Africa. *Human Rights in Ethiopia, 1987*. Washington, D.C.: USGPO, 1987.

Vanderlinden, Jacques. *Introduction au Droit de l'Éthiopie Moderne*. Paris: Librairie Générale de Droit et de Jurisprudence, 1971.

——. "A Further Note on an Introduction to the Sources of Ethiopian Law." *JEL*, 3 (2) (1966): 635–39.

——. "An Introduction to the Sources of Ethiopian Law, from the 13th to the 20th Century." *JEL*, 3 (1) (1966): 227–83.

Vestal, Theodore M. "An Analysis of the New Constitution of Ethiopia and the Process of Its Adoption." *NAS*, 3 (2) (1996): 21–38.

Vosikis, Nicolas. *Le Trust dans le Code Civil Éthiopien: Étude de Droit Éthiopien avec Référence au Droit Anglais*. Genève: Librairie Droz, 1975.

Yacob Haile Mariam. "The Quest for Justice and Reconciliation: The International Criminal Tribunal for Rwanda and the Ethiopian High Court." *International and Comparative Law Review*, 22 (4) (1999): 667–745.

Yonas Kebede. "Legal Aspects of the Ethiopian-Somali Dispute." *HA*, 1 (1) (1978): 26–31.

Zack, Arnold M. "The New Labour Relations Law in Ethiopia." *Bulletin of International African Labour Institute*, 12 (1965): 223–33.

Zakir Ibrahim. "Legal Aspects of Ethiopia's Deportation of Undesirable Eritrean Citizens." *Ethioscope*, 5 (1) (1999): 14–22.

Government and Politics

Aaron Tesfaye. "Political Power and Democratization in Ethiopia." Ph.D. diss., Claremont Graduate University. 1996.

Abbink, Jon G. "Breaking and Making the State: The Dynamics of Ethnic Democracy in Ethiopia." *Journal of Contemporary African Studies*, 13 (2) (1995): 149–63.

——. "New Configurations of Ethiopian Ethnicity: The Challenge of the South." *NAS*, 5 (1) (1998): 59–81.

——. "Violence and the Crisis of Conciliation: Suri, Dizi and the State in South-West Ethiopia." *Africa*, 70 (4) (2000): 527–50.

Abdi, Said Yusuf. "Self-Determination for the Ogaden Somalis." *HA*, 1 (1) (1978): 20–25.

Abebe Zegeye and Siegfried Pausewang (eds.). *Ethiopia in Change: Peasantry, Nationalism and Democracy*. London: British Academic Press, 1994.

Acheson-Brown, Daniel G. "The Ethiopian Revolution: An Ideological Analysis." *HA*, 15 (1–4) (1997): 92–109.

Alem Asres. "History of the Ethiopian Student Movement: Its Impact on Internal Social Change, 1960–1974." Ph.D. diss., University of Maryland College Park, 1990.

Alemseged Abbay. *Identity Jilted or Re–imaging Identity? The Divergent Paths of the Eritrean and Tigrayan Nationalist Struggles*. Lawrenceville, N.J.: RSP, 1996.

Alemu Mekonnen. "Efficiency of Ethiopian Public Manufacturing Enterprises and the Policy Environment." *Ethiopian Journal of Economics*, 1 (2) (1992): 38–52.

Arthur, Pamela Ann. "The Ethiopian Revolution: A Revolution from Above and Its Outcomes." Ph.D. diss., Northwestern University, 1982.

Asafa Jalata. "The Emergence of Oromo Nationalism and Ethiopian Reaction." *Social Justice*, 22 (3) (1995): 165–89.

——. *Oromia and Ethiopia: State Formation and Ethnonational Conflict, 1868–1992*. Boulder, Colo.: LR, 1993.

——. *Oromo Nationalism and the Ethiopian Discourse: The Search for Freedom and Democracy*. Lawrenceville, N.J.: RSP, 1998.

——. "The Question of Oromia: Euro–Ethiopian Colonialism, Global Hegemonism and Nationalism, 1870s–1980s." Ph.D. diss., State University of New York at Binghamton, 1990.

——. "Two National Liberation Movements Compared: Oromia and the Southern Sudan." *Social Justice*, 27 (1) (2000): 152–74.

Asamenew G. W. Gebeyehu. "The Background to the Political Crisis in Ethiopia." *Ufahamu*, 18 (1) (1990): 25–40.

Asamenew G. W. Gebeyehu. "Background to the Political Crisis in Ethiopia: The Post-Monarchy Predicament." *Ufahamu*, 18 (2) (1990): 2–12.

Asmarom Legesse. *Oromo Democracy: An Indigenous African Political System*. Lawrenceville, N.J.: RSP, 2000.

Asmelash Beyene. "Civil Service Reform in Ethiopia." *African Administrative Studies*, 51 (1998): 97–115.

Asmelash Beyene, and John Markakis. "Representative Institutions in Ethiopia." *JMAS*, 5 (2) (1967): 193–219.

Assefa Negash. *The Pillage of Ethiopia by Eritreans and Their Tigrean Surrogates*. Los Angeles: Adey Publishing Company, 1996.

Bahru Zewde and Siegfried Pausewang (eds.). *Ethiopia: The Challenge of Democracy from Below*. Uppsala: Nordiska Afrikainstitutet, 2002.

Brons, Maria, Martin R. Doornbos, and M.A. Mohamed Salih. "The Somali-Ethiopians: The Quest for Alternative Futures." *Eastern Africa Social Science Research Review*, 11 (2) (1995): 45–70.

Brüne, Stefan. "Ideology, Government, and Development: The People's Democratic Republic of Ethiopia." *NAS*, 12 (2/3) (1990): 189–99.

Busha J. Taa. "The Ethiopian Revolution and the Challenge of Tradition, 1974–1991." M.A. thesis, University of Western Ontario (Canada), 1997.

Campbell, Will. *The Potential for Donor Mediation in NGO-State Relations: An Ethiopian Case Study*. Brighton: University of Sussex Institute of Development Studies Working Paper, 1996.

Chege, Michael. "The Revolution Betrayed: Ethiopia, 1974–9." *JMAS*, 17 (3) (1979): 359–80.

Clapham, Christopher. *Haile Selassie's Government*. New York: Frederick A. Praeger. 1969.

——. "Imperial Leadership in Ethiopia." *AA* (1968) 68 (271) (1969): 110–20.

——. "The Institutions of the Central Ethiopian Government." D.Phil. diss., Oxford University, 1966.

——. *Nationalism, Nationality, and Regionalism in Ethiopia*. John Hack Memorial Lecture at Lancaster University, November 1995.

——. "Revolutionary Socialist Development in Ethiopia." *AA*, 86 (343) (1987): 151–65.

——. "The Socialist Experience in Ethiopia and its Demise." *Journal of Communist Studies*, 8 (2) (1992): 105–25.

——. "State, Society, and Political Institutions in Revolutionary Ethiopia." *Institute of Development Studies Bulletin*, 21 (4 (1990): 35–45.

——. *Transformation and Continuity in Revolutionary Ethiopia*. Cambridge: Cambridge University Press, 1988.

Cohen, John Michael. "Analysing the Ethiopia Revolution: A Cautionary Tale." *JMAS*, 18 (4) (1980): 685–91.

——. "Decentralization and 'Ethnic Federalism' in Post–Civil War Ethiopia." In K. Kumar (ed.). *Rebuilding Societies after Civil War: Critical Roles or International Assistance*. Boulder: LR, 1997: 135–53.

——. "Ethnic Federalism in Ethiopia." *NAS*, 2 (2) (1995): 157–88.

——. *"Ethnic Federalism" in Ethiopia*. Cambridge, Mass.: Harvard Institute for International Development, 1995.

——. Forrest D. "The People's Democratic Republic of Ethiopia: Masking and Unmasking Tragedy." *World Politics*, 43 (4) (1991): 570–86.

Copley, Gregory R. *Ethiopia Reaches Her Hand unto God: Imperial Ethiopia's Unique Symbols, Structures, and Role in the Modern World*. Alexandria, Va.: Defense and Foreign Affairs, 1998.

Courlander, Harold. "The Emperor Wore Clothes: Visiting Haile Selassie in 1943." *American Scholar*, 58 (2) (1989): 271–81.

Crummey, Donald. "Society, State, and Nationality in the Recent Historiography of Ethiopia." *JAH*, 31 (1) (1990): 103–19.

Dabala Olana. "Success and Survival in Rural Oromia: Aspects of Contending with an Empire State." Ph.D. diss., University of Calgary, 1996.

Dessalegn Rahmato. "The Political Economy of Development in Ethiopia." In Edmond J. Keller and Donald Rothchild (eds.). *Afro-Marxist Regimes: Ideology and Public Policy*. Boulder: LR, 1987: 155–79.

Donham, Donald L. *Marxist Modern: An Ethnographic History of the Ethiopian Revolution*. Berkeley: University of California Press, 1999.

D'Silva, Brian and Peter Koehn. "Analysing the Ethiopian Revolution: A Rebuttal." *JMAS*, 20 (3) (1982): 513–19

Ellis, Gene. "Questions about Socialism in Ethiopia: A Preliminary Inquiry." *NAS*, 2 (3) (1980/1981): 181–88.

Eshete Taddesse. "The State and Performance of Public Enterprises in Ethiopia." *Ethiopian Journal of Economics*, 4 (1) (1995): 1–38.

Ethiopia. Ministry of Information. *Important Utterances of H.I.M. Emperor Haile Selassie I 1963–1972*. Addis Ababa: Imperial Ethiopian Ministry of Information, 1972.

——. *Selected Speeches of His Imperial Majesty Haile Selassie I, 1918–1967*. Addis Ababa: Imperial Ethiopian Ministry of Information, 1967.

——. *Speeches Delivered by His Imperial Majesty Haile Selassie Ist Emperor of Ethiopia on Various Occasions, May 1957–December 1959*. Addis Ababa: Ministry of Information, 1960.

Ethiopian Human Rights Council. *EHRCO's 1st Report on May General Election: Problems of the Registration Process*. Addis Ababa: Ethiopian Human Rights Council, 2000.

Ethiopian Students Union in North America. "The National Democratic Revolution in Ethiopia." *Challenge*, 12 (1) (1972): 1–102.

Fentahun Tiruneh. *The Ethiopian Students: Their Struggle to Articulate the Ethipian Revolution*. Chicago: Nyala Type, 1990.

Gaitachew Bekele. *The Emperor's Clothes: A Personal Viewpoint on Politics and Administration in the Imperial Ethiopian Government 1941–1974*. East Lansing: Michigan State University Press, 1993.

Gebru Tareke. "Resistance in Tigray (Ethiopia): From Weyane to TPLF." *HA*, 6 (4) (1983/1984): 15–29.

Ghelawdewos Araia. *Ethiopia: The Political Economy of Transition*. Lanham, Md.: University Press of America, 1995.

Giday Degefu Koraro. *Traditional Mechanisms of Conflict Resolution in Ethiopia*. Addis Ababa: Ethiopian International Institute for Peace and Development, 2000.

——. "Ethiopia: A Real Revolution?" *WT*, 31 (1) (1975): 15–23.

Girma Negash. "Language and Politics: A Comparative Analysis of Revolutionary Rhetoric of Regime Leaders and Power Contenders between 1974 and 1977." Ph.D. diss., University of Colorado Boulder, 1982.

Greenfield, Richard David. *Ethiopia: A New Political History*. New York: Praeger, 1965.

Guebre-Heywet Baykedagne. *L'Empereur Menelik et l'Ethiopie*. Addis Ababa: Maison des Etudes Ethiopiennes, 1993.

Gupta, Vijay. "The Ethiopian Revolution: Causes and Results." *India Quarterly*, 34 (2) (1978): 158–74.

Halliday, Fred and Maxine Molyneux. *The Ethiopian Revolution*. London: Verso, 1981.

Hamdesa Tuso. "Ethiopia: New Political Order—Ethnic Conflict in the Post Cold War Era." *Africa*, 52 (3) (1997): 343–64.

Harbeson, John Willis. "Elections and Democratization in Post-Mengistu Ethiopia." In Krishna Kumar (ed.). *Post-Conflict Elections, Democratization, and Democratic Assistance*. Boulder, Colo.: LR, 1998: 111–32.

——. "The Ethiopian Crisis: Alternative Scenarios for Change." *HA*, 13/14 (3/4 and 1/2) (1990/1991): 121–31.

——. *The Ethiopian Transformation: The Quest for the Post-Imperial State*. Boulder, Colo.: WP, 1988.

——. "The Future of the Ethiopian State after Mengistu." *CH*, 92 (574) (1993): 208–12.

——. "Is Ethiopia Democratic? A Bureaucratic Authoritarian Regime." *Journal of Democracy*, 9 (4) (1998): 62–69.

——. "Perspectives on the Ethiopian Revolution." *EN*, 1 (1) (1977): 1–8.

——. "Perspectives on the Ethiopian Transformation: Variations on Common Themes." *NAS*, 12 (2/3) (1990): 65–89.

——. "Socialism, Traditions, and Revolutionary Politics in Contemporary Ethiopia." *CJAS*, 11 (2) (1977): 217–34.

——. "Socialist Politics in Revolutionary Ethiopia." In Carl G. Rosberg and Thomas M. Callaghy (eds.). *Socialism in Sub-Saharan Africa: A New Assessment*. Berkeley: Institute of International Studies, University of California, 1979: 345–417.

——. "State, Revolution, and Development in Ethiopia." *African Studies Association Papers*, 28 (49) (1985): 1–36.

——. "Whither the Revolution?" *AR*, 21 (4) (1976): 48–54.

Harris, Myles F. *Breakfast in Hell: A Doctor's Eyewitness Account of the Politics of Hunger in Ethiopia*. New York: Poseidon Press, 1987.

Harsch, E. *The Ethiopian Revolution*. New York: Pathfinder Press, 1978.

Henze, Paul Bernard. "Communism and Ethiopia." *Problems of Communism*, 30 (3) (1981): 55–74.

——. *Communist Ethiopia: Is It Succeeding?* Santa Monica, Calif.: Rand Corporation, 1985.

——. *The Defeat of the Derg and the Establishment of New Governments in Ethiopia and Eritrea*. Santa Monica, Calif.: Rand Corporation, 1992.

——. *Ethiopia in Early 1989*. Santa Monica, Calif.: Rand Corporation, 1990.

——. *Ethiopia in 1990: The Revolution Unraveling*. Santa Monica, Calif.: Rand Corporation, 1991.

——. *Ethiopia in 1991: Peace Through Struggle*. Santa Monica, Calif.: Rand Corporation, 1991.

——. *Ethiopia: The Fall of the Derg and the Beginning of Recovery under the EPRDF (March 1990–March 1992)*. Santa Monica, Calif.: Rand Corporation, 1995.

——. "Ethiopia: Post-Communist Transition and Adjustment to Eritrean Independence." *Problems of Post-Communism*, 42 (5) (1995): 40–49.

——. *The Ethiopian Revolution: Mythology and History*. Santa Monica, Calif.: Rand Corporation, 1989. Also, in *NAS*, 12 (2/3) (1990): 1–17.

——. *Glasnost about Building Socialism in Ethiopia*. Santa Monica, Calif.: Rand Corporation, 1990.

——. "Marxism-Leninism in Ethiopia: Political Impasse and Economic Deterioration." In Michael Clough (ed.). *Reassessing the Soviet Challenge in Africa*. Berkeley: Institute of International Studies, University of California, 1986: 31–47.

——. "Marxist Disaster and Cultural Survival in Ethiopia." *Problems of Communism*, 39 (6) (1990): 66–80.

——. *Mengistu's Ethiopian Marxist State in Terminal Crisis*. Santa Monica, Calif.: Rand Corporation, 1990.

——. "A Political Success Story." *Journal of Democracy*, 9 (4) (1998): 40–54.

Hess, Robert Lee. "Ethiopia." In Gwendolen M. Carter (ed.). *National Unity and Regionalism in Eight African States*. Ithaca: Cornell University Press, 1970: 441–538.

——. *Ethiopia: The Modernization of Autocracy*. Ithaca and London: Cornell University Press, 1970.

Hess, Robert Lee, and Gerhard Loewenberg. "The Ethiopian No-Party State: A Note on the Function of Political Parties in Developing States." *American Political Science Review*, 58 (4) (1964): 947–50.

Hinterwirth, E. M. "Ethiopia, 1974–1991: Chronicle of a Revolution. Implementation of State Power by Socialist-Oriented Leadership." Ph.D. diss., Universitaet Wien, 1992.

Holcomb, Bonnie K. "The Tale of Two Democracies: The Encounter between USA-Sponsored Ethiopian 'Democracy' and Indigenous Oromo Democratic Forms." *JOS*, 4 (1/2) (1997): 47–82.

Howard, William Edward Harding. *Public Administration in Ethiopia: A Study in Retrospect and Prospect*. Groningen: Wolters, 1955.

Huntington, Samuel P. *Political Development in Ethiopia: A Peasant-Based Dominant-Party Democracy?* Addis Ababa: Report to USAID/Ethiopia, 1993.

Joireman, Sandra Fullerton. "Opposition Politics and Ethnicity in Ethiopia: We Will All Go Down Together." *JMAS*, 35 (3) (1997): 387–407.

Joseph, Richard. "Oldspeak vs. Newspeak." *Journal of Democracy*, 9 (4) (1998): 55–61.

Kassahun Ber Hanu. "Ethiopia Elects a Constituent Assembly." *ROAPE*, 22 (63) (1995): 129–35.

Kassim Shehim. "Ethiopia, Revolution, and the Question of Nationalities: The Case of the Afar." *JMAS*, 23 (2) (1985): 331–48.

Katz, Donald R. "Children's Revolution: A Bloodbath in Ethiopia." *HA*, 1 (3) (1978): 3–11.

Keller, Edmond J. "Ethiopia: Revolution, Class, and the National Question." *AA*, 80 (321) (1981): 519–49.

——. "The Ethiopian Revolution at the Crossroads." *CH*, 83 (491) (1984): 117–21, 137–38.

——. "Ethiopian Revolution: How Socialist Is It?" *JAS*, 11 (2) (1984): 52–65.

——. "The Ethnogenesis of the Oromo Nation and Its Implications for Politics in Ethiopia." *JMAS*, 33 (4) (1995): 621–34.

——. "Remaking the Ethiopian State." In I. William Zartman (ed.). *Collapsed States: The Disintegration and Restoration of Legitimate Authority*. Boulder, CO: LR, 1995: 125–39.

——. "Revolution and the Collapse of Traditional Monarchies, Ethiopia." In Barry M. Schutz and Robert O. Slater (eds.). *Revolution and Political Change in the Third World*. Boulder, Colo.: LR, 1990: 81–98.

——. "Revolution and State Power in Ethiopia." *CH*, 87 (529) (1988): 217–23.

——. "Revolution, Class, and the National Question: The Case of Ethiopia." *NAS*, 2/3 (3/1) (1980/1981): 43–68.

——. *Revolutionary Ethiopia: From Empire to People's Republic*. Bloomington: Indiana University Press, 1988.

——. "Revolutionary Ethiopia: Ideology, Capacity, and the Limits of State Autonomy." *Journal of Commonwealth Comparative Politics*, 23 (1985): 112–39.

——. "The Revolutionary Transformation of Ethiopia's Twentieth-Century Bureaucratic Empire." *JMAS*, 19 (2) (1981): 307–35.

——. "State, Party, and Revolution in Ethiopia." *ASR*, 28 (1) (1985): 1–18.

Keller, Edmond J., and Barbara Thomas-Wooley. "Majority Rule and Minority Rights: American Federalism and African Experience." *JMAS*, 32 (3) (1994): 411–27.

Kidane Mengisteab. "New Approaches to State Building in Africa: The Case of Ethiopia's Ethnic-Based Federalism." *ASR*, 40 (3) (1997): 111–32.

Kiflu Tadesse. *The Generation: The History of the Ethiopian People's Revolutionary Party, Part I: From the Early Beginnings to 1975.* Trenton, N.J.: RSP, 1993.

——. *The Generation Part II: Ethiopia Transformation and Conflict. The History of the Ethiopian People's Revolutionary Party.* Lanham, Md.: University Press of America, 1998.

Klein, K. *Pre-Election Technical Assessment Report.* Washington, D.C.: International Foundation for Election Studies, 1994.

Knife Abraham. *Ethiopia: From Bullets to the Ballot Box—The Bumpy Ride to Democracy and the Political Economy of Democracy.* Lawrenceville, N.J.: RSP, 1994.

Koehn, Peter. "Ethiopian Politics: Military Intervention and Prospects for Further Change." *AT*, 22 (2) (1975): 7–21.

Kumssa Asfaw. "Ethiopia, Revolution, and the National Question: The Case of the Oromos." *JAS*, 15 1/2 (1988): 16–22.

Lefort, Rene. *Ethiopia: An Heretical Revolution?* London: ZB, 1981.

Legesse Lemma. "Political Economy of Ethiopia 1875–1974: Agricultural, Educational, and International Antecedents of the Revolution." Ph.D. diss., University of Notre Dame, 1980.

Legum, Colin. *Ethiopia: The Fall of Haile Selassie's Empire.* New York: Africana Publishing, 1975.

——. "Realities of the Ethiopian Revolution." *WT*, 33 (8) (1977): 305–12.

Leenco Lata. *The Ethiopian State at the Crossroads: Decolonization and Democracy or Disintegration?* Lawrenceville, N.J.: RSP, 1999.

Levine, Donald Nathan. "Ethiopia: Identity, Authority, and Realism." In Lucian W. Pye and Sidney Verba (eds.). *Political Culture and Political Development.* Princeton, N.J.: Princeton University Press, 1965: 245–81.

Lewis, William. "Ethiopia: The Quickening Pulse." *CH*, 54 (318) (1968): 78–82, 114.

——. "The Ethiopian Empire: Progress and Problems." *Middle East Journal*, 10 (3) (1956): 257–68.

Logan, Rayford W. "Ethiopia's Troubled Future." *CH*, 44 (257) (1963): 46–50, 54.

Lyons, Terrence. "Closing the Transition: The May 1995 Elections in Ethiopia." *JMAS*, 34 (1) (1996): 121–42.

Major Asseged. "Ethiopia: Revolution and War, 1974–1978." Ph.D. diss., University of Denver, 1982.

Markakis, John. *Ethiopia: Anatomy of a Traditional Polity*. London: Oxford University Press, 1974.

——. "Nationalities and the State in Ethiopia." *TWQ*, 10 (4) (1989): 118–47.

——. "Social Formation and Political Adaptation in Ethiopia." *JMAS*, 11 (3) (1973): 361–81.

——. "The Somali in the New Political Order of Ethiopia." In Hussein M. Adam and Richard Ford (eds.). *Mending Rips in the Sky*. Lawrenceville, NJ: RSP, 1997: 497–513.

Markakis, John, and Nega Ayele. *Class and Revolution in Ethiopia*. Trenton, N.J.: RSP, 1986.

McClellan, Charles W. "State Transformation and Social Reconstitution in Ethiopia: The Allure of the South." *IJAHS*, 17 (4) (1984): 657–75.

McDonald, Steve. "Learning a Lesson." *AR*, 37 (5) (1992): 27–29.

Meheret Ayenaw. "Public Administration in Ethiopia, 1974–1991: Administrative and Policy Responses to Turbulence." Ph.D. diss., State University of New York at Albany, 1997.

Meldrum, Andrew. "Mengistu's Golden Parachute." *AR*. 36 (4) (1991): 42–44.

Mengistu Haile Mariam. "Ethiopia Under Fire." *The African Communist*, (71) (1977): 92–97.

——. "Our Fight Is with Those Opposed to the Masses." *Africa*, (79) (1978): 12–16.

——. *Replies to Questions from* Time *Magazine*. Addis Ababa: CCWPE Press Section. July 1986.

Mesfin Araya. "Preliminary Notes on State and Society: The Current Crisis in Ethiopia." *NAS*, 11 (3) (1989): 41–49.

Messay Kebede. *Survival and Modernization: Ethiopia's Enigmatic Present— A Philosophical Discourse*. Lawrenceville, N.J.: RSP, 1999.

Messing, Simon David. "Changing Ethiopia." *Middle East Journal*, 9 (4) (1955): 413–32.

Michaelson, Marc. "Ethnic Federalism in Ethiopia." *Institute of Current World Affairs Letters*, (1999): 1–10.

Moore, W. Robert. "Coronation Days in Addis Ababa." *NGM*, 59 (6) (1931): 738–46.

National Democratic Institute for International Affairs and the African American Institute. *An Evaluation of the June 21, 1992 Election in Ethiopia*. New York: African American Institute, 1992.

Nega Mezlekia. *Notes from a Hyena's Belly: An Ethiopian Boyhood*. New York: Picador USA, 2000.

"The Oromos: Voice against Tyranny." *HA*, 3 (3) (1980): 15–23.

Ottaway, Marina (ed.). "Ethiopia: The Fifteenth Year of the Revolution." *Comparative Politics*, 23 (2) (1991): 239–48.

——. "The Ethiopian Transition: Democratization or New Authoritarianism?" *NAS*, (NS) 2 (3) (1995): 67–84.

——. (ed.). *The Political Economy of Ethiopia*. New York: Praeger, 1990.

——. "Social Classes and Corporate Interests in the Ethiopian Revolution." *JMAS*, 14 (3) (1976): 469–86.

Ottaway, Marina, and David Ottaway. *Ethiopia: Empire in Revolution*. New York: Africana Publishing, 1978.

Norwegian Institute of Human Rights. *Local and Regional Elections in Ethiopia 21 June 1992*. Oslo: Norwegian Institute of Human Rights. 1992.

Pankhurst, Richard. "Tribute, Taxation, and Government Revenues in Nineteenth and Early Twentieth Century Ethiopia" Part I, *JES*, 5 (2) (1967): 37–87; Part II, 6 (1) (1968): 21–72; and Part III, 6 (2) (1968): 93–118.

Pausewang, Siegfried. *The 1994 Election and Democracy in Ethiopia*. Oslo: Norwegian Institute for Human Rights, 1994.

Pausewang, Siegfried, Kjetil Tronvoll, and Lovise Aalen (eds.). *Ethiopia since the Derg: A Decade of Democratic Pretension and Performance*. London: Zed Books, 2002.

Perham, Margery. *The Government of Ethiopia*. Evanston: Northwestern University Press, 1969.

Pliny the Middle-Aged (pseud.). "The Lives and Times of the Dergue." *NAS*, 5 (3) (1983/1984): 1–41.

——. "The PMAC: Origins and Structure." Part 1 *EN*, 2 (3) (1978/1979): 1–18.

——. "The PMAC: Origins and Structure." Part 2 *NAS*, 1 (1) (1979): 1–20.

Poluha, Eva. "Conceptualizing Democracy: Elections in the Ethiopian Countryside." *NAS*, 4 (1) (1997): 39–70.

Prendergast, John, and Mark Duffield. "Liberation Politics in Ethiopia and Eritrea." In Taisier M. Ali and Robert O. Matthews (eds.). *Civil Wars in Africa: Roots and Resolution*. Montreal: McGill-Queen's University Press, 1999: 35–51.

Roberts, John. "Seignorage and Resource Mobilization in Socialist Ethiopia." *Development Policy Review*, 10 (3) (1992): 271–88.

Rock, June. "Ethiopia Elects a New Parliament." *ROAPE*, 23 (67) (1996): 92–102.

Schwab, Peter. *Decision-Making in Ethiopia: A Study of the Political Process*. London: Hurst, 1972.

Seyoum Hameso (ed.). *Ethiopia: Conquest and the Quest for Freedom and Democracy*. London: TSC Publications, 1997.

Sherr, E. M. "Political Structure of Ethiopia." *NAS*, 12 (2/3) (1990): 177–88.

Silberman, Leo. "Ethiopia: Power of Moderation." *Middle East Journal*, 14 (2) (1960): 141–52.

Southard, Addison E. "Modern Ethiopia." *NGM*, 59 (6) (1931): 679–738.

Steffanson, Borg G., and Ronald Starrett. *Documents on Ethiopian Politics. Volume I, The Decline of Menelik II to the Emergence of Ras Tafari, Later Known as Haile Selassie 1910–1919*. Salisbury, N.C.: Documentary Publications, 1976.

Steiner, H. Arthur. "The Government of Italian East Africa." *The American Political Science Review*, 30 (5) (1936): 884–902.

Tarekegn Adebo. "Democratic Political Development in Reference to Ethiopia." *NAS*, 3 (2) (1996): 53–96.

Tecola W. Hagos. *Democratization? Ethiopia (1991–1994): A Personal View*. Cambridge: Khepera Publishers, 1995.

Teferra Haile-Selassie. *The Ethiopian Revolution 1974–1991: From a Monarchical Autocracy to a Military Oligarchy*. London: Kegan Paul International, 1997.

Tesema Ta'a. "The Political Economy of Western Central Ethiopia: From the Mid–Sixteenth to the Early Twentieth Centuries." Ph.D. diss., Michigan State University, 1986.

Teshale Tibebu. "Ethiopia: The 'Anomaly' and 'Paradox' of Africa." *Journal of Black Studies*, 26 (4) (1996): 414–30.

Teshome Mulat. "Trends in Government Finance." *Ethiopian Journal of Economics*, 2 (1) (1993): 73–100.

Tibebe Eshete. "The Root Causes of Political Problems in the Ogaden, 1942–1960." *NAS*, 13 (1) (1991): 9–28.

Tronvoll, Kjetil. "Voting, Violence, and Violations: Peasant Voices on the Flawed Elections in Hadiya, Southern Ethiopia." *JMAS*, 39 (4) (2001): 697–716.

Tronvoll, Kjetil, and Ø. Aadland. *The Process of Democratisation in Ethiopia: An Expression of Popular Participation or Political Resistance?* Oslo: Norwegian Institute of Human Rights, 1995.

Tseggai Isaac. "Policy Efforts of a Weak State: Ethiopia before and after the 1974 Revolution." Ph.D. diss., University of Missouri Columbia, 1991.

United States. House of Representatives. Committee on Foreign Affairs. Subcommittee on Africa. *Ethiopia: The Challenges Ahead*. Washington, D.C.: USGPO, 1994.

——. *Looking Back and Reaching Forward: Prospects for Democracy in Ethiopia*. Washington, D.C.: USGPO, 1993.

Vaughan, Sarah. *The Addis Ababa Transitional Conference of July 1991: Its Origins, History and Significance*. Edinburgh: Centre of African Studies, Edinburgh University, 1994.

Waal, Alex de. "Ethiopia: Transition to What?" *World Policy Journal*, 9 (4) (1992): 719–37.

Walle Engedayehu. "Ethiopia: Democracy and the Politics of Ethnicity." *AT*, 40 (2) (1993): 29–52.

——. "Ethiopia: Pitfalls of Ethnic Federalism." *AQ*, 34 (2) (1994): 149–92.

Warr, Michael. "There's a Revolution in Ethiopia." *HA*, 2 (3) (1979): 4–10.

Yohannes Petros. "A Survey of Political Parties in Ethiopia." *NAS*, 13 (2/3) (1991): 141–64.

Young, John. "Development and Change in Post-Revolution Tigray." *JMAS*, 35 (1) (1997): 81–99.

——. "Ethnicity and Power in Ethiopia." *ROAPE*, 23 (70) (1996): 531–42.

——. "Regionalism and Democracy in Ethiopia." *TWQ*, 19 (2) (1998): 191–204.

——. "The Tigray and Eritrean Peoples Liberation Fronts: A History of Tensions and Pragmatism." *JMAS*, 34 (1) (1996): 105–20.

Anthropology, Ethnology, Local History, and Paleoanthropology

Abbink, Jon. "The Deconstruction of 'Tribe': Ethnicity and Politics in Southwestern Ethiopia." *JES*, 24 (1991): 1–21.

——. "Ethnic Conflict in the 'Tribal Zone': The Dizi and Suri in Southern Ethiopia." *JMAS*, 31 (4) (1993): 675–82.

——. "Ritual and Political Forms of Violent Practice among the Suri of Southern Ethiopia." *CEA*, 38 (2/4) (1998): 271–95.

——. "Settling the Surma: Notes on an Ethiopian Relief Experiment." *Human Organization*, 51 (2) (1992): 174–80.

——. "Tribal Formation on the Ethiopian Fringe: Toward a History of the 'Tishana'." *NAS*, 12 (1) (1990): 21–42.

——. "Violence, Ritual, and Reproduction: Culture and Context in Surma Dueling." *Ethnology*, 38 (3) (1999): 227–42.

Abdussamad H. Ahmad. "Priest Planters and Slavers of Zage." *IJAHS*, 29 (3) (1996): 543–56.

Almagor, Uri. "Alternation Endogamy in the Dassanetch Generation-Set System." *Ethnology*, 22 (2) (1983): 93–108.

——. "The Social Organization of the Dassanetch of the Lower Omo." Ph.D. diss., Manchester University, 1971.

——. "The Year of the Emperor and the Elephant." *NAS*, 7 (1) (1985): 1–22.

Alula Abate and Fekade Gedamu. *The Afar in Transition: Some Critical Issues in Pastoral Rehabilitation and Development*. Addis Ababa: Ethiopian Red Cross Society, 1988.

Alvisini, Alesia. "I Rapporti Politico-Economici Fra Gli Oromo e l'Italia: Alleanze e Ambiquita." *Africa*, 55 (4) (2000): 489–521.

Ayele Gebre Mariam. "Labour Inputs and Time Allocation among the Afar." *Nomadic Peoples*, (23) (1987): 37–56.

Bahru Zewde. "The Aymallal Gurage in the Nineteenth Century: A Political History." *TJH*, 2 (2) (1972): 54–68.

Bartels, Lambert. *Oromo Religion: Myths and Rites of the Western Oromo of Ethiopia: An Attempt to Understand*. Berlin: Dietrich Reiner, 1983.

——. "The Western Oromo: Some Important Aspects of Their Religion." *Quaderni di Studi Etiopici*, 3/4 (1982/1983): 122–62.

Bassi, Marco. "The Complexity of a Pastoral African Polity: An Introduction to the Council Organization of the Borana-Oromo." *JES*, 32 (2) (1999): 15–33.

———. *The Borana: An Ethiopian Society of Consentaneity*. London: Haan Associates, 1999.

Bauer, Dan Franz. "Land, Leadership, and Legitimacy Among the Inderta Tigray of Ethiopia." Ph.D. diss., University of Rochester, 1973.

Baxter, Paul T. W. "Ethiopia's Unacknowledged Problem: The Oromo." *AA*, 77 (308) (1978): 283–96.

Baxter, Paul T. W., Jan Hultin, and Alessandro Triulzi (eds.). *Being and Becoming Oromo: Historical and Anthropological Enquires*. Lawrenceville, N.J.: RSP, 1996.

Beckwith, Carol, and Angela Fisher. "The Eloquent Surma of Ethiopia." *NGM*, 179 (2) (1991): 76–99.

Bender, M. Lionel (ed.). *Peoples and Cultures of the Ethio-Sudan Borderlands*. East Lansing: Michigan State University, 1981.

Berhane Asfaw, et al. "Australopithecus Garhi: A New Species of Early Hominid from Ethiopia." *Science*, 284 (5414) (1999): 629–35.

———. "The Earliest Acheulean from Konso-Gardula." *Nature*, 360 (6406) (1992): 732–35.

Blackhurst, Hector. "A Community of Shoa Galla Settlers in Southern Ethiopia." Ph.D. diss., Manchester University, 1974.

———. "Ethnicity in Southern Ethiopia: The General and the Particular." *Africa*, 50 (1) (1980): 54–65.

———. "The Konso of Ethiopia." *Africa*, 45 (1) (1975): 96–97.

Blakely, Clarence L. *The Ethiopians*. New York: Independence Publishing Company, 1931.

Boaz, Dorothy Dechant. "Modern Riverine Taphonomy: Its Relevance to the Interpretation of Plio-Pleistocene Hominid Paleoecology in the Omo Basin, Ethiopia." Ph.D. diss., University of California Berkeley, 1982.

Boaz, Noel Thomas. "Paleoecology of Plio-Pleistocene Hominidae in the Lower Omo Basin, Ethiopia." Ph.D. diss., University of California Berkeley, 1977.

Bobe, Rene. "Hominid Environments in the Pliocene: An Analysis of Fossil Mammals from the Omo Valley, Ethiopia." Ph.D. diss., University of Washington, 1997.

Braimah, J. A., H. H. Tomlinson, and Osafroadu Amankwatia. *History and Traditions of the Gonja*. Calgary: University of Calgary Press, 1997.

Brogger, J. "Spirit Possession and Management of Aggression among the Sidamo." *Ethnos*, 40 (1975): 285–90.

Brooke, Charles Harding. "The Galla of North-Eastern Africa." *Geographical Review*, 47 (1957): 275–77.

——. "Settlements of the Eastern Galla, Hararge Province, Ethiopia." Ph.D. diss., University of Nebraska, 1956.

Cappelli, Vanni. "The Oromo of Ethiopia: Africa's Nation Manque." *HA*, 15 (1–4) (1997): 81–91.

Cerulli, Ernesta. *Peoples of South-West Ethiopia and Its Borderland*. London: IAI, 1956.

Chiatti, Remo. "The Politics of Divine Kingship in Wolaita, 19th and 20th Centuries." Ph.D. diss., University of Pennsylvania, 1984.

Clamons, Cynthia Robb. "Gender in Oromo." Ph.D. diss., University of Minnesota, 1992.

Clark, J. D. et al. "African Homo Erectus: Old Radiometric Ages and Young Oldowan Assemblages in the Middle Awash Valley, Ethiopia." *Science*, 264 (5167) (1994): 1907–10.

Clarke, John Desmond. "Short Notes on the Stone Age Sites at Yavello, South Abyssinia." *Transactions of the Royal Society of South Africa*, 31 (1) (1945): 29–37.

Clarke, John Desmond, and G. R. Price. "Use-Wear on Later Stone-Age Microliths from Laga Oda, Hararghi, Ethiopia, and Possible Functional Interpretations." *Azania*, 13 (1978): 101–10.

Clarke, John Desmond, and H. Kurashina. "New Pleistocene Archaeological Occurrences from the Plain of Gadeb, Upper Webi Shebele Basin, Ethiopia, and a Statistical Comparison of the Gadeb Sites with Other Early Stone Age Assemblages." *Anthropologie*, 18 (2/3) (1980): 161–87.

Clarke, John Desmond, and M. A. J. Williams. "Recent Archaeological Research in Southeastern Ethiopia: Some Preliminary Results." *Annales d'Ethiopie*, 11 (1978): 19–42.

Cotter, George. *Salt for Stew: Proverbs and Sayings of the Oromo People with English Translations*. Debre Zeit: Maryknoll Fathers, 1990.

Coon, Carleton S. *Measuring Ethiopia and Flight into Arabia*. Boston: Little, Brown, and Company, 1935.

——. "A Realist Looks at Ethiopia." *The Atlantic Monthly*, 156 (3) (1935): 310–15.

De Heinzelin, Jean, et al. "Environment and Behavior of 2.5-Million-Year-Old Bouri Hominids." *Science*, 284 (5414) (1999): 625–29.

Donham, Donald L. "An Archeology of Work among the Maale of Ethiopia." *Man* (29) (1) (1994): 147–59.

——. "A Note on Space in the Ethiopian Revolution." *Africa*, 63 (4) (1993): 583–90.

——. "Revolution and Modernity in Maale, Ethiopia, 1974 to 1987." *Comparative Studies in Society and History*, 34 (1) (1992): 28–57.

Englebert, Victor. "The Danakil: Nomads of Ethiopia's Wasteland." *NGM*, 137 (2) (1970): 186–211.

Evans-Pritchard, E. E. *The Nuer: A Description of the Modes of Livelihood and Political Institutions of a Nilotic People.* New York and Oxford: OUP, 1940.

Feibel, Craig S. et al. "Stratigraphic Context of Fossil Hominids from the Omo Group Deposits: Northern Turkana Basin, Kenya and Ethiopia." *American Journal of Physical Anthropology*, 78 (4) (1989): 595–622.

Fellman, Jack. "Ethiopian–Semitic: The Situation in Gurage Land." *Anthropos*, 96 (1) (2001): 206–7.

Ferenc, A. "Myths and Traditions Concerning the Origin of the Oromo People." *Africana Bulletin*, (35) (1988): 59–65.

Freeman, Dena. *Initiating Change in Highland Ethiopia: Causes and Consequences of Cultural Transformation.* Cambridge: Cambridge University Press, 2002.

Gabreyesus Hailemariam. *The Gurage and Their Culture.* New York: Vantage Press, 1991.

Gadaa Melbaa. *Oromia: An Introduction to the History of the Oromo People.* Minneapolis: Kirk House Publishers, 1999.

Gamst, Frederick C. *The Qemant: A Pagan-Hebraic Peasantry of Ethiopia.* New York, Holt, Rinehart and Winston, 1969.

Gebre Yintiso. *The Art of Southwestern Ethiopia: An Exploratory Study of Production Practices.* Addis Ababa: AAU, 1995.

Getachew Kassa. "A Note on the Finaa (Fimaa) Institution among the Pastoral Afar of the Middle Awash Valley, North Eastern Ethiopia." *JES*, 30 (2) (1997): 1–26.

Gezahegn Petros. *The Karo of the Lower Omo Valley.* Addis Ababa: AAUP, 2000.

Giday Wolde Gabriel et al. "Ecological and Temporal Placement of Early Pliocene Hominids at Aramis, Ethiopia." *Nature*, 371 (6495) (1994): 330–33.

Giel, R., Y. Gezahegn, and J. N. van Luijk. "Faith Healing and Spirit Possession in Ghion, Ethiopia." *SSM*, 32 (2) (1968): 203–9.

Girma Getahun. "Ancient Customary Laws of the Gafat People." *JES*, 30 (2) (1997): 27–88.

Gollo Huqqaa. *The 37th Gumii Gaago Assembly: The Oromo Traditional, Economic, and Socio-Political System.* Addis Ababa: Norwegian Church Aid, 1996.

Grant, John Cameron. *The Ethiopian: A Narrative of the Society of Human Leopards.* New York: Black Hawk Press, 1935.

Greenfield, Richard and Mohammed Hassan. "Interpretation of Oromo Nationality." *HA*, 3 (3) (1980): 3–14.

Griaule, Marcel. *Burners of Men: Modern Ethiopia.* Philadelphia: J. B. Lippincott, 1935.

Hallpike, Christopher Robert. *The Konso of Ethiopia: A Study of the Values of a Cushitic People.* Oxford: CP, 1972.

——. "Religion and Society: A Study of the Konso of Ethiopia." D.Phil. diss., Oxford University, 1968.

——. "The Status of Craftsmen among the Konso of South-West Ethiopia." *Africa*, 38 (3) (1968): 258–69.

Hamer, John H. "Commensality, Process, and the Moral Order: An Example from Southern Africa." *Africa*, 64 (1) (1994): 126–44.

——. *Humane Development: Participation and Change among the Sadama of Ethiopia*. Tuscaloosa, Ala.: University of Alabama, 1987.

——. "Inculcation of Ideology among the Sidama of Ethiopia." *Africa*, 66 (4) (1996): 526–51.

——. "Sidamo Generational Class Cycles: A Political Gerontocracy." *Africa*, 40 (1) (1970): 50–70.

——. "The Sidama of Ethiopia and Rational Communication Action in Policy and Dispute Settlement." *Anthropos*, 93 (13) (1998): 137–53.

Hamer, John H., and Irene Hamer. "Spirit Possession and Its Socio-Psychological Implications among the Sidamo of South-West Ethiopia." *Ethnology*, 5 (4) (1966): 392–408.

——. "Impact of a Cash Economy on Complimentary Gender Relations among the Sadama of Ethiopia." *Anthropological Quarterly*, 67 (4) (1994): 187–202.

Hecht, Elisabeth-Dorothea. "Spirit Possession Cults in a Comparative Perspective": A Modern Amhara Village and Ancient Greece." *African Study Monographs*, 17 (1) (1996): 1–34.

Hinnant, John T. "The Gada System of the Guji of Southern Ethiopia." Ph.D. diss., University of Chicago, 1977.

——. "Guji Trance and Social Change: Symbolic Response to Domination." *NAS*, 12 (1) (1990): 65–78.

——. "Spirit Possession, Ritual, and Social Change: Current Research in Southern Ethiopia." *RA*, (11) (1970): 107–11.

Hoben, Allan. "The Role of Ambilineal Descent Groups in Gojam Amhara Social Organization." Ph.D. diss., University of California, Berkeley, 1963.

——. "Social Anthropology and Development Planning: A Case Study in Ethiopian Land Reform Policy." *JMAS*, 10 (4) (1972): 561–82.

Hogg, Richard. *Pastoralists, Ethnicity, and the State in Ethiopia*. London: Haan, 1997.

Huntingford, George W. B. *The Galla of Ethiopia: The Kingdoms of Kafa and Janjero*. London: IAI, 1953.

James, Wendy. "A Crisis in Uduk History." *Sudan Notes and Records*, 49 (1968): 17–44.

——. '*Kwanim Pa: The Making of the Uduk People: An Ethnographic Study of Survival in the Sudan-Ethiopian Borderlands*. Oxford: CP, 1979.

Johanson, Donald. "The Dawn of Humans: Face-to-Face with Lucy's Family." *NGM*, 189 (3) (1996): 96–117.

Johanson, Donald, and Blake Edgar. *From Lucy to Language.* New York: Simon and Schuster, 1996.

Johanson, Donald, and Maitland A. Edey. *Lucy: The Beginnings of Humankind.* New York: Simon and Schuster, 1981.

Johanson, Donald, and Maurice Taieb. "Plio-Pleistocene Hominid Discoveries in Hadar, Ethiopia." *Nature*, 260 (5549) (1976): 293–97.

Johanson, Edward Augustus. *Adam vs. Ape Man in Ethiopia.* New York: Little and Ives Company, 1931.

Kaplan, Steven. *The Beta Israel (Falasha) in Ethiopia: From Earliest Times to the Twentieth Century.* New York: New York University Press, 1992.

——. "The Beta Israel (Falasha) Encounter with Protestant Missionaries: 1860–1905." *Jewish Social Studies*, 49 (1) (1987): 27–42.

Kenney, Nathaniel T. "Ethiopian Adventure." *NGM*, 127 (4) (1965): 548–82.

Kessler, David. *The Falashas: The Forgotten Jews of Ethiopia.* London: George Allen and Unwin, 1982.

Kimbel, William H., et al. "The First Skull and Other New Discoveries of Australopithecus Afarensis at Hadar, Ethiopia." *Nature*, 368 (6470) (1994): 449–51.

——. "Systematic Assessment of Homo from Hadar, Ethiopia." *American Journal of Physical Anthropology*, 103 (2) (1997): 235–62.

Lange, Werner J. "Cultural Integration of Ethiopian Highlands." *NAS*, 3 (2) (1981): 1–24 and 3 (3) (1981/1982): 17–42.

——. *History of the Southern Gonga.* Wiesbaden: FS, 1982.

LeBel, Philip. "On Gurage Architecture." *JES*, 7 (1) (1969): 21–30.

——. "Oral Tradition and Chronicles on Gurage Immigration." *JES*, 12 (2) (1974): 95–106.

Lee, Sunga Agnes. "The Sidamo, Their Cattle, and Ensete: A Study towards an Understanding of Agropastoralism and Sustainability." Ph.D. diss., University of Colorado at Boulder, 2000.

Lewis, B. A. *The Murle: Red Chiefs and Black Commoners.* Oxford: CP, 1972.

Lewis, Herbert S. "Gada, Big Man, K'allu: Political Succession among the Eastern Mech'a Oromo." *NAS*, 12 (1) (1990): 43–64.

——. *A Galla Monarchy: Jimma Abba Jifar, Ethiopia, 1830–1932.* Madison: University of Wisconsin Press, 1965.

——. *Jimma Abba Jifar: An Oromo Monarchy in Ethiopia 1830–1932.* Lawrenceville, N.J.: RSP, 2001.

——. "Neighbors, Friends, and Kinsmen: Principles of Social Organization among the Cushitic-Speaking Peoples of Ethiopia." *Ethnology*, 13 (1974): 145–57.

———. "Wealth, Influence, and Prestige among the Shoa Galla." in Arthur Tuden and Leonard Plotnicov (eds.). *Social Stratification in Africa*. New York: Free Press, 1970: 163–86.

Locke, Robert. "The First Human?" *Discovering Archaeology*, 1 (4) (1999): 32–39.

Lord, Edith. *Queen of Sheba's Heirs: Cultural Patterns of Ethiopia*. Washington, D.C.: Acropolis Books, 1970.

Lydall, Jean, and Ivo Strecker. *The Hamar of Southern Ethiopia*. 3 vols. Hohenschäftlarn: Klaus Renner Verlag, 1979.

MacDermot, Brian Hugh. *Cult of the Sacred Spear: The Story of the Nuer Tribe in Ethiopia*. London: Robert Hale, 1972.

Means, S. M. *Ethiopia and the Missing Link in African History*. Harrisburg: Atlanta Publishing Company, 1980.

Mengesha Rikitu. *Oromia Recollected: Culture and History*. London: Biiftuu Diirama Oromo Assoc., 1998.

Messing, Simon David. "Group Therapy and Social Status in the *Zar* Cult of Ethiopia." *American Anthropologist*, 60 (6) (1958): 1120–5.

———. *Highland-Plateau Amhara of Ethiopia*. New Haven: HRAF Files, 1985.

———. "Role Differentiation in the Amhara Family in Ethiopia." *Journal of Human Relations*, 8 (3/4) (1960): 388–93.

———. *The Story of the Falashas: "Black Jews" of Ethiopia*. Brooklyn: Balshon Printing and Offset, 1982.

Mohammed Hassen Ali. "The Oromo of Ethiopia, 1500–1850: With Special Emphasis on the Gibe Region." Ph.D. diss., University of London, 1983.

———. *The Oromo of Ethiopia: A History 1570–1860*. Cambridge: CUP, 1990.

———. "A Short History of Oromo Colonial Experience: Part 1, 1870–1935." *JOS*, 6 (1/2) (1999): 109–98.

———. "A Short History of Oromo Colonial Experience: Part 2, Colonial Consolidation and Resistance 1935–2000." *JOS*, 7 (1/2) (2000): 109–98.

Naty, Alexander. "The Thief-Searching (Leba Shay) Institution in Aariland, Southwest Ethiopia, 1890s–1930s." *Ethnology*, 33 (3) (1994): 261–72.

Negaso Gidada. *History of the Sayyoo Oromoo of Southwestern Wallaga, Ethiopia, from about 1730–1886*. Frankfurt: Johann Wolfgang Goethe-Universität, 1984.

Nicolas, Gildas E. F. "The Dizzu of Southwest Ethiopia: An Essay in Cultural History Based on Religious Interactions." Ph.D. diss., University of California, Los Angeles, 1976.

Osgood, Wilfred Hudson. "Nature and Man in Ethiopia." *NGM*, 54 (2) (1928): 121–76.

Osterlund, David Conrad. "The Annuak Tribe of South Western Ethiopia: A Study of Its Music within the Context of Its Sociocultural Setting." Ph.D. diss., University of Illinois Urbana-Champaign, 1978.

Park, James Loder. "Life's Tenor in Ethiopia." *NGM*, 67 (6) (1935): 783–93.

Pankhurst, Alula. "'Caste' in Africa: The Evidence from South-Western Ethiopia Reconsidered." *Africa*, 69 (4) (1999): 485–509.

Pankhurst, Alula, and Dena Freeman (eds.). *Living on the Edge: Marginalised Minorities of Craftworkers and Hunters in Southern Ethiopia.* Addis Ababa: AAUP, 2001.

Quirin, J. A. *The Evolution of the Ethiopian Jews.* Philadelphia: University of Pennsylvania, 1992.

Radosevich, Stefan C., et al. "Reassessment of the Paleoenvironment and Preservation of Hominid Fossils from Hadar, Ethiopia." *American Journal of Physical Anthropology*, 87 (1) (1992): 15–27.

Reminick, Ronald A. "The Manze Amhara of Ethiopia: A Study of Authority, Masculinity, and Sociality." Ph.D. diss., University of Chicago, 1973.

Salole, Gerry. "Who're the Shoans." *HA*, 2 (3) (1979): 20–9.

Schoenberger, M. "The Falasha of Ethiopia: An Ethnographic Study." M.A. thesis, Cambridge University, 1975.

Shack, William A. *The Central Ethiopians: Amhara, Tigrina, and Related Peoples.* London: IAI, 1974.

——. *The Gurage: A People of the Ensete Culture.* London: OUP, 1966.

——. "On Gurage Judicial Structure and African Political Theory.: *JES*, 5 (2) (1967): 89–101.

——. "Some Aspects of Ecology and Social Structure in the Ensete Complex in South-West Ethiopia." *Journal of the Royal Anthropological Institute of Great Britain and Ireland*, 93 (1) (1963): 72–79.

Sileshi Semaw. "Late Pliocene Archaeology of the Gona River Deposits, Afar, Ethiopia." Ph.D. diss., Rutgers University, 1997.

Stauder, Jack. *The Majangir: Ecology and Society of a Southwest Ethiopian People.* Cambridge: CUP, 1971.

Susman, Randall L. "Who Made the Oldowan Tools? Fossil Evidence for Tool Behavior in Plio-Pleistocene Hominids." *Journal of Anthropological Research*, 47 (2) (1991): 129–51.

Taddesse G. Berisso. "Traditional Warfare among the Guji of Southern Ethiopia." M.A. thesis, Michigan State University, 1988.

Taddesse Tamrat. "Ethnic Interaction and Integration in Ethiopian History: The Case of the Gafat." *JES*, 21 (1988): 121–54.

——. "Processes of Ethnic Interaction and Integration in Ethiopian History: The Case of the Agaw." *JAH*, 29 (1) (1988): 5–18.

Teferi A. Abate. "Government Intervention and Socioeconomic Change in a Northeast Ethiopian Community: An Anthropological Study." Ph.D. diss., Boston University, 2000.

Teshale Tibebu. "Ethiopia: The 'Anomaly' and 'Paradox' of Africa." *Journal of Black Studies*, 26 (4) (1996): 414–30.

Tippett, Alan R. *Peoples of Southwest Ethiopia*. Pasadena, Calif.: William Carey Library, 1970.

Triulzi, Alessandro. "Trade, Islam, and the Mahdia in Northwestern Wallagga, Ethiopia." *JAH*, 16 (1) (1975): 55–71.

Turton, David. "Referees and Leaders: A Study of Social Control among the Mursi of South-Western Ethiopia." Ph.D. diss., London School of Economics and Political Science, 1973.

——. "'We Must Teach Them to Be Peaceful': Mursi Views on Being Human and Being Mursi." *Nomadic Peoples*, 31 (1992): 19–33.

Van de Loo, Joseph. *Guji Oromo Culture in Southern Ethiopia*. Berlin: Dietrich Reiner, 1991.

Vecchiato, Norbert L. "Illness, Therapy, and Change in Ethiopian Possession Cults." *Africa*, 63 (2) (1993): 176–96.

Waldman, M. *The Jews of Ethiopia: The Beta Israel Community*. Jerusalem: Joint Distribution Committee, 1985.

Waldron, Sidney. "The Political Economy of Harari-Oromo Relationships, 1559–1874." *NAS*, 6 (1/2) (1984): 23–39.

Weedman, Kathryn Jane. "An Ethnoarchaeological Study of Stone Scrapers among the Gamo People of Southern Ethiopia." Ph.D. diss., University of Florida, 2000.

Weissleder, Wolfgang. "The Political Ecology of Amhara Domination." Ph.D. diss., University of Chicago, 1965.

Werner, A. "The Galla of East Africa." *JRAS*, 13 (50) (1914): 121–42 and 13 (51) (1914): 262–87.

Wesselman, Henry Barnard, III. "Pliocene Micromammals from the Lower Omo Valley, Ethiopia: Systematics and Paleoecology." Ph.D. diss., University of California Berkeley, 1982.

Westheimer, R. and Steven Kaplan. *Surviving Salvation: The Ethiopian Jewish Family in Transition*. New York: New York University Press, 1992.

White, Tim D., et al. "Australopithecus Ramidus: A New Species of Early Hominid from Aramis, Ethiopia." *Nature*, 371 (6495) (1994): 306–12.

——. "Jaws and Teeth of Australopithecus Afarensis from Maka, Middle Awash, Ethiopia." *American Journal of Physical Anthropology*, 111 (1) (2000): 45–68.

——. "New Discoveries of Australopithecus at Maka in Ethiopia." *Nature*, 366 (6452) (1993): 261–65.

Wood, Bernard. "The Oldest Hominid Yet." *Nature,* 371 (6495) (1994): 280–82.

Woolbert, Robert Gale. "The Peoples of Ethiopia." *FA*, 14 (2) (1936): 340–44.

Yayehe, Qes Asres. *Traditions of the Ethiopian Jews*. Thornhill, Ont.: Kibur Asres, 1995.

Architecture, Arts, Language, Literature, and Music

Abdurahman Mohamed Korram. "Oromo Proverbs." *JES*, 7 (1) (1969): 65–80; Part II, *JES*, 10 (2) (1972): 105–26.

Aboneh Ashagrie. "Popular Theatre in Ethiopia." *Ufahamu*, 24 (2/3) (1996): 32–41.

Abraham Demoz. "Moslems and Islam in Ethiopic Literature." *JES*, 10 (1) (1972): 1–11.

Aleme Eshete. *Songs of the Ethiopian Revolution*. Addis Ababa: Central Printing Press, 1979.

Alone, J. P. H. M., and D. E. Stokes. *Short Manual of the Amharic Language*. London: Macmillan and Company Ltd., 1946.

Aregga Hailemichael. "A Thematic Analysis of the Afar Camel Folk Literature: An Ethnography-of-Communication Approach." *JES*, 28 (1) (1995): 1–22.

Ashenafi Kebede. "The Music of Ethiopia: Its Development and Cultural Setting." Ph.D. diss., Wesleyan University, 1971.

Ayele Bekerie. *Ethiopic: An African Writing System—Its History and Principles*. Lawrenceville, N.J.: RSP, 1997.

Bach, Emmon. "Is Amharic an SOV Language?" *JES*, 8 (1) (1970): 9–20.

Bachrach, Shlomo. *Ethiopian Folk-Tales*. Addis Ababa: Oxford University Press, 1967.

Beke, Charles Tilstone. "On the Languages and Dialects of Abyssinia." *Proceedings of the Philological Society*, 2 (33) (1845): 89–107.

Bender, Marvin Lionel. "The Languages of Ethiopia: A New Lexicostatistic Classification and Some Problems of Diffusion." *Anthropological Linguistics*, 13 (5) (1971): 165–288.

——. *The Non-Semitic Languages of Ethiopia*. East Lansing: African Studies Center, Michigan State University, 1976.

——. "Notes on Lexical Correlations in Some Ethiopian Languages." *JES*, 4 (1) (1966): 5–16.

——. "The Origin of Amharic." *Journal of the Institute of Language Studies*, 1 (1) 91983): 41–52.

Bender, Marvin Lionel, et al. (eds.). *Language in Ethiopia*. London: Oxford University Press, 1976.

Berry, LaVerle. "Architecture and Kingship: The Significance of Gondar-Style Architecture." *NAS*, 2 (3) (1995): 7–19.

Bliese, Loren F. "Afar Songs." *NAS*, 4 (3) (1982/1983): 51–76.

Cassiers, Anne. "Handicrafts and Technical Innovation in Ethiopia." *Cultures*, 2 (3) (1975): 103–18.

Cerulli, Enrico. "Folk-Literature of the Galla of Southern Abyssinia." In *Harvard African Studies*, 3 (1922): 11–228.

Cervicek, Pavel, and Ulrich Braukämper. "Rock Paintings of Laga Gafra." *Paideuma*, 21 (1975): 47–60.

Chojnacki, Stanislaw. "Ethiopian Artist Berhane Mehary." *EO*, 14 (2) (1971): 140–48.

——. *Ethiopian Icons: Catalogue of the Collection of the Institute of Ethiopian Studies Addis Ababa University*. Milan: Skira Editions, 2000.

——. "A Hitherto Unknown Foreign Painter in 18th-Century Ethiopia: The Master of Arabic Script and His Portraits of Royal Donors." *Africa*, 40 (4) (1985): 577–610.

——. "The Iconography of Saint George in Ethiopia." *JES*, 11 (1) (1973): 57–73; 11 (2) (1973): 51–92; and 12 (1) (1974): 71–132.

——. *Major Themes in Ethiopian Painting: Indigenous Developments, The Influence of Foreign Models, and Their Adaptation, from the 13th to the 19th Century*. Stuttgart: FS, 1983.

——. "The Nativity in Ethiopian Art." *JES*, 12 (2) (1974): 11–56.

——. "Nimbi in Ethiopian Painting: Their Chronology and Significance." *Paideuma*, 36 (1990): 13–36.

——. "Note on the Early Iconography of St. George and Related Equestrian Saints in Ethiopia." *JES*, 13 (2) (1975): 39–55.

——. "Notes on Art in Ethiopia in the 15th and Early 16th Century: An Inquiry into the Unknown." *JES*, 8 (2) (1970): 21–65.

——. "Notes on Art in Ethiopia in the 16th Century: An Enquiry Into the Unknown." *JES*, 9 (2) (1971): 21–97.

——. "Notes on Lesser-Known Marian Iconography in 13th- and 14th-Century Ethiopian Painting." *Aethiopica: International Journal of Ethiopian Studies*, 5 (2002): 42–66.

——. "Short Introduction to Ethiopian Painting." *JES*, 2 (2) (1964): 1–11.

Colby, James G. "Notes on the Northern Dialect of the Afar Language." *JES*, 8 (1) (1970): 1–8.

Crummey, Donald E. *African Zion: The Sacred Art of Ethiopia*. New Haven: YUP, 1993.

——. "Tewodros in Ethiopian Historical Fiction." *JES*, 16 (1983): 115–28.

Dillman, August. *Ethiopic Grammar*. Amsterdam: Philo Press, 1974.

Ethiopia. Ministry of Culture and Sport. *Afework Tekle: Short Biography and Selected Works*. Addis Ababa: Artistic Printers of Ethiopia, 1987.

Ethiopia. Ministry of Information. *Patterns of Progress: Music, Dance, and Drama*. Addis Ababa: Ministry of Information, 1968.

"Ethiopian Art." In *Encyclopedia of World Art*. Vol. 5. New York: McGraw Hill, 1961: 82–100.

Eyayu Lulseged. "Social, Economic, and Political Discontent in Ethiopia as Reflected in Contemporary Amharic Songs (mid 1950s–mid 1970s)." *JES*, 27 (2) (1994): 21–43.

Falceto, Francis. *Abyssinie Swing: A Pictorial History of Modern Ethiopian Music*. Addis Ababa: Shama Books, 2001.

Falgayrettes, C. *Aethiopia: Vestiges de Gloire*. Paris: Musée Dapper, 1987.

Fekade Azeze. "Ethiopian Creative Writing and Criticism in English: A Review and Bibliography." *JES*, 18 (1985): 34–50.

Ford, Carolyn M. "Notes on the Phonology and Grammar of Chaha-Gurage." *JES*, 19 (1986): 41–80.

Ferguson, Charles A. "The Ethiopian Language Area." *JES*, 8 (2) (1970): 67–80.

Gerard, Albert G. "Amharic Creative Literature: The Early Phase." *JES*, 6 (2) (1968): 39–59.

Getie Gelaye. "Contemporary Amharic Oral Poetry from Gojjam: Classification and a Sample Analysis." *Aethiopica: International Journal of Ethiopian Studies*, 2 (1999): 124–43.

Girma Kidane and Richard Wilding. *The Ethiopian Cultural Heritage*. Addis Ababa: Artistic Printers, 1977.

Grierson, Roderick (ed.). *African Zion: The Sacred Art of Ethiopia*. New Haven: YUP, 1993.

Gutt, E. A. "Studies in the Phonology of Silti." *JES*, 16 (1983): 37–73.

Hayward, Richard. "The Challenge of Omotic." *HA*, 16 (1/2/3/4) (1998): 1–30.

Hecht, Elisabeth-Dorothea. "Basketwork of Harar." *African Study Monographs* (Kyoto University) 18 (1992): 1–39.

Hecht, Elisabeth-Dorothea, Brigitta Benzing, and Girma Kidane. *The Hand Crosses of the Institute of Ethiopian Studies Collection*. Addis Ababa: AAU, 1990.

Heldman, Marilyn E. "Creating Religious Art: The Status of Artisans in Highland Christian Ethiopia." *Aethiopica: International Journal of Ethiopian Studies*, 1 (1998): 131–47.

——. "Fre Seyon: A Fifteenth-Century Ethiopian Painter." *African Arts*, 31 (4) (1998): 48–55, 90.

——. *The Marian Icons of the Painter Fre Seyon: A Study in Fifteenth-Century Ethiopian Art, Patronage, and Spirituality*. Wiesbaden: Harrassowitz, 1994.

——. "The Sacred Art of Ethiopia." *Historian*, 57 (1) (1994): 35–42.

Henze, Paul Bernard (ed.). *Aspects of Ethiopian Art Form from Ancient Axum to the Twentieth Century*. London: Jed Press, 1993.

Hetzron, Robert. *Ethiopian Semitic: Studies in Classification*. Manchester: Manchester University Press, 1972.

Hudson, Grover. "Ethiopian Semitic Overview." *JES*, 33 (2) (2000): 75–86.

Huntsberger, Paul E. *Highland Mosaic: A Critical Anthology of Ethiopian Literature in English*. Athens: Ohio University Center for International Studies, 1973.

Kane, Thomas L. *Amharic-English Dictionary*. 2 vols. Wiesbaden: Otto Harrassowitz, 1990.

———. *Ethiopian Literature in Amharic*. Wiesbaden: Otto Harrassowitz, 1975.

Kaplin, Steven, and Chaim Rosen. "Created in Their Own Image: A Comment on Beta Israel Figurines." *CEA*, 36 (1/2) (1996): 171–82.

Kiros Teodros. "Claude Sumner's Classical Ethiopian Philosophy." *NAS*, 3 (2) (1996): 39–52.

Krapf, Johann Ludwig. *An Imperfect Outline of the Elements of the Galla Language*. London: Church Missionary Society, 1840.

———. *Vocabulary of the Galla Language*. London: Church Missionary Society, 1842.

Lambdin, Thomas. *Introduction to Classical Ethiopic (Ge'ez)*. Cambridge, Mass.: Harvard University Press, 1978.

Lamberti, M., and R. Sottile. *The Wolaytta Language*. Köln: Rudiger Koppe, 1997.

Lange, Werner. "Cultural Integration of Ethiopian Highlands." *NAS*, 3 (2) (1981): 1–24 and 3 (3) (1981/1982): 17–42.

———. *Domination and Resistance: Narrative Songs of the Kafa Highlands*. East Lansing: Michigan State University, 1979.

Langmuir, Elizabeth Cross, et al. *Ethiopia: The Christian Art of an African Nation*. Salem, Mass.: Peabody Museum of Salem, 1978.

Leroy, Jules. *Ethiopian Painting in the Late Middle Ages and under the Gondar Dynasty*. London: Merlin Press, 1967.

———. et al. *Ethiopia: Illuminated Manuscripts*. Greenwich, Conn.: UNESCO World Art Series, 1961.

Leslau, Wolf. "Amharic Love Songs." *Paideuma*, 36 (1990): 157–72.

———. "Arabic Loanwords in Selti." *Aethiopica: International Journal of Ethiopian Studies*, 2 (1999): 103–23.

———. *Ethiopians Speak: Studies in Cultural Background Harari*. Berkeley: University of California Press, 1965.

———. "The Languages of Ethiopia and Their Geographical Distribution." *EO*, 2 (3) (1958): 116–21.

———. "The Present State of Ethiopic Linguistics." *Journal of Near Eastern Studies*, 5 (1946): 215–29.

———. "Toward a History of the Amharic Vocabulary." *JES*, 2 (2) (1964): 12–20.

Longenecker, Martha (ed.). *Ethiopia: Folk Art of a Hidden Empire*. La Jolla, Calif.: Mingei International Museum of World Folk Art, 1983.

Matthews, Derek H. "Ethiopian Monastery Church of Debra Damo." *Antiquity*, 12 (1949): 188–200.

Mercier, Jacques. *Ethiopian Magic Scrolls*. New York: George Braziller, 1979.

Mekuria Bulcha. "The Politics of Linguistic Homogenization in Ethiopia and the Conflict over the Status of Afaan Oromoo." *African Affairs*, 96 (384) (1997): 325–52.

Mercier, Jacques. *Art That Heals: The Image as Medicine in Ethiopia*. New York: The Museum of African Art, 1997.

Molvaer, Reidulf Knut. *Black Lions: The Creative Lives of Modern Ethiopia's Literary Giants and Pioneers*. Lawrenceville, N.J.: RSP, 1997.

——. *Tradition and Change in Ethiopia: Social and Cultural Life as Reflected in Amharic Fictional Literature ca. 1930–1974*. Leiden: E. J. Brill, 1980.

Mulugeta Seyoum. "The Development of the National Language of Ethiopia: A Study of Language Use and Policy." Ph.D. diss., Georgetown University, 1985.

Munro-Hay, Stuart C. "Aksumite Pottery from Medebai." *Aethiopica: International Journal of Ethiopian Studies*, 2 (1999): 183–89.

Negaso Gidada. "Oromo Historical Poems and Songs: Conquest and Exploitation in Western Wallago, 1886–1927." *HA*, 5 (3) (1982): 32–40.

Negussay Ayele. *Wit and Wisdom of Ethiopia*. Hollywood, Calif.: Tsehai Publishers, 1998.

Niguse Abbebe, and M. L. Bender. "The Ethiopian Language Academy, 1943–1974." *NAS*, 6 (3) (1984): 1–7.

Olmstead, Judith, and James A. Sugar. "Ethiopia's Artful Weavers." *NGM*, 143 (1) (1973): 125–41.

Pankhurst, Richard. "Ethiopia, the Aksum Obelisk, and the Return of Africa's Cultural Heritage." *AA*, 98 (391) (1999): 229–39.

——. "Ethiopian Manuscript Illumination: Some Aspects of the Artist's Craft as Revealed in 17th and 18th Century Manuscripts in the British Library." *Azania*, 19 (1984): 105–14.

——. "Ethiopian Manuscript Illustration: The Four Evangelists." *EO*, 9 (2) (1965): 100–12.

——. "Fear God, Honor the King: The Use of Biblical Allusion in Ethiopian Historical Literature, Part 1." *NAS*, 8 (1) (1986): 11–30.

——. "Fear God, Honor the King: Use of Biblical Allusion in Ethiopian Historical Literature, Part 2." *NAS*, 9 (1) (1987): 25–88.

——. "Gallery of Ethiopian Art: Mohammed Ali." *EO*, 14 (3) (1971): 207–18.

——. "A History of the Axum Obelisk Return Struggle." *HA*, 16 (1/2/3/4) (1998): 127–43.

——. "Some Notes for a History of Ethiopian Secular Art." *EO*, 10 (1) (1966): 5–80.

——. "Traditional Ethiopian Art." *EO*, 5 (1962): 291–301.

Pankhurst, Richard, and Leila Ingrams. *Ethiopia Engraved: An Illustrated Catalogue of Engravings by Foreign Travellers from 1681 to 1900*. London and New York: Kegan Paul International, 1988.

Parker, E. M. "Afar Stories, Riddles, and Proverbs." *JES*, 9 (2) (1971): 219–87.

Parker, E. M., and R. J. Hayward. *An Afar-English-French Dictionary*. London: School of Oriental and African Studies, University of London, 1985.

Pavillon des Arts. *L'Arche Ethiopienne: Art Chrétien d'Ethiopie*. Paris: Paris-Musees, 2000.

Playne, Beatrice. *St. George for Ethiopia*. London: Constable, 1954.

Powne, Michael. *Ethiopian Music: An Introduction*. Oxford: OUP, 1966.

Proceedings of the First International Conference on the History of Ethiopian Art. 2 vols. London: Pindar, 1989.

Rufin, Jean-Christophe. *The Abyssinian*. New York and London: W. W. Norton and Company, 2000.

Savard, Georges C. "War Chants in Praise of Ancient Afar Heroes." *JES*, 3 (1) (1965); 105–8.

Shelemay, Kay K. "The Liturgical Music of the Falasha of Ethiopia." Ph.D. diss., University of Michigan, 1977.

——. "The Music of the Lalibeloc: Musical Mendicants in Ethiopia." *JAS*, 9 (3) (1982): 128–38.

——. *Music, Ritual, and Falasha History*. East Lansing: African Studies Center, Michigan State University, 1986.

——. "The Musician and Transmission of Religious Tradition: The Multiple Roles of the Debtara." *Journal of Religion in Africa*, 22 (3) (1992): 242–60.

Silverman, Raymond A. (ed.) *Ethiopia Traditions of Creativity*. East Lansing: Michigan State University Museum, 1999.

——. "Zerihun Yetmgeta." *African Arts*, 30 (1) (1997): 52–57.

Sumner, Claude. *Ethiopian Philosophy: The Fisalgwos*. Addis Ababa: AAUP, 1982.

——. *Ethiopian Philosophy: The Treatise of Zar'a Ya'eqob and of Walda Heywat*. Addis Ababa: AAUP, 1978.

——. *Oromo Wisdom Literature*. Vol. I, *Proverbs: Collection and Analysis*. Addis Ababa: Gudina Tumsa Foundation, 1995.

——. *Oromo Wisdom Literature*. Vol. II, *Songs: Collection and Analysis*. Addis Ababa: Gudina Tumsa Foundation, 1997.

——. *Oromo Wisdom Literature*. Vol. III, *Folktales: Collection and Analysis*. Addis Ababa: Gudina Tumsa Foundation, 1996.

——. *Proverbs, Songs, Folktales: An Anthology of Oromo Literature*. Addis Ababa: Gudina Tumsa Foundation, 1996.

Sumner, Claude, and Lemma Guya. *Oromo Folktales: An Illustrated Album*. Addis Ababa: Gudina Tumsa Foundation, 1997.

Taddese Beyene (ed.). *Proceedings of the First International Conference on Ethiopian Art*. London: Warburg Institute, 1987.

Taddesse Adera and Ali Jimale Ahmed (eds.). *Silence Is Not Golden: A Critical Anthology of Ethiopian Literature*. Lawrenceville, N.J.: RSP, 1999.

Taddesse Tamrat. "A Short Note on Ethiopian Church Music." *Annales d'Ethiopie*, 13 (1985): 137–43.

Takkele Taddese. "Issues in Language Policy and Language Choice: A Sociolinguistic Profile of the Major Ethiopian Languages." *JES*, 18 (1985): 80–90.

Taye Assefa. "Detective Fiction in Amharic." *NAS*, 11 (3) (1989): 13–33.

———. "Dreams in Amharic Prose Fiction." *JES*, 21 (1988): 155–83.

———. "The Narrative Architecture of *The Thirteenth Sun*." *JES*, 33 (1) (2000): 1–48.

———. "Tewodros in Ethiopian Historical Fiction." *JES*, 16 (1983): 115–28.

Taye Assefa and Shiferaw Bekele. "The Study of Amharic Literature: An Overview." *JES*, 33 (2) (2000): 27–73.

Taye Taddesse. *Short Biographies of Some Well-Known Ethiopian Artists, 1869–1957*. Addis Ababa: Kuraz Publishing Agency, 1991.

Taylor, N. "Gamo Syntax." Ph.D. diss., University of London, 1994.

Tilahun Gamta. *Oromo-English Dictionary*. Addis Ababa: AAUP, 1989.

Tosco, Mauro. "Cushitic Overview." *JES*, 33 (2) (2000): 87–121.

Tsehaye Teferra. "A Sociolinguistic Survey of Language Use and Attitudes towards Language in Ethiopia: Implications for Language Policy in Education." Ph.D. diss., Georgetown University, 1977.

Ullendorff, Edward. *The Semitic Languages of Ethiopia*. London: Taylor's (Foreign) Press, 1955.

———. "The Semitic Languages of Ethiopia and Their Configuration to General Semitic Studies." *Africa*, 25 (2) (1955): 154–60.

Unseth, Peter. "Gumuz: A Dialect Survey Report." *JES*, 18 (1985): 91–114.

Vadasy, Tibor. "Ethiopian Folk-Dance." *JES*, 8 (2) (1970): 119–46.

———. "Ethiopian Folk-Dance II: Tegre and Gurage." *JES*, 9 (2) (1971): 191–218.

———. "Ethiopian Folk-Dance III: Wallo and Galla." *JES*, 11 (1) (1973): 213–31.

Walker, Craven Howell. *English-Amharic Dictionary*. London: The Sheldon Press, 1928.

The Walters Art Museum. *Ethiopian Art*. Lingfield, Vic: Third Millennium Publishing, 2001.

Wright, William. *Lectures on the Comparative Grammar of Semitic Languages*. Cambridge: CUP, 1890.

Yigazu Tucho. "An Examination of Language Policy and Strategies for the Dissemination of Amharic in Ethiopia between 1942 and 1974." Ph.D. diss., Ohio University, 1992.

Yonas Admassu. "Narrating Ethiopia: A Panorama of the National Imaginary." Ph.D. diss., University of California, Los Angeles, 1995.

Zelealem Leyew. "Code-Switching: Amharic-English." *Journal of African Cultural Studies*, 11 (2) (1998): 197–216.

Zenebe Bekele. *Music in the Horn: A Preliminary Analytical Approach to the Study of Ethiopian Music*. Stockholm: Evrfattares Bokmaskin, 1987.

Health, Medicine, and Welfare

Aadland, Oyvind. "Introducing a Tuberculosis Control Program in Sidama: A Case Study in Cross-Cultural Communication." Ph.D. diss., Northwestern University, 1996.

Abate Mammo. "Childlessness in Rural Ethiopia." *Population and Development Review*, 12 (3) (1986): 533–46.

——. "Factors Responsible for Childhood Mortality Variation in Rural Ethiopia." *Journal of Biosocial Science*, 25 (2) (1993): 223–38.

——. "Mortality in Rural Ethiopia: Levels, Trends, Differentials." Ph.D. diss., University of Pennsylvania, 1988.

Abebe Salelesh. "Physician-Patient Interaction in a Prenatal Clinic in Addis Ababa, Ethiopia: A Study to Assess the Communications Style of the Physicians and Its Effect on Patient Outcome." Ph.D. diss., Johns Hopkins University, 1996.

Alemayehu Geda. "Quantitative Measurement of Poverty in Ethiopia." *Ethiopian Journal of Development Research*, 15 (2) (1993): 17–52.

Asfaw Desta. "National Health Planning in Ethiopia." Ph.D. diss., Johns Hopkins University, 1971.

Aydagnehum Geleta. "Problems of Pharmaceutical Production in Ethiopia." *Science, Technology and Development*, 11 (1) (1993): 26–35.

Baarkhuus, Arne. "Public Health in Ethiopia." *Ciba Symposia*, 9 (7) (1947): 698–709.

Bevan, P. and Sandra Fullerton Joireman. "The Perils of Measuring Poverty: Identifying the 'Poor' in Rural Ethiopia." *Oxford Development Studies*, 25 (1) (1997): 315–41.

Bhattacharyya, Karabi, and John Murray. "Community Assessment and Planning for Maternal and Child Health Programs: A Participatory Approach in Ethiopia." *Human Organization*, 59 (2) (2000): 255–66.

Bishaw, M. "Attitudes of Modern and Traditional Medical Practitioners Toward Cooperation." *Ethiopian Medical Journal*, 28 (1990): 63–72.

——. "The Implications of Indigenous Medical Beliefs to Biomedical Practice." *Ethiopian Journal of Health Development*, 3 (2) (1989): 75–89.

——. "Promoting Traditional Medicine in Ethiopia and Eritrea: A Brief Historical Review of Government Policy." *SSM*, 33 (2) (1991): 193–200.

Buschkens, W. F. L., and L. J. Slikkerveer. *Health Care in East Africa: Illness Behaviour of the Eastern Oromo in Hararghe, Ethiopia*. Assen: V. Gorcum, 1982.

Chang, Wen-Pin. "Development of Basic Health Services in Ethiopia." *Journal of the Formosan Medical Association*, 68 (6) (1969): 306–21.

——. "Health Manpower Development in an African Country: The Case of Ethiopia." *Journal of Medical Education*, 45 (1) (1970): 29–39.

Collier, Paul, Stefan Dercon, and John Mackinnon. "Density versus Quality in Health Care Provision: Using Household Data to Make Budgetary Choices in Ethiopia." *The World Bank Economic Review*, 16 (3) (2002): 425–48.

Conacher, D. G. "Medical Care in Ethiopia." *Transactions of the Royal Society of Tropical Medicine and Hygiene*, 70 (2) (1976): 141–44.

Croppenstedt, Andre, and Christophe Muller. "The Impact of Farmers' Health and Nutritional Status on Their Productivity and Efficiency: Evidence from Ethiopia." *Economic Development and Cultural Change*, 48 (3) (2000): 475–502.

Curtin, Philip D. "The March to Magdala." In Philip D. Curtin, *Disease and Empire: The Health of European Troops in the Conquest of Africa*. Cambridge: CUP, 1998: 29–48.

Damen Haile Mariam. "The Effect of Extended Family Support on the Demand for Health Care in Ethiopia." Ph.D. diss., University of California, Berkeley, 1996.

Dercon, Stefan, and Pramila Krishnan. "In Sickness and in Health: Risk Sharing within Households in Rural Ethiopia." *The Journal of Political Economy*, 108 (4) (2000): 688–727.

Egge, Kari Noel. "Food for Work: Is There a Nutritional Impact? An Analysis of USAID-Sponsored Title II Development Programming in Ethiopia." Ph.D. diss., Tulane University, 2000.

Fletcher, M., and Awash Teklehaimanot. "*Schistosoma Mansoni* Infection in a New Settlement in Metekel District, North-Western Ethiopia." *Transactions of the Royal Society of Tropical Medicine and Hygiene*, 83 (6) (1989): 793–97.

Fisseha Wegayehu. "Analysis and Evaluation of Housing Programs in Ethiopia: 1976–1986." D.Architecture diss., Rice University, 1987.

Gabre–Emanuel Teka. *Water Supply—Ethiopia: An Introduction to Environmental Health Practice*. Addis Ababa: AAUP, 1977.

Gatti, S., et al. "A Survey of Amoebic Infection in the Wonji Area of Central Ethiopia." *Annals of Tropical Medicine and Parasitology*, 92 (2) (1998): 173–79.

Gebre ab Barnabas and Anthony Zwi. "Health Policy Development in Wartime: Establishing the Baito Health System in Tigray, Ethiopia." *Health Policy and Planning*, 12 (1) (1997): 38–49.

Gundersen, S. G. "Delayed Reinfection of Schistosoma Mansoni in the Blue Nile Valley of Western Ethiopia 10 Years after Mass Chemotherapy." *Acta Tropica*, 70 (1) (1998): 35–42.

——. "Leprosy and Tuberculosis in the Blue Nile Valley of Western Ethiopia." *Leprosy Review*, 58 (2) (1987): 129–40.

Gundersen, S. G., A. Schmitt-Lechner, and B. Bjorvatn. "Onchocerciasis in the Blue Nile Valley of Western Ethiopia." *Transactions of the Royal Society of Tropical Medicine and Hygiene*, 82 (1) (1988): 122–27.

Habtemariam, R., T. Seyoum, and S. Byadijev. "Mental Illness Treated in Ethiopian Hospitals, 1977–81." *EJAS*, 4 (2) (1987): 53–70.

Hodes, Richard, and Helmut Kloos. "Health and Medical Care in Ethiopia." *New England Journal of Medicine*, 319 (14) (1988): 918–24.

Howarth, F. "The Faculty of Medicine of the Haile Selassie I University." *Israel Journal of Medical Sciences*, 1 (5) (1965): 1038–44.

Kirk, R. "Medical Report on the Kingdom of Shoa." *Transactions of the Medical and Physical Society of Bombay*, 7 (1843): 3–31.

Kloos, Helmut. "Health Aspects of Resettlement in Ethiopia." *SSM*, 30 (6) (1990): 643–56.

——. "Health Impact of War in Ethiopia." *Disasters*, 16 (4) (1992): 347–54.

——. "The Geography of Pharmacies, Druggist Shops, and Rural Medicine Vendors, and the Origin of Customers to Such Facilities in Addis Ababa." *JES*, 12 (2) (1974): 77–94.

——. "Medicine Vendors and Their Products in Markets in the Ethiopian Highlands and Rift Valley." *EN*, 2 (1) (1978): 47–69.

——. "Primary Health Care in Ethiopia: From Haile Selassie to Meles Zenawi." *NAS*, 5 (1) (1998): 83–113.

——. "Primary Health Care in Ethiopia under Three Political Systems: Community Participation in a War-Torn Society." *SSM*, 46 (4/5) (1998): 505–22.

——. "Schistosomiasis and Irrigation in the Awash Valley of Ethiopia." Ph.D. diss., University of California Davis, 1977.

——. "Utilization of Selected Hospitals, Health Centres, and Health Stations in Central, Southern, and Western Ethiopia." *SSM*, 31 (2) (1990): 101–14.

——. "Water Resources Development and Schistosomiasis Ecology in the Awash Valley, Ethiopia." *SSM*, 20 (6) (1985): 609–25.

Kloos, Helmut, and Zein Ahmed Zein (eds.). *The Ecology of Health and Diseases in Ethiopia*. Boulder, Colo.: WP, 1993.

Kloos, Helmut, et al. "Illness and Health Behaviour in Addis Ababa and Rural Central Ethiopia." *SSM*, 25 (9) (1987): 1003–19

Lindtjorn, Bernt. "Cancer in Southern Ethiopia." *Journal of Tropical Medicine and Hygiene*, 90 (4) (1987): 181–87.

——. "Xerophthalmia in the Gardula Area of Southwest Ethiopia." *Ethiopian Medical Journal*, 21 (1983): 169–74.

Makonnen Bishaw. "Integrating Indigenous and Cosmopolitan Medicine in Ethiopia." Ph.D. diss., Southern Illinois University, Carbondale, 1988.

——. "Promoting Traditional Medicine in Ethiopia: A Brief Historical Review of Government Policy." *SSM*, 33 (2) (1991): 193–201.

Mammo Beshah. "Health Care Delivery Systems in Underdeveloped Countries: Ethiopia, A Case Study." Ph.D. diss., University of Missouri Columbia, 1980.

Marcus, Harold Golden. "Disease, Hospitals, and Italian Colonial Aspirations in Ethiopia, 1930–35." *NAS*, 1 (1) (1979): 21–26.

Messing, Simon David. "Traditional Healing and the New Health Centers." *Conch*, 8 (1/2) (1976): 52–64.

The National AIDS Council Secretariat. *National Guidelines for Voluntary HIV Counseling and Testing in Ethiopia*. Addis Ababa: The National AIDS Council Secretariat, 2000.

Nerayo Teklemikael and Eyob Azaria. "Problems of Health Service Delivery in Eritrea." *Eritrean Medical Journal*, 1 (3) (1983): 3–11 and 2 (1) (1984): 12–24.

O'Brien, Henry R. "Mapping a Program of Public Health for Ethiopia." *Public Health Reports*, 68 (10) (1953): 976–83.

Pact Ethiopia. *Assessment Study of HIV/AIDS Implementing Organizations*. Addis Ababa: Pact Ethiopia, 2000.

Pankhurst, Estelle Sylvia. "The Gandhi Memorial Hospital, an Indian Gift." *EO* 4 (10) (1960): 333–36.

Pankhurst, Richard. "The Beginnings of Modern Medicine in Ethiopia." EO, 9 (2) (1965): 114–60.

——. "The Great Ethiopian Influenza Epidemic of 1918 (Ye Hidar Beshita)." *Ethiopian Medical Journal*, 27 (1989): 235–42.

——. "The Hedar Baseta of 1918." *JES*, 13 (2) (1975): 103–31.

——. "An Historical Examination of Traditional Medicine and Surgery." *Ethiopian Medical Journal*, 3 (4) (1965): 151–72.

——. "A Historical Note on Influenza in Ethiopia." *Medical History*, 21 (2) (1977): 195–200.

——. "The History and Traditional Treatment of Rabies in Ethiopia." *Medical History*, 14 (4) (1970): 378–89.

——. "The History and Traditional Treatment of Smallpox in Ethiopia." *Medical History*, 9 (4) (1965): 343–55.

——. "The History of Cholera in Ethiopia." *Medical History*, 12 (3)(1968): 262–69.

——. *The History of Famine and Epidemics in Ethiopia Prior to the Twentieth Century*. Addis Ababa: Relief and Rehabilitation Commission, 1985.

——. "The History of Leprosy in Ethiopia to 1935." *Medical History*, 28 (1) (1984): 57–72.

——. *An Introduction to the Medical History of Ethiopia*. Trenton, N.J.: RSP, 1990.

——. "The Medical Activities in Eighteenth-Century Ethiopia of James Bruce the Explorer." *Medizin Historisches Journal*, 17 (1982): 256–87.

——. "Old-Time Cures for Syphilis, Seventeenth to Twentieth Centuries." *Journal of the History of Medicine and Allied Sciences*, 30 (3) (1975): 199–216.

——. "Some Factors Influencing the Health of Traditional Ethiopia." *JES*, 4 (1) (1966): 31–70.

——. "Some Notes for the History of Typhus in Ethiopia." *Medical History*, 20 (4) (1976): 384–93.

Parisis, N. *L'Abissinia*. Milan: Brigola, 1888.

Pavlica, Dusan. "Analysis of Medical Admissions to the Armed Forces Hospital in Addis Ababa from January 1966 to January 1970." *EMJ*, 8 (4) (1970): 193–200.

Rivers, John P. W. "Lessons for Epidemiology from the Ethiopian Famine." *Annales Société Belgique Médicine Tropicale*, 56 (1976): 345–57.

Rosa, Franz W. "Training Health Workers in Gondar, Ethiopia." *Public Health Reports*, 77 (1962): 595–601.

Ross, D., and C. Moreno. *Health Care in Tigray: An Evaluation of Primary Health Care Services in the Central Region of Tigray, Ethiopia*. Oxford: OXFAM, 1985.

Saba Woldemichael Masho. "Cost Analysis and Attitudinal Study of Abortion among Health Workers and Women Admitted to Hospitals in Addis Ababa, Ethiopia." D.P.H. diss., University of California, Berkeley, 1997.

Seelig, John Michael, and Andargatchew Tesfaye. "Child Welfare Issues in Ethiopia." *International Social Work*, 37 (3) (1994): 221–37.

Shousha, A. T. "The First Public Health College and Training Center in Ethiopia: Gondar College." *Journal of the American Women's Medical Association*, 12 (1957): 209–11.

Slikkerveer, Jan Leendert. "Rural Health Development in Ethiopia." *SSM*, 16 (21) (1982): 1859–72.

Solomon Ayalew. "Macro Evaluation of Health Expenditure in Ethiopia." *EO*, 16 (3) (1973): 204–15.

Stommes, Eileen, and Seleshi Sisaye. "The Development and Distribution of Health Care Services in Ethiopia: A Preliminary Review." *CJAS*, 13 (8) (1980): 487–95.

Tadesse Mammo Bantirgu. "Psychological Effects of Prolonged Stress on Ethiopian Expatriates in the United States." Ph.D. diss., University of Cincinnati. 1995.

Teshai Berhane Selassie. "An Ethiopian Medical Text Book." *JES*, 9 (1) (1971): 95–180.

Tirussew Teferra. "Problems and Prospects of Persons with Disabilities in Ethiopia." *Ethiopian Journal of Development Research*, 15 (1) (1993): 67–88.

Torrey, Edwin Fuller (ed.). *An Introduction to Health and Health Education in Ethiopia*. Addis Ababa: Berhanena Selam Printing Press, 1966.

Tsegaye Habtemariam. "A Study of African Trypanosomiasis Using Epidemiologic Models: The Case of Ethiopia." Ph.D. diss., University of California, Davis, 1979.

Turshen, Meredeth. "Medical Aid to Ethiopia, 1950–1970." *NAA*, 7 (1) (1985): 49–61.

Vecchiato, Norbert L. "Culture, Health, and Socialism in Ethiopia: The Sidamo Case." Ph.D. diss., University of California, Los Angeles, 1985.

——. "Ethnomedical Beliefs, Health Education, and Malaria Eradication in Ethiopia." *International Quarterly of Community Health Education*, 11 (4) (1991): 385–97.

——. "Sociocultural Aspects of Tuberculosis Control in Ethiopia." *Medical Anthropology Quarterly*, 11 (2) (1997): 183–201.

Von Massow, Fra. *Access to Health and Education Services in Ethiopia*. Oxford: OXFAM Working Papers, 2001.

Walley, J. B., B. Teferra, and M. A. McDonald. "Integrating Health Services: The Experiences of NGOs in Ethiopia." *Health Policy and Planning*, 6 (4) (1991): 327–35.

Webb, A. H. "Beginnings of Medical Education in Ethiopia." *Journal of the National Medical Association*, 49 (1957): 160–64.

World Bank. *Ethiopia: Population, Health, and Nutrition Sector Review*. Washington, D.C.: World Bank, 1985.

Young, Allan. "The Practical Logic of Amhara Traditional Medicine." *RA*, (26) (1974): 79–89.

Zahn, W. *Adami Tullu: Apotheker, Pionier und Zauberer im Lande des Negus*. Stuttgart: Deutsche Volksburcher, 1951.

Zahra Ibrahim. "Notes from a Barefoot Doctor." *Eritrean Medical Journal*, 2 (1) (1984): 56–67.

Education

Abebe Asefa Yirgou. "Secondary Technical/Vocational Education Program in Ethiopia, 1983–1992." Ph.D. diss., University of Texas, Austin, 1995.

Abebe Fisseha. "Education and the Formation of the Modern Ethiopian State, 1896–1974." Ph.D. diss., University of Illinois, Urbana–Champaign, 2000.

Abir, Mordechai. "Education and National Unity in Ethiopia." *AA*, 69 (274) (1970): 44–59.

Abraham, H. "A Comparative Study on the Preparation of Senior Secondary School Teachers in Ethiopia." *EJE*, 12 (1) (1991): 1–40.

Alme Eshete. "Foreign-Educated Ethiopians before 1889." *EJE*, 6 (1973): 115–48.

Amanuel Gebru and Mulugeta Gebreselassie. "Gender Equity in Education in Ethiopia: Hurdles, Initiatives, and Prospects." *Ethiopian Journal of Development Research*, 21 (1) (1999): 1–34.

Andargachew Tesfaye. "The Training and Development of Manpower for Social Sciences in Ethiopia." Ph.D. diss., University of Michigan, 1973.

Asafa Jalata. "The Struggle for Knowledge: The Case of Emergent Oromo Studies." *ASR*, 39 (2) (1996): 95–123.

Assefa Bequele. "The Educational Framework of Economic Development in Ethiopia." *EO*, 11 (1) (1967): 49–58.

Assefa Gabre–Marian. "The Amharic Language Academy." *Journal of the Language Association of Eastern Africa*, 1 (1) (1970): 26–30.

Ayalew Gebre Selassie. "An Institute of Education: A Proposal for a Mechanism for Supervision and Improvement of the Instructional Program in Ethiopian Schools." Ph.D. diss., Columbia University, 1970.

Ayalew Kanno. "Systems Application to Education Planning." *EJE*, 7 (1) (1974): 39–53.

Bairu Tafla. "Education of the Ethiopian Mäkwanent in the Nineteenth Century." *EJE*, 6 (1) (1973): 18–27.

Bergtold, Gary D., and David C. McClelland. *The Impact of Peace Corps Teachers on Students in Ethiopia*. Cambridge: Human Development Foundation, 1968.

Beyene Negewo. "The Impact of University Education on the Formation of Political Attitudes: Sources of Negative Political Attitudes of Ethiopian University Students." Ph.D. diss., Stanford University, 1977.

Bhola, H. S. "Adult Literacy for Development in Ethiopia: A Review of Policy and Performance at Mid-Point." *Africana Journal*, 16 (1994): 192–214.

Caulk, Richard Alan. "Ernest Work on Ethiopian Education." *Ethiopian Journal of Education*, 8 (1) (1975): 1–14.

Colburn, Forrest D. "The Tragedy of Ethiopia's Intellectuals." *Antioch Review*, 47 (2) (1989): 133–45.

Dejene Aredo. "The Brain Drain from Ethiopia." *Ethiopian Development Forum*, 1 (3) (2000): 1–19.

Desta Asyeghn. "Schooling and Inequality in Pre-Revolutionary Ethiopia." *EN*, 2 (2) (1978): 1–14.

——. "A Socioeconomic Analysis of Schooling in Ethiopia." *NAS*, 4 (2) (1982): 27–46.

——. "Student Alienation: A Study of High School Students in Ethiopia." Ph.D. diss., Stanford University, 1977.

Elleni Tedla. "Indigenous African Education as a Means for Understanding the Fullness of Life: Amhara Traditional Education." *Journal of Black Studies*, 23 (1) (1992): 7–26.

Erku Yimer. "Literacy Programs in Ethiopia: A Comparative Study of Pre- and Post-February, 1974 Revolution Periods." Ph.D. diss., University of Wisconsin, Madison, 1987.

Fassil R. Kiros. *Implementing Educational Policies in Ethiopia*. Washington, D.C.: World Bank, 1990.

Fisseha Haile. "A Study of Institutionality: Addis Ababa University, 1961–1981." D. Ed. diss., Indiana University, 1984.

Fitzgerald, M. A. "Education for Sustainable Development: Decision-Making for Environmental Education in Ethiopia." *International Journal of Educational Development*, 10 (4) (1990): 289–301.

Gebeyehu Ejigu. "Educational Planning and Educational Development in Ethiopia: 1957–1973." Ph.D. diss., University of Wisconsin, Madison, 1980.

Germa Amare. "Aims and Purposes of Ethiopian Church Education." *EJE*, 1 (1) (1967): 1–11.

———. "An Appraisal of an Ongoing Literacy Campaign in Ethiopia." *NAS*, 13 (2/3) (1991): 69–100.

———. "Current Trends in Higher Education in Ethiopia." *NAS*, 10 (1) (1988): 47–68.

———. "Education and Society in Prerevolutionary Ethiopia." *NAS*, 6 (1/2) (1984): 61–80.

———. "Government Education in Ethiopia." *EO*, 1 (2) (1962): 335–42.

———. "Trends in Higher Education in Post-Revolutionary Ethiopia." In A. Irele (ed.). *African Education and Identity: Proceedings of the International Congress of African Studies, Ibadan 1985*. Oxford: Hans Zell Publishers, 1991: 109–25.

Gizaw Altaye. *Problems of Overcrowding and Space Utilization in Government Primary Schools of Addis Ababa*. Nairobi: African Studies in Curriculum Development and Evaluation, 1985.

Gould, W. *Problems of Secondary School Provision in African Cities: The Example of Addis Ababa*. Liverpool: Department of Geography, University of Liverpool, 1973.

Greenfield, Richard. "Afro-Ethiopia: A Note on the Current State of Higher Education and University Research in Ethiopia." *Makerere Journal*, (8) (1963): 1–16.

Grey, Robert Daniel. "Education and Politics in Ethiopia." Ph.D. diss., Yale University, 1970.

Gudeta Mammo. "The National Literacy Campaign in Ethiopia." *Prospects*, 12 (2) (1982): 193–99.

Gumbel, Peter, Kjell Nyströem, and Rolf Samuelsson. *Education in Ethiopia 1974–1982: The Impact of Swedish Assistance— An Evaluation*. Stockholm: Swedish International Development Agency, 1983.

Habtamu Wondimu. "Socio-Economic Problems of the Ethiopian Youth: With a Focus on Education, Training, and Work." *Ethiopian Development Forum*, 1 (3) (2000): 31–53.

Haile Woldemichael. *The Maximization of Resources Utilization in Institutions of Higher Learning in Africa: The Case of Addis Ababa University*. Addis Ababa: AAUP, 1983.

Hanson, John W. *Secondary Level Teachers: Supply and Demand in Ethiopia*. East Lansing: Michigan State University, Institute for International Education and African Studies Center, 1970.

Hedlund, Robert L. "Higher Education in Ethiopia." *EO*, 2 (6) (1959): 195–223.

———. "Teachers and the Teaching Profession in Ethiopia." Ph.D. diss., University of Utah, 1975.

Hoben, Susan J. *The Language of Education in Ethiopia: Empowerment or Imposition?* Boston: Boston University, African Studies Center, 1995.

———. "Literacy Campaigns in Ethiopia and Somalia: A Comparison." *NAS*, 10 (2/3) (1988): 111–25.

Hough, J. R. "Educational Development in Ethiopia." *Compare*, 17 (2) (1987): 157–66.

Hultin, Mats. *Ethiopia: Post Evaluation Report, First Education Project*. Washington, D.C.: World Bank, 1973.

———. *Ethiopia: Staff Appraisal Report: An Education Project*. Washington, D.C. World Bank, 1966.

Jacobson, G. S. "The Organization and Administration of Public Schools in Ethiopia." *EJE*, 1 (1) (1967): 12–17.

Kapeliuk, Olga. "A New Generation of Ethiopian Students." *NAS*, 10 (2/3) (1988): 105–10.

Love, Robert S. "Education and Manpower Planning in Ethiopia." *EJE*, 4 (2) (1971): 68–78.

Maaza Bekele. "A Study of Modern Education in Ethiopia: Its Foundation, Its Development, Its Future, with Emphasis on Primary Education." Ph.D. diss., Columbia University Teachers College, 1966.

McCann, James Craig. *Orality, State Literacy, and Political Culture in Ethiopia: Translating the Ras Kassa Registers*. Boston: Boston University, African Studies Center, 1991.

McNab, Christine. "Language Policy and Language Practice: Implementing Multilingual Literacy Education in Ethiopia." *ASR*, 33 (3) (1990): 65–82.

Mehret Ayenaw. "The Teaching and Study of Public Administration: The Experiences at Addis Ababa University." In Walter O. Oyugi (ed.). *The Teaching and Research of Political Science in Eastern Africa*. Addis Ababa: Organization for Social Science Research in Eastern Africa, 1989: 171–89.

Mekuria Bulcha. "Modern Education and Social Movements in the Development of Political Consciousness: The Case of the Oromo." *African Sociological Review*, 1 (1) (1997): 30–65.

Melaku Mekonnen. "Factors Influencing School Dropouts in a Sub-Saharan African Nation: Perceptions of Ethiopian Educators." Ph.D. diss., Texas A&M University, 1990.

Mellesse Amossa Taddesse. "The Role of Education in Combating Famine and Promoting Development in Ethiopia." Ed.D. diss., Columbia University, 1990.

Mulugeta Emebet. "Against the Odds: The Educational Experiences and Coping Strategies of Female Students in Rural Ethiopia." Ed.D. diss., University of Cincinnati, 1998.

Mulugeta Gebreselassie and Amanuel Gebru. "Salient Socio-Economic and Demographic Aspects of School Enrollment: The Case of Primary Schooling in Ethiopia." *Eastern Africa Social Science Research Review*, 16 (2) (2000): 1–24.

Mulugeta Wodajo. "Ethiopia: Some Pressing Problems and the Role of Education in Their Resolution." *Journal of Negro Education*, 30 (3) (1961): 232–40.

———. "The State of Educational Finance in Ethiopia." *EJE*, 1 (1) (1967): 18–26.

Niguse Abbebe and M. Lionel Bender. "The Ethiopian Language Academy: 1943–1974." *NAS*, 6 (3) (1984): 1–7.

Pankhurst, Estelle Sylvia. *Education in Ethiopia*, Woodford: New Times and Ethiopia News, [1946].

———. "Education in Ethiopia: Secondary Education." *EO*, 2 (5) (1958): 162–64.

———. "History of Ethiopian Schools." *EO*, 2 (4) (1958): 130–37.

———. "Imperial College of Agriculture and Mechanical Arts." EO, 1 (10) (1957): 312–17.

———. "Jimma Agricultural School." *EO*, 1 (10) (1957): 318–24.

Pankhurst, Richard. "Education in Ethiopia during the Italian Fascist Occupation." *IJAHS*, 5 (3) (1972): 361–96.

———. "The Foundations of Education, Printing, Newspapers, Book Production, Libraries, and Literacy in Ethiopia." *EO*, 6 (3) (1962): 241–90.

Paulos Milkias. "Political Linkage: The Relationship between Education, Western Educated Elites, and the Fall of Haile Selassie's Feudal Regime." Ph.D. diss., McGill University, 1982.

———. "Traditional Institutions and Traditional Elites: The Role of Education in the Ethiopian Body-Politic." *ASR*, 19 (3) (1976): 79–93.

"Recent Developments in Ethiopian Education." *Ethiopian Economic Review*, (6) (1963): 67–79.

Rydland, Inge Herman. "Adult Education as Realization of Development: A Critical Analysis of Development Paradigms in Ethiopia." D.Ed. diss., Northern Illinois University, 1993.

St. George, Eileen Sarah. "Textbooks as a Vehicle for Curriculum Reform." Ph.D. diss., Florida State University, 2001.

Saunders, Will P. "Schools for Rural Transformation in Africa." *EJE*, 3 (1) (1969): 15–23.

"Schools (Harar)." *EO*, 2 (2) (1958): 81–99.

Searle, Chris. *A Blindfold Removed: Ethiopia's Struggle for Literacy.* London: Karia Press, 1991.

Seyoum G. Selassie. *Development of Social Policy in Ethiopia.* Dire Dawa: Seyoum Selassie, 1983.

Seyoum Teferra. "The Causes and Magnitude of Brain Drain in Higher Education Institutions with a Particular Reference to AAU." *Ethiopian Development Forum*, 1 (3) (2000): 20–30.

Shack, William. "Organization and Problems of Education in Ethiopia." *Journal of Negro Education*, 28 (4) (1959): 405–20.

Sjöström, Margareta, and Rolf Sjöström. *How Do You Spell Development? A Study of a Literacy Campaign in Ethiopia.* Uppsala: SIAS, 1983.

Sjöström, Rolf. *YDLC: A Literacy Campaign in Ethiopia; An Introductory Study and a Plan for Further Research.* Uppsala: SIAS, 1973.

Solomon A. Getahun. "Brain Drain and Its Effect on Ethiopia's Institutions of Higher Learning, 1970s–1990s." *African Issues*, 30 (1) (2002): 52–6.

Solomon Inquai. "Adult Literacy in Ethiopia: A Profile." *JES*, 7 (1) (1969): 55–63.

——. "The Application of Radio in Community Education in Ethiopia." Ph.D. diss., Ohio State University, 1963.

Summerskill, John. *Haile Selassie I University: A Blueprint for Development.* New York: Ford Foundation, 1970.

Tadesse Negash. "Implications of Decentralization for Educational Planning in a Transition from a Centralized to a Federal State: The Case of Ethiopia." Ph.D. diss., University of Pittsburgh, 1999.

Tamrat Mereba. "Education, Mass Participation, and the Impact of Communication on the Rural Development Campaign in Ethiopia: 1974–1978." Ph.D. diss., University of Wisconsin, Madison, 1983.

Techeste Ahderom. "The Development of Asmara University." *EJAS*, 1 (1) (1981): 79–147.

Teffera Betru. "A Study of the Organization and Operational Strategies to Link Research and Extension in the Agricultural Higher Education Institutions in Ethiopia." Ed.D. diss., Oklahoma State University, 1994.

Tekeste Negash. *The Crisis of Ethiopian Education: Some Implications for Nation-Building.* Uppsala: University of Uppsala, Department of Education, 1990.

———. *Rethinking Education in Ethiopia*. New Brunswick, N.J.: Transaction Publishers, 1996.

Tekle Ayano. "Effects of Training on Teachers' Acquisition of Complex Teaching Strategies and Student Achievement: Evaluation of Grade 10 Mathematics Teaching in Addis Ababa." Ph.D. diss., University of Toronto, 1993.

Teshome G. Wagaw. "Access to Haile Selassie I University." *EO*, 14 (1) (1971): 31–46.

———. *The Development of Higher Education and Social Change: An Ethiopian Experience*. East Lansing: Michigan State University Press, 1990.

———. *Education in Ethiopia: Prospect and Retrospect*. Ann Arbor: University of Michigan Press, 1979.

———. *The Role of Adult Literacy in the Development of Africa: A Case of Ethiopia*. Waltham, Mass.: African Studies Association, 1977.

Tilahun Beyene. "The Kind of School Supervision Needed in Developing Countries: Case Study; Ethiopia." Ed.D. diss., University of Maryland College Park, 1982.

Tilahun Workeneh. "Ethiopian Pioneering in Adult Education: Berhane Zare New Institute (1948–1978)." *EJE* 12 (2) (1991): 36–87.

———. "The Evolution of a Continuing Teacher Education Program at Ethiopia's Haile Sellassie I University: A Case Study with a Proposed Model." Ph.D. diss., University of Southern California, 1979

———. "The Road to Literacy: An Assessment of Some Aspects of the Ethiopian National Literacy Campaign." *EJE*, 11 (2) (1989): 79–92.

———. "Thirty Years of University Based In-Service Teacher Education." *EJE*, 11 (2) (1990): 85–128.

Trudea, E. "A Survey of Higher Education in Ethiopia, with Implications for Future Planning and Development." Ph.D. diss., Columbia University, 1964.

Tsehaye Teferra. "A Sociolinguistic Survey of Language Use and Attitudes towards Language in Ethiopia: Implications for a Language Policy in Education." Ph.D. diss., Georgetown University, 1979.

Verhaagen, A. "Les Structures d'Enseignement et Leur Rôle dans l'Histoire de l'Ethiopie Impériale." *Civilisations*, 41 (1/2) (1993): 459–81.

Wolde Yesus Gebre-Mariam. "Education and Economic Growth in Ethiopia." D.Ed. diss., Columbia University, 1981.

Yalew Ingidayehu. "Provision and Organisation of Continuing Professional Education in Ethiopia." D.Phil. diss., New University of Ulster, 1985.

Environment, Fauna, Flora, Geography, Nile Waters, Population, and Tourism

Abbadie, Antoine d'. "Note on Some Names of Places on the Shores of the Red Sea." *JRGS*, 9 (1839): 317–24.

d'Abbadie, Antoine. *Géographie de l'Ethiopie*. Paris: Gustave Mesnil, 1890.

Akinyemi, Nurudeen B. "Sources of Future Conflict in the Horn: Water Management and Interstate Relations among Egypt, Sudan, and Ethiopia." *The Journal of African Policy Studies*, 1 (3) (1995): 23–43.

Alemneh Dejene. *Environment, Famine, and Politics in Ethiopia: A View from the Village*. Boulder, Colo.: LR, 1990.

Amin, Mohamed, and Duncan Willetts. *Ethiopia: A Tourist Paradise*. Nairobi, Camerapix, 1996

Amin, Mohamed et al. *Journey through Ethiopia*. Nairobi: Camerapix Publishers, 1997.

Asmerom Kidane. "Demographic Consequences of the 1984–1985 Ethiopian Famine." *Demography*, 26 (3) (1989): 515–22.

——. "The Quality and Consistency of the Addis Ababa Demographic Census and Surveys 1961–84." *Sinet Ethiopian Journal of Science*, 10 (1/2) (1987): 19–39.

——. "Reestimating the Ethiopian Population by Age and Geographical Distribution, 1935–1985." *NAS*, 9 (3) (1987): 59–73.

Assefa Bequele. "Population and Labour Force Projections for Ethiopia, 1968–1983." *Ethiopian Journal of Development Research*, 1 (1) (1974): 17–30.

Atkins, Richard Alan. *A Geography of Ethiopia*. Addis Ababa: Sudan Interior Mission Printing Press, 1970.

Aubert, Mark. *Ethiopia*. Hong Kong: Local Colour Ltd., [2001].

Austin, Herbert H. "A Glimpse of Western Abyssinia." *JRAS*, 37 (148) (1938): 348–65.

Aynalem Adugna and Helmut Kloos. "Two Population Distribution Maps for Ethiopia Based on the 1984 Census." *NAS*, 9 (1) (1987): 89–95.

Azbaha Haile. "Fertility Conditions in Gondar, Northwestern Ethiopia: An Appraisal of Current Status." *Studies in Family Planning*, 21 (2) (1990): 110–18.

Azene Bekele-Tesemma et al. *Useful Trees and Shrubs for Ethiopia: Identification, Propagation, and Management for Agricultural and Pastoral Communities*. Nairobi: Regional Soil Conservation Unit, Swedish International Development Authority, 1993.

Badege Bishaw. "Determining Options for Agroforestry Systems for the Rehabilitation of Degraded Watersheds in Alemaya Basin, Hararghe Highlands, Ethiopia." Ph.D. diss., Oregon State University, 1993.

Bahru Zewde. "Forests and Forest Management in Wallo in Historical Perspective." *JES*, 21 (1) (1998): 87–121.

Bangs, Richard. *The Lost River: A Memoir of Life, Death, and Transformation on Wild Water*. San Francisco: Sierra Club Books, 1999.

Bard, Kathryn A. (ed.). *The Environmental History and Human Ecology of Northern Ethiopia in the Late Holocene: Preliminary Results of Multidisciplinary Project*. Naples: Istituto Universitario Orientale, 1997.

——. "The Environmental History of Tigray (Northern Ethiopia) in the Middle and Late Holocene: A Preliminary Outline." *African Archaeological Review*, 17 (2) (2000): 65–86.

Baum, James Edwin. *Savage Abyssinia*. London: Cassell and Company Ltd., 1928.

Beke, Charles Tilstone. "Communications Respecting the Geography of Southern Africa." *JRGS*, 12 (1842): 84–101.

Belay Tegene. "Indigenous Soil Knowledge and Fertility Management Practices of the South Wallo Highlands." *JES*, 21 (1) (1998): 123–58.

——. "Land-Cover/Land-Use Changes in the Derekolli Catchment of the South Welo Zone of Amhara Region, Ethiopia." *Eastern Africa Social Science Research Review*, 18 (1) (2002): 1–20.

Berhanu Abegaz. "Papers in Ethiopian Demography I: Population Growth, Composition, and Distribution." *NAS*, 6 (3) (1984): 19–46.

——. "Papers in Ethiopian Demography II: Levels and Patterns of Fertility and Mortality." *NAS*, 7 (2) (1985): 1–21.

——. "Papers in Ethiopian Demography III: Labor Force Structure, Migration, and Poverty." *NAS*, 7 (3) (1985): 1–20.

Beyene, Doilicho. "Rural Urban and Regional Variations in the Sex Structure of Ethiopia's Population." *Eastern and Southern Africa Geographical Journal*, 4 (1) (1993): 35–49.

Blanchard, Dean Hobbs. *Ethiopia: Its Culture and Its Birds*. San Antonio: Naylor Company, 1969.

Blanford, William T. *Observations on the Geology and Zoology of Abyssinia, Made During the Progress of the British Expedition to That Country in 1867–68*. London: Macmillan, 1870.

Bland Sutton, John. *Man and Beast in Eastern Ethiopia*. London: Macmillan, 1911.

Blower, John H. "The Wildlife of Ethiopia." *Oryx*, 9 (1968): 276–85.

Bolton, Melvin. *Ethiopian Wildlands*. London: Collins and Harvill, 1976.

Brander, Bruce. *The River Nile*. Washington, D.C.: National Geographic Society, 1966.

Brietenbach, F. von. *The Indigenous Trees of Ethiopia*. Addis Ababa: Ethiopian Forestry Association, 1963.

Briggs, Philip. *Guide to Ethiopia*. Bucks: Bradt Publications 2002.

Brown, Leslie H. *Conservation for Survival: Ethiopia's Choice*. Addis Ababa: HSU, 1973.

——. *Ethiopian Episode*. London: Country Life, 1965.

Buer, Curtis. *Report on a Survey of the Bale Mountains 1969–1971*. Addis Ababa: Wildlife Conservation Organization, 1971.

Butzer, Karl W. *Recent History of an Ethiopian Delta: The Omo River and the Level of Lake Rudolf*. Chicago: University of Chicago Department of Geography, 1971.

Cain, Chester Robert. "Animals at Axum: Initial Zooarchaeological Research in the Later Prehistory of Northern Ethiopian Highlands." Ph.D. diss., Washington University, 2000.

Campbell, J. "Land or Peasants? The Dilemma Confronting Ethiopian Resource Conservation." *AA*, 90 (358) (1991): 5–21.

Camerapix. *Spectrum Guide to Ethiopia*. Nairobi: Camerapix Publishers International, 1995.

Cartledge, Daniel M. "Taming the Mountain: Human Ecology, Indigenous Knowledge, and Sustainable Resource Management in the Doko Gamo Society of Ethiopia." Ph.D. diss., University of Florida, 1995,

Chaffey, D. R. *South-West Ethiopia Forest Inventory Project: A Glossary of Vernacular Plant Names and a Field Key to the Trees*. Surbiton: Land Resources Development Centre, 1980.

Chang, Wen Pin. "Knowledge, Attitudes, and Practice of Family Planning in Ethiopia." *Studies in Family Planning*, 5 (11) (1974): 344–48.

——. "Population Studies in Ethiopia: Knowledge, Attitudes, and Practice Surveys in Population and Health." *JES*, 12 (1) (1974): 25–69.

Chojnacki, Stanislaw. "Drought and Deforestation." *Bulletin of the Horticultural Society of Ethiopia*, 3 (6) (1976): 10–12.

——. "Forests and the Forestry Problem as Seen by Some European Travellers in Ethiopia." *JES*, 1 (1) (1963): 32–39.

Chorowicz, Jean, et al. "Northwest to North-Northwest Extension Direction in the Ethiopian Rift Deduced from the Orientation of Extension Structures and Fault-Slip Analysis." *Geological Society of American Bulletin*, 106 (12) (1994): 1560–70.

Ciampi, Gabriele. "Cartographic Problems of the Eritreo-Ethiopia Border." *Africa*, 56 (2) (2001): 155–89.

Constable, M., and D. Belshaw. *A Summary of Major Findings and Recommendations from the Ethiopian Highlands Reclamation Study*. Addis Ababa: Ministry of Agriculture, Land Use Planning and Regulatory Department/Food and Agriculture Organisation, 1985.

Conway, Declan. "The Climate and Hydrology of the Upper Blue Nile River." *GJ*, 166 (1) (2000): 49–62.

——. "The Development of a Grid-Based Hydrologic Model of the Blue Nile and the Sensitivity of Nile River Discharge to Climate Change." Ph.D. diss., University of East Anglia, 1993.

Conway, Declan, et al. "Historical Climatology and Dendrocclimatology in the Blue Nile Basin, Northern Ethiopia." In E. Servat, et al. (eds.). *Water Resources Variability in Africa during the XXth Century*. Wallingford: International Association of Hydrological Sciences, 1998: 243–51.

Cook, Henry. "Notes on the Climate and Geology of Abyssinia, with a Table of Heights." *PRGS*, 14 (1869): 158–67.

Cooley, William Desborough. *Cladius Ptolemy and the Nile*. London: John W. Parker and Sons, 1854.

Crummey, Donald. "Deforestation in Wallo: Process or Illusion?" *JES*, 31 (1) (1998): 1–41.

Decaux, H. *Chasses en Abyssinie*. Paris: Delagrave, 1904.

Dessalegn Rahmato. "Environmentalism and Conservation in Wallo before the Revolution." *JES*, 31 (1) (1998): 43–86.

Dupuis, C. E. "Lake Tana and the Nile." *JRAS*, 35 (138) (1936): 18–25.

Erlich, Haggai, and Israel Gershoni (eds.). *The Nile: Histories, Cultures, and Myths*. Boulder, Colo.: LR, 2000.

Ethiopia. Chamber of Commerce. *Guide Book of Ethiopia*. Addis Ababa: Berhanenna Selam Printing Press, 1954.

Ethiopian Mapping Agency. *National Atlas of Ethiopia*. Addis Ababa: Ethiopian Government, 1981.

——. *National Atlas of Ethiopia*. Addis Ababa: National Mapping Agency, 1988.

Farran, C. D. O. "The Nile Waters Question in International Law." *Sudan Notes and Records*, 41 (1960): 88–100.

Federal Democratic Republic of Ethiopia. *Environmental Policy of Ethiopia*. Addis Ababa: Environmental Protection Authority with Ministry of Economic Development and Cooperation, 1997.

——. *The 1994 Population and Housing Census of Ethiopia Results at the Country Level, Analytical Report*. Addis Ababa: Central Statistical Authority, 1999.

——. *The 1994 Population and Housing Census of Ethiopia Results at the Country Level, Statistical Report*. Addis Ababa: Central Statistical Authority, 1998.

Feyisa Demie. "Population Growth and Sustainable Development: The Case of Oromia in the Horn of Africa." *JOS*, 4 (1/2) (1997): 153–78.

Flinton, Fiona and Imeru Tamrat. "Spilling Blood over Water? The Case of Ethiopia." In Jeremy Lind and Kathryn Sturman (eds.) *Scarcity and Surfeit: The Ecology of Africa's Conflicts*. Pretoria: Institute for Security Studies, 2002: pp. 243–319.

Food and Agriculture Organisation. *Ethiopian Highlands Reclamation Study*. 2 vols. Rome: Food and Agriculture Organisation, 1986.

Friedmann, Herbert. *Birds Collected by the Childs Frick Expedition to Ethiopia and Kenya Colony, Part I. Non Passeres*. Washington: Smithsonian Institution, 1930.

Fuertes, Louis Agassi. *Abyssinian Birds and Mammals*. Chicago: Field Museum of Natural History, 1930.

Fuertes, Louis Agassi, and William Hudson Osgood. *Artist and Naturalist in Ethiopia*. Garden City, N.J.: Doubleday, Doran, 1936.

Galperin, Georgi. *Ethiopia: Population, Resources, Economy*. Moscow: Progress Publishers, 1981.

Gamachu, Daniel. *Aspects of Climate and Water Budget in Ethiopia*. Addis Ababa: AAUP, 1977.

Garstin, William Edward. "The Blue and White Niles." *Edinburgh Review*, 190 (1899): 267–308.

"Geography of Ethiopia." *Edinburgh Review*, 41 (1824): 181–94.

Getaneh Assefa. "Stratigraphy and Sedimentology of the Mesozoic Sequence in the Upper Abbay River Valley Region, Ethiopia." Ph.D. diss., University of Minnesota, 1975.

Giday Woldegabriel et al. "Geology, Geochronology, and Rift Basin Development in the Central Sector of the Main Ethiopia Rift." *Geological Society of America Bulletin*, 102 (4) (1990): 439–58.

Girma Amare. "The Nile Issue: The Imperative Need for Negotiation on the Utilization of the Nile Waters." *Ethiopian International Institute for Peace and Development Occasional Papers*, 2 (6) (1997): 3–15.

——. "The Nile Waters." *Ethioscope*, 3 (2) (1997): 3–12.

Girma Zenebe. *Discover the Age-Old Virgin Attractions of the Amhara Region (Addis Ababa-Woldia Road)*. Bahir Dar: The Amhara National Regional State Culture, Tourism and Information Bureau, 1997.

Gobena Huluka. "Environmental Impacts of Gold Mining in Oromia." *JOS*, 6 (1/2) (1999): 159–72.

Gordon, Frances Linzee. *Lonely Planet Guide to Ethiopia, Eritrea, and Djibouti*. Melbourne: Lonely Planet Publications, 2000.

Gouin, Pierre. *Earthquake History of Ethiopia and the Horn of Africa*. Ottawa: International Development Research Center, 1979.

Graham, John. *Ethiopia: Off the Beaten Trail*. Addis Ababa: Shama Books, 2001.

Griffiths, J. F. "Ethiopian Highlands." In H. E. Landsberg (ed.). *World Survey of Climatology*. Amsterdam: Elsevier, 1972: 369–88.

Haile Wolde Emmanuel. "Awash River Basin." *Ethiopian Geographical Journal*, 4 (2) (1966): 17–25.

Hancock, Graham, et al. *Under Ethiopian Skies*. Nairobi: Camerapix Publishers, 1983.

Hecht, Elisabeth-Dorothea. "Ethiopia Threatens to Block the Nile." *Azania*, 23 (1988): 1–10.

Hoben, Alan. *Paradigms and Politics: The Cultural Construction of Environmental Policy in Ethiopia*. Boston: Boston University: African Studies Center, 1995.

Hillawi Tadesse. "The Nile River Basin." *Ethioscope*, 4 (1) (1998): 13–23.

Hoben, Allan. "The Cultural Construction of Environmental Policy: Paradigms and Politics in Ethiopia." *Ecologist*, 27 (2) (1997): 55–62.

——. "Paradigms and Politics: The Cultural Construction of Environmental Policy in Ethiopia." *WD*, 23 (6) (1995): 1007–22.

Hodson, Arnold Wienholt. *Where Lion Reign: An Account of Lion Hunting and Exploration in S. W. Abyssinia.* London: Skeffington and Son, 1928.

Horvath, Ronald J. "Addis Ababa's Eucalyptus Forest." *JES*, 6 (1) (1968): 13–19.

Howell, J. P. and J. A. Allen (eds.). *The Nile: Resources Evaluation, Resource Management and Hydropolitics and Legal Issues.* London: School of Oriental and African Studies and Royal Geographical Society, 1990.

——. (eds.). *The Nile: Sharing Scarce Resources.* Cambridge: CUP, 1994.

Hunri, Hans. "Degradation and Conservation of Soil Resources in the Ethiopian Highlands." *Mountain Research and Development*, 8 (1988): 123–30.

——. *Soil Conservation Manual for Ethiopia.* Addis Ababa: Ministry of Agriculture, 1986.

Hunri, Hans, and I. Perich. *Towards a Tigray Regional Environmental and Economic Strategy.* Berne: Group for Environment and Development, University of Berne, 1992.

Huntingford, George Wynn Brereton. *The Historical Geography of Ethiopia from the 1st Century AD to 1704.* Oxford: Oxford University Press, 1989.

Johns, Chris. *Valley of Life: Africa's Great Rift.* Charlottesville, Va.: Thomson-Grant, 1991.

Johnson, Peggy, and P. Douglas Curtis. "Water Balance of Blue Nile River Basin in Ethiopia." *Journal of Irrigation and Drainage Engineering*, 120 (3) (1994): 573–90.

Keeley, James, and Ian Scoones. "Knowledge, Power, and Politics: The Environmental Policy-Making Process in Ethiopia." *JMAS*, 38 (1) (2000): 89–120.

Kendie, Daniel. "Egypt and the Hydro-Politics of the Blue Nile River." *NAS*, 6 (1) (1999): 141–69.

Kerisel, Jean. *The Nile and Its Masters: Past, Present, Future.* Cape Town: A. A. Balkema, 2001.

Kinfe Abraham. "The Nile Issue: The Psycho-Political Hurdles to an Agreement and the Way Forward to a Rapprochement." *Ethiopian International Institute for Peace and Development Occasional Papers*, 3 (7) (1997): 5–29.

Kloos, Helmut and Aynalem Adugna. "The Ethiopian Population: Growth and Distribution." *GJ*, 155 (1) (1989): 35–51.

Kloos, Helmut, et al. "Social and Ecological Aspects of Resettlement and Villagization among the Konso of SW Ethiopia." *Disasters*, 14 (4) (1990): 309–21.

Langer, William L. "The Struggle for the Nile." *FA*, 14 (2) (1936): 259–73.

Lanz, Tobias J. "Environmental Degradation and Social Conflict in the Northern Highlands of Ethiopia: The Case of Tigray and Wollo Provinces." *AT*, 43 (2) (1996): 157–82.

Last, Geoffrey. "Some Notes on the Scenery of the Ethiopian Rift Valley." *EO*, 5 (3) (1961): 194–202.

Lee, R. "Ethiopia: The Environmental Implications of Industrial Technology." Ph.D. diss., University of Strathclyde, 1997.

Lee, R., and G. Zwadie. "Population Growth, Environmental Stress, and Innovation in Ethiopian Peasant Agriculture." *Science, Technology and Development*, 15 (1) (1997): 104–26.

Le Roux, H. *Chasses et Gens d'Abyssinie*. Paris: Calmann-Levy, [1903].

Lobo, Jerome. *A Short Relation of the River Nile, of Its Sources and Current*. London: John Martin, 1669.

Logan, Walter Ewart Miller. *An Introduction to the Forests of Central and Southern Ethiopia*. Oxford: Imperial Forestry Institute, University of Oxford, 1946.

Ludwig, Emil. *The Nile: The Life Story of a River*. New York: Viking Press, 1937.

Mageed, Yahir Abdel. "Integrated River Basin Development: A Challenge to the Nile Basin Countries." *Sudan Notes and Records*, 52 (1981): 69–81.

Markham, Clements Robert. "Geographical Results of the Abyssinian Expedition." *JRGS*, 38 (1868): 12–49.

Maydon, Hubert Conway. *Simien, Its Heights and Abysses: A Record of Travel and Sport in Abyssinia, with Some Account of the Sacred City of Aksum and Ruins of Gondar*. London: H. F. and G. Witherby, 1925.

Mayo, D. R. W. Bourke. *Sport in Abyssinia*. London: John Murray, 1876.

McCann, James Craig. *A Tale of Two Forests: Narrative of Deforestation in Ethiopia, 1840–1996*. Boston: Boston University, African Studies Center, 1998.

Mekete Belachew. "A Spatio-Temporal Analysis of Deforestation in Ethiopia: With Particular Reference to the Environs of Addis Ababa." *JES*, 32 (1) (1999): 89–131.

Mengistu Woube. "Ethnobotany and the Economic Role of Selected Plant Species in Gambela, Ethiopia." *JES*, 28 (1) (1995): 69–86.

——. *The Geography of Hunger: Some Aspects of the Causes and Impacts of Hunger*. Uppsala: University of Uppsala, 1987.

——. *Resource Use and Conflicts along the Blue Nile River Basin*. Monograph. Uppsala: Uppsala University Geographics Laboratory, 1995.

——. "Southward-Northward Resettlement in Ethiopia." *NAS*, 2 (1) (NS) (1995): 85–106.

Mesfin Wolde Mariam. *An Atlas of Ethiopia*. Addis Ababa: n.p., 1970.

——. "An Estimate of the Population of Ethiopia." *EO*, 5 (2) 91961): 135–41.

——. *The Geography of Ethiopia*. Addis Ababa: Berhane Selam Press, 1972.

——. *An Introductory Geography of Ethiopia*. Addis Ababa: Berhanena Selam Printing Press, 1972.

——. *Preliminary Atlas of Ethiopia*. Addis Ababa: Department of Geography, University College, 1962.

——. *Suffering under God's Environment: A Vertical Study of the Predicament of Peasants in North-Central Ethiopia*. Bern: African Mountains Assoc. and Geographica Bernensia, 1991.

Miressa Duffera Garoma. "Biogeochemistry of Phosphorus in the Highland Plateau Soils of Ethiopia." Ph.D. diss., North Carolina State University, 1996.

Mohamed, Omer Mohamed Ali. "The International Regime of the River Nile." Ph.D. diss., University of Southern California, 1982.

Mohr, Paul A. *The Geology of Ethiopia*. Addis Ababa: HSU Press, 1971.

Mooney, Herbert Francis. *A Glossary of Ethiopian Plant Names*. Dublin: Dublin University Press, 1963.

——. *The Need for Forestry in Ethiopia*. Addis Ababa: University College Press, 1959.

——. *Report on the Bamboo Forests of Wallega Province with a View to their Possible Utilization for Paper Pulp*. Addis Ababa: British Middle East Development Division, 1959.

——. *Report on the Bamboo Forests of Southern Balé in Harrar Province of Ethiopia*. Addis Ababa: British Middle East Development Division, 1961.

——. *Report on the Bamboo Forests of Kaffa and Illubabor*. Addis Ababa: British Middle East Development Division, 1960.

——. *A Note on the Forests in and around Aruanna Mounts in Bale Sub-Province and on Forestry Cooperatives*. Addis Ababa: British Middle East Development Division, 1958.

Morell, Virginia. "Kings of the Hill." *NGM*, 202 (5) (2002): 100–21.

Morton, Bill. *A Field Guide to Ethiopian Minerals, Rocks and Fossils*. Addis Ababa: AAUP, 1978.

Nagelkerke, Leo A. J., et al. "In Lake Tana, a Unique Fauna Needs Protection." *BioScience*, 45 (11) (1995): 772–75.

Nardos Fissaha. "Systematics of Hadar (Afar, Ethiopia) Syudae." Ph.D. diss., Howard University, 1999.

Newcombe, Kenneth. *Ethiopia: An Economic Justification for Rural Afforestation; The Case of Ethiopia*. Washington, D.C.: World Bank, 1984.

Nicol, Clive W. *From the Roof of Africa*. New York: Alfred A. Knopf, 1972.

Nomachi, Kazuyoshi. *Bless Ethiopia*. Tokyo: Odyssey Publications, 1998.

Office of the Population and Housing Census Commission. *Population and Housing Census 1984: Analytical Report on Shewa Region*. Addis Ababa: People's Democratic Republic of Ethiopia, 1989.

Pankhurst, Richard. "The History of Deforestation and Afforestation in Ethiopia Prior to World War I." *NAS*, (NS) 2 (1) (1995): 119–33.

——. "Some Notes on the Historical and Economic Geography of the Mesewa Area (1520–1885)." *JES*, 13 (1) (1975): 89–116.

——. "Wild Life and Forests in Ethiopia." *EO*, 7 (1964): 241–48.

Pease, Alfred E. *Travels and Sport in Africa*. 3 vols. London: Arthur L. Humphreys, 1902.

Population and Housing Census Commission. *Ethiopian Census 1984*. Vol. I Addis Ababa: Population and Housing Census Commission, 1984.

Poschen-Eiche, P. *The Application of Farming Systems Research to Community Forestry: A Case Study in the Harage Highlands, Eastern Ethiopia*. Werksheim: Josef Margraf, 1989.

Posni, Frank. "Available Demographic Data and the Level and Patterns of Population Concentration in Ethiopia: An Assessment." *Ethiopian Journal of Development Research*, 1 (1979): 11–32.

Powell-Cotton, Percy Horace Gordon. *A Sporting Trip through Abyssinia*. London: Rowland Ward, 1902.

Roberts, Leo B. "Traveling in the Highlands of Ethiopia." *NGM*, 68 (3) (1935): 296–328.

Rubenson, Sven. "Conflict and Environmental Stress in Ethiopian History: Looking for Correlations." *JES*, 24 (1991): 71–96.

Rushdi, Said. *The River Nile: Geology, Hydrology and Utilization*. New York: Pergamon Press, 1993.

Rzóska, Julian. *The Nile: Biology of an Ancient River*. The Hague: Dr. W. Junk Publishers, 1976.

Sebsebe Demissew. "A Study of the Vegetation and Floristic Composition of Southern Wallo, Ethiopia." *JES*, 31 (1) (1998): 159–92.

"Settler Migration during the 1984/85 Resettlement Programme in Ethiopia." *Geojournal*, 19 (2) (1989): 113–27.

Shahin, M. *Hydrology of the Nile Basin*. Amsterdam: Elsevier, 1985.

Shiferaw Bekele and S. Holden. "Soil Erosion and Smallholders' Conservation Decisions in the Highlands of Ethiopia." *WD*, 27 (4) (1999): 739–52.

Shimelis Beyene Gebru. "Role of Female Mating Behavior in Hybridization between Anubis and Hamadryas Baboons in Awash, Ethiopia." Ph.D. diss., Washington University, 1998.

Smith, Scot E., and Hussam M. Al-Rawahy. "The Blue Nile: Potential for Conflict and Alternatives for Meeting Future Demands." *Water International*, 15 (4) (1990): 217–22.

Stahl, M. "Environmental Rehabilitation in the Northern Ethiopian Highlands: Constraints to People's Participation." In D. Ghai and J. M. Vivian (eds.). *Grassroots Environmental Action*. London: Routledge, 1992: 281–303.

Stitz, V. "The Amhara Resettlement of Northern Shewa during the 18th and 19th Centuries." *RA*, (1) (1970): 70–81.

Sutcliffe, J. P. "Soil Conservation and Land Tenure in Highland Ethiopia." *Ethiopian Journal of Development Research*, 17 (1) (1995): 63–88.

Sutcliffe, J. V., and Y. P. Parks. *The Hydrology of the Nile*. Wallingford: International Association of Hydrological Sciences, 1999.

Swain, Ashok. "Ethiopia, the Sudan, and Egypt: The Nile River Dispute." *JMAS*, 35 (4) (1997): 675–94.

———. "The Nile River Basin Initiative: Too Many Cooks, Too Little Broth." *SAIS Review*, 22 (2) (2002): 293–307.

Swain, E. H. F. *Ethiopia: Forest Policy, Legislation, and Development*. Addis Ababa: Ministry of Agriculture, 1953.

Taddesse Berisso. "Deforestation and Environmental Degradation in Ethiopia: The Case of Jam Jam Province." *NAS*, (NS) 2 (2) (1995): 139–55.

Tadiwos Chernet. "Petrological, Geochemical, and Geochronological Investigation of Volcanism in the Northern Main Ethiopian Rift Southern Afar Transition Region." Ph.D. diss., Miami University, 1995.

Thomas Tolcha. "Result of Soil Conservation Experiments and the Scope for Implementation: The Case of the Chercher Highlands." *Ethiopian Journal of Development Research*, 20 (2) (1998): 25–63.

Transitional Government of Ethiopia. *National Conservation Strategy*. 4 vols. Addis Ababa: National Conservation Secretariat, 1994.

Tsegaye Gabre-Medhin and Alberto Tessore. *Ethiopia, Footprint of Time*. Addis Ababa: Ethiopian Tourism Commission, 1984.

Twenty One-Day Trips from Addis Ababa. Norwich, England: University of East Anglia, 1997.

United Nations Economic Commission for Africa. *Problems and Prospects for Intercountry Cooperation for Integrated Water Resources Development of the Nile River Basin*. Addis Ababa: UNECA, 1995.

United States. Department of the Interior. *Land and Water Resources of the Blue Nile Basin: Ethiopia*. 17 vols. Washington, DC: USGPO, 1964.

Urban, Emil Karl, and L. Brown. *A Checklist of the Birds of Ethiopia*. Addis Ababa: APP, 1971.

Urban, Emil Karl, L. Brown, and J. Poole. *Endemic Birds of Ethiopia*. Addis Ababa: Ethiopian Tourist Commission, 1980.

Van Perlo, Ber. *Illustrated Checklist to the Birds of Eastern Africa*. London: Collins, 1995.

Vivero, Jose Luis. *The Endemic Birds of Ethiopia and Eritrea*. Addis Ababa: Shama Books, 2001.

Waterbury, John. *Hydropolitics of the Nile Valley*. Syracuse: Syracuse University Press, 1979.

———. "Is the Status Quo in the Nile Basin Viable?" *The Brown Journal of World Affairs*, 4 (1) (1997): 287–98.

———. *The Nile Basin: National Determinants of Collective Action*. New Haven: YUP, 2002.

Waterbury, John, and Dale Whittington. "Playing Chicken on the Nile? The Implications of Microdam Development in the Ethiopian Highlands and Egypt's New Valley Project." *Natural Resources Forum*, 22 (3) (1998): 155–63.

Weld-Blundell, Herbert. "The Blue Nile and Irrigation." *JRAS*, 27 (106) (1928): 97–103.

White, J. G. *Report on Lake Tana: Outlet Control Work and Ethiopian Highway from Addis Ababa to Lake Tana*: New York: The J. G. White Engineering Corporation, 1932.

Whittington, Dale, and E. McClelland. "Opportunities for Regional and International Cooperation in the Nile Basin." *Water International*, 17 (1992): 144–54.

Williams, M. A. J., and H. Faure. *A Land between Two Niles*. Rotterdam: A. A. Balkema, 1980.

Woien, H. "Deforestation, Information, and Citations: A Comment on Environmental Degradation in Highland Ethiopia." *Geojournal*, 37 (4) (1995): 501–12.

Wood, A. "Natural Resource Conflicts in South-West Ethiopia: State, Communities, and the Role of the National Conservation Strategy in the Search for Sustainable Development." *Nordic Journal of African Studies*, 2 (2) (1993): 83–102.

——. "Population Redistribution and Agricultural Settlement Schemes in Ethiopia." In J. L. Clark et al. (eds.). *Population and Development Projects on Africa*. Cambridge: CUP, 1985: 84–111.

Wood, A., and Michael Ståhl. *Ethiopia: National Conservation Strategy: Phase One Report*. Gland: International Union for the Conservation of Nature, 1989.

Wood, T. G. "Termites in Ethiopia: The Environmental Impact of Their Damage and Resultant Control Measures." *Ambio*, 20 (3/4) (1991): 136–38.

World Bank. *Ethiopia: Forestry Project*. Washington, D.C.: World Bank, 1986.

Yntiso Deko Gebre. "Population Displacement and Food Insecurity in Ethiopia: Resettlement, Settlers, and Hosts." Ph.D. diss., University of Florida, 2001.

Zanettin, Bruno. *Evolution of the Ethiopian Volcanic Province*. Roma: Academia Nazionale dei Lincei, 1992.

Zewde Gabre-Sellasie. *The Nile Question 1955–1964: The Ethiopian Perspective*. Monograph. (May 1997).

General And Collected Works

Abdussamad H. Ahmad and Richard Pankhurst (eds.). *Adwa: Victory Centenary Conference 26 February–2 March 1996*. Addis Ababa: Institute of Ethiopian Studies and AAUP, 1998.

Ahmed Zekaria et al. (eds.). *Proceedings of the International Symposium on the Centenary of Addis Ababa, November 24–25, 1986*. Addis Ababa: AAU, Institute of Ethiopian Studies, 1987.

Bahru Zewde. "A Century of Ethiopian Historiography." *JES*, 33 (2) (2000): 1–26.

——. *A Short History of Ethiopia and the Horn*. Addis Ababa: Bahru Zewde, 1998.

Bahru Zewde et al. "From Lund to Addis Ababa: A Decade of Ethiopian Studies." *JES*, 27 (1) (1994): 1–28.

Bahru Zewde, Richard Pankhurst, and Taddese Beyene (eds.). *Proceedings of the XIth International Conference of Ethiopian Studies, Addis Ababa 1991*. 2 vols. Addis Ababa: Institute of Ethiopian Studies, 1994.

Beckingham, C. F., and Edward Ullendorff (eds.) *Ethiopian Studies: Papers Read at the Second International Conference of Ethiopian Studies (Manchester University, [8–11] July, 1963)*. Manchester: Manchester University Press, 1964.

Berhanou Abebe. *Histoire de l'Ethiopie: D'Axoum à la Révolution: (c. IIIe Siècle Avant Notre Ère–1974)*. Paris: Maisonneuve et Larose, 1998.

Buxton, David Roden. *The Abyssinians*. New York: Praeger, 1970.

Center for the Study of the Horn of Africa. *Proceedings: First International Conference on the Horn of Africa*. New York: Center for the Study of the Horn of Africa, 1987.

——. *Proceedings: Second International Conference on the Horn of Africa*. New York: Center for the Study of the Horn of Africa, 1988.

——. *Proceedings: Third International Conference on the Horn of Africa*. New York: Center for the Study of the Horn of Africa, 1989.

——. *Proceedings: Fourth International Conference on the Horn of Africa*. New York: Center for the Study of the Horn of Africa, 1990.

——. *Proceedings: Fifth International Conference on the Horn of Africa*. New York: Center for the Study of the Horn of Africa, 1991.

——. *Proceedings: Sixth International Conference on the Horn of Africa*. New York: Center for the Study of the Horn of Africa, 1992.

——. *Proceedings: Seventh International Conference on the Horn of Africa*. New York: Center for the Study of the Horn of Africa, 1993.

Congresso Internazionale di Studi Etiopici, 1972. *IV Congresso Internazionale di Studi Etiopici (Roma 10–15 Aprile, 1972)*. 2 vols. Rome: Accademia dei Lincei, 1974.

Convegno Internazionale di Studi Etiopici, Rome, 1959. *Atti del Convegno Internazionale di Studi Etiopici (Roma 2–4 Aprile, 1959)*. Rome: Accademia dei Lincei, 1960.

Dunn, P. (ed.). *Quo Vadis Ethiopia Conference Proceedings*. Washington, D.C.: Howard University, 1983.

Ege, S. (ed.). *Development in Ethiopia: Proceedings from a Conference at the University of Trondheim, 9–10 March, 1987.* Trondheim University, College of Arts and Science, 1988.

Ethiopia. Ministry of Information. *Our Land.* Addis Ababa: Ministry of Information, c. 1960.

Ethiopia: Peuples d'Ethiopie: Histoire, Populations, Croyances, Art et Artisanat. Brussels: Gordon and Breach Arts International, 1996.

Fukui, Katsuyoshi, and David Turton (eds.). *Warfare among East African Herders: Papers Presented at the First International Symposium, National Museum of Ethnology.* Osaka: National Museum of Ethnology, 1979.

Fukui, Katsuyoshi, Eisei Kurimoto, and Masayoshi Shigeta (eds.). *Ethiopia in Broader Perspective: Papers of the 13th International Conference of Ethiopian Studies.* 3 vols. Kyoto: Shokado Book Sellers, 1997.

Gerard, Bernard. *Ethiopie.* Paris: Editions Delroisse, 1973.

Goldenberg, Gideon. (ed.). *Proceedings of the Sixth International Conference of Ethiopian Studies, Tel Aviv, 14–17 April, 1980.* Rotterdam: Balkema, 1986.

Great Britain. Naval Intelligence Division. *A Handbook of Abyssinia.* London: HMSO, 1917.

Gromyko, A. A. (ed.). *Proceedings of the Ninth International Congress of Ethiopian Studies, Moscow, 26–29 August 1986.* 6 vols. Moscow: Nauka Publishers, 1988.

Hess, Robert Lee. (ed.). *Proceedings of the Fifth International Conference of Ethiopian Studies, Session B, April 13–16.* Chicago: University of Illinois at Chicago Circle, 1979.

Hinnant, John Thomas, and B. Finne. *Proceedings of the Sixth Michigan State University Conference on Northeast Africa, April 23–25, 1992.* East Lansing: Michigan State University, 1992.

Hotten, J. C. *Abyssinia and Its People.* Westport, Conn.: Greenwood Press, 1986.

International Conference of Ethiopian Studies. *Proceedings of the Third International Conference of Ethiopian Studies, Addis Ababa, (3–7 April), 1966.* 3 vols. Addis Ababa: HSU, Institute of Ethiopian Studies, 1969/1970.

Jesman, Czeslaw. *The Ethiopian Paradox.* London: OUP, 1963.

Jones, Arnold Hugh Martin and Elizabeth Monroe. *A History of Abyssinia.* Oxford: OUP, 1935.

Kaplan, Irving et al. *Area Handbook for Ethiopia.* Washington, D.C.: American University, 1971.

Kaula, Edna Mason. *The Land and People of Ethiopia.* Philadelphia: J. B. Lippincott Company, 1965.

Kebbede Mikael. *Ethiopia and Western Civilization.* Addis Ababa: Berhanenna Selam, 1949.

Lepage, C., et al. (eds.). *Études Ethiopiennes. Actes de la Xe Conférence Internationale des Études Ethiopiennes, Paris, 24–28 Août 1988*. Paris: Société Français des Études Ethiopiennes, 1994.

Levine, Donald Nathan. *Greater Ethiopia: The Evolution of a Multiethnic Society*. Chicago: University of Chicago Press, 1974.

——. *Wax and Gold: Tradition and Innovation in Ethiopian Culture*. Chicago: University of Chicago Press, 1965.

Lipsky, George A. et al. *Area Handbook for Ethiopia*. Washington, D.C.: American University, 1964.

——. *Ethiopia, Its People, Its Society, Its Culture*. New Haven: HRAF Press, 1962.

Marcus, Harold Golden. *A History of Ethiopia*. Berkeley: University of California Press, 1994.

——. (ed.). *New Trends in Ethiopian Studies. Papers of the 12th International Conference of Ethiopian Studies, Michigan State University, 5–10 September 1994*. 2 vols. Lawrenceville, N.J.: RSP, 1994.

——. (ed.). *Proceedings of the First United States Conference on Ethiopian Studies, 1973*. East Lansing: African Studies Center, Michigan State University, 1975.

Mathew, David. *Ethiopia: The Study of a Polity, 1540–1935*. London: Eyre and Spottiswoode, 1947.

Melake G. Ghebrehiwet. "The Role of Selected Historic Leaders in Meeting Social Needs in Ethiopia: From Ezana to Haile Selassie." Ph.D. diss., United States International University, 1994.

Mulatu Wubneh and Yohannis Abate. *Ethiopia: Transition and Development in the Horn of Africa*. Boulder, Colo.: WP, 1988.

Munro-Hay, Stuart. *Ethiopia: The Unknown Land; A Cultural and Historical Guide*. London: I. B. Tauris Publishers, 2002.

Nelson, Harold D., and Irving Kaplan (eds.). *Ethiopia: A Country Study*. 3rd ed. Washington, D.C.: USGPO, 1981.

Ofcansky, Thomas P., and LaVerle Berry (eds.). *Ethiopia: A Country Study*. 4th ed. Washington, D.C.: USGPO, 1993.

Pankhurst, Richard. *The Ethiopians*. Oxford: Blackwell, 1998.

——. (ed.). *The Ethiopian Royal Chronicles*. Addis Ababa: OUP, 1967.

Pankhurst, Richard, Ahmed Zekaria, and Taddese Beyene (eds.). *Proceedings of the First National Conference of Ethiopian Studies, Addis Ababa, April 11–12, 1990*. Addis Ababa: Institute of Ethiopian Studies, 1990.

Pankhurst, Richard, and Taddese Beyene (eds.). *Silver Jubilee of the Institute of Ethiopian Studies: Proceedings of the Symposium, Addis Ababa, November 24–26, 1988*. Addis Ababa: AAU, Institute of Ethiopian Studies, 1990.

Peacock, George. *Hand-Book of Abyssinia*. London: Longmans, Green, Reader and Dyer, 1867.

Pilger, A., and A. Rösler (eds.). *Proceedings of an International Symposium on the Afar Region and Related Rift Problems, Held in Bad Bergzabern, F. R. Germany, April 1–6, 1974*. 2 vols. Stuttgart: E. Schweizerbartische Verlagsbuchhandlung, 1974/1976.

Proceedings of the Fourth Seminar of the Department of History (Awasa, 8–12 July 1987). Addis Ababa: AAUP, 1989.

Proceedings of the Third International Conference of Ethiopian Studies, 1966. Addis Ababa: HSU, 1969.

Rubenson, Sven. "Ethiopia and the Horn." In John E. Flint (ed.). *The Cambridge History of Africa*. Vol. 5, *From c. 1790 to c. 1870*. Cambridge: CUP, 1976: 51–98.

——. (ed.). *Proceedings of the Seventh International Conference of Ethiopian Studies, University of Lund, 26–29 April, 1982*. Uppsala: SIAS, 1984.

Schwab, Peter. *Ethiopia*. London: Frances Pinter, 1985.

Taddesse Beyene (ed.). *Proceedings of the Eighth International Conference of Ethiopian Studies, University of Addis Ababa, 1984*. 2 vols. Huntingdon: Elm Publications, 1988, 1989.

Taddesse Beyene, Richard Pankhurst, and Shiferaw Bekele (eds.). *Kasa and Kasa: Papers on the Lives, Times, and Images of Téwodros II and Yohannes IV (1855–1889)*. Addis Ababa: AAUP, 1990.

Taddesse Beyene, Taddesse Tamrat, and Richard Pankhurst (eds.). *The Centenary of Dogali: Proceedings of the International Symposium, Addis Ababa–Asmara, January 24–25, 1987*. Addis Ababa: AAUP, 1988.

Talbot, David Abner. *Contemporary Ethiopia*. New York: Philosophical Library, 1952.

Tegegne Gebre Egziabher et al. (eds.). *Aspects of Development Issues in Ethiopia: Proceedings of a Workshop on the 25th Anniversary of the Institute of Development Research*. Addis Ababa: AAU, Institute of Development Research, 1999.

Tsehai Berhane Selassie (ed.). *Gender Issues in Ethiopia: Proceedings of the First University Seminar on Gender Issues in Ethiopia, Addis Ababa, December 24–26, 1989*. Addis Ababa: AAU, Institute of Ethiopian Studies, 1991.

Tubiana, Joseph (ed.). *Modern Ethiopia, from the Accession of Menelik II to the Present: Proceedings of the Fifth International Conference of Ethiopian Studies, 19–22 December, 1977, Nice, 19–22 December 1977*. Rotterdam: Balkema, 1980.

Ullendorff, Edward. *The Ethiopians: An Introduction to Country and People*. London: OUP, 1960.

Warsaw University. Institute of Oriental Studies, Department of African Languages and Cultures. *Ethiopia Studies*. Warsaw University. Institute of Oriental Studies, Department of African Languages and Cultures, 1988.

Communications, Media, Post, Press, and Transport

Abel, Alfred, and M. Pasteau. "The Arrival of the First Aeroplane in Ethiopia." *JES*, 10 (2) (1972): 97–103.

Adams, Phillip L., and Benjamin V. Andrews. *Improvement of Ethiopian Ports*. Menlo Park, Calif.: Stanford Research Institute, 1968.

Adler, Ivan. *Handbook of the Postage Stamps of the Empire of Ethiopia, and Her Postal System*. Stockholm: Broborg, 1961.

Aleme Eshete. "A Page in the History of Posts and Telegraphs in Ethiopia." *JES*, 13 (2) (1975): 1–16.

Alem Mezgebe. "Ethiopia: The Deadly Game." *Index of Censorship*, 7 (1978): 16–20.

Baker, J. "Developments in Ethiopia's Road System." *Geography*, 59 (2) (1974): 150–54.

Bekure Woldesemait. "Accessibility of East African Ports to Ethiopia." *Ethiopian Journal of Development Research*, 15 (1) (1993): 29–54.

"A Brief History of the Imperial Highway Authority." *EO*, 5 (2) (1961): 101–10.

Christopher, John Barrett. "Ethiopia, the Jibuti Railway, and the Powers, 1899–1906." Ph.D. diss., Harvard University, 1942.

Cohen, R. "Censorship Costs Lives." *Index on Censorship*, 16 (5) (1987): 15–8.

Coles, R. L. and Jules J. Heierle. "International Civil Aviation in Ethiopia." *EO*, 2 (9) (1958): 309–12.

Collier, Owen P. C., and K. M. A. Perkins. "History of the Franco-Ethiopian Railway from Djibouti to Addis Ababa." *Transport History*, 10 (3) (1979): 220–48.

Doig, Ken. "Gambella-Gambela-Gambeila." *Menelik's Journal*, 5 (1) (1989): 323–30.

——. "Gambella-Gambela-Gambeila: Part II Postal History." *Menelik's Journal*, 7 (2) (1991): 511–16.

Ethiopia. Ministry of Posts, Telegraphs and Telephones. *Ethiopian Stamp Catalogue*. Addis Ababa: Post Office, 1969.

——. *A Short History and Description of the Postage Stamps of the Empire of Ethiopia*. Addis Ababa: APP, 1956.

Ethiopian Airlines. *Bringing Africa Together: The Story of Ethiopian Airlines*. Addis Ababa: Ethiopian Airlines, 1988.

"Ethiopian Airlines: Fifty Years of Reliable Service." *Africa*, (177) (1986): 45–52.

614 • BIBLIOGRAPHY

6

Garretson, Peter P. "Ethiopia's Telephone and Telegraph System, 1897–1935." *NAS*, 2 (1) (1980): 59–71.

Geiger, Theodore. *TWA's Services to Ethiopia: Eighth Case Study in an NPA Series on United States Business Performance Abroad*. Washington, D.C.: National Planning Association, 1959.

Gilmour, T. Lennox. *Abyssinia: The Ethiopia Railway and the Powers*. London: Alston Rivers Ltd., 1906.

Gulelat Gebre Mariam. *A Survey on the History and Problems of the Franco-Ethiopian Railways*. Addis Ababa: Land Transport Department, 1973.

Gupta, S. "Use of Mass Media for Education in Ethiopia." *Communication Review*, 1 (1) (1995): 101–10.

Hailu Wolde Amanuel. "Major Ports of Ethiopia: Aseb, Jibuti, Mesewa." *EGJ*, 3 (1) (1965): 35–47.

Head, Sydney W. "The Beginnings of Broadcast Audience Research in Ethiopia." *JES*, 6 (2) (1968): 77–92.

"Heights of Excellence." *Selamta*, 18 (2) (2001): 8–14.

Italian Library of Information. *The Jibuti–Addis Ababa Railroad*. New York: Italian Library of Information, 1939.

Janas, J. *History of the Mass Media in Ethiopia*. Warsaw: University of Warsaw, Institute of Oriental Studies, 1991.

Kaplan, Nachum. "Ethiopian Flights and Air Mail Service 1929–35." *Menelik's Journal*, 6 (3) (1990): 446–57.

——. "The Napier Expedition October 1867–July 1868." *Menelik's Journal*, 9 (3) (1993): 687–99.

——. "Postal History 1867–1893." *Menelik's Journal*, 3 (1) (1987): 5–12.

Killion, Tom C. "Railroad Workers and the Ethiopian Imperial State: The Politics of Workers' Organization on the Franco-Ethiopian Railroad, 1919–1959." *IJAHS*, 25 (3) (1992): 583–602.

Lee, William F. "From Bush Telegraphy to Microwave Systems: Telecommunications in Ethiopia 1897–1973." *Ethiopia Mirror*, 1 (3) (1973): 28–41.

——. "Press Freedom in Ethiopia." *Ethiopia Mirror*, 2 (4) (1974): 32–4.

Loepfe, Willi. *Alfred Ilg und die Äthiopische Eisenbahn*. Stuttgart: FS, 1974.

Lovelace, A. E. "Ethiopian Airlines and Tourism." 5 (3) (1961): 236–44.

——. "The History of Ethiopian Airlines." *EO*, 5 (3) (1961): 228–32.

Marcus, Harold Golden. "The British and the Ethiopian Railway." *African Dimensions*, (1975): 29–51.

Mikal Baissa. "Radio Ethiopia: Broadcasting in a Multi-Ethnic Society 1928–1974." Ph.D. diss., Northwestern University, 1982.

Pankhurst, Estelle Sylvia. "The Beginning of Modern Transport in Ethiopia: The Franco-Ethiopian Railway and Its History." *EO*, 1 (12) (1957): 376–90.

——. "Ethiopian Aviation, Past and Present." *EO*, 2 (1) (1957): 13–23.

——. "To Kenya by Ethiopian Airlines." *EO*, 2 (12) (1959): 394–99.

Pankhurst, Richard. "The Franco-Ethiopian Railway and Its History." *EO*, 6 (4) (1963): 342–79.

——. "The Genesis of Photography in Ethiopia and the Horn of Africa." *British Journal of Photography*, 123 (41) (1976): 878–82; 123 (42) (1976): 910–13; 123 (43) (1976): 933–35; and 123 (44) (1976): 953–35, 957.

——. "Road Building during the Italian Fascist Occupation of Ethiopian (1936–1941)." *AQ*, 15 (3) (1976): 21–63.

——. "Transport and Communications in Ethiopia, 1800–1935." *Journal of Transport History*, 5 (1961/1962): 69–66, 166–81, 233–54.

Payne, Eric. *Ethiopia: The Issues of 1894–1903*. Ethiopian Stamps Booklet No. 1. Berkshire, England: Philip Cockrill, 1982.

Ram, K. V. "British Government, Finance Capitalists, and the French Jibuti–Addis Ababa Railway, 1898–1913." *JICH*, 9 (2) (1981): 146–68.

Rayner, N. "Rural Roads and Economic Development in Ethiopia." *Logistics and Transport Review*, 16 (4) (1980): 313–24.

Rosso, Max. *Le Rail Franco-Éthiopien en Détresse*. Paris: Pensée Universelle, 1983.

Schimberg, A. W. "Highways in Ethiopia." *EO*, 5 (2) (1961): 100–134.

Sciaky, Roberto. *Ethiopia 1867–1936: History, Stamps, and Postal History*. Vignola, Italy: Vaccari, 1999.

——. *Ethiopia 1867–1936: History, Stamps, and Postal History—Addendum*. Vignola, Italy: Vaccari, 2001.

——. *Ethiopia Tewodros to Menelik: Postal History from the Napier Expedition to the Independent Imperial Post 1867–1908*. Vignola, Italy: Vaccari, 2002.

——. "The Italo-Ethiopian War Years of 1935–1936: Stamps, Mail, and Censorship." *Menelik's Journal*, 28 (4) (2002): 11–16.

Seawall, John Patrick. "Mass Communications in Ethiopia: Blunted Instrument of Government." M.A. thesis. University of Texas, Austin, 1971.

Seed, William H. *Ethiopia's Iron Curtain*. Chicago: Ethiopian Freedom Committee, 1955.

Seyoum Tegegn Worq. "The Ethiopian Ports." *EO*, 12 (4) (1969): 242–43.

Sheckler, Annette C. "Evidence of Things Unseen: Secrets Revealed at the Voice of America." *HA*, 16 (1/2/3/4) (1998): 31–51.

Shiferaw Bekele. "The Ethiopian Railway and British Finance Capitalism, 1896–1902." *Africa*, 46 (2) (1991): 351–74.

——. "The Railway Trade and Politics: A Historical Survey." M.A. thesis. AAU, 1982.

Solheim, Espen. "A Philatelic Journey in Ethiopia: February 2002." *Menelik's Journal*, 18 (3) (2002): 12–17.

Stromböm, Donald A. "Highway Planning in Ethiopia." *Traffic Quarterly*, 20 (1) (1966): 147–56.

Tesfaye Tafesse. "The Patterns and Problems of Work Trips in Addis Ababa." *JES*, 22 (1989): 75–96.

Tristant, Henri. "Ethiopian Postal Exchanges with Foreign Countries Prior to 1908." *Postal History Journal*, 14 (25) (1970): 17–25.

——. *Postal History of Ethiopia: During the Reign of Emperor Menelik II.* Parts I and II. Paris: Huguette Gagnon, 1977.

Willigs, J. A. *Ethiopia: Mass Media, Education, and Development.* Paris: UNESCO, 1969.

Worq Aferahu Kebede. "The Franco-Ethiopian Railways." *Addis Reporter*, 1 (37) (1969): 15–18.

Cities and Urban Affairs

Ababu Aligaz. "The History of Yergalem Town and Its Environs from 1933 to 1974." M.A. thesis. AAU, 1995.

Akalou Wolde-Michael. "Some Thoughts on the Process of Urbanization in Pre–Twentieth Century Ethiopia." *EGJ*, 5 (2) (1967): 23–34.

——. "Urban Development in Ethiopia (1889–1925): Early Phase." *JES*, 11 (1) (1973): 1–16.

——. "Urban Development in Ethiopia in Time and Space Perspective." Ph.D. diss., UCLA, 1967.

Albertis, E. A. d'. *Una Gita all'Harrar.* Milano: Treves, 1906.

Alula Abate. "Urbanization and Regional Development in Ethiopia." *Colloquium Geographicum*, 18 (1985): 242–71.

Andargatchew Tesfaye. "The Social Consequences of Urbanization: The Addis Ababa Experience." *Ethiopian Journal of Development Research*, 14 (1) (1992): 1–43.

Assefa Damte. "Urbanization in Ethiopia: Pre- and Post-Revolution Experience." Ph.D. diss., University of Wisconsin, Milwaukee, 1993.

Baker, Jonathan. "The Growth and Functions of Small Urban Centres in Ethiopia." In Jonathan Baker (ed.). *Small Town Africa: Studies in Rural-Urban Interaction.* Uppsala: SIAS, 1990: 209–27.

——. *The Rural-Urban Dichotomy in the Developing World: A Case Study from Northern Ethiopia.* London and Oslo: Norwegian University Press, 1986.

Baker, Jonathan, and Tsion Dessie. *Rural Towns Study in Ethiopia.* Stockholm: SIAS, 1994.

Barker, W. C. "Extract Report on the Probable Geographical Position of Harrar; With Some Information Relative to the Various Tribes in the Vicinity." *JRGS*, 12 (1842): 238–44.

Bekure W. Semait. "Industrial Development in Addis Ababa Area: A Miniature Capitalist Penetration." *JES*, 17 (1984): 37–61.

Benti, Getahun. "The Dynamics of Migration to Addis Ababa (Ethiopia) and the Overurbanization of the City, c. 1941–c.1974." Ph.D. diss., Michigan State University, 2000.

Berhanu Tereke. "Urbanization in Ethiopia." Ph.D. diss., Institute of Social Studies, 1994.

Bigsten, A., and N. Makonnen. "The Anatomy of Income Distribution in Urban Ethiopia." *African Development Review*, 11 (1) (1999): 1–30.

Brotto, E. "Il Regime delle Terre nel Governo de Harar." *Rivista di Diritto Coloniale*, 2/3 (1939): 349–65 and 4 (1939): 589–608.

Caulk, Richard Alan. *Harar in the Nineteenth Century and the Loss of Its Independence*. Addis Ababa: HSU, Faculty of Arts, 1968.

——. "Harar Town and Its Neighbors in the Nineteenth Century." *JAH*, 18 (3) (1977): 369–86.

Cohen, John M., and Peter H. Koehn. "Rural and Urban Land Reform in Ethiopia." *African Law Studies*, 14 (1977): 3–61.

Comhaire, Jean L. "Urban Growth in Relation to Ethiopian Development." *Cultures et Developpement*, 1 (1) (1968): 25–39.

Dierig, Sandra. *Urban Environmental Management in Addis Ababa: Problems, Policies, Perspectives, and the Role of NGOs*. Hamburg: Institut für Afrika-Kunde, 1999.

Di Lauro, R. *Tre Anni a Gondar*. Milano: A. Mondadori, 1936.

Ellis, Gene. "In Search of a Development Paradigm: Two Tales of a City." *JMAS*, 26 (4) (1988): 677–83.

Fuller, Mia. "Wherever You Go, There You Are: Fascist Plans for the Colonial City of Addis Ababa and the Colonizing Suburb of EUR '42." *Journal of Contemporary History*, 31 (2) (1996): 397–418.

Garretson, Peter P. "A History of Addis Ababa from Its Foundation in 1886 to 1910." Ph.D. diss., University of London, 1974.

Gibb, Camilla C. T. "Religion, Politics, and Gender in Harar." D.Phil. diss., University of Oxford, 1997.

——. "Sharing the Faith: Religion and Ethnicity in the City of Harar." *HA*, 16 (1/2/3/4) (1998): 144–62.

Habtemariam Tesfaghiorghis. "Ethiopia." In J. D. Traver (ed.). *Urbanization in Africa: A Handbook*. Westport, Conn.: Greenwood Press, 1994: 181–97.

——. "The Growth of Urbanization in Ethiopia." *East African Economic Review*, 2 (2) (1986): 157–67.

Hecht, Elisabeth-Dorothea. "The City of Harar and the Traditional Harar House." *JES*, 15 (1982): 57–78.

Horvath, Ronald J. "Language, Migration, and Urbanization in Ethiopia." *Anthropological Linguistics*, 15 (5) (1973): 221–43.

——. "The Process of Urban Agglomeration in Ethiopia." *JES*, 8 (2) (1970): 81–8.

——. "The Wandering Capitals of Ethiopia." *JAH*, 10 (2) (1969): 205–19.

Koehn, Peter Harold. "The Municipality of Addis Ababa, Ethiopia: Performance, Mobilization, Integration, and Change." Ph.D. diss., University of Colorado at Boulder, 1973.

——. "Urban Origins and Consequences of National and Local Political Transformation in Ethiopia." In John Walton and Louis H. Masotti (eds.). *The City in Comparative Perspective: Cross National Research and New Directions in Theory*. New York: John Wiley, 1976: 155–78.

Koehn, Peter Harold, and Sidney R. Waldron-Maxwell. *Afocha: A Link Between Community and Administration in Harar, Ethiopia*. Syracuse, N.Y.: Syracuse University Press, 1978.

Krishnan, Pramila. "Family Background, Education, and Employment in Urban Ethiopia." *Oxford Bulletin of Economics and Statistics*, 58 (1) (1996): 167–83.

Lalor, K. J. "Victimisation of Street Children in Addis Ababa: Factors of Resilience and Susceptibility." Ph.D. diss., University College, Cork, 1997.

McClellan, Charles W. "Articulating Modernization and National Integration at the Periphery: Addis Ababa and Sidamo's Provincial Centers." *ASR*, 33 (1) (1990): 29–54.

Mengistu Woube and Orjan Sjoberg. "Socialism and Urbanization in Ethiopia, 1975–90: A Tale of Two Kebeles." *International Journal of Urban and Regional Research*, 23 (1) (1999): 26–44.

Mulatu Wubneh. "A Multivariate Analysis of Socio-Economic Characteristics of Urban Areas in Ethiopia." *African Urban Quarterly*, 2 (4) (1987): 425–33.

——. *A Spatial Analysis of Urban-Industrial Development in Ethiopia*. Syracuse: Syracuse University, 1982.

——. "Urban Growth and Absorptive Capacity of Cities in Ethiopia." *African Studies Association Papers*, 28 (141) (1985): 1–18.

Munro-Hay, Stuart C. "State Development and Urbanism in Northern Ethiopia." In T. Shaw et al (eds.). *The Archaeology of Africa: Food, Metals, and Towns*. London: Routledge, 1993: 609–21.

Pankhurst, Estelle Sylvia. "Addis Ababa Today." *EO*, 1 (2) (1957): 45–55.

——. "Ancient Harar in Legend and History." *EO*, 2 (2) (1958): 44–5.

——. "Changing Face of Addis Ababa." *EO*, 4 (5) (1960): 134–76.

Pankhurst, Richard. "The City Fifty Years Ago." *EO*, 1 (2) (1957): 60–6.

——. "The Foundation and Growth of Addis Ababa to 1935." *EO*, 6 (1) (1962): 33–61.

——. "Harar at the Turn of the Century." *EO*, 2 (2) (1958): 62–6.

——. "Harar in the Old Days." *EO*, 2 (2) (1958): 47–55.

——. "The History of Dabra Tabor (Ethiopia)." *Bulletin of the School of Oriental and African Studies*, 40 (2) (1977): 235–66.

——. *History of Ethiopian Towns. Vol. I From the Middle Ages to the Early 19th Century*. Wiesbaden: FS, 1982.

——. *History of Ethiopian Towns. Vol. II From the Mid 19th Century to 1935*. Stuttgart: FS, 1985.

——. "Menelik and the Foundation of Addis Ababa." *JAH*, 2 (1) (1961): 103–17.

——. "Notes on the Demographic History of Ethiopian Towns and Villages." *EO*, 9 (1) (1965): 60–80.

Pankhurst, Richard, and Graham Hancock. "Addis Ababa." *Selamta*, 2 (3) (1985): 6–13.

Paulitschke, P. *Harar*. Leipzig: F. A. Brockhaus, 1888.

Raven-Roberts, Angela. "Notes from the Field: Strategies for Street Children of Addis Ababa; Defining the Issues." *NAS*, 13 (2/3) (1991): 1–6.

Robecchi Bricchetti, L. *Nell-Harar*. Milano: Galli, C. Chiesa, F. Omodei-Zorini e Fuindani, 1896.

Rosen, Charles Bernard. "Warring with Words: Patterns of Political Activity in a Northern Ethiopian Town." Ph.D. diss., University of Chicago, 1974.

Santagata, Fernando. *L'Harrar*. Rome: Garzanti Editore, 1940.

Shack, William. "Notes on Voluntary Associations and Urbanization in Africa, with Special Reference to Addis Ababa, Ethiopia." *African Urban Notes*, (1974/1975): 5–10

Solomon Gebre. "The Condition of the Poor in Addis Ababa: A Social Problem Not Yet Addressed." *Dialogue*, 2 (1) (1993): 1–34.

Solomon Mulugeta. "Housing for Low and Moderate Income Workers in Addis Ababa, Ethiopia: Policy versus Performance." Ph.D. diss., Rutgers University, 1995.

Teketel Haile-Mariam. "To Awasa, a Future City, Farming and Cadastral Survey." *EO*, 4 (12) (1961): 395–402.

Tessema Ta'a. "The Process of Urbanization in Wollega, Western Ethiopia: The Case of Nekemte." *JES*, 26 (1) (1993): 59–72.

Wagner, Ewald. "The Arabic Documents on the History of Harar." *JES*, 12 (1) (1974): 213–24.

Waldron, Sidney. "Social Solidarity and Social Cohesion in the Walled City of Harar." Ph.D. diss., Columbia University, 1974.

Yohannes Kinfu. "Demographic Characteristics of Poor Households in Urban Ethiopia: The Case of Dire Dawa Town." *Ethiopian Journal of Economics*, 4 (2) (1995): 67–86.

Women

Alem Habtu. "Women's Education in Ethiopian Historical Perspective and the (1979–1991) National Literacy Campaign." Ph.D. diss., New School for Social Research, 1996.

Anbessa Teferra. "Ballissa: Women's Speech among the Sidama." *JES*, 20 (1987): 44–59.

Appleton, Simon, John Hoddinott, and Pramila Krishnan. "The Gender Wage Gap in Three African Countries." *Economic Development and Cultural Change*, 47 (2) (1999): 289–312.

Bairu Tafla. "Marriage as a Political Device: An Appraisal of a Socio-Political Aspect of the Menelik Period 1889–1916." *JES*, 10 (1) (1972): 13–22.

Balaba, I. K. K. *The Role of Women in National Development*. Addis Ababa: Ethiopian Women's Welfare Association, 1969.

Bauer, Dan F. *Household and Society in Ethiopia*. East Lansing: African Studies Center, 1977.

Beauregard, Erving E. "Two Ethiopian Empresses: Menen and Taitu." *HA*, 6 (3) (1983/1984): 35–39.

Betemariam Berhanu and Michael White. "War, Famine, and Female Migration in Ethiopia, 1960–1989." *Economic Development and Cultural Change*, 49 (1) (2000): 91–113.

Cassiers, Anne. "Mercha: An Ethiopian Woman Speaks of Her Life." *NAS*, 5 (2) (1983): 57–81.

Crummey, Donald. "Women and Landed Property in Gondarine Ethiopia." *IJAHS*, 14 (3) (1981): 444–65.

Dejene Aredo. *The Gender Division of Labour in Ethiopian Agriculture: A Study of Time Allocation in Private and Cooperative Farms in Two Villages*. New York: Social Science Research Council, Project on African Agriculture, 1992.

Duncan, M. E., et al. "STDs in Women Attending Family Planning Clinics: A Case Study in Addis Ababa." *SSM*, 44 (4) (1997): 441–54.

Eshetu Wencheko and Habtamu Ashenafi. "The Influence of Selected Social and Demographic Factors on Fertility: The Case of Bahirdar Town." *Ethiopian Journal of Development Research*, 20 (1) (1998): 1–21.

Fekerte Haile. "Women Fuelwood Carriers and the Supply of Household Energy in Addis Ababa." *CJAS*, 23 (3) (1989): 442–51.

Farnyhough, Timothy Derek. "The Traditional Role and Status of Women in Imperial Ethiopia." *Journal of the Steward Anthropological Society*, 13 (2) (1982): 69–81.

Gettleman, Jeffrey. "Women, War, and Development in Ethiopia." *Cultural Survival Quarterly*, 19 (1) (1995): 39–42.

Haile Bubbamo Arficio. "Some Notes on Traditional Hadiya Women." *JES*, 11 (2) (1973): 131–56.

Hammond, Jenny. *Sweeter than Honey, Ethiopian Women and Revolution: Testimonies of Tigrayan Women*. Trenton, N.J.: RSP, 1990.

Holcomb, Bonnie K. "Oromo Marriage in Wallaga Province, Ethiopia." *JES*, 11 (1) (1973): 107–42.

Kuwee Kumsa. "The Siiqqee Institution of Oromo Women." *JOS*, 4 (1/2) (1997): 115–52.

Laketch Dirasse. *The Commodatitsation of Female Sexuality: Prostitution and Socio-Economic Relations in Addis Ababa, Ethiopia*. New York: AMS Press, 1991.

Molvaer, Reidulf Knut. "Siniddu Gebru: Pioneer Woman Writer, Feminist, Patriot, Educator, and Politician." *NAS*, 4 (3) (1997): 61–75.

Olmstead, Judith. *Women between Two Worlds: Portrait of an Ethiopia Rural Leader*. Urbana and Chicago: University of Illinois Press, 1997.

Pankhurst, Estelle Sylvia. "Three Notable Ethiopia Women." *EO*, 1 (3) (1957): 85–7, 89–90.

Pankhurst, Helen. *Gender, Development, and Identity: An Ethiopian Study*. London: ZB, 1992.

Pankhurst, Richard. "Employment of Women." *EO*, 1 (3) (1957): 98–102.

——. "The History of Prostitution in Ethiopia." *JES*, 12 (2) (1974): 159–78.

Pankhurst, Rita. "Women in Ethiopia Today." *AT*, 28 (4) (1981): 49–51.

Ponzanesi, Sandra. "Post-Colonial Women's Writing in Italian: A Case Study of the Eritrean Ribka Sibhatu." *NAS*, 5 (3) (1998): 97–115.

Rosenfeld, Chris P. "Eight Ethiopian Women of the Zemene Mesafint (c. 1769–1855)." *NAS*, 1 (2) (1979): 63–85.

Spadacini, B., and P. Nichols. "Campaigning against Female Genital Mutilation in Ethiopia Using Popular Education." *Gender and Development*, 6 (2) (1998): 44–52.

Tesfu Baraki. *Culture, Society, and Women in Ethiopia*. Addis Ababa: Ethiopian Women Lawyers Association, 1996.

Van Kesteren, Jose. "Female Workers in Addis Ababa." *Eastern Africa Social Science Research Review*, 4 (1) (1988); 17–32.

Williams, Larry, and Charles S. Finch. "The Great Queens of Ethiopia." *Journal of African Civilization*, 6 (1984): 12–35.

Wilson, Amrit. *Women and the Eritrean Revolution: The Challenge Ahead*. Trenton, N.J.: RSP, 1991.

World Bank. *Implementing the Ethiopian National Policy for Women: Institutional and Regulatory Issues*. Washington, D.C.: World Bank, 1998.

Yehieli, Michele Kathleen. "Factors of Acculturation Associated with Breast-feeding Practices among Resettled Refugees: A Case Study of Ethiopian Immigrants in Northern Israel." D.P.H., diss., University of California, Los Angeles, 1995.

Travel and Exploration

Abbadie, Antoine d'. *Douze Ans dans la Haute-Ethiopie (Abyssinie)*. Paris: Hachette, 1868.

Allen, William Edward David. "Ethiopian Highlands." *GJ*, 101 (1) (1943): 1–15.

Alvares, Francisco (Charles Fraser Beckingham and George Wynn Brereton Huntingford, eds.). *The Prester John of the Indies: A True Relation of the Lands of the Prester John being the Narrative of the Portuguese Embassy to Ethiopia in 1520*. 2 vols. London: HS, 1961.

Annaratone, C. *In Abissinia*. Roma: Enrico Voghera, 1914.

Annesley, George (Viscount Valenta). *Voyages and Travels to India, Ceylon, the Red Sea, Abyssinia, and Egypt in the Years 1802, 1803, 1804, 1805, and 1806*. 3 vols. London: W. Miller, 1809.

Athill, Lawrence F. "Through South-Western Abyssinia to the Nile." *GJ*, 56 (5) (1920): 347–70.

Audon, Henry. "Voyage au Choa." *Le Tour du Monde*, 58 (1889): 113–60.

Austen, Herbert H. "Survey of the Sobat Region." *GJ*, 17 (5) (1901): 495–512.

Baker, Samuel White. "Journey to Abyssinia in 1862." *JRGS*, 33 (1863): 237–41.

——. *Exploration of the Nile Tributaries of Abyssinia*. Hartford: O. D. Case and Company, 1868.

——. *Ismailia*. 2 vols. London and New York: Macmillan and Company, 1874.

——. *The Nile Tributaries of Abyssinia, and the Sword Hunters of the Hamran Arabs*. London: Macmillan and Company, 1867.

——. "On the Tributaries of the Nile in Abyssinia." *PRGS*, 10 (1866): 279–95.

Baratti, Giacomo. *The Later Travels of S. Giacomo Baratti, an Italian Gentleman, into the Remote Countries of the Abissins, or of Ethiopia Interior*. London: Billingsley, 1670.

Barois, M.–J. "Impressions de Voyage en Abyssinie." *Bulletin de l'Institut Égyptien*, 11 (1908): 13–36.

Bartleet, Eustace John. *In the Land of Sheba*. Birmingham: Cornish Brothers, 1934.

Beccari, C. *Il Tigrè da un Missionario Gesuito del Secolo XVII*. 2nd ed. Rome: Edmanno Loescher, 1912.

Beckingham, Charles Fraser, and George Wynn Brereton. *Some Records of Ethiopia, 1593–1646*. London: HS, 1954.

Beke, Charles Tilstone. "Abyssinia: Being a Continuation of Routes in that Country." *JRGS*, 14 (1844): 1–64

——. "Appendix to Messers. Isenberg and Krapf's Journal Routes to Abyssinia and the Neighboring Countries, Collected from Natives." *JRGS*, 10 (1841): 580–86.

——. "On the Countries South of Abyssinia." *JRGS*, 13 (1843): 254–69.

——. *The Sources of the Nile*. London: Madden, 1860.

Bernatz, John Martin. *Scenes in Ethiopia*. London: F. G. Moon, 1852.

Bianchi, G. *Alla Terra dei Galla*. Milan: Treves, 1884.

Bieber, F. J. *Kaffa*. 2 vols. Vienna: Anthropos Administration, 1920–1923.

Blanc, Henry Jules. "From Metemma to Damot, along the Western Shores of the Tana Sea." *PRGS*, 13 (1868/1869): 39–51.

Blashford-Snell, John N. "Conquest of the Blue Nile." *GJ*, 136 (1) (1970): 42–60.

———. *Where the Trails Run Out*. London: Hutchinson and Company, 1974.

Blundell, Herbert Weld. "A Journey through Abyssinia to the Nile." *GJ*, 15 (2) (1900): 97–121 and 15 (3) (1900): 264–72.

———. "Exploration in the Abai Basin, Abyssinia." *GJ*, 27 (6) (1906): 529–53.

Borelli, Jules. *Ethiopie Méridionale*. Paris: Librairies-Imprimeries Réunies, 1890.

Boyes, John. *My Abyssinian Journey*. Nairobi: W. Boyd, [1941].

Bredin, Miles. *The Pale Abyssinian: A Life of James Bruce, African Explorer and Adventurer*. London: HarperCollins Publishers, 2000.

Bruce, James. *Travels to Discover the Source of the Nile in the Years 1768, 1769, 1770, 1771, 1772, and 1773*. 8 vols. Edinburgh: A. Constable and Company, 1813.

Buchholzer, John. *The Land of Burnt Faces*. London: Arthur Barker, 1955.

Bulatovich, Alexander Xavieryerich (ed. and trans. Richard Seltzer). *Ethiopia through Russian Eyes: Country in Transition 1896–1898*. Lawrenceville, N.J.: RSP, 2000.

Burdette, Henry A. *A Visit to King Theodore*. London: J.C. Hotten, 1868.

Burton, Richard Francis. *First Footsteps in East Africa*. 2 vols. London: Longmans, 1856.

———. "Narrative of a Trip to Harar." *JRGS*, 25 (1855): 136–50.

———. *The Nile Basin*. London: Tinsley Brothers, 1864.

Busk, Douglas. *The Fountain of the Sun: Unfinished Journeys in Ethiopia and the Ruwenzori*. London: Max Parrish, 1957.

Buxton, David. *Travels in Ethiopia*. London: Lindsay Drummond, 1949.

Cecchi, Antonio. *Da Zeila alla Frontiera des Caffa. Viaggi di Antonio Cecchi nel'Africa Equatoriale, 1876–1881*. 3 vols. Rome: Ermanno Loescher and Company, 1886.

Celarie, Henriette. *Ethiopia XX Siecle*. Paris: Librairie Hachette, 1934.

Cerulli, Enrico. *Etiopia Occidentale*. 2 vols. Rome: Sindicato Italiano Arti Grafici, 1930–1933.

Cheesman, Robert Ernest. *Lake Tana and the Blue Nile: An Abyssinian Quest*. London: Macmillan, 1936.

———. "The Upper Waters of the Blue Nile." *GJ*, 71 (4) (1928): 358–76.

Chojnacki, Stanislaw. "Dr. Zagiell's 'Journey' to Abyssinia: A Piece of Polish Pseudo-Ethiopica." *JES*, 2 (1) (1964): 25–32.

———. "Some Notes on Early Travellers in Ethiopia." *University College Review*, 1 (1) (1961): 71–89.

——. "William Simpson and His Journey to Ethiopia 1868." *JES*, 6 (2) (1968): 7–38.

Chojnacki, Stanislaw, and Innes Marshall. "Colonel Milward's Abyssinia Journey, 2 December 1867 to 13 June 1868." *JES*, 7 (1) (1969): 81–118.

Cipolla, A. *Pagine Africaine di un Esploratore*. Milan: Alpes, 1927.

Citerni, C. *Ai Confini Meridionali dell'Etiopia*. Milan: Ulrico Hoepli, 1913.

Combes, Edmond, and Maurice Tamisier. *Voyage en Abyssinie*. 4 vols. Paris: Louis Desessart, 1838.

Crawford, Osbert Guy Stanhope. *Ethiopian Itineraries, circa 1400–1524*. Cambridge: HS, 1958.

Crosby, Oscar T. "Abyssinia: The Country and Its People." *NGM*, 12 (3) (1901): 89–102.

——. "Notes on a Journey from Zeila to Khartoum." *GJ*, 18 (1) (1901): 46–61.

Crummey, Donald. "French Travelers in Ethiopia." *JAH*, 16 (4) (1975): 530–31.

Cumming, Duncan. *The Gentleman Savage*. London: Century, 1987.

DaCosta, M. G. (ed.). *The Itinerario of Jeronimo Lobo*. London: HS, 1984.

Darley, Henry Algernon Cholmley. *Slaves and Ivory in Abyssinia: A Record of Adventure and Exploration among the Ethiopian Slave Raiders*. New York: Robert M. McBride, 1935.

De Castro, L. *Nella terra dei Negus*. Milan: Treves, 1915.

De Cosson, Emilius Albert. *The Cradle of the Blue Nile: A Visit to the Court of King John of Eihiopia*. 2 vols. London: John Murray, 1877.

D'Esme, Jean. *A Travers L'Empire de Menelik*. Paris: Librairie Plon, 1928.

De Monfreid, Henry. *Vers les Terres Hostiles de l'Ethiopie*. Paris: Bernard Grasset, 1933.

De Prorok, Byron. *Dead Men Do Tell Tales*. New York: Creative Age Press, 1942.

Drury, Bob, Innes Powell, and Jim Mallinson. "Ethiopia: The Land Where Time Began." *Cross Country Edition*, 74 (2001): 64–68.

Duchesne-Fournet, Jean. *Mission en Éthiopie (1901–1903)*. 3 vols. Paris: Masson et Cie Éditeurs, 1909.

Dufton, Henry. *Narrative of a Journey through Abyssinia in 1862–3*. London: Chapman and Hall, 1867.

Dunckley, Fan C. *Eight Years in Abyssinia*. London: Hutchinson and Company, 1935.

Emily, J. *Mission Marchand*. Paris: Hachette, 1913.

Escherich, G. *Im Lande des Negus*. Berlin: Georg Stilke, 1912.

Faïtlovitch, J. *Notes d'un Voyage chez les Falachas*. Paris: Ernest Leroux, 1905.

——. *Quer durch Abessinien*. Berlin: M. Poppelauer, 1910.

Fays, Pierre-Etienne. *Voyages d'Abyssinie en Ethiopie*. Brussels: Migrations, Beauchevain, Nauwelaerts, 1998.

Ferguson, L. *Into the Blue: The Lake Tana Expedition 1953*. London: Collins, 1955.
Ferret, Pierre Victor Adolphe, and Joseph-Germain Galinier. *Voyages en Abyssinie, dans les Provinces de Tigré, Samen et de l'Amhara*. 3 vols. Paris: Paulin, 1847.
Forbes, Duncan Charles. *The Heart of Ethiopia*. London: Robert Hale, 1972.
——. *Rimbaud in Ethiopia*. Hythe: Volturna Press, 1979.
Forbes, Rosita. *From Red Sea to Blue Nile: A Thousand Miles of Ethiopia*. New York: Lee Furman, 1935.
Fouyas, Panayiotis G. "James Bruce of Kinnaird and the Greeks in Ethiopia." *Abba Salama*, 2 (1971): 161–78.
Franchetti, R. *Nella Dancalia Etiopica*. Verona: A. Mondadori, 1930.
Girard, A. *Souvenirs d'un Voyage en Abyssinie (1868–1869)*. Cairo: Ebner, 1873.
Gold, Joel Jay. "Samuel Johnson's Epitomizing of Lobo's 'Voyage to Abyssinia,'" Ph.D. diss., Indiana University, 1962.
Graham, Douglas Cunningham. (Lady Erskin, ed.). *Glimpses of Abyssinia*. London: Longmans, Green, Reader and Dyer, 1867.
Graham, John. *Ethiopia: Off the Beaten Trial*. Addis Ababa: Shama Books, 2001.
Greenfield, Richard David. "Ethiopian Itineraries: Some Routes in Northern Ethiopia." *EO*, 6 (4) (1963): 313–35.
Griaule, Marcel. *Abyssinian Journey*. London: John Miles, 1935.
Grühl, Max. *The Citadel of Ethiopia: The Empire of the Divine Emperor*. London: Jonathan Cape, 1932.
Guadalupi, Gianni. *The Discovery of the Nile*. New York: Stewart, Tabori and Chang, 1997.
Gwynn, Charles William. "A Journey in Southern Abyssinia." *GJ*, 38 (2) (1911): 113–39.
Halevy, Joseph. *Travels in Abyssinia*. London: Wertheimer, 1878.
Hallé, Clifford. *To Menelik in a Motor Car*. London: Hurst and Blackett, 1913.
Halls, John James. *The Life and Correspondence of Henry Salt, H. B. M. Late Consul-General in Egypt*. London: Richard Bentley, 1834.
Harlan, Henry V. "A Caravan Journey through Abyssinia." *NGM*, 47 (6) (1925): 613–63.
Harmsworth, Geoffrey. *Abyssinian Adventure*. London: Hutchinson and Company, 1935.
Harris, William Cornwallis. *The Highlands of Ethiopia*. 3 vols. London: Longman, Brown, Green and Longmans, 1844.
Hartlmaier, Paul. *Golden Lion: A Journey through Ethiopia*. London: Geoffrey Bles, 1956.
Hayes, Arthur J. *The Source of the Blue Nile: A Record of a Journey through the Soudan to Lake Tsana in Western Abyssinia, and of the Return to Egypt by the Valley of the Atbara with a Note on the Religion, Customs, etc. of Abyssinia*. London: Smith, Elder and Company, 1905.

Hayter, Frank Edward. *In Quest of Sheba's Mines*. London: Stanley Paul, 1935.

Head, Francis Bond. *The Life and Adventures of Bruce, the African Traveller*. New York: Harper and Brothers, 1840.

Henze, Paul Bernard. *Ethiopian Journeys: Travels in Ethiopia 1969–72*. London: Ernest Benn Ltd., 1977.

Héricourt, Rochet de. *Voyage sur la Côte Oriental de la Mer Rouge, dans le Pays d'Abel et le Royaume de Choa*. Paris: Arthur Bertrans, 1841

Heuglin, T. von. *Reisen in Nord-Ost Afrika*. Gotha: Justus Perthes, 1857.

——. *Reisen nach Abessinien*. Jena: Hermann Costenoble, 1868.

Hindlip, Charles Allsop. *Sport and Travel: Abyssinia and British East Africa*. London: T. Fisher Unwin, 1906.

Hodson, Arnold Wienholt. "Journeys from Maji, South-West Abyssinia." *GJ*, 73 (5) (1929): 401–28.

——. "Notes on Abyssinian Lakes." *GJ*, 60 (1) (1922): 65–67.

——. *Seven Years in Southern Abyssinia*. London: T. Fisher Unwin, 1927.

——. "Southern Abyssinia." *GJ*, 53 (2) (1919): 65–83.

Hoskins, George Alexander. *Travels in Ethiopia above the Second Cataract of the Nile*. London: Longman, Rees, Orme, Brown, Green and Longman, 1835.

Hutchinson, Thomas J. *Ten Years' Wanderings among the Ethiopians*. London: FC, 1967.

Imperato, Pascal James. *Arthur Donaldson Smith and the Exploration of Lake Rudolf*. New York: Medical Society of the State of New York, 1987.

——. *Quest for the Jade Sea: Colonial Competition around an East African Lake*. Boulder, Colo.: WP, 1998.

James, Wendy, Gerd Baumann, and Douglas H. Johnson (eds.). *Juan Maria Schuver's Travels in North East Africa 1880–1883*. London: HS, 1996.

Jessen, Burchard Heinrich. "South-Western Abyssinia." *GJ*, 25 (2) (1905): 158–71.

Johnson, Isaac C. *Sport on the Blue Nile; Or Six Months of a Sportsman's Life in Central Africa*. London: Robert Banks and Son, 1903.

Johnston, Charles. *Travels in Southern Abyssinia, through the Country of Adal to the Kingdom of Shoa*. 2 vols. London: J. Madden and Company, 1844.

Johnston, Harry Hamilton. *The Nile Quest*. London: Lawrence and Bullen, Ltd., 1903.

Jonveaux, Emile. *Two Years in East Africa: Adventures in Abyssinia and Nubia, with a Journey to the Sources of the Nile*. London: T. Nelson and Sons, 1875.

Juel-Jensen, Bent and Geoffrey Rowell (eds.). *Rock-Hewn Churches of Eastern Tigray: An Account of the Oxford University Expedition to Ethiopia, 1974*. Oxford: Oxford University Exploration Club, 1975.

Koettlitz, Reginald. "A Journey through Somaliland and Southern Abyssinia to the Shangalla or Berta Country and the Blue Nile and through the Sudan to Egypt." *SGM*, 16 (1900): 467–90.

Kulmer, Friedrich von. *Freiherr. im Reiche Kaiser Meneliks*. Leipzig: Klinkhart and Biermann, [1911].

Landor, A. H. S. *Across Wildest Africa*. 2 vols. London: Hurst and Blackett, 1907.

Lauribar, Paul de. *Douze Ans en Abyssinie*. Paris: Ernest Flammarion, 1898.

Lefebvre, Théophile. *Voyages en Abyssinie Exécuté Pendant les Années 1839, 1840, 1841, 1842, 1843*. 6 vols. Paris: Arthus Bertrand, 1845–51.

Lejean, Guillaume. *Voyage en Abyssinie Exécuté de 1862 à 1864*. 2 vols. Paris: Hachette et Cie, 1872.

Le Roux, H. *Ménélik et Nous*. Paris: Nilsson, Per Lamm, 1902.

Leymarie, H. *Un Dieppois en Abyssinie*. Dieppe: Vigie de Dieppe, 1898.

Licata, G. B. *Assab e i Danachili: Viaggio e Studi*. Milan: Treves, 1885.

Lobo, Jerome. *A Voyage to Abyssinia by Father Jerome Lobo*. London: A. Bettesworth and C. Hitch, 1735.

MacCreagh, Gordon. *The Last of Free Africa*. New York: Century, 1928.

Makin, William J. *Red Sea Nights*. New York: National Travel Club, 1933.

Manley, Deborah, and Peta Rée. *Henry Salt: Artist, Traveller, Diplomat, Egyptologist*. London: Libra, 2001.

Marcus, Harold Golden, and Melvin E. Page. "John Studdy Leigh: First Footsteps in East Africa?" *IJAHS*, 5 (3) (1972): 470–78.

Markham, Clements Robert. "The Portuguese Expeditions to Abyssinia in the Fifteenth, Sixteenth, and Seventeenth Centuries." *JRGS*, 38 (1868): 1–12.

Marsden-Smedley, Philip. *A Far Country: Travels in Ethiopia*. London: Century, 1990.

Martini, G. *Nell'Affrica Italiana: Impressioni e Recordi*. Milan: Treves, 1891.

Massaja, G. *I miei Trentacinque Anni di Missione nell'alta Etiopia: Memorie Storiche di Fra Guglielmo Massaja*. 12 vols. Rome: Tipografia Poliglotta di Propaganda Fide; Milan: S. Giuseppe, 1885–1895.

Matteucci, P. *In Abissinia*. Milan: Treves, 1880.

Maud, Philip. "Exploration in the Southern Borderland of Abyssinia." *GJ*, 23 (5) (1904): 552–79.

Maydon, M. C. "Across Eritrea." *GJ*, 63 (1) (1924): 45–56.

Mérab, Pierre. *Impressions d'Éthiopie: L'Abyssinie sous Ménélik II*. 3 vols. Paris: Éditions Ernest Leroux, 1921, 1922, and 1929.

Middleton, Dorothy. *Baker of the Nile*. London: Falcon Press, 1949.

Montandon, G. *Au Pays Ghimirra: Récit de mon Voyage à Travers le Massif Éthiopien (1909–1911)*. Neuchâtel: Attinger, 1913.

Moorehead, Alan. *The Blue Nile*. London: Hamish Hamilton, 1962.

Morell, Virginia. *Blue Nile: Ethiopia's River of Magic and Mystery*. Washington, D.C.: National Geographic Society, 2001.

Munzinger, Werner. "Journey across the Great Salt Desert from Hanfila to the Foot of the Abyssinian Alps." *PRGS*, 13 (1868): 219–23.

——. "Narrative of a Journey through the Afar Country." *JRGS*, 39 (1869): 188–232.

Murphy, Dervla. *In Ethiopia with a Mule*. London: John Murray, 1968.

Murray, Alexander. *An Account of the Life and Writings of James Bruce*. Edinburgh: A. Constable, 1808.

Nantet, Bernard, and Edith Ochs. *A la Découverte des Falasha: Le Voyage de Joseph Halévy en Abyssinie (1867)*. Paris: Payot and Rivages, 1998.

Natsoulas, Theodore. "Arthur Rimbaud: Trade and Politics in Northeast Africa 1881–1891." *NAS*, 3 (2) (1981): 49–68 and (3) (3) (1981/1982): 43–60.

Nesbitt, Ludovico Mariano. "Danakil Traversed from South to North in 1928." *GJ*, 76 (4) (1930): 298–315; 76 (5) (1930): 391–414; and 76 (6) (1930): 545–57.

——. *Desert and Forest: The Exploration of the Abyssinian Desert*. London: Jonathan Cape, 1934. Published in America as *Hell-Hole of Creation: The Exploration of the Abyssinian Danakil*. New York: A. A. Knopf, 1935.

——. "From South to North through Danakil." *GJ*, 73 (6) (1929): 529–39.

Neumann, Oscar. "From the Somali Coast through Southern Ethiopia to the Sudan." *GJ*, 20 (4) (1902): 373–401.

Norden, Hermann. *Africa's Last Empire: Through Abyssinia to Lake Tana and the Country of the Falasha*. Philadelphia: Macrae Smith Company, 1930.

Orléans, Henri d'. *Une Visite à l'Empereur Ménélick: Notes et Impressions de Route*. Paris: Dentu, 1898.

Pakenham, Thomas. *The Mountains of Rasselas: An Ethiopian Adventure*. London: Weidenfeld and Nicholson, 1998.

Pankhurst, Richard (ed.). *Travellers in Ethiopia*. London: OUP, 1965.

Pankhurst, Richard, and Leila Ingrams. *Ethiopia Engraved: An Illustrated Catalogue of Engravings by Foreign Travellers from 1681 to 1900*. London and New York: Kegan Paul International, 1988.

Pankhurst, Richard, and Denis Gerard. *Ethiopia Photographed: Historic Photographs of the Country and Its People Taken between 1867 and 1935*. London: Kegan Paul International, 1996.

Pariset, D. *Al Tempo di Menelik*. Milan: V. Bombiani, 1937.

Parkyns, Mansfield. *Life in Abyssinia: Being Notes Collected during Three Years' Residence and Travels in That Country*. 2 vols. London: John Murray, 1853.

Pearce, Nathaniel (J. J. Hall, ed.). *The Life and Adventures of Nathaniel Pearce*. 2 vols. London: Henry Colburn and Richard Bentley, 1831.

Peck, Edward. "A Swiss Pasha of Massawa: Werner Munzinger (1832–1875)." *ESR*, 3 (1) (1999): 127–38.

Pennazzi, L. *Dal Po ai due Nile*. 2 vols. Milan: Treves, 1882.

Perret, M. "James Bruce en Ethiopie." In *Colloque International Voyage et Voyageurs*. Brussels: Foundation Nicolas-Claude Fabri de Peiresc, 1985: 61–80.

Piazza, G. *Alle Corte de Menelik*. Ancona: Giovanni Puccini, 1912.

Plowden, Walter Chichele. *Travels in Abyssinia and the Galla Country, With an Account of a Mission to Ras Ali in 1848*. London: Longmans, Green, 1868.

Poncet, Charles-Jacques. "A Journey to Abyssinia." *General Collection of the Best and Most Interesting Voyages and Travels*, 15 (1814): 61–107.

——. *A Voyage to Ethiopia, Made in the Years 1698, 1699 and 1700*. London: W. Lewis, 1709.

Powell, E. Alexander. *Beyond the Utmost Purple Rim: Abyssinia, Somaliland, Kenya Colony, Zanzibar, the Comoros, Madagascar*. New York: Century Company, 1925.

Prutky, Remedius (J. H. Arrowsmith, trans. and ed.). *Prutky's Travels in Ethiopia and Other Countries*. London: HS, 1991.

Raffray, A. *Afrique Orientale: Abyssinie*. Paris: E. Plon, 1876.

Rava, M. *Al Lago Tsana (Il Mar Profondo d'Etiopia)*. Rome: Reale Società Geografica, 1913.

Reid, James Macarthur. *Traveller Extraordinary: The Life of James Bruce of Kinnaird*. London: Eyre and Spottiswoode, 1968.

Remond, G. *La Route de l'Abbaï Noir: Souvenirs d'Abyssinie*. Paris: G. Crès, 1924.

Rey, Charles Fernand. "Abyssinia and Abyssinians of To-Day." *GJ*, 60 (3) (1922): 177–94.

——. "Abyssinia of To-Day." *JRAS*, 21 (84) (1922): 279–90; 22 (85) (1922): 17–29; and 22 (86) (1923): 109–20.

——. *In the Country of the Blue Nile*. London: Duckworth, 1927.

——. *The Real Abyssinia*. London: Seeley, Service and Company, 1935.

——. "A Recent Visit to Gudru and Gojjam." *GJ*, 67 (6) (1926): 481–506.

——. *Unconquered Abyssinia as It Is To-Day*. London: Seeley, Service and Company, 1923.

Rimbaud, Arthur. *Lettres de J. A. Rimbaud: Egypt, Arabie, Ethiopie*. Paris: Société du Mercure de France, 1899.

——. *Voyage en Abyssinie et au Harrar*. Paris: La Centaine, 1928.

Rittlinger, Herbert. *Ethiopian Adventure: From the Red Sea to the Blue Nile*. London: Oldhams Press, 1959.

Roberts, Leo B. "Traveling in the Highlands of Ethiopia." *NGM*, 48 (9) (1935): 297–328.

Rohlfs, G. *Meine Mission nach Abessinien auf Befehl Sr. Maj. des Deutschen Kaiers im Winter 1880/81*. Leipzig: F. A. Brockhaus, 1883.

Romitti, Antonio. "Carlo Piaggia's Sojourn around Lake Tana: 1871–1875." *JES*, 19 (1986): 113–39.

Rosen, Felix. *Eine Deutsche Gesandtschaft in Abessinien*. Leipzig: Von Veit, 1907.

Ross, Emory Denison. "Early Travellers in Abyssinia." *JRAS*, 21 (84) (1922): 268–78 and 21 (85) (1922): 5–16.

Royal Geographical Society. *The Source of the Nile: Explorers' Maps A.D. 1856–1891*. London: Royal Geographical Society, 1964.

Rüppell, Eduard. *Reise in Abyssinien*. 3 vols. Frankfurt: Siegmund Schmerber, 1838–1840.

Rushby, Kevin. *Eating the Flowers of Paradise: A Journey through the Drug Fields of Ethiopia and Yemen*. London: Constable, 1998.

Salt, Henry. *A Voyage to Abyssinia and Travels into the Interior of That Country*. London: FC, 1967.

Sancaeu, Elaine. *The Land of Prester John: A Chronicle of Portuguese Exploration*. New York: Alfred Knopf, 1944.

——. *Portugal in Quest of Prester John*. London: Hutchinson and Company, 1943.

Schoff, Wilfred H. (ed.). *The Periplus of the Erythraean Sea*. New York: Longmans, Green and Company, 1912.

Silverberg, Robert. *Bruce of the Blue Nile*. New York: Holt, Rinehart and Winston, 1969.

Simon, G. *Voyage en Abyssinie et chez les Gallas-Raias*. Paris: Challamel, 1885.

Smith, Harrison. *Through Abyssinia: An Envoy's Ride to the King of Zion*. New York: A. C. Armstrong and Son, 1890.

Snailham, Richard. *The Blue Nile Revealed: The Story of the Great Abbai Expedition, 1968*. London: Chatto and Windus, 1970.

Soleillet, Paul. *Voyages en Éthiopie (Janvier 1882–Octobre 1884)*. Rouen: Imprimerie d'Espérance Cagniard, 1886.

Southworth, Alvan S. *Four Thousand Miles of African Travel: A Personal Record of a Journey up the Nile through the Soudan to the Confines of Central Africa*. New York: Baker, Pratt and Company, 1875.

Starkie, Enid. *Arthur Rimbaud in Abyssinia*. Oxford: CP, 1937.

Stern, Henry Aaron. *Wanderings among the Falashas in Abyssinia; with a Description of the Country and Its Various Inhabitants*. London: Werthaim, Macintosh and Hunt, 1862.

Steuben, Kuno. *Alone on the Blue Nile*. London: Travel Book Club, 1973.

Stewart, Julia. *Eccentric Graces: Eritrea and Ethiopia through the Eyes of a Traveler*. Trenton, N.J.: RSP, 1998.

Stigand, Chauncey Hugh. *To Abyssinia through an Unknown Land: An Account of a Journey through Unexplored Regions of British East Africa by Lake Rudolf to the Kingdom of Menelik*. Philadelphia: J. B. Lippincott Company, 1910.

Tedesco-Zammarano, Lieutenant-Colonel. *Alle Sorgenti del Nila Azzuro*. Rome: Alfieri and Lacroix, 1922.

Telles, Balthazar. *The Travels of the Jesuits in Ethiopia*. London: J. Knapton, A. Bell, and J. Baker, 1710.

Thesiger, Wilfred. "The Awash River and the Aussa Sultanate." *GJ*, 85 (1) (1935): 1–23.

——. *The Danakil Diary: Journeys through Abyssinia 1930–34*. London: HarperCollins, 1996.

——. *The Life of My Choice*. London: HarperCollins Publishers, 1988.

Thomas, Henry (ed.). *The Discovery of Abyssinia by the Portuguese in 1520*. London: British Museum, 1938.

Toy, Barbara. *In Search of Sheba: Across the Sahara to Ethiopia*. London: John Murray, 1961.

Toynbee, Arnold J. *Between Niger and Nile*. London: Oxford University Press, 1965.

Turton, E. R. "Lord Salisbury and the Macdonald Expedition." *JICH*, 5 (1) (1976): 35–52.

Udal, John O. *The Nile in Darkness: Conquest and Exploration 1504–1862*. Wilby: Michael Russell, 1998.

Vanderheym, J. G. *Une Expédition avec le Négous Ménélik: Vingt Mois en Abyssinie*. Paris: Hachette, 1896.

Vayssiere, Alexandre. *Souvenirs d'un Voyage en Abyssinie*. 2 vols. Brussels: Schnee, 1857.

Vigoni, P. *Abissinia: Giornale di un Viaggio*. Milan: Ulrico Hoepli, 1881.

Vivian, Herbert. *Abyssinia: Through the Lion-Land to the Court of the Lion of Judah*. New York: Longmans, Green, 1901.

Von Hohnel, Ludwig. *Discovery of Lakes Rudolf and Stefanie: A Narrative of Count Samuel Teleki's Exploring and Hunting Expedition in Eastern Equatorial Africa in 1887 and 1888*. 2 vols. London: FC, 1968.

Waddington, George, and Bernard Hanbury. *Journal of a Visit to Some Parts of Ethiopia*. London: John Murray, 1822.

Wakefield, Thomas. *Footprints in Eastern Africa, or Notes of a Visit to the Southern Gallas*. London: W. Reed, 1866.

——. "Fourth Journey in the South Galla Country in 1877." *PRGS*, 4 (1882): 358–72.

Waugh, Evelyn. *Remote People*. London: Duckworth, 1985.

Wellby, Montagu Sinclair. "A Journey to the Abyssinian Capital." *Harper's Magazine*, 110 (1900): 141–52.

——. "King Menelik's Dominions and the Country between Lake Gallop (Rudolf) and the Nile Valley." *GJ*, 16 (3) (1900): 292–364.

——. *'Twixt Sidar and Menelik: An Account of a Year's Expedition from Zeila to Cairo through Unknown Abyssinia*. London and New York: Harper and Brothers, 1901.

Whiteway, Richard Stephen. (ed.). *The Portuguese Expedition to Abyssinia in 1541–1543*. London: HS, 1902.

Winstanley, William. *A Visit to Abyssinia: An Account of Travel in Modern Ethiopia*. London: Hurst and Blackett, 1881.

Wylde, Augustus Blandy. *'83 to '87 in the Soudan: With an Account of Sir William Hewett's Mission to King John of Abyssinia*. 2 vols. London: Remington and Company, 1888.

About the Authors

David H. Shinn was a foreign service officer in the State Department for 37 years. He served at U.S. embassies in Lebanon, Kenya, Tanzania, Mauritania, Cameroon, and Sudan and as the American ambassador to Ethiopia from 1996 to 1999. He was director of East African affairs in the Department of State from 1993 to 1996 and had separate responsibility earlier for Somalia, Djibouti, Ethiopia, Tanzania, and Uganda. He has a Ph.D. from George Washington University and currently teaches there as an adjunct professor in the Elliott School of International Affairs.

Thomas P. Ofcansky received a Ph.D. in East African history from West Virginia University (1981). He held several academic posts and is currently with the State Department. He has published numerous books and articles about East Africa, including *Paradise Lost: A History of Game Preservation in East Africa* (2002). He has traveled widely throughout East Africa.